OUR TIMES

America at the Birth of the Twentieth Century

EDITED AND WITH NEW MATERIAL BY

DAN RATHER

BASED ON THE LANDMARK STUDY BY

MARK SULLIVAN

A LISA DREW BOOK

SCRIBNER

New York   London   Toronto   Sydney   Tokyo   Singapore

SCRIBNER
1230 Avenue of the Americas
New York, NY 10020

SCRIBNER and design are trademarks of Simon & Schuster Inc.

Set in Adobe Janson Text
Designed by Jenny Dossin

Manufactured in the United States of America

1   3   5   7   9   10   8   6   4   2

Library of Congress Cataloging-in-Publication Data
Sullivan, Mark, 1874–1952.
Our times : America at the birth of the twentieth century / edited with new material by
Dan Rather : based on the landmark study by Mark Sullivan. —Abridged ed.
p.   cm.
Abridged ed. of: Our times, 1900–1925. 1926–1935.
"A Lisa Drew book."
Includes index.
1. United States—History—1865–1921. 2. United States—Civilization—1865–1918.
3. United States—Civilization—1918–1945. 4. World War, 1914–1918—United
States. I. Rather, Dan. II. Sullivan, Mark, 1874–1952. Our times, 1900–1925. III. Title.
E741.S88   1996
973.91—dc20   95-30055
CIP

ISBN 0-684-81573-7

This book is lovingly dedicated to our own contributions to American history: daughter Robin, son Danjack, and daughter-in-law Judy.

Contents

Acknowledgments

The assistance of Steven H. Biel, Ph.D., of Harvard University, has been invaluable. Without his guidance, I would have had neither the ability nor the audacity to attempt this edition. It was Dr. Biel who devised a method of editing that was both efficient and intellectually defensible. He contributed his seemingly limitless reserves of scholarly expertise in full measure. I relied heavily but confidently on his recommendations in reducing *Our Times* from six volumes to one. My gratitude must extend as well to his wife, Jean Kolling, and their son Jacob, who helped Dr. Biel to help me. Of his capacities as a teacher and historian, the least I can say is this: I envy his students.

For helping this book into existence, William Madison deserves more praise and appreciation than can be expressed. In this undertaking, as in so many others, he has been an incomparable aide, confidant, tutor, and all-around good right arm. Among his many contributions was leading me to Dr. Biel. Without Bill, the book never would have been begun, much less finished. As he continues on his way to becoming a great novelist, he once again set aside his own writing to help with mine. For this, and so much more, the gratitude of all Rathers runs deep.

My wife, Jean Grace Goebel Rather, gets me through this life. Without you, my fighting-heart partner, there would be no book, there would be no reason to get up in the morning. I can never forget that "our times" together are the ones that matter most.

Carlo DeVito, formerly with Scribner, initiated this project and first invited me to participate. My editor Lisa Drew took over the project and has shown her customary patience, good humor, and wisdom at every step.

The heirs of Mark Sullivan, through their kind cooperation, have helped make this edition a reality. I hope they will feel as I do, that their grandfather would be glad of this opportunity to teach new generations, as he must once have taught his grandchildren.

I am as ever deeply indebted to my colleagues at CBS News, among them Peter Lund, Eric Ober, Catherine Lasiewicz, Linda Mason, Lane Venardos, Ted Savaglio, Steve Glauber, Al Ortiz, Allen Alter, Margery Riker, Jeffrey Fager, Al Berman, Patricia Shevlin, Michael Fountain, Eric Shapiro, Kathleen Biggins, Toby Wertheim, Janis Kinzie Culhane, Deborah Margolis Rubin, James Moore, Joe Peyronnin, Susan Zirinsky, and Donna Dees.

The support and friendship of Kim Akhtar, Duncan Macauley, and Suzanne and Bob Nederlander continue to uplift me at home and at work.

Richard and Carole Leibner, David and Susan Buksbaum, Tom and Claire Bettag, Eunice Martin, Bill and Carolyn Johnston, Perry and Betsy Smith, Sam and Mary Ann Quisenberry, Howard Stringer and Jennifer Patterson, Jody and Andrew Heyward, Toby and Joel Bernstein, Pam and Martin Anisman, Charles and Mary Catherine Ball, Don and Gayle Canada, Terri and Tim Vanackern, make my life a joy.

Susan Cipollaro, Amy Bennett, Sakura Komiyama, Allison Zarinko, Allen Zelon, Jeff Wilson, Ethel Goldstein, Renee Itzkowitz, Eve Bartlett, Sylvia Ellis, Will Schwalbe, A.J. Warren, Terri Belli, and Susan Shackman Adler have my enduring gratitude and affection.

Editor's Introduction

W hen Mark Sullivan set out to write the history of his times, many scoffed at the idea that he could attempt such a thing, and said that he would be better off not trying. Indeed, the attempt was more than a little audacious; at the time it was considered impossible to record any kind of history so soon after the fact. *Our Times* covers the years 1900–1925, and the first volume appeared in 1926. That's fast work, even for someone who's paying attention as closely as Mark Sullivan. But the means whereby Sullivan paid attention were also audacious. Mark Sullivan was a journalist. Journalists, or so went the conventional wisdom, were the least capable of writing serious history.

That view may have changed somewhat in our own day. Elizabeth Drew gets the credit for saying, "Journalism is the first draft of history"; yet it's no slight to Ms. Drew to suggest that others before her have had the same idea and have tried to express it. Reporters may not be trained historians, but few are completely unaware when history takes place before their very eyes, as it does quite often for the luckier ones. Still, in 1926, "mere reporters" such as Mark Sullivan, even those who, as he did, studied at Harvard, didn't go around attempting a serious record of the recent history of the United States. Most of them were just trying to beat the deadline for the next morning's edition. The thought of Sullivan and his history must have called to his critics' minds images of Don Quixote and his windmill.

Yet Sullivan did succeed, and in the process changed many of the rules for those who followed. In his sweeping portrait of America as it had been only moments before, Sullivan incorporated documentary evidence the likes of which no one had ever contemplated. Schoolbooks, popular music, newspaper headlines, even advertisements told him a tremendous amount about daily life—a subject into which serious, academic historians did not deign to delve. But Mark Sullivan was determined that *Our Times* warrant its "our." This is a truly democratic work (though not in the partisan sense, since Sullivan was an ardent Republican, about which more later). *Our Times* is a survey of the times of Theodore Roosevelt and Woodrow Wilson, yes, but it is also the times of Mark Sullivan and the men and women who would be his readers.

I had heard of Sullivan, vaguely, back there somewhere, perhaps when I attended Sam Houston State Teachers College in Texas, perhaps even earlier from my parents, who were voracious readers and would have likely read any of the magazines to which he contributed. Years later, in the early 1990s, Sullivan's name came up in the course of conversation, and I asked, "Who, exactly, was he?" The answer was, "Well, he was kind of the Dan Rather of his day."

This, naturally enough, piqued my interest. I'd like to believe this is how most people would have responded if their name had been mentioned in such a way, whether they were in the egocentric television business or not. So I set out to do a little research and reporting of my own. Who *was* this character, this Mark Sullivan, this "Dan Rather of his day"? (My motives were far from disinterested, of course: finding out about "the Dan Rather of his day" was a good way to find out what the speaker thought about the Dan Rather of *this* day.) What I found out was humbling in extremis. Mark Sullivan was one of the best reporters and most widely respected journalists of his time. Mark Sullivan was one hell of a lot better reporter than Dan Rather ever has been or can be.

He was, first of all and always foremost, a "vacuum sweeper" of a re- porter, as journalists later became fond of saying about any reporter who always seemed to get it all: all the salient facts, all the key quotes, all the big trends and all the telling details—and get it all right, all the time, on every story. Mark Sullivan was one of the original "vacuum sweepers," as maga- zine journalism—like the country—was exploding, expanding, and improv- ing just around the turn of the century. One of the originals and the best among them. He seldom seems to have missed anything, and he wrote it fast and well.

Which leads to the second inescapable trait: he could write so well. Readers had no trouble understanding him; and because he wrote so inter- estingly, readers tended to be riveted. Being a combination "vacuum sweeper" reporter and high-quality writer, especially in the grinder that is daily, weekly, even monthly journalism, is rare—then and now. This is the core of what made Sullivan great and has made his work last. Around that core, and adding to it, was his work ethic and his access to sources. He was an indefatigable work horse, up early, staying late, all hours, all days. With Sullivan, one has only to review the tremendous volume of his journalism to know what a hard worker he was.

After more than a quarter of a century as a superb, widely read, widely acclaimed magazine writer, he set out to write a history of his times. The first of six volumes appeared in 1926, the last in 1936. The books attracted a tremendous readership and highly complimentary reviews. Every one was a best-seller, most appeared on the "best of the year" lists of the most influential critics, and Sullivan was regularly considered a shoo-in for a Pulitzer Prize. The compacted publication schedule meant that Sullivan wrote furiously and hard against deadline, turning out one book roughly every eighteen months or so—not to mention his journalistic writing, which he continued to produce without missing a beat. The quality of *Our Times* is stunning for many reasons, not the least of which is that it is so consistent. And that is all the more impressive because he wrote so well, so fast, against so many deadlines over such a long period.

Perhaps one should not be surprised. After all, Sullivan had spent an adult lifetime writing hard against newspaper and magazine deadlines, and the quality of all that work was always superior. Yet the world has been and is filled with good, even great reporters who falter when it comes to writing a book—any book, even one book. And it is not uncommon for a good reporter to turn out *one* good book, then tail off when it comes to later efforts in the longest form. Just another challenge Sullivan met and brushed away.

Respect for Sullivan's crowning achievement, the series of books published under the title *Our Times*, has grown over the years. As each book hit the market in the years after 1926, each was a sensation. The breadth and depth, the sweep and the power of Sullivan's narrative made them best-sellers. It was like an ongoing serial, a national soap opera, but with a difference: all of it was true and fresh in the minds of many readers who, with Sullivan, had actually lived the times, who knew and felt the pulse of those times. It is fair to say that no series of nonfiction books, all on the same general subject and written by the same author over such a short period, ever captured the country so completely, sold so well, was so widely read and acclaimed, and had such a lasting, growing reputation for excellence as Mark Sullivan's *Our Times*.

Since their heyday, the books have become known and respected among historians worldwide as an invaluable authority on one of the most important periods of American history: when, as Sullivan saw it, the United States stepped onto the world stage, triumphed in the Great War, and then ducked back into the wings, into the materialism and self-absorption of the Roaring Twenties.

Who could quibble with Sullivan's access to sources? He had, even by late-twentieth-century standards—perhaps even especially by those standards—absolutely stunning access. He talked personally to presidents and paupers, to inventors and poets, robber barons and labor leaders, and a dizzying array of others who made history. Teddy Roosevelt? Knew him well, was a confidant of T.R. Henry Ford? Ditto. And the list goes on, of those who made America and made history during the period in which America emerged as a world leader.

With *Our Times*, Sullivan planned to write a *second* draft of the history of the United States in the first twenty-five years of this century. Among the many impressive things about Sullivan and his reporting is that he recognized what was happening and why it was important *as it was happening*. He recognized it as a long-running story, tackled it, and plunged into it with zeal and stamina. He eyeballed great events, interviewed key players, took notes, got it all down, and got it right.

And not just "Great Men and Great Events." He concentrated on daily life as well. He reported on and noted the songs of the day, the best books, what ordinary people liked and disliked; he spotted fashion and cultural trends and was constantly on the lookout for changes in daily life. His essay on dog ownership at the turn of the century is still cited both as an indication of his eye for the telling detail—and his ability to turn established historical writing practice on its head.

And how American daily life had changed! Electricity, films, radio, advertising, automobiles, and airplanes, among many, many other developments, were changing America, and the world. The acceleration of change in America was phenomenal in the years 1900 to 1925, and Sullivan was its premier chronicler.

As I began to study Sullivan and read *Our Times*, my interest and excitement level grew. Here was perhaps the greatest combination reporter and writer America ever produced, yet even among American journalists he was, by the last quarter of this century, barely known by the kind of audience he most sought. A few historians remember and revere him and his work, but to practically everyone else among the great American public Sullivan loved and admired, he was unknown.

Part of the problem, obviously, was that *Our Times* covered six thick volumes. And from that was born the idea of the present edition: All right, take it down, get it down to *one* volume (hopefully readable), then try to write some new material around it, and present the marvel of Sullivan's work to new generations of Americans. This volume is the result.

I have not rewritten *Our Times*. I have removed material but not revised, and in the very few cases where it was necessary to provide transition or to distill into a few lines what Sullivan had originally written over several pages, I have retained the key elements of Sullivan's original language. I have been managing editor of the "CBS Evening News" since 1981 and am pretty well acquainted by now with the delicate requirements of editing another reporter's work. Especially in Mark Sullivan's case, to rewrite him would have been to tamper with the strength and clarity of his language—and to do that would have interfered with the lessons he has to teach.

And how much Sullivan has to teach us! What valuable insights and information there are in *Our Times*. The reader will get a taste of what the great events were in America in a defining moment in the country's history and get real insights into what daily life was like and how it changed. *Our Times* is jam-packed with compelling characters. Not just Teddy Roosevelt and Henry Ford and Woodrow Wilson, but a literal cross-section of those who made America what it was and laid the groundwork for what it has become. You will read the testimony of eyewitnesses, both famous and little known. It is testimony gathered *by* a man who was himself an eyewitness—testimony gathered through personal interviews, but also testimony solicited by mail. Sullivan was not only a prolific writer of news and magazine copy and of books, he was also was a prolific letter writer. While writing his chapters on early aviation, he wrote to military experts, manufacturers, the surviving Wright Brother—and the Wright *Sister*. Each of whom provided anecdotes, observations, and rich detail for Sullivan's history. A newspaperman at heart, Sullivan wrote to editors at major papers around the country, asking for their assessment of the most important national *and* local stories of the period. He wanted to ensure that the perspective of *Our Times* was truly representative of the country as a whole; for this he needed help, especially from outside the Northeast, where he made his home. Sullivan also knew that newspaper editors are in the business of clarity. He asked them to send headlines, articles, and advertisements they thought might help readers to understand this history.

His first draft complete, Sullivan checked, rechecked, and checked again. He specialized in fact-checking, demonstrating what journalists of integrity are supposed to do, but too seldom do (then and now). I have never read anything by any reporter who went to more efforts to check his reporting for accuracy than Sullivan. For example, time and again, while writing *Our Times*, he would mail a draft chapter back to his eyewitness correspondents, to the Wright sister, for example, and to others who knew the subject well, for comment and assistance. If his correspondents didn't think he was getting the story quite right, Sullivan would make changes. But if perchance Sullivan disagreed with those comments, he'd note his disagreements. This is one of the reasons for his widespread reputation for fairness as well as accuracy.

This combination of first-rate, first-person reporting and writing, together with a passion for accuracy and fairness, conveyed through so many compelling characters taking part in so many great events, is what makes Sullivan and *Our Times* so unique—and so valuable. No historian writing about America, American history, and the American experience in any language can afford not to read Sullivan, and neither can anyone else, especially any American who seeks to understand, *really* understand, what this nation is and how it got this way. Many of the strongest, deepest traits in the American character were forged in the furnace of rapid change that was the United States in the first quarter of the twentieth century. Sullivan and *Our Times* are and will forever be the best original source material for knowing about that era.

Neither Sullivan nor his books were perfect. To say that they are the best, which I do, is far from claiming they are perfect, or anything near that.

Certainly hindsight makes it easier to see that while Sullivan displayed remarkable aptitude for identifying consensus (most of his interpretations of even the most recent events would find their match in most schoolbooks in history classrooms for a couple generations), he did skip a few items, and sometimes he overlooked what now seems to us essential.

History writing is necessarily arbitrary: Did Lee's surrender have a greater effect on the country than Lincoln's assassination? Where then do you end a history of the Civil War? How can we distinguish the demarcations between eras? How can we say when one trend begins and another ends, except arbitrarily? That's the way Sullivan latches on to his quarter century—yet he can't resist sneaking back as much as thirty years to explain origins, influences, and antecedents, especially in his section on education; in his section on the literature of the twenties, he sneaks over in the other direction. We may now be inclined to ask, "Well, all right, why not simply make this a history of America from 1870 to 1928?" In cases where his overstepping the limits doesn't provide a sufficient answer to that question, I have held Sullivan to his original, arbitrary line.

History writing is also storytelling, and especially popular history, such as *Our Times*, demands some observance of the conventions of storytelling: characters, suspense, and satisfaction, beginning, middle, and end. (I have noticed this in some of the "histories" of the company where I work, in which factual accounts are blended with more dramatically or even novelistically satisfying storylines: how surprised the readers must be to put down their books, turn on the television set, and find CBS News still going about its business, having neither lived happily ever after nor dropped dead.) We see an arc of a story through the writing of *Our Times*, a story that in the living was visible perhaps to no one else but Sullivan: that story is the rise of Teddy Roosevelt, his promise, and its betrayal.

Sullivan was a self-described Progressive and an openly avowed Republican Party voter. Neither the term "Progressive" nor "Republican" may mean the same thing today as it did then, but the point is that Sullivan had his biases, and he made no secret of most of them. What he tried to do, and in my opinion succeeded in the main, was to let his readers know of them, then go on and make a maximum effort to be accurate and fair. But these biases did sometimes affect his judgment and his writings, in ways that even he perhaps was unaware of or neglected to pay enough attention to.

I think of this particularly when considering some of the omissions in *Our Times*: There is little to nothing on Theodore Roosevelt's foreign policy (Sullivan barely even mentions the legendary "Big Stick" policy) or on Woodrow Wilson's domestic policies (as a Republican, Sullivan couldn't admit that any Democrat could be a Progressive). And there is a bitterness to the writing in the final chapters, which can come only from a man whose fondest hopes for his country have been disappointed.

Candidly, what I miss most in *Our Times* is reporting on race relations and World War I. Sullivan offers little reporting about race relations at all, and what he does give shows a woefully weak understanding of their importance in America throughout its history. The whole sorry influence of the Ku Klux Klan as it developed in the late nineteenth and early twentieth century, the culture that Mark Twain called "The United States of Lyncherdom," is never dealt with by Sullivan. This is a glaring omission. There is some absolutely marvelous reporting by Sullivan about the home front during World War I, but he never went to the war. For the events that took place in the war overseas, among and with Americans, Sullivan depends on the great war correspondent, the father of modern war correspondence, Richard Harding Davis. We can only guess what Sullivan, with his keen observation and generous sensibilities, might have written of life as it was lived by callow Americans who changed the world's destiny from the trenches in France.

In reading and enjoying—then whittling, paring, and reducing—Mark Sullivan's monumental popular history of the United States, I have been confronted by a number of, if not outright obstacles, then speed bumps at least on the road to understanding.

The first and most obvious is simply this: *Our Times* is not Our Own Times. I have been unable to escape the thought that this history brings the reader right up to, but not beyond, the time of my own birth, so that my birthday becomes a clear delineation between past and present. This is reassuring in one sense: I must not be very old. I postdate history.

Sullivan's Times, that first quarter century of the modern era, are far removed from most of today's readers, at best a flat backdrop against which grandmother's anecdotes were played. Our impressions of Sullivan's Times may resemble early movies in their herky-jerky, sepia-tinted quaintness. Reading this book may bring greater dimension to those impressions, but Sullivan and his presumptuous editor can make *Our Times* seem more immediate only if the reader possesses a large measure of understanding—and forgiveness.

This is because Sullivan operates with a number of suppositions that present an entire range of additional speed bumps to the modern reader. Some now strike us as quaint: for example, Sullivan's continued belief, despite these many years, that his reader is living in a time of prohibition of alcohol under the provisions of the Eighteenth Amendment. Other suppositions are more troublesome.

Because I feel strongly that Sullivan deserves a fair hearing, quite apart from the outdated cultural baggage he carries, I have tried to jettison the worst of his chauvinism while retaining a representative vision of the era. But the reader must be aware that I have removed some material, and that Sullivan is not a "sensitive man" of the 1990s. We cannot escape or alter the fact that Mark Sullivan lived very much in a white male world and often ignored the rest. He isn't yet capable of understanding the changes in the lives of American women, who at the beginning of *Our Times* couldn't vote, smoke, wear short hair or short skirts, or work outside the home except in a few, mostly menial, jobs. Even worse is Sullivan's patronizing attitude toward African Americans (whom he calls "Negroes," then the only term in polite use) and other American minorities—when he remembers that they exist. Sullivan writes freely of "the dominant white race" in the United States. Such a locution might possibly be excused in some academic circles today, and, as his early citations from Senator Albert Beveridge indicate, there were many worse offenders during Their Times. But for the modern reader, in the era of "political correctness" and widespread attempts to consider the needs and experience of every demographic group, Sullivan's words, attitudes, and narrow scope may understandably startle or dismay.

In those cases where I believe the extremity or insensitivity of Sullivan's language might interfere with an ideally balanced reading of the work, I have made cuts. I have been quick to remove the ethnic jokes, which wouldn't have added much even to Sullivan's original readers' comprehension. But elsewhere, I have let Sullivan's phrasing and perspective stand. The word "Negro" is used, without any further disclaimer from this editor. The prohibition of liquor remains in effect, without repeated reminders from me.

Sullivan has other, less pernicious shortcomings. He is probably the first (although by no means the last) popular historian to rely on the American humorist Finley Peter Dunne's character "Mr. Dooley" as the ultimate authority on all questions of popular interpretation of the events of the era. No harm in this, except that modern readers won't hold "Mr. Dooley" in reverent nostalgia and are far less accustomed to reading transliterated burlesques of dialect. In the main, I have been impressed that "Mr. Dooley" has aged better than his best-known descendant, Will Rogers, whose humor often leaves younger audiences scratching their heads in wonder. I have omitted most of Sullivan's citations from "Mr. Dooley," but retained enough to give today's reader a clear sense of "Dooley's" perspective and the esteem in which he was held by his contemporaries.

We may perceive limitations, but Sullivan's complete confidence in his scope (and why wouldn't he be confident—as a white male?) propels his chronicle with enthusiasm. Sullivan adores his subject. He loves America: he revels in the events and prizes the leaders and the colorful characters who people his country. The reader can almost picture Sullivan chuckling to himself as he resuscitates the old jokes and beloved eccentrics of the era. In the course of six weighty volumes, Sullivan never abandons his sense of humor. He brims over with prices, statistics, anecdotes, and, a great novelty in history-book publishing at the time, pictures. His history is shod with abundant, amusing, digressive footnotes whose relevance Sullivan himself frequently calls into question; most of these this editor has reluctantly excised in consideration of length and narrative drive. Ultimately, the impact of Sullivan's many tittles and jots is exhilarating, and like a pointillist painting winds up rendering a dazzling portrait of the Average American.

In reading this history, it may be useful to think of Sullivan himself as an Average American. Of course there is no such thing as an Average American, and if there were, it wouldn't have been Mark Sullivan: Harvard-educated world traveler, esteemed journalist, confidant of presidents and congressmen. Even his more humble origins can't be considered average. But on occasion Sullivan himself, despite his awareness of the exceptional role he plays, encourages the reader to consider the author's experience as representative, for example, in the many technological changes he witnessed personally from childhood to maturity. So we may consider Sullivan a useful guide who comes to us with a number of representative views, with lessons that are neither irreproachable nor easily dismissed.

Our Own Times are perilously close to the turn of the next century, which is also the turn of the millennium. We are told that at the last turn of the millennium, Europeans went crazy for several years, seeing omens in everything and awaiting the apocalypse at every minute; they calmed down only when they were certain the next millennium had begun. Slightly less superstitious than those Europeans, we may seek our turn-of-the-millennium guidance from something other than comets and two-headed calves. We may turn to history, and the tricky, sometimes elusive, lessons history teaches.

And Sullivan's Times have many lessons to offer us. In Our Own Times, America has been the preeminent world player for most of the century, and in the aftermath of the cold war, it is now reassessing its role. There is value in examining events and opinions at the moment when the United States confidently entered the world arena—and then pulled back.

Why didn't Americans capitalize on their strength and influence after the Great War? Why didn't America join the League of Nations that had been the brainchild of the American president Woodrow Wilson? Why did America squander so many of the opportunities that were handed over by war-fatigued Europe? Mark Sullivan himself raised these questions but couldn't answer them. Even writing so soon after the fact, he found the isolationism and consumerism of the Roaring Twenties to be bewildering and even shameful. The America that Mark Sullivan dreamed of, the America that Teddy Roosevelt promised, was not an America that would consider retreating in victory. Yet that, in Sullivan's point of view, is exactly what happened. When Sullivan wrote, he knew of course that the twenties were only the prelude to the Great Depression; he didn't, and couldn't, know that the Great War would one day be known as World War I.

Today the United States still flirts with isolationism and xenophobia, as it has always done. Geography and a good part of our heritage permit such attitudes. At its heart, this country does not believe in self-absorption or fear, and will always move outward, with the best of intentions, even into space. But the tendency to pull back, to look away from the rest of the world, has existed at least since George Washington warned of "entangling foreign alliances," and it endures today. Mark Sullivan thought that tendency was a mistake. This book may tell us why.

But that is only one of the lessons Mark Sullivan has to teach us. It is easy to pick a quarter century and call it definitive, decisive, revolutionary: what aspect of human life *doesn't* change in twenty-five years? During what twenty-five years are the seeds *not* sown for the next generations? Yet the case can be made that the major characters of *Our Times* did nothing so much as draw the blueprints for what would be called "The American Century," the period from the Spanish-American War to the end of the cold war (and perhaps beyond).

Mark Sullivan shows us the workshop in which Our Own Times were designed. During *Our Times*, Theodore Roosevelt invented the modern presidency, Franklin Roosevelt entered politics, and John Kennedy and Ronald Reagan were born and sent to school. During *Our Times*, the Wright Brothers invented the airplane, Hollywood became something other than a real estate development, and Marconi's radio began to cast broadly the first strands of its network among the peoples of the global village. Those are just a few of the political, technological, and cultural changes. The more important change you will find as you read is this: During *Our Times*, Americans will cease to be characters in a book, will cease to be shadows of forgotten ancestors, and will cease to be our remembered grandparents; gradually, these Americans will become recognizable as ourselves. What we do, what we think, who we are, is due to them.

When Mark Sullivan writes of "Our Times," he means to include you and me.

DAN RATHER
New York and Austin,
Spring 1995

Author's Foreword

A vondale is a village in southeastern Pennsylvania, in Chester County; it is about 40 miles west of Philadelphia and about 8 miles north of the Mason and Dixon line, where that historic boundary curves in an arc to the north, to make room for the "hundreds" of Delaware. (A "hundred" as the name for the smallest unit of government goes back to pre-Norman England; Delaware is, I think, the only place in America where it is preserved.) The streams about Avondale flow south into Delaware Bay; a little to the west is a slight rise in the land, a plain just high enough to make a watershed, beyond which the streams flow into the Susquehanna River and Chesapeake Bay.

It is a countryside of soft, rolling hills and tranquil winding creeks; of old, well-tilled farms, many of them long held by the same families, with practically every farm preserving a woodlot, a bit of the primeval wilderness, made up mainly of oaks, with some poplars and an occasional hickory, and, until a blight that came in the early 1900s, many chestnuts, out of which the farmers split the posts and rails for their fences, which here still resist the invasion of the iron post and steel wire. If the woodlot is on low ground, there are beeches; on the edges, the dogwood salutes the spring with broad white petals. Along the streams are many willows, thriftily preserved to guard against loss of the soil by flood. In the meadows stand occasional black walnuts, some locusts, and here and there a gum tree; the gum tree is the herald of autumn: When its leaves begin to show red, the farmer knows that corn-cutting time is just ahead. The crops are much the same as those first planted on the virgin soil; wheat, corn, and potatoes remain staples; clover and timothy for hay have given way to alfalfa; oats has diminished in proportion as the horse has retired before the automobile—when gasoline first appeared, local jest called it "oats for the car." By the side of each fat barn a tall silo is a comparative modernism; milk has become a principal "money crop."

It is a fertile land; a township near Avondale was named by the early settlers "New Garden." Those early settlers must have escaped a part, at least, of the pangs of homesickness, for the Avondale countryside looked, and still looks, much like some parts of the rural England from which they came. Their origin, and some of their institutions, are commemorated by the local place-names: Chatham, Oxford, Nottingham, Chesterville, London Grove, Penn Green, Kennett Square, Marlborough. (Two of the nearby villages kept Indian names, Toughkennamon and Hockessin.) Within 5 miles of Avondale are seven Quaker meetinghouses, nearly all dating back to the early settlement, some now disused but all kept up in simple dignity, brooding upon the burying-grounds that surround them, in the older of which, according with Quaker tradition, the headstones rise no more than nine or ten inches above the trimmed grass. Like the churches, the farmhouses are well kept up, many of solid stone or brick. Three tall evergreens in front of the house is a local custom almost universally maintained. It is a lovely country, soft to the eye and sweet to the spirit, with appealing suggestions of comfort, security, a wholesome way of life, a tempo attuned to nature's own, traditions, affectionate attachment to the local soil. Had it happened to have, in its two and a half centuries, as many poets as New England, it might have been as well known. No part of America is more American, none more dependable to serve as the type of a settled, working, time-tested order of society.

On an old farm about a mile west of Avondale, I write these words in the room in which I was born. Through the south window, some 10 miles away, I can see, and, when the wind is right, faintly hear, the airplanes whir by on their ten daily flights between Washington and New York. Yet as a boy I saw, on the road at the end of our lane, as a familiar spectacle, an institution now as extinct as the drover, he and his helpers, with many a "ho" and "hi," driving cattle "on the hoof" to the Eastern city markets. On the road—still dirt, improved enough to accommodate the automobile but not enough to incautiously invite the through bus or the speeding tourist—the first vehicle I saw not drawn by a horse was a steam "traction engine" (pronounced "en-gyne"), an amazing novelty which, at a pace much slower than a horse, though more powerful, drew the threshing machine from farm to farm; ahead of it, at a distance of a 100 yards, rode a mounted man with a red flag to warn of danger. Of one form of transportation I have seen the complete cycle; the trolley car came in the early 1880s, grew for a decade or two, was undermined by the automobile and bus, and, by the time I was fifty, was on the way to desuetude. In the field in front of the house I saw my father reap the wheat with a "cradle." When, at the end of one harvest, he hung the cradle beside the flail on a rafter of the barn, it remained there permanently, for the next year he drove a mechanical marvel called a "reaper." By the time the startling "reaper and binder" came, I was a schoolboy well grown.

Completing this foreword as the short winter afternoon wanes, I turn on the electric light. But this morning, in the attic, I fingered the candle mold into which, as a boy, I saw my mother pour melted tallow; that was just before kerosene, which we preferred to call, less pretentiously, "coal oil." With a finger and thumb I turn on the steam heat, but in the kitchen is still the fireplace that once was the only source of warmth; on the inner sides are the hooks from which hung the crane.

But not all the span can be described by comparison of new with old. For some of the new is so utterly new that it had no predecessor. In the year in which I was born, there was no telephone, nor any other means of carrying the human voice farther than could be accomplished by a good pair of lungs in a favoring wind. There was no radio, no motion picture. The coming of these, and others like them, with the changes in point of view that accompanied them, composes a part of the theme of this history. Of much else with which it deals, the patient reader will be aware as he turns the pages. I hope that he will find as much pleasure in the reading, as I in the writing, of an America that was only yesterday, yet much of which is one with Nineveh and Tyre.

MARK SULLIVAN,
Avondale,
December 8, 1935

PART I

The Turn of the Century

CHAPTER I
The Turn of the Century

The purpose of this narrative is to follow an average American through a quarter century of his country's history, to re-create the flow of the days as he saw them, to picture events in terms of their influence on him, his daily life and ultimate destiny. The aim is to appraise the actors of history and their activities according to the way they affected the average man, the way he felt about them, the ways in which he was influenced by his leaders, and in which he influenced them.

As democracy in America has expressed itself, the period 1900–1925 is unparalleled in the importance of the role played by the average man. He was the principal spectator; indeed, he was the whole audience. He not only watched the performance, but largely determined the actions of those who from time to time were upon the stage, regulated the length of their tenure in the spotlight, retired them to the wings, or summoned them back. It was his will or his whim, his applause, his disapproval or his indifference, that dictated the entrances and the exits. He himself was one of the performers—was in fact the principal performer in a more fundamental sense and more continuously than any of the actors; for the drama consisted essentially of the reactions of the average man to the actors and of the actors to him. This average man, this audience, was also in a true sense the author and the stage manager. In short, he was, as he himself would express it, "pretty near the whole show."

In habitat, this average American is universal. He may slur his r's in Georgia or grind them in Illinois; drawl the gentle r's of the Lone Sta' State, or describe himself as living in the Green Mount-in State. Geographically, he has no boundaries. But if the reader prefers to personify him and give him a local habitat, if he wishes to pick out one average American who shall typify all average Americans, he may take advantage of that statistical accident whereby every decade some small American community is elevated to a curious and, though irrelevant, nevertheless proud and interest-provoking conspicuousness, by emerging as the resultant of the labors of some hundreds of clerks in the Census Bureau. The town determined as the center of population of the United States in 1900 was named, as it happens, Columbus, in Indiana. It would be squeezing the last drop of significance out of a statistical coincidence to suggest that the town which happened to be the center of population was also the typical dwelling place, and had the typical surroundings, of the man who in the same year was the typical American. Yet a fair case might be made out to the effect that the typical American of 1900 had possibly more points of identity with the typical inhabitant of an Indiana community than with most other persons in other backgrounds. Socially, Indiana provided the dramatis personae of the novels and plays of that American writer who, more nearly than any other during the period this history covers, reflected typical American life, Booth Tarkington of Indianapolis. Politically, this average Indianan, with his neighbor in Ohio, determined the occupant of the White House for nearly half of all the years from the Civil War to 1925. In politics, the representativeness, so to speak, of the citizen of Indiana and Ohio was universally recognized, and won for him something close to omnipotence; for his ideas, his prejudices, his economic interests were universally considered and generally deferred to.

However, this suggestion is merely casual, and has no more purpose than to give some slight flesh-and-blood concreteness to what otherwise might be a rather indefinite abstraction, the average American. And in this narrative the average American is not a formless conception; he is the principal character. The reader may seem to lose sight of him for considerable stretches, but he is there, on every page.

II

If the American, reading the papers of New Year's Day, 1900, was more than commonly reflective over the serious aspects of the news, it was only partly because the sporting page and the comic strip had not yet arrived to overbalance the American newspaper on the side of the merely di-

Western movement of the center of population as determined by the Census Bureau for the decades 1790–1900. In 1900, the center was 6 miles west of Columbus, Indiana. By 1920, the center had moved farther west, to the village of Whitehall, Indiana.

verting. It was due also to the presence in the newspapers of that day and in the sermons of the day before, of a spirit of solemnity, occasioned by the coming of a new year and, as some said, a new century.

Throughout 1899 there had been much discussion as to what day and year marked the close of the nineteenth century and the beginning of the twentieth. It was recognized by everybody as a turning point, a 100-mile stone. There was a human disposition to sum things up, to say who had been the greatest men of the century just closed, what had been the greatest books, the greatest inventions, the greatest advances in science. Looking forward, there was a similar disposition to forecast and predict. This appealed to nearly everybody, and to find people disputing the correctness of the date you chose for harking back or looking forward was an irritation. Wherever men met they argued about it. Editorials dealt with it, seriously or facetiously. Contentious persons wrote letters to the papers. Schoolchildren were set to figuring.

The learned editor of *The Review of Reviews*, Dr. Albert Shaw, settled the question for the readers of his magazine in January 1900. With somewhat the air of an Olympian so wise he can afford to be tolerant, he gently rebuked those who were disputing about so clear a thing: "There has been a curious misapprehension in the minds of many people, and even in print there has been a good deal of allusion to the year now ending [1899] as the closing one of the nineteenth century."

Having thus, in his capacity of commentator on events, recorded a dispute, which, because it existed, one must take account of, Dr. Shaw proceeded with an air becoming to unassailable authority, an air which seemed to say: "Of course, you understand I'm not arguing with you; I'm merely telling you":

> A half-minute's clear thinking is enough to remove all confusion. With December 31 we complete the year 1899—that is to say, we round out 99 of the 100 years that are necessary to complete a full century. We must give the nineteenth century the 365 days that belong to its hundredth and final year, before we begin the year 1 of the twentieth century. The mathematical faculty works more keenly in monetary affairs than elsewhere; and none of the people who have proposed to allow ninety-nine years to go for a century would suppose that a $1,900 debt have been fully met by a tender of $1,899.

III

Among the more scintillating facets of the surface of life as reflected in the newspapers on January 1, 1900, the *Indianapolis Journal* recorded that "A. P. Hurst, a drygoods salesman from New York, interviewed at the Bates Hotel last night," assured the world that "The shirtwaist will be with us more than ever this summer. Women are wearing shirtwaists because

The shirtwaist vogue of 1900. Three patterns "specially designed" for the Ladies' Home Journal *of May 1899.*

they are comfortable, because they can be made to fit any form, and because they are mannish. Sleeves will be smaller, but still not tight.

"The shirtwaist," the confident Mr. Hurst assured a world too supine in its submission to the dogma that change is a cosmic law, "the shirtwaist has come to stay."

Concerning another institution there was an equally confident assertion of secure optimism as to the present and future state of trade. The advertisement of Budweiser—a name potent and far-flung in those days—took the form of a congratulatory telegram from the manufacturer:

NEW YEAR GREETING. IMPORTANT TELEGRAM
St. Louis, Mo., Dec. 31, 1899.

J. L. Bieler, Indianapolis, Ind.

Prediction of our last year's message pale [*sic*] in the presence of our trade reports for 1899. We have reached the highest point in our history. Our motto "Nothing is too good for the American people" has found prompt and generous response. In return we send with a hearty goodwill our wishes for a Happy New Year.

ADOLPHUS BUSCH, President,
Anheuser-Busch Brewing Association.

Nobody in 1900 could have imagined that it would become necessary twenty-five years later to explain that the reference was to beer, real beer; to Budweiser, a brand name that blazed ornately before Prohibition in the windows of 10,000 saloons and blurred the landscape with its billboards; which was a national institution in much the same sense as baseball, ice cream, or the Ford automobile; which was the subject, during World War I, of a popular song:

Bud Budweiser's a friend of mine, friend of mine; yes, a friend of mine.
What care I if the sun don't shine while I've got Budweiser?
That's the reason I feel so fine, feel so fine; yes, I feel so fine;
For though Bill the Kaiser's a friend of Budweiser's,
Budweiser's a friend of mine.

Liquor in various aspects occupied a good deal of the attention of the newspapers of January 1, 1900. The *Boston Transcript* sedately deplored the city's record of 26,000 drunks in a year, but believed that "an evil sure to exist under any circumstances can better be kept within bounds by restriction than by prohibition." The Raleigh, North Carolina, *News and Observer* reported the sudden death from impure whiskey of "eight prime young negroes"—a phrase recalling slavery. (There were localisms such as that all over the not yet standardized America of 1900.) The *Wichita Beacon* recorded that burglars in Davidson's sa-

ESTABLISHED 1823.

WILSON

Whiskey.

THAT'S ALL!

Liquor advertisements in the newspapers and magazines of 1900 were as common as those of any other business.

loon had robbed the slot machine of $8, but "did not disturb the stocks of liquor"—a discrimination which did not at that time necessarily reflect extreme abstemiousness but which in 1925 would have been inexplicable on any commercial basis. In Utica, New York, a liquor-dealer offered through *The Press*, "rye, bourbon, and Canada malt whiskey, $2 per gallon; strictly pure California wines, 75 cents per gallon." The Portland *Oregonian* reported a New Year's sermon: "The agitation against side entrances to saloons has not attained permanence and the recent organization of liquor-dealers to defeat reform has revealed the saloon in its true light as an institute of vice."

As an antidote to organization and money on the side of the liquor sellers, there was just getting under way an organization on the other side, destined to be the nemesis of the saloon. The Washington, Pennsylvania, *Reporter* carried the announcement that "A meeting is called for Tuesday evening, January 2, 1900, at 7:30 at the First Presbyterian Church, to consider the question of the organization of an Anti-Saloon League."

The *Omaha World-Herald* printed advertisements of "sugar, 4c. lb.; eggs, 14c. a dozen." The Williamsport, Pennsylvania, *Gazette and Bulletin*, "potatoes 35c. to 45c. a bushel, butter 24c. to 25c. a pound." The *Dallas News*, "top hogs $4.15." Wheat was 70 cents a bushel; corn, 33 cents; Texas steers, $4.25 a hundred.* The *Boston Herald:* "Boarders Wanted; turkey

---

*While Texas readers may understand this terminology of the cattle market, it seems wise, for the benefit of the startled New York proofreader who queries the word "hundred," to explain that in this connection it means hundredweight.

dinner, 20 cents; supper or breakfast, 15 cents." In the *Trenton Times*, the United States Hotel quoted rates of "$1 per day; furnished rooms 50 cents—horse sheds for country shoppers." In the Chicago Tribune, Siegel, Cooper & Co. advertised: "Ladies' muslin nightgowns, 19c.; 50-inch all-wool sponged and shrunk French cheviots, water and dust proof serges, all high-class fabrics, warranted for color and wear, 79c." In the same paper The Fair offered "women's shoes, worth $3, for sale at $1.97; misses' and children's shoes, $1.19." In the Decatur, Illinois, *Review* was advertised: "A good well-made corset in long or short style, all sizes; our price, 50 cents." Gingham was 5 cents a yard; men's box-calf shoes $2.50; "Stein-Bloch suits that were $13 to $17, now $10"; men's suits that were $8 to $13, for $5.50. "Ten dollar overcoats for six dollars." In the Los Angeles *Express* an advertisement said: "Wanted, Jan. 8, lady cashier for store; salary $8 a week; name 2 or 3 references."

The *St. Louis Post-Dispatch* received within twenty-four hours 725 answers to an advertisement that had read:

> NIGHT WATCHMAN WANTED—Must be fairly well educated, neat of appearance, able-bodied, and if necessary be ready to furnish bond; none but those who can show absolute proofs of their honesty and sobriety in all senses of the word need apply; hours, 6 to 6, Monday to Friday (off Saturday nights); 1 P.M. Sunday to 6 A.M. Monday; salary $15 per week; state whether married or single and inclose references. Address in own handwriting, H 789, *Post-Dispatch*.

In the *Chicago Tribune* a patent-medicine advertisement proclaimed: "General Joe Wheeler Praises Peruna." Similar testimonials were by three U.S. senators. One, from a senator from Mississippi, read: "For some time I have been a sufferer from catarrh in its most incipient stage. So much so that I became alarmed as to my general health. But hearing of Peruna as a good remedy, I gave it a fair trial, and soon began to improve. I take pleasure in recommending your great catarrh cure. Peruna is the best I have ever tried."

Help Wanted—Female.

GIRLS WANTED, over 14, to label samples, $2.50. The National Cloak Co., 112 W. 24th st.

Help Wanted—Male.

STENOGRAPHER and typewriter for a downtown commercial house; salary about $10 per week; preference given to one who can read and write Spanish. Address, giving age and reference, D. F. C., Export, P. O. box 2301, N. Y.

BOY WANTED to work in saloon & learn bartending. Apply 23 E. 17th st.

HELP WANTED—FEMALE.

Household Help Wanted—Female.
CHAMBERMAID wanted for nurses' training school; to live out; hours 7.30 A .M. to 2.30 P. M.; $40 per month. Apply 1086 Lexington av. (near 76th).

GIRL, white, housework, plain cooking; small Christian family; afternoons and evenings only; sleep out. M 504 World, Harlem.

HELP WANTED—MALE

CLERK, with time-keeping experience, hours 6.30 A. M. to 2.30 P. M.; $110 month; state age, experience; religion. F. 846 World.

A contrast between 1900 and 1925. The advertisements in the left-hand column, offering such wages as $10 a week and less for stenographers, are reproduced from the New York World *of January 4, 1900. Those in the second column appeared in the same paper just twenty-five years later, January 1, 1925.*

In 1900, Tulsa, Oklahoma, was a straggling one-street town. Eleven years before it did not exist. This photograph was taken in 1893.

The *Duluth News-Tribune* advertised a brand of tobacco as "not made by a trust," a form of commendation frequent in trade slogans of that time of antimonopoly sentiment. The West Chester, Pennsylvania, *Local News* reflected the preammonia, preelectric method of storing up coolness for the summer: "Horace Sinclair and William Tanguy are filling their ice-

Tulsa, Oklahoma, in 1924, a city of 110,000. The president of the Exchange National Bank (in the tall building at the left of the photograph) is James J. McGraw. As a boy, Mr. McGraw saw Oklahoma when, in the entire length and breadth of it, there was not one white man. He participated with his family in the first rush of settlers to the Cherokee strip in 1893.

houses to-day with six-inch ice from the Brandywine." A Trenton, New Jersey, store, daringly unconventional, advertised a skirt, specially made for skating, "short enough to avoid entanglement with the skates." The fashion notes of the New Orleans *Item* praised lightweight skirts, "as they can be gathered up in the hand and kept clear of muddy pavements." The *Tacoma News-Tribune* described the preparations of many Tacomans to join the rush to the new Alaska goldfield, at Nome. The *Wichita Beacon* recorded a heated fight between those who wanted the proposed Arkansas River bridge wide enough to carry the streetcar tracks, and those who claimed the streetcars would frighten the horses. In all the advertising pages of the *Baltimore Sun* the word "automobile" did not appear, but there were columns of advertisements for broughams, rockaways, Germantowns, opera wagonettes, phaetons, buggies, runabouts, and tally-hos.

The Tulsa (then Indian Territory, now Oklahoma) *Democrat*, at the time a weekly, had no January 1 issue, but on January 7, 1900, it devoted itself to some self-congratulatory statistics. The population had reached 1,340; President Kurn of the Frisco Railroad was quoted as saying Tulsa had become the biggest point of traffic origin in the Territory; the carload business for the week was given as: "Receipts: 1 car bran; shipments: 2 cars hogs, 1 car sand, 1 car mules." In the world of matters less exclusively commercial, the *Democrat* chronicled the approaching nuptials of Mary, daughter of Chief Frank Corndropper, the ceremony to include a transfer of several hundred ponies to the bride's father by the bridegroom (who must be a full-blood).

IV

In his newspapers of January 1, 1900, the American found no such word as "radio,"* for that was yet twenty years from coming; nor "movie," for that, too, was still mainly of the future; nor "chauffeur," for the automobile was only just emerging and had been called "horseless carriage," when treated seriously, but rather more frequently "devil-wagon," and the driver, the "engineer." There was no such word as "aviator"—all that that word implies was still a part of the Arabian Nights. Nor was there any mention of income tax or surtax, no annual warnings of the approach of March (later April) 15—all that was yet thirteen years from coming. In 1900, doctors had not heard of insulin; science had not heard of relativity or the quantum theory. Farmers had not heard of tractors, nor bankers of the Federal Reserve System. Merchants had not heard of chain stores nor "self-service"; nor seamen of oil-burning engines. Modernism had not been added to the common vocabulary of theology, nor futurist and "cubist" to that of art. Politicians had not heard of direct primaries, nor of the

---

*The number of new words added to the dictionary between 1900 and 1925, and new uses of old words, is a reflection of the expanding intelligence and the increasing complexity of civilization. Nearly 1,000 were used to adjust the radio to the language. Hundreds were required for the automobile, its parts and associations; yet more hundreds for the popular and technical terminology of aviation.

commission form of government, nor of city managers, nor of blocs in Congress, nor of a League of Nations, nor of a World Court. They had not heard of "muckrakers," nor of "Bull Moose" except in a zoological sense. Neither had they heard of "dry" and "wet" as categories important in vote-getting, nor of a Volstead Act; they had not heard of an Eighteenth Amendment, nor a Nineteenth, nor a Seventeenth, nor a Sixteenth—there were but fifteen amendments in 1900, and the last had been passed in 1869.

In 1900, woman suffrage had only made a beginning, in four thinly peopled western states. A woman governor or a woman congressman was a humorous idea, far-fetched, to be sure, yet one out of which a particularly fertile humorist, on the stage or in the papers, could get much whimsical burlesque.

The newspapers of 1900 contained no mention of smoking by women, nor of "bobbing," nor "permanent wave," nor vamp, nor flapper, nor jazz, nor feminism, nor birth control. There was no such word as "rum-runner"; nor "hijacker"; nor "bolshevism," "fundamentalism," "behaviorism," "Nordic," "Freudian," "complexes," "ectoplasm," "brainstorm," "Rotary," "Kiwanis," "blue-sky law," "cafeteria," "automat," "sundae"; nor "mah-jongg"; nor "crossword puzzle." Not even military men had heard of camouflage; neither that nor "propaganda" had come into the vocabulary of the average man. "Over the top," "zero hour," "no-man's land" meant nothing to him. "Drive" meant only an agreeable experience with a horse. The newspapers of 1900 had not yet come to the lavishness of photographic illustration that was to be theirs by the end of the quarter century. There were no rotogravure sections. If there had been, they would not have pictured Boy Scouts, nor state constabularies, nor traffic cops, nor Ku Klux Klan parades; nor women riding astride, nor the nudities of the Follies, nor one-piece bathing suits, nor advertisements of lipsticks, nor motion picture actresses, for there were no such things.

In 1900, "short-haired woman" was a phrase of jibing; women doctors were looked on partly with ridicule, partly with suspicion. Of prohibition and votes for women, the most conspicuous function was to provide material for newspaper jokes. Men who bought and sold lots were still real estate agents, not "realtors." Undertakers were undertakers, not having yet attained the frilled euphemism of "mortician." There were "star-routes" yet—rural free delivery had only just made a faint beginning; the parcel post was yet to wait thirteen years. For the deforestation of the male countenance, the razor of our grandfathers was the exclusive means; men still knew the art of honing. The hairpin, as well as the horseshoe and the buggy, were the bases of established and, so far as anyone could foresee, permanent businesses. Ox teams could still be seen on country roads; horse-drawn streetcars in the cities. Horses or mules for trucks were practically universal; livery stables were everywhere. The blacksmith beneath the spreading chestnut tree was a reality; neither the garage mechanic nor the chestnut blight had come to retire that scene to poetry. The hitching post had not been supplanted by the parking problem. Croquet had not given way to golf. "Boys in blue" had not yet passed into song. Army blue was not merely a sentimental memory, had not succumbed to the invasion of utilitarianism in olive green. G.A.R. were still potent letters.

In 1900, the Grand Army of the Republic was still a numerous body, high in the nation's sentiment, deferred to in politics, their annual national reunions and parades stirring events, and their local posts* important in their communities. Among the older generation the memories and issues of the Civil War still had power to excite feeling, although the Spanish War, with its outpouring of a common national emotion against a foreign foe, had come close to completing the burial of the rancors of the War Between the States. Such terms as "Rebel," "Yank," and "damn Yankee," "Secesh" were still occasionally used, sometimes with a touch of ancient malice. A few politicians, chiefly older ones, still found or thought they found potency in "waving the bloody shirt." Negro suffrage was still a living and, in some quarters, acrimonious issue.

The passing of the questions arising out of the Civil War, and the figures associated with it, as major incidents of politics and life, was one of the most marked of the many respects in which 1900 was a dividing year.

V

In 1900, America presented to the eye the picture of a country that was still mostly frontier of one sort of another, the torn edges of civilizations' first contact with nature, man in his invasion of the primeval. There were some areas that retained the beauty of nature untouched: the Rocky Mountains, parts of the western plains where the railroads had not yet reached, and some bits of New England. There were other spots, comparatively few, chiefly the farming regions of eastern Pennsylvania, New York State, and New England, where beauty had come with the work of man—old farms with solid well-kept barns, many of heavy stone or brick; substantial houses with lawns shaded by evergreen trees that had been growing for more than a generation, fields kept clean to the fence corners—areas that to the eye and spirit gave satisfying suggestions of a settled order, traditions, crystallized ways of life, comfort, serenity, hereditary attachment to the local soil.

Only the eastern seaboard had the appearance of civilization having really established itself and attained permanence. From the Alleghanies to the Pacific Coast, the picture was mainly of a country still frontier and of a people still in flux: the Alleghany mountainsides scarred by the ax, cluttered with the

---

*By 1917, there was but a tottering handful of them left to contribute a pathetic blessing to the ceremonies with which their grandsons, under the name American Expeditionary Force, left to fight in France, grandsons destined to substitute, in the newer generation's experiences, Belleau Wood for Gettysburg, St. Mihiel for Bloody Angle. In April 1918, passing through Peru, Indiana, on a train, I saw what was left of the local G.A.R. post come down to the station to see the local "draftees" off. The veterans, the youngest of whom necessarily were at least seventy, wore their army uniforms, and evidently had been at pains to get together what was left of the fife and drum corps that had played them off to war some fifty years before. Now once more it played "Rally 'Round the Flag, Boys," to old men who could no longer rally. As one watched them saying good-bye to the younger men, one wondered how much the furtive tears in their eyes were for their own long-gone youth, and how much for the fates that might await their grandsons.

Group photograph taken at Omaha Exposition, 1897. The older type of American Indian could still be seen in 1900. Geronimo, seated third from the right, was the last of the fighting Indian leaders.

rubbish of improvident lumbering, blackened with fire; mountain valleys disfigured with ugly coal-breakers, furnaces, and smokestacks; western Pennsylvania and eastern Ohio an eruption of ungainly wooden oil derricks; rivers muddied by the erosion from lands cleared of trees but not yet brought to grass, soiled with the sewage of raw new towns and factories; prairies furrowed with the first breaking of sod. Nineteen hundred was in the flood tide of railroad-building: long fingers of fresh dirt pushing up and down the prairies, steam shovels digging into virgin land, rock-blasting on the mountainsides. On the prairie farms, sod houses were not unusual. Frequently there were no barns, or, if any, mere sheds. Straw was not even stacked but rotted in sodden piles. Villages were just past the early picturesqueness of two long lines of saloons and stores, but not yet arrived at the orderliness of established communities; houses were almost wholly frame, usually of one story, with a false top, and generally of a flimsy construction which suggested transiency; larger towns with a marble Carnegie Library at Second Street, and Indian tepees at Tenth. Even as to most of the cities, including the eastern ones, their outer edges were a kind of frontier, unfinished streets pushing out to the fields; sidewalks, where there were any, either of brick that loosened with the first thaw or wood that rotted quickly; rapid growth leading to rapid change. At the gates of the country, great masses of human raw materials were being dumped from immigrant ships. Slovenly immigrant trains tracked westward. Bands of unattached men, floating labor, moved about from the logging camps of the winter woods to harvest in the fields or to railroad-construction camps. Restless "sooners" wandered hungrily about to grab the last opportunities for free land.

One whole quarter of the country, which had been the seat of its most ornate civilization, the South, though it had spots of melancholy beauty, presented chiefly the impression of weedy ruins thirty-five years after the Civil War, and comparatively few years after Reconstruction—an ironic word.

CHAPTER 2
America in 1900

In 1900, the United States was a nation of just under 76 million people, with dependencies in the West Indies, off the coast of Asia, near the Arctic Ocean, and in the mid-Pacific, all acquired recently, except Alaska. The area of the mainland was 3,026,789 square miles. This expanse of territory reached from 25° north latitude to 49°. Its temperature varied from a winter extreme of 45° below zero in Bismarck, North Dakota, to a summer extreme of 117° in Phoenix, Arizona, its elevation from the 14,501 feet of Mount Whitney to the sea-level savannas of the Gulf Coast; its climate from the four months of immunity from frost that was good for hard wheat in North Dakota, to the practically frostless lands that would raise oranges in Florida and California.

Within this scope of land and climate there was such an abundance and variety of food and other natural resources as made it the most nearly self-sustaining compact nation that then was or ever had been. Within its own borders it reaped every variety of edible grain; raised every kind of vegetable food in common use, except bananas and a few condiments and stimulants, such as cocoa, coffee, tea, and pepper—and even some of these were raised to some extent, and practically all could be raised in any emergency. It produced every kind of meat for common use. From its streams, lakes, and shores it was supplied with nearly every kind of fish or fish product except a few epicurean delicacies, such as caviar from Russia and sardines from the Mediterranean.

Of material for clothing, it had five times as much cotton as all the rest of the world, as much wool as the people desired to raise, and while it imported

BISMARCK, N. DAK.
45° BELOW ZERO

EXTREME TEMPERATURE RANGE
OF THE UNITED STATES

PHOENIX, ARIZ.
117° ABOVE ZERO

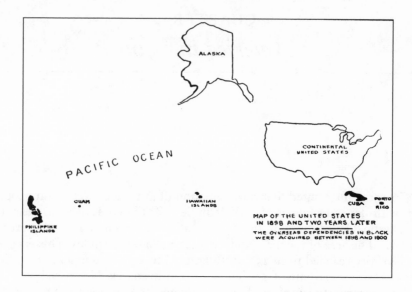

MAP OF THE UNITED STATES
IN 1898 AND TWO YEARS LATER
THE OVERSEAS DEPENDENCIES IN BLACK
WERE ACQUIRED BETWEEN 1898 AND 1900

silk and some linen, it could produce these in any quantity necessary for its own use. Of the raw materials for shelter and for the most exacting and complex needs of modern manufacture of every kind, it had teeming stores. Of woods it had an abundance of all, except a few minor and dispensable ones like mahogany, teak, and balsa. Of minerals it had an abundance of all the more important ones, and also some supplies of tin, manganese, vanadium, and platinum, though it imported most of these. Of vegetable products needed on any large or essential scale for manufacture, it had all except rubber, and it had the soil and climate to produce this if desired.

Not only did this nation have supplies of every kind of natural resource and raw materials abundant for its own use; of most of them, it had stores far greater than those of any other nation; and of many, more than all the rest of the world. Measured by annual output, in 1900, America produced more than half the world's cotton, corn, copper, and oil; more than a third of its steel, pig iron, and silver; and substantially a third of its coal and gold.

Of the physical facts about this country, two had more bearing on its welfare than any others. Externally, it was widely separated from the two old and densely populated continents of the world—from Europe by the Atlantic Ocean, from Asia by the Pacific. Internally, within this nation's whole immensity of territory, there was no boundary, no customs barrier, no variation of currency or fundamental law, no impediment to the free interchange of goods and ideas.

The parts of this country were bound together for the purposes of trade and mutual intercourse by almost 200,000 miles of railroad, more than 200,000 miles of telegraph lines, and more than a million miles of telephone wire in service.

Though some portions of this country were not as well adapted to the propagation of human stock, especially to the preservation of infants in their early years, as some European countries less subject to violent extremes of heat and dryness; yet in this respect the people inhabiting this territory had practiced much ingenuity in the inventing and perfecting of devices for making artificial ice, pasteurizing milk, heating their homes in winter, and otherwise overcoming local handicaps of climate; and also had equipped themselves generously with physicians and nurses, and institutions for training them, and with hospitals; so that on the whole this territory was admirably adapted to the physical well-being of the human stock that inhabited it.

This human stock was of the white (Caucasian) race, except: about 9 million in whole or part of black (Ethiopian) blood, descendants of a strain originally brought to the country as slaves and later set free and made citizens; about 114,000 of Mongolian stock (90,000 Chinese and 24,000 Japanese); and 237,000 who were in whole or part of the aboriginal Indian blood.

A most important fact about the stock of this nation—for which there was no parallel or precedent among great nations, either of its own time or of the past; an aspect that had many advantages, but which came to be regarded during this quarter century as having possible perils in excess of its advantages—was the fact that alone among great nations its stock was not indigenous to the soil, was not homogeneous, had no long common history nor any body of common institutions arising out of its own experiences. Its people had come from other countries, either immediately or through near ancestors, all within a period of less than 300 years, and most within a much shorter period. Also, this people recruited its population as much through additions from overseas as through births in its native stock.

As respects the origins of the white race: in 1900, 41 million were reckoned roughly as "native white stock," meaning descendants of those who had been in America for at least one whole generation. Of this native white stock a large majority derived from the early settlers, who had been chiefly British. Twenty-six million, or 40 percent, of the total whites had come very recently from Europe—either as direct immigrants or the children of immigrants. Of this class of recent increments, about 30 percent were of British stock, 31 percent of German stock, 4 percent Swedish, 4 percent Russian, 4 percent Austrian, 3 percent Italian. At this time, however, and for several years after 1900, immigration from Russia, Poland, and Italy was increasing very rapidly; whereas immigration from northwestern Europe was not. Consequently there was a measurable tendency for the British and other northwest European portions of the stock to decline from their numerical superiority in the composition of this people as a whole.

II

Most of the institutions of this people, their language, their religion, their fundamental laws, their point of view regarding organized society, the relations of the sexes, education, and the like, were derived from the same European countries that were the sources of the people them-selves. To a great extent, their institutions were based on British models. English was the common language, universal and mandatory in legislative proceedings, legal documents, and the like; and practically universal in daily use. Exceptions consisted of a few spots in Pennsylvania, where the language in daily use was "Pennsylvania Dutch," a patois derived from the early German settlers of those communities and modified by contact with the English tongue; some communities in the Southwest, where Spanish was in common use, a heritage from the early Spanish settlers of Mexico; a few spots, like part of the Gulf coast of Louisiana, where a remnant of Aca-dian exiles retained their French tongue after 140 years; a few other locali-ties, chiefly in New England, where more recent immigrants from French Canada retained their French tongue. Some of the late immigrants from Europe continued to use their native tongues in a few settlements: Italian and Yiddish in New York and other cities of the East; German in some communities in the Northwest, as well as Swedish, Finnish, Polish, Greek. Indian tribal languages were in use in a few scattered places.

In jurisprudence the origin was wholly English, except in Louisiana, where the Napoleonic code of the early settlers was retained. The legisla-tive institutions were based wholly on English models.

In education the traditions were prevailingly British, except that in higher university education there had been for some years a disposition to turn to German models and to import German teachers. Of the modern languages taught in high schools and colleges, other than English, there was more of German than of all others combined.

As respects literature, including poetry and the drama, the origins were al-most wholly British. A few Latin and Greek classics were read in high schools and colleges. There was some literature from the French, chiefly nov-els and philosophy, with a few dramas; some from the Germans, mostly philosophical; little from the Spanish, except one or two classics; some from Italy; and the beginnings of a literature transplanted from Russia and the Scandinavian countries.

Classical music was an exception to the prevailingly British origins of this people's culture. The only British contributions that could be regarded as within the category "classic" were the comic operas of Gilbert and Sulli-van. In this field there was a strong infusion from the German, chiefly the operas of Wagner and the instrumental music of Beethoven, Brahms, and some others. There was also a strong infusion from the Italian, consisting of such operas as Verdi's *Il Trovatore, La Traviata,* and *Aïda.* There was some classic music of French origin, some of Russian, and a little of Span-ish. A few experiments had been made, chiefly by Edward MacDowell, to-ward building up a characteristic American music based on Indian strains.

Popular music was largely British in origin, and more from Scotland and Ireland than from England. A considerable number of the melodies in pop-ular use came from Negro sources or were based on Negro themes and the Negro imagination. In this particular year, 1900, there was, in instrumental popular music, a vogue for a type known as "ragtime" and the "cake-walk."

*   *   *

The religious attachments of this people were almost wholly to denominations accepting the doctrine of the divinity of Jesus Christ. The exceptions, which differed utterly from each other and had nothing essential in common except nonacceptance of the divinity of Jesus Christ, were about 1,050,000 Jews, about 75,000 Unitarians, and a few hundred believers in Buddhism or some other Oriental religion. A few Indians still followed their original rites.

Within the Christian religion about 12 million were attached to the Roman Catholic faith; about 700,000 to the Episcopal; a few hundreds to the Greek Catholic. The remainder belonged to one or another evangelical or reformed denomination—about 6 million Methodists, 5 million Baptists, 1.5 million Lutherans, 1.5 million Presbyterians, 350,000 Mormons, 80,000 followers of Christian Science. Except the Mormons and the followers of Christian Science, which sects had originated in America, most of these denominational affiliations had accompanied immigrants to America or been inherited from immigrants. All the immigrant stocks, except the Negro, tended to maintain the religions of the countries from which they came.

III

The distinctive characteristics of the American people, marking them off from some or all other nations, included: a determined faith in the democratic organization of society and the representative form of government; a taboo against kings and aristocracy; separation of church and state; zeal for universal education; an indisposition to maintain a large standing army; and a prevailing and growing trend toward the abolition of alcoholic drinks. There was a freedom—at that time—from much of the regulation by government that was common in many other countries, and a vigilance against encroachment by government on the individual, a trait derived from the comparatively recent experiences of most of these people as voluntary exiles from monarchical and other exacting forms of government.

There was a freedom from stratification into castes, social or industrial, accompanied by the absence from the country's political system of any permanent or important labor or otherwise radical political party. Freedom from stratification also led to sociability, an easy approachableness and informality in human relations, not common in nations having one degree or another of caste.* The people had independence of spirit, accompanied by the concession of equal independence to others—a trait due to exemption from caste, to the nature of the people, most of whom had been pioneers themselves or in their recent ancestors, and to immunity from great anxiety about making a livelihood, an immunity made possible by the natural wealth of the country. Another national trait was a responsiveness to ideal-

*While exemption from caste was characteristic of the white race, it is also true that between whites and blacks there was a greater separation than characterized race relations in most other countries.

ism, greater than was common among older nations where the economic pressure of numbers made unselfishness less easy and where experience had brought disillusionment. The American temperament included adaptiveness, a willingness more prompt than among other peoples to dismiss the old and try the new, a freedom from enthrallment to the familiar, which accounted for much of the rapidity of their progress, especially in machinery.

Some minor distinctive institutions included: the celebration of a national holiday known as Thanksgiving; rocking chairs; a greater fastidiousness about personal cleanliness as measured by the commonness of bathtubs as compared with other countries; ice water, pie, New England boiled dinner, chewing gum; baseball, a game calling for unusually quick reactions intellectually and prompt and easy cooperation muscularly; a diversion called poker, indigenous to this nation and containing definite elements of the interplay of psychology not found in ordinary card games.

IV

Of all the characteristics of this people the most important was freedom of opportunity for the individual, which provided the nation with a constant, rapid, and generous supply of leadership in every line from its own ranks. A national habit of mind, social organization, and education made it as easy for the individual to arrive at leadership from the lowest ranks as for those in the highest ranks to keep it. Certain handicaps, partly legal and partly in the intangible world of social point of view, denied to those already highly placed in wealth or position any great hereditary advantages or rights, or any other security of tenure except what they and their descendants could provide through energy or talent. The same national point of view and practice, together with the great natural wealth of the country and the system of universal free education, made it easy for the talented and the energetic to rise.

William McKinley, president 1897–1901, taken at his desk in the White House. (From a photograph by Underwood & Underwood)

In 1900, the president of the United States, William McKinley, was the son of a country lawyer. The greatest ironmaster, Andrew Carnegie, was the son of a weaver—he had come to the United States as an immigrant and had spent his youth as a telegraph messenger boy. Of the two men who were making the largest contributions to applied science, one, Michael Pupin, had been a shepherd boy in Serbia, had come to America as an immigrant, and worked as a farmhand in Delaware; the other, Thomas A. Edison, had spent his youth as a newsboy and telegraph operator. One of

Mark Twain in front of his boyhood home. Taken on the occasion of his last visit to Hannibal, Missouri, 1902. (From a photograph copyrighted by Tomlinson)

the outstanding geniuses in electricity, Charles P. Steinmetz, had come to America to escape persecution for his socialistic beliefs, and had had difficulty, because of physical defects, in passing the immigration authorities, who feared he might become a public charge. The leading railroad operator, James J. Hill, had begun as a clerk in a village store. The richest man in the country, John D. Rockefeller, had been a clerk in a commission house. One of the leaders of literature, Mark Twain, had got his pen name from his experience as a pilot on a Mississippi River steamboat. A noted journalist, Joseph Pulitzer, had entered America as an immigrant, literally without dry clothes on his back, for he had leaped from a ship in Boston Harbor and swum ashore in order to take advantage, for himself, of the bounty offered to volunteers in the Civil War.

At the same time, this American system provided abundant opportunity for those who had been born in the higher ranks to remain there, if they had the character, talent, and energy to endure the competition. In 1900, the man who was just becoming one of the leaders in public life, Theodore Roosevelt, had been born to wealth and in the social environment of the old Dutch families of New York. The man who in 1900 was entrusted with carrying our institutions to our new imperial possession, the Philippines, and who was later to be president of the United States and chief justice of

William H. Taft in 1900.   *Calvin Coolidge just before 1900.*   *Herbert Hoover in 1900.*

the Supreme Court, William H. Taft, was the son of a man who had been secretary of war and attorney general in cabinets a generation before. The leading educator, Charles W. Eliot, president of Harvard University, had been born in the higher social and business circles of New England. The leading banker, J. Pierpont Morgan, although his power was due to the salience of his personality, had inherited the banking house of which he was head. One of the leading businesses, the du Pont Company, had been in the hands of one family since its foundation, more than 100 years before.

Among those who had not yet emerged in 1900 to leadership but were destined to supply it within the quarter century to follow, who in the opening year of the century were being incubated for leadership through some of the processes which this democracy provided, was Woodrow Wilson, a professor at Princeton who had yet to write his history of the American people. In 1900, Herbert Hoover, then twenty-five years old and five years out of Leland Stanford University, through which he had worked his way, was making in China the beginnings of what was to be, before he was thirty-five, a worldwide reputation as an engineer. And Calvin Coolidge was still an obscure lawyer in a small New England town, making his beginnings in politics in fellowship with a local shoemaker.

CHAPTER 3
Some Contrasts and Changes:
1900 to 1925

On January 10, 1900, America read in its newspapers the accounts, heralded with grandiose headlines, of a speech delivered in the Senate the day before by Albert J. Beveridge of Indiana. Because of the speaker's youth—he was thirty-seven—because of certain qualities that went with his youth, because it was his first speech as a senator, and because of the aggressive policy he advocated, his speech received nationwide attention. Senator Beveridge had just returned from a trip to the scene of the American army operations in the Philippines. His speech dealt with the question of annexing and retaining that distant archipelago, and, broadly, with the whole policy of territorial expansion for America, the leading political issue of the day. Some sentences (selected chiefly from his peroration) read:

> . . . We will not renounce our part in the mission of the race, trustee, under God, of the civilization of the world. . . . Mr. President, self-government and internal development have been the dominant notes of our first century; administration and the development of other lands will be the dominant notes of our second century. . . . He has made us [our race] the master organizers of the world to establish system where chaos reigns. . . . He has made us adepts in government that we may administer government among savage and senile peoples. . . . And of all our race, He has marked the American people as His chosen Nation to finally lead in the regeneration of the world. This is the divine mission of America, and it holds for us all the profit, all the glory, all the happiness possible to man. We are trustees of the world's progress, guardians of its righteous peace. The judgment of the Master is upon us: "Ye have been faithful over a few things; I will make you ruler over many things." What shall history say of us? Shall it say that we renounced that holy trust, left the savage to his base condition, the wilderness to the reign of waste, deserted duty, abandoned glory, forgot our sordid profit even, because we feared our strength and read the charter of our powers with the doubter's eye and the quibbler's mind? Shall it say that, called by events to captain and command

the proudest, ablest, purest race of history in history's noblest work, we declined that great commission? . . . Pray God the time may never come when mammon and the love of ease will so debase our blood that we will fear to shed it for the flag and its imperial destiny.

The tone of Beveridge's speech was in the spirit of the times. It was a day of expansion and expansiveness: Great Britain pushing into Africa from north and south; France contesting Great Britain's advance at Fashoda and elsewhere; Russia pressing down into China; even Italy looking to get a foothold in Africa; Belgium beginning to exploit the Congo; Germany picking up unconsidered trifles everywhere. It was a day also of young men: Cecil Rhodes, Kitchener of Khartoum. Just a few months before, Kipling had given out his poem about taking up the White Man's Burden. So much was America infected by ideas about far-flung lines of empire that even the gentle, amiable William Allen White added a high-pitched note to the chorus about Anglo-Saxon "manifest destiny." On March 20, 1899, he wrote in the Emporia *Gazette:* "Only Anglo-Saxons can govern themselves. The Cubans will need a despotic government for many years to restrain anarchy until Cuba is filled with Yankees. Uncle Sam the First will have to govern Cuba as Alphonso the Thirteenth governed it. . . . It is the Anglo-Saxon's manifest destiny to go forth as a world conqueror. He will take possession of the islands of the sea. . . . This is what fate holds for the chosen people. It is so written. . . . It is to be."

The American people listened to Senator Beveridge's speech (it was a keynote of the Republican administration's policy and platform) and to

An antiexpansion cartoonist protests against Uncle Sam's following the counsels of Senator Beveridge. (From the Brooklyn Daily Eagle, *January 1900)*

Raising the flag over Santiago. Drawn by F. C. Yohn from photographs and sketches made during the ceremony. Showing the squadron of Second U.S. Cavalry and Ninth U.S. Infantry and the group of general officers and their staffs.

American officers in the Philippines in 1900. The tall man at the extreme left of the second line is Major, later General, John J. Pershing. (Courtesy of U.S. Signal Corps)

General Wood and other officials at the review of the Street Cleaning Department on the Alameda.

other similar speeches as part of what guidance they could get in a new relation to the world that had been thrust on them unexpectedly by the Spanish-
American War. They set up the policies involved in that new relation as a
political issue in the presidential campaign of 1900, under the name "expansion," as it was called by the Republicans, who favored it, or "imperialism"
and "militarism," as it was called by the Democrats, who opposed it. They
debated it, and heard it debated. They decided, apparently, in favor of expansion by electing the Republican ticket, William McKinley and
Theodore Roosevelt, over William Jennings Bryan and Adlai Stevenson, and
proceeded to the business of making adjustments with their new possessions
and with the world in a manner that seemed at the time to constitute the kind
of answer Senator Beveridge's rhetorical questions pleaded for.

During 1900, the United States: maintained in the Philippines an army
of 60,000 officers and men, employed in putting down a rebellion led by
Emilio Aguinaldo, and at the same time sent there William H. Taft and
four others as a commission to set up civil government; maintained in
Cuba a temporary governor-general in the person of General Leonard
Wood, and began the work of fixing the permanent relations of that island
with the United States; devised a form of civil government for Puerto Rico,
and otherwise cleaned up the debris of the Spanish-American War. The
United States also brought 1,280 Cuban schoolteachers to Boston to study
at Harvard University; abolished polygamy in the Island of Guam; ordered

the Sultan of Sulu to liberate his slaves; adopted a territorial form of government for Hawaii; ratified the annexation of the Island of Tutuila in the Samoas; carried on negotiations for the purchase of the Danish West Indies; made inquiries looking to the purchase of the Galapagos Islands; negotiated with

Uncle Sam: "By gum, I rather like your looks." (From the Rocky Mountain News, *Denver, 1900)*

England, France, Germany, Italy, Russia, and Japan for the open-door policy in China, and secured adoption of it; sent 2,400 troops to China to participate with the troops of European nations and Japan in the suppression of the Boxer Rebellion; negotiated the Hay-Pauncefote Treaty looking to the construction of an isthmian canal by the United States; entered into trade treaties with Germany and Italy; entertained President McKinley's recommendation that Congress take "immediate action on the promotion of American shipping and foreign trade"; sent 5,000 tons of corn to relieve a famine in India; sent more exhibits to the Paris Exposition than any other nation; and won sixteen out of the twenty-one contests in the international athletic (Olympic) games at Paris.

All this America did in the year 1900. These events having to do with America's relation to the world, and especially the ones having to do with expansion, with the new possessions that came to us as a result of the Spanish War, constituted the most important activity of the United States in that year. Reading them in the impressiveness of their aggregate, or witnessing them at the time, one might have assumed that they marked a new departure in American history. And from the standpoint of the past, they did. But so far as one might have inferred something about the future, so far as one might have assumed—as many in 1900 did—that this striking coincidence of many activities in the field of foreign relations was an augury of further expansion overseas, and that we were about to add ourselves to history's long procession of empires—so far as that was assumed, the forecast was not borne out. It so happened that these various annexations, in all of which important steps were taken in 1900, were the only annexations of land off our own continent that America had ever made, excepting only the four diminutive islands of Samoa, and distant Guam, all taken two years before, in 1898; and none were made thereafter. We completed later the purchase of the Danish West Indies, and we completed the steps for the ownership of the Panama Canal Zone, but we never made another annexation.

The entire history of American overseas expansion is compressed practically within the year 1900 and the two years preceding. We took the path of

The expansion rooster. Cartoon of America during the period of its expansion ambition, 1900. (From the San Francisco Chronicle)

Senator Beveridge's "imperial destiny" far enough to complete the commitments we had become involved in, as unanticipated and rather disturbing incidents of a war we had begun only to rescue the Cuban people from the cruelties of Spanish rule. Then we stopped. For the change of emotion we went through, the cooling down from a hectic and rather artificially stimulated ardor, there is no phrase that conveys the picture quite so precisely as: We concluded to forget it. The American people, after about 1902, not only had a distinct disinclination for further expansion but were inclined to regard the annexations we had already made as embarrassing liabilities. By 1919, so great was our disinclination for responsibilities that when they were strongly urged upon us by other nations in the form of "mandates" over some of the former German dependencies, we rejected them with an emphasis that was clear evidence of an overwhelming and definitely crystallized public opinion in favor of America remaining at home.

II

The change in the relation of America as a nation to the rest of the world was only one of the undreamed changes that came to the United States and its people during the period 1900 to 1925. The elevation of America internationally was important, but it entered less into the daily life of the average man than some other advances during the same period—advances that came not through political leaders, nor wars, nor the other agencies that constitute the materials of most histories, but from men of science and practical industry.

The World War, and all that accompanied it and resulted from it, was not the most important thing that happened during this period, except as respects international relations. Undoubtedly, the war was a supreme adventure to the millions who went to fight, and had a profound influence on the other millions who remained at home. But even measured by the yardstick of human life, the losses occasioned by the war were far outbalanced by the salvaging of life effected by new discoveries of medical science and the application of new principles in sanitation. Due chiefly to medical progress between 1900 and 1925, man was enriched in the thing he prizes most—his security of tenure on life, his defense against disease and death. The average age of the people who died in 1900 was forty-nine, of those who died in 1925, fifty-five. A dozen Great Wars could not counteract the beneficence of this progress. The Great War thrust upon us world leadership, economic, financial, and, to the extent that we accepted it, political; but this elevation had little concrete effect on the life of the individual, compared with the blessings showered on him by medical science.

At the beginning of 1900, it had not yet been proved that yellow fever was transmitted by a mosquito, typhus by a louse, bubonic plague by a flea. William Crawford Gorgas had not yet demonstrated that mosquitoes may be eliminated from any portion of the earth's surface and man's only weapon against malaria was quinine. Neither these facts nor the fundamental fact underlying them was known, and these plagues were as uncontrollable, except by the expedient of isolation, as they had been since the beginning of history. It was not known that typhoid and cholera come from germs in unclean water and milk; these diseases were still the scourges they always had been. Insulin for diabetes, vaccination against typhoid, emetin for dysentery, adrenaline—all were still unknown. Antitoxin for diphtheria and the X-ray were only just coming into use. Paul Ehrlich had not yet made those 606 patient experiments that resulted in the remedy for syphilis. Radium had not yet been used in the treatment of cancer. All these and many other advances in medicine, surgery, and sanitation came between 1900 and 1925. They effected a six years' postponement of death, and that was but one enrichment among many.

Man was enriched in the outward reach of his senses. It is true by 1900 the telephone had been developed to a point where one man could talk to another over 1,400 miles of space, from New York to Omaha. That was already a marvel. But in 1900, men still under middle age could remember the time when the farthest distance one man could throw his voice was limited to what a good pair of lungs could do in a favoring wind, hands cupped megaphonelike, and "a whoop or a holler." In 1921, when President Harding delivered his speech at the burial of the unknown soldier, the distance his voice could carry was multiplied by the De Forest tube 3,000,000,000,000,000,000,000,000,000 times; by 1925, the radio made the human voice audible halfway around the world.

Man was similarly enriched in the outward reach of his sight, or in the number of things that were brought within his vision, and the facility with which they were brought by increases in the capacity of the telescope, through which more of the universe was brought within his understanding; by increased power of the microscope, through which man's knowledge of the minute forms of life was multiplied; by the perfection of the motion picture and its use in education and entertainment.

Man was enriched in the quantity of power brought to his service and by the lowered cost of this power, brought about partly by increased production and partly by the growing efficiency of the engines devised for converting coal, gas, petroleum, and waterfalls into power. One advance alone, the perfection and widespread application of the internal-combustion engine, which is the outstanding single achievement of this quarter century in the field of mechanical advance, added to the service of man not less than half a billion horsepower. In 1900, the average American farmer had, as the only supplement to his own muscles, the power of two or three horses to carry on his work. By 1925, practically every progressive farmer had an automobile of at least 20 horsepower. Many had tractors of between 20 and 50 horsepower, stationary gas engines of from 2 to 10 horsepower, and electrical connection with nearby generating plants which put at their command practically unlimited power. By the harnessing of rivers for the development of electrical power, by immense increases in the size of the units of steam and electricity man could now manufacture and control, the quantity of power brought to his service was multiplied enormously. In 1900, there was but one generating station exceeding 5,000 horsepower; in 1925, there were more than fifty stations exceeding 100,000 horsepower. In the total electric power produced in the country, the growth was from an aggregate of 3,343 million horsepower hours in 1902 to 74,576 million horsepower hours in 1923, a twentyfold increase.

Man was enriched in his knowledge of the universe. In one field of pure science, understanding the nature of matter, the advances made between 1900 and 1925 were greater than the sum of all the advances made in all time before.

Man was enriched in his leisure. In 1900, the Saturday half-holiday was practically unknown, and the ten-hour working day for six days a week was still common. It was in 1901 that the federal government gave sanction to the eight-hour day by decreeing it for work on government contracts. In 1900, golf was a diversion for the rich, somewhat under disapproval as being effete. A winter trip to Florida or California was yet more exclusively a rare prerogative of the well-to-do. Even the two-week summer holiday had barely begun to get under way.

Man was enriched—fabulously enriched—in his access to material goods—comforts, conveniences, luxuries. In 1900, the automobile was a dubious novelty. There were in all less than 8,000 in the United States; by 1925, there were more than 17 million. In 1900, there were less than 10 miles of concrete road; by 1925, more than 20,000. In 1900, there was but one telephone for every 66 people; by 1925 it was of practically universal access, with one for every 7 people. In 1900, it was recorded that the number of silk stockings sold in the United States was 12,572 dozen pairs, one pair for one out of every 2,000 of the population; in 1921, the number of pairs of silk or artificial silk was 18,088,841—one for every 6 of the people—an increase of access to luxury which, expressed in percentages, almost invades higher mathematics—and destroyed the ancient significance of "a silk stocking."

Man was enriched in his knowledge of the surface of the earth. During this period both the North Pole and the South Pole were reached. By 1925, there remained no considerable portion of the earth's surface that had not been explored. By the airplane, man achieved his age-long ambition to fly; by the submarine, he achieved the capacity to remain under water and direct his movements there at will. By the wireless, he was enriched in his safety on the sea.

In 1900, the great Texas oil fields were still undiscovered. Radium, helium, the use of vanadium in steel, argon gas, electrolytic waterproofing, high-speed tool steel, the long-distance transmission of photographs were undiscovered or undeveloped. The Marconi wireless was unperfected. The "loading coil" for long-distance telephoning, the multiplex telephone, the vacuum-tube amplifier were unknown. The tungsten electric light was not yet made. In 1900, there were no oil-burning locomotives, no flotation process for recovering copper, no vacuum cleaners, no self-starter, no electric cook-stoves or electric irons, no fireless cookers, no disk phonographs.

(This section has dealt only with the material enrichment of man. Whether he was also spiritually enriched, what use man made of his increased years upon the earth, his increased leisure, the energies released by machinery from the need of getting a livelihood—the whole question of the spiritual experiences of man during this period is one about which it is not possible to speak so broadly or so confidently.)

III

The years 1900 to 1925 included the greater part of the activities of Bryan, almost all the national career of Roosevelt, and all the public life of Wilson. It comprised the whole of the stirring history of the birth, growth, and death of the Progressive Party. It covered practically all the national career of William H. Taft, and all that of Warren G. Harding, who, when the quarter century began, was an obscure editor in a little Ohio town. These were the years of the principal activities of Robert M. La Follette and Henry Cabot Lodge; they included the periods of two picturesque speakers of the House of Representatives, Joseph G. Cannon and Champ Clark. Elihu Root, Charles Evans Hughes, and Philander Chase Knox all made the beginnings of their national careers after 1900. This period saw the apotheosis of the political boss in Senators Mark Hanna (who first defined Republican policy as "stand pat"), Matthew S. Quay, Arthur Pue Gorman, Thomas C. Platt, and Nelson W. Aldrich—and the passing of that type with the death, at midnight of the closing day of 1922, of Senator Boies Penrose, high-stand graduate, first of Harvard College and later of Pennsylvania politics, who in the first edition of Bryce's *American Commonwealth* was mentioned as an eminent leader of municipal reform, and in the second edition was discreetly unmentioned.

Into some or all of the years of this quarter century overlapped several whose early achievements became so familiar that by 1925 they already seemed almost legendary: Thomas Edison, whose early invention gave promise to his own phrase, "press the button"; Alexander Graham Bell, inventor of the telephone; Collis P. Huntington, the transcontinental railroad-builder, whose epitaph was that he had reduced the breadth of the American continent from six weeks to six days; John D. Rockefeller; Mary Baker Eddy, one of the two Americans who have founded considerable religions.

The year 1900 saw Dr. Walter Reed's determination of the cause of yellow fever, and Dr. William Gorgas's discovery and practice of the means of exterminating it—by 1925, these two pioneers of science and sanitation had already reached whatever is science's equivalent of canonization. Theirs were only two of the many advances in medical science which made that field one as to which, indisputably, this could be said to be the golden age.

The years 1900 to 1925 included the riper years of J. Pierpont Morgan, and the complete history, so far, of the most striking of his promotions, the United States Steel Corporation, the largest unit of organized business in the world. It included practically all the publicly noticed career of Edward H. Harriman, who, because of the greater public attention focused on his financial operations, and because of his failure to see the light of a new day in the relations between capital and politics, was called, inadequately, a mere manipulator; he was also one of the ablest practical railroad men of his generation, an outstanding example of rich constructive imagination coupled with the capacity for execution on as large a scale as human minds often comprehend.

Other characters were in the crowded and varied gallery of 1900 to 1925: Samuel Gompers, whose lifetime coincided with the whole history of successful labor organization in America; James J. Hill, Admiral George Dewey, Admiral Robert E. Peary, Carry A. Nation, Ben Tillman, Billy Sunday. But one may fall back on the words in which Saint Paul, similarly pressed, took refuge when he found himself unable to complete, fully, the "roll-call of the worthies," and of some not so worthy: "For the time would fail me to tell of Gideon, and of Barak, and of Samson, and of Jephthah; of David also and of Samuel, and of the prophets: . . . Wherefore seeing we also are compassed about with so great a cloud of witnesses, let us lay aside every weight . . . and let us run with patience the race that is set before us."

And, finally, in the way that play producers sometimes put the name of the principal actor in the emphasis of heavy type at the end of the list of dramatis personae, let us recall that character who is often ignored but never should be, the average American, who in this narrative plays the principal role. Professor William G. Sumner of Yale once published a lecture about the average American, entitled "The Forgotten Man," which, in spite of some high-pitched overstatement, has become a familiar passage, in a sense a classic, in American political economy:

> Wealth comes only from production, and all that the wrangling grabbers, loafers, and robbers get to deal with comes from somebody's toil and sacrifice. Who, then, is he who provides it all? Go and find him, and you will have once more before you the Forgotten

Man. You will find him hard at work because he has a great many to support. Nature has done a great deal for him in giving him a fertile soil and an excellent climate, and he wonders why it is that, after all, his scale of comfort is so moderate. He has to get out of the soil enough to pay all his taxes, and that means the cost of all the jobs and the fund for all the plunder. The Forgotten Man is delving away in patient industry, supporting his family, paying his taxes, casting his vote, supporting the church and school, reading his newspaper, and cheering for the politician of his admiration, but he is the only one for whom there is no provision in the great scramble and the big divide. Such is the Forgotten Man. He works, he votes, generally he prays—but he always pays—yes, above all, he pays.

This forgotten man, the principal character in this narrative, had come, just preceding the period of this history, to think he was being forgotten entirely too much, and arrived at a resolution destined, with other factors, to carry him far. The enrichment that subsequently came to him was less dependent on politics than on some other forces, but that purpose of the average man to make himself heard was part of a mood which determined much of the political and social history of this quarter century; a mood in which the average American thought of himself as the underdog in a political and economic controversy, in which he was determined to fight for himself, but also felt the need of a big brother with a stick.

CHAPTER 4

1900: *Looking Backward and Looking Forward*

In 1900 and 1901, in the flood of newspaper and periodical literature evoked by the ending of one century and the beginning of another, there was much pointing with pride, much looking back a hundred years to the beginning of the preceding century, to 1800, to find data upon which could be set a glorified contrast. Most of these contrasts emphasized material achievements.

There were compilations showing the advances in population, area, machinery, industry, invention, and finance; reviews of the extension of the western boundary of settlement from the Appalachian Range to the Pacific Ocean; and of the number of states from fifteen to forty-five. There was much recalling of the time when Ohio, Indiana, Illinois, Michigan, and Wisconsin had been largely a wilderness unpeopled except by Indians and a few frontier settlements. There were grandiose recitals of the growth from the time when Philadelphia had been the largest city in America, with 66,000 people; New York second, with 60,000; Baltimore third, with 26,500; Boston fourth, with 25,000; and Charleston, South Carolina, fifth, with 19,000—and Chicago had not existed. There were detailed descriptions of the advances from the time when there had been no railroads, no telegraph, no telephone, no steamboat, no streetcar, no electricity, no kerosene, no mower or reaper; when it had taken two days to go from New York to Philadelphia; when cooking-stoves, carpets, and window glass had been luxuries.

Some of those who, in 1900 and 1901, wrote of the changes during the century then closing, included in their reflections aspects of American life other than material. The Reverend Newell Dwight Hillis spoke of the century just passed as "one of the most fascinating chapters in the story of man's upward progress," because "for the first time government, invention, art, industry, and religion have served all the people rather than the patrician classes. . . . Now, fortunately, the millions join in the upward march."

This same note, the elevation of the common man, appeared in most of the discriminating discussions of what had been accomplished. The *Indianapolis Journal* for January 7, 1900, said: "No single feature of nineteenth-century progress has been more remarkable or more significant of advancing civilization than the improvement in the condition of the working classes"; and called attention to the fact that 100 years before, "slavery existed in the whole of South America, all of the West Indies, and most of North America."

People generally, reviewing the century then just passed, were quite self-congratulatory, even self-laudatory. "Laws," recited Dr. Hillis, "are becoming more just, rulers humane; music is becoming sweeter and books wiser; homes are happier, and the individual heart becoming at once more just and more gentle. . . . For to-day, art, industry, invention, literature, learning, and government—all these are captives marching in Christ's triumphant procession up the hill of fame."

The writers who pointed out these contrasts for the delectation of the reader of 1900 had the air of regarding the country as having done marvelously, and not a little the manner of one who thinks not much else needs to be done.

II

Even more than recounting the marvels of the 100 years just ended, there was an outflow of predictions about the future. The newspapers and periodicals solicited it from persons whose eminence in various lines seemed to qualify them for visualizing the coming years. Inasmuch as it was chiefly persons of fairly luxuriant imagination who would be either inclined or qualified to forecast the future, the results were usually grandiose. Occasionally, however, the invitations to prophesy reached persons whose temperament led them to believe the world had done very well up to date, and that change was inadvisable and therefore improbable. One of these, dealing with transportation and communication, wrote confidently: "Within the memory of this generation, the earth has been girdled with iron and steel, and the electric telegraph and the cable have practically annihilated terrestrial space; these modes of communication have come to stay, and they are ultimate."

Another of those whose temperaments enabled them to speak with confident definiteness about finality, wrote in the *Literary Digest:* "The ordinary 'horseless carriage' is at present a luxury for the wealthy; and altho* its price will probably fall in the future, it will never, of course, come into as common use as the bicycle." In this same field, the future trend of automobile development, an advertisement for the Mobile Company of America, in the *Cosmopolitan Magazine,* declared with axiomatic confidence that "it may be laid down as a fact that the operation of a gasoline machine requires the employment of an expert of high intelligence and thorough training. . . . The steam machine represents a power that is absolutely understood, and its reliability known beyond all question."

There were even men of preeminent and unassailable position in sci-

---

*This is the way the word was spelled. The *Literary Digest* was one of the very few organs of the English language that had consented to use that language in the manner devised by Andrew Carnegie's project for "simplified spelling."

Life, *in June 1901, looked forward nine years and published this prophetic picture with the caption: "An intruder on the Speedway in 1910."*

ence, whose temperament, or whose preoccupation with exactness, whose distrust of imagination, led them into skepticism about mechanical advances, and caused them to fix limits for the creative genius of man. Simon Newcomb, the astronomer, head of the Nautical Almanac Office of the U.S. Naval Observatory at Washington, wrote:

> The example of the bird does not prove that man can fly. . . . There are many problems which have fascinated mankind since civilization began, which we have made little or no advance in solving. . . . May not our mechanicians . . . be ultimately forced to admit that aerial flight is one of that great class of problems with which man can never cope, and give up all attempts to grapple with it? . . . Imagine the proud possessor of the aeroplane darting through the air at a speed of several hundred feet per second! It is the speed alone that sustains him. How is he ever going to stop? . . . The construction of an aerial vehicle which could carry even a single man from place to place at pleasure requires the discovery of some new metal or some new force. Even with such a discovery we could not expect one to do more than carry its owner.

Passing of the horse. An unusual example of accurate forecasting by a prophetic cartoonist, Homer Davenport. Published in the New York Journal *in 1899, when hardly anyone believed that the horse would really be supplanted.*

A scientist who ventured to be more imaginative than Dr. Newcomb was chided for his rashness. Dr. S. P. Langley, secretary of the Smithsonian Institution at Washington, had conducted some experiments looking toward aviation—they now rank as a milestone in that art—and had said that his experiments convinced him that "the great universal highway overhead is now soon to be opened," and that "airplanes may be built . . . to travel at speeds higher than any with which we are familiar."

Whereupon the *Popular Science Monthly* observed:

> Doctor Langley seems to claim too much. . . . The secretary of the Smithsonian Institution should be the representative of American science and should be extremely careful not to do anything that may lend itself to an interpretation that will bring injury on the scientific work of the government or of the country. . . . He could have placed his scientific knowledge at the disposal of army officers and expert mechanicians, and this would have been better than to attempt to become an inventor in a field where success is doubtful

and where failure is likely to bring discredit, however undeserved, on scientific work.

The prophecy of limitation was much less in quantity, however, than the prophecy of expansiveness. Within the field of transportation, much of the forecasting dealt with subways for cities, a kind of prophecy that did not call for much boldness, because it was in 1900 that the earliest projects for underground transportation in New York began to take form. The builder of the first, John B. MacDonald, wrote that "surface travel will be an oddity [in New York] twenty years from now"; and William Baldwin, president of the Long Island Railroad, predicted that "Philadelphia will be a suburb of New York in twenty years." Charles M. Skinner wrote:

> . . . much of local travel in the future will be over elevated roads—not in the public streets, where they have no place, but through yards, where they have bought a right of way—and through tunnels. Economy of facilities suggests the tunnel. . . . With good roads, and with trolley-cars to carry one to the shop, the prayer-meeting, the library, the school, the sewing-circle, the village improvement society, country industries will be made easier, touch with the markets more rapid, amusements more generous, and life will be broader, freer, more diverse.

Thomas A. Edison, in an interview in the *New York Times*, was quoted as saying: "Next year I will wager I can take a car of my own design fitted with my motor and battery, and go to Chicago and return in less time, and with more pleasure, than any other machine in existence. There will be no breakdown, no explosion of gas or gasoline, and the trip will be made at an even twenty-five miles an hour."

The *Providence Journal* said: "The day is coming when practically every household will have a telephone, just as it has other modern facilities. This may seem a broad statement, but no one can read the figures of the last few years without seeing how general the use of the instrument is getting to be."

A prophecy that included two rather extraordinary details came from an odd figure at the time, John Jacob Astor, one of the three or four richest men in America, who combined with his custody of the largest amount of New York City real estate under one ownership, a really earnest, if occasionally naive, preoccupation with some forms of art and science. Mr. Astor wrote that

> as zoology shows us the amphibian metamorphosed into the land vertebrate, followed by the bird, so history reveals the aborigine's dugout, the Fifth Avenue omnibus, and the ox-cart, followed by the automobile, which is preparing the light and powerful engine that will soon propel the flying-machine. This will be a happy dawn for earth-dwellers, for war will become so destructive that it will probably bring its own end; and the human caterpillar, already mechani-

cally converted into the grasshopper, will become a fairly beautiful butterfly. Street pavements will, of course, be smooth and easily cleaned—asphalt, bituminous macadam, or sheet steel; and keeping horses in large cities will doubtless be prohibited by the Board of Health, as stabling cows, pigs, or sheep is now. Second-story sidewalks, composed largely of translucent glass, leaving all the present street level to vehicles, are already badly needed, . . . and will doubtless have made their appearance in less than twenty years.

There was widely read in America, and rather more sympathetically in America than in his own country, the really remarkable *Anticipations* of H. G. Wells. He exhorted his countrymen to "strip from their eyes the most blinding of all influences, acquiescence in the familiar." He was zealously interested in the "numerous experimental motors to-day." About these new vehicles the least pretentious of his predictions was that "their exasperating trail of stench will soon be fined away." He asked his skeptical readers to take his word for it that there would soon be "a light, powerful engine, smooth-running, not obnoxious to sensitive nostrils, and altogether suitable for high-road traffic. . . . It will be capable of a day's journey of 300 miles or more." As for the airplane, Wells believed it would come, but said: "I do not think it at all probable that aeronautics will ever come into play as a serious modification of transport and communication."

Even Wells, however, balked at the submarine: "I must confess that my imagination, in spite even of spurring, refuses to see any sort of submarine doing anything but suffocate its crew and founder at sea."

Aside from mechanics, within the field of social organization and control, one of the most striking of Wells's anticipations included an attitude toward persons afflicted with a craving for strong drink, markedly different from the attitude of those residents of the United States who, after the passage of the Eighteenth Amendment in 1918, felt that deprivation of access to the means of intoxication was the denial of a fundamental human right. Wells foresaw a New Republic, whose people

> will hold, I anticipate, that a certain portion of the population—the small minority, for example, afflicted with indisputably transmissible diseases, with transmissible mental disorders, with such hideous incurable habits of mind as the craving for intoxication—exists only on sufferance, out of pity and patience, and on the understanding that they do not propagate; and I do not foresee any reason to suppose that they will hesitate to kill when that sufferance is abused. And I imagine also the plea and proof that a grave criminal is also insane will be regarded by them, not as a reason for mercy, but as an added reason for death.

Dr. Albert Shaw predicted in the *Review of Reviews* that "the twentieth century in future ages will be famous for the expanded and altered nature of international relations. It is not improbable that, when the events of the twentieth century fall into their true places in the perspectives of history, the work of the Hague Peace Conference will appear as the crowning achievement of the period and its best legacy to its successor." Andrew Carnegie was even more definite. He was hopeful "that ere the twentieth century closes, the earth will be purged of its foulest shame, the killing by men in battle under the name of war."

There were not wanting the prophets of pessimism. The year 1900 was about the beginning of the importation of various literary missionaries from Russia, one of whom said:

> One fears for the future of mankind. The most ominous sign is not the fact that the cook, servant-girl, and lackey want the same pleasures which not long ago were the monopoly of the rich alone; but the fact that all, all without exception, rich and idle as well as poor and industrious, seek and demand daily amusements, gaiety, excitement, and keen impressions—demand it all as something without which life is impossible, which may not be denied them.

The *New York World* gathered together a kind of symposuistic town meeting of the prophets of evil by inviting them to say what they believed to be the greatest menace of the new century. William Jennings Bryan said: "The increasing influence of wealth will lead to increasing disregard of the inalienable rights of man." President Schurman of Cornell feared most the "exaltation, worship, and pursuit of money as the foremost good of life." Samuel Gompers was concerned about Oriental competition against American labor. Dean Farrar declared "the chief social danger is the dominance of drink." President Hadley of Yale thought it was "legislation based on the self-interest of individuals, or classes, instead of on public sentiment and public spirit." Ellen Terry, the growing artificiality of our social life. The Bishop of Gloucester, "self-advertising vanity." Sir Arthur Conan Doyle said "an ill-balanced, excitable, and sensation-mongering press." Max Beerbohm expressed the same apprehension in two words: "jumpy journals."

One man, the Archbishop of Canterbury, when asked what was the chief danger threatening the coming century, replied: "I have not the slightest idea."

CHAPTER 5
More Contrasts and Changes: 1900 to 1925

O f all changes, the most momentous to a country are, obviously, any that take place in the physical composition of the people. There were such changes in America: first, in a direction different from the past; and then, toward the end of the period, back to the old direction. The changes were slight, in proportion to the population as a whole, but at the time they were arrested they had a rapid momentum.

Always up to 1900 the largest strain by far in the ethnic composition of the American people had been that from northern and western Europe: from Great Britain, Germany, the Scandinavian countries. But in 1900, and for about twenty years preceding, the additions to the American stock from this strain, by immigration, were falling off. At the same time, immigrants from the south and east of Europe, from Latin and Slavic countries, had begun to come in rapidly increasing numbers.

This tendency toward a change in the fundamental composition of the American stock was stopped by an act of Congress in 1921, followed by another in 1924. By that time the country had become uneasy, partly over the increase in immigration as a whole, and partly over the excessive proportion that was coming from sources different from the earlier sources of immigrants. These acts of Congress reflected a mood of doubt that came to the American people about the desirability of being "the melting pot."* The act of 1924 limited the number of immigrants that could legally be admitted to 164,677 (as compared with 1,197,892

1900 $567,241,000
1923 $3,847,046,000
TAXES LAID BY NATIONAL GOVERNMENT

1900 $40,160,000
1922 $1,055,088,000
INTEREST ON PUBLIC DEBT

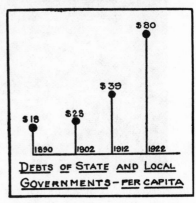

$80
$39
$18 $23
1890   1902   1912   1922
DEBTS OF STATE AND LOCAL
GOVERNMENTS – PER CAPITA

---

*"The melting pot" was a phrase used by Israel Zangwill to describe America as it was about 1900. At the time, the implications of sentiment and altruism in the phrase rather pleased America.

who had come during the last year of normal, unrestricted immigration).
Within this total the number permitted to come from each country was 2
percent of the natives of that country already in America in 1890. The aim
was to keep the proportions of the different strains in America the same in
the future as they had been in the past. This decision, made by the American people and put into effect through Congress, to exercise a deliberate
control over the additions to their stock, to keep those additions in confor-

*Fifth Avenue in New York City as it was in 1900 and as it was in 1924. Examination will
reveal one automobile among the horse-drawn vehicles of 1900, and one horse-drawn vehicle among the automobiles of 1924. Nothing in history is comparable to this rapid change in
transportation. (Courtesy of the U.S. Bureau of Public Roads)*

1900   *1925*
Evolution in bathing costumes. The illustration on the left is from Vogue, *June 21, 1900.*

mity to the proportions already here, to maintain the degree of homogeneity already existing—this decision, because it went to the roots of the composition of the people, may reasonably be called the most far-reaching change that occurred in America during the course of this quarter century.

II

Of changes on the outward surface of American life, one of the most marked was in women's dress and adornment. Just before 1900, in the decade of the nineties, the vogue of the bicycle had begun a revolutionary innovation, which, after 1900, was carried farther by a greater participation in athletics by women in colleges, by increased employment of women in business, and by certain curious consequences of the war.

The judgment of the authorities on this subject who have been consulted by the writer agrees with common recollection, that the bicycle started the revolution. In the late eighties and early nineties, when the high wheel was supplanted by the "safety," women began timorously to ride. Previous to that, almost the only sport freely permitted to women by old-fashioned convention had been croquet. Women had ridden horseback, but only on sedate side-saddles and in a costume, the "riding habit," in which the amount of covering and cloth was even greater than in the long trains of ordinary dress.

Manufacturers began to adapt a safety bicycle for women using nets to protect skirts from becoming tangled in the whirling wire spokes. Gradually and daringly a few women began to wear shorter skirts, weighting the hems down with little strips of lead.

The next insurgency against the stiff-laced conventionality of the Victo-

1900   1925   1900   1925

1900   1925

Upper row, from left to right, the illustrations are from Vogue, *February 8, 1900;* Pictorial Review, *September 1925;* Vogue, *January 11, 1900;* Scribner's Magazine, *September 1925. Lower row, left, sport clothes,* Vogue, *for February 22, 1900, recommended this skirt: "There is nothing so sensible, comfortable, and clean. . . . The skirt just escapes the ground, or perhaps a little more." Right, from* Good Housekeeping, *August 1925.*

From the Ladies' Home Journal, *May 1899.*

From the Ladies' Home Journal, *September 1925. With this change disappeared hat pins, hair pins, hair combs, false hair, and most of the natural hair.*

rian period was lawn tennis, accompanied by modification of stays and corsets. That met with outraged criticism. Ministers exhorted their congregations to eschew the ungraceful, unwomanly, and unrefined game which offended against all the canons of womanly dignity and delicacy. But sports for women began to be adopted in women's colleges, then beginning to expand. For various sports, including basketball, the more daring began to appear in bloomers, which were in reality trousers cut full and gathered at the knee to resemble a skirt. These garments were ridiculed in the press and denounced from the pulpit, and suffered once more the same reviling as had the bloomer of 1851.

It took years for the changes in dress to pass from specialized costumes for sport into ordinary wear. A timorous start toward skirts ending at the ankles for street wear in bad weather was ridiculed, if not more gravely condemned, in the term, applied to dress and to wearers, "rainy-daisies."

In 1900, the standards of style in appearance and dress ran to "smallness," and called for high, tight-laced corsets, tight kid gloves, and shoes usually a size or more too small. The standard of beauty in waists called for one that could be "easily clasped with two hands." Some women reduced their waists from a normal measurement of twenty to twenty-four inches, to eighteen or twenty. This was opposed by reformers and physicians, but they did not make much headway until years later. Kathleen Norris has described the conventionally dressed woman of 1900:

> She wore a wide-brimmed hat that caught the breezes, a high choking collar of satin or linen, and a flaring gored skirt that swept the street on all sides. Her full-sleeved shirt-waist had cuffs that were eternally getting dirty, her stock was always crushed and rumpled at the end of the day, and her skirt was a bitter trial. Its heavy "brush binding" had to be replaced every few weeks, for constant contact with the pavement reduced it to dirty fringe in no time at all. In wet weather the full skirt got soaked and icy. Even in fair weather its wearer had to bunch it in great folds and devote one hand to nothing else but the carrying of it.

With the other changes, dresses that required ten yards of material were supplanted by some requiring less than three. Cotton stockings almost disappeared, and silk took their place. The long sleeves of 1900 receded to none at all in 1925. Skirts receded to the knees, stockings below them. If a woman who had come to maturity in 1900 should have spent the subsequent twenty years in a Rip Van Winkle sleep, she would probably have been less startled by an airplane than by garters worn visibly below the knee. The high boned collar passed. With it went tight lacing, and almost the corset itself. In evening wear there was a change reflected in a Mutt and Jeff joke: Mutt had gone to a party and Jeff asked him what the ladies had on. Mutt replied: "I don't know; I didn't look under the table." Another newspaper picture of the change was compressed into four lines of verse in the *Washington Star* for July 4, 1925:

I haven't anything to wear
Friend Wife of yore would oft declare.
And, as she dons her modern dress,
Her argument is proved, I guess.

While many of the innovations in woman's appearance began with the bicycle and other sports as early as 1900, none made really rapid headway, and some did not start at all until after 1914. As late as May 1909, the *Ladies' Home Journal* said:

A man has always been told that a woman's hair is her crowning glory. And he has believed it. In the eyes of many a man a woman's hair and the contour of her head have typified feminine beauty. But recently he has been puzzled to see the hair of his womankind increase amazingly in quantity until he has wondered why feminine hair should so suddenly have acquired the habit of growth. It has confused him. But simultaneously, with his wonderment he heard whisperings of "rats" and "puffs."

Alice, daughter of Theodore Roosevelt, shortly after her marriage, in 1906, to Nicholas Longworth, later, in 1925, Speaker of the House of Representatives. The dress, typical of the early 1900s, presented difficulties in connection with the roads and the mode of conveyance of that period. (From a photograph by Paul Thompson)

The World War brought a need and a demand for women at the front as nurses, stretcher bearers, ambulance drivers, workers in ammunition plants, factory hands—occupations always before filled by men, and regarded as impossible for women. Women at the front discovered that under the limitations of time and otherwise, work and care for appearance, as well as defense against vermin, would be facilitated by short hair. Women in ammunition factories found that powder got into their hair and was dangerous. The changes in dress and customs brought about by these and other conditions became one of the controverted subjects of the day; they were the occasion of sermons and furnished material for the comic sheet. The wartime newspapers carried photographs of women wearing overalls, knickers, and with hair bobbed. Other women, learning of the comfort and time-saving qualities of short hair, soon took up the practice. Finally it became a fad. At the end of

A cartoon by Berryman, in the Washington *(D.C.)* Star, *for August 31, 1924.*

the war it showed some signs of dying out, but was revived by moving-picture actresses. By the beginning of 1924, bobbed hair was practically universal. Nearly all the new spring hats were so small that only bobbed

Even the barber shops have changed. What prophet of 1900 would have dared predict that woman would elbow man from the barber's chair? (By courtesy of Franklin Simon)

heads could get into them. Many women were forced to join the vogue. It was almost impossible to find a hat large enough for a woman with long hair. New and attractive styles of bobbing were invented. Flappers, middle-aged women, even gray-haired grandmothers invaded man's last retreat, the barber shop; men complained that instead of finding the *Sporting Times* and the *Police Gazette* to pass the time while waiting for the call of "next," they were more likely to pick up *Vogue* or the *Ladies' Home Journal*. An ingenious barber in California put out a sign: "BARBER SHOP FOR MEN ONLY."

III

Many changes that came in the women's world were associated with Edward Bok. For certain elevations in the taste of houses and house furnishings, he is more to be thanked than any other one man. Bok was editor of the *Ladies' Home Journal* from 1889 to 1919, and he took the magazine from a circulation of 440,000 copies when he took over to 2 million when he retired. During most of that time, especially the early part of it, the *Ladies' Home Journal* was frequently spoken of, sometimes jeeringly yet with a measure of allegorical truth, as the monthly bible of the American home. Bok gave advice to women, very positive advice, for he was a didactic man, with some of the crusader and much of the schoolteacher in his temperament. Some of his counsel was in areas of extraordinary intimacy, affairs of the heart, proper decorum, and the like, such that the spectacle of this especially masculine man offering guidance to women in matters extremely feminine gave rise to astonishment, and to humor when the astonishment was not too great for levity. He and his periodical came to be a favorite subject for the newspaper comedians. In the period about 1900, there were as many Bok jokes as there came later to be Ford jokes. Bok

This guide to "The right and wrong ways of holding skirts" was printed in the New York Pictorial *as late as December 27, 1908. But which is right and which is wrong?*

smiled with those that smiled at him, and went his successful way. The outstanding characteristic of his editing was intimate and personal service; he employed physicians and nurses of the highest standing, experts on cooking, and authorities in other lines, for duties of which their printed contributions were only a fraction; their chief function was to answer letters which the subscribers were solicited to send. Through the aggregate of all this, the best standards of cooking, nursing, and household management, as well as higher standards of taste in houses, furniture, and decoration, were carried into homes throughout the length and breadth of the land.

Bok rendered an immense service to American women and American homes, though in some respects his leadership was rejected. He was conservative, and never took up the feminist movement, which became important on the intellectual side of the life of women. As to women's dress, also, he was unsuccessful. Some kind of tide, deeper than he knew, was running against him. His preaching about clothes was chiefly in the direction of austerity of appearance, and of the completeness of covering which, in the early 1900s, was supposed to be either a cause or an outward evidence of inner rectitude. His teaching about dress was in the opposite direction from the lipsticks, the bobbed hair, the short stockings, and the other brevities that arose in spite of him. Once his crusading spirit led him to really try to revolutionize American dress. He started a formidable movement to get away from Paris as the source of styles and models, and to substitute New York and American designs, harking back to American themes, such as Indian costumes. He began his campaign with the slogan "American Fashions for American Women." He had three designers visit the Metropolitan Museum for new and artistic ideas. They worked for months; the designs were passed on by a board of New York women whose judgment in clothes was good, after which pages of them were published. The attempted innovation was widely advertised, and conventions of dressmakers were called to discuss American-made fashions. But in spite of all the formidable energy, the idea did not "take." Commercial forces and feminine tastes were too much for Bok.

In many aspects of the life of women, Bok worked a revolution in the direction of simplicity and utility. His editorial genius lay largely in his realization of the superiority of the concrete and the visual, to mere abstractions. He knew that a picture can tell more than a page of text. Once he said that the way to lead women to the appreciation of beauty was not to print an essay by Ruskin but to tell them how many packages of flower seeds you can buy for fifteen cents, and print a diagram of how to plant them. He conducted competitions that brought in thousands of photographs of gardens in bloom, and printed many pages of them. By this, and a department entitled "Floral Hints and Helps," he stimulated the beautifying of lawns. In a department entitled "Beautiful America" he showed contrasting photographs of localities "before and after" the removal of offensive advertising signs and billboards. Another department, "How Much Can Be Done with Little," showed photographs of backyards before and after they were improved by planting vines, flowers, and trees.

He carried on campaigns against patent medicines, and printed photographs and plans showing how to get rid of mosquitoes. By these and similar methods in other fields he promoted simplicity and the other attributes of better taste. He used to print photographs side by side, labeling one "This chair is ugly" and the other "This chair is beautiful." Month after month he carried these comparisons through tables, beds, draperies, table decorations.

Bok played a large role in transforming the American house from the rather stark and boxlike thing that was common in the nineties, and American interiors from standards of furniture and decoration which, so far as there were standards at all in the earlier period, were overbalanced on the side of tawdry ornateness. The American parlor of 1900 was furnished, usually, with "three-piece" sets, upholstered in red or green plush, gaudy successor to the horsehair, then just beginning to be looked on with disapproval. On the walls of typical American homes were large framed pictures in colors, landscapes, groups of idyllic children. For the bedroom and dining room suites, golden oak was in vogue. On the floor was an ingrain carpet, with huge, highly colored floral designs, underlaid with padding and tacked down. In the banishing of these, Bok may have been helped by the fact that during and after the Spanish War, many thousands of American soldiers, tourists, businessmen, and schoolteachers, visiting our newly acquired overseas dependencies, had the opportunity to be impressed with the aesthetic and hygienic qualities of bare floors.

By 1925, the once common boxlike or L-shaped house had given way to a new and distinctly American type built on simpler and lovelier lines. Cupolas, balconies, fancy windows were discarded. Iron deer, dogs, and cupids ceased to adorn the lawns. Untidy backyards and old sheds gave way to sod lawns, walks of cement, and brick or metal garages. (Bok caused a good deal of commotion by printing a series of photographs of the more squalid parts of American cities in the spirit of a search to determine preeminence in municipal ugliness.) Interiors likewise became simpler and more attractive. Pantries gave way to built-in cupboards. Kitchens became more compact and were arranged to save labor and steps for the housewife. Kitchen sinks, which at first were made low because they were the successor of washtubs into which the water had to be lifted and poured by hand, came to be built high when architects and contractors were compelled to realize that with water carried by pipes the need was to save back-bending. Cheerful colors were introduced on kitchen walls, linoleum in attractive designs on the floor. Part of the front porch was changed into a sunroom, heated in winter, screened in summer. The hat rack gave way to the built-in closet. Other built-in features included buffets, bookcases, and beds. People began to buy and manufacturers to supply "period" furniture: styles of Adam, Louis XV, and Queen Anne periods. Colonial designs became popular. The old wooden folding beds, which by day acted as desks and bookcases, disappeared. The brass bed arrived, and later the imitation-wood bed of steel.

IV

An interesting and accurate index to changes in clothes, ornaments, fur-nishings, tools, and ways of American life is supplied by the business records of the great mail-order houses. They had existed before 1900, but their great growth was made possible chiefly by two innovations, of which one, rural free delivery, came in 1896, and the other, parcel post, in 1913. These mail-order houses supplied customers in literally every hamlet and on almost every farm in America with a greater variety and volume of things in common use than any other merchants in the world. They sold by mail everything from a paper of pins to a nine-room house. They received as many as 200,000 letters a day, and sold upward of 100,000 different kinds of articles, including food, clothing, implements for farming, decora-tions for houses, tools for barns—even the houses and barns themselves. Their successive yearly catalogues from 1900 to 1925 constitute a social history of America. Through the helpfulness of the head of one of them, Julius Rosenwald, and his associates of Sears, Roebuck & Company, the writer was, in 1925, supplied with data about changes in popular taste and ways of life as revealed by the records of that company's contacts with up-ward of 6 million customers, who, with their families, included over a quar-ter of the population of the country. How curiously close a touch the mail-order houses had with American life is illustrated by their ability to prophesy that almost twice as many babies would be born in 1920 as in 1919, their forecast being based on their sales of maternity corsets—an in-dex that public statistics could not have supplied.

In the Sears, Roebuck catalogue of 1900 there was no mention of auto-mobiles or automobile accessories. By 1925, this was one of the largest de-

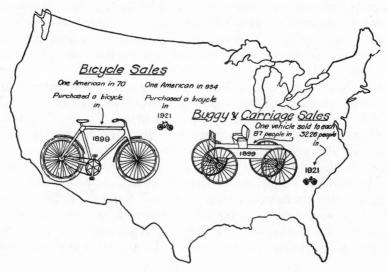

The eclipse of the bicycle and buggy.

Old and new types of factory buildings. The first plant and the 1925 plant of the Victor Talking Machine Company.

partments. The 1900 catalogue carried sixty-seven pages devoted to buggies, harness, saddles, and horse blankets; the catalogue of 1925 had a scant eight. Stoves that the housewife used to take a pride in polishing with her own hands gave way to enamel surfaces. Wood-burning stoves and baseburners fed with hard coal gave way to a system of hot-air tubes from a furnace in the cellar, and these in turn to pipes carrying hot water or steam to radiators. The bathroom came to be an adjunct that every house could have, and the daily bath a common institution.* The old-fashioned "rock-a-bye" cradle, theme of song and poem, was replaced by a crib with rubber-tired wheels, enclosed sides and top, with wire screens to protect the tiny occupant from flies and mosquitoes. By 1925, cradles were eagerly sought as antiques. New and indestructible toys made their appearance: gyroscope tops, educational toys. Teddy bears, Charlie Chaplin toys, character dolls, able to say "Mama" and made to withstand rough handling, replaced the dolls with china heads, which were often broken between Christmas and New Year's.

Pages of the mail-order catalogues record the early existence and later passing of a fad for a man to wear the emblem of his trade—the blacksmith hung a gold anvil or horseshoe from his watch chain, the bartender a jeweled beer keg, the sailor a miniature anchor or compass, the railroad engineer a small locomotive, the conductor a caboose. Gold-headed canes and umbrellas were a mark of solid affluence. Heavy, thick, gold watches—

*It was about 1900 that a joke became current which recorded a small-town visitor to a city hotel writing home to his family: "The bathroom here is so nice I can hardly wait for Saturday night."

Left, an American soldier in the war with Spain. The uniform was poorly adapted to tropical wear. The blue woolen shirts, being dark, attracted mosquitoes, and being of wool, multiplied the discomforts of campaigning in tropical swamps. The trousers were full-length, and when worn with leggings made the wearer appear uncouth. Right, uniform and equipment of the American soldier during the Great War. (By courtesy of U.S. Signal Corps)

"turnips" they were sometimes called—were an indication of prosperity in the individual, and the common choice for a testimonial of esteem when a group of men wanted to honor one of their fellows.

The changes in men's clothing, though not as marked as in women's, were in the same direction, toward lighter weight and greater attention to appearance. In 1900, durability and wearableness were the prized qualities; by 1925, it was style and comfort. The 1900 man when "dressed up" wore a derby hat, a wool suit of dark color, the coat with padded shoulders, collar and cuffs stiffly laundered, and the shirt held together at the bosom with studs; toothpick shoes; fleece-lined underwear; and heavy socks. Only the "dude" wore garters to hold his socks in place. There was no differentiation between summer suits and winter ones: The "second-best" did service on weekdays the year round, and the Sunday suit was resurrected once a week, good weather or bad. Between 1900 and 1925, men ventured into grays, light shades of brown, powder blues; wore soft felt hats, soft collars and cuffs, and socks of silk or lisle or other lightweight material. Plain dark-blue serge, which provided 50 percent of men's wear in 1900, gave way to weaves and colors less simple. Substantial overcoats of heavy broadcloth, designed to last for years, were supplanted by lighter and flimsier materials designed to conform to rapidly changing styles, and to the expectation of not more than one season's use. There was a steady tendency to inconspicuousness in scarf pins, cuff links, and watch chains.

Changes occurred in the types of literature ordered from mail-order houses. In 1900, the "best-sellers" of the mail-order houses had to do with fortune-telling, palm-reading, dream books,* after-dinner toasts. By 1925, books of this type had practically disappeared from stock. Bibles were steady sellers throughout the entire period, a marked increase taking place after the war.

Musical instruments changed. In 1900, the Sears, Roebuck catalogue displayed two full pages of mouth organs, an instrument capable of giving forth inspiring melody when puffed by an expert, but in 1925, there were few mouth-organ virtuosos. Along with the mouth organ into obscurity went the Jew's harp, an inexpensive mechanism whose simple note was drowned out by the saxophone that was popular in the 1920s. Something more happened in popular music than the crowding out of the mouth organ and Jew's harp by the saxophone and the ukulele. The coming of "canned" music, the Victrola; the phonograph and its variations was the true blight of the older and simpler instruments. Mechanical music brought versions of the classics, and the reproduced voices of artists, to masses who otherwise would never have heard them. But the Jew's harp and the mouth organ had the virtue that they required, and enabled, people to produce their own music. There was a greater quantity of music abroad in the America of 1925, but less making of music by the people.

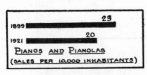

Piano and pianola production did not increase. They were overwhelmed first by the phonograph and then by the radio.

One necessity forced upon the mail-order houses reflected a change that ran through American life. In 1900, they selected most of their fall lines a year in advance. In 1925, they were obliged to delay the selection so as to include every possible new idea, and sometimes, at the last moment, to add a bulletin of new styles. Farm customers came to be almost as close to the trend of styles as city customers.

This experience of the mail-order houses was a characteristic that ran all through American life. Increasing emphasis on style was practically universal. Nearly everything was affected by it, nearly everybody succumbed to it. It was hard to resist, for once a style was established it flooded the retail shops, and the older models became difficult to be got by the few purchasers whose individualism, or loyalty to old ways, was

---

*The relative disappearance of such books reflected, fundamentally, a wider diffusion of knowledge of the laws of nature, of the acceptance of logic, and the true relations of cause and effect. It is true that in 1925 dreams were looked upon as having significance by a type of person very different from those who in 1900 looked upon them as "signs." In 1925, there was a genuine effort to find significance in dreams, but this effort attempted to be consistent with science, with laws of psychology; there was a cult for the theory of dream psychology put out by Freud and other physicians. The relative disappearance of a primitive point of view about arbitrary relations between "signs" and coming events was an outstanding feature of the period. The disappearance, however, was far from complete. In the 1920s, the wife of President Harding used to consult a Washington astrologer.

A change in military uniforms and ornamentation. Left, General Nelson A. Miles, between 1895 and 1903 commanding general of the U.S. Army, and right, General John J. Pershing, head of the American troops in the Great War.

stronger than their servitude to vogue. It had deep-reaching effects on taste, even on character. Manufacturers and dealers ceased to strive for durability. Once they fell into the swing of making for style, they felt it was useless to produce goods that would wear well for more than a season. Consumers who were drummed and herded into fear of being out of style as to clothes and hats came to fear being out of style in thought. Individualism, strength of personality, came to be more rare. The advertising pages of the newspapers and periodicals became dedicated to making people feel that to be out of style was to be ridiculous. To the extent the reading matter reflected the spirit of the advertisements, there was the same

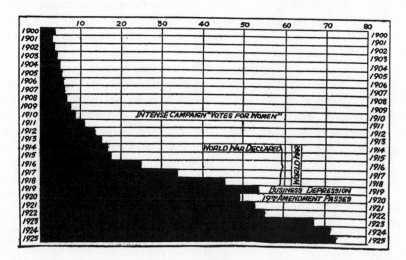

The growth of cigarette consumption for twenty-five years.

urge to follow the vogue. Merchants, with the aid of the newspapers, adopted ingenious devices for shortening the period between styles; actually, in some cities a man who wore a straw hat after October 1, or a felt one after May 1, was subjected to a jeering hardly short of rough handling.

It is little wonder if the spirit of quick change from style to style came to affect some of life's spiritual and aesthetic aspects, and practically every one of its material aspects. Who could have supposed that the owners of dogs would yield to style, or that the dog itself could be made to conform to style? But it was.

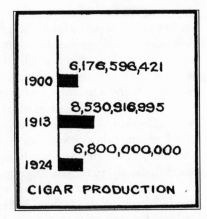

Cigar production started to increase in a normal proportion to population but was overwhelmed by the cigarette, of which the production increased 1,500 percent.

V

I n the pages of this work there are many allusions to changes in taste. These records of the passing vogues will give rise to one kind of reflection or another, depending on whether the reader's years and temperament are those which think the age just past was the golden one, or that every aspect of the world that is new is also good. There is one field of change as to which, for most persons, the reproduction of the vogues of an earlier day will recall sentiments associated with childhood, such that it will be difficult for any reader upward of twenty-one to admit that the dogs of today are the equal to those of yesterday.

A pioneer of "bobbed hair," and an early advanced "feminist" in all respects, Dr. Mary Walker. She was authorized by Congress to wear male dress. Taken in 1914. (From a photograph by Edmonston)

Fashion has passed through changes about dogs as it has about clothes, shoes, hats, hair cuts, facial forestation, automobiles, drama, and fiction. I put it this way: "Fashion has passed through changes." But perhaps a diligent historian would be able to prove that most of these changes, which are described as arising in the taste of the people, really came about through the initiative and energy of commercial persons who had a shrewdly pecuniary realization that if the old could be made to seem passé (through propaganda, advertising, or what-not), then the new could be sold in profitable quantities. Certainly this motive has played a part in the changes in fashions in women's clothes and automobiles as well as in some other fields. In the case of man's most loyal friend, some of the changes will take a good deal of proof to show they have been for the best—the change, for example, from the Newfoundland to the Pekinese. Many a fine breed of dog, whose worth had been known through generations, was elbowed gradually into the back corners and garrets of man's affection. Was there ever a finer animal than the Newfoundland, prized, among other reasons, for gentleness with children? In 1900, and some years before, he guarded nearly every porch door, dozed on almost every hearthstone. By 1925, you might pass through the entire year, travel far up and down the country, without seeing one, although a few professional breeders kept the strain alive, either out of sentiment—lest the Newfoundland join the messenger pigeon and the bison—or in the vague hope that the agencies of vogue would spin the wheel and bring the old favorite back.

Almost as numerous as the Newfoundland in 1900 was the humorous, ludicrous, but intelligent pug. Readers of sufficient years will see in imagination that fat, familiar form with the upturned nose and the tail curled so absurdly in a circle, wheezing and puffing along, often towed by a youngster. The favor the pug enjoyed as a household pet was due largely to his gentleness and scrupulous cleanliness. By 1925, he was hardly to be found except occasionally in the possession of some ancient lady, loyal to youthful affection, sleepy, yawning, wheezing beside a footstool in front of a fireplace. Just why the honest, homely pug fell away in popularity is as inexplicable as a good many other changes in style. Possibly he was unable to reduce his waistline to the fashionable slenderness of the Boston terrier or the sleek Borzoi of 1925. We could more easily have spared the noisy, yapping Pomeranian or the snuffling Pekinese.

Of the dogs that succeeded the Newfoundland and the pug, many were aliens, exotics. They were introduced to America, as a rule, at the top of the world of fashion. Some became popular and familiar, others had a brief vogue in dog shows but never came in contact with the wider dog world of collies, setters, pointers, beagles. The chow is one dog whose origin as an American fashion could probably be traced with fair accuracy. His vogue came after the American expedition to China at the time of the Boxer rebellion in 1900. Among those who brought back chows as souvenirs of that then very strange land was Richard Harding Davis, the war correspondent and popular author. Descendants of Davis's importation were given to his friends and found their way into the New York Dog Show. Their oddity instantly attracted attention. They became the vogue of the elite for a few years and later were fairly common.

Appearance counts for much in popular taste. No doubt that same ludicrousness that had something to do with the eclipse of the pug accounted also for the brevity of the reign of the friendly, awkward dachshund. There can be nothing in the theory that the war brought his eclipse, for he had begun to lose ground long before the Kaiser brought misfortune to a good many things German.

If the dachshund suffered for his ancestry, the poodle should have come into high favor, for he was French from his blunt nose to the tip of his curling tail. On the contrary, the poodle, after the war, came to be rarely seen. The poodle, too, suffered from a touch of absurdity of appearance, for which the fault lay not with him but with the style adopted for clipping his

John Drew (top left), when the Old English sheepdog was in vogue.

The dog that had the longest and greatest vogue of all, the mongrel; and the truest of dog lovers, the American boy (top center).

Rex Beach with English setter (top right).

Booth Tarkington and his French poodle (center).

Dachshund, popular in 1900 (left lower).

A Newfoundland, common in the 1890s. "Polaria" was imported from England by J. A. Graydon in an effort to reestablish the breed in America (right lower).

coat. The King Charles spaniel and the Skye terrier, both of long-haired breeds, had a brief vogue and passed, as well as the dalmation and the sleek greyhound, the oldest dog man knows, dating back 7,000 years. The smooth-haired fox terrier, an admirable dog, gave way to his cousin, the popular—for a brief while—wire-haired fox terrier.

The breeds unknown in 1900 which by 1925 had passed through the stages of dog show and fashion, and had begun to come into really popular favor, included the so-called police dog. One met them everywhere; in town, where one felt rather sympathetic to see them tugging at the leash, and in the country, where, as excellent watchdogs, they rightfully belonged. They had a style, a presence, which seemed to be the quality that counted most in the 1920s.

VI

In the year 1900, the writer of this history was twenty-five years old. In the year in which this is written, 1925, the writer, therefore, had lived through the last quarter of the nineteenth century and the first quarter of the twentieth. In the beginning of the earlier period, many of the oldest ways of life were still common. The earliest lantern I carried as a boy was of a model as old, at least, as Shakespeare, a cylinder of tin with little jagged holes punched through it, large enough to let thin glimmers of light come through, and small enough not to let the wind blow out the candle, which stood in a socket inside the cylinder. Candles were still in frequent use, the candle mold, twelve long tubes of tin or zinc joined together, still a common household article. About that time, however, the coal-oil lamp was beginning to overcome the prejudice against novelty and the fear, not infrequently justified, that it was dangerous, liable to explosion. The earliest ones were of plain glass with a wick of red flannel; later came ornate ones of painted china, wall lamps with reflectors, and, finally, an exaltation of convenience and adornment, the hanging lamp, suspended from the ceiling at the middle of the room, and raised or lowered by a small chain on pulleys.

Many of the tools for farming were still the same as they had been for a thousand years. I have seen grain threshed from the straw by a flail, two long sticks joined end to end by a leather thong six or eight inches long. The thresher used one as a handle and swung the other down on the straw spread on the barn floor. That steady drum beat was a rainy day sound on many a thrifty small farm. In the 1880s, however, the large mechanical thresher had come into use as a community institution. It went the rounds from farm to farm with a professional threshing crew. The earlier ones took their power from horses in a treadmill; in the eighties, the power came to be supplied by portable steam engines. It was not until the nineties that these engines could move from farm to farm under their own power. In the early part of the period, the primitive hand-"cradle" for mowing wheat, oats, and rye was still to be found on every farm, though it was being displaced by the horse-drawn reaper. In the eighties, there came a marvel, the "reaper-and-binder," which cut the grain, accumulated it in bundles, and tied them with twine, all in one process. The horse-drawn mowing machine had already supplanted the scythe for everything except fence corners and small lots. It was during the eighties that the "hayfork" became common, a mechanism of steel tines, rope, and pulleys, which lifted the hay from the wagon to the mow by horsepower.

Many of the changes during this period came from one cause: the spread of the railroads. As late as the eighties and even into the nineties there survived a self-contained unit of society every few miles. On the little streams of the East there were gristmills. The farmer hauled his wheat to the mill, saw it ground, and received in return flour which he used for his family, bran for the animals in the barn, and middlings for the poultry. Presently the railroads, and the rise of great flour mills manufacturing on an immense scale, brought it about that the farmer sold his wheat outright at the railroad station and then bought his flour from the local store as he needed it, both wheat and flour, meantime, having traveled hundreds or thousands of miles.

In the earlier period, butchering day, usually a cold day in late November or early December, was a universal institution on the farms. One or two hogs and a beef animal were killed. For pork, the operation began with the heating of stones in an outdoor fire. When sufficiently hot, the stones were thrown into a barrel of water into which, later, the slaughtered hog was sunk to soften his bristles for shaving. In due course the hams were salted and hung from hooks in the kitchen, together with one or two quarters of the slaughtered steer, which for a year to follow provided food as dried beef. This institution, too, succumbed to the railroads and the rise of

Before refrigeration and refrigerator cars, packers stored their barreled pork in mountainous piles adjacent to the slaughtering houses. Hence the work "packer." Slaughtering was done only in the winter months. (By courtesy of Armour and Company)

the great packinghouses. The farmer
came to sell his hogs and cattle at the
railroad station for shipment to
Chicago or the nearest packinghouse
elsewhere, and bought his meat from
time to time as he needed it from the
nearest meat dealer. In lumber, the
railroads brought the same transformation. As late as the eighties a
farmer, about to build a barn, went
into his woodlot, chopped down the
oaks, and trimmed them with his

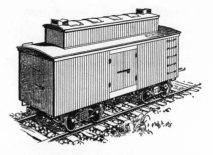

*The first refrigerator car. (By courtesy of
Armour and Company)*

broadax. When he had enough for the frame of the barn, there was a "raising," to which the neighbors came to help lift the heavy timbers and join
them (often with a jollification afterward, that included hard cider). To a
considerable extent even the boards were still sawed by local sawmills on
the nearby streams. Presently that, too, gave way to the custom of buying
lumber already cut, brought from a distance, and to the specialized labor of
the building contractor.

The buggy, which to the youth of 1900 was the equivalent, not of the
Ford, but of the $2000, or $3,000 car of 1925, was, in the eighties, still
largely a product of local makers who would build them to order at $150 to
$200. The wheelwright shop, often combined with the blacksmith shop,
still held sway with the local gristmill as a community institution. On the
timbers beneath the roof of every blacksmith shop one could see the strips
of hickory, curved ones for the wheels,
drying in the slow warmth from the
forge, a method of seasoning considered to be more desirable and durable
than the quicker drying practiced in
factories.

The farmer's wife, too, was still largely
independent of the distant cannery.
"Preserving" was a household rite that
followed the season from strawberry-
time through raspberries to blackber-
ries and on to peaches and pears. In
the fall, as one drove along the country roads, one sniffed the agreeable
scent of drying fruit, and on lean-to
roofs saw frames in which the sliced
apples were drying in the autumn sun.
In October or November, applesauce
making was an event like butchering
day. Apple butter making involved, for

*The meat wagon of the 1890s. Every-
thing is shown except the flies that accompanied it and were regarded as both
unavoidable and harmless. (By courtesy
of Armour and Company)*

some of the household, or for relays of them, a romantic night in the open. The apples, pared and sliced, together with cider, were put into a large copper-lined pot that hung on a frame over an outdoor fire. The fire had to be kept going as much as forty-eight hours, and some one had to steadily keep the mixture moving with a long-handled wooden stirrer specially made for this work.

Every housewife had her own coffee grinder, sausage grinder, and apple parer. Ancient custom, and also a kind of pride, caused both wife and husband to seek to produce and preserve as much of their food as possible—a workmanlike individualism destined to be overcome by the ease of railroad transportation, by the cheapness of quantity production in factories, by refrigerator cars that lengthened the seasons for fresh fruit, and by cold-storage warehouses. In the earlier day, the farmer depended on the local store for little more than sugar, usually the soft brown kind (much more delectable to children sent to carry it from the store than granulated sugar); molasses, drawn from a barrel into a jug; coffee, unground; tea and spices—all bought, often, not with cash but through the barter of chickens, eggs, and butter.

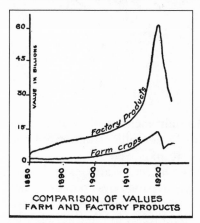

COMPARISON OF VALUES
FARM AND FACTORY PRODUCTS

One may have a feeling for the greater economic independence of that day, even the romance of its greater simplicity and individuality, but one must admit that cleanliness, sanitation, and health had an advance in the transition from country store, fly-smitten sugar bins and molasses barrels, from the dried cod and herring that hung like bronzed mummies from hooks or wires, and the pickle barrel in the cellar, open alike to the storekeeper's hand and to adventurous insects—from these and other aspects of the old-time country store, to the cartons and bottles which, during the eighties and nineties, began to come on the railroads from distant factories, to be retailed by the local store, later by chain stores.

Hand in hand with the changes brought by the railroads went others that reflected the universal trend toward specialization of labor. In the closing decades of the nineteenth century, on many farms, the milk was separated by the farmer's wife, through methods that had not changed much since the days of Jael. It was allowed to stand in pails in the cool water of the springhouse until the cream rose to the top, when it was removed with a "skimmer," a thin, saucer-shaped bit of metal, and put in crocks, large vessels of coarse gray earthenware, sometimes ornamented with blue. (The farmer's wife of 1880 bought them at the village store for five to twenty cents each; in 1925, they were on sale in antique shops at $5 to $10 each.) The week's accumulation of cream was turned to butter with an old-fashioned churn, the operation calling for several hours of hard work by wife or children. All this began to give way during the eighties to local

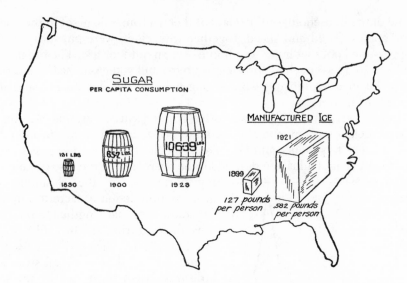

"creameries" to which the farmer took his milk each morning and where the separation into cream and the residue of skim milk or buttermilk was made by centrifugal separators operated by steam power.

On any average farm of the nineties one could see, as articles of daily or seasonal use, knee-high leather boots—the ones for boys frequently had copper reinforcement at the toes; earmuffs, bits of velvet on a wire framework large enough to slip over the ear. Buffalo robes in the early eighties could be bought for fifty cents or a dollar; by 1900, they, with the buffalo itself, had practically disappeared; by 1925, you counted it an adventure if you came across one at country "public sales" of the household goods of old farm families. There were sleighs, the bodies made sometimes of wood, sometimes of woven willow withes; those of unusual distinction of style were called "cutters." In winter, the wheels of farm wagons were replaced

Another institution that has passed. In 1925 one could search for months in the most backward districts before finding such an outfit as this. (By courtesy of U.S. Bureau of Public Roads)

with sled runners, and small bells were attached to the harness. The journey of such an equipage to the "crossroads store" or the village was attended with an agreeable glamour unknown to a generation inured to the automobile. Oxen were still common. "Buck" and "Berry" were as familiar as Mr. Ford's "Lizzie" later came to be; every boy knew what an ox or horse should do when ordered to "gee" or "haw." Speed was accelerated by a vocal cluck or "git ep," the 1890 equivalent of "step on the gas."

Among farmers and workers elsewhere, underwear made of bright-red flannel was in widespread favor, based on the presumed possession of a kind of superstitious virtue additional to its warmth. A harvest field of the eighties or early nineties presented a picture almost like men in uniform—each harvester stripped to the waist except for the bright-red flannel undershirt. It was worn in winter for the sake of the warmth, and a popular idea that it was dangerous to change led to its retention throughout the summer, a prejudice with somewhat the same sanitary results as the one against night air. Fly screens had not become general; there was a theory that the high, fringy bushes of the asparagus plant would either repel flies or attract them—I forget which. In any event, such bushes were hung close to the ceiling over the dining room table. Drains for reducing lowland to cultivation were made as the earliest farmer must have made them: At the bottom of the ditch, two rows of flat stones were set on edge and covered with other flat stones. During the eighties, the railroads began to bring porous brick tile. Either on the old-time individual farms or in the communities were lime kilns; they, together with the local bone mill, and the product of the barn and chicken yards, supplied the fertilizer.

Within the usual American home, Monday was always "wash day," attended by a soapy, steamy scent of suds. Water frequently had to be carried in buckets from a well some distance from the house. The clothes were "put to soak" the night before, and washing was begun as early as four in the morning. It was a matter of pride with housewives to have the washing hung before breakfast, and neighbors would vie with one another in seeing whose washing appeared earliest on the line. Tuesday was "ironing day." The irons were heated on a hot stove. Men's "boiled" shirts, linen collars, and cuffs and women's and children's dresses and underwear with many yards of ruffles, starched to a wooden inflexibility, were "done up" at home. Wednesday was sewing and mending day. Women's and children's clothing was made at home, and usually the shirts of the men of the household. Darning huge piles of socks and stockings so perfectly that the darning could hardly be detected was a prized accomplishment of a good housewife. The best silk dress was often turned and remade to serve for a few more years. No man was ashamed to wear an honest patch. Thursday was a kind of midweek rest day; so far as it had fixed tasks, they were usually crocheting or embroidering, quilting, making rag carpets. Friday was cleaning day. The thick carpets had to be swept with a broom; the housewife usually wore a dust cap or towel wrapped around her head to protect her hair. Af-

This photograph of the last horse-drawn fire engine in Washington, D.C., was taken on the occasion of its last public appearance, in 1925.

ter a thorough sweeping of rooms and stairs, furniture was dusted. Kitchen floors and porches were scrubbed, usually on hands and knees. The stoves were brightly polished. Saturday was "baking day." All the bread and pastries were made in the home, large solid loaves, pies, cakes, doughnuts, and that delicacy most prized by the small boy—cookies, usually made with a coating of white sugar and with a solitary raisin set like a jewel in the center and kept in a crock on an inaccessible shelf of the pantry to be doled out for good behavior or withheld for discipline. To use much "baker's bread" was

A modern gasoline-motor fire engine. (From a photograph by Underwood & Underwood)

an indictment, at once, of a housewife's industry and of her pride in her calling. Sunday was called the day of rest, but for the housewife it meant, often, the arrival of "company" and extra cooking. It was at this period that the old adage was most apt: "A man may work from sun to sun, but woman's work is never done."

To the relief of this routine of industry there came first the Chinese laundry and later the community laundry as a business institution; the dry cleaner; the electric washing machine and wringer, the electric iron; the vacuum sweeper; the electric sewing machine; and the fireless cooker. Housework was completely revolutionized. The adaptations of electricity for housework began to arrive about 1900 in the cities. By 1925, the long antennae of the power stations had begun to reach out along country roads, and the conveniences that the city woman had been enjoying were now made available to the farmer's wife. For regions isolated from transmission lines, compact generators driven by small gasoline or kerosene motors were devised, which furnished light for buildings, helped the housewife in her daily tasks, and pumped water for domestic uses. Electricity or gasoline began to milk the cows, curry the horses. In 1925, a list of devices sold by the New York Edison Company, with the cost per hour of current used by each, included:

Dishwasher	2 cents	Waffle iron	5 cents
Ironing machine	7 cents	Toaster	3 cents
Sewing machine	½ cent	Chafing dish	7 cents
Vacuum sweeper	1 cent	Table stove	5 cents
Washing machine	2 cents	Fireless cooker	2½ cents

The installation of these electrical devices* cost, of course, much more than the primitive tools of the earlier day; but once installed, the labor that came from the powerhouse cost much less than the hand labor that before had been the only way.

A picture of an electric wire in a modern house excels a fairy story. It comes through conduits or on poles. Once inside the walls it divides into a score of tentacles that burrow, climb, and reach, each ending in some separate service. In any house, at the same hour, electricity might be producing heat in one room, cold in another, light in a third. To yet another it brought the voices of friends from thousands of miles away. It heated water, it cooked, it froze ice in the refrigerator, it carried healing through ingenious pads that curved on aching backs; it swept, sewed, ironed—and it provided heat for the curling iron with which the housewife beautified herself for the evening's gaiety, a housewife who in the preceding generation would have accepted old age at forty and been much too occupied with the work, now done for her by electricity, to give much thought to adornment

*Light was practically the only common household use of electricity in 1900. Almost all the others—kitchen range, vacuum cleaner, refrigerator, dish washer, floor polisher—came after 1900.

or gaiety. "Modern woman," said the *Waco News Tribune* in June 1925, "may have faults, but she doesn't look as bent and worn as a 'dutiful wife' did in the old days."

By electricity and other sources of mechanical energy, life was made much less burdensome. In a sense, too, it was made more simple. To turn a switch was a long distance from the annual candle-dipping or the weekly task of filling the kerosene lamps. To turn a radiator valve was very different from the daily work of filling the wood box. Doubtless something attractive, something possibly of essential value, was missed by the generation of children who thought of light as something you made with the pressure of a finger and thumb on a switch; of heat as something that came through pipes; of milk as something that appeared on the table by the agency of a milkman, whose visit was so early that many a child grew up without even seeing one. The vogue of the Boy Scout movement, designed to recover, at much pains, the arts of chopping wood and making a fire, seemed to recognize that something had been lost with the disappearance of the household chores of earlier childhoods.

1899	$71.10
1921	$196.20

REFRIGERATORS
SALES PER THOUSAND INHABITANTS

1899	$1.16
1921	$4.43

ELECTRICAL MACHINERY
PER CAPITA PURCHASES

1899	$61.20
1921	$257.20

GAS AND OIL STOVES AND APPLIANCES
EXPENDITURES PER 1000 INHABITANTS

1899	$2.34
1921	$6.31

BREAD AND OTHER BAKERY PRODUCTS
CONSUMPTION PER CAPITA

1899	$10.10
1921	$28.50

ELECTRIC FLATIRONS
SALES PER 1000 INHABITANTS

The coming of electricity and the gasoline motor might have given men and women such a freedom from labor and constant care as would have seemed, to the earlier generation, an Arabian Night's dream. Release from much hard physical labor actually came, but life did not become more simple. New needs, new desires, were stimulated. Luxuries became necessities. Man, instead of regarding the new invention as releasing him from just that much labor, allowed it to add to the number of things he thought he must have, or his family thought they must have: radio, automobile, scores of articles that did not retain the status of novel luxuries but became familiar needs almost overnight. The average man conceded almost nothing to be beyond his wants or means. Instead of comparing his state with the past, instead of reflecting that he was far richer in material comforts and conveniences than George Washington, who was the richest American of his generation—instead of that, the average man made his comparison with the richest of his own generation. He usually wanted as many conveniences; and through the beneficences of science, invention, and the social organization of America, was enabled to approximate what would otherwise have seemed his preposterous wishes. He got more goods, more things, but also he became more enmeshed in the anxieties of a complex and hurried way of life. He missed the chance of making a possibly more

An old-fashioned housewife's daily task, before the coming of electricity. (By courtesy of the Edison Company)

satisfying use of the release from physical labor that electricity brought, the chance for leisure, repose, simplicity of life, and the spiritual qualities that can go with simple living.

But the common generalization that compares the present unfavorably with the past, that pictures the earlier day as golden, is subject to a good deal of qualification. The anxiety to share the latest and highest standard of living may keep modern man's nose to the grindstone of his family's presumed needs. But that is a fault of inner philosophy, of the individual's management of his personal existence. In any event, worry about meeting the installments on the automobile is hardly to be compared with the anxiety that attended, as late as 1895, the presence, for example, of diphtheria in the family, or any of many other terrors that science banished.

CHAPTER 6
The Automobile Emerges

On the streets of Chicago, in September 1892, appeared a strange vehicle. "Ever since its arrival," said a contemporary account, "the sight of a well-loaded carriage moving along the streets at a spanking pace with no horses in front and apparently with nothing on board to give it motion, was a sight that has been too much, even for the wide-awake Chicagoan. It is most amusing to see the crowd gather whenever the vehicle appears. So great has been the curiosity that the owner when passing through the business section has had to appeal to the police to aid him in clearing the way."

The owner of this novelty of 1892, William Morrison of Des Moines, Iowa, is credited with having been the first man in America to make an electric automobile—electric as distinguished from steam and gasoline. In the automobile industry the word "first" is perilous to use; for there is no one person, as there is in the field of older inventions, to whom can be ascribed the credit of being either the indisputable pioneer or, as yet, the popularly accepted one. If it were desired to set up a monument to the man primarily responsible for the presence, in the year 1925, of 17 million automobiles in the United States, as there are monuments to inventors in other fields, it would be necessary, in this case, for the monument to be a composite figure, the features of which would need to be equitably distributed in the proportions of the claims made by many rivals and their partisans. If any schoolboy is asked who invented the steamboat, he replies "Fitch"; if asked about the cotton gin, he replies "Whitney"; if about the sewing machine, "Howe"; if about the reaper and binder, "McCormick"; if about the steam locomotive, "Stephenson." But no schoolboy, and not even any authority within the automobile world, is able, with equally instant certainty, or within the compactness of a single name, to say that any one man is the inventor of the automobile. Or, if any name is set up as entitled to priority of time or credit, the claim is hotly disputed by the partisans of others. Not only as to the automobile as a whole, but even as to most of its fundamental parts, there is no accepted certainty in the allocation of credit for invention.

Doubtless one reason for the greater glibness with which we name the inventors of older mechanisms, like the sewing machine and the steamboat, is the distance in time since the older machines were perfected. Doubtless it is partly due also to the fact that at the times when these older machines were invented there was less setting down of things in print—history was more generally in the custody of word-of-mouth tradition, and tradition usually exalts personality. Probably a more discriminating truth would say that in the case of these older inventions there were contributions from many different pioneers. And possibly, also, the schoolboy of a hundred years ahead of us, when asked who invented the automobile, may say "Henry Ford."

The best reason why no name is associated with the invention of the automobile is that it was not an invention. Nobody invented it. Certainly nobody in America invented it. The automobile, in America especially, was an assembling, an adapting. Almost every adjunct to the automobile, as it was in 1900, had long been in use in other devices. The transmission, in one form or another, was an essential part of the lathes in every machine shop and of the driving wheel of most stationary engines. The frictionless bearing had been developed for the bicycle. The acetylene light was familiar to everybody. In short, the automobile was no more than a coordination and adaptation of old ideas and inventions, some of which, like the wheel, mingled their origins with the mists of antiquity. Possibly, in making such a comprehensive statement, we should except the electric spark used first by Benz in 1886 to ignite the explosive mixture in the cylinder of an engine, but even here it should be remembered that long before the human race had evolved intelligible speech, it was known that lightning could start fires: Certainly Benjamin Franklin during a June thunderstorm in 1752 produced a real jump-spark with kite and key and his own good knuckles.

II

What really happened in America during the eighties and early nineties was that news and photographs trickled over from Europe of "horseless vehicles" that had been made there. Whereupon, in nearly every village and town in America, especially in the Midwest, the local mechanical genius devoted his whole being to this new device. This activity was typical also of what composed the first stage of the automobile industry in America, isolated persons making a single machine. Sometimes it was the local mechanical genius, sometimes the local crank.

In many respects this was the American spirit at its best, a feverish ferment of intellectual curiosity, mechanical ingenuity, and cleverness of adaptation. Bicycle manufacturers, makers of baby carriages, wagon makers, toy makers, mechanics, bicycle repairmen, perpetual-motion cranks—all put their minds on the new idea from Europe. Of the Americans who later became manufacturers to any successful degree, Alexander Winton had been a bicycle repairman; Franklin a die caster; Henry Ford a mechanic in an electric powerhouse; Pierce a manufacturer of bird cages, bicycles, and refrigerators; Elwood Haynes had been field superintendent of a natural gas company. The Studebaker car came out of a wagon factory, the Peerless from a clothes wringer factory, the Stanley from a photographic dry-plate factory.

A suggestion by Life *in the early nineteen hundreds.*

All this American activity was adaptation, not invention. Such invention as there was, and most of the pioneering, was done in Europe. It is one of the commonest beliefs in America, and one of the most agreeable to national self-satisfaction, that we made the automobile. But we did not. An American historian of the industry, James Rood Doolittle, wrote: "We did not invent the first car that ran, we did not invent the internal-combustion hydrocarbon motor that is universally used to-day, we did not invent the first tires; but we have taught our teachers almost everything modern they know about such things." That is a frank admission, and there is even more truth in the admission than in the qualification at the close. In all respects—except salesmanship and quantity manufacture, which came later as American contributions—the automobile was a European product. Up to 1905, there were more motor vehicles in Great Britain than in America. Bearing in mind the difference in population and the difference in purchasing power of the people, the evidence of Europe's leadership is indisputable. The American contribution was one of adaptation almost wholly. It is true that the process of adaptation to American conditions included a few advances that had the dignity of true originality. Because there were no good roads in America, the cars for use here had to be built so as to stand more strain. The American adapters worked out new equations, new chemical compounds, new tables of metal stress, and new springs, which could at once ensure ease on asphalt pavements, comparative comfort on cobblestones, and at the same time accommodate themselves to the very rough roads that were about the only kind America then had.

III

The second stage of the automobile in America was composed of the efforts of a comparatively small number, out of the many that tinkered at it, who had the wish to make a business of it, or whom circumstances permitted to get that far. In this stage, the ambition of the pioneers did not go beyond making one machine at a time, by hand, on order from such patrons as they could find.

Of the many scores of cranks and near-geniuses who in the late eighties and early nineties were experimenting with "horseless carriages," relatively few were successful enough to impress their names and their creations on the public of their day. Only those who persevered year after year, undismayed by the jibes of their neighbors, are remembered at all.* In the newspapers of that period one saw references to builders of self-propelling vehicles who were utterly unknown in 1925. Of those who persevered and came to be regarded as indisputably connected with the beginning of the automobile in America, three names stand out.

Charles E. Duryea, of Chicopee, Massachusetts, in the late eighties was engaged in the then booming bicycle business. By 1891, he had come to be such an expert that he did nothing but design bicycles, which were built by the Ames Manufacturing Company. With the summer letup in business in 1891, Duryea found time to design a gasoline motor, with the idea of using it to drive a vehicle. He was helped by his brother Frank, a toolmaker, whose advice proved invaluable. After many tribulations the first Duryea machine was finished in September 1892. The brothers, fearing the ridicule they well knew would follow a breakdown on the public roads, decided to try out the machine indoors. The test was a success, but it was found that the engine was not quite strong enough. Encouraged, the brothers set to work to build a stronger engine. Almost a full year passed before they had finished. In the summer of 1893 everything was ready, and the machine was tried out on the roads. This time the engine proved powerful enough, and the weird hodgepodge of steel and wood and brass, after being cranked from the rear, started off at a good 10 miles an hour—a speed it maintained until stopped, as there was no way for the driver to regulate the velocity by varying the quantity of gasoline fed to the motor. In the following year, Duryea built another and better car. During 1894, 1895, and 1896, he won most of the races held in America, and was easily the outstanding figure in the automobile world. In 1896, his production rose to ten cars, each one better than the last. He was still designing automobiles in 1925, and threatening, with an idea for applying propelling force at the rim of a driving wheel instead of at the shaft, to revolutionize the industry he did so much to start.

Another of the pioneers, one who at his death in May 1925 was termed by many the "Father of the automobile in America," was Elwood Haynes.

*Fifteen companies which started in the early days of the automobile were still in existence in 1925. Over a thousand that started had failed. The fifteen that lasted to 1925 are listed below, with the dates of their first cars:

Apperson	1901	Cadillac	1902	Franklin	1900	Locomobile	1899
Olds	1897	Packard	1902	Pierce-Arrow	1901	Studebaker	1898
Buick	1903	Ford	1903	Haynes	1896	Maxwell	1904
Overland	1902	Peerless	1900	Stearns	1900		

Haynes, in 1890, was the field superintendent of a natural-gas company in Kokomo, Indiana. His interest in the automobile was not merely that of a crank inventor. Rather, it was due to dissatisfaction at losing so much time in his constant trips with a horse and buggy over the rough roads around Kokomo. As a substitute for the horse, he studied the possibilities of steam, electricity, and gasoline. In 1893, he purchased a small gasoline engine, which he set up on blocks and started. The vibration was excessive, but Haynes figured it was no worse than the jars and jolts he was accustomed to in driving a buggy. He made rough sketches of the vehicle he had in mind,

The Buggyaut of Charles Duryea, preserved in the Smithsonian Institution at Washington, is credited as being the second gasoline car made in America. It was built by Charles Duryea of Chicopee Falls, Massachusetts, in 1892–93, and made 7 to 8 miles an hour. (Courtesy of the Smithsonian Institution)

The first car built by Elwood Haynes. Equipped with pneumatic tires and a small one-cylinder gasoline engine, it ran at a speed of 8 to 10 miles per hour, on July 4, 1894, at Kokomo, Indiana. (Courtesy of the Smithsonian Institution)

An early type of electric car, photographed by Harris and Ewing, at Washington, about 1909. The woman wearing the white hat is the wife of Senator William E. Borah. (From a photograph by Harris & Ewing)

Henry Ford at the wheel of his first car. It continues to occupy a place of honor in a special room of the Dearborn factory. (Courtesy of Ford Motor Company)

and with these went to see Elmer Apperson, who ran a small machine shop in Kokomo. Apperson studied the sketches and listened to Haynes's explanations. The idea appealed to him, as it did to almost every American mechanic with a flair for "making things go." In the end he agreed to construct the "horseless carriage." Many of the parts that went into the first Haynes car could be bought in the open market and did not need to be studied out in detail and laboriously manufactured—such as clutches, bicycle tires, wheels, and chains. Other parts, however, had to be built new. As the work went on, difficulties cropped up which necessitated varying the original plans. When such crises occurred, Apperson's brother Edgar, a bicycle repairman, was called in. A good bicycle repairman of those days could solve any mechanical tangle amenable to rule-of-thumb settlement, and Edgar Apperson was one of the best. With a bolt here, a shim there, and a bit of curved wire somewhere else, he nonchalantly overcame difficulties that had taxed the brains of his brother and Elwood Haynes. Finally the great day came when the vehicle was ready for trial. It is indicative of the moral fiber of the three builders and their confidence in their work that the trial was to be public, and that the date decided on was the Fourth of July, 1894, a day on which it was certain that the streets of Kokomo would be overflowing with holiday crowds predisposed and eager to jeer at failure. But no jeers were heard. The queer carriage, drawn by a horse through Kokomo to an outlying road, was followed by an avidly curious crowd. With the proud but nervous Haynes at the steering rod, and the path cleared of onlookers, a crank was projected between the spokes of a rear wheel and the engine started. In a silence broken only by the puffing of the fretful motor, the car dashed away between the rows of awed watchers at a speed about twice as fast as a man's walk.

The third of the Americans who in the early nineties persisted in their attempts to build motor-driven vehicles was Henry Ford of Detroit. Ford was regarded by his neighbors as a visionary who hadn't sense enough to work the forty acres of land given him by his father as a bribe to leave the city and return to the broader opportunities of farm life. As a boy, Ford had been interested in machinery, cheap watches, threshers and binders, and mowing machines. Before reaching his twenties, he left the farm and went to Detroit to work in a powerhouse. In his spare time he tinkered at a gasoline engine of his own contrivance, making a cylinder out of an old gas pipe, a flywheel out of wood, and other parts out of odds and ends. Of the great moment in Ford's life, the day when his first automobile actually ran, there is a brief but vivid description in Dr. Samuel S. Marquis's book *Henry Ford*:

> I have heard from him and Mrs. Ford the story of the last forty-eight hours that he worked on that first car. Forty-eight hours without sleep. The second night Mrs. Ford sat up waiting the outcome of his efforts. The machine was nearing completion. Would it run? It was about 2 A.M. when he came in from the little shop that stood in the rear of the house. The car was finished and ready for a try-out. It was raining. Mrs. Ford threw a cloak over her shoulders and followed him to the shop. He rolled the little car out into the alley, started it, mounted the seat and drove off. The car went a short distance and stopped. The trouble was a minor one. The nut of a bolt had come off. It seems that there was some vibration in that first machine, which has been handed down to its millions of offspring.

IV

The gasoline automobile was not the first to get under way. In the first real automobile show ever held in America, in New York in 1900, more than a third of the space was taken up by displays of various electric cars; of the rest of the space, nearly all was consumed by steam cars. Only a minor fraction was devoted to the type of car that later got the lead.

The electric car lost out largely because its power could only be renewed at electric charging stations, and as these were only to be found in cities, its radius of motion was limited. The steam car fell behind for a variety of reasons, among which was the greater expert knowledge required to operate it, the necessity the operator of a steam car was under of securing a steam engineer's license—a process not to be compared with the perfunctory examination of applicants for a driver's license as practiced universally as late as 1925—and the rather well-founded fear in the public mind of the dangerous aspects of the steamer. (In the Glidden Tour of 1906, two steam cars caught fire and burned.) The public was afraid of mishaps—in winter when undrained boilers and tanks were wrecked by the formation of ice, at all times because of the danger of explosions from leaking gasoline reservoirs. By 1925, these defects had been largely eliminated, but in that year only one company of any importance was producing steam cars in America, and

Maxwell's car of the early 1900s arriving at Mt. Washington on one of the Glidden Tours.

the output of that company was in the neighborhood of only 1,000 cars yearly.

The electric car that was the favorite in the early years of the century was, in many respects, more comfortable than its gasoline rival. It was smoother, less noisy, less smelly, easier to control. And as to the steam car, which, essentially, was the refinement of the railroad locomotive, many believe that if its development had not been restricted, it might have been more popular than the gasoline car. Possibly an additional reason for the gasoline machine leaving the others behind may have been some accident

Testing an electric car in the Automobile Show of 1900, in Madison Square Garden, New York.

of personality, a greater aggregate of aggressive energy in those manufacturers who concentrated on gasoline.

V

In 1895 there were 300 motor vehicles in more or less continuous operation in America. The qualification "more or less" is used advisedly. The occasional exhilarating periods, when the possessor of one of these 300 could dash along the cobbled thoroughfares of our cities at a continuing pace, were interspersed with hours of laborious "tinkering" and adjusting. Particularly exasperating was the process of starting the motor, which frequently entailed the draining of the victim's last reserve of strength, patience, and self-command. Nor, once the motor was started, did the autoist's lot become easy. Switches had to be pressed, and a complexity of pedals and levers had to be operated simultaneously by drivers woefully inexperienced. Frequently when the driver wished to go one way, the car went another. Not infrequently brakes or pedals refused to function, and terror-stricken drivers were carried helplessly along by iron steeds indifferent alike to prayers and curses from behind or obstacles in front. Even when the machines were not in use they were not out of the minds of their harassed owners. As public garages had not yet appeared, the cars were kept, as a rule, in livery stables, the personnel of which had scant sympathy for "man's new servant." Arousing in the breasts of the general public sentiments of curiosity and derision, their delicate mechanisms were subjected to the pryings of small boys and stable hangers-on. Under such circumstances the great masses of the people were quite content to leave the automobile to the "bugs" who seemed to enjoy the struggle, and to the rich whose interest in the ownership of a horseless carriage outweighed the many inconveniences which possession entailed.

In spite of the not very encouraging position of the automobile at this period, there were not lacking those who foresaw its future. Among these optimistic prophets was a contributor to the *Eclectic Magazine* in 1895:

> I name ten years as the time within which we may see the railways given up to business traffic and persons in a hurry; the country dotted with airy vehicles flying along on roads that continental nations might be proud of. . . . Electric trams and electric cabs shall have worked wonders in our cities, which now will be clean and sweet instead of foul and muddy. As traffic becomes gentler, rates will diminish. Heads will no longer throb with disagreeable sights and sounds. The busy man will be able to think as he drifts along on wheels of softest motion; not agitated by thoughts of the wretched beast in front, nor distraught by noises round him. Modern life will have lost a few of its worst terrors.*

*He failed to predict that by 1925 one of the "worst terrors" of "modern life" was death by automobile.

The ten years allowed by this prophet came and went without seeing much more than the beginning of the revolutionary changes in living conditions and transportation that he predicted. The "roads that continental nations might be proud of" had as yet hardly begun to emerge from the mud of 1900, and heads still throbbed from the smells and sounds produced by mankind's varied mediums of transportation. Nevertheless, progress was being made daily, and on an immense scale. The new industry called irresistibly to alert, adventurous young men. To them it mattered little that in its early period of development the automobile was a hapless

The coming of good roads. The same car, the same man, and the same place. (By courtesy of U.S. Bureau of Public Roads)

thing, awkward, erratic, and ugly, compared with the trim rubber-tired carriages that sped along behind well-cared-for horses; or that it was destined, by almost unanimous popular opinion, to be relegated shortly to the oblivion from which it had emerged. These men—Pope, Winton, White, Whitney, Prescott, Gaeth, Lane, Farmer, Wilkinson, Moon, Pierce, Packard, Ford, Marmon, to mention but a few—took enthusiastic hold of the infant industry, with the result that by 1905 the number of cars under registry had grown to the impressive total of 77,988, compared with the 300 that had been in existence in America in 1895, ten years before.

This progress was doubly notable since it was made in the face of popular distrust of the automobile; and because important advances had to be made in the design and construction of cars to enable them to compete with the more advanced products of European factories. In the July 1899 issue of *McClure's Magazine*, Ray Stannard Baker summed up the progress that had been made when the last century was coming to a close:

> . . . Between the 1st of January and the 1st of May, 1899, companies with the enormous aggregate capitalization of more than $388,000,000 have been organized in New York, Boston, Chicago, and Philadelphia for the sole purpose of manufacturing and operating these new vehicles. At least eighty establishments are now actually engaged in building carriages, coaches, tricycles, delivery-wagons, and trucks, representing no fewer than 200 different types of vehicles, with nearly half as many methods of propulsion. Most of these concerns are far behind in their orders, and several of them are

Allowing fifteen feet for each of the motor vehicles in use in the United States during 1924, and placing one behind another, a traffic line would be formed stretching twice around the globe.

working day and night. A hundred electric cabs are plying familiarly on the streets of New York, and 200 more are being rushed to completion in order to supply the popular demand for horseless locomotion. At least two score of delivery-wagons, propelled chiefly by electricity, are in operation in American cities, and the private conveyances of various makes will number well into the hundreds. A motor-ambulance is in operation in Chicago; motor-trucks are at work in several different cities; a motor gun-carriage for use in the army will be ready in the summer. . . . At least two cities are using self-propelled fire-engines. A trip of 720 miles, from Cleveland to New York, over all kinds of country roads, has actually been made in a gasoline carriage, and an enthusiastic automobile traveler is now on his way from New England to San Francisco.

The sum Mr. Baker mentions, $388 million, was capitalization, not cash. Had the automotive industry been fed any such sum of real money early in 1899, the row subsequently hoed would have been easier. Until 1907, capital held aloof. Until 1905 or thereabouts, the automobile was a toy of the mechanically inclined and a luxury of the well-to-do. On the streets of well-paved cities it was finding a limited employment by sharing with the horse the delivery service of department stores, and to an even more limited extent it vied with the now obsolete hansom and closed cab as a public conveyance. But it suffered from the odium of being an ostentatious luxury of the rich. The following stanzas of a parody appeared in *Life* as late as 1904 under the caption "The Charge of the Four Hundred":

> Half a block, half a block,
>   Half a block onward,
> All in their motobiles
>   Rode the Four Hundred.
> "Forward!" the owners shout,
> "Racing-car!" "Runabout!"
>   Into Fifth Avenue
>   Rode the Four Hundred.
>
> "Forward!" the owners said.
> Was there a man dismay'd?
> Not, though the chauffeurs knew
>   Some one had blundered.
> Theirs not to make reply,
> Theirs not to reason why,
> Theirs but to kill or die.
>   Into Fifth Avenue
>   Rode the Four Hundred.

Being a luxury, and so seductive a luxury as to tempt some people of moderate means to mortgage their homes and waste their substance in the purchase and maintenance of "devil wagons," as they were then facetiously called, it was but natural that they should be regarded askance by bankers and capitalists. Plenty of other reasons existed why capital should not flow into the industry. There was trouble over the early patents and many suits about infringements; revolutionary changes were being made in the designs of cars at short intervals. What conservative custodian of capital would face his associates with the proposal that they invest heavily in an industry that was the butt of every jokesmith in the land? To readers accustomed to the ubiquity and the foolproof quality of the automobile, a joke from *Life* in 1904 will suggest the earlier attitude toward the new invention:

> "Yes, I enjoy my automobile immensely."
> "But I never see you out."
> "Oh, I haven't got that far yet. I am just learning to make my own repairs."

VI

While Americans did not invent the automobile, nor have any serious share in the improvement of it, they did make one immense contribution, and that constituted the third stage of the automobile in this country. It was Americans who made the automobile available to the average man. It is often assumed that the automobile industry was the pioneer of "quantity production," and that among automobile makers Ford was the earliest to use this system. Neither assumption is correct. The automobile manufacturers merely took up an idea evolved a century earlier by Eli Whitney and elaborated on it to a stupendous, amazing degree. By 1925, "quantity production" had become an essential of American industry, and of importance far beyond its place in business, as being a long step in the enrichment of man, in making goods available to him at a price within his reach.

The early European manufacturers made automobiles "to order" and chiefly for the rich, as did the early American manufacturers. In 1900, some American manufacturers turned to the idea of making cars in quantities to be offered for sale as a standard article, and at a price that average men could pay. This necessitated abandonment of the fine handwork of European machines. What these American pioneers of "quantity production" did was to select such parts of European models as were capable of being made in large quantities by machine. This involved the rejection of some of the best features of the European models. If the thing did not lend itself to machine manufacture, it was passed by. As a result, the Americans did not make the best machines, nor anything near the best; but they did make an acceptable machine that would start, go somewhere, and return, with a minimum of mechanical trouble, at small expense, and at a cost such that great numbers of people could buy.

In 1900, the Olds Motor Works erected in Detroit what was then the

Onlookers parked in nearby fields to see the Vanderbilt Cup Race.

largest automobile factory in the country. They concentrated their entire equipment and abilities on a single model—and that was a fundamental step in developing the theory and practice of quantity production. For the first time in automobile history, parts were ordered in thousand lots: 2,000 sets of transmission gears from Dodge Brothers; 2,000 motors from Leland and Faulkner. They sold the car first for $600, then for $650. The first year, they made 400 machines; the second, 1,600; the third, 4,000. The capitalization of the firm was $350,000, but $200,000 was all the cash that ever went into the company. The first two years they paid out 105 percent in cash dividends. That was the indisputable demonstration that the automobile could be more than a rich man's toy. This event, in the year 1900, was the birth of the automobile as a commercial reality.

The innovation of "mass production," "quantity production," "repetitive processes," as it is variously called, was the beginning of the second stage of the automobile, the stage of diffusion, which made it available to all. Mass production was accompanied by a new and enormously expanded development of advertising and marketing. Both mass production and advertising became fundamentally important American institutions, not only as respects the automobile but in the widest sense.

CHAPTER 7
The Airplane Emerges, Too

About the time of the turn of the century, the most alert and authoritative of the popular magazines in America was *McClure's*. Its policy expressed itself in a serious effort to say the last word, and in another sense the final word, on current developments in all fields. *McClure's*, wishing to give its readers the most unimpeachable thought on the possibility of human flight, procured an article from Simon Newcomb, Ph.D., LL.D. Newcomb was a scientist of the best standing. He had been professor of mathematics at the U.S. Naval Academy and at Johns Hopkins University, had been editor of the *American Journal of Mathematics*, had supervised the erection of the Lick Observatory telescope, had made important discoveries in the field of the velocity of light, and had been given honors by many distinguished scientific societies of the world and by American universities and by Oxford, Cambridge, and Dublin.

Newcomb's article, in the September 1901 issue of *McClure's*, reveals the distinguished mathematician divided between two emotions: irritation that aviation should be taken seriously by sensible persons, and patience in the purpose of making his readers see, as clearly as he did, how futile the notion was. He seemed determined to explain in a step-by-step manner the fundamental and eternal reasons from which even the unerudite reader could make the inevitable deduction. He gave his article the title "Is the Airplane Coming?"

Professor Newcomb did not quite say "no"; rather, he said "no" in a manner meant to carry greater conviction than that small word could:

> No builder of air castles for the amusement and benefit of humanity could have failed to include a flying-machine among the productions of his imagination. The desire to fly like a bird is inborn in our race, and we can no more be expected to abandon the idea than the ancient mathematician could have been expected to give up the problem of squaring the circle. . . . As the case stands, the first successful flyer will be the handiwork of a watchmaker and will carry nothing heavier than an insect.

Farther on Professor Newcomb's suppressed impatience burst through his inhibitions for a moment and betrayed him into a more nearly explicit negation: "The example of the bird does not prove that man can fly. . . .

Imagine the proud possessor of the aeroplane darting through the air at a speed of several hundred feet per second! It is the speed alone that sustains him. How is he ever going to stop?"

Finally, Professor Newcomb lost entirely, for a careless moment, the pose of making an open-minded inquiry, and came out with a statement positive enough to assure him a place among those skeptical philosophers he derided because they had set limits to man's inventiveness: "I have shown that the construction of an aerial vehicle which could carry even a single man from place to place at pleasure requires the discovery of some new metal or some new force."

This was the prevailing attitude of the printed word, in the popular sense, toward aviation. It had the effect of confirming the average man's age-long conviction that human flight belonged in the world of fable and increased his disbelief in the possibility of it.

II

There was a scientist of the highest standing, Professor Samuel P. Langley, secretary of the Smithsonian Institution, who believed human flight was possible, who spent the major part of his mature lifetime trying to make it an actuality—and had the tragic fate of deepening in a spectacular way the average man's conviction that human flight could never be.

On May 6, 1896, one of Langley's models, weighing about twenty-six pounds, having wings measuring fourteen feet from tip to tip, and equipped with a miniature steam engine, was set going on the banks of the Potomac River at Washington. It sustained itself in the air about a minute and a half and traveled a distance of about half a mile, dropping gently into the river when the fuel and water in the tiny engine were exhausted. Later that same year, on November 28, a similar model traveled about three-fourths of a mile at a speed of 30 miles an hour.

The U.S. War Department had been impressed. The Board of Ordnance and Fortifications urged Langley to attempt a machine capable of carrying a man. Langley consented, reluctantly. With a subsidy of $50,000 from the board, with the support and help of the army, with the backing of the Smithsonian, with the confidence of so much of the scientific world as believed aviation possible at all, Langley, with an assistant, Charles M. Manly, built an engine really remarkable, considering the state at that time of progress in internal-combustion engines. Weighing but 124 pounds, it developed under test 52.4 horsepower, a record best understood when it is realized that Europe and America had been scoured for a 12 horsepower engine weighing in the neighborhood of 100 pounds, and none had been found. This engine Langley and Manly placed in a man-size airplane having two sets of wings placed tandem fashion—a replica of the early smaller models in every respect save the engine.

Delay followed delay, but on October 7, 1903, seven years after the

Charles M. Manly and Samuel P. Langley.

Board of Ordnance and Fortifications had made its appropriation, preparations were complete for the first trial flight.

The scene was at Widewater, Virginia, at a point where the Potomac River broadens out into a kind of bay some 4 miles wide. In this spacious background, about a mile from the Maryland side of the river, were set up paraphernalia as novel as the expected event. For a parent-ship, Dr. Langley had built a huge, long, arklike houseboat; on its top, from stern to bow, was a runway of two rails seventy feet long; on the runway, at the stern, backed tightly against coiled springs, was what Langley called a "catapult car" designed to hurl the airplane into space. Atop the "catapult car" rested the airplane itself.

About what happened that day, so far as it had to do with the scientific and expert mechanical aspects of the experiment, there was disagreement at the time. Manly, who was in the airplane, seemed not to have been able to follow the rapidity of the events with sufficient calmness of observation. Langley, the inventor, who was not present, had a theory about what had happened differing from Manly's. The airplane, as well as parts of the catapult car and the runway, was so damaged as to make postmortems uncertain in their findings.

The whole country yelled. It was a day of triumph for every faithful defender of the immutability of what is. Practically every headline and news story seemed to reflect smug satisfaction in the proof that man's conviction about the impossibility of human flight was still sound and right, seemed almost savagely gratified that an impious professor questioning the law of gravity had been so sensationally rebuked and humiliated. The news stories seemed to reflect, too, the suspicion, partly condescending, partly truculent, of laymen against scientists, an attitude commoner then than now. The stories actually seemed to gloat in affirmation and repeated reaffirmation of the unqualified completeness of the failure. They became almost delirious when Langley failed again in December.

However Langley the scientist may have remained confident about aviation, Langley the man was desperately hurt, hurt to the point of physical illness, by the tornado of ridicule. It came from high and low. One specimen which, because of the elevation of its source, is worth reviving for posterity came from the well-known writer Ambrose Bierce: "I don't know how much larger Professor Langley's machine is than its flying model was—about large enough, I think, to require an atmosphere a little denser than the intelligence of one scientist and not quite so dense as that of two."

By the newspaper accounts of Langley's failure, by the editorial jeers about it, by the quips in comic periodicals and the skits in the vaudeville theaters, the struggling new science Langley had striven so earnestly to advance was discredited; and the skeptical multitudes were given spectacular confirmation of their conviction that human flight could not be, flattering approval for their steadfastness of belief that what has not been, cannot be.

III

We leap, as the old-fashioned melodramatists used to say, nine short, December days. Langley's final failure had taken place December 8, 1903. By one of the most ironic coincidences ever staged by the "twin impostors," there occurred on December 17, 1903, the culmination of the experiments of two men who, in every detail of their background and nearly every material circumstance attending their efforts, were as far removed from Langley as if the contrast had been deliberately arranged by some cosmic deity in an exceptionally sardonic mood. Where Langley was known to the whole world as one of its foremost scientists, Orville and Wilbur Wright were known merely as practical mechanics—in the very limited circle where they were known at all. Where Langley had the prestige of a great scientific institution, the Smithsonian, the Wrights had only the background of a bicycle shop. Where Langley had the backing of a U.S. government subsidy of $50,000, the Wrights had only the resources of a small manufacturing and repair business. Langley's work had been car-

ried out under the observation of learned societies and the U.S. Army, and
had been watched by newspapers and magazines; the total number of persons who had seen or heard about any part of what the Wrights had been
doing for five years was probably less than 100, a few helpers and friends,
and casual callers at their shop. The final trials of the Langley machine had
taken place under the fierce glare of the mechanisms for publicity concentrated at the nation's capital, and had been followed by practically every
newspaper reader in the United States and many in Europe; the test by the
Wrights of their machine took place at one of the most inaccessible spots
in America, without a newspaperman present, nor anyone else except the
Wrights themselves and a few coast guards. Between the pageant-attended
publicity-charged atmosphere of Washington on December 8, 1903,
and the remote sand dunes of Kitty Hawk, North Carolina, on December
17, the literal difference was nine days in time and 200 miles in space. By
all the attending circumstances, including the outcome, the difference was
immeasurable.

One evening, in the summer of 1896, Wilbur Wright, reading a newspaper
after his day in the brothers' bicycle shop, chanced upon an account of the
death of a German engineer, Otto Lilienthal, who had been killed by the
fall of a "glider." Orville was at home convalescing from an attack of typhoid fever. Wilbur kept the newspaper and showed it to his brother after
Orville had completely recovered. By the impression that chance newspaper article made on two minds intellectually curious and inclined toward
experiment, the Wrights were drawn into that web of which an earlier ex-
perimenter had written:

> If there be a domineering, tyrant thought, it is the conception
> that the problem of flight may be solved by man. When once this
> idea has invaded the brain it possesses it exclusively. It is then a
> haunting thought, a walking nightmare, impossible to cast off. If
> now we consider the pitying contempt with which such a line of re-
> search is appreciated, we may somewhat conceive the unhappy lot
> of the poor investigator whose soul is thus possessed.

   The Wrights, reading whatever literature they could find, discussing it,
finding analogies for some of the principles in their own experience as bicycle experts, arrived at conclusions characteristic of original minds, minds
accustomed through their daily work to test theory by practice. They observed that the aeronautical enthusiasts fell into two groups. One gave
chief attention to machines equipped with power, the other to gliders. The
Wrights chose to align themselves with the second group, "partly," wrote
Wilbur Wright, "from impatience at the wasteful extravagance of mounting delicate and costly machinery on wings which no one knew how to
manage."
   Having decided that soaring in a glider should be the immediate step,

they reached another conclusion equally characteristic of their instinct for reality. The essential need was practice.

In scientific terms, the problem of remaining safely afloat in the air consists in causing the center of gravity to coincide with the center of pressure. But in actual practice, as Wilbur Wright put it, there is "an almost boundless incompatibility of temper which prevents their remaining peaceably together for a single instant, so that the operator, who in this case acts as peacemaker, often suffers injury to himself while attempting to bring them together."

While the Wrights were pondering over this problem, it happened that one evening in 1899 Orville went with his sister to the home of some friends, Wilbur remaining at the shop. Business was slack and Wilbur, to pass the time, idly picked up an empty cardboard box which had been left on the counter by a customer who had bought an inner tube for his bicycle. This box was oblong in shape and not dissimilar in outline to the biplane glider the brothers were planning to build. Wilbur noticed he could twist the box between his hands, distorting its surfaces. Holding it before him, he observed that with slight exertion he could warp it so that simultaneously the surface on the right side forward had a downward inclination, and that on the left side forward an upward inclination. The idea occurred to him: Could not the surfaces of a glider be warped in the same manner, thus achieving a method for lateral balancing based on the application of varying vertical wind pressures on either wing as desired? Keeping on an even keel had been the problem that had defeated all previous experimenters. It was the greatest of all the problems to be solved before man could fly. Did the twisted tire box give the clue to its solution?

When Orville returned he found Wilbur sketching a system for warping the glider wings in the manner suggested by the tire box. The idea was explained to Orville; he thought it good; and a discussion began which lasted far into the night.

That forgotten evening in a humdrum bicycle shop in a quiet Dayton street, when two earnest men became excited over a twisted cardboard box, marks, more than any other event, the moment when the secret of flight was discovered. It is a milestone in history, aviation's equivalent to Newton's observation of the falling apple.

In the summer of 1900, the brothers built their first large glider, incorporating in it the best ideas that had come from their years of reading and discussing, including their own wing-warping principle.

While the glider was taking shape in their hands, the Wrights wrote to the Weather Bureau at Washington, asking where in the United States they could find the best conditions for gliding experiments; that is, a combination of hilly country with fairly constant winds of rather high velocity. They did not say in their specifications that the hills should be of such a material as to do the minimum of damage to a falling structure of wood and cloth or to a falling man, but doubtless they were pleased when their correspondence with the Weather Bureau, and later with a North Carolina postmaster, resulted in the suggestion of Kitty Hawk, a region of rolling hills, but hills made of sand, dunes built up by the strong winds blowing steadily from the sea.

That first season at Kitty Hawk (1900) was disappointing. The hours and hours of practice they had hoped to obtain finally dwindled down to about two minutes of flying the glider as a kite, with no one aboard. But they acquired one assurance. While their new wing-warping device for lateral stability did not solve the problem completely, it nevertheless worked sufficiently well to give them reason to believe that with modification it would do what they hoped.

This encouragement, however, was more than balanced by a distrust that began to undermine their confidence in the mathematical tables on which they had based their calculations of wind pressures and "drift." These tables had been worked out by others before the Wrights became interested in aviation; on their accuracy depended all progress that could be achieved by anybody.

"We saw," the brothers wrote later, "that the calculations upon which all flying-machines had been based were unreliable, and that all were simply groping in the dark. Having set out with absolute faith in the existing scientific data, we were driven to doubt one thing after another, till finally, after two years of experiment, we cast it all aside. . . . Truth and error were everywhere so intimately mixed as to be indistinguishable."

What faced them now was no less than the job of working out new tables—doing the scientific part of aviation from the ground up. The task was one for trained mathematicians—indeed trained mathematicians had already done it, and done it wrong. The brothers had left high school at seventeen.

The job would not have dismayed them too much had they not been obliged to take their personal circumstances into account. Up to this time they had regarded their experimenting as a diversion; now it began to be a serious matter. Further progress was highly problematical and could only be attained by experimenting on an ambitious scale. For their expenses they had to rely on the bicycle business. To continue their experiments on the scale now necessary meant a greater drain on their resources, at all times scanty. It meant also their absence from Dayton for months on end, during which their business must suffer.

In the winter of 1901–1902, in their Dayton shop, they built an ingenious wind tunnel, designed to give results free from the errors in measurements and calculations of their predecessors. Under the necessity of learning the mathematical part of aviation from the rudiments up, they made preliminary measurements of many different shaped surfaces, and, later, systematic measurements of standard surfaces so varied in design as to bring out the underlying causes of differences in pressures.

By the fall of 1902 they had tables of their own making. Again they went to Kitty Hawk, and now, for the first time, the glider performed according to calculations. In September and October (1902) nearly 1,000 flights were made, several covering distances of over 600 feet. Some, made against a wind of 36 miles an hour, proved the effectiveness of the new device for control.

The Wrights had now reached substantially the end of the glider phase of their progress. They had carried out the program they had laid out years before, to learn to fly by getting on a glider and flying. In the course of that, they had of necessity done what they had never anticipated being obliged to do, had dismissed the entire accumulation of scientific data, had explored the scientific basis of aviation from the ground up, and had written it anew. They had found by scientific experiments what elements were needed to give a glider the maximum of lifting power and how to maneuver it in flight. They had learned—and this was most important—the personal, physical art of flying, what to do in the air as a swimmer learns what to do in water.

That the Wrights, in their joint study and experiment, accomplished more than the aggregate of all their predecessors is accounted for chiefly by a factor in their association which is so unique, so distant from anything with which the average man is familiar, that one cannot assume it will dawn upon the reader unless attention is called to it.

It was not that the Wrights, being two, had an advantage over lone workers—though, to be sure, that was a contributing element in their success. Other men working alone had learned some of the secrets of flight, but their knowledge had been snuffed out when, as frequently happened, they succumbed to the risks that are inseparable from experimentation. Had one of the Wrights been killed, there would have been no loss to the sum of the world's knowledge of flight; the surviving brother could have carried on with at least a chance to succeed.

Nor was the sentimental aspect of the brothers' relations of fundamental importance in their success. Their affection for each other did not differ from what is frequent between brother and brother and between close friends.

It was something else. An intellectual kinship grew up between them—more than a kinship, a twinship—more even than a twinship, a unity.

From early youth the Wrights had the same tastes, the same interests, the same likes and dislikes. They worked together, lived together, played together. A bond of this kind between brothers is usually dissolved at adolescence, by separation in high school or college, by marriage and the earning of a living. In the case of the Wrights it was never broken.

From their constant association throughout more hours of the day than human beings are together ordinarily, from their continuing presence together under the same sets of circumstances, a curious phenomenon developed: The associative thinking of both came to be identical. Their trains of thought ran on parallel tracks and their automatic reactions became the same. Again and again it happened that, having spent an evening discussing a problem, they would appear at breakfast the next morning with identical solutions. Frequently, when the brothers were near each other in the bicycle shop or elsewhere, both at the same moment would start singing the chorus of the same popular song or, again, both would break a silence by uttering the same remark. As the years went on and these coincidences became more frequent, the brothers' curiosity was stirred. After some characteristically impersonal analysis, they decided their lifelong association must have brought their minds into a state of synchronization, so that events oc-

Top, the first Wright glider, being flown as a kite, Kitty Hawk, North Carolina, 1900. Center, one of the later Wright gliders in flight. Bottom, the Wright airplane that made the first flight in history, December 17, 1903.

curring in their vicinity had identical reflexes in their minds and led to identical mental and physical reactions. Almost their minds became as one, and their muscles responded as to the same brain. In any emergency each brother knew just what the other would do. More accurately, they did not go through any process of "knowing." Each acted instinctively and automatically as if the other were himself. In a crisis, if Wilbur happened to be in the machine and Orville on the ground, Orville sensed instinctively what Wilbur would do to avert disaster, and Orville automatically applied the compensatory motion.

This quality of the Wrights, in a curious way, ran counter to a law of matter, and enabled them to triumph over matter. Mathematical law affirms that the whole is equal to the sum of its parts, that one and one make two, and never more. But this particular union of the Wrights brought an element outside of and above calculations of quantity.

For two men to cooperate toward an intellectual end is not unusual; in modern research laboratories as many as a score of men work together toward a single invention. But the Wrights were not merely two workers. They were not two at all; they were parts of one; they were, in effect, one Wright raised to an nth power, which is a different thing and much greater.

This twinship, multiplied, was the unique feature of the Wrights. Through it they invented the airplane, as neither of them alone would have. Through it they brought flight to the world at least a generation before it would have come but for them.

In 1903, the Wrights were ready for the final stage, the application of power to their glider, the construction of a power-driven airplane. Little time was lost deciding the engine must be of the internal-combustion type, but when they applied to automobile manufacturers and other makers of gasoline engines, they found no one willing to contract to provide them with the sort of engine they required. Thrown on their own resources, they

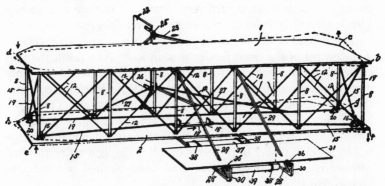

Orville and Wilbur Wright made their first patent application on March 23, 1903. This drawing, which accompanied their application, illustrated the working of the wing-wrapped device for lateral stability and, together with the specifications which they prepared themselves, sufficiently answers the belittling phrase often applied to them—"just practical mechanics."

built the engine themselves. Even more difficult was the task of finding the perfect propeller. Again, they designed and built their own.

On Wednesday, September 23, 1903, the Wrights, with their glider, their engine, and their propellers, left Dayton again for Kitty Hawk. Arriving there, they began fitting their engine and propellers to their plane. They were ready on December 17, 1903. That was nine days after Langley had made his final spectacular failure at Washington, and after the newspapers had flooded the country with the conviction of conclusive proof that human flight could not be.

Of what happened at Kill Devil Hill that day, there was a newspaper account in a local paper which a fair number of readers must have seen, but which practically none took in.

Of that inaccurate account, printed in the local *Norfolk Virginian-Pilot*, condensed versions were sent by its authors to newspapers in New York and some other cities. Such metropolitan papers as printed it at all did so inconspicuously. Possibly managing editors may have been moved by a realization that, for them, the situation presented difficulties; newspapers which on December 9, 1903, the day after Langley's failure, had told the world that aviation was not and could not be, could not consistently explain on December 18 that aviation was.

For an account of the first flight ever made by man in a power-driven plane, more technical if less picturesque than the ones in the newspapers, we may turn to Orville Wright himself:

> Wilbur, having used his turn in the unsuccessful attempt on the 14th, the right to the first trial now belonged to me. Wilbur ran at the side, holding the wing to balance it on the track. The machine, facing a 27-mile wind, started very slowly. Wilbur was able to stay with it till it lifted from the track after a forty-foot run.
>
> The course of the flight up and down was exceedingly erratic. The control of the front rudder was difficult. As a result the machine would rise suddenly to about ten feet, and then as suddenly dart for the ground. A sudden dart when a little over 120 feet from the point at which it rose into the air, ended the flight. This flight lasted only 12 seconds, but it was nevertheless the first in the history of the world in which a machine carrying a man had raised itself by its own power into the air in full flight, had sailed forward without reduction of speed, and had finally landed at a point as high as that from which it started.
>
> Wilbur started the fourth and last flight at just 12 o'clock. The first few hundred feet were up and down as before, but by the time three hundred feet had been covered, the machine was under much better control. The course for the next four or five hundred feet

had but little undulation. However, when out about eight hundred feet the machine began pitching again, and, in one of its darts downward, struck the ground. The distance over the ground was measured and found to be 852 feet; the time of the flight 59 seconds.

The Wright brothers dismantled their machine, packed it in "two boxes and a barrel," and returned to Dayton. They had invented the flying machine indisputably.

IV

The Wrights continued to fly, again and again; they remained in the air as much as thirty-eight minutes and covered as great a distance as 24 miles. But the world did not know it, refused to believe anybody who said it had happened, and remained unaware of it until more than four years after the first flight occurred.

The explanation lay partly in the circumstances of the Wrights' flights: the lack of publicity about their experiments, the absence of reporters when their flights were made, the fact that just before their first flight the world had been flooded with accounts of the spectacular failure of Langley; the fact that newspapers which, on December 8, 1903, had described Langley's failure as proof of the impossibility of flight, could not readily eight days later convince the world if they tried, nor even themselves, that human flight had actually taken place.

But to a much greater extent, the explanation lay in the fixed state of mind of the average man about aviation—an incredulity so great that to resurrect it now, after it has so completely gone, to re-create for the reader of today the attitude of the average man prior to 1908, is one of the major difficulties of the writing of this history.

So firmly embedded in man's deepest consciousness was his conviction of the impossibility of human flight, that hardly any printed account could convince him it had actually been accomplished. The experience of believing had to wait, for each man, until he actually looked up with his own eyes and saw an airplane flying. Only then did he get the sensation of conviction, the thrill.

Awareness by the world that human flight had actually been accomplished did not come until 1908, when the Wrights again went to Kitty Hawk for another series of flights.

In that year, a newspaper stringer, D. Bruce Salley, covered a beat beginning at Norfolk, Virginia, and stretching south for 100 miles along the deeply indented coastline of Virginia and North Carolina. Salley had a roving assignment from the Norfolk *Landmark* to wander up and down this lonely region of drifting sand dunes in quest of maritime news, and in addition had the usual query man's relation to outside newspapers, including the *New York Herald,* to which he sent dispatches dealing with shipwrecks and other local events having sufficient national importance to justify the attention of the metropolitan press.

From Salley, on the evening of May 6, 1908, about the hour when the Broadway theaters were filling and the staffs of the New York papers were gathering for their work, came a telegram saying that at Kitty Hawk, North Carolina, two brothers named Wright had flown almost 1,000 feet at a height 60 feet above the ground in a flying machine without a balloon attachment.

To the managing editors, whose function it is to pass instant judgment upon the probable news value of the query man's information, to determine how much weight shall be given to it, and to decide whether it is sufficiently important to call for subsequent treatment by reporters dispatched from the home office—to them, the reports from North Carolina presented a problem serious and delicate.

Aviation, to managing editors, was vexation. Hardly a week passed without its report or "tip" about an inventor, usually in some remote part of the world, who had a wonderful new idea for overcoming gravitation, or who had built, or was going to build, a machine that would fly. None of these stories, so far as the managing editors knew, had ever been convincingly substantiated; indeed, scores of them when run down had turned out to be hoaxes, or attempts to deceive, or the impractical dreams of irresponsible visionaries.

To managing editors, walking their careful tightrope between not being misled by irresponsible rumors and not missing authentic news, the reports from North Carolina presented one more opportunity to be damned if they did and damned if they didn't. Should they print the story without first verifying it, their reward might be unbelief and ridicule. On the other hand, they had to consider the possibility that Salley might be right, in which event, if they should let pass the opportunity to treat the report with the conspicuousness it deserved, their position would be even more unhappy.

These editorial dubieties lasted less time than it takes to tell them. The decision reached was midway between caution and daring, closer to the former than to the latter. One can read the editors' mood in the yellowed pages of the *New York Herald* for May 7, 1908. Salley's flying-machine story is on the first page, but not at the top of a column. It occupies a position less prominent than two other dispatches—"Republicans to Push Currency Bill" and "Deposed Emperor of Korea to Be Exiled to Japan." In headlines, it is on a parity with a front-page story about a retired sea captain who "possesses a formula by which one may live a hundred years."

This cautious restraint in the printing of Salley's dispatch was one side of the policy usual with newspapers in such cases; the other side was the prompt dispatching of the paper's own staff correspondents.

These correspondents two days later descended upon Salley in somewhat the mood of generals summoned from the comforts of staff headquarters by an outlying sentinel with information he deems important. If the sentinel's report proves correct, he will be given approval touched with condescension; otherwise he will hear extremely unpleasant remarks about his credulity, veracity, sobriety, and other traits of intelligence and character.

The correspondent of the *New York Herald*, Byron R. Newton, whether moved by skepticism of his own about Salley's veracity, or by consciousness of the public's skepticism about the whole subject of flying, decided to practice safety first, by using in his early dispatches a phrase of disavowal: "according to Salley." But two days after his arrival, Newton's doubts vanished. From Kill Devil Hill he watched the Wright brothers fly and reported their achievement to the world:

> There was something weird, almost uncanny, about the whole thing. Here on this lonely beach was being performed the greatest act of the ages, but there were no spectators and no applause save the booming of the surf and the startled cries of the sea birds. Often, as the machine buzzed along above the sand plains, herds of wild hogs and cattle were frightened from their grazing grounds and scurried away for the jungle, where they would remain for hours looking timidly out from their hiding-places. Flocks of gulls and crows, screaming and chattering, darted and circled about the machine as if resentful of this unwelcome trespasser in their hitherto exclusive realm. There was something about the picture that appealed to one's poetic instincts—the desolation, the solitude, the dreary expanse of sand and ocean and in the centre of the melancholy picture two solitary men performing one of the world's greatest wonders.

PART II

America
Finding Itself

CHAPTER I
Educating the American Mind

Editor's Note: At this point, Mark Sullivan wrote a very long section he proudly called "The American Mind," and for which he made a grand claim: "Through study of the history of education in America, especially the elementary schools, more than by any other process, will understanding be gained of the American mind, of the reasons an American was American." We may not recognize this for the revolutionary statement it was at the time. In recent years, our politicians and moral leaders have focused so much attention on public elementary school curriculum, on every aspect from prayer to poetry, that we are fairly well used to the idea that what we learn as children contributes mightily to who we become as adults. In Sullivan's times, no serious historian would have dreamed of turning to old schoolbooks to find the seeds of the nation's character—precisely what Sullivan sets out to do.

In many ways, serious historians have caught up with and surpassed Sullivan. Being at once too broad and too narrow in its scope, "The American Mind" simply doesn't live up to its title—but it does wonderfully portray much of American daily life, both as it was lived and as it was recalled by the former students Sullivan consulted. The modern reader won't fail to appreciate the hegemony of the educational system that allowed for the distribution of presumptions and generalizations our "multicultural" world would never tolerate. And the modern reader may recognize echoes of the present day as century-old voices claim that the education of their childhood was more sound, more moral, more lasting than that offered to children "today."

For its shortcomings, I briefly considered omitting "The American Mind." Yet for its insight into daily life then and now, I have decided to offer a modestly retitled "Educating the American Mind." Frankly, I have a duty to the man whose work I am editing. I believe Mark Sullivan was proud of the work he did here; no matter the standards of his new audience, he would be terribly offended if I were to omit the section altogether.

*   *   *

The aim of this chapter is to survey the average American's stock of ideas, so far as those ideas came to him through his early education. Without undertaking to assign relative importance to the various channels, education

A country school in upstate New York, about 1870.

is treated at this point merely because of convenience in the arrangement of this volume. It is tenable to say, however, that schools provided a larger proportion of the average American's stock of ideas than was the case with other nationalities. Education in America was much emphasized and practically universal. Wherever education is general, it tends to modify or supplant oral tradition, overlaps religion, and is apt to be more potent than reading, because education has a sanction of authoritativeness and comes when the mind is plastic.

For an obvious reason education is treated, not as it was during the period with which this history mainly deals, but as it was during the generation immediately antecedent. The average mature American of 1900–1925 had gone to school during the decades preceding. To a large extent the ideas he held as an adult, which he expressed through the men whom he

Cold morning in a country school. (From Harper's Young People, *an illustrated weekly)*

elected to office, through the leaders he chose or accepted in all lines of thought, and the principles and issues he supported or opposed, had been formed, or at least the foundation for them had been acquired, in the American schools as they were during the generation in which he was a child. For the great majority of Americans, formal education ended with what they got from the common schools.

The survey that follows has made use of the obvious sources, including a large number of the textbooks. These springs have been supplemented by personal recollections from a large number of persons who were school-children at one time or another during the decades from 1860 to 1900, and who were still living during the years when these chapters were composed.

II

The nature of American education was always a subject of earnest attention from thoughtful persons. The books written about it compose a considerable library; the speeches were innumerable. Of the books, one, published in 1906 and again in 1918, by the American historian and philosopher Henry Adams (1838–1918), was adjudged by some exalted authorities to be the most important work published in America during so much of the twentieth century as had then passed. Time has shown *The Education of Henry Adams* was overrated, but the theme was formidable: What should be the educational equipment for "man as a unit in a unified universe"?

Adams reviewed his own education, both that which he had received from schools and universities, and that which came to him from other sources and other experiences, with the purpose of determining what part of it turned out, "in his personal experience, to be useful, and what not"; to what degree his education had equipped him to function "as a consciously assenting member in full partnership with the society of his age." Adams's conclusion, as to his own education, was seriously adverse:

> Pondering on the needs of the Twentieth Century . . . in the essentials like religion, ethics, philosophy; in history, literature, art; in the concepts of all science except, perhaps, mathematics, the American boy of 1854 stood nearer the year 1, than the year 1900. The education he had received bore little relation to the education he needed. Speaking as an American of 1900 he had no education at all.

In this complaint, Adams was not quite fair to his teachers. He was able to "ponder on the needs of the twentieth century" after that century had arrived; his teachers were not. Moreover, if it were true that Adams's deprecatory estimate of what education did for him was applicable to everybody, we should be obliged to be more than a little appalled. For the education that Adams received was, according to standards commonly accepted, the best the world afforded. Certainly it was the most elaborate

The great bulk of education in the United States was provided by the common schools. High schools were late in coming and slow in growing. The map above (adapted from Cubberley's History of Education, *and based on figures from the U.S. Department of Education) shows approximately the only high schools existing in America in 1860. There had been about thirty more than are here shown, chiefly in the southern states, where education was interrupted by the Civil War. The total number was only 321, of which more than half were in three states—Massachusetts (78), New York (41), and Ohio (48).*

that pains had devised or money could purchase. If that kind of education did nothing for Adams, if it failed to equip him for the world of 1900 in which he lived, then we should be obliged to suffer from disquiet when we think of the more ordinary and casual education available to average men who lacked Adams's advantages of fortune and background.

Perhaps we shall be more comfortable if we concede that Adams was a very unusual personality, and that his failure to derive satisfaction from his education was due not wholly to the nature of the education he received but partly to his own unusualness. Probably by this assumption we shall be more accurate also, for the clear fact is that the ordinary education which America provided for average men gave satisfaction and enjoyment to great numbers of them; and produced from among them many who are fairly to be described as able to cope with the conditions in which they spent their mature lives; not only to cope with them, but to master them.

The common schools, which provided the average American with education, must be judged as what they were. The one outstanding ideal they had was less in the world of education than in the world of democracy. They were founded and maintained on the principle that all the people should have some learning, that the entire nation should be literate.

Schools dedicated to so high and difficult a purpose of democracy, necessarily, could not have pretentious curriculums. So far as their teaching had direct purposes, they aimed to make their pupils good men and women, and to equip them with some facility and indispensable fundamentals—reading, writing, and arithmetic.

Possibly, even with so titanic a burden as giving some education to all, the schools might have done more. Some earnest persons thought they could, and worked diligently to enlarge their scope.

The one conspicuous lack in the schools of 1865–95 was science.* In that field the only subject generally taught was physiology, and that was taught not as a science, and not in the scientific method, but for a reason apart from science, for a moral purpose. The method was memory work wholly; the pupils learned by heart the names, in Latin, of the bones, arteries, veins, viscera, valves of the heart. Of the 250 paragraphs of summary at the ends of the chapters in one widely used textbook, Blaisdell's *Our Bodies and How We Live*, 50 dealt with the injurious effect of alcohol and tobacco on the organs and processes of the body. The preface had a footnote saying the work had been revised by an official of the Women's Christian Temperance Union. To Albert Mordell, who went to school in Philadelphia in the 1890s, "it seemed as if the reason for studying about the organs and skin was to learn the effects of alcohol and tobacco on them."

The absence of science teaching in the schools would have justified, if anything would, Henry Adams's complaint of ill-equipment for life in the twentieth century. The schoolboy of the 1880s was destined to spend his mature life in a world in which science and its applications affected his existence vitally, but the common schools taught him not even the elementary facts of physics** and chemistry. He was destined to see the automobile substituted for the horse; to see electricity take the place of his former means of providing himself with light, and become a large source of his supply of heat and power; to have daily familiarity with the telephone and radio, to come in contact with the laws of refraction as expressed in the camera, to see the X-ray and radium in the hands of his doctor; to see chemistry, by the devising of rayon and other products, flout one of the most infallible maxims in his schoolbooks: "You cannot make a silk purse out of a sow's ear."

For all that transformation, the schoolboy of the seventies and eighties had no preparation—for the very good reason that the scientists themselves did not anticipate it. Had the children studied *Natural Philosophy*, written by William G. Peck in 1881, they would have learned, about electric power, that "Attempts have been made, and with partial success, to employ electro-magnetism as a motor for the propulsion of machinery, but in all cases the expense has been so great as to preclude its economical use."†

*Even in the high schools, little science was taught, and this as late as the nineties was available to only an insignificant proportion of children of school age. In 1890, there were in the whole country only 2,256 public high schools, with 202,968 pupils. In 1922, the corresponding figures were 14,056 and 2,319,407. In 1890, less than one-third of one percent of the country's population were enrolled in high schools; in 1922, the percentage was 2.04, a sevenfold increase.
**There was no physics, but two young men whose education stopped with the high school in Dayton, Ohio, invented the airplane.
†By 1925, electricity was generated and used in the United States to the extent of 31.5 million horsepower. The industry represented an investment of over $7 billion.

A generation ago children walked long distances to school. (From McGuffey's Second Eclectic Reader*)*

Perhaps it is just as well the schoolchildren did not learn much of what science thought it knew in the 1870s and 1880s. Not only would they have had to get rid of it, but they would have been worse handicapped than if they had known nothing of science, except as respects what they learned of science's methods and standards. They would have known a good deal that was not so, would have had their minds set against the amazing revelations that science was bringing about. It was difficult enough for some who followed science as a career to adjust their minds to the changes.

Had the schoolchildren of the 1880s been taught what science then thought it knew, they would have learned the principle of the immutability of the chemical elements—and would have lived to see it overturned by the discovery of radioactivity. They would have learned the principle of the conservation of mass—and would have lived to see that principle vanish with the experimental discovery of the increase in mass of the electron with speed as the velocity of light is approached. They would have learned the principle of the conservation of energy—and would have lived to see that principle suffer a material change "when both experimental and theoretical evidence came forward that energy and mass are interconvertible terms related by the Einstein equation $mc^2=E$, since in that discovery the ideas of energy and of mass became completely scrambled."* They would have learned the principle of conservation of momentum—and would have seen it denied universality by the subsequent formulation of the quantum theory.

In short, what science a student could have learned, even as late as 1895, was to be subjected to revolutionary changes such as had never before taken place and were at that time inconceivable.

*Quoted from Dr. R. A. Milliken's paper read to the American Philosophical Society in 1926. All the changes in science summarized above rest on the authority of this paper.

In the 1920s, motor-buses collected and carried children to consolidated schools. This bus served a school in Hopewell Township, New Jersey. (From a photograph by Ewing Galloway)

The decay of the country school began about 1900. Not only did the rural population become too small to support them, but families that remained on the farms felt the instruction in the nearby town schools was better—at least it conformed to the modern idea. Farmers who were prosperous enough, and ambitious for their children, sent them to the town schools, paying a fee the towns exacted from outsiders, and continuing to pay the usual tax to support the rural schools they did not patronize.

Then came the incitement, universal in American life, to centralization, consolidation, "bigger and better." Rural school boards, infected by the vogue of statistics, estimated that five separate schools with thirty pupils each, and one teacher to each school, was more expensive than one central school. Also, the central school would be more efficient—that was another word that came into vogue. The process was hurried by the automobile and improved roads. Consolidated schoolhouses were built near the center of the district. Buses, provided by the school board, went about the district, gathering up the children each morning and returning them each evening. With that innovation went a subtle psychological change—the difference between, on the one hand, of going to school, or being sent by parents, and, on the other, of being picked up by the state-owned bus and carried. In 1927, a publication of the University of North Carolina recorded, with pride, that the state had 2,317 school buses, carrying an average of 87,000 children daily to 814 consolidated schools, a use of the new system exceeded only by Indiana and Ohio.

III

The backbone of education in the common schools of America—so far as it aimed to impart ideas, standards of individual and social conduct, and the like—was the "Readers." They were to the last two-thirds of the nineteenth century what the New England Primer had been to the eighteenth. The Readers were the only textbooks used in all schools that bore directly and positively upon the formation of character, or that provided ethical guidance. History and geography dealt mainly with facts; arithmetic and spelling were designed for mental discipline.

The Readers came in series, usually six, graduated to meet the needs of pupils of all ages—the First Reader dealing with the alphabet and words of one syllable, the Sixth adapted to pupils of fifteen and older. The beginning of the Readers was more or less simultaneous with the beginning of public education at the expense of the state. The Readers reflected, as this conception of education did, a liberalizing spirit, a tendency to teach more than religion and ethics. As we shall see, the tendency did not become extravagant, judged by modern standards.

When people could not read, who wrote the ballads of a nation may have been more important than who made the laws. After literacy and schools became general, the authorship of school textbooks became important. Thus the author of the Reader of Readers became one of the most influential Americans of the century: William Holmes McGuffey.

A quibbler might point out that McGuffey was merely the compiler of the selections so fondly remembered, and that only the authors of them, Shakespeare and Milton and the others, are important—all that is easy. But

William H. McGuffey. (From A History of the McGuffey Readers, *by Henry H. Vail)*

is it safe to underestimate the man who, for millions of Americans, just at the right moment in their fleeting adolescence, opened the gate to literature? To open the gate in just the right way, to lead the child in, to cause him to want to go in; to point the way and to make it seem alluring, calls for inspiration and understanding little short of authorship itself. How many of us would have learned to know any of the English poets if we had been left to begin at the first page and try to find our own discouraged ways to the passages that would thrill us? We cannot be sure; in any event, it was McGuffey's compilations that reached the mind of young America.

The certain importance of McGuffey is seen most clearly by reflecting

(Reprinted by Henry Ford in 1925 from McGuffey's Second Eclectic Reader*)*

on men of ordinary circumstances. To millions of others, to probably nine out of ten average Americans, what taste of literature they got from McGuffey's was all they ever had; what literature the children brought into the home in McGuffey's Readers was all that ever came. Broad classical reading was decidedly not general. McGuffey, in short, because of the leverage of his Readers, played a large role in forming the mind of America. A compiler who selects, from the entire body of English literature, enough to fill six small books, may put into the process as much personality as many an author of original works. The principles, ideals, and rules of conduct that McGuffey held are clearly revealed in the stories and passages he selected to illustrate them and drive them home.

IV

In 1836, McGuffey compiled, for a firm of publishers in Cincinnati, a First and Second Reader; and in 1837, a Third and Fourth. In 1841, with the assistance of his brother, he compiled the Fifth, first known as *McGuffey's Rhetorical Guide*. In 1851, the five Readers were made into six. The series was revised five times. The last revision was copyrighted in 1901. They were still being sold in 1927. Their vogue endured from the presidency of Martin Van Buren to that of Theodore Roosevelt. Children studied McGuffey's, grew up, had children who in turn studied McGuffey's; these again had children who read McGuffey's sixty years after their grandparents had begun with them. In a country prone to change, McGuffey's had permanence for a strikingly long time.

Of the earlier editions there are no sales records, but of one revised edition more than 8 million copies of the First Reader were used. Of the Sixth Reader, which, being for mature pupils, had the least sale, over a million copies were distributed. One feels justified in estimating that, taking into account all the editions, as many as 70 or 80 million McGuffey's Readers must have been used by American schoolchildren. This should be qualified by remembering that some children used more than one Reader, depending on how long they remained at school. Taking everything into account, it would not be surprising if at least half the schoolchildren of America, from 1836 to 1900, drew inspiration from McGuffey's Readers. When America sent expeditions of schoolteachers to carry American culture to the Philippines and Puerto Rico, McGuffey's Readers were translated into Spanish; when Japan felt an urge to experiment with American ways, McGuffey's was translated and carried its democratic point of view into the background of a crystallized feudalism centuries old.

The comprehensive purpose of McGuffey's Readers is to be found in sentences from the prefaces: ". . . to obtain as wide a range of leading authors as possible, to present the best specimens of style, to insure interest in the subjects, to impart valuable information, and to exert a decided and healthful moral influence."*

McGuffey's was the source of that stock of points of view and tastes held in common, which constituted much of America's culture, its codes of morals and conduct, its standards of propriety, its homely aphorisms, its "horse-sense" axioms. In this field McGuffey's embodied, of course, some points of view common to civilization everywhere, but McGuffey's also taught and accounted for mental attitudes and ethical concepts which dif-

*From the 1879 revised editions of the Fifth and Sixth Readers.

"George is kind to Jack and Jack loves him, be-cause he is kind. The kind and good are al-ways loved." (From McGuffey's First Eclectic Reader*)*

ferentiated America from other peoples, or were more emphasized in America than elsewhere. In this respect, McGuffey was a kind of American Confucius, the latter, like the former, taking his sayings from the accumulated lore of the people. Some fables came from as far back as Aesop; others retold bits of homely truth that had been crystallized generations before by British people—many of the scenes of the McGuffey's stories had a British setting. Yet other stories and aphorisms were indigenous to America, lessons learned by pioneer contact with the frontier of a new country, experiences with Indians and wild animals. At all times and in every respect, McGuffey's Readers had a strong flavor of religion; much of its contents was Puritan and evangelical, none was inconsistent with the religion of Calvin and Knox.

Incitement to consideration for animals was taught by a story about a lame dog who, when cured, brought another lame dog to be doctored. That story, incidentally, imputed to dogs a mutual helpfulness, a so-to-speak philanthropic caninitarianism that calls for a good deal of proof. McGuffey, when bent on teaching a moral lesson, was conspicuously indifferent to details of natural history.

In McGuffey's Second Reader was the story of George Washington and the mutilated cherry tree, ending:

> "George," said his father, "do you know who killed that fine cherry-tree yonder in the garden?" This was a hard question; George was silent for a moment; and then, looking at his father, his young face bright with conscious love of truth, he bravely cried out: "I can't tell a lie, father; you know, I can't tell a lie. I did cut it with my hatchet."
>
> "Come to my arms, my dearest boy!" cried his father, in transports; "come to my arms! you killed my cherry-tree, George, but

The sad fate of a boy who stopped to play in a pond on his way to school, and was drowned.
(*From* McGuffey's First Eclectic Reader)

you have now paid me for it a thousandfold. Such proof of heroic truth in my son is of more value than a thousand trees, though they were all of the purest gold."

By the 1920s, youth doubted whether that story accorded with what they—or their fathers—would have done under similar circumstances, decided it was inconsistent with their own observations of life—and passed on to raise doubts about some other orthodox statements of history and rules of conduct.

So far as the Readers gave a noticeable proportion of space to any particular mood, one sensed a greater emphasis on melancholy than was characteristic of the more light-minded generation that followed. That, however, was no more a trait of the compilers of Readers than of the spirit of the times. It was a part of decorum and piety, even of propriety, to be a little melancholy. That went with a philosophy common to McGuffey's dour Scotch Presbyterian ancestors and to the Puritan forebears of New England as well. From the two, expressing themselves in education and religion, it infected nearly all America. The "hair shirt" was a hardship physically, but because of that, a luxury spiritually. Sheer enjoyment, of poetry or anything else, was not to be indulged except with the accompaniment of the recalling of death.

In those days, wherever American life was touched by either the school or the church, it heard a note of "Hark from the tombs a doleful cry." With a curious combination of consistency and inconsistency, there was equal assertion that death was a happy state.

Space proportionate to melancholy, and having the effect of balancing it, but only of balancing it, was given to passages having the note of joy in nature, usually accompanied by a prudent reminder that joy is fleeting and death certain.

It was the way of many of the selections to hold out, in the first few lines, the bait of joy in order to get in, at the conclusion, the castor oil of pious admonition—enjoyment as bait for enjoinment.

Other selections came straight to the point. "Somebody's Mother" began:

> The woman was old and ragged and gray . . .
> She stood at the crossing and waited long,
> Alone, uncared for, amid the throng.

Scores passed her without offering to help. Boys out of school ran by, careless of her. At last, however, came one youth, "gayest laddie of all the group," who did not need to have had the instruction, later available to Boy Scouts, that he should do one good deed a day:

> He paused beside her and whispered low,
> "I'll help you cross if you wish to go."

The youth, like the Boy Scouts, believed not only in doing good but in reporting it:

> Then back again to his friends he went,
> His young heart happy and well content.
> "She's somebody's mother, boys, you know,
> For all she's aged and poor and slow."

Frequently, the pious lesson was presented without placebo or sweetening. To be resigned to what was called "God's will" was part of the philosophy of the age. "Little Victories," in McGuffey's Fifth Reader, was the story of a boy who had lost his limb. "Limb" was the word—no polite little boy would have spoken of his "leg" in that generation. And the baddest boy would not have been equal to the diabolical audacity of standing in front of a mixed company of boys and girls, and using the word "leg." A thunderbolt would have been expected from the heavens, and if that source were inattentive, the teacher would have supplied one.

Possibly, speculation by youthful minds as to whether everything their elders called "God's will" was really the will of a benevolent deity, or

(Published by Van Antwerp, Bragg & Co.)

whether a more accurate bookkeeping should charge some of it against something less benign and hardly Divine—possibly that may also have had a part in causing some of the questioning doubt that was characteristic of that generation when it grew up, and of a later generation. The expectations aroused by the lessons in the Readers may not have been borne out in later experience.

The complete contents of McGuffey's Sixth Reader consisted of 138 selections from 111 different authors. From Shakespeare were more than from any other author, nine, including "Hamlet's Soliloquy" and "Fall of Cardinal Wolsey." Sir Walter Scott and Henry Wadsworth Longfellow stood next, with four each. There were three each from the Bible, Bryant, Washington Irving, and Daniel Webster.

It is this aspect of McGuffey's, as a collection of well-chosen selections from the best English and American literature, that inspired the most affectionate recollections of it. Rev. Joseph Fort Newton wrote that "for many a boy of the older West, McGuffey's varied and wise selections from the best English authors were the very gates of literature ajar."

The tie that McGuffey's made between American schoolboys and Shakespeare, Milton, and Byron was strong. It accounted, in part, for the role America played in the Great War. The racial and national psychologies attending that conflict gave rise to much intellectual controversy, and are not to be disentangled with temerity. One can readily believe that millions of Americans must have been moved subconsciously by the feeling, not always identified by themselves, that they were one with the race of Shakespeare and Milton. Every little prairie schoolhouse in America was an outpost of English literature, hardly less potent to inspire recruits when the time came than the British drumbeat itself. Had American schoolchildren been brought up on Goethe and Heine, as they were on Shakespeare and Milton, is it certain America's role in the Great War would have been the same?*

V

Next to the Readers, which aimed directly at implanting principles, the subject that did most to give American schoolchildren ideas about their relation to the universe was history. As taught in American common schools during the 1870s and 1880s, it meant American history, and American history meant chiefly the Revolutionary War, the Declaration of Independence, the founding of our government, and other events associated with our separation from Great Britain. History, as such, had not been taught at all until about 1850; when the need for textbooks arose, they were built largely on Revolutionary War legends—handed down, many of them, by oral tradition—and on the laudatory narratives and biographies of Rev-

*I realize this argument runs counter to another, on page 144, but I think both are correct.

olutionary War events and heroes. Through this material, and consequently through the history textbooks, ran one clear thread.

Although the education of Henry Adams was far distant from that of the average American, the schooling of both had at least one common characteristic, which led to one common quality in the generation from 1900 to 1925, especially in the political standpoint of that generation. "Resistance to something," Adams wrote, "was the law of New England nature; the boy looked out on the world with the instinct of resistance."

It seems startling to say, but is easily provable, that the American schoolboy of the 1870s and 1880s lived in an atmosphere as close to the Revolutionary War as if it had taken place a decade before, instead of a century. Our American resistance to economic and political oppression by Great Britain was the one great epic of our history, our one great adventure as a nation in its relation to other nations; and the writers of schoolbooks gave it proportionate emphasis. Many of the writers of the textbooks had had the story of the Revolution direct from the lips of fathers or grandfathers who had fought in it. Benjamin F. Butler, a politician who was powerful in Congress and in Massachusetts politics as late as 1890, used to describe the visits two old Revolutionary soldiers made to his father's home on winter nights. Fortified with hot cider, they would rehearse the times they beat the British tyrants. To a small boy, such a story was to have a dominating influence. Many of the American authors whose writings were quoted in the schoolbooks and memorized by the pupils had their principal inspiration out of such memories.

Among the textbooks on American history surviving in the memories of those who went to school in the seventies and eighties, one of the most frequently mentioned was John Clark Ridpath's *History of the United States, Prepared Especially for Schools*, published in 1879. In that book, the outstanding chapter begins: "The American Revolution was an event of vast importance. . . . The result has been the grandest Republican government in the world."

Such statements were indisputably accurate, yet they were also capable of leaving a disproportionate sense of cosmic values in the minds of youths whose study of history ended with this one volume. Literally, many an American boy knew every battle and detail of the American Revolution, who never heard or read the phrase "French Revolution," or, if he had heard it, regarded it as an ungallant appropriation by a foreign people of a word whose true brand was American.

Jefferson reading the Declaration in committee. (From Quackenbos's American History for Schools, *published by Appleton)*

Many an American youth knew all about the Boston Tea Party but never heard of the ultimatum of the barons at Runnymede. An American school-boy of the 1880s, if asked to name the eighteen decisive battles of history and left to the resources of his common school education, might possibly have included Waterloo; aside from that, he probably would have named half a dozen from the Revolution, half a dozen more from the Civil War, would have thrown in one or two each from the War of 1812 and the Mexican War, and would have stopped, patriotically, at his own shores.

Always, in the histories, the emphasis was on liberty, freedom, independence. Ridpath's account of the American nation began:

> The cause of the Revolution was the passage by Parliament of laws destructive of colonial liberty. . . . In 1765 the English parliament passed the Stamp Act. The news of the hateful act created great wrath in America. The bells of Philadelphia and Boston rung a funeral peal. In New York a copy of the Stamp Act was carried through the streets with a death's head nailed to it. The Sons of Liberty was organized. The colonists were few and feeble but they were men of iron wills who had made up their minds to die for liberty.

The histories gave to minor episodes of the Revolutionary War a lofti-ness of treatment to which authorities on military science would have hesi-tated to assent. Battles and skirmishes were described in phrases which one might explain, perhaps, on the quite worthy theory that the writer of text-books had to compete with the dime novels which the boys sometimes read surreptitiously behind the camouflaging covers of the textbooks.

Ridpath romantically described the capture of Fort Ticonderoga by the Vermont patriot, Ethan Allen:

> With this mere handful, Allen made a dash and gained the gate-way of the fort. The sentinel was driven in, closely followed by the patriot mountaineers. Allen rushed to the quarters of the comman-dant, and cried out: "Surrender this fort instantly!"
> "By what authority?" inquired the officer.
> "In the name of the great Jehovah and the Continental Con-gress," said Allen, flourishing his sword.*

Histories printed soon after the Civil War, for use in the North, treated the Confederates in a spirit far from historical or judicial. Charles Goodrich's *His-tory of the United States of America; for the use of Schools*, published in 1867, seemed to gloat in dragging in such words as "rebel" and "treason":

> The rebellious States seized the forts, arsenals, mints, ships, and national property of whatever description within their boundaries.

---

*In Sullivan's time, a Yale professor attacked Ridpath's scene, insisting that Allen really said, "Open up here, you damned bastard sons of bitches!" Sullivan admired the accuracy but couldn't bring himself to use the words, at which I had to guess. —D.R.

First cheer for the Stars and Stripes (1777). (From Quackenbos's American History for Schools, *published by Appleton)*

> In Washington but little was done to stem the tide of treason. . . . Most of the members of Congress from the seceding States resigned their seats, and, defiantly exulting in their treason, would listen to no terms of accommodations. [Cabinet members] resigned from sympathy with secession, and were permitted, like the rebel delegations in Congress, to leave Washington and return to their own States, to plot treason there. Robert E. Lee took command of the State Forces of Virginia, in opposition to the nation which had educated and honored him, and which he had sworn to support.

This note of violence toward the South soon softened, and in a comparatively short time disappeared. While it lasted, the South adopted textbooks of its own. But the treatment of the British as the stock villains of American history continued to be a fundamental theme of our textbooks until more than a century and a quarter after the Revolution. The effect on generation after generation of American youth was inescapable.

B. L. Eddy, of Roseburg, Oregon, comparing his own schooldays with the present ones, was moved to say:

It seems to me that the United States History and other books that told us about our country gave us the impression that it had

been founded and led by men of virtue and wisdom—and that no other country could compare with ours in liberty, enlightenment, or progress. . . . We have much taught in the schools nowadays [1927] in the way of patriotism, but it seems to me, as I look back,

Mount Vernon. (From Quackenbos's American History for Schools, *published by Appleton)*

that patriotism was just our native atmosphere then; whereas now we have to use a ventilator fan to force it in. The country has too many highbrows writing text-books and holding university chairs who haven't much use for the Constitution or the flag or our great statesmen. Such chaps hadn't been pupped in the '70's!

In the testimony of former students, there is a running implication that the spirit of resisting tyranny, of fighting for liberty, in the education of the generation that went to school in the seventies and eighties, accounted for the fight the same generation made, when they became mature men and voters, against economic oppression. The American trait of resistance was not merely patriotic or military. The British oppression in its beginning was chiefly economic, having to do with tea, ships, and taxes; America acquired a tradition of resistance to oppression, whether political or economic.

However, assigning specific causes to national traits is perilous.* Some historians, and other authors, do it with a manner in which debonair assurance is substituted for logical proof. Each reader had best do it for himself, using such insight as he has and such information as comes to him. But probably one indisputable assertion can be made: The treatment of the British in American schoolbooks accounted for the sympathy Americans had for the Boers in 1899, for much of the sympathy Americans always had for the Irish in their struggle for independence, and accounted generally for a prevailing anti-British strain in American thought and feeling. As late as 1927, Mayor William H. Thompson of Chicago found it politically profitable to denounce King George—not the Third, but the Fifth.

---

*In fact, assigning traits to nations is perilous. Are all British stolid? Or all Frenchmen like Chanticleer?

VI

Pride of country, dominant strain in the histories, characterized the geographies as well. The *Primary Geography*, compiled by James Cruikshank, LL.D.,* in 1867, and current for a decade after, assured young America that "There are now more than 30,000,000 of people and the United States are the freest, most enlightened, and powerful government on earth."

Toward peoples other than American, Cruikshank had the spirit of generous tolerance that can only accompany assured superiority: "France is celebrated for its manufacturers; especially of silks. . . . Education is not universal, but the better classes are refined and cultivated."

This teaching, that America was "God's country," may have accounted for a certain air of condescension, not always tolerant, which American doughboys carried with them through the Great War, to the puzzlement of some of their Allies who had not learned relative values of nations from the same schoolbooks. The same cause may lie behind America's attitude of self-sufficiency in international relations, its unwillingness to join the League of Nations, the readiness with which American politicians can stir the people into insistence upon isolation.

Toward Prussia (then a separate country) Cruikshank was inclined to be gracious: "Prussia is a large and powerful kingdom . . . one of the first powers in the world. It is more than twice as large as the State of New York. Every child is compelled to attend school. The people are intelligent."

Toward some other outlander nations, Cruikshank was definite in the assertion of their inferiority: "Half-civilized peoples, like the Chinese and Mexicans, have towns and cities, cultivate the soil, and exchange products; but have few arts** and little intelligence."

A log cabin. (From A Primary Geography, *by James Cruikshank, published by Wm. Wood & Co.)*

Colton's conceded a little more to China, though it found some grave defects: "The Chinese are in-

*Editor of the *New York Teacher* and assistant superintendent of schools, Brooklyn, New York. Cruikshank's geography was published in 1867, by William Wood and Company, New York. It, like all the geographies, was in use for many years after the date of its publication. J. H. Colton's geography was published in 1863, by Ivison, Phinney & Co., New York; G. W. Colton's geography in 1877, by Sheldon & Co., New York; Guyot's, 1868, Charles Scribner & Co., New York; Monteith's, 1885, A. S. Barnes & Co., New York and Chicago; Cornell's, 1867, D. Appleton and Co., New York; Swinton's, 1875, Ivison, Blakeman, Taylor and Co., New York and Chicago; Warren's, 1877, Cowperthwait & Co., Philadelphia.

**It would be interesting to compare, as of the decade (1867–77) when this geography provided instruction to American youth, the relative amounts of art in China and in the United States.

Traveling among the Andes. (From Warren's Common School Geography, *published by Cowperthwait & Co.)*

genious, industrious, and peaceful; but miserably conceited. They cling to the customs of their ancestors."

The geographies, in a way different from the histories but having the same effect, recalled to the child of the 1880s the youthfulness of his country, how near its beginnings in pioneer life and Indian wars. Many included in their illustrations pictures of wigwams, palisades for defense against Indians, log cabins, and maps showing Indians and buffaloes on territory which, to many schoolchildren of the seventies, was next door. The West was usually called the "Far West." It was pictured by Guyot's *Elementary Geography*, published in 1868:

> Nearly all parts of the East are occupied by a busy people. The larger part of the West has few inhabitants, except Indians. [In] Kansas, Nebraska, and Texas, the people . . . employ themselves chiefly in raising cattle and horses. Great herds of these animals roam wild over the plains of Texas. When they are wanted by their owners, men go out on very swift horses and surround them.

Standard geographies published between 1867 and 1877, and studied during one or two decades later, said of the West that "large herds of buffalo roam over the prairies. . . ." "Most of the Indians within the United States inhabit this section; several tribes maintain almost constant hostilities against the whites. . . ." "Santa Fé is the principal point in the wagon-train route from North to South. . . ." "The wild horses, known as mustangs, are commonly taken with the lasso." Colton's geography, published twenty years before the discovery of the relation between disease and mosquitoes, said that "in nearly all parts of the West intermittent chills with fevers are more or less common; the air is rendered malarious by the frequent disturbance of the rich virgin soil." Of the territories then still existing Cruikshank said: "They are very thinly settled by whites, and contain many Indian tribes. They are divided into sections, called, Indian Territory, New Mexico, Dakotah, Montana, Idaho, Washington, Utah, and Arizona."

The geographies, unable to keep step as fast as Congress conferred statehood, were always several years behind. It was difficult, indeed, for textbooks or anything else to keep pace with the swiftness of the changes

Miners at work. (From Cornell's Intermediate Geography, *published by Appleton & Co.)*

that were taking place. All Cruikshank had to say to the schoolchildren of the seventies about Florida was: "Tallahassee is the capital. Key West is the largest and most important city. Many vessels are wrecked here. Much salt is made by evaporation of sea water, and exported."

To the children who studied those old geographies, doubtless the information seemed as permanently dependable as everything else they learned. But in the nature of things, many of the facts of geography are bound to be ephemeral, and the transiency of the picture of the earth's political divisions was greater over the past fifty years than at any time before. Beginning in 1870, something like three-fourths of the earth's surface, and about two-thirds of its population, slid out from under kings and emperors, becoming republics of one kind or another. All in all, possibly it was just as well that the memories of pupils of the 1870s held the solemn facts less tenaciously than various whimsical impressions, picked out and stored away by the not-to-be-guessed selectiveness of childish minds. The residuum left with Newton D. Baker was probably similar to that retained by many another youth: "I am not certain that my mind has not always been defaced with the notion, which I got out of Mitchell's Geography, that the various countries were yellow, pink, green, or red splotches on a piebald globe."

Unsatisfactory though this might be, as a basis for knowledge of the world of 1927, Mr. Smith found one reason for recalling Colton's with affection and gratitude, as having a specific usefulness: "Colton's Geography was an understandable book, admirably conceived as to size. Behind its ample pages one could read the *Fireside Companion* with its never ended tales of blood and romance, or the *Nickel Library* or *Ole Cap Collier*, without fear of detection."

* * *

Scene in Polynesia. (From A Complete Course in Geography, *by Wm. Swinton, pub-lished by Ivison, Blakeman, Taylor Co.)*

A village scene in Europe.   *Traveling in Russia.*

Ostrich-hunting on the Sahara. (From Elementary Geography for Primary Classes, *by A. H. Guyot, published by Charles Scribner & Co.)*

In teaching the facts of geography, an almost universal practice was to take advantage of rhyme and harmony, to sing them. Apparently this was a folk method, begun by someone so long ago that it is impossible to identify him, and passed by word of mouth from one generation to the next, and from one part of the country to another. The chants and rhymes that were evolved constituted one of America's very small number of oral traditions. The simplest version of it—there were difficulties of meter and rhyme in achieving simplicity—consisted of the name of the state, the name of the capital city, and the name of the river on which it was located. This, as sung, was repeated for each state, with no change in the words, but with a rising inflection at the end of the first line, and falling at the end of the second. On this, which presumably was the original form, were built scores of variations, many of them reflecting the inventiveness of teachers or others musically or poetically endowed. The names of the rivers in the first two states happened to approximate a rhyme:

> Maine, Augusta, on the Kennebec.
> New Hampshire, Concord, on the Merrimac.

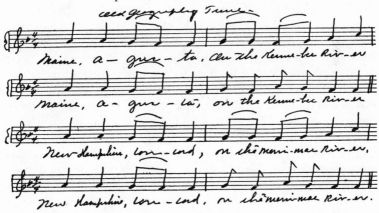

One old chant to which geography was sung. Sent by Mrs. J. N. Allen, Muskogee, Oklahoma.

With this start, many tried to introduce rhyme, as well as meter, throughout—an ambition made sadly difficult or wholly balked by disinclination of the names of rivers to agree with each other euphonically, by an equally arbitrary refusal of geographical names to have the same numbers of syllables, and by other recalcitrancies of geographical facts.

On any schoolday morning, in schoolhouses all over America, hundreds of thousands of children were sending out one variation or another of that old chant in waves which, in the aggregate, reached from the Atlantic to the Pacific, a kind of radio by relays long before radio was invented. While it might almost be said that there were hours when practically all the childish voices in America were singing in unison, the methods were as various as the words. Practically every detail of state, American, and world geography was put into rhyme of a sort, and sung to tunes ranging from "Old Grimes Is Dead" to "Yankee Doodle," from "Go Tell Aunt Rhody" to an air which students in Boonesboro, Iowa, called "the India-rubber tune," because of the elasticity enforced by failure of the names of states and cap-

itals to have uniform numbers of syllables. (The alphabet and multiplica-
tion tables, also favorite singing lessons, scanned better.) Correspondents
sent dozens of examples of songs, for which they expressed great affection
and an equal insistence that this was a good way to learn geography: "It was
hard for some of us youngsters to make the words and metre harmonize—
but we learned geography. . . . To this very day when I wish to ascertain
what river a capital is located on, I immediately run over in my mind the
old chant till I reach the one I want."

                                    VII

During a period ending about 1912, and ranging backward more than
sixty years, a wave of amendments to state constitutions throughout
America inserted into the fundamental law statutes of religious freedom,
providing for universal education at the expense of the state, aiming to ensure complete and rigid separation of church and state, and forbidding the
use of state funds for sectarian religious teaching. In a common interpretation of these phrases, it is customary to say, but as misleading as many familiar sayings, that the constitutional provisions ended the connection
between the schools and religion, that thereafter the public schools of
America were secular. That is far from true. The religious spirit and tradition were more powerful than the secular form. In practice, all that was
ended or prevented by the constitutional amendments was any sectarian or
religious teaching that should run counter to the dogmas or practices of
any important* sect or creed. Religion remained in the schools to practically as great an extent as immediately before the amendments. What happened was that the states carried on a system of education in which
practically all the traditions and most of the influences were religious. The
spirit of the schools was religious and continued so. So deeply embedded
was the spirit of religion in the common schools of America that nothing
short of a revolution, or a trend immensely long, could have uprooted it.

From the earliest beginning, in every section of America, education started
as a religious conception, its sole purpose to enable the child to read the
Bible; that continued to be the sole purpose, and religion continued to be
the dominant note in education until the period with which this chapter
deals, the last quarter of the nineteenth century.

As we have seen, McGuffey's and other Readers conformed to tradition
by making up much of their contents of stories with religious or ethical
morals. As education broadened, with the addition (in about the following
order) of arithmetic, grammar, geography, and history, the religious tradition was carried on in all the textbooks in which it could be included appropriately.

*The religious teaching that continued in the schools often ran counter to the tenets of denomina-
tions relatively unimportant in numbers, such as Unitarians and Mormons.

J. D. Steele's introduction to *Fourteen Weeks of Chemistry* in 1873 began with a direct affirmation: "Each tiny atom is . . . watched by the Eternal Eye and guided by the Eternal Hand, all obey immutable law. When Christ declared the very hairs of our head to be numbered, he intimated a chemical truth which we can now know in full to be that the very atoms of which each hair is composed are numbered by that same watchful Providence."

Chemical Physics, published in 1877, said that "no science furnishes more . . . convincing proofs of the existence of God" than chemistry. Peter Mark Roget put the orthodox affirmation into the title of his *Animal and Vegetable Physiology, as Exhibiting the Power, Wisdom, and Goodness of God*. The great American botanist Asa Gray, in his *Botany for Young People and Common Schools*, published in 1858, introduced a quotation from the Bible as the opening passage of his book; and, for himself, began: "This book is intended to teach Young People how to begin to read, with pleasure and advantage, one large and easy chapter in the open Book of Nature; namely, that in which the wisdom and goodness of the Creator are plainly written in the Vegetable Kingdom."

In the American public schools during the period from about 1865 to 1900 and later, the geographies contained all that was then taught about the origin of man, and the other subjects which in the later schools of a more complex age came to be called geology, zoology, and biology; so far as these subjects were differentiated from ordinary geography, it was sometimes called "physical geography." These textbooks were not only 100 percent orthodox, they were even a little complacent about man's place in the cosmos. Cruikshank's *Primary Geography* gave assurance: "God made the world for man to live on, and has fitted it for man's convenience and comfort; giving the food that is best for him to eat; the air to breathe; and making storms and tempests to purify the air."

The geographies of the period were serenely confident about the inferiority of religions other than Christian. Colton's geography said that

> Mohammedanism or Islamism is the religion taught by Mohammed, an imposter who recorded his doctrines in a book called the Koran. It consists of a confused mixture of grossly false ideas and precepts with Judaism and Christianity. . . . Most systems of religion, while professing to cultivate virtue, often encourage vice; and thus injure both spiritual and worldly interests. Christianity is the only system which elevates man to a true sense of his moral relations, and adds to his happiness.

To the child of the seventies and eighties, the spirit of religion in the schools gave a sense of definite relation to the universe, of eternity of personality; caused his mind to dwell frequently on things of the spirit and gave him a personal sense of spirituality; and caused him to have reverence. Most important of all, it provided him with comfort-bringing definiteness of rules in the otherwise difficult area of right and wrong—in short, supplied him with standards. The unsettlement of standards, the uncertainty about moral anchorages, the weakening of authoritative criterions of ethics and taste, were the unhappiest of the consequences that attended the decline of religion that came during the nineteen twenties, in the schools and elsewhere.

VIII

Americans, as individuals, were not, in their personal relations, a histrionic people, hardly even a declamatory one; they were, indeed, inclined to the suppression of personal emotion. They were a people not prone to loquaciousness, yet, in their schools, they put emphasis on elocution. For the explanation we must consider, therefore, conditions of American life. The United States, with a Congress, forty or more state legislatures, and thousands of town and city councils, had more forums for lawmaking, and hence for public speaking, than other nations. Public life was the most prized career, until close to the end of the nineteenth century, when the service of corporations became extravagantly remunerative.

Political campaigns were frequent and the people took interest in public debate. When there were no motion pictures and the theater was taboo to a considerable portion of the people, political debate was at once public business and also entertainment; an attractive political orator had some of the glamour that heroes of the stage and the movies came to have later. When neither mechanical music nor celluloid reels were shipped from cities, smaller communities created their own amusements, in which the lyceum and the "literary society," with local speakers and reciters, were the principal feature.

Among the professions, the two respected most were law, which involved mainly courtroom forensics (until the "office-lawyer" came, with aggregations of organized wealth), and the pulpit, which still held some of the authority that attended the Puritan clergyman of the eighteenth century. Some religious sects made much use of lay speakers; Quakers, having no official clergy, were addressed only by members, who spoke when "the spirit moved" them; other sects heard the official "circuit-rider" only once in so often—for the most part, the congregations were led by members. To be able to expound a gospel at one of the Sunday or midweek religious services—at least three a week were the usual routine—or to take charge of the Sunday school or prayer meeting, or to say the prayer at a funeral, was a duty that might come to almost anybody.

To equip youth for a function, at once a public duty and an opportunity to stand out, which might come to any one, either as career, avocation, or emergency, the schools gave formal training at least once a week, many schools oftener. The pupils as a rule made their own selections, though frequently the teacher directed students to memorize and recite specific "pieces." The universal source of the selections was either the textbook

Remorse.
Oh, wretched state! Oh, bosom
black as death!

Denying—rejecting.
A proposition so infamous should
instantly be voted down.

Repulsion.
Avaunt! Richard's himself again.

(From the Delsarte Speaker, *edited by Henry Davenport Northrop, published by National Publishing Company, Philadelphia)*

formally called a "Speaker," or the other textbook called "Reader." In the earlier days, the Readers were relied upon chiefly. In the 1880s and 1890s, a tendency to expand the number of textbooks for specific subjects, accompanying a tendency toward specialization in all fields of life, expressed itself in books designed exclusively for elocution. Among the earlier ones were McGuffey's *New Juvenile Speaker,* 1860; *Young America Speaker,* 1870; *Young Folks Speaker,* 1882; the *Manual of Elocution and Reading,* 1882. In the nineties came the *Star Speaker,* 1892; *Uncle Herbert's Speaker,* 1896; and the *Delsarte Speaker,* 1896. The last was named after a French singer and teacher who evolved and made popular an intricate philosophy of "correspondence" of the parts of the body, which came to be widely known in America as the system of "Delsarte gestures." If the Delsarte System,* as practiced by schoolchildren and other amateurs, gave occasion sometimes for critical amusement, the fact remains that Delsarte was a pioneer in analyzing the movements of the body that accompany various emotions. The "law of correspondence" he based on nature—a mother desiring to show affection for a child presses it to her breast, not to her head. According to other laws, a gesture of mentality takes the point of departure from the head, one of moral value from the chest. All this, the *Delsarte Speaker* illus-

---

*The "Delsarte System" was not only for elocution, but for carriage and bearing, while walking, sitting, or standing. So general was it in the nineties that Joseph Newman wrote a popular song, which did not take Delsarte as seriously as many did, "Since Birdie Commenced Her Delsarte":

> Her right hand goes this way, her left one goes that,
> And she flings them high into the air,
> To show her improvement she gives the "wave" movement
> And impersonates Hate and Despair. . . .
> There's lots of sleep-walking, also dumb talking,
> Since Birdie's commenced her Delsarte.

trated with pictures. There were full-page drawings showing appropriate poses and gestures for "Accusation"—"Thou art the man"; "Remorse"— "Oh, wretched state! Oh, bosom black as death"; and so on through the gamut, "Meditation," "Defiance," "Easy Repose," "Exaltation," "Horror," "Invocation."

Another textbook was the *Star Speaker*. Being explicit, this book did not leave the pupil to depend on the illustration, vivid though it seems; but gave specific instructions for just the mobilization of legs, feet, arms, and eyes best adapted to convince the audience that the reciter was in a mood of loving his country:

Gesture for beginning recitation.

> PATRIOTISM. DESCRIPTION OF FIGURE
>   The right foot a slight space in advance; the form elevated to full height; the right arm extended, and the hand just raised to a level with the eyes; the left arm extended, so that the wrist is on a level with the waist; the hand open, the palm horizontal.

Such an attitude, the *Star Speaker* suggested as an example, would be suitable while delivering:

> Breathes there the man with a soul so dead,
> Who never to himself hath said,
> This is my own, my native land!

For the pose of "Cursing," also, there was specific and minute instruction about the disposition of feet, arms, fingers, and palms, including "shoulders well back; head erect; lips wearing a fierce expression, eyes glancing malignantly."

The Speakers and Readers had formal lessons on "Articulation, Pronunciation, Inflection, Accent and Emphasis, Pitch and Compass of the Voice"; including "faults to be remedied," such as to avoid saying "par-ticular" for "par-tic-u-lar."

For the attainment of this elegance, Brooks's *Manual of Elocution and Reading* provided "Exercises for Elocutionary Practice," gymnastic exercises for the lips and tongue, and also the mind.

Theophilus Thistle, the successful thistle-sifter, in sifting a sieve full of unsifted thistles, thrust three thousand thistles through the thick

Patriotism.

Cursing.
(From the Star Speaker*)*

of his thumb. Now, if Theophilus Thistle, the successful thistle-sifter, in sifting a sieve full of unsifted thistles, thrust three thousand thistles through the thick of his thumb, see that *thou*, in sifting a sieve full of unsifted thistles, thrust not three thousand thistles through the thick of *thy* thumb. Success to the successful thistle-sifter.

For boys, the favored selections were those through which they could give expression to the patriotic sentiments about America, the spirit of heroic resistance they had learned from the histories. Practically every boy declaimed at least once, and certainly every pupil heard many times, the speech of Patrick Henry ending: "I know not what course others may take; but as for me, give me liberty, or give me death."

There was no humor in the earlier "Speakers"; they were still under the preoccupation that education is an incident of religion. By the 1880s, however, they began to include selections which at once expressed the particular sense of humor called "American," and, by impressing it on schoolchildren, perpetuated it—Mark Twain's account of his experiences as a farmer, his tale of an ambitious dog which overestimated its capacity to catch up with a confident coyote, and his "Funeral of Buck Fanshaw." Some of the more simple humorous selections, designed for younger children, were direct enough to be looked down upon a little by a later generation, which would call them "slap-stick." Some of the pieces were humorous and are funny. I use both the past and the present tenses because of a vague feeling that, as to some of these pieces, the reasons for which they seemed humorous in 1896, when the *Delsarte Speaker* was published, are not the same reasons for which the generation of 1927 will concede they are funny. *Uncle Herbert's Speaker* gave text and minute directions for what modern comedians would call "putting over the 'laugh line'":

A LITTLE BOY'S LECTURE

Ladies and gentlemen: Nearly four hundred years ago the mighty mind of Columbus, traversing unknown seas, clasped this new continent in its embrace. A few centuries later arose one here who now lives in all our hearts as the Father of his Country. Christopher Columbus was *great*. George Washington was *great*. But here, my friends, in this glorious nineteenth century is—a *grater!* (Exhibiting a large, bright tin grater. The large kind used for horseradish could be most easily distinguished by the audience.)

The *Pathetic Recitations* usually included Dickens's "Death of Little Nell." An expression of this aspect of popular taste was "Nobody's Child," published in the *Schoolday Magazine*, and "noticed and copied and sung and spoken almost everywhere":

A humorous recitation. (From the Delsarte Speaker, *published by National Publishing Company, Philadelphia)*

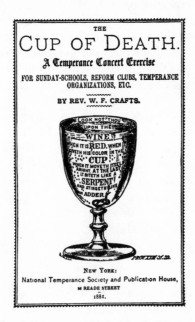

(From The Sunday-School Concert, *published by the National Temperance Society and Publication House)*

Alone in the dreary, pitiless street,
With my torn old dress, and bare, cold feet,
All day I have wandered to and fro,
Hungry and shivering, and nowhere to go;
The night's coming on in darkness and dread,
And the chill sleet beating upon my bare head.
Oh! why does the wind blow upon me so wild?
Is it because I am nobody's child?

All the six stanzas were sheer gloom. There was no story, nothing happened, and no comfort for the child was suggested except in the concluding three lines a hope of a future "home above."

Tragedies of the sea were favorites, including Longfellow's "Wreck of the *Hesperus*" and Southey's "Inchcape Rock." Zealous temperance leaders organized a practically universal inculcation in schoolchildren of detestation of the liquor traffic—ultimately leading to the National Prohibition Act of 1919. Schoolroom recitations encouraged students never to touch lips that touched liquor, or to sign the temperance pledge.

Many pieces formally marked off in the Speakers as "Selections for Boys and Girls" had the note that in a later generation came to be called "inspirational"; these recommended virtue over vice, and in some cases were considered preparation for future missionaries.

Penmanship was the especial study, the particular aspect of the schools, in which pupils with latent capacities for the ornate, the artistic, and the elegant could exercise their aspirations—the nearest to pictorial art they were permitted to come, the only outlet for artistic expression. Penmanship had the virtue of being useful, as well as ornamental—the accomplishment had

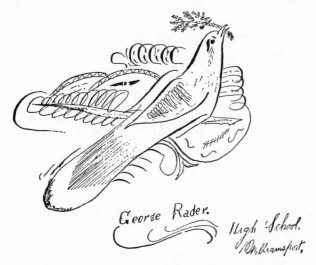

This is a sample of the work of an assiduous student of penmanship.

Virtue has its own reward.

In every schoolbook, emphasis was placed on the moral lesson. The copybook did not escape, for what better way could a maxim be impressed on the mind than by writing it over and over on the twenty ruled lines on the page? The maxim here reproduced is from Potter & Hammond's Synthetical, Analytical and Progressive System of Penmanship. Other copybook maxims were: "It is never too late to mend." "Judge not at first sight." "Quit not a certainty for hope." "Being upright in all things, we gain a reputation." "Pleasant words with pleasant tones will accomplish much."

a value in the marketplace. Teachers and parents thought "drawing" was a waste of time but admired the "harmony of curve and slope" in the penmanship flourishes portraying birds and flowers.

The teacher of penmanship was the center around which grew up a vogue of "business colleges," Spencerian* schools, commercial schools. Several in different parts of the country were conducted by members of the Spencer family; others by Pierce, Eastman, Bryant, and Stratton. These were the "schools of business" until after 1900, when Harvard University appropriated the term for a more pretentious treatment of the subject.

The emphasis which the common schools of the 1870s, 1880s, and 1890s put upon handwriting and allied subjects reflected a social point of view and an economic condition. Parents, farmers or others, who toiled with their hands, wanted their children to have "white-collar" jobs. To be a bookkeeper in a business house, or a clerk in a government office, was at once genteel and more remunerative than what was called "labor." Many who achieved the ambition lived to see the overalls-worker pass far above them in remuneration and economic standing. About 1890, $1.25 a day was good wages for workers in steel mills, while bookkeepers could make $15 a week. By 1925, bookkeepers and clerks could make $20 to $35 a week, while carpenters, bricklayers, and plasterers made $10 to $15 a day.

Alas for the Spencerian system, the invention of the typewriter doomed the Spencerian glory.

IX

The study of arithmetic was intended to impart mental discipline. Mental arithmetic was real drill—to stand on your feet and think fast and accurately, before the eye of a minatory teacher, and under the gaze of the whole school, and to answer such problems as:

> How many square inches in a piece of paper six inches long and four inches wide?

*After Platt Rogers Spencer, an Ohio schoolteacher and originator of the "Spencerian Style and System of Penmanship," hugely influential for generations. Eventually, the Spencer family also manufactured pens.

Reduce to their lowest terms: $\dfrac{12}{16}$, $\dfrac{24}{36}$, $\dfrac{16}{28}$, $\dfrac{28}{49}$, $\dfrac{32}{36}$.

Henry paid ¼ of all his money for a knife, ⅛ for a ball, and ⅙ for a necktie: What part of his money had he left?

A harness was sold for ¾ of ⅖ of what it cost. What was the loss percent?

Many of the examples in written arithmetic would be stiff to the average adult with a college education:

The fore wheel of a carriage is 9 feet, and the hind wheel 10½ feet in circumference; how many times will each turn round in running from Boston to Andover, 20½ miles?

The salary of the president of the United States is $25,000 per annum; what sum may he expend daily and yet save $41,560 in one term of office, viz., 4 years?

Those problems are from Eaton's *Common School Arithmetic*, the contents of which included: Compound Interest; Discount; Banking and Bank Discount; Insurance; Stocks; Commission and Brokerage; Taxes; Custom House Business; Exchange; Equation of Payments; Profit and Loss; Partnership; Compound Proportion; Alligation Medial; Involution; Evolution; Arithmetical Progression; Annuities; Permutation; Tare and Tret.

Problems in arithmetic were "figured out" on slates, the pupils using pencils of soft stone sharpened at one end. The slate has given way almost everywhere before the scratch pad, but in the seventies, eighties, and nineties it was the commonest article in a schoolchild's equipment. Slates were fragile and liable to break if let fall, but with care could be made to last several years, being passed down, in that economical age, from older brother to younger. The cheapest, selling for ten cents, were about the size of this page, were made of poor material, and with smooth places where no pencil could make a mark; they were framed in a plain wooden border, poorly mortised, forever coming apart. Better grades of slates were almost as large as a tabloid newspaper, had double panels hinged in the back, and about their borders a protective strip of bright red or blue flannel.

The strongest argument against slates was hygienic and was doubtless one reason why they lost their former ubiquity. Fastidious teachers showed their pupils how to erase writing by wiping it off with a damp cloth or a sponge, but to schoolchildren this seemed a long-way-around method for achieving results that could just as efficaciously be attained by saliva and a brisk rubbing with the coat sleeve.

The slate is gone, and with it has gone the gleeful practice of the mischievous youth of forty years ago, of drawing caricatures of the teacher or the girl with pigtails across the aisle—caricatures that, when danger of approaching authority threatened, could be deftly swept into oblivion by the stroke of a moistened thumb.*

American schools strongly emphasized spelling, the "test of scholarship in the district school," as one former student recalled. Most correspondents recalled oral drills, usually with some form of competition, such as the group spelling-bee. Neighboring schools were pitted against each other. Often whole communities took part. Senator Simeon Fess of Ohio recalls some so heated that they lasted beyond midnight.

The mute umpire of these matches was a book, one of the most widely known ever printed in America. *The Blue-Back Speller,* or *Webster's Blue-Back Speller,* was a universal textbook in the schools, yet it was more than that. "We all began life on Webster's spelling-book," wrote a resident of Buffalo, New York. It became the master-book on spelling everywhere, a standard article of commerce, like sugar and salt, kept in the stores, alongside the gingham and the calico.

More than five generations learned from it. They first studied it before there was any United States, as early as 1787; and it was still being used in schools as late as the early 1900s. Boys learned from the *Blue-Back Speller,* grew up, became presidents of the United States, died, and were relatively forgotten, while the presses of D. Appleton & Company ground out new editions for second, third, and fourth generations. The first edition was printed on a handpress, the last on the most modern Hoe; the first antedated the presidency of Washington, the last was contemporary with Roosevelt.

The compiler was Noah Webster, who called the earliest one, printed in 1783, *First Part of a Grammatical Institute of the English Language.* That too ponderous title, destined to be simplified by five generations of schoolchildren into *The Blue-Back Speller,* must have struck old Noah Webster himself as cumbersome, for by 1789 apparently he was calling it a *Spelling-Book.*

For nearly half a century, Noah Webster lived upon the profits of his *Speller.* As it was his only means of livelihood and he needed protection from piracy, Webster visited many states and secured the enactment of copyright statutes, "so that," says Grant Overton, "he may be the instigator of American copyright protection." Webster, using the profits of his *Speller* as his means of livelihood, devoted himself to compiling his dictionary, which yielded him no profit at all, although it has been a valuable estate to his family. In 1855, the plates of the *Speller* were taken over by another company for a further half-century of publication.

Neither the *Speller* nor any other schoolbook of the early days of the nineteenth century could confine itself to the branch of learning it taught. It had to be semireligious. The *Blue-Back Speller* had its quota of moral lessons of the usual type.

*New math and pocket calculators likewise deny such simple pleasures to more recent generations of schoolchildren—who have doubtless discovered substitute diversions. —D.R.

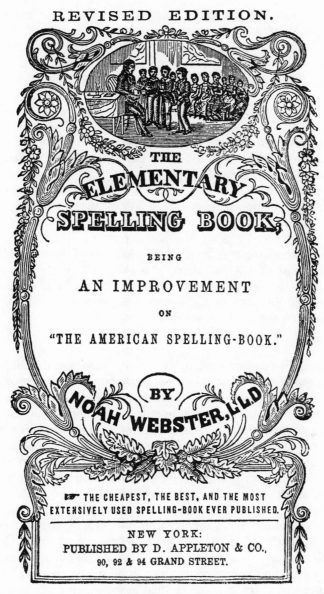

This spelling book was in common use during the 1890s, and still used in schools after 1900.

*   *   *

In the teaching of spelling, a difficulty lay in the fact that before the teachers had time to give sufficient drill in spelling, the pupils, as they took up other subjects, were obliged to make daily use of some words that to them were new and very formidable. There would be regrettable lack of balance in having pupils studying, for example, arithmetic but not knowing how to spell the word. To give young minds a shortcut to the spelling of polysyllabic words, there was an ingenious device with which one learned to spell the word "Arithmetic" by memorizing a sentence "A rat in the house may eat the ice cream." The initial letters of the words in the sentence spell "Arithmetic." A similar expedient was:

G   E   O   G   R A P H   Y
George Eliot's Old Grandmother Rode a Pig Home Yesterday

Osgood's *American Advanced Speller* stood up bravely for the desirability of learning to spell long words, and, in that spirit, began at Lesson I with "a-m am" and by easy stages led up to

| lat i tu di na ri an | su per nat u ral i ty |
| pu sil la nim i ty | in com mu ni ca bil i ty |

Nearly all who have sent me their recollections of their schooldays have shown pride and affectionate approval for the proficiency in spelling that the old schools developed; have had the air of saying: "Those were the days when boys and girls could *spell*"—with a manner of confidently inviting comparison with the modern generation.

Arithmetic really produced exactness of the processes of thinking. Spelling could only produce, at best, exactness of memory. Spelling was a kind of memory marathon, the mental equivalent of six-day bicycle races, or endurance contests in dancing. Arithmetic led to intellectual skill. No one could speak of such a thing as skill in spelling. You either remembered how the word was spelled or you did not. If memory training were the object, it would be better accomplished by the memorizing of good poetry, which would give rise to worthy and agreeable emotions in the process, and leave in the mind a valuable residue, which spelling did not.

Ranking with spelling and arithmetic, as studies good for mental discipline, was grammar; and ranking with McGuffey's Readers and Noah Webster's Speller in ubiquity and venerableness was Murray's *Grammar of the English Language*, first issued by Lindley Murray in 1795, regarded as the standard textbook on its subject throughout England and America for nearly a hundred years, and still studied in some American schools as late as the 1870s. Another familiar grammar was Greene's grammar, which in 1868 contained a record of, and reflection upon, some familiar American locutions:

> The following are actual expressions collected from a large number of schools. They should be carefully corrected.
> 'Taint no good. I hain't got no writin' pen. I've got some on t'other side of me slate. You said 'twas yourn. Mine was writ better'n hisn, only he writ more nor I did. You be's telling on him. He done it, too, marm. I can't git it no way. Be them two right? I

cotched the ball. Hullo, teacher! Florie and me went out and drove
hoop. She jawed her mother.

Grammar, especially parsing, was regarded by one correspondent, Albert Mordell, as an unhappy denaturing device for taking the poetry out of
poems. "We would be given selections from poems and told to find the
subject, which might be half a dozen lines away from the predicate, with
dependent clauses strung all around. Prose was not used for parsing because the subject was before the predicate where it belonged, and therefore
provided no puzzle to sharpen our wits—or confuse them."

Important as discipline were the chores, outside the school, the farm and
household tasks concerned with food and heat and light, in the days before
"press the button"; when heat meant, for the boys, chopping wood and carrying it in and filling the woodbox; and light meant, for the girls, filling the
lamps; water meant pumping and carrying in buckets; milk meant milking
the cows; butter meant churning. The countless other chores: rising early
to help feed the animals, cleaning the stables and providing fresh straw in
the evening, turning the grindstone, supplying muscle-power for the corn-
sheller and the grain-fan. Many a boy was led to give thought to the value
of school by being taken from it in the early spring to help with the plow-
ing and planting.

Most important of all in imparting the discipline of forgoing the unat-
tainable, was poverty. A story told of Calvin Coolidge as a schoolboy at
Plymouth, Vermont, in the fall of 1880, said he requested a penny of his father, a country-store keeper and farmer, a "man of means" according to the
standards of that time and place; the father replied: "Well, if the Democrats win, we'll have hard times, but if the Republicans win, times will be
good; come back after the election."*

No aspect of those early schools will surprise, and probably dismay, the
America of 1927 so much as the extent to which teachers expressed their
disapproval by physical means. Apparently it was not merely frequent but
almost universal, and wholly accepted as a thing to be taken for granted.

In 1927, correspondents remembered the blows of hickory switches,
rulers, rawhide strips, outright beatings, and numerous other forms of what one
termed "torture." Of Iowa during the 1880s, one correspondent recalled:

> The culprit was led out of the room into the hall and there the
> punishment was administered. We were not permitted to be eye-
> witnesses, but care was taken, evidently, not to remove the scene of
> activity far away from the student body that the resounding whacks
> did not reach our ears. It was a dull hour when from some room or

*May this have been parental propaganda, designed to make young Coolidge the kind of conserva-
tive Republican he became?

"What has he done? He laughs and talks in school. He loves to be idle. Does he not look bad?" (From McGuffey's First Eclectic Reader*)*

other a culprit was not dragged out into the hall and physically admonished.

Some of the pupils who in their mature years contributed these recollections felt that their conduct called for some kind of punishment, and they did not seem to object because it was physical. Some concede that there was frequently a spirit which called for physical forcefulness in the teacher.

Alfred Holman, long editor of the San Francisco *Argonaut*, wrote of a school in Oregon:

> In our own school, and pretty much every other, there was a new teacher at the beginning of each school term, and it was necessary for him to establish himself in authority as against the two or three big boys who were found in every such school. I recall that one of our teachers, a frail young chap, summoned our prize bully to the platform. When he refused to come, the teacher gathered him by the collar and dragged him the whole length of the room. Thereafter the bully ate out of his hand, so to speak. This was a common experience and it explains, in part, why it was necessary that the pioneer schools should be taught by men rather than women.

Even where overt rebelliousness was lacking, pupils seem to have looked upon whipping as part of the accepted order.

Dr. W. D. Howe, who went to school in southern Indiana in the 1880s, dissented strenuously from tolerance about corporal punishment:

> I think nothing has left such an impression on me as the floggings which we youngsters in our seats in the next room could hear going

At work. (From Old-Time School Books, *by Clifton Johnson, the Macmillan Company)*

on, given to certain boys who had to have them regularly and who were of an inferior mental calibre. I am sure that others had the same impression that I had—a sort of sickening disgust after the teacher took the big switch from over his desk and went into the next room to give the beating. You can talk all you please about the value of such punishment; as I remember it, it didn't mean anything; indeed, I hardly know of a boy who was constantly whipped that way who ever amounted to anything later in life.

About the change—from the things here described to the modern condition, in which a teacher who "lays hands" on a pupil is liable to find himself in the criminal courts—there could be more discussion than there is space for in this history.

CHAPTER 2
Roosevelt

A seer of the 1860s, looking through the census roll for the one who forty to sixty years later would become the champion of the average American and lead him in a struggle against economic oppression, might readily have arrived last upon the name which in the census of 1860 figured as, Theodore Roosevelt, age 2. By his birth, because his father was a well-to-do New York City merchant of the oldest Dutch lineage and because his mother belonged to the "southern aristocracy," Roosevelt's preordained lot was to pass his life in the rather supercilious detachment of that stratum of American society for which the common term at that time was "the upper crust." By his inherited fortune—not large but yet substantial—he belonged, in Carlyle's famous classification, with the "haves," and not with the "have-nots"; and was destined to leisure, or to a career of further moneymaking in the family business. Through his education at Harvard, he might have shared the mental attitude known as "Harvard indifference." His puniness as a youth would have excused ease. His taste for writing books called for the cloister rather than the forum. The zest for outdoor life that he cultivated should have been satisfied, according to the standards of his class, by riding in a red coat after trained hounds across the sunny fields of Long Island. Had he ventured into anything so indecorous as politics, he should have had the role of the upper classes doing their duty, played in the costume with which the humorists of the early 1880s actually robed him, the typical "dude in politics."

But why try to picture this contrast, between the Roosevelt that might have been and the Roosevelt that was, through the clumsiness of repetitive detail? It was put once by William Hard, in the obituary tribute he wrote, and it need never be put again: "He might have been the greatest dilettante of his day. He might have been, in mind and body, its greatest dandy. He might have been the most promiscuous absorber of its offerings. He became the most girded pursuer of its activities."

II

Roosevelt, returning to his New York home after his graduation from Harvard in 1880, inquired of some of his family's associates—who

Roosevelt and his brother Eliot playing with Edith Carow, whom he later married, and his sister Corinne, later Mrs. Douglas Robinson. About 1875. (Courtesy of the Roosevelt Memorial Association)

were naturally "the men in the clubs of social pretension, men of cultivated tastes and easy life"—about the location of the district Republican Association and how to go about joining it.

These men—and the big business men and lawyers also—laughed at me, and told me that politics were "low"; that the organizations were not controlled by "gentlemen"; that I would find them run by saloon-keepers, horse-car conductors, and the like, and not by men with any of whom I would come in contact outside; and, moreover, they assured me that the men I met would be rough and brutal and unpleasant to deal with. I answered that if this were so it merely meant that the people I knew did not belong to the governing class, and that the other people did—and that I intended to be one of the governing class; that if they proved too hard-bit for me I supposed I would have to quit, but that I certainly would not

quit until I had made the effort and found out whether I
really was too weak to hold
my own in the rough and
tumble.*

Roosevelt, joining the local Republican club, was noticed by one
of the minor captains, "Joe" Murray, a party workhorse fitting in
most respects the familiar type,
but with more insight and character. Murray thought young Roosevelt, as a scion of wealth and
social position, would be a good
vote-getter in what the political
argot of New York called the "dia-
mond-back" district, the wealthi-
est in the city, with a constituency
that included Columbia University and the principal "brownstone
fronts" of the city.** Roosevelt accepted the suggestion that he run
for the state assembly.

*Roosevelt on a vacation in the Maine woods in
1879. (Courtesy of the Roosevelt Memorial
Association)*

III

I n his early days in the assembly, Roosevelt quickly found that not all the
corruption in politics consisted of ballot-box stuffing and getting offices
for friends; or rather, found that these forms of political corruption were
merely the small change which active politicians get from a bigger divide.
He discovered for himself, in short, the existence of a superior force, symbolized later in a vivid appellation, "the man higher up."

This discovery Roosevelt blurted out, to the dismay of some who had
promoted his entry into politics, in a speech in the assembly attacking "the
infernal thieves who have those railroads in charge . . . with their hired
stock-jobbing newspaper, with their corruption of the judiciary, and with
their corruption of this House." The passage ended with a phrase then new
and seriously shocking, "the wealthy criminal class."

The phrase was quoted again and again, often in connotations in which
a hundred prophets were ready to swear it would be Roosevelt's valedictory
in politics.

Theodore Roosevelt: An Autobiography.
**Meaning, in the early 1880s, the homes of wealth and social position.

Roosevelt's home while a student at Harvard, from 1876 to 1880.

The phrase did not end Roosevelt's political career; but—for reasons other than those the prophets had in mind—it marked the highest point his antagonism toward big business reached until two decades passed. From 1883 until 1902, Roosevelt measurably receded from that early impulse. His shock at the corruption of big business was overlaid by apprehension about the radicalism of some of the manifestations of social unrest, and the violence of some others. When Henry George, the single-tax advocate, ran for mayor of New York in 1886, Roosevelt ran against him. When members of the international anarchists' organization in Chicago, sentenced to death for throwing bombs that killed several policemen, were pardoned by Governor Altgeld, Roosevelt was shocked at the condoning of violence. When another anarchist tried to murder Henry C. Frick during the 1892 Homestead Riots, Roosevelt seriously feared the spirit of revolution might spread far enough to undermine the government. When Bryan ran for the presidency on a platform demanding the so-called free coinage of silver, Roosevelt felt that national honesty was on the defensive.

Roosevelt, believing these were a more fundamental menace than the corrupt practices of corporations, fell back from his early assault. During two decades, he not only "laid-off" the anti-big-business movements but excoriated the leaders of them. Of Bryan he said in a letter to his sister in September 1896: "His utterances are as criminal as they are wildly silly. All the ugly forces that seethe beneath the social crust are behind him."

By his recession from his early impulse to fight big business, Roosevelt for nearly twenty years was reduced to the rank of a political reformer of the ordinary type. His instinct for better things he expressed, between 1889 and 1895, in a struggle for civil service reform, a role pretty distant

Roosevelt on the round-up, 1885. (Courtesy of the Roosevelt Memorial Association)

from high-rank warfare—fighting petty politicians, not big business—at that time civil service reformers were looked upon as meddlesome cranks, more annoying than formidable.

From 1895 to 1897, he threw his vigor for decency into service as police commissioner of New York City, where he helped Jacob A. Riis in his enterprise for improving the conditions of the poor in New York. He wrote essays and made speeches about purity in politics. But he was, during this

Roosevelt at Oyster Bay about the time he was police commissioner. (Courtesy of the Roosevelt Memorial Association)

President Roosevelt on a bear hunt in April 1905. (Copyright Charles Scribner's Sons)

period, wholly a political reformer, and in no sense an economic reformer.

In 1897, as assistant secretary of the navy, he made a record of vigorous preparedness for the Spanish War. In 1898, as lieutenant-colonel of the Rough Riders regiment, he appealed romantically to the country. In 1900 and 1901, as governor of New York, he managed the business of the state competently, enlisted popular support of ideals of decency in politics, compelled the public service corporations to pay reasonable taxes, and resisted the state "boss," Thomas C. Platt, who, to get rid of him, "kicked him upstairs" into the vice-presidency.

Roosevelt's fame was great. It did not, however, include any general expectation that he would become a leader of the excited opposition stirred up by the trusts. The recollection of his early assault on "the criminal wealthy" was twenty years old and had become faint. People thought of him as personally independent, as cleanly and utterly free from the polluting alliance between politics and big business; but they did not commonly think of him as sharing the mood of those who sought to reform government, nor as among those who had a crusading conviction against "the world's real rulers, those who control the concentrated portion of the money supply." They did not think of him as a "trust-buster"; on the contrary, in the campaign of 1900, when he was the Republican candidate for vice-president, he had spoken ironically of the attitude of Bryan and the Democrats about the trusts. One of Roosevelt's friends, writing a campaign biography, with every wish to give Roosevelt as many titles to distinction as his career to that time warranted, described him as "that amiable and gifted author, legislator, field-sportsman, soldier, reformer, and executive."

IV

The newspaper writers and cartoonists of the early 1880s, complacently or cynically reflecting the spirit of that period, saw Theodore Roosevelt as an impetuous boy beating puny fists against the impregnable walls of what is. They dressed him in a high hat, a coat of the smart style called "cutaway," and the skin-tight trousers that were the fad of the day. His teeth they did not notice, concealing them under a rather too carefully tended mustache. They completed their pictures with labels usually synonymous with "dude reformer."

Roosevelt, making his maiden speech as an officeholder, was pictured by the *New York Sun:* "Young Mr. Roosevelt of New York, a blond young man with eye-glasses, English side-whiskers and a Dundreary drawl in his speech." The drawl was illustrated by eccentric typographical treatment of a phrase from the speech—"r-a-w-t-h-e-r r-e-l-i-e-v-e-d." Equal belittlement, coupled with a hint of advice to Roosevelt's constituency, was expressed, after another of Roosevelt's speeches, by another New York paper: "The popular voice of New York will probably leave this weakling at home hereafter." One newspaper called him "Oscar Wilde,"* and others repeated the epithet. The Albany correspondent of *The Observer* in his despatches customarily referred to Roosevelt as "the little man" and "His Lordship," and pictured him as strutting about with his nose in the air, and comporting himself with more than a touch of condescending superiority toward his rustic and East Side colleagues. The most tireless among Roosevelt's newspaper detractors was the *New York World.* Throughout Roosevelt's three terms in the assembly, whenever he made a speech or gave out an interview or otherwise came into public notice, the *World* aimed at him barbs dipped in poison. His youth, his wealth, his appearance, his speech, his associates—all served as pretexts for ridicule. One day, the *World* dispatch from Albany began: "Young Mr. Roosevelt, having recovered from his recent attack of the croup . . ." Another time the jeering took the form of verse:

> His strong point is his bank account,
> His weak point is his head.

---

* The original of the name was then at the height of his aesthetic vogue.

Roosevelt as the cartoonists saw him during the 1900s. (From the Philadelphia Inquirer*)*

Roosevelt was not the sort to take the *World*'s abuse lying down. Even this early he had a well-stocked vocabulary of scorching invective. Nothing the *World* ever printed about Roosevelt was half so devastating in brutal directness, or so pungent with innuendo as the characterization he delivered on the floor of the assembly: "The New York *World*, a local stock-jobbing sheet of limited circulation, of voluble scurrility and versatile mendacity—owned by the arch-thief of Wall Street and edited by a rancorous kleptomaniac with a penchant for trousers."

Some of the deprecation of Roosevelt was a reflection of partisanship among the New York papers—the *World*'s was a direct expression of the interests that then owned it, Jay Gould and his associates, railroad and public utility promoters, and monopolists. But the same note is to be found in newspapers published outside New York State. The *Boston Herald*, with an air of artistic objectivity, gave this portrayal of the young Roosevelt: "He has a very light colored, slight mustache, wears jaunty clothes, and his head is topped by a small straw hat with a straight rim dyed blue on the under side. . . . He looks for all the world like a young college graduate hunting for a place on the editorial staff of some newspaper."

Even as late as 1890, newspapers used such phrases as "a Jane dandy," "punkin-lily," "scion of a diluted ancestry," "Terrapin Teddy," "descendant of the wayback Roosevelts from Rooseveltville," "Rosy Roosy," "Tintinnabulating Ted," and a strange epithet, mysterious as to its derivation, and cryptic as to meaning, but clearly devised to convey derogation, "Mr. Theossehos Roosevelt."

Roosevelt as the cartoonists saw him during the 1900s. (Homer Davenport in the New York Evening Mail*)*

Even such newspapers as wished to be friendly to Roosevelt gave him, so to speak, discouraged encouragement; spoke of him in terms of giving a pat on the back to a well-meaning young man who one hopes will stay in politics but who one expects hardly will. An oasis of not too hopeful approval was published on the editorial page of the *New York Times:*

> Mr. Roosevelt has a most refreshing habit of calling men and things by their right names, and in these days of judicial, ecclesiastical, and journalistic subserviency to the robber barons of the Street, it needs some little courage in any public man to characterize them and their acts in fitting terms. There is a splendid career open for a young man of position, character, and independence like Mr. Roosevelt.

"He has been called a swell," said a New England journal, "but it would be well if every State had just such swells." "Let them all come to the front and take part in the government," added a western paper encouragingly.

Doubtless Roosevelt, wearing the clothes a young man of his background would naturally receive from his tailor, stood out from the older members of the New York Assembly, and from the rural type as well as the usual city type. His energetic forthrightness set him apart also, as well as his spontaneousness, his lack of youth's ordinary disposition toward self-effacement in the presence of elders. Roosevelt was not a dude, either in meticulousness of dress, or in vacuity of mind, or in indolence. Neither at that time, nor at any time was he self-conscious about dress or manner. As a youth at Harvard, he paid considerably less than the normal young man's attention to clothes. His mother, with presumably accurate knowledge, used to speak of him as her "young berserker." The newspapers assumed that a young man who came from a wealthy old family and had been educated at Harvard must have the characteristics that newspapers commonly attributed to that caste. Or they seized upon foppishness as the most convenient trait with which to identify a new and conspicuous figure in public life. Or they used this means of expressing the contemptuous superiority of the "hard-boiled," among both newspapermen and politicians, toward the young and the idealistic. Or they thought of "dude" as a symbol for the futility of attacking the accepted order. All motives combined to fasten upon Roosevelt the tag that became practically universal during the early years of his public life.

By the rule that usually governs, that early conception of Roosevelt should have remained to the end. The public's initial impression, the role the newspapers give a man when he first appears in the news, almost always sticks. To alter the public's first conception of a man is almost more difficult than to alter personality itself.

Nevertheless, Roosevelt changed the picture. More accurately, the times changed, the mood of the people changed, and the newspapers reflected the transition. In the

Roosevelt as the cartoonists saw him after he had attacked the trusts.

Roosevelt as the cartoonists saw him during his presidency. (From the New York World*)*

Roosevelt as the cartoonists saw him during the 1900s. (Macauley in the New York World)

Roosevelt when he was elected president—as seen by Bernard Partridge, the cartoonist of Punch.

early 1880s, the forces Roosevelt attacked were seen as those that had fought the Civil War, abolished slavery, preserved the Union; that were resisting the inflationary economic heresies of greenbackism and free silver; and, as business leaders and railroad builders, were opening up the country. By the early 1900s, "opening up the country" was called "stealing the public land," and in all respects the forces Roosevelt opposed were seen in a very different light. The writers and cartoonists of the 1900s portrayed Roosevelt at the height of his presidency as the fighting champion of the people, a combination of Rough Rider and fire-eater, fists clenched, chin thrust forward, hair bristling, eyes glaring, and—final touch of belligerency—teeth made to symbolize a steam shovel biting into an ogre labeled "The Trusts," teeth gnashing defiance at Wall Street, or gloating in triumph over it—the outstanding, incomparable symbol of virility in his time. Of the elements that entered into the transformation, comparatively little is to be ascribed to a change in Roosevelt's personality. Much more potent was a change that came in the conditions of the times and the mood of the people.

CHAPTER 3
A Picture, a Poem, and the Times

During Christmas week of the year 1898, California schoolteacher Edwin Markham, living on the heights back of Oakland, in a cottage that looked down upon the bay and city of San Francisco and the Golden Gate, utilized his vacation to complete a poem. For years he had been haunted by the memory of a painting he had seen reproduced in *Scribner's Magazine* in 1886, "The Man With the Hoe," by the French peasant-artist Millet. Then he had the great joy of seeing the original painting in San Francisco. He described the experience subsequently:

> I sat for an hour before the painting and all the time the terror and power of the picture was growing upon me. I saw that this creation of the painter was no mere peasant, no chance man of the fields, but he was rather a type, a symbol of the toiler, brutalized through long ages of industrial oppression. I saw in this peasant the slow but awful degradation of man through endless, hopeless, and joyless labor.

The poem was first published in the *San Francisco Examiner* on January 15, 1899.

THE MAN WITH THE HOE

By Edwin Markham
(Written after Seeing Millet's World-Famous Painting)

Bowed by the weight of centuries he leans
Upon his hoe and gazes on the ground,
The emptiness of ages in his face,
And on his back the burden of the world.
Who made him dead to rapture and despair,
A thing that grieves not and that never hopes,
Stolid and stunned, a brother to the ox?
Who loosened and let down this brutal jaw?
Whose was the hand that slanted back this brow?
Whose breath blew out the light within this brain?
Is this the Thing the Lord God made and gave

To have dominion over sea and land;
To trace the stars and search the heavens for power;
To feel the passion of Eternity?
Is this the dream He dreamed who shaped the suns
And pillared the blue firmament with light?
Down all the stretch of Hell to its last gulf
There is no shape more terrible than this—
More tongued with censure of the world's blind greed—
More filled with signs and portents for the soul—
More fraught with menace to the universe.

What gulfs between him and the seraphim!
Slave of the wheel of labor, what to him
Are Plato and the swing of Pleiades?
What the long reaches of the peaks of song,
The rift of dawn, the reddening of the rose?
Through this dread shape the suffering ages look;
Time's tragedy is in that aching stoop;
Through this dread shape humanity betrayed,
Plundered, profaned and disinherited,
Cries protest to the Judges of the World,
A protest that is also prophecy.

The Man with the Hoe. (This reproduction of Millet's painting is printed through the courtesy of William H. Crocker, of San Francisco, owner of the original)

O masters, lords and rulers in all lands,
Is this the handiwork you give to God,
This monstrous thing distorted and soul-quenched?
How will you ever straighten up this shape;
Touch it again with immortality;
Give back the upward looking and the light;
Rebuild in it the music and the dream;
Make right the immemorial infamies
Perfidious wrongs, immedicable woes?

O masters, lords and rulers in all lands,
How will the Future reckon with this Man?
How answer his brute question in that hour
When whirlwinds and rebellion shake the world?
How will it be with kingdoms and with kings—
With those who shaped him to the thing he is—
When this dumb Terror shall reply to God
After the silence of the centuries?

The poem flew eastward across the continent, like a contagion. As fast as the mails carried it, newspapers printed it as a fresh focus of infection, first California and the Pacific Coast, then the Mississippi Valley, on into New York and New England, over the line into Canada. Within a week, phrases and couplets from it were on every lip. Newspaper editions containing it were exhausted and publishers reprinted it, together with editorials about

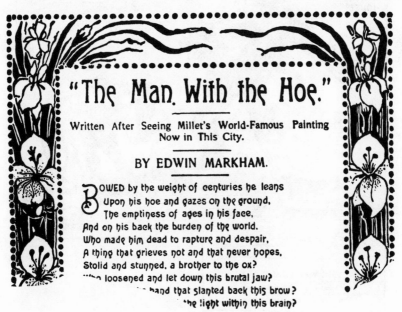

(*Reproduced from the original publication of* "The Man With the Hoe," *in the* San Francisco Examiner, *January 15, 1899*)

it, and the hundreds of manuscripts of comment received from the public. The newspapers, a historian of the day remarked, as a unique phenomenon, "gave as much space to 'The Man With the Hoe' as to prize-fights and police stories. The clergy made the poem their text, platform orators dilated upon it, college professors lectured upon it, debating societies discussed it, schools took it up for study."

Sociologists, editors, political leaders, all who were close to the heart of the crowd or concerned with it, seized upon "The Man With the Hoe" as an expression of the prevailing mood of the American people. William Randolph Hearst, with true journalistic instinct, realizing that William J. Bryan was the outstanding spokesman of the sort of protest the poem expressed and appealed to, asked Bryan to write about it for the *New York Journal.* Bryan made the poem the text for a characteristic summing up of the complaints of the times. Ominously, he quoted Victor Hugo's description of the mob as "the human race in misery." On his own account Bryan said:

THE WAR CHANT
Every time I come to town
    The boys keep a-kickin' my dawg aroun.
Makes no diff'rence if he is a houn'——
    They gotta quit kickin' my dawg aroun'!

"Common People's" insurgency, after growing for many years, became acute during the Taft administration. (Herbert Johnson, in the Philadelphia North American)

It is not strange that "The Man With the Hoe" created a profound sensation. It is a sermon addressed to the heart. It voices humanity's protest against inhuman greed. There is a majestic sweep
to the argument; some of the lines pierce like arrows. How feeble
in comparison have been the answers to it.

The extremes of society are being driven further and further
apart. Wealth is being concentrated in the hands of a few. At one
end of the scale luxury and idleness breed effeminacy; at the other
end, want and destitution breed desperation. . . .

Markham himself had not anticipated the kind of acclaim that came to
his poem, and certainly not the volume of it. He had looked upon Millet's
powerful painting, he had been moved to an ecstasy, and had written a
poem. Apparently it took time for him to find just the significance that the
country saw in the poem instantly.

It was Bryan who tied Markham's poem directly to existing American
conditions, translated Markham's generalizations into an indictment with
specific counts. Some of Bryan's accusations were aimed at conditions already passed or passing; others pointed straight at the heart of conditions
that were causing widespread discontent. When Bryan asked: "Is it the
fault of God or Nature . . . that our tax laws are so made . . . that the poor
man pays more than his share and the rich man less?" he was referring to
the Supreme Court's invalidation, in 1895, of the attempt to have an in-
come-tax law, an attempt that had to wait for success until 1913.

But when Bryan asked: "Is it the fault of God or of Nature that children
are driven into factories?" he was referring not only to child labor (then
coming to be generally looked upon as deplorable), but, in a broader sense,
to the increase of factory life in America, the economic condition that was
increasingly taking American families from the farm to the factory—a transition which, in connection with what had previously been the ideal of life
in America, was a principal cause of social fretfulness.

And when Bryan asked: "Is God or Nature responsible for the . . . trust?
Is God or Nature responsible for private monopolies?" he was putting his
hand on the name for the particular institution which, in that year, and for
fifteen years afterward, was the country's outstanding political issue, regarded as its outstanding social menace.

Indictment of the times was not confined to Markham's poetry or Bryan's ex-
egesis. Men of different temperaments, from a variety of fields, described the
condition in phrases no less strong. A message sent to Congress by one of the
most solid of conservatives, Grover Cleveland, had asserted that

the gulf between employers and the employed is constantly widen-
ing, and classes are rapidly forming, one comprising the very rich
and powerful, while in another are found the toiling poor. . . . The
communism of combined wealth and capital, the outgrowth of

overweening cupidity and selfishness, which insidiously undermine
the justice and integrity of free institutions, is not less dangerous
than the communism of oppressed poverty and toil, which, exas-
perated by injustice and discontent, attacks with wild disorder the
citadel of rule.

Theodore Roosevelt, shortly before the presidential elections of 1904,
in a conversation with a journalist, painted a word picture not less somber
than Markham's:

> Corporation cunning has developed faster than the laws of na-
> tion and State. Corporations have found ways to steal long before
> we have found that they were susceptible of punishment for theft.
> Sooner or later, unless there is a readjustment, there will come a ri-
> otous, wicked, murderous day of atonement. There must come, in
> the proper growth of this nation, a readjustment. If it is not to
> come by sword and powder and blood, it must come by peaceful
> compromise. These fools in Wall Street think that they can go on
> forever! They can't!
>
> I would like to be elected President of the United States to be
> the buffer between their foolishness and the wrath that is surely to
> come—unless they sober up.

Chief Justice Edward G. Ryan, of the Supreme Court of Wisconsin, addressing the University of Wisconsin as early as 1873, had foreseen an arrogance of corporate wealth which came promptly upon his prediction of
it, and continued for more than thirty years:

> There is looming up a new and dark power. I cannot dwell upon
> the signs and shocking omens of its advent. The accumulation of in-
> dividual wealth seems to be greater than it ever has been since the
> downfall of the Roman Empire. The enterprises of the country are
> aggregating vast corporate combinations of unexampled capital,
> boldly marching, not for economic conquests only, but for political
> power. For the first time really in our politics money is taking the
> field as an organized power. . . . Already, here at home, one great
> corporation has trifled with the sovereign power, and insulted the
> State. There is grave fear that it, and its great rival, have confeder-
> ated to make partition of the State and share it as spoils. . . . The
> question will arise, and arise in your day, though perhaps not fully in
> mine: "Which shall rule—wealth or man; which shall lead—
> money or intellect; who shall fill public stations—educated and pa-
> triotic freemen, or the feudal serfs of corporate capital?"

President Schurman, of Cornell, in his June 1906 commencement address offered a menacing description of the America of the day that was no
less menacing than Markham's:

A conception of organized society in America, visualized by Opper in the New York Journal *during the McKinley administration.*

This cartoon by Herbert Johnson, in the Philadelphia North American, *pictured "The Common People" being victimized by the power that "predatory wealth" had in politics, as symbolized by "Uncle Joe" Cannon, then Speaker of the House of Representatives. The series of cartoons in which "The Common People" figured as always downtrodden, always "put upon," ran for many years, and were especially trenchant about the time of the Insurgent Progressive party movements.*

To get and to have is the motto not only of the market, but of the altar and of the hearth. We are coming to measure man—man with his heart and mind and soul—in terms of mere acquisition and possession. A waning Christianity and a waxing Mammonism are the twin spectres of our age. The love of money and the reckless pursuit of it are undermining the National character.

The condition that caused such excited utterances and the condition that explained the furor over "The Man With the Hoe" were one. The year of the publication of Markham's poem, 1899, and the following year, saw the publication of twenty-eight books about "Trusts," and more than 150 magazine articles, in addition to several of the nineteen volumes of the official report of the U.S. Industrial Commission, which had spent many months hearing testimony about monopolies.

"Is God or Nature," Bryan asked, "responsible for the trust? Is God or Nature responsible for private monopolies?" By implication, he answered, the trust was wholly man-made. (And to Bryan's way of thinking, wholly evil.) In this Bryan was only partly right. That simple believer that black is all black, and white all white, did not always understand those more complex fields of truth where black shades into white. The complete truth about the rise of the trusts was that some of the responsibility lay in one quarter, some in another. Concretely, the trusts were partly a phase of normal industrial evolution, partly a product of the greed of individual men. To understand the trust, we had best begin with the part industrial evolution had in it.

CHAPTER 4

From Old to New in Industry

Throughout America, during the latter half of the nineteenth century, continued a process of little shops closing down, big factories growing bigger; little one-man businesses giving up, great corporations growing and expanding; rural communities becoming stagnant, big cities pulsing forward; farm districts thinning out, cities growing denser; fewer shopkeepers able to buy where they would, more compelled to take what a monopoly gave them, and at a monopoly's price; fewer craftsmen, more factory operatives; fewer workers known by name to their employers, more carried on big factory payrolls as numbers identified by brass checks.

In this gradual consolidation of industry into larger units, in the doom of the small local manufacturer and the older order of industry of which he was the unit, the most potent cause was the railroad, and the use made of the railroads by those who controlled them. If the effect of the railroads on industry had been restricted to the necessary consequence of lower cost of railroad transportation compared to older forms, many a small local manufacturer would have been doomed anyhow; but he would have submitted to his extinction as an economic inevitability, as something not to be averted, like the visitation of a storm or some other influence of nature. Without

This photograph of Henry Ford's first factory is typical of old-time industry.

rancor, he might have decided
to go himself to the city, or to
unite with another manufacturer, or otherwise to adjust
himself as dictated by his years,
his temperament, and the other
circumstances. Neither he, nor
his neighbors, nor the public
generally would have seen the
process as justification for a
sense of outrage and occasion
for political protest.

But we cannot think of the
railroads as if they came by nature, like the phenomena of
weather. The railroads were
made by men—were conceived
and built for gain, and managed
for gain. The planning for gain
took in every possibility that
self-interest could envisage.
Had the effort for gain been restricted to the normal profit on
carrying goods and passengers,
those who were affected would
have had no justification for re-

*Reece's Mills in Ohio, built in the early years of
the nineteenth century. A good type of the old-
time "off-the-railroad" industry.*

sentment. But in the use made of the railroads by their owners and managers, the legitimate profit on transportation was often a relatively
unimportant motive. The power to fix freight rates carried opportunities
compared to which reasonable return for services rendered was inconse-
quential. It opened the door to schemes and conspiracies. Frequently, there
was common ownership of the railroads and of some industries, or community of interest between them. In such cases railroad rates were fixed to
give advantage to the favored industry and to handicap its rivals. Often, low
rates were given to the favored industry and high rates imposed on its competitor, with the deliberate, specific purpose of driving the victim out of
business or compelling him to sell out to the favored rival. Sometimes the
motive of the railroad managers for making low rates was competition of
railroad against railroad. In such cases, all the manufacturers had the role
of pawns, sometimes elevated to temporary advantage, sometimes destroyed. Occasionally there was competition of community against community, with the railroad manager giving the advantage of low freight rates
to the community with which his personal interest was identified, and fatally high ones to the rival.

The power to fix freight rates was the power of life and death over industries, and often over whole communities. The individuals possessing
that power were unrestrained (there was no Interstate Commerce Com-

mission or other regulation until 1887, and no effective regulation until 1906), and they used it ruthlessly.

It was not merely that they destroyed individual businesses and bankrupted individual businessmen; by their arbitrary exercise of uncurbed power, bodies of workmen were forced out of employment, families dislocated, whole communities laid prostrate and disrupted. The average man came to think of the power of the railroads as a malevolent influence manipulated secretly by persons distant and mysterious. He came to think of the railroad as having a more essential power over his happiness than the government, and to feel that the equality guaranteed to him by the Constitution was a small thing, if he had not equality before the railroads.

Akron, Ohio, a city whose phenomenal growth was made possible by the revolution in industry and transportation brought by the railroad. The upper photograph shows the city as it was in 1865, when much of its commerce was carried in canal boats. The lower view is of a busy Akron street in 1925.

CHAPTER 5
Oil

Nearly all the varieties of attempts to achieve monopoly in the modern sense are illustrated, many in the extreme degree, in the career of one American industry, oil. Men still living in 1927 had witnessed the whole history of that industry, from its birth just before the Civil War to its position in 1927. As this is written there still lived the man who, watching the industry's spectacular beginning, had dreamed its useful developments and participated in them; had devised or shared in some of its practices that the courts called iniquitous; had come to dominate it and to be known throughout the world as the symbol of it; had become, through it, the richest individual of all time—John D. Rockefeller.

As late as the 1840s, little was known about the substance which by 1925 was to enable humans to move about on the surface of the earth at more than 50 miles an hour; to go above the clouds and beneath the waters and direct their movements there at will; to cross the Atlantic Ocean either through the air above, or in a submarine; which was to drive 20 million automobiles, thousands of railroad engines, and hundreds of ships. By 1925, the raw material of the leering little patent-medicine business of 1840 was to be the sixth of the country's industries and indispensable to the first, the automobile business; was to be the basis of an industry which, in the aggregate, expressed as the total value of oil and its products in 1925, was more than $2 billion. Who can overstate the romance of its beginnings, a gift of nature urging itself upon the world, pressing out of cracks in rocks, clamoring for the attention of man—who responded by cursing it as a nuisance! Who can exaggerate the drama of its growth, which is the story of what man did about a great new natural resource, of how he refined it, adapted it, and how he arranged the division of it among those who could use it or had need of it!

Individuals here and there, men of exceptional initiative, used rock oil to soften leather or quiet the squeak of wooden axles. A few others made torches of it. In 1854, a graduate of Dartmouth College, George H. Bissell, leased some land from which rock oil was seeping, sent a specimen to Professor Silliman of Yale for analysis, and was informed: "You have a raw material from which by simple and not expensive process [you] may manufacture very valuable products."

The following year, 1855, a young farmer boy whose family had shortly before moved from New York State began work as a bookkeeper in Cleve-

Crude tank cars of 1863. (From The History of the Standard Oil Company, *by Ida M. Tarbell. Courtesy of the author)*

land. Out of his $25 a month he saved enough to become partner in a produce commission firm; out of that he saved enough to be able, in 1862, when he was twenty-three years old, to invest, with his partner and a daring young mechanical engineer, $4,000 in a business that people were beginning to speak of as "oil-refining." There, with his bookkeeper training, with his instinct for system that made him probably the first man in America deserving to be called an expert accountant, with his repugnance to gambling and his habit of orderly ways that expressed itself in regularly conducting a Sunday school class, with his prudent, frugal temperament—he now found himself engaged in the least organized and most chaotic industry in the world, for which the only precedent—and that an inadequate one—was the California gold rush of thirteen years before; an industry characterized by a lack of orderliness which to Rockefeller's mind was akin to lack of Godliness; a prince-today-and-pauper-tomorrow industry, for which the popular personification was a character known as "Coal-Oil Johnny," familiar for a generation as the symbol of splurging wealth alternating with utter poverty; an industry in which chance was the largest element, in which calamity was forever just around the corner and did not always keep itself there; an industry whose susceptibility to fire seemed symbolic of its fundamental characteristics—"When the fire-bell rang,"

Roby Frank, cabinet maker, bds 17 Johnson
ROBY E. W. & CO. (Edward W. Roby and William H. Keith), wood and coal, C. & P. R. R. Coal Pier, and Merwin n Columbus St. Bridge
Rochert Conrad, h 175 St Clair.
Rock John, bar keeper. bds 11 Public Square
ROCKAFELLOW JOHN J., coal, C. & P. R. R. Coal Pier, h 183 Prospect
Rockefeller John D., book-keeper, h 35 Cedar
Rockefeller William, physician, h 35 Cedar av
Rockett Morris, rectifier, h 182 St Clair
Rockwell Edward, Sec. C. & P. R. R., bds Weddell House

John D. Rockefeller in the role in which he appeared in the Cleveland city directory in the 1850s. (From The History of the Standard Oil Company, *by Ida M. Tarbell. Courtesy of the author)*

said Rockefeller, "we would all rush to the refinery and help put it out, and while the blaze was still burning, I would have my pencil out, making plans for rebuilding"; an industry half at the economic mercy of wells that ran dry with a suddenness whimsical and disastrous, and half at the mercy of new wells and new fields; an industry in which, in 1859, the raw material, crude oil, sold at $20 a barrel, and in 1861 at fifty-two cents. To every fundamental trait in Rockefeller's character, the instability was abhorrent.

But while he had a strong distaste for mere chance such as the gambling nature of many of the other oil men loved for its own sake, while he had extreme aversion to being at the mercy of circumstances, at the same time his nature rose and expanded to the prospect of adventure of a different kind, had marked boldness for enterprise when it was predicated on careful thinking by himself and plans thoroughly prepared. With his intellectual sure-footedness he had studied the industry carefully, had not entered it until he had acquired confidence that in time it

WM. ROCKEFELLER & CO.—The co-partnership heretofore existing between Wm Rockefeller, John D Rockefeller and Samuel Andrews, under the firm name of Wm Rockefeller & Co., is this day dissolved by mutual consent, having sold our entire interest in the Refining business to Messrs Rockefeller, Andrews & Flagler. Cleveland, February 28, 1867.

THE UNDERSIGNED DO HEREBY certify that they have formed a special partnership under the act of the General Assembly of the State of Ohio, entitled "an act to authorize and regulate limited partnerships," passed January 24th, 1846; that said partnership is to be conducted, and its business done under the name of Rockefeller, Andrews & Flagler; that Stephen V. Harkness, of East Cleveland, in the County of Cuyahoga, and State of Ohio, is the special partner, and has contributed seventy thousand ($70,000) dollars in money as capital to the stock of said partnership, and that John D. Rockefeller, Henry M Flagler and Samuel Andrews, of Cleveland, in the County of Cuyahoga and State of Ohio, and Wm. Rockefeller, of the city, county and State of New York, are the general partners; that the business to be transacted is the manufacture of and dealing in crude Petroleum and its products; That the principal place of Business of said firm is to be at the said city of Cleveland and that said partnership is to commence on the twenty-eighth day of February, 1867, and terminate on the first day of March, 1872.
　　JOHN D. ROCKEFELLER, [L S]
　　WILLIAM ROCKEFELLER, [L S]
　　SAMUeL ANDREWS, [L S]
　　HeNRY M. FLAGLER, [L S]
　　STEPHEN V. HARKNESS. [L S]
　　　CLEVELAND, February 28, 1867.
　State of Ohio, } ss
Oounty of Cuyahoga. }
　Before me George Hester, a Justice of the Peace, appeared John D. Rockefeller, William Rockefeller, Samuel Andrews, Henry M. Flagler, and Stephen V. Harkness, who acknowledged the signing and sealing the foregoing instrument to be their own free act and deed.
　In witness I have hereunto subscribed my name this 28th day of February. A D 1867.
　　　　GEORGE HESTER,
　　　　Justice of the Peace.
feb 0 408

Partnership notices about Rockefeller's first firm, published in Cleveland newspapers in 1867.

would be worldwide, would be carried on on a big scale, would ultimately be like steel or copper. Once in it, he brought to his own unit (Rockefeller, Andrews, and Clark) his qualities of careful planning, system, order; his instinct for economies; and also a high degree of intent devotion. The day he married, he celebrated in his refinery, with a dinner for the twenty-six employees, after which, on departing, he called the foreman aside and directed him: "Keep them all at work. Keep them all busy. But don't ask anybody to do anything for nothing."

By January 1870, Rockefeller was the leading figure in the Cleveland oil trade, doing, with his partners, about a fifth of all the business. In that month, he and his brother William, with some associates, organized the Standard Oil Company, consisting of two refineries at Cleveland and a selling agency at New York. The capital was $1 million, divided into 10,000 shares at $100 each.

The offices of Rockefeller & Andrews in Cleveland, in 1865. (From The History of the Standard Oil Company, *by Ida M. Tarbell. Courtesy of the author)*

Rockefeller had done well in his own unit of the oil industry, but deplored the state of the industry as a whole, its ups and downs, its waste, the recurrent periods of opulence and distress, the overproduction alternating with underproduction, the violent fluctuations in price. Much of this Rockefeller attributed to the competition the oil men practiced against each other, the throat-cutting competition of virile, rather reckless men struggling for advantage in a new and not yet organized industry.

Rockefeller abhorred competition, not only abhorred it in the industry in which he was engaged, but abhorred it as a principle of business. In a private conversation during his later years, he once spoke of the old-time competition as entailing "idiotic, senseless destruction," and explained:

> Competition had existed for generations. In all lines of industry, history had repeated itself over and over, in cycles every ten or twelve years. Excessive production, followed by loss with failure and bankruptcy to the weaker concerns. The strong ones, the survivors, finding themselves in control of the trade, remembering the losses they had suffered, took advantage of the opportunity to recoup themselves by charging higher prices, and also picked up the wrecks along the shore, buying out the ruined competitors. For a while, business was good and profitable. Presently, outsiders, seeing the prosperity, set up new competition, and once more the experience was repeated, with consequent loss and bankruptcy.

The competition thus described by Rockefeller, from his point of view, was the universal order in industry. No one conceived any other. Economists regarded it as the underlying principle of trade; business men accepted it as that. When Rockefeller proposed an alternative system to a Cleveland businessman, the latter said, in conservative puzzlement: "It looks all right on paper, but it's too 'scope-y.'" Rockefeller called his plan "co-operation and conservation"; a variation of it practiced later in Germany was called the "cartel" system; by 1927, it came to be advocated by many American business leaders as "stabilization." At all times, opponents of the idea and believers in competition called it monopoly, or the equivalent of monopoly.

Rockefeller's wish was to bring all the units of the industry into a group under one leadership, to eliminate less economical plants, to use combined strength for bringing about improvements and economies, to curtail pro-

William Smith, who drilled the first oil well for Colonel Drake, in 1850. (From The History of the Standard Oil Company, *by Ida M. Tarbell. Courtesy of the author)*

duction and hold oil off the market when there was oversupply, and to stabilize prices. His frank and sincere purpose was, in short, to end competition, to end the free working of the law of supply and demand, and to substitute for it an artificial control. His ideal took forms of varying rigidity from time to time, and the methods he practiced in pursuit of it led to a resistance and outcry which, during more than fifty years, consumed more of the time of legislatures and courts, and more of the space of newspapers, than any other controversy in American business.

Rockefeller, throughout his long life, at times when he was the most criticized man in the world, and his company the most subpoenaed, never thought of himself as having done wrong to any man; always thought of his critics among the general public as excusable because they were uninformed or misinformed; and of his enemies in the oil business as inspired by envy. Much of the criticism, he said, "came from those who having been offered their choice to take cash or stock in our company for their business, had not faith enough to take stock. They took the cash; when the stock became many times increased in value, they blamed us for their own bad choice. They had no spirit for the adventure."

This man, the subject of discussion and speculation to an extent hardly equaled in his generation, can be understood by interpreting him in the spirit of the strain of New England religion he had through his mother. His mind was impregnated with the old doctrine of "election." To his competitors he gave the opportunity to be saved—they could elect to take stock in the Standard Oil Company. If they failed to elect that salvation, they were responsible for their own fate, and Rockefeller looked upon them as Jonathan Edwards would have looked upon a man who declined to accept spiritual salvation, with regretful disapproval, tempered with tolerant pity.

Risks in the oil business when John D. Rockefeller entered it—a tank of stored oil on fire.

Once, in his old age, he was asked, "What did you do with those who refused to come in with you?" and replied: "We left them to the mercy of time; they could not hope to compete with us."

Rockefeller's own conviction that he was always fair and even generous with his competitors and that the methods he used to gain a monopoly in oil were ethical, is beyond dispute. The shrewd "Mr. Dooley"—the popular newspaper character created by Finley Peter Dunne—once said of him: "There's wan thing sure fr'm what I can see, an' that is that Jawn D. hasn't an idea that he iver did wrong to annywan."

By the eighties, it had become common knowledge that the Standard Oil Company controlled more than 90 percent of the country's refining business. How this control had been secured, how it was exercised, and whether the mechanism of control was within the law were mysteries. Long since, government had created checks on firms, partnerships, corporations, and other business organizations; it was evident the Standard Oil Company had found something entirely new, some novel form of compact, some mechanism for monopoly too elusive for the laws as they then existed to catch. What it was, where it was kept, by what authority it lived, nobody knew.

A committee of investigation from the New York State Senate sought in 1888 to find out. It put Rockefeller on the stand. From testimony sometimes plausible, sometimes apparently willing, sometimes evasive, at all times subtle, the committee learned that

> thirty-nine corporations had turned over their affairs to an organization having no legal existence, independent of all authority, able to do anything it wanted anywhere; and to this point working in absolute darkness. Under their agreement, which was unrecognized by the State, a few men had united to do things which no incorporated company could do. It was a situation as puzzling as it was new.

"This," wrote the committee, "is the original *trust*."

That word, as the name for combination aiming at monopoly, first came into the language about 1882, three years after the device had been adopted by the Standard Oil Company. Thereafter, both the word and the thing it stood for spread through the country.

CHAPTER 6
Titans at War

As Rockefeller became preeminent in oil, Andrew Carnegie became preeminent in steel. Rockefeller was the outstanding exponent of combination, Carnegie of ruthless competition. Rockefeller, thinking in terms similar to European "cartels," would go to other men in the oil business, would talk to them about the desirability of combination and stabilization; would argue against the wastes of competition, would ask his competitor to unite with him, would offer to give either cash or stock in the Standard Oil Company for his competitor's plant. If the competitor declined, he would be subject to the Standard's competition, and likely to find himself sooner or later a casualty.

Carnegie did nothing like that. He scorned cooperation with his competitors. Although he occasionally participated in pools, he disdained them. Of price-fixing agreements between competitors, he said: "artificial arrangements, strengthening the other fellow as much as they strengthen you . . . bad business." That is the key to Carnegie's point of view, an outstanding individualist in his era. To his board of managers of the Carnegie Steel Company, he wrote: "We should look with favor upon every combination of every kind upon the part of our competitors; the bigger they grow, the more vulnerable they become." Though he acquired two plants, Homestead and Duquesne, by purchase, Carnegie as a rule rarely tried to persuade or force a competitor to sell out to him, rarely entertained any notion of buying him out. Carnegie generally paid no attention to rivals except to gloat when his methods made them squirm, or succumb. Carnegie managed his business as an utterly ruthless individualist, and as the ablest manufacturer in his field. He made good steel, at a lower cost than anybody else, and sold it at such prices as, under the conditions, would give him the best advantages. When conditions called for the cutting of prices, Carnegie cut, murderously.

By these methods Carnegie had become,

Andrew Carnegie.

by 1900, the greatest steelmaker in America. The entire steel and iron business of America in that year was composed of the Carnegie Company—and the others. "The others" consisted chiefly of seven fairly large companies, each less efficient than the Carnegie Company, all harried by Carnegie's hard-driving competition.

II

Carnegie, by 1900, had had his fill of business. For fifty years, from the age of thirteen, he had lived a life of ever-increasing pressure and strain. His dominance in steel had been achieved by unceasing battle, against his competitors, against his workmen, against all who got in his way. The pace he had maintained was a killing one, and he was tired. He wanted time to live up to the doctrine he had formulated: "The man who dies rich dies disgraced." He had interested himself in a large variety of avocations, including many philanthropies and some harmless, even laudable, social and literary vanities; and wished to devote himself to them exclusively.

But he feared merely to retire, leaving his capital in the business, and permitting it to be managed by others. No one of his partners was his equal in ruthlessness or resourcefulness, the two qualities which, as the steel business was at that time, were alone capable of keeping the Carnegie interests at the top. Steel then, as it had been from the discovery of the Bessemer process, knew no such thing as stable prosperity. Carnegie feared that unless he himself were at the helm during the famine years, his companies would suffer. He was troubled, anxious, tired. His mind went back in his sixties to the memorandum for personal guidance he had jotted down one Christmastime during his thirties, the longing to cast aside business, to become a figure in the world of education, literature, and public affairs. In spite of his pride in the company that bore his name, he was willing to sell out—"willing," indeed, is too weak word.

To dispose of so huge a property as the Carnegie Steel Company and its allied interests, could not be a mere matter of offering it for sale. Probably—one need hardly say "probably"—there was only one possible purchaser, only one man in all America who combined the necessary requirements. To buy the Carnegie company meant, under the conditions of the time, to form a steel trust. There was only one man of such potent influence and ample financial backing as to command the confidence of investors in the plants to be combined and of the public generally; only one man who could "put over" the trust in the sense of buying the competing plants from their owners and also in the sense of getting the public to buy shares in the trust.

III

The man thus fixed by conditions as the objective, the "prospect," of Carnegie's salesmanship was J. Pierpont Morgan. When Carnegie put out the tentacles of his business art to draw Morgan into a "dicker," he brought into temporary juxtaposition, though decidedly not into union in any sense, two of the greatest industrial Joves since Vulcan and Midas. By every aspect of their respective settings, they were fitted to have no relation to each other except that of rivalry. One difference between them was sufficiently suggested by the fact that when occasion brought them together, observers noticed Carnegie address Morgan as "Pierpont," and saw Morgan wince—there is no record that any one ever heard Morgan call Carnegie "Andy."

Carnegie did not wield absolute power over Morgan, but he did make him do what he wanted. Morgan's qualifications for the role to which Carnegie now proposed to assign him were not confined merely to his greater command of money than any other man or firm in America. As Carnegie was the leading exponent of competition, so was Morgan a leading exponent of combination—he had just concluded a decade devoted to the reorganization of the country's railroads into a group of systems, rescuing them from the rapidly recurrent bankruptcies that had accompanied their earlier phase. He had just combined a number of small steel companies, rescuing them from distress into which they had been driven chiefly by the ruthless competition of the Carnegie Company. In the Wall Street jargon of the day, to "reorganize" was to "re-Morganize."

Fear of Carnegie provided Morgan with one motive for forming a steel trust which should at once take the Carnegie Company in and by the same act get Carnegie personally into private life. Another motive, the desirability, on the broadest grounds, of stabilizing the steel business, the general benefits which consolidation would bring to the steel industry and to the country's whole industrial structure, had already been urged upon Morgan by Carnegie's friend and associate Elbert H. Gary. Steel had been, as Carnegie once expressed it, "always either prince or pauper"; violent expansion and high prices alternated with deep depressions and prices so low that only the unit most advantageously situated could survive; alternations of feast and famine distressed not only the owners but the workmen, whose customary characterization of dull times in the steel trade was "soup-house days"; values were periodically upset and investors made timid; consumers of steel could not count confidently on future prices. All this was recited to Morgan by Gary, but in vain, until Carnegie brought his kind of pressure.

Carnegie's salesmanship was a double art in which threat was balanced with allurement. The whole of it was described in a picture taken from the field of religion: "In the conversion of the heathen, missionaries have found it useful to describe the condition of the damned before presenting a picture of the joys of the blessed. It was on some such principle that the threat of industrial war was thus made by Carnegie, before the blessings of the co-operation and consolidation were set out before the alarmed financier."*

IV

The plan for organizing the United States Steel Corporation was made public March 3, 1901, through an advertisement signed by J. P. Morgan and Company. The reaction was instantaneous. Some of it was pride, a superficial national egotism inspired by the grandiosity of the biggest trust in the world. But much more of the spontaneous response was alarm, alarm of several different kinds, caused by contemplating different aspects of the trust. Much took the form of apprehension of socialism. Should the movement toward combination continue, the *Boston Herald* thought that "if a limited financial group shall come to represent the capitalistic end of industry, the perils of socialism, even if brought about by a somewhat rude, because forcible, taking of the instruments of industry, may be looked upon by even intelligent people as possibly the lesser of two evils."

Similarly, the *Philadelphia Evening Telegraph* considered that "If a grasping and unrelenting monopoly is the outcome, there will be given an enormous impulse to the growing antagonism to the concentration of capital, which may lead to one of the greatest social and political upheavals that has been witnessed in modern history."

Once Morgan determined to form the merger, it was characteristic of his whole career that he entered into no argument about price with the owners of the merged companies, but paid the first figures asked. He capitalized the new company at

Bonds	$303,450,000
Preferred stock	550,000,000
Common stock	550,000,000

In paying off the constituent companies, Morgan showed clearly his chief motive for organizing the combination. To all the smaller companies he gave stock, which would permit them to have a proportionate voice in management. But to the Carnegie Company he gave chiefly bonds, the total bond issue of the new corporation, $303,450,000, plus 98,277,120 in preferred stock, plus $90,279,040 in common stock. Carnegie's version of this was that he insisted on having bonds because he regarded the stock as not merely water but air. Morgan's version was that he wanted to get Carnegie out of the management and out of the steel business, completely out, with no leverage through which he could have a hand in the management of the United States Steel Corporation, and no motive or excuse to destabilize Morgan's stabilization.

*From *History of the Carnegie Steel Company*, by James Howard Bridge.

Of the securities that went to the Carnegie Company, the lion's share went to Carnegie personally. It was commonly reckoned, and probably true, that Carnegie, as he retired, was worth $250 million, measured in cash. Carnegie went to Europe for a rest and shortly afterward began a career of giving, the magnificence of which was an ironic comment on those who thought one result of "big business" in America would be the setting up of a caste of hereditary plutocrats. (Carnegie retained so little of his fortune for his heirs that after he died in August 1919, his widow found herself inconvenienced when the postwar period of high taxes continued.)

J. Pierpont Morgan.

Morgan, for himself and his associates in the underwriting syndicate, took 648,988 shares of the preferred stock and 648,987 of the common, valued, at the lowest price at which the shares were sold in the ensuing stock market campaign, at $77,987,640. This profit, however, was mere "paper," mere stock certificates, until the shares could be sold to the public.

To "make a market," Morgan employed a celebrated market manipulator of the day, James R. Keene. The time was propitious. Fundamental conditions were right, and the necessary superficial conditions, the atmosphere, could be made to order. The country had just finished a victorious war and acquired great overseas possessions. "Empire" was in the air, and the psychology that went with it. Industrial enterprise, held back by the prolonged depression of the early nineties, had begun to pulse forward. Investors, who had been made timid by the threat of free silver, were reassured by the second defeat of Bryan in 1900 and the formal adoption of the gold standard by Congress that same year. The discovery of a new gold supply, the Yukon, had at once stimulated the spirit of adventure and added more gold to the base of currency, causing wages to rise, as well as the prices of commodities. The creation of the trusts, the vogue of the promoters, their Monte Carlo prodigality and picturesqueness, the bigness of the extraordinary sums of money constantly mentioned in newspaper headlines and the rapidity with which such profits were made, dazzled men's minds, so that they became drunk with the passion of money-getting, and blind to all other standards and ideals. Everybody thought and spoke in millions, and the Napoleons of finance became, in a sense, heroes and demigods. Men and women and even children all over the country drank in thirstily every scrap of news that was printed in the press about these so-called captains of industry, their successful "deals," the offhand way in which they converted slips of worthless paper into guarantees of more than princely wealth, and all the details concerning their daily lives, their personal peculiarities, their virtues, and their vices. To the imagination of millions of Americans, the financial centers of the country seemed to be spouting streams of gold into which any one might dip at will. All the conditions combined to compose an ideal time in which to "make a market" and unload stock on the public. Daily transactions on the New York Stock Exchange, many of them "wash" sales manipulated for psychological effect, reached totals never before approached—on one day over 3 million shares changed hands, and in one week over 10 million. The public was kept advised, alluringly, of the winnings made in stocks by some of the spectacular figures of the new era. As a result, thousands of the public became ephemeral customers of the brokerage house. A stenographer, coming late in the morning, explained she had been to her broker to buy "a hundred Steel common." Barbers told customers of tips they had had from promoters they shaved, on which they had made thousands. A slogan ran through New York, not only downtown but in shops, on streetcars, on commuter trains: "Buy A. O. T.—Any Old Thing." Everything was going up. No tip could fail.

The Steel Corporation's shares were put out as carrying dividends of 4 percent on the common and 7 percent on the preferred. Sales were started on the exchange at 38 for the common and 82¾ for the preferred; and were advanced to 55 and 101⅞, respectively.

Morgan, seeing this advance satisfactorily under way, in April 1901, a little over a month after he had organized the Steel Corporation, took a trip to Europe for what the newspapers commonly designated as "a well-earned rest." On his return, Morgan, with Edward H. Harriman, organized a new and gigantic holding company with a capital of $400 million, the Northern Securities Company, taking in the three great railroad systems of the Northwest: the Great Northern, the Northern Pacific, and the Burlington.

To the sensational outcry that had attended Morgan's organization of the greatest industrial holding company, the United States Steel Corporation, six months before was now added a new explosion of clamor over his creation of the greatest railroad holding company.

Toward the end of this period, in September 1901, an event occurred that was as remote from the calculations of steel and railroad giants as imagination can conceive. A crazy Pole named Czolgosz went into the tailor shop of a Chicago friend and said that after weighty reflection about the state of the world he had decided to kill a priest. "Why kill a priest?" asked the tailor. "There are so many priests; they are like flies—a hundred will come to his funeral." On considering this argument, Czolgosz decided it was better to kill a president. He went to Buffalo, New York, and on September 6, shot and fatally wounded President McKinley.

This utterly irrelevant, mad act brought to an end the presidency of the man of whom the journalist Herbert Croly said: "When Mr. McKinley was re-elected, big business undoubtedly considered that it had received a license to do very much as it pleased."

McKinley's successor, however, would surprise big business—and nearly everyone else.

CHAPTER 7
Waiting

Roosevelt's first three months in the presidency were interesting, even spectacular; the infectiousness of his exuberant vitality made the country realize there was a new man in the White House; indeed, a new kind of man. His high spirits, his enormous capacity for work, his tirelessness, his forthrightness, his many striking qualities, gave a lift of the spirits to millions of average men, stimulated them to higher use of their own powers, gave them a new zest for life.

But there was no light on what the new president would do about McKinley's essential policy, benevolence toward big business. Roosevelt's early assurance that he would "continue McKinley's policy," was believed to be meant not as a pledge but rather as a gesture of calm appropriate to the circumstances, the natural impulse and act of any vice-president on succeeding to power as an incident of national tragedy, designed to bring confidence to a country made nervous by an act of violence. The assassination of McKinley had caused, among other expressions of apprehension, a sharp drop in the stock market, followed by a stalemate, during which business watched for fulfillment—or disappointment—in its hope that Roosevelt would be a "pale copy of McKinley" (Roosevelt's own phrase for the role many urged on him). The more important leaders of business, long dependent on McKinley's mentor and adviser Mark Hanna as their friend in the high places of politics, besought him for light, but Hanna had no light. Roosevelt treated Hanna, whom he really liked, not only with sincere cordiality but with the affectionate deference due an older man who for five years had been the most powerful political figure in the country, and had just been bereaved, at one blow, of his most intimate friend and of the leverage that had made his power secure. Roosevelt knew what Hanna's attitude toward him had been, but

"To Mark Hanna, with McKinley in the Presidency, God was in His Heaven and the world was good." Hanna was shorn of his power when McKinley died and Roosevelt succeeded to the presidency.

could afford to be generous. His was the rising star; Hanna's the falling. He went out of his way to be cordial to the heartbroken power broker, writing him a kindly letter asking for an early conference.

Hanna was touched. But it was characteristic of his impulsive optimism, which always expected the best, to take rather too much for granted. He replied: "There are many important matters to be considered from a political standpoint and I am sure we will agree upon a proper course to pursue. Meantime 'go slow.' You will be besieged from all sides and I fear in some cases will get the wrong impression. Hear them all patiently but RESERVE YOUR DECISION."

Hanna acted as if he thought Roosevelt's request for friendship and counsel called for a public gesture of appreciation; but with characteristic simplicity he did it a little too bluntly, and in a way not best adapted to promote his purpose. To a correspondent of the *New York World* Hanna gave an interview, meant to be eulogistic of Roosevelt to the last degree, intended to express what Hanna thought was the finest thing he could possibly say. Roosevelt must have grinned when he read: "Mr. Roosevelt is an entirely different man to-day from what he was a few weeks since. He has now acquired all that is needed to round out his character—equipoise and conservatism. The new and great responsibilities so suddenly thrust upon him have brought about this change."

II

The tone of Hanna's interview was duplicated by the conservative press, as if moved by a strategy which says the way to make a child be what you want him to be is to act as if he already is so and praise him. The *Washington Star* spoke of the new president as "a man of unquestioned courage and of widespread popularity," and in the same breath reminded him that he was "thoroughly and conscientiously committed to the policies of the party in power as represented by Mr. McKinley." The *New York Tribune* felt no doubt that "President Roosevelt must be well aware that his temperament has been regarded as less cautious and conservative than that of his predecessor," but, fearful lest the reader should get a disquieting impression, added: "Mr. Roosevelt has been in perfect sympathy with the triumphant policies of Mr. McKinley . . . whose beneficent administration he will assiduously endeavor to continue and perpetuate."

The *New York Sun*, outstanding exponent of the conservative interests, and intimately close to J. P. Morgan, threw overboard every lifesaver of caution that it might need later on and went out on the extreme end of the fragile limb of confident prophecy. On September 15, 1901, the *Sun* ended a column of almost fulsome tribute to the new chief executive with the words: "He is the most striking embodiment of contemporary Americanism; is of spotless honor and unconquerable fidelity to the loftiest and sternest ideals of public duty. . . . Theodore Roosevelt is a man on whom the American people can rely as a prudent and a safe and sagacious successor to William McKinley."

III

The earliest sign, the first occasion on which Roosevelt must make official utterance of policies, would be his message on the assembling of Congress, December 5, 1901. The message was awaited with curiosity and, when published, was greeted with almost universal newspaper comment which said that apparently Roosevelt was not going to break any big-business china. Some newspapers, having hoped that Roosevelt would hit out in his characteristically vigorous fashion, were even a little disappointed: "There are no fireworks in it"; "Anything but a sensational document"; and "Not exactly the kind of message it was natural to expect from a man of Mr. Roosevelt's temperament." From the conservative press generally came the relief which attends the ending of apprehension: "'The Rough Rider' and the 'Jingo,' the impetuous youth of a year ago, has disappeared, and instead we have in the White House a President who, to judge from his first communication to Congress, might be a man of sixty, trained in conservative habits." And: "The country will draw a deep sigh of satisfaction."

Such passages as Roosevelt's message had about the trusts were embedded in a mass of more than 10,000 words, dealing with more than twenty topics, including international peace, the Monroe Doctrine, civil service, conservation, game protection, and immigration. Such surroundings would have deadened almost any utterance about the trusts, even had it been decisive. But Roosevelt's allusions to the trusts were not decisive. His mind was not decisive about them. He was still under the spell of the influences that for nearly twenty years had kept him away from this question; his mind was still under a momentum it had acquired in the campaigns of 1896 and 1900. In the first of these the issue had been currency; in the second, territorial expansion. As to both, Roosevelt had felt strongly that the Republicans were right and that Bryan and the Democrats were "utterly and hopelessly wrong." He had thrown himself so completely into those fights that when he became president he had not yet returned to equilibrium.

Moreover, Bryan and the Democrats were now making the trust question their chief issue; Roosevelt unconsciously tended to associate them with error on that question as he had on the previous ones; and tended also to be hesitant about taking up any position upon which Bryan and the Democrats had fixed their brand. Just the year before, in the campaign of 1900, he had jeered at the Democrats: "They have raved against trusts, they have foamed at the mouth, prating of impossible remedies they would like to adopt." Moreover, Roosevelt was a Republican, the Republicans were the businessmen's party, and reactionary business controlled it. Roosevelt, so long as he had been a subordinate, could conform or get out. Now he was chief and had to consider his responsibility.

As a result of all these influences, Roosevelt had never focused his mind

Roosevelt's cabinet. From left to right are Taft, Wilson, Straus, Root, Hitchcock, Cortelyou,
Bonaparte, Metcalf, Roosevelt, Shaw. (From a photograph by Brown Bros.)

on the trust issue, had never been intellectually convinced or emotionally moved about it. Consequently, his treatment of the question in his first message to Congress was the sort that expresses itself inconclusively, tepidly, and in balanced sentences: "There have been abuses connected with the accumulation of great fortunes, *yet* it remains true that [such accumulations] confer . . . immense incidental benefits upon others." "It is not true that as the rich have grown richer, the poor have grown poorer; *on the contrary* . . ." Our "serious social problems" associated with great corporate fortunes are not due "to the tariff nor to any other governmental action, *but* to natural causes in the business world. . . . Much of the antagonism to these fortunes is wholly without warrant." "The mechanism of modern business is so delicate that extreme care must be taken not to interfere with it in a spirit of rashness or ignorance."

In introducing such suggestions for remedy as he had to offer, he preserved the balanced form: "All this is true; and *yet* it is also true that there are real and grave evils." By a device that was frequent with him, he weighted one end of a sentence with reproof for business, the other with reproof for labor: "It should be as much the aim of those who seek for social betterment to rid the business world of crimes of cunning as to rid the entire body politic of crimes of violence." His specific recommendation said that "publicity is the only sure remedy which we can now invoke."

Balanced and cushioned though this was, it contained substantially the whole of Roosevelt's philosophy about big organizations of business. To the end, even when his name was a worldwide symbol for belligerent attack

Roosevelt's occasional coupling of labor unions with the trusts, in his castigations, inspired this cartoon by Maybelle in the Brooklyn Eagle.

against corporate power, he always maintained a distinction between the evil men who managed some trusts, and the good men who managed others. He never shared, indeed, he deliberately and conspicuously avoided, both the Bryan practice of denouncing all big business and the Wilson principle of insistence upon competition. Roosevelt would allow units of business to grow as large as economic conditions might permit, but would subject them to continuous supervision by the government. This last, that the government should have the right to regulate, and especially that the government should be recognized as above all business and above all businessmen, big or little—that was the heart of Roosevelt's doctrine, the point on which he fought his great controversies.

That Roosevelt's first message to Congress put its discussion of the trusts in the form of balanced sentences was part of his conscious art of politics. The balanced sentence, used by a public man who never conspicuously uses anything else, may reflect a cautious "trimmer," or a man habitually verbose, or one temporarily tired. But Roosevelt essentially was the most forthright public character of his time—a man who could hurl, when the occasion demanded, such epithets as "malefactor of great wealth" and "out-patient of bedlam" was in no danger of being called timid. With Roosevelt, use of the balanced sentence was usually a precaution against misunderstanding; an insistence upon clearness; the reflection of a love of fair-dealing that will not leave a proposition half-stated; unwillingness to let one kind of evil escape censure while the public is stirred by another. His approval of the right of labor to organize for its own protection was always coupled with a reminder that this right does not justify the commission of violence. When his trust policy exposed him to attack as an enemy of capital, his answer was: "We shall find it necessary to shackle cunning as in the past we have shackled force."

The country, especially the newspapers and critics, not yet familiar with the precise place the balanced sentence had in Roosevelt's use of language, interpreted his allusions to the trusts in his first message to Congress as one of the class of his performances which *Blackwood's Magazine* characterized: "With splendid ingenuity he proved how [to] take both sides in any dispute at one and the same time; . . . [to] fight with the same hand for rich and poor." Or, as "Mr. Dooley" put it:

> "Th' trusts," says he [Roosevelt], "are heejous monsthers built up be th' inlightened intherprise iv th' men that have done so much to advance progress in our beloved counthry," he says. "On wan hand I wud stamp thim undher fut; on th' other hand not so fast. What I want more thin th' bustin' iv th' thrusts is to see me fellow counthrymen happy an' continted. I wudden't have thim hate th' thrusts. Th' haggard face, th' droopin' eye, th' pallid complexion that marks th' inimy iv thrusts is not to me taste. Lave us be merry about it an' jovial an' affectionate. Lave us laugh an' sing th' octopus out iv existence."

That view of Roosevelt's first message to Congress was shared by those who were disappointed with it and by those whom it relieved from anxiety. Wall Street slept well.

CHAPTER 8
Roosevelt Goes into Action

Less than three months later, on the evening of February 18, 1902, J. P. Morgan, entertaining business associates at dinner at his home on Madison Avenue, in New York, was summoned to the telephone by a friend in a newspaper office, who told him the press dispatches had just

A famous cartoon, "The Soap-and-Water Cure," signalizing the beginning of Roosevelt's enforcement of the Sherman Anti-Trust Act.
PRESIDENT ROOSEVELT: *During the next sixteen months of my term of office this policy shall be persevered in unswervingly.*
AMERICAN EAGLE: *"Je-hosaphat!"*
(Reproduced by permission of the proprietors of Punch. *Cartoon by Bernard Patridge)*

When Roosevelt began to enforce the Sherman Anti-Trust law, it was pictured as the dead returned to life, by Bartholomew in the Minneapolis Journal.

brought from Washington an announcement given out by the attorney general, which, in spite of the shock-absorbing tortuousness of official phraseology, conveyed appallingly the information that Morgan's latest merger, the Northern Securities Company, was to be prosecuted by the government—with the implication inherent that the action was the beginning of a policy of enforcing the Sherman law against all trusts.

Morgan turned from the telephone to his associates at the dinner table, his countenance showing appalled dismay but little anger. In telling the news to his guests, he dwelt on what he felt was the unfairness of Roosevelt's action. Roosevelt, he said, ought to have told him, ought to have given him a chance to make over the Northern Securities Company, if necessary, so as to conform to whatever Roosevelt thought was right. Or, if the company must be dissolved, Roosevelt ought to have given him an opportunity to dissolve it voluntarily. That alternative, Morgan felt, should have been afforded him by any one, most of all by Roosevelt. He had regarded Roosevelt as a gentleman, reared in his own social setting.

Morgan hurried to Washington. "If we have done anything wrong," he said to Roosevelt, "send your man [meaning Attorney General Knox] to my man [naming one of his lawyers] and they can fix it up." "That can't be done," said the president. "We don't want to fix it up," added Knox, who assisted at the interview, "we want to stop it." Morgan inquired: "Are you going to attack my other interests, the Steel Trust and the others?" "Certainly not," replied the president, "unless we find out that in any case they have done something we regard as wrong." As Morgan went away Roosevelt remarked: "That is a most illuminating illustration of the Wall Street point of view. Mr. Morgan could not help regarding me as a big rival operator, who either intended to ruin all his interests or else could be induced to come to an agreement to ruin none."

II

Roosevelt, having started the Northern Securities suit on its slow way through the courts, took, during the summer of 1902, trips through the country, in the course of which he explained what his policy about the trusts was to be, always keeping the serenity of balanced sentences and, as used by him, their forcefulness; always prefacing statements of his determination to enforce the law with assurances of his wish to preserve the economic good that there might be in large units of business. At Cincinnati, he said: "The biggest corporation, like the humblest private citizen, must be held to strict compliance with the will of the people." At Philadelphia, at a banquet of the Union League Club, he said:

Theodore Roosevelt and Niagara Falls were the two outstanding natural phenomena of America, observed John Morely after a visit to this country during Roosevelt's presidency. (From a photograph by Henry Miller)

> The question of the so-called trusts is but one of the questions we must meet in connection with our industrial system. There are many of them and they are serious; but they can and will be met. Time may be needed for making the solution perfect; but it is idle to tell this people that we have not the power to solve such a problem as that of exercising adequate supervision over the great industrial combinations of to-day. We have the power and we shall find out the way. We shall not act hastily or recklessly, and a right solution shall be found, and found it will be.

At which, one witness noticed, some representatives of "large and prosperous public-utility companies shook their heads, as if to say 'that won't do.'"

In the meantime, in another quarter, another form of capitalistic assumption of divine right had come to a head, in a form that constituted a challenge to Roosevelt, which asked him, as he saw it, whether any individual or group of individuals could be permitted to be more powerful than the government.

III

The bituminous coal miners of the country had been brought into a union for the first time in 1890, and in 1899 had been joined by the anthracite miners, the two groups composing a nationwide union, the United Mine Workers of America, destined to remain compact and successful, and to figure in a good deal of history under an able leader. John Mitchell, by studying in his spare hours, had risen from a laborer in the coal mines to a position of affectionate respect hardly attained by any other labor leader in America. His tact, intelligence, organizing ability, integrity, and personal charm had won for him the love and confidence of union men, and made him a popular figure with the public.

In 1900, the anthracite miners struck for a 10 percent increase in wages. Whether or not they chose their time with consciousness of the strategy of striking during a political campaign, Mark Hanna quickly saw that aspect of it. He, as national chairman of the Republican Party, responsible for the success of McKinley, went to Wall Street, saw the operators and bankers of the industry, and told them they had better add 10 percent to the miners' wages, rather than run the risk of Bryan getting into the White House. The coal presidents and bankers shivered at the warmed-over scare of Bryan's free silver platform and yielded.

John Mitchell, leader of the United Mine Workers of America.

The miners' union, soon after the campaign-year victory, began to press for further advantage. Its demands, as phrased in public announcements and discussions, were "for an increase in wages, a decrease in time, and payment . . . by weight [and not] by car." But as the Anthracite Coal Strike Commission (appointed later) reported, with an understanding not common in official documents, "The cause lies deeper than the occasion, and is to be found in the desire for the recognition by the operators of the miners' union." That was more repugnant to the operators and the bankers associated with them than almost any conceivable demand for wages. It involved treating the miners' union officials as equals, and carried with it the principle of collective bargaining. What now followed was an epochal step in the evolution of that system.

On May 12, 1902, the entire body of anthracite miners, 147,000, left the mines. Throughout the summer no work was done; in the fall, the coal yards, depleted by the previous winter's consumption and not restocked during the summer, were at famine level. Yards in New York which in other years at this time had an average of 2,000 tons in storage now had less than a tenth of that amount. On September 1, the price of anthracite, normally about $5 a ton, was at $14. The poor, buying it by the bucket or the bushel, paid one cent a pound, $20 a ton. Toward the end of September, several schools in New York were closed in order to conserve their scanty fuel; as the weather grew colder, people bought oil, coke, and gas stoves—poor substitutes for anthracite. In the West, mobs seized coal cars passing through the towns on the railways. By September 30, stocks were practically exhausted; for what little coal there was, $20 a ton was asked. A day later the price in New York jumped to $28 and then to $30 a ton.

IV

On October 1, 1902, Roosevelt invited the operators and the miners' leaders to Washington to consult with him for the purpose of trying to reach a settlement. From the conservative newspapers a storm arose. The *New York Sun* said the president's action was "extraordinary," "unprecedented," and "dangerous."

On October 3, both parties arrived in Washington, the operators in an offensively belligerent mood. Roosevelt was plainly on the defensive. He had absolutely no authority over them, and he knew it. He was acting with no more power than any leading citizen in private life, and frankly said so as he opened the conference:

> I disclaim any right or duty to intervene in this way upon legal grounds or upon any official relation that I bear to the situation; but the urgency and the terrible nature of the catastrophe impending requires me to use whatever influence I personally can to . . . end a situation which has become literally intolerable. With all the earnestness there is in me I ask that there be an immediate resumption of operations in the coal mines in some such way as will, without a day's unnecessary delay, meet the crying needs of the people. I appeal to your patriotism, to the spirit that sinks personal consideration and makes individual sacrifices for the general good.

No sooner had Roosevelt concluded his punctiliously phrased appeal than the miners' leader, John Mitchell, rose. Mitchell's rather romantic personality never appeared to better advantage. His natural distinction of person and manner was accentuated by his affecting the sober garb and the "reversed" collar of the clergyman. In this gathering of strong men, he stood out easily the most intelligently forceful of all, save Roosevelt.

Mitchell spoke in a loud, clear voice. He did not make the mistake of berating his opponents or of voicing the complaints of his followers. Had he done that he would have lost Roosevelt's sympathy. Instead, he made a proposal which the operators could not ignore without drawing upon themselves public condemnation. He said: "I am much pleased, Mr. President, with what you say. We are willing that you shall name a tribunal which shall determine the issues that have resulted in the strike; and if the gentlemen representing the operators will accept the award or decision of such a tribunal, the miners will willingly accept it, even if it be against our claims."

One of the lawyers the operators brought with them read a long prepared argument which told President Roosevelt his true duty was to instruct his attorney general to bring suit to dissolve the miners' union as a violator of the Sherman Anti-Trust law. The operators evidently intended to rouse the president to an outburst of anger and thereby put him in the wrong; but he kept his temper perfectly, as did also the labor leaders throughout. The tone of the operators was one of studied insolence toward the president and animosity toward the miners' leaders. They intimated that Roosevelt had failed in his duty, that he should long since have broken the strike by the employment of the regular army, and that the responsibility for the existing situation rested largely upon him. They said the government was "a contemptible failure if it can secure the lives and property and comfort of the people only by compromising with the violators of law and the instigators of violence and crime." "Are you asking us to deal with a set of outlaws?" one of the operators, John Markle, inquired of the president; and the other operators commonly spoke of the members of the union as criminals and anarchists. The operators were quoted by a *New York Sun* reporter as saying, after the conference, that they regarded the president's action as "a grand-stand play," and an "intrusion upon a situation that in no wise concerned him."

That evening Roosevelt wrote to Hanna: "Well, I have tried and failed. I feel downhearted. . . . But I am glad I tried, anyhow. I should have hated to feel that I had failed to make any effort. What my next move will be I cannot yet say."

V

Secretary of War Elihu Root, although the strike was not within his official responsibility, felt deeply that something extremely serious was ahead. With a thoroughness and orderliness characteristic of his mind, he asked for and made a study of the statements made and positions taken by the two opposing sides at the fruitless conference of October 3. From his study, and from his experience in many a tense lawsuit, Root sensed that the difficulty lay in the stage the controversy had reached, the stage where men are made stubborn, more by reluctance to seem to "back down" than by the principle involved. Root went to Roosevelt, told him he thought he saw a possible way by which the thing Roosevelt wanted could be accomplished, without humiliation to anybody, and asked Roosevelt's permission to try his hand at a suggestion for getting out of the impasse. The understanding between Root and Roosevelt was that the former was not committing the president in any way, but was acting on his individual responsibility.

With Roosevelt's permission, Root wrote a note to J. P. Morgan, asking if he would care to have a talk with him about the situation. Root found Morgan as willing as himself to see the public aspect of the situation and to try to find a way to end it. (Morgan throughout had never shared the recalcitrancy of the operators; on the contrary, his position had always been one of trying to persuade the operators to arbitrate, but of being resisted.)

On October 14, Morgan telephoned for a special train, went to Washington (accompanied by one of his junior partners, Robert Bacon, a friend and classmate of Roosevelt and bound to him by special ties); he called on Root, with him walked to the temporary White House* on Jackson Place, and presented to Roosevelt a document signed by the six biggest operators—a document which when read closely suggests among other things how great may be the difference, often, between the document the public sees and the negotiations and forces that bring it about. The document read, in part:

> We suggest a Commission be appointed by the President of the United States (if he is willing to perform that public service) to whom shall be referred all questions at issue between the respective companies and their own employees, whether they belong to a union or not, and the decision of that Commission shall be accepted by us.
>
> The Commission to be constituted as follows:
>
> 1. An officer of the engineer corps of either the military or naval service of the United States.
>
> 2. An expert mining engineer, experienced in the mining of coal and other minerals and not in any way connected with coal-mining properties, either anthracite or bituminous.
>
> 3. One of the judges of the United States Court of the Eastern District of Pennsylvania.
>
> 4. A man of prominence eminent as a sociologist.
>
> 5. A man who by active participation in mining and selling coal is familiar with the physical and commercial features of the business.

That carefully specified list of five classes from which arbitrators must be chosen is less important for what it includes than for what it excludes. It admitted no person who by any stretch of the imagination could be described as a representative of a labor union. That careful exclusion reflected what was at the very bottom of the operators' hearts, dislike of recognizing the right of labor men to have a union, distaste for admitting equality between labor unions and them. So far as they could, they wanted it to appear as if, for them, labor unions did not exist, or at least that they had no place in any sphere so elevated as arbitration. The miners, on the other hand, specified nothing, tried to dictate nothing. They merely told

* The White House was being repaired.

Roosevelt they would like very much to have on the board Bishop Spalding of the Catholic diocese of Peoria, Illinois, and someone—they did not give any name—representing union labor. They did not ask that he be a member of the miners' union—any organized-labor man would do. They were willing either that the two be added to the operators' five, or included among them. But the operators would not relent. They refused to permit labor to be officially represented on the board.

At length it dawned on Roosevelt what was in the operators' minds. The operators were not willing that anybody *described as a labor man* should be added to their list of specified classes. "They did not mind my appointing any man, whether a labor man or not, so long as he was not appointed *as* a labor man, or *as* a representative of labor. They did not object to my exercising any latitude I chose in the appointments so long as they were made under the headings they had given."

The words, including the italicized *as*'s are Roosevelt's. He added:

> I shall never forget the mixture of relief and amusement I felt when I thoroughly grasped the fact that while they would heroically submit to anarchy rather than have Tweedledum, yet if I would call it Tweedledee they would accept it with rapture; it gave me an illuminating glimpse into one corner of the mighty brains of these "captains of industry." In order to carry the great and vital point and secure agreement by both parties, all that was necessary for me to do was to commit a technical and nominal absurdity with a solemn face. This I gladly did. I announced at once that I accepted the terms.

Thereupon Roosevelt conducted, so to speak, one of the most rapid courses in higher education that ever raised the scholastic standing of a humble and modest man. Among his appointees to the arbitration commission was one upon whom he conferred the honorary degree of "eminent sociologist," a gentleman who up to that time had been known only as Grand Chief of the Order of Railway Conductors, E. E. Clark.

In giving out the list for publication, Roosevelt let the public in on the joke, so far as he could, by adding after Clark's name a parenthetical explanation that he had been appointed "as a sociologist—the President assuming that for the purposes of such a Commission, the term sociologist means a man who has thought and studied deeply on social questions and has practically applied his knowledge."

But "the relief of the whole country was so great that the sudden appearance of the head of the Order of Railway Conductors as an 'eminent sociologist' merely furnished material for puzzled comment on the part of the press."

On October 23, the miners resumed work. On November 10, Roosevelt went on a bear hunt in Mississippi, with equally historic result for the American toy industry.

*   *   *

Cartoon by Berryman, drawn in 1902, which started a Teddy-bear vogue lasting as long as Roosevelt lived. The original is in the National Press Club at Washington.

Roosevelt, ten years later, fixed October 1902 and the settlement of the coal strike as the time he "struck his own note" about big business. Lawrence F. Abbott had written in a newspaper article a sentence fixing November 1904, the month Roosevelt was elected president in his own right, as the time "he began to shape the government upon the policies, in contradistinction to those of McKinley, which have now become historically associated with his administration." On the margin of the newspaper clipping Roosevelt wrote: "No, the mere force of events had made me strike absolutely my own note by October 1902, when I settled the coal strike and started the trust-control campaign."

VI

In the 1904 campaign between Roosevelt and Alton B. Parker, the business interests that hated the former followed a course reflected by the outstanding journalistic exponent of them. The *New York Sun* had begun its treatment of Roosevelt when he became president by the flattering assumption that his great good sense and solid character would of course cause him to follow the steps of McKinley and to abide faithfully by the orthodox principles of the Republican Party, including the party's protective guardianship of the interests of business. When Roosevelt compelled the coal operators to arbitrate the strike of 1902, and when he started suit against the Northern Securities Company, the *Sun* attacked him with a trenchant force rarely exceeded in political controversy. As the question of Roosevelt's renomination by the Republicans approached, the *Sun* demanded that it be denied him, and that the standard be given to Mark Hanna. When Roosevelt's nomination became inevitable, the *Sun* continued protesting.

After Roosevelt was nominated and after the Democrats had nominated Parker, the *Sun*, and the financial interests it represented, surveyed the alternatives. Their emotions clamored that they oppose Roosevelt; their intellects told them that while Parker personally was a satisfactory conservative, it was still clear that fully half the Democratic Party had the attitude of Bryan toward big business. In this dilemma, the *Sun*, after five weeks' reflection, printed one of the briefest editorials that ever expressed a great newspaper's position in a campaign, a compact triumph of the qualities of intellect and humor that caused the *Sun* to be universally admired, even by those who most strongly disagreed with it. The *Sun*'s announcement of its choice read simply: "Theodore! will all thy faults——"

As the campaign went on, the *Sun* explained its conversion in later editorials: "We prefer the impulsive candidate of the party of conservatism to the conservative candidate of the party which the business interests regard as permanently and dangerously impulsive."

The campaign ended in victory for Roosevelt by an unprecedented majority, the Democrats carrying not one state north of the Mason and Dixon line, and not all those south of it, the most disastrous defeat suffered by any major party since the 1872 campaign of Horace Greeley. Missouri went Republican for the first time since Civil War and Reconstruction days.

VII

Roosevelt, elected, said to Mrs. Roosevelt: "I am no longer a political accident." To the newspapers he gave out a memorable statement designed to assure the public that his presidency would be influenced by no consideration of his personal political fortunes, but that his actions would be determined on principle, and could be judged on merit:

> I am deeply sensible of the honor done me by the American people in thus expressing their confidence in what I have done and have tried to do. I appreciate to the full the solemn responsibility this confidence imposes upon me, and I shall do all that in my power lies not to forfeit it. On the 4th of March next I shall have served three and one-half years, and this three and one-half years constitutes my first term. The wise custom which limits the President to two terms regards the substance and not the form. Under no circumstances will I be a candidate for or accept another nomination.

THE MYSTERIOUS STRANGER.

"The Mysterious Stranger," a famous cartoon by John McCutcheon, published by the Chicago Tribune, *November 10, 1904, the day after the election returns showed Missouri had gone Republican.*

CHAPTER 9
The Crusade for Pure Food

In 1906, Upton Sinclair, a young man devoted to romantic philosophy, realistic literature, and experimental socialism, finished a novel, named it *The Jungle*, carried the manuscript to five different publishers who rejected it, decided to print it as he could, and asked his friend, fellow Socialist and fellow author Jack London, to write the announcement. London, seeing the novel as what the author meant it to be, described it as an appeal for socialism, a protest against "wage slavery," and wrote:

> CIRCULATE "THE JUNGLE"
> Dear Comrades: . . . The book we have been waiting for these many years! It will open countless ears that have been deaf to Socialism. It will make thousands of converts to our cause. It depicts what our country really is, the home of oppression and injustice, a nightmare of misery, an inferno of suffering, a human hell, a jungle of wild beasts. . . . What "Uncle Tom's Cabin" did for the black slaves "The Jungle" has a large chance to do for the white slaves of to-day.

London's most troubling apprehension was that the book might encounter a "conspiracy of silence" on the part of "capitalism," by which he meant merely that he feared it might not be read; that it might make no more noise and get no more circulation than is the usual and normal fate of more than ninety-nine new books out of every hundred. Hence he warned his Socialist comrades: "Remember, this book must go out in the face of the enemy. . . . The most dangerous treatment it will receive is that of silence. For that is the way of capitalism. Comrades, do not forget the conspiracy of silence. Silence is the deadliest danger this book has to face."

The Jungle was one of the earliest examples of Tolstoyan pessimism and other Russian influences on American fiction, and, as a novel, was measurably comparable to the best of its Slavic models. It told the epic tragedy of Jurgis, a Lithuanian peasant who saw in his native village one of the posters with which American industrial corporations and steamship companies lured immigrants to America. Jurgis came to Chicago, and got a job in the stockyards—which Sinclair called "Packingtown," a name that had been used locally, and which *The Jungle* caused to become familiar nationally and to endure for several years. In Packingtown, the immigrant came into contact with about every evil that American industry and politics contained. He had to pay graft to get his job, and more to keep it; he lived in a lodging house where the keeper "would rent the same bed to double shifts of men, one working every day and using it at night, the other working by night and using it by day"; he was cheated by the real estate man who sold him a house on the installment plan under a contract the Lithuanian could not read; he and his family were infected by hideous diseases, and by moral ulcers as well, from the conditions under which they toiled; he was "speeded up" beyond his strength by "pace-makers"; he found the company he worked for had secret mains through which they stole water from the city; he saw his neighbors used as pawns and victims of the worst practices of municipal politics; he was blackmailed into paying high prices for adulterated beer because "the saloonkeeper 'stood in' with all the big politicians in the district"; he went through the familiar experiences of being "laid off," of striking, and of being "blacklisted"; he was persecuted by "spotters"; he lost his savings through a bank failure; when an intolerable grievance led him to "beat up" the foreman over him, he found the company "stood in" with the courts, and he was sent to jail unjustly. Hardly a solitary American influence, institution, or individual that this immigrant-laborer met failed to cheat him, exploit him, brutalize him.

Not only was Jurgis the victim of constant tragedy, but every human being that had any important part in the book was a tragedy. And not only the human beings. The animals were portrayed by Sinclair as tragedies. As one result, the workmanship of the book was like the picture it aimed to convey of the stockyards, a welter of the terribly grim, together with some other things that Sinclair meant to be terribly grim, but which to the average American reader were almost comically trivial. In the spirit of his Russian models, Sinclair, giving souls to the unhappy pigs, wrote:

> One could not stand and watch very long without becoming philosophical, without beginning to deal in symbols and similes, and to hear the hog-squeal of the universe. Was it permitted to believe that there was nowhere upon the earth, or above the earth, a heaven for hogs, where they were requited for all this suffering? Each one of these hogs was a separate creature. Some were white hogs, some were black; some were brown, some were spotted; some were old, some were young; some were long and lean, some were monstrous. And each of them had an individuality of his own, a will of his own, a hope and a heart, a desire; each was full of self-confidence, of self-importance, and a sense of dignity. And trusting and strong in faith he had gone about his business, the while a black shadow hung over him and a horrid Fate waited in his pathway. Now suddenly it had swooped upon him, and had seized him by the leg. Relentless, remorseless it was; all his protests, his screams, were nothing to it; it did its cruel will with him, as if his wishes, his feelings, had simply no existence at all; it cut his throat and watched him gasp out his life. And now was one to believe that there was

nowhere a god of hogs, to whom this hog-personality was precious, to whom these hog-squeals and agonies had a meaning? Who would take this hog into his arms and comfort him, reward him for his work well done, and show him the meaning of his sacrifice?

The squeals of the pigs, as their throats were slit, seemed to Sinclair a symphony of tragedy:

> A most terrifying shriek . . . followed by another, louder and yet more agonizing—for once started upon that journey the hog never came back—at the top of the wheel he was shunted off upon a trolley, and went sailing down the room. And meantime another was swinging up, and then another, and another, until there was a double line of them, each dangling by a foot and kicking in frenzy— and squealing. The uproar was appalling; one feared there was too much sound for the room to hold—that the walls must give way or the ceiling crack. There were high squeals and low squeals, grunts, and wails of agony.

One wondered, as one read, just what did this particular detail of Packingtown prove. A pig, one felt, would have squealed just as loudly, would have been just as reluctant to be killed by an old-time individual butcher in a sylvan village as by a trust in Chicago, and was otherwise indifferent to the economic and social aspects of the ceremony. As for the reader to whose sympathies Sinclair appealed, it was rather common knowledge that the initial step in the process of providing bacon for breakfast is accompanied by sounds dissonant to sensitive ears.

But let no one think *The Jungle* was a book to smile at. As a picture of America taking peasants from the fields of Europe and throwing them into the crucible of American industry, like ore or any other raw material; as the reality of what idealism called the "melting pot," *The Jungle* was a not too greatly exaggerated bit of truth about American industrial life as it was at that time—a *Jungle* could have been written about he coal mines, the street mills, and many other industries.

Sinclair's vagarious excitability always left the reader of his books uncertain how far the author's intention was art, and how far propaganda. So far as Sinclair had in mind propaganda for reform, he meant his book to show the process by which workers became, and in Sinclair's judgment ought to become, Socialists.

But all this passed over the public's head. The public ignored the tragedy of Jurgis the man, neglected the sociological jeremiad, was unmoved by the plea and propaganda for socialism. Sinclair's picture of the sausage-making machines, for example, was meant by him to make readers feel sad about the number of handworkers displaced. But what most impressed the public was something unappetizing about the stuffing process: "There was a sort of spout, a stream of sausage-meat would be shot out . . . a wriggling snake of sausage of incredible length."

What the public took hold of avidly and excitedly were some adventitious allusions to the food they were buying and eating; casual passages which Sinclair intended as mere bits of local color, as minor in the whole picture as the squeals of the pigs; offhand details which vivified the impression made upon some of the more sensitive senses by the modern mass manufacture of food. One was the stockyards smell, which Sinclair described quite mildly: "a strange pungent odor, that you caught in whiffs; you could literally taste it as well as smell it—you could take hold of it, almost, and examine it at your leisure . . . an elemental odor, raw and crude; it was rich, almost rancid, sensual and strong."

That was the most innocuous of Sinclair's bits of description. It, alone, would have made no commotion. The stockyards smell was an old story; newspapers had made jokes about it for years. But Sinclair went farther.

He pictured a meat inspector, a government official, so agreeably engaged in chatting with a visitor about the deadliness of the dangers inherent in eating tubercular pork, that he let a dozen carcasses pass him without testing them. Another inspector, more meticulously conscientious, had proposed, as a means of saving frugal packers from temptation, that tuber-

A sausage-making machine. (From a photograph by Underwood & Underwood)

cular carcasses be treated with an injection of kerosene—and had been dropped from the government's inspection service, quickly and mysteriously—an incident not only raising disagreeable doubts about the wholesomeness of the meat every one was eating, but implying that the packers had a political pull which enabled them to get rid of overconscientious inspectors.

"There was said to be two thousand dollars a week hush-money from hogs that had died of cholera on the trains," and which "were . . . hauled away to a place in Indiana where they made a fancy grade of lard." Old cattle, and diseased ones, made into canned beef. "Potted chicken" made of "tripe, the fat of pork, beef suet, hearts of beef, and waste-ends of veal."

> Devilled ham . . . made out of the waste-ends of smoked beef that were too small to be sliced by the machines; and also tripe dyed with chemicals so that it would not show white.
>
> Old rancid butter "oxidized" by a force-air process, to take away the odor, rechurned with skim-milk, and sold in the cities. A good part of what the public buys for lamb and mutton is really goat's flesh! . . . The rats were nuisances; the packers would put poisoned bread out for them; they would die, and then rats, bread, and meat would go into the hoppers together. . . . Men worked in the tankrooms, full of steam, in some of which there were open vats near the level of the floor . . . [when] they fell into the vats, sometimes they would be overlooked for days, till all but the bones of them had gone out to the world as Durham's Pure Leaf Lard.*

The passages giving these bits of local color in the Odyssey of Jurgis, as he worked his tragic way through Packingtown, were not more than eight pages in the 308 of *The Jungle;* but it was those eight pages the public seized upon.

Sinclair complained that he had wished to appeal to the hearts of the people, but had only succeeded in reaching their stomachs: "I had not been nearly so interested in the 'condemned meat' as in something else, the inferno of exploitation. I realized with bitterness that I had been made a

---

*In order that the reader of this volume may escape the error, practically universal, of classifying Sinclair and his *Jungle* with the "Muckrakers" who made much history during this period, it should be understood that *The Jungle* was a novel, fiction; and that these charges about conditions in the stockyards did not purport to have any more than the loose standard of accuracy that fiction demands for local color and background. Moreover, Sinclair as artist was so submerged by Sinclair as propagandist, that accuracy about background was even less compelling on him than on artists who are artists wholly. As fiction, the charges in *The Jungle* are to be taken as faithful to the broad picture, the impression. Sinclair gave many of them as portions of the offhand conversation of stockyard workers among themselves. He did not pretend to have seen these things, nor to have verified them, nor to have taken them from official records. There was truth in them, but not necessarily literal truth.

The "Muckrakers"—Lincoln Steffens, Ida Tarbell, Ray Stannard Baker, and others—were utterly different from Sinclair in their methods. They put out their product as *fact*, and asked the public to accept it and test it as such. The Muckrakers spent months of investigation before printing a brief article of 5,000 or 6,000 words. They investigated everything, confirmed everything. (Samuel S. McClure, who was editor of *McClure's Magazine* when that periodical was the pioneer

'celebrity,' not because the public cared anything about the workers, but simply because the public did not want to eat tubercular beef." The disappointed author started a cooperative boardinghouse in New Jersey, called Helicon Hall (the name led to some ribald puns), in which the boarders were supposed to take turns at the dish washing. The boardinghouse failed to cooperate, conspicuously, and Sinclair joined an "individualist-anarchist single-tax" colony at Arden, Delaware. Later, he lived near Los Angeles, California, where he ran for Congress on the Socialist ticket and for governor as a Democrat and spent his later career as writer of pamphlets and books (none of them attaining the fame of *The Jungle*) expressing acute dissatisfaction with the way the world was run.

For the effect *The Jungle* had on the average American, hygienic rather than spiritual or social, we can rely on that incomparably astute exponent of the typical American point of view, "Mr. Dooley":

> Dear, oh dear, I haven't been able to ate annything more nourishin' thin a cucumber in a week. . . . A little while ago no wan cud square away at a beefsteak with betther grace thin mesilf. To-day th' wurrud resthrant makes me green in th' face. How did it all come about? A young fellow wrote a book. Th' divvle take him f'r writin' it. Hogan says it's a grand book. It's wan iv th' gr-reatest books he iver r-read. It almost made him commit suicide. The hero got a fancy job poling food products out iv a catch-basin, an' was promoted to scrapin' pure leaf lard off th' flure iv th' glue facthry. Th' villain fell into a lard-tank an' was not seen again ontil he turned up at a fash'nable resthrant in New York. Ye'll see be this that 'tis a sweetly sintimintal little volume, to be r-read durin' Lent. I see be th' publishers' announcements that 'tis th' gr-reatest lithry hog-killin' in a peryod iv gin'ral lithry culture. If ye want to rayjooce ye'er butcher's bills buy "The Jungle." It shud be taken between meals, an' is especially ricomminded to maiden ladies contimplatin' their first ocean voyage.

and the best of the muckraking publications, verifies my own recollection that a single magazine article by Lincoln Steffens or Miss Tarbell often represented six months of investigation and upward of $3,000 of expense, aside from the writer's salary.) The Muckrakers took their material from what they themselves saw, or from sworn testimony in lawsuits or in legislative investigations. They made it a point to talk with everybody who had legislative investigations. They made it a point to talk with everybody who had important, firsthand information. Almost always they discussed their material with the man accused, or the head of the corporation they were investigating. Since most of the articles and books written by the Muckrakers would have been libelous if incorrect, the manuscripts were almost always subjected to scrutiny by lawyers.

The fictional character of Sinclair's *Jungle* bothered President Roosevelt when he came to use it as the basis of a demand for pure-food legislation. While there was abundant truth in *The Jungle* (and more in some conditions Sinclair did not mention) to justify the legislation, it was embarrassing to be unable to find proof for some details of Sinclair's charges.

For the public, the impression Sinclair conveyed was as much as was needed; the public made no meticulous inquiry into details, but sensed strongly that there was something rotten in Packingtown, literally.

To the packers, *The Jungle* came as a proof, peculiarly convincing and peculiarly painful, of several ancient adages, including the two which say that troubles never come singly, and that it never rains but it pours. Seventeen of the heads of the beef industry had recently fallen into a form of trouble with the federal government which included serious menace of jail, on the charge that they had combined into a monopoly. In defending themselves against that charge, the packers, distracted souls, were already using all their resources of lawyers and press agents, at the moment when they were hit by the storm aroused by *The Jungle*. Gallantly they stiffened their legal and literary sinews for the extra effort the situation called for. The best known of the packers, J. Ogden Armour, wrote a series of articles for the *Saturday Evening Post*. (Sinclair charged that the hard-pressed Armour had saved himself the labor of actually writing the articles by employing a literary hack.) A well-known publicist of the day, Elbert Hubbard, who had begun his writing career as a radical iconoclast and ended it as a composer of laudatory panegyrics about big business, wrote a defense of the packers, in which he said *The Jungle* was "a libel and an insult to intelligence." This the packers put into plate-matter for newspapers, and also mailed out a million copies throughout the country. These efforts they supplemented with the leverage of widespread newspaper advertising.

But much more than the effects of *The Jungle* entered into the storm that arose throughout the country. The things Sinclair suggested with his bits of impressionistic painting about beef were paralleled by conditions known with exactness about the large-scale preparation of other foods. *The Jungle*, indeed, was merely the final, spectacular, fictional climax to a long agitation that had been carried on in solid and convincing ways by patient investigators, food chemists in the employ of the state and federal governments, journalists of the exact-minded Muckraker type, leaders of women's clubs, and other reformers and altruists.

II

It was a decade or so after the Civil War that the old-time, simple, unorganized, one-man purveying of food began to give way to an overpowering new philosophy that was getting into business generally—bigness in operations, bigness in the number of workers employed, bigness in profits. The mechanism for it was supplied or made possible by the railroads; the motive was supplied by the zest for profits. The railroads made it practicable at once to collect the raw materials over a large territory and to supply customers over a territory equally extended. When the expansion reached its height, it could happen that a steer might be bought near a little village, be shipped several hundred miles to Chicago, be butchered there, and then be shipped back as dressed meat to be bought by the same man who raised the steer—passing, in the process, through the hands of scores of men who had no acquaintance with each other and no sense of responsibility toward

the others in the chain—and who, especially, had no sense of personal relation to the consumer, or responsibility to him.

In this process of immense expansion, the more enterprising among the
small establishments doubled, quadrupled, multiplied to a hundred times
the size of the old-time business units. The less aggressive, and those less
endowed with imagination, succumbed. So did those whose consciences or
temperaments made them disinclined to sell a product unless it had been
made by their own hands, or under their own eyes. All who had any defect
in adaptability to the new order in its raw early stages, succumbed. In the
meatpacking business, the growth of the big went on until, in 1905, about
thirty years after the tendency began, seventeen men, composing the heads
of five corporations, were indicted by the federal government as having
monopolized the meat business of the country.

The new order of business was insatiable in its reaching out for means of
aggrandizement. Any new idea that promised to increase sales, reduce
costs, and multiply profits was eagerly seized. The promoter, the banker,
the lawyer, were drawn into its service—not omitting the politician and the
lobbyist; the advertising man and the expert accountant; the inventor and
the chemist—especially, in the food business, the chemist.

The shipment of food over long distances, the selling of it many months or
even more than a year after it had been prepared, involved preservation.
Some of the arts of overcoming distance and time, which the philosophy of
bigness required of the chemist and of the inventor, were legitimate. They
developed and perfected the art of refrigeration, and the results of that
constitute one of the most conspicuous of those enrichments that have
come to the average man in our times. Refrigeration, including the refrigeration car, with other inventions, brought to the average man by 1925
such an abundance and variety of food, such a freedom from limitations of
season, time, or distance, as enabled him to smile at his deprived ancestors.

After artificial refrigeration, refrigerator cars, and cold storage, and after
the mass organization of food purveying that accompanied them, an average man, even a poor man, might eat meals including oranges from California or Florida, lemons from Sicily, olives from Italy, new potatoes from
Bermuda, bananas from Central America, grapefruit from the Isle of Pines,
and fresh meats and fish from hundreds of miles away.

The chemists and inventors employed by the big food-purveying organizations devised ingenious containers of glass, tin, and paper or oiled paper, by which food of many varieties could be packed or preserved in large
quantities, could be shipped great distances and marketed conveniently.
These containers—indeed, the whole system of selling by the package—
ensured cleanliness in transit and cleanliness in retail stores. If there were
impurities in some of the food purveyed by some corporations it was solely
the impurities that went in at the time of packing. Once goods were sealed
into their containers of tin, glass, and paper, they were marketed under
conditions more conducive to public health than had formerly been the

Courtesy of Armour & Co.

Sketch showing the ingenious economy of space in refrigerator cars. (Courtesy of Armour & Co.)

case; were secure against contaminations sometimes associated with keeping goods in bulk, as they were kept and sold in the old-time stores—bins with only a hinged lid, bins of sugar, of beans, of coffee; barrels, usually with the top off, containing fish or meat in brine.

One other advantage came with organized business, its inventors and chemists. Drugs could be shipped from every quarter of the world, their volatile oils preserved for an indefinite time by airtight packing. Before

Interior of a chain grocery store, 1925.

that, the medical resources of the old-time home had consisted of a very small number of "store-bought" drugs, a paper package of dried leaves of senna, a few lumps of alum, a few more of camphor, perhaps a bottle of turpentine. The greater reliance of the family was on home-gathered herbs—bone-set, pennyroyal, St. Johnswort—plucked in the autumn along the weedy edges of the fields, and hung in dry wisps from the attic rafters, where they imparted a pungent fragrance to the upper rooms of the house; mustard seeds, sassafras roots. Access to a greater variety of drugs, and more intelligent use of them were made possible by invention and chemistry, though these benefactions were destined to be attended by evils, as we shall see.

III

Some of the services of the inventor and chemist to bigness were definitely not services to the public. Refrigeration was asked to do more than its stage of development at that time was able to do. Presently the chemist was solicited to do by his arts what ice could not do; more accurately, what nature meant never should be done. The chemist was asked not merely to eke out nature, not merely to adapt nature; he was asked to make an impossible bridge between nature and the new philosophy of bigness; he was asked to cheat, deliberately and flagrantly. In the case of some products of nature, fruits, vegetables, or what not, the chemist was asked to, and actually did, devise artificial substitutes.

Chemists suggested substances which, added to foods, prevented their too early decomposition, and coloring matters which concealed decomposition that had already taken place; and still other substances possessing the magic property of restoring foods, already deteriorated, to a deceiving simulation of freshness. Stale, rancid, soiled, and unsalable butter, in various degrees of putrefaction, was made over and sold for fresh. Eggs, which the passage of time had made a little more than mellow, and which for that reason had been theretofore unusable; eggs that would have ruined the reputation of any old-time grocer selling them to an old-time housewife whose senses were experienced in recognizing the more advanced phases of nature—such eggs, in the new impersonality of big business, its complexities and the secrecies of its chemistry, were deodorized with formaldehyde, became a standard commodity of commerce, and were sold in enormous quantities for cake-making. In the earlier period of the use of cold storage, the word "fresh" when used in connection with eggs as well as meat, conveyed no necessary guarantee of nearness in time to the living animal. Apples, of which the succulence, in their pristine stage, had proved overalluring to some of the smaller invertebrates; and other apples in a condition that represented too great a zeal for conservation, were made into a jelly which, mixed with flavoring substances derived by chemistry from coal tar, appeared on the market labeled "currant," "blackberry," "plum jam," "pure apple butter."

Chemicals, or adulterants, or substitutes, came to appear in much of the food that average persons ate. At the annual meeting of the National Association of State Dairy and Food Departments at St. Paul, Minnesota, in 1903, a report on "The Use of Coloring Matter and Antiseptics in Food Products" was read by the State Analyst of South Dakota, James H. Shepard, to whom training in chemistry had given a bent for austere truth, as well as a convincing way of setting out proof. That extraneous substances appeared in most of the articles in common use for food, he took for granted—to his audience of food officials, that did not need proof. What he was intent on showing was the aggregate of such substances absorbed in a day by the average person, and the effect of such an aggregate on the human body. This was his answer to some food manufacturers who, unable to conceal their use of chemicals or other adulterants, claimed the amount in the portion for a single meal was so small as to be harmless.

"In order," said Professor Shepard, "to bring this matter out more forcibly, I have prepared a menu for one day such as any family in the United States might possibly use, and I am not sure but the working man in our cities would be quite likely to use it." Professor Shepard's menu, omitting the few articles not commonly adulterated, such as potatoes, was:

BREAKFAST
Sausage, coal-tar dye and borax.
Bread, alum.
Butter, coal-tar dye.
Canned cherries, coal-tar dye and salicylic acid.
Pancakes, alum.
Syrup, sodium sulphite.
   This gives eight doses of chemicals and dyes for breakfast.

DINNER
Tomato soup, coal-tar dye and benzoic acid.
Cabbage and corned beef, saltpetre.
Canned scallops, sulphurous acid and formaldehyde.
Canned peas, salicylic acid.
Catsup, coal-tar dye and benzoic acid.
Vinegar, coal-tar dye.
Bread and butter, alum and coal-tar dye.
Mince pie, boracic acid.
Pickles, copperas, sodium sulphite, and salicylic acid.
Lemon ice cream, methyl alcohol.
   This gives sixteen doses for dinner.

SUPPER
Bread and butter, alum and coal-tar dye.
Canned beef, borax.
Canned peaches, sodium sulphite, coal-tar dye, and salicylic acid.
Pickles, copperas, sodium sulphite, and formaldehyde.

Catsup, coal-tar dye and benzoic acid.
Lemon cake, alum.
Baked pork and beans, formaldehyde.
Vinegar, coal-tar dye.
Currant jelly, coal-tar dye and salicylic acid.
Cheese, coal-tar dye.
　　This gives sixteen doses for supper.

　"According to this menu," said Professor Shepard, "the unconscious and unwilling patient gets forty doses of chemicals and colors per day."

On a table in the House of Representatives, when the Pure Food bill came up for discussion in 1906, were displayed several hundred food samples—bottles, cans, and cartons purchased at grocery stores throughout the country. Attached to each was an analysis made by chemists of state and municipal health and food bureaus. A few among them were:

Maple syrup. Adulterated with a large percentage of cane syrup.
Honey. Largely glucose and bugs.
Plum preserves. Very largely adulterated with glucose, colored with a coal-tar dye.
Pineapple jelly. Made up largely of glucose and preserved with benzoic acid.
Olive oil. This is a sample of oil claimed to have been made in France; largely cotton-seed oil and sesame oil.
Extract of lemon. Purely an artificial product.
Apple-cider extract. Prepared from ethers and alcohol.
Carbonated soda water. Artificially colored with coal-tar dye.
Alfalfa seed. Picked out of raspberry jam.
Filler for cayenne pepper. Ground wood and corn meal.
Mustard filler. Wheat flour and turmeric.

　The extent of the adulteration of food, of the use of chemicals and artificial dyes, as set out in official statements supported by carefully attested analyses, was so great as to be practically universal.

It was not that American merchants and manufacturers were especially vicious or dishonest. They had as high an average of uprightness as any other class. Human nature had not suddenly changed. The trouble had its roots in the evolution that had taken place in business, the substitution of the corporation for the individual, and the injection of distance and middlemen between producer and consumer. That evolution had done away with checks which, operating between man and man, has stiffened the standards of indigenous human nature. The corporation threw about business a cloak of impersonality behind which practices could be carried on which under the older system would have brought odium to their perpetrators, which enabled men who wanted to be dishonest to be so, and to put their honest competitors under a disadvantage. There was no way for the consumer to differentiate between good and bad merchandise. There was no federal law to compel manufacturers to use only wholesome materials in their food products, or to prepare them with a decent regard for the health of the public. Nor was there any way by which consumers could distinguish between honest manufacturers and others. This condition was insidiously demoralizing to business and brought about a general lowering of standards. Wholesome, properly prepared food products were subjected to commercial disadvantage by counterfeits, selling more cheaply. Conscientious manufacturers found it difficult if not impossible to compete with their less ethical business rivals, and were driven in self-defense to emulate their meretricious trade practices. Many manufacturers gave sympathetic support to the movement for a pure-food law, so far as they could do so without incurring too much animosity from others in their trades.

Along with the rest went the adulteration of liquor and other drugs; the sale of medicines under false, misleading, or incomplete labels; the use, without restrictions, in patent medicines of opium, morphine, cocaine, laudanum, and alcohol; the preposterously false and cruelly misleading curative qualities claimed. These patent medicines were sold in every drugstore in the land, and in many rural general stores. It was an immense traffic; in 1900, the total volume of business was $59,611,355. The patent-medicine manufacturers comprised, at that time, the largest single user of advertising space in newspapers. Farmers living remote from physicians and, in the towns and cities, persons of modest means, to whom a physician's fee was an item to be considered, used patent medicines as practically the sole remedy for every kind of sickness.

In the patent-medicine business, the essential art was not medicine, nor chemistry. The fundamental genius for it was psychological. It consisted of skill in playing on the credulity of the simpleminded and the trusting. The patent-medicine man and the quack doctor were holdovers from primitive man's belief in magic—the belief that diseases could be cured by irrelevant specifics—a stick or a root from the forest, incantations, the fingernail of your enemy, "hair of the dog that bit you." They were atavistic "throwbacks" to the time when man was not able to reason, or at least did not reason in this field—remaining in a time when knowledge of the relation between cause and effect, the nature of disease, its source, prevention, and cure had been brought to the status of a science.

The patent-medicine manufacturers made an art of describing the symptoms of diseases in such a way as to terrorize the reader of their pamphlets and advertisements into believing he had one or more of the ailments they pretended to cure; and in describing their cure-alls in terms to convey the conviction of hope. Some of the largest solicited the public, especially women, to write to the eminent physician whom they represented to be the head of the concern, and whom they often referred to in a manner meant to suggest vast experience and inspire confidence, "Old Doctor ——." The patent-medicine business was the one in which the modern device of adaptable "form letters" was developed. The letters of the sick, of the hypochondriac, and of the sympathy-seeking rarely reached the eye of any doctor, but went to great staffs of clerks and stenographers, who gave them just enough attention to classify them as having to do with "cancer," or "consumption," or whatever the ailment might be, and then typed the standardized form of reply, usually beginning unctuously with "Dear Friend." The letters from the "suckers" were saved and became an important part of the stock in trade of many quacks. When the concern to whom the letter had been originally directed had sold as much medicine to the patient as his credulity would absorb, his letter and others, made up into bundles of thousands, were sold as "prospects" to other concerns.

The secrets of the patent-medicine business were made known to the public by a series of exposures conducted by Edward W. Bok in his widely circulated *Ladies' Home Journal* in 1904–1905, and by a similar series written by Samuel Hopkins Adams and others in *Collier's Weekly* in 1905. Bok, moved by discovering the extent to which his women readers medicated themselves by mail, dosed themselves and their children with dubious concoctions, and wrote trustingly intimate letters to concerns that made them articles of commerce, dug to the roots of the whole system. He reproduced an advertisement of Lydia E. Pinkham's Vegetable Compound, which said: "Mrs. Pinkham, in her laboratory at Lynn, Mass., is able to do more for the ailing women of America than the family physician. Any woman, therefore, is responsible for her own suffering who will not take the trouble to write to Mrs. Pinkham for advice."

Alongside this benevolent invitation Bok printed the photograph of a tombstone in Pine Grove Cemetery at Lynn, the picture large enough to show the lettering which recited the death of Lydia E. Pinkham twenty-two years before. Bok reproduced the label of Mrs. Winslow's Soothing Syrup, a medicine for quieting the fret of teething babies, as it was sold in America, and alongside it the label of the same medicine as sold in England, the two being identical except that the English label, under the requirements of the British law, informed mothers that "This preparation, containing, among other valuable ingredients, a small amount of morphine, is, in accordance with the Pharmacy Act, hereby labeled 'Poison.'"

This illustrated Bok's objective, and the objective of the whole crusade for the truthful labeling of medicine, food, and liquor; namely, that there should be a law in America requiring that the bottle, carton, or package should bear a label stating exactly what drugs and chemicals were in the medicine, and what chemicals, coloring matter, or preservatives had been added to the food. Bok printed chemical analyses of twenty-seven widely advertised patent medicines—very surprising the contents of some were—and argued for a law which should require the analysis to be printed on the label of every bottle of patent medicine sold to the American public.

The *Collier's Weekly* articles by Samuel Hopkins Adams, under the frank

title "The Great American Fraud," discussed the curative claims, as compared with the chemical analyses, of scores of patent medicines. Peruna, for
example, was purported to cure a good many things—Adams thought the
only thing it would really and infallibly cure was acute thirst for alcoholic
liquor in Prohibition territory; he reprinted an order forbidding Peruna on
Indian reservations, issued by an official who wanted to carry out the government's purpose of saving its wards from intoxication.

To each of the patent medicines Adams paid what he deemed to be its
just deserts. Some contained dangerous drugs; some were no worse than
innocuous. To some, whose principal content was alcohol, Adams even
conceded what virtue was supposed, in pre-Prohibition days, to lie in a
small dose of tonic or bitters, plus the psychological virtue of permitting
earnestly naive temperance folks to drink a little liquor under the comfort-
ing and harmless delusion that they were not violating their total-absti-
nence pledges but merely taking medicine. Some patent medicines made
utterly impossible claims to curative properties, others were more restrained. Adams analyzed and discussed, among others: "Dr. King's New
Discovery for Consumption—Greatest Discovery of the Nineteenth Century," "Dr. Kline's Great Nerve Restorer—Fits Permanently Cured,"
"Shiloh's Consumption Cure—the Cure That Is Guaranteed . . . ,"
"Warner's Safe Cure—Does Your Back Ache? It's Your Kidneys," "Swamp-
Root—Thousands Have Kidney Trouble and Don't Know It," "Wine of
Cardui—Take Cardui and You Will Soon Be Well," and "Hydrozone—
Positive Preventive of Yellow Fever."

In addition, Adams stuck his penetrating lance under the secret formulas

One of the reproductions with which Collier's Weekly *illustrated its campaign against
patent medicines, July 8, 1905.*

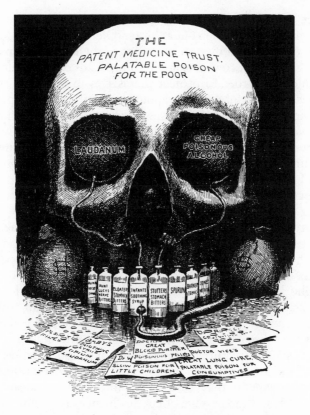

One of the series of drawings that accompanied Samuel Hopkins Adams's articles for Collier's *on "The Great American Fraud." The patent-medicine business was not a trust, but at that time "trust" was a brick hurled by cartoonists, editors, and clergymen at any businesses they regarded as undesirable. (From* Collier's, *June 3, 1905)*

of "the opium-containing soothing syrups, which stunt or kill helpless infants; the consumption cures, perhaps the most devilish of all, in that they destroy hope where hope is struggling against bitter odds for existence; the headache powders which enslave so insidiously that the victim is ignorant of his own fate; the catarrh powders which breed cocaine slaves." Four widely advertised "catarrh powders" were picked out by Adams as "the ones most in demand." "All of them," he wrote, "are cocaine; the other ingredients are unimportant."

IV

The suspicion that something very wrong was going on in food, drink, and medicines; the resentment against it; and the effort to overcome it began with the farmers. Farmers made butter, which came from cows. Beef packers manufactured oleomargarine, which came from cows also, though not via the lacteal teats. Oleomargarine was just as good as butter, but many of the makers, as if they had some native preference for indirection, wanted to sell oleo not as oleo but as butter. Oleo, naturally almost as white as lard, was colored with dyes so as to give to the consumer an exceptionally vivid suggestion of cows grazing in sunny fields of buttercups.

The farmers, in order to protect themselves in the states where they were politically powerful, brought about the institution of departments of agriculture in the state governments, with chemists and law officers whose business it was to ferret out and pursue imitations of butter, as well as adulterated butter. This function led naturally to an official and minatory curiosity about other adulterated or artificially colored food products and substitutes for food products, and ultimately about drugs and medicines. By 1900, several states had official departments of food and drugs devoted to analyzing products on sale in the state.

This farmer movement was the beginning of food analysis in the United States—of food analysis, that is, by public officials and in the interest of the public. The state chemists were, so to speak, counterchemists, devoting themselves to unearthing the practices of those chemists who had sold themselves into the service of the food adulterators. The state chemists, and the little staffs they built up around them, had several especially pregnant effects; they developed a technique of food analysis, of discovering adulteration and identifying the adulterants; they induced state legislatures to enlarge the pure-food statutes to include all kinds of food, in addition to butter, and secured increasing appropriations for enforcement; they caused the formation of local, municipal boards of health and the passage of city ordinances requiring higher standards of purity, especially for milk. By all their activities they stimulated popular interest in sanitation.

In 1898, the official chemists of as many states as had then adopted the institution formed the National Association of State Dairy and Food Departments. The earliest result of the organization of the state chemists into a national association, with annual meetings, was realization that they must have, in addition to their state laws, a national one. Under the federal Constitution, the shipment of food from one state into another could be controlled adequately and practicably only by a federal law. Moreover, the state laws varied greatly in the standards they set up. There was essential unfairness to the manufacturers of food in having different requirements in different states. The need of a national law, uniform throughout the country, was imperative.

One of the earliest of the state chemists, one of the first men to take an interest in food sanitation, and easily the outstanding figure in the crusade for pure food, was Dr. Harvey Washington Wiley, a very mountain among men, a lion among fighters. In 1874, when Purdue University was founded, Dr. Wiley was appointed its first chemist, and later was made state chemist of Indiana. In 1883, he was appointed chief chemist of the Department of Agriculture at Washington. There he remained until 1912, a period of twenty-nine years, at once the major portion of his mature life, and the whole period of the fight for pure food in the United States.

Wiley, watching with the eye of an expert the metamorphosis of the food industries of the country, saw clearly the evils and abuses that accompanied the change. Endowed by nature with a capacity for passionate indignation, having the spiritual zeal of a crusader and the physique to endure hard fighting, he dedicated himself to waging war on the evils and to this end launched out on a campaign of public education. Let the consumers once become fully aware of what the food manufacturers were doing, he reasoned, and there would surely follow an irresistible demand for a statutory corrective.* Wiley brought to his task of popular education an unusual array of talents. He could write and speak interestingly and authoritatively. He was convincing and persuasive. He, better than anyone else, knew the intimate details of the partnership that had come into being between the preserved-food manufacturer and the commercial chemist—and the harmful effects it was having on the digestive organs of the American people. And he, better than anyone else, knew how to tell about it. As time went on, there arose a demand for his services as a lecturer. On the platform the forcefulness and originality of his utterances gained from the impressiveness of his appearance: his large head capping the pedestal of broad shoulders and immense chest, his salient nose shaped like the bow of an ice-breaker, and his piercing eyes, compelled attention. He had a keen instinct for the dramatic. In 1903, he caught and held the attention of the entire country through the so-called poison-squad experiments, in which he fed volunteers, from the employees of his bureau, foods containing preservatives, with the object of determining whether or not they were injurious to health—an episode which caused Dr. Wiley to be called, jeeringly or affectionately, according to the point of view, "Old Borax."

Wiley came to have increasingly the confidence of the public, as, indeed, of all who wanted pure-food legislation. He was frequently called on for technical advice by Congress and by the pure-food workers. With the jeopardized private interests, however, and with the press and politicians who were friendly to them or otherwise skeptical about the need of reform, Wiley was anathema. The *New York Sun* bestowed on him the title "chief janitor and policeman of the people's insides."

Hardly any man in the United States, excepting only Roosevelt himself, had a larger or more powerful group of enemies than Wiley. In time, it came to be said of him, as is usually said of crusaders, that he was extreme. The adjective caused no abatement of Wiley's crusading belligerency. He gave as good as he got. Manufacturers who used chemicals the harmfulness of which was as yet unproved; those who used a comparatively small percentage of dubious preservatives; those who claimed, as many then did, that it was impossible to preserve foods without chemicals; those who said there was no harm in making food more alluring by the use of dyes—all

*The same idea was used in other fields by Presidents Roosevelt and Wilson, who gave it the familiar names "publicity" and "pitiless publicity."

fought Wiley, in the press so far as they had access to it, through association of chemists where they could, through the use of political influence with Congress and with Dr. Wiley's superiors and associates in the Department of Agriculture. All of which the grim old doctor met with his Puritan challenge: "Tell the truth on the label and let the consumer judge for himself."

Wiley, on one of his trips through the country, speaking before the Village Improvement Association of Cranford, New Jersey, stirred a latent crusading zeal in one of the members, Alice Lakey, who became a leading spirit in the reform. She infected the New Jersey State Federation of Women's Clubs, and later the General Federation of Women's Clubs and the National Consumers' League.

Lakey was moved by one of the most dynamic of forces, the indignation of a woman against evils practiced, as the adulteration of food partly was, for profit at the expense of the health and happiness of children. She, becoming, so to speak, Dr. Wiley's apostle among the women, procured an exhibit of impure or otherwise adulterated foods, with which she lectured up and down the land, transforming the suspicious disquiet of the women into outraged resentment and strenuous action.

The women of the country were ripe for the crusade. Enough of them had lived through the transition from home and village food industry, to large-scale corporation food industry, to know the taste, odor, and sight of pure products of nature; and to recognize that in what they were now obliged to buy, and what they could not avoid feeding to their children, there were elements new and mysterious, and therefore disquieting. These women, by the support they gave Dr. Wiley, by the pressure they brought upon Congress, did important political work years before they were allowed to vote.

The groups fighting for the Pure Food law staged, at the St. Louis Exposition of 1904, one of the most effective bits of propaganda ever achieved, for pure food or for any other purpose.

A large space had been allotted there to manufacturers of preserved foods, who put on display practically every brand and variety of canned and bottled goods manufactured in the United States. The pure-food workers, chiefly from the Association of State Food and Dairy Departments, secured from the Exposition officials permission to open a booth nearby. Then the state chemists of Illinois, Massachusetts, Michigan, Ohio, Kentucky, North Carolina, Minnesota, Utah, Oregon, Connecticut, South Dakota, and Nebraska set to work. They took samples of well-known artificially colored foods. From each they extracted the dye. With the extracted colors, they dyed pieces of wool and silk. To each bit of cloth they attached a properly attested chemist's certificate, explaining the nature of the dye, and giving the name of the food sample from which it had been taken. Then they shipped the whole exhibit to the pure-food booth at the St. Louis Exposition.

When the exposition opened, visitors by the thousands filed by the beautifully arranged display of the food manufacturers—and then paused at the pure-food booth. Here they saw duplicated many of the cans and bottles on view in the food manufacturers' booth, each having a placard naming the deleterious substances used in its coloring and preservation. On a table, in a brilliantly hued layout, were the silk and woolen cloths that had been colored with dyes extracted from the foods. The subtle purpose was that the passerby would reason that silk and wool are animal tissues, that a human being's intestines are animal tissues also, and that a dye which would bring a brilliant green, or carmine, or yellow to wool and silk, might, when swallowed in food, bring the same color to the passerby's insides.

Many Americans felt an acute disquiet about any departure from the conventional in the coloring of the internal organs. In short, the average American examined that display in the aisles of the St. Louis Exposition with intentness and minuteness, and passed on with a readiness to listen favorably to any agitator who thought Congress ought to do something about the use of artificial coloring in food.

V

In February 1905, a committee of six from the organized workers for pure food, headed by Robert M. Allen, secretary of the National Association of State Dairy and Food Departments, called on President Roosevelt. Roosevelt was sympathetic, promised to look into the need for the law, and told them to come back in the fall. During the summer he talked with Dr. Wiley, with Dr. Ira Remsen of Johns Hopkins University, and with his personal physician, an exceptionally wise man, Dr. Samuel W. Lambert. In November 1905, when the committee called again, Roosevelt told them, as recounted by Robert M. Allen in 1927: "I, of course, want to be the first to make my message to Congress public, but I am going to trust you and tell you that it will contain a recommendation for a law to stop interstate traffic in adulterated foods and drugs. But it will take more than my recommendation to get the law passed, for I understand that there is some very stubborn opposition."

Roosevelt in his annual message, delivered to Congress December 5, 1905, fulfilled his promise in three brief, forceful sentences:

> I recommend that a law be enacted to regulate interstate commerce in misbranded and adulterated foods, drinks, and drugs. Such law would protect legitimate manufacture and commerce, and would tend to secure the health and welfare of the consuming public. Traffic in foodstuffs which have been debased or adulterated so as to injure health or to deceive purchasers should be forbidden.

Previous attempts to pass such a bill had been frustrated by influential lobbyists and conservative legislators. This time, with the powerful friend in the White House, and with the support of the sentiment that had been built up, the bill could no longer be headed off by mere obstruction. The Senate Republican leader, Nelson W. Aldrich of Rhode Island, had to fight in the open, an extremely unusual experience, for his art of leadership lay partly in his minute knowledge of the political and business affiliations of the senators and of what strings to pull, partly in the power to command Republican senators which went with his official position as leader, and partly in his skill in parliamentary procedure. Because he had those stronger leverages of power, and also because he was one of the least eloquent of senators, Aldrich rarely made speeches. Now, he broke his rule of silence, the action being partly justified by the fact that as a wholesale grocer (among other large interests) he had expert knowledge of the subject matter. He based his argument, however, not on the private interest of food purveyors but on public interest—the "liberty of the people":

> Is there anything in the existing condition that makes it the duty of Congress to put the liberty of all the people of the United States in jeopardy? . . . Are we going to take up the question as to what a man shall eat and what a man shall drink, and put him under severe penalties if he is eating or drinking something different from what the chemists of the Agricultural Department think desirable?

That specious fallacy was too glaring to escape exposure. The Pure Food bill put no regulation on any consumer; all its regulations were on makers and sellers. The only prohibitions in the bill were few: against selling diseased meat, or decomposed food, or dangerously adulterated food. The bulk of the provision of the bill did not prohibit the sale of anything, but merely demanded that the label should truthfully describe the contents, a regulation which, far from limiting the consumer's freedom, enlarged it.

About the middle of February 1906, the American Medical Association brought direct pressure on Aldrich. Dr. Charles A. L. Reed of Cincinnati, chairman of the Association's Legislative Council, told Aldrich he had back of him some 135,000 physicians, all organized locally into about 2,000 county units, each member instructed not only to act himself but to ask his patients and friends to bring pressure on the Senate. Dr. Reed told Aldrich further that he and the members of the American Medical Association were determined to carry this issue of the Pure Food bill into partisan pol-

Senator Nelson W. Aldrich (February 1905), who argued that the Pure Food law was a curtailment of liberty.

itics if necessary. The opposition in the Senate collapsed a few days later, on February 15, 1906. On February 21 the bill passed the Senate 63 to 4.

The hurdle of the Senate was now passed—after seventeen years. The bill went to the House and was referred to the appropriate committee. There it slept. And it slept. Furtive obstruction, the chloroform of the lethal committeeroom, was now what the bill had to fear. There was not a doubt that, if it came to a vote, it would pass.

In a few weeks the friends of the bill observed a disconcerting sign: the professional lobbyists, carrying their packed grips out of Washington hotels on their way home. They asked a friendly journalist, Henry Beach Needham, to see what he could find out. Needham diplomatically approached one of the Republican leaders of the House, who told him that the business interests affected by the bill were so large, and there would be so much controversial debate on it, that the leaders had decided not to bring the bill out of committee at that session.

VI

It was at this stage, March 1906, that one of the repercussions of Sinclair's *Jungle*, published the preceding month, reached Roosevelt. Roosevelt was disgusted by *The Jungle*, as most consumers were, but also in the sense that he regarded Sinclair as having made an overdrawn picture. The aspect of *The Jungle* that stirred Roosevelt was its reflection on the U.S. government and his administration of it. There were government inspectors in the packinghouses; if bad beef were being sold, the government inspection service was at fault. Roosevelt, though confident the conditions could not be as bad as Sinclair painted them, determined to get the facts. He called *The Jungle* to the attention of Secretary of Agriculture Wilson, whose department was entrusted with meat inspection at the packinghouses. Wilson sent a committee of three officials from his department to Chicago to investigate. With that, Roosevelt, for the moment, dropped the matter, turning to the Railroad Rate bill and the other preoccupations of his busy winter. Within a very short time, his attention was called back to the beef packers.

The publishing firm of Doubleday, Page & Company, at the time Sinclair had submitted to them the manuscript of *The Jungle*, had taken the precaution, before deciding to publish it, of sending a lawyer to Chicago to determine if conditions at the packinghouses were really as Sinclair pictured them. The lawyer reported that they were, and wrote an article describing what he had seen. This article and two others, one by a former city bacteriologist of Chicago and the other by a physician whose practice was among the stockyard workers—all three only slightly less sensational than *The Jungle*—the firm decided to publish in the magazine it owned, *The World's Work*, edited by Walter Hines Page. Before printing the articles, the firm sent proofs of them to Roosevelt.

Instantly Roosevelt became "all act." Allegations made in fiction by a writer for whose mind Roosevelt had qualified respect was one thing; allegations made by a serious and responsible magazine were quite different. Roosevelt decided the investigation already initiated by Secretary Wilson was not enough, because those investigators, being from the same department as the meat-inspection service, being, indeed, the men responsible for the administration of the inspection service, might be regarded by the public as insufficiently eager to uncover derelictions of fellow workers and subordinates. Roosevelt determined to have an investigating commission free from any possible suspicion of temptation to make a "whitewashing" report.

In the early oral report the commission made to Roosevelt, the detail that most disturbed him was the fact that the government label on the prepared products of the packers was being flagrantly misused. The products carried, conspicuously, the legend: "Inspected and passed by the United States Government." Actually, the only inspection done by the government was confined to the killing-floors, where carcasses were examined and, if found diseased or otherwise unfit, were condemned. No government inspector saw, or was required by the law to see, the later stages of preparation of products put out with the assurance of the government's O.K. The government inspectors saw the killing of the hog, but saw nothing of the many processes that took place between the killing and the shipment of "potted ham."

Roosevelt's immediate impulse was to direct that the use of the government labels be discontinued forthwith. He realized, however, that this would create a sensation which, added to the furor already ablaze because of Sinclair's book and the *World's Work* magazine articles, would do immense damage to the packers' business, not only throughout America but in Europe, especially Germany, where the apparent guarantee of the U.S. government was relied upon to meet official German standards.

Roosevelt felt that with the report of his commission in his hands, and with the publicity raging over the charges from other sources, he could surely secure the enactment of a law which would extend government inspection to all the processes of preparing meat. His intention was not to make public the report of his commission, but merely to take the leaders of Congress into his confidence, and hurry through a proper measure. He had Senator Beveridge of Indiana prepare a carefully worded measure, which was made a rider to the Agricultural Appropriation bill and became known as the Beveridge Amendment. This was introduced into the Senate on May 22, 1906, and three days later, May 25, passed without debate, without the formality of reference to a committee, and without a dissenting vote. Only action by the House remained.

But the packers, panic-stricken by the avalanche of trouble that had struck them, committed the incredible folly of fighting the one measure which could rescue them, which would assure the world that henceforth the government of the United States would inspect every process of packing and by its stamp guarantee the purity of the products. If they had been calm enough to analyze their emotions, they would have realized their panic was caused less by fear of the Meat Inspection bill than by fear of the publication of the commission's report, now in the president's hands. Roosevelt was quite willing to suppress the report—in fact preferred to suppress it—but only on condition of consent to the passage of the Meat Inspection rider.

The packers were too frantic to understand where their own interest lay. Sinclair, taking advantage of the new uproar, printed several articles in newspapers repeating and amplifying the charges in *The Jungle*. The packers in their desperation had some western senators demand that Roosevelt cause his commissioners to issue a public statement saying that some of the worst of Sinclair's charges were unfounded. In their frantic panic the packers wanted to stop everything, quickly. They came on to Washington; they inspired more than a thousand telegrams to Roosevelt protesting against publication of the commission's report; they dragooned the livestock raisers of the country into supporting them, on the theory that the ruin to the packinghouses was already beginning to back up on the livestock raisers; they tried to intimidate Roosevelt's commissioners; surest sign of all that they had lost their heads, they tried, through themselves and their friends in Congress, to intimidate Roosevelt.

Roosevelt responded by sending Congress the commission's preliminary report. In part the report read:

> Usually the workers toil without relief in a humid atmosphere heavy with the odors of rotten wood, decayed meats, stinking offal, and entrails. . . . In a word, we saw meat shovelled from filthy wooden floors, piled on tables rarely washed, pushed from room to room in rotten box carts, in all of which processes it was in the way of gathering dirt, splinters, floor filth, and the expectoration of tuberculous and other diseased workers. . . . Some of these meat scraps were dry, leathery, and unfit to be eaten; and in the heap were found pieces of pigskin and even bits of rope strands and other rubbish. Inquiry evoked the frank admission from the man in charge that this was to be ground up and used in making "potted ham."

From Washington, the commission's report was telegraphed to the press. Everybody read it. As the standing indictment against the packing industry, it supplanted *The Jungle*. Everywhere indignation flamed. The subject was not one the nuances of which could most fittingly be expressed in rhyme, but newspaper versifiers found it inspiring. The *New York Evening Post* parodied a familiar rhyme:

> Mary had a little lamb,
> And when she saw it sicken,
> She shipped it off to Packingtown,
> And now it's labelled chicken.

A sudden drop in sales brought to the packers a receptiveness of mind in which they were willing to listen to those who counseled that the Meat Inspection amendment might have a virtue, that the stamp of the government on their products would be a certificate of character, much needed as the only thing that could restore public confidence and bring back their lost trade. With this realization by the packers came willingness to accept government inspection. The prospect was so bright with new hope that it caused them to forget their previous conviction that the amendment was unconstitutional. In their reversed state of mind, their objection on principle to paternalism and to encroachment of federal jurisdiction on state functions was obscured by the appreciation of its usefulness to them. What was utilitarian to them could not be populistic. They about-faced and became earnest advocates of an inspection law—not exactly the pending measure, but a modification of it strong enough to still public clamor, while not so drastic as to inconvenience them too greatly.

Eventually the Wadsworth substitute, with its provision that the cost of meat inspection be paid by the government, prevailed in the Senate. The momentum of the Meat Inspection amendment carried with it the Pure Food bill, which, its enemies thought, had been safely chloroformed in the committee. "It was amusing," Robert M. Allen wrote in 1927, "to see the lobbyists come hurrying back from their vacations, to the Raleigh and the Willard," prominent Washington hotels.

In the end, the exposures of the packers by Roosevelt's commission, of the patent medicines by the *Ladies' Home Journal* and *Collier's*, of food adulteration and food dyeing by Dr. Wiley and state and city food officials—the aggregate of all these investigations worked into the strengthening of Roosevelt's hand and was invincible. Congress passed the Pure Food and the Meat Inspection bills in June 1906.

VII

There were several sequels, reflections, and conclusions. Organized women had learned that organized liquor is not invincible. The liquor interests, which had been among the most vehement opponents of the purity measures, had met their first important defeat. Partly because of incautious boasting of their power, they broke their own backs. Once defeated, they were weakened permanently. "I have often thought," R. M. Allen wrote in 1927, "in the light of subsequent events, that this defeat hastened the independence of Congress toward the Prohibition question. If that interest had supported a strict bill against adulteration and misbranding of liquors and then supported its enforcement, they would probably have gained enough public sentiment to have successfully postponed national Prohibition."

Another conclusion was in the words of Walter H. Page, editor of *World's Work*. It was, he said, having in mind the passage of both the Railroad Rate bill and the Pure Food and Meat Inspection measures, the most "ferocious, . . . the most loquacious, one of the most industrious, and at times one of the most exciting sessions of recent years. A stimulating breeze was blowing over the national government all through the session."

The "stimulating breeze" was Roosevelt.

The defeat of the "Old Guard" Republican leaders on the pure-food issue led to defeats at the polls. In its implications, sinister to Roosevelt's opponents in Congress, it constituted a mark in the elevation of the president's power—led to recognition that a congressman or senator who resisted legislation advocated by Roosevelt ran the risk of loss of confidence by his own constituents.

PART III

Roosevelt's America

CHAPTER I
Roosevelt's Power

It is simple history to say that the relation Roosevelt had to America at this time, the power he was able to wield, the prestige he enjoyed, the affection he received, the contentment of the people with him—their more than contentment, their zesty pleasure in him—composed the lot of an exceptionally fortunate monarch during a particularly happy period of his reign. The basis of it was the fights Roosevelt made against organized wealth—the sum of which was that he had, in the plain sight of the common man, presented spectacle after spectacle in which business, capital, corporate power took off its hat in the presence of the symbol and spokesman of government.

Some serious folk, thinking this triumph was the whole of the attraction Roosevelt had for the people, wrote exalted tributes in which they pictured him as St. George slaying the dragon. But that kind of service, if it stood alone, would have made Roosevelt not a king but rather an austere Cromwell destroying kings. The battles Roosevelt fought, had they been waged by a LaFollette or a Bryan, or even a Grover Cleveland, might have had the somber sourness of a Puritanical crusade. What brought to Roosevelt the affection that few kings have had, and gave gay delight to the people, was, in addition to his valiance in high affairs, certain qualities of his temperament, facets of his scintillating personality, which included his methods of combat, and the agreeable excitement that accompanied them: the din, the alarums, the thunderclaps of his denunciations, the lightning strokes of his epithets, his occasional ruthlessness of attack, his grinning acceptance of occasional setbacks, the quickness of his rally, the adroitness of his parry; "the fun of him," as one of his New York police captains remarked after his death—"It was not only that he was a great man, but, oh, there was such fun in being led by him." Roosevelt in battle, which was Roosevelt most of the time, was a huge personality endowed with energy almost abnormal, directed by an acute intelligence, lightened by a grinning humor, engaged in incessant action. The spectacle, occupying the biggest headlines in the daily newspapers, gave to the life of that day a zest and stimulus and gaiety such that average Americans who lived through the period carried it as a golden memory, sighing "there'll never be another Roosevelt," and telling their grandchildren that once they saw a giant.

Roosevelt's fighting was so much a part of the life of the period, was so tied up to the newspapers, so geared into popular literature, and even to

President Roosevelt at Inspiration Point, Yosemite, April 1903. (From a photograph by Underwood & Underwood)

the pulpit (which already had begun to turn from formal religion toward civic affairs), as to constitute, for the average man, not merely the high spectacle of the presidency in the ordinary sense but almost the whole of the passing show, the public's principal interest. It caused the people to take delight in Roosevelt as president, to wish nothing better than that he should go on being president, and to be willing, if Roosevelt himself would not run, to accept whomever Roosevelt might choose.

II

Roosevelt in his political battles used many arts. He neglected no old maneuver, and devised several new ones, of which the characteristic was that they were carried out before the public eye, making of the average man always an excited spectator, usually an ardent partisan.

The heart of Roosevelt's method was to inspire headlines. He was the first public man to realize and adapt himself to the relative ebbing of the power of the editorial compared to the news despatch and the cartoon, the first to have a technique for getting the advantage of the headline. Probably, presidents before him had known the thing that Roosevelt meant when he said, "The White House is a bully pulpit," but no president before him or after used the White House so frequently or effectively for pulpiteering and other forms of promotion of his policies and purposes. More than any other president he understood that everything coming out of the White House is news, and turned that fact to his advantage. He was the earliest American public man to grasp the syllogism that on Sunday all normal business and most other activi-

Speaking at Boise City, Idaho, May 28, 1903. (From a photograph by Underwood & Underwood)

ties are suspended; that Sunday is followed by Monday; and that, therefore, the columns of the Monday papers present the minimum of competition for public attention—whence many of the public statements, epithets, and maledictions with which Roosevelt conducted his fights were timed to explode in the pages of the Monday-morning newspapers.

Cartoons—these Roosevelt inspired as the morning sun awakens life. At any gusty word from him, cartoons filled the air like autumn leaves in a high wind. The cartoon, as a method of political combat, was not new; but until the 1890s it had been confined to weekly periodicals, and was handicapped therefore by some remoteness from instant timeliness; the process of reproduction had involved time-consuming tooling on wooden blocks by handworking engravers. About the time Roosevelt became an important figure in American life, a photoengraving process had been invented which permitted the making of a chemically etched zinc block within a few minutes after completion of the artist's pen drawing. Thus the daily newspapers were enabled to use cartoons freely, thus cartoonists were able to make their drawings within an hour of receipt of the current news, and thus the newspapers were able to present them to the public a few hours later.

Into this new development, Roosevelt, with his incessant activity, fitted like a Heaven-devised engine. A cartoonist, going to his office in the late afternoon, need hardly worry about finding a topic for his cartoon; Roosevelt would have been sure to have done something or said something. Some essential quality in Roosevelt's temperament and in his characteristic

actions was kin to the spirit in which cartoons had to be made, lent itself to the
nervous tension that was a condition of
the cartoonist's art. Upon the inspiration
of a phrase from him, cartoonists' pencils
swung to paper like a needle to the north.
His teeth, grim in contest or grinning in
triumph, were Heaven-made for the cari-
caturist's art, and likewise his thick-lensed
glasses, happily adapted to portraying
glaring looks—his whole physical makeup,
as well as his temperament, ideal for both
the subject and the spirit of the cartoonists' technique.

Roosevelt, in a quiet academic address
about international relations, said: "Speak
softly—but carry a big stick," and a myriad
cartoons pictured him as a mighty fighter
swinging a hundred variations of a war
club against the dragon railroads. He said
"strenuous life," and a thousand pencils
drew him riding at top speed in pursuit of
some malefactor of great wealth. He said
"the spear that knows no brother," and in
a hundred newspapers, harassed amassers
of money shrank from a spear held in
Roosevelt's burly fist. He said "square
deal" and cowering figures with dollar
signs upon their foreheads and labeled

*Postcard of 1907. During Roo-
sevelt's presidency the "Teddy Bear"
was, to older people, a symbol of the
president's fun-loving and playful
qualities and, to children, a welcome
and beloved addition to the menagerie of toyland—no doll family
was complete without its snow-
white, awkward, laughter-provok-
ing bear.*

"trusts" listened to doom from an avenging god that had big teeth and
wore glasses. He demanded regulation of the railroads, and the newspapers
blossomed with pictorial melodrama, in which the railroads played the role
of villain. A railroad train emerging from a tunnel lending itself to the suggestion of a maddened wild animal at the mouth of his den, while Roosevelt, always in the role of a hero, facing the dragon, provided the kind of
dramatic action the cartoonists loved to picture. At the end of a fight he
once said "delighted," and on a hundred million newspaper pages, pleased
teeth purred "dee-lighted" over some conquest of a trust.

Nine times out of ten the cartoon was of Roosevelt in combat; always,
almost without exception, it was Roosevelt in action. From having lived
through the period and from having searched the files during the preparation of this history, I venture to say that not among the literally myriads of
Roosevelt cartoons are half a dozen in which he sleeps, or even rests. Once,
seeking to symbolize his retirement from the presidency, I worked for days
with an artist to devise a picture in which Roosevelt, his labors over, should
enjoy repose. We gave it up. The thing could not be done, was contrary no
less to art than to nature.

"*I am the State!*" Puck *and some of Roosevelt's other critics felt or pretended that they felt alarms lest he should constitute himself Theodore I, King of America. (From* Puck, *1904)*

Roosevelt "rough-riding" the world. (L. D. Bradley in the Chicago Daily News)

His favorite author. This cartoon of a farmer reading one of Roosevelt's messages was a favorite with the latter, who had it framed and hung above the mantel of his study. (Lowry in The Chronicle *[Chicago])*

III

Roosevelt realized the power inherent in the popular magazines, and took pains to keep in touch with the editors and writers of them, young men, as a rule, as ardent as himself. By reading the periodicals diligently, and by more intimate contacts, he knew the personnels of their staffs, knew the individual traits and biases of the writers, knew even the office politics of the periodicals as adequately as he followed the internal politics of his own party committees. If there was in a magazine office an owner, editor, or writer unsympathetic to his policies, Roosevelt took especial pains to maintain a balancing friendliness with others of the staff, doing it all with the habitual directness and casual boldness of his spirit. If a magazine printed an article with which he disagreed, he would write a letter to the author or editor, or have a talk with him, in which he would express his dissent with the forcefulness that was customary with him, a letter in which belligerency and graciousness were so mingled as to seem to say, "You can print this if you want to and we will fight it out before the public; or you can come to see me in fair friendliness and I will give you the facts that will enable you to see the light." The more direct acquaintance of the writer of this history with Roosevelt began with a not wholly approving editorial allusion I had written about one of Roosevelt's judicial appointments, which drew from Roosevelt a letter of eleven typewritten pages, with many interlineations, in which he reviewed every one of the judicial appointments he had made in the six years of his presidency, detailing, as to each, the considerations that had determined the selection. If a new author wrote something helpful to one of Roosevelt's fights, or otherwise interesting to him, the writer was likely, soon, to glow at a White House luncheon, at which his experience was apt to be that described by one such author: "You go into Roosevelt's presence, you feel his eyes upon you, you listen to him, and you go home and wring the personality out of your clothes."

This cartoon typifies the conception great masses of the people had of Roosevelt during his presidency. (From the Pittsburgh Gazette-Times*)*

It would be inaccurate historically, and unfair to Roosevelt, to imply that his cultivation of magazine writers was merely a cold technique for advancing his causes. His relations with authors, while they were of advantage to him, were a spontaneous incident of the enormous range of his interest in varied kinds of human beings. Roosevelt was interested in, and therefore had the power of stimulating, every sort of writer and artist—poets like Edwin Arlington Robinson and Bliss Carman, novelists like Owen Wister and Kathleen Norris, historians like James Ford Rhodes and the English G. M. Trevelyan, naturalists like John Muir and John Burroughs, artists like Augustus Saint-Gaudens and Frederic Remington.

All these—artists, writers, poets, and sculptors—were stimulated by Roosevelt to new endeavor. And not only they. Everybody in America, in every sort of career, from teachers and naturalists to cowboys and prize-fighters, seemed to derive from Roosevelt in the White House a lift toward higher functioning. Partly the widespread stimulus arose from the number of representatives of diverse lines of work or art with whom Roosevelt had contact—during no presidency did the White House visiting list contain so many names, or reflect interest in so wide a gamut of human activity. Partly the increased elation with which nearly everybody in America went to his job in the morning arose from awareness of the obvious delight that Roosevelt had in his own job. Partly the stimulus Roosevelt radiated to the average man arose from consciousness that Roosevelt was making the fight for the common man, for the preservation of individuality against the irking chains of organization, corporate power.

Writers, functioning at joyous speed upon ignition from the emanations of Roosevelt's personality, kept the pages of the popular magazines glowing with support of Roosevelt's crusades. The friendly writers who took inspiration direct from him were sometimes called, jeeringly, Roosevelt's "fair-haired boys." A wider group who took their inspiration from many sources, and who as frequently inspired Roosevelt as they were inspired by him, came to be recognized as a definite school of writing, sometimes called the "literature of exposure," which historically has a fairly important place in both the letters and the politics of the early part of this century. "Exposure," said George W. Alger in the *Atlantic Monthly* for August 1907 "forms the typical current literature of our daily life. . . . They expose in countless pages the sordid and depressing rottenness of our politics; the hopeless apathy of our good citizens; the remorseless corruption of our great financiers and business men. . . . They show us our social sore spots, like the three cheerful friends of Job. They show us the growth of business 'graft,' the gangrene of personal dishonesty among an honorable people, the oppressing increase in the number of bribe-takers and bribe-givers. They tell us of the riotous extravagance of the rich, and the growth of poverty. . . . The achievement of the constructive elements of society has been neglected to give space to these spicy stories of graft and greed."

The media for these jeremiads consisted chiefly of low-priced maga-

zines, made possible by innovations in the art of printing—glazed paper
made from wood pulp, much cheaper than rag paper, and an advance in
photography followed by improvement in the art of printing photographs.
The inexpensiveness, accompanied by attractiveness, thus made possible
was first utilized to print, at a price of ten or fifteen cents, magazines which
aimed at entertainment alone, and achieved it, in typical cases, by liberal
extravagance with photographs accompanying casually improvised articles

PRESIDENT ROOSEVELT IS RESTING AT OYSTER BAY

First he chops down a few trees.

Then takes a cross-country canter.

And a twenty-minute brisk walk.

After which he gives the children a wheel-barrow ride.

He then rests for a moment

By which time he is ready for breakfast.

*Cartoons always emphasized Roosevelt in action. This one is by John T. McCutcheon of the
Chicago Tribune.*

about actresses or queens, or persons deemed socially important. Then the greatest magazine genius America has ever known, Samuel S. McClure, created a fifteen-cent magazine which, in its influence upon public opinion, was hardly less important than Roosevelt himself, and of which Roosevelt took advantage.*

McClure, without particularly intending to, as a spontaneous expression of his personality, achieved a union of what is interesting and what is important by commissioning writers with a background of scholarship and mental habits of accuracy and thoroughness, such as Ida M. Tarbell, to make clear to the understanding of the average man the intricacies and chicaneries which lie

Samuel S. McClure, founder of the school of literature of exposure.

in the area where business comes in contact with politics. Tarbell's "History of the Standard Oil Company," starting in *McClure's* during 1902, followed, in the same magazine, by Lincoln Steffens's "Shame of the Cities" and Ray Stannard Baker's "The Railroad on Trial," presently inspired other writers to follow and other magazine publishers to imitate.

<h1 style="text-align:center">IV</h1>

After the literature of exposure had enjoyed its remarkable vogue for some five or six years, it passed into a phase that not only impaired the value of it to Roosevelt and his reforms, but gave concern to him in his role of watchful guardian of the nation's good.

The public appetite for exposure continued eager as ever. Because of that, inevitably, as always, promoters arose to commercialize it, imitators to cheapen it and to offer the public a decidedly inferior brand. Magazines very different from the originating *McClure's* stridently adopted exposure as a specialty; writers very distant in background and method from Tarbell hurried to the market with wares for which the description "inferior" would be eulogistic. A sensational stock market operator, Thomas W. Lawson, who had been a handyman for captains of industry in some of their more sordid adventures, wrote the secrets he had shared with them, under the heading "Frenzied Finance," and added a new name, "the System," to the phrases of odium, with which were designated the interlocking chicaneries of big business. That Lawson's motive might have been something less than conscientious scholarship is suggested by the contract he made

*McClure was Sullivan's sometime employer. —D.R.

Thomas W. Lawson, of Boston, who turned, for a brief period, from the practice of "Frenzied Finance" to the exposure of it. (Courtesy of the New York World)

with a theretofore obscure magazine, *Everybody's,* in which he asked for no compensation, stipulating only that the publishers should spend at least $50,000 in advertising the articles, to which Lawson on his own account added at least five times the sum, with the result that the circulation of *Everybody's Magazine* multiplied in one year from less than 150,000 to more than five times that. What Lawson may have lacked in experience as a writer, or in conformity to conventional standards in his own decidedly bizarre business practices, he made up for in a most extraordinary vividness of characterization, which caused crowds to clamor at newsstands for the monthly installments of *Everybody's*—the crowds, including the financiers whom Lawson exposed, eager to end the suspense in which during thirty days of every month they wondered what ghastly secret of the underworld of high finance Lawson would tell next. There was plenty of fact in Lawson's narrative—the evidence was intrinsic and was also to be found in collateral exposures of an official sort—but Lawson's facts were so mingled with fantastic emanations from his extraordinarily ebullient personality, and Lawson's own performances in the field of stock speculation were so inconsistent with the role of soldier for the common good, as to cause newspapers justly to belittle him. The public became satiated—by the end of four years of it, Lawson felt called upon, as in 1908 he went back to his stock speculation, to turn his extraordinary powers of vituperation upon the ungrateful public themselves, calling them "gelatine-spined shrimps,"

ONE LAST WORD

If it should happen that my reports arrive to-day and you should read them in my to-morrow's advertisement, with the word "Buy," I will advise the purchase of Nevada-Utah only up to 20 for the present. This will not mean that I advise buying orders to be limited at 20, as I advise that under no circumstances should any one buy at over five points above the closing to-night. That is, if Nevada-Utah closes to-night at 10, see to it that your broker is instructed to-night to buy at not over 15 to-morrow—if my advertisement says "Buy." If, after the excitement of the first two hours has subsided—I predict a new "Wildest two hours in stocks," with transactions of 200,000 to 300,000 shares for the day—the price is still above 15, I will advise further as to price limit in my advertisement of the following day.

THOMAS W. LAWSON

A section of a Lawson advertisement in one of his many stock manipulation campaigns.

"saffron-blooded apes."

William R. Hearst, expanding from daily newspapers into periodicals, bought the *Cosmopolitan Magazine* and announced, in the month in which Roosevelt's railroad rate bill was launched in the Senate, February 1906, a series of exposures which, he told the world, would be "the most vascular and virile" thus far printed. Condescendingly, Hearst's announcement said of his predecessors: "Well-meaning and amazingly industrious persons writing without inspiration . . . have been able to pile before magazine readers indiscriminate masses of arid facts." From such prosaic

William R. Hearst.

tedium Hearst promised to steer clear; his exposures would be "by the masterly hand of David Graham Phillips."

Phillips was a novelist. In the articles he wrote for Hearst, which he called "The Treason of the Senate," he demonstrated that in senses more subtle than the obvious one, fiction may be far from fact. He was unfamiliar with his material and with the background of the picture he purported to paint. Instead of the austere setting down of fact, which had been the very essence of the literature of exposure, and which had carried conviction to the reader, Phillips substituted tawdry literary epithets, "the Senate's craftily convenient worship of the Mumbo-Jumbo mask and mantle of its own high respectability." For the stark citation of documents that had given convincing force to Tarbell's exposures of railroad rebates, Phillips substituted—sure sign, in a writer, of haste and paucity of fact—lavish exclamation points. "The treason of the Senate!"

It was part of Roosevelt's art of winning the decision before the court of public opinion to dissociate himself from the more extreme among his own partisans and followers—from what he himself later called the "lunatic fringe" that rushes into the comet's tail of every reform movement. This course he followed now. Not forgetful of the help the responsible writers of exposure were to him, to the railroad rate bill, and to many other good causes, he took care that his rebuke should apply only to the irresponsible ones. The time and the occasion for his rebuke were determined by his reading "with great indignation a certain magazine," containing a loose diatribe, just before a private dinner of the Gridiron Club on March 17, 1906. At the dinner, Roosevelt took as the theme for his speech a passage from Bunyan's *Pilgrim's Progress:* "the Man with the Muckrake, the man who could look no way but downward with the muckrake in his hand; who was offered a celestial crown for his muckrake but who would neither look up nor regard the crown he was offered but continued to rake to himself the filth of the floor."

Although the speech, following Gridiron Club tradition, was not published, gossip about Roosevelt's allusion got around. In the amount of comment he heard, he realized the potentiality in the chance inspiration that had led him to revive Bunyan's generally forgotten figure of speech. With Roosevelt, to recognize opportunity was to put Fboth arms around it, quickly and firmly, and so he installed the term "muckraker" in the American language.

Gleefully the conservative portion of the press fastened the name "muckraker" on each and all, good and bad, among the writers in behalf of reform. With equal promptness, and equal glee—and with a good deal of generosity, considering the circumstances—all the writers of exposure accepted the epithet that was meant for some of them, and in the eyes of most of the public "muckraker" became a term of approval.

V

On his fourth day in the presidency, Roosevelt, in an hour's talk with the Washington correspondent of the *New York Evening Post*, revealed as much of his plans for his administration as he had had time to make. The correspondent, in one of those "indirect discourse" despatches that sometimes follow confidential talks between presidents and newspapermen, emphasized an ambition close to Roosevelt's heart, one that he was especially eager to achieve. Roosevelt wanted to "see the South back in full communion" with the rest of the nation. Whenever a Republican administration was in power at Washington—and with the exception of Cleveland's two terms there had been none but Republican administrations since before the Civil War—the South, partly from its own choice and partly from lingering hostility toward it, remained "standing on the outside." This Roosevelt deplored. He wanted to see the South as much at home in Washington under all conditions, as the North and West, and he "would take great pride" in bringing about this final step of reconciliation. In the carrying out of his purpose, he told the correspondent, he would, in making appointments to office in southern states, take sympathetic account of the South's peculiar problems and its point of view. Naturally, as a party man, Roosevelt would feel obliged to give preference to Republicans over Democrats, but "if it came to a question between an unfit Republican and a fit Democrat," he would "not hesitate a moment to choose the Democrat."

Had Roosevelt been timid, or expedient; had his good impulses been limited by political caution, his advanced policy toward the South could have stopped with the recognition of Democrats. But Roosevelt's restlessly

*Theodore Roosevelt and Booker T. Washington at Tuskegee, Alabama, October 24, 1905.
(Courtesy American Press Assn.)*

adventurous mind proposed to deal with the South's great incubus, the in-
termeshed social and political issue of race. The Negro in the South, Roosevelt said, "must take his chances like the rest; if he be a man who has
earned the respect of his white neighbors . . . he has nothing to fear from
President Roosevelt because of his color." At the same time, a Negro who
has failed to live up to this standard "will have no favor because he is black
or because he is a Republican. By this measure [the respect of his white
neighbors] every negro who aspires to office will be tested."

"The standard of personal character and civic virtue which the President
will set up for the negro's emulation"—so he told the correspondent—"is
best embodied in Booker T. Washington."

It was a statesmanlike wish, to heal the forty-year sore of sectionalism, to
show the South that a Republican administration could have the same attitude toward it as toward other sections. For this aim, Roosevelt had, besides the ordinary motive of patriotism, the not overlooked one of doing a
service to the Republican Party. In addition, Roosevelt had toward the
South a personal relation which at once partly inspired his purpose and
equipped him to carry it out: His mother had been a southerner, from
Georgia; two of his mother's brothers had fought on the Confederate side
in the Civil War; and his father, rather than bear arms against his wife's
family, had refrained from enlisting with the Union troops, had confined
himself to the Civil War equivalent of Red Cross work.

Roosevelt began by making appointments that electrified the South with
hope of a new day, of a place in the nation's councils comparable to what it

had had before the Civil War. Incredulously at first, and then warmly, the South applauded. From the best papers in the North and from thoughtful persons everywhere, came praise. Roosevelt was not a man to have grandiose visions about his place in history, but it is not surprising that there came to him his earliest glimpse of what every president sometimes thinks about if he has any imagination at all, the realization that he has got hold of something with which to "mark his administration in history." Roosevelt consciously set the political regeneration of the South as the first of his ambitions.

Then, suddenly, on October 18, 1901, only five weeks after taking office, his whole policy toward the South encountered devastating contretemps. Unexpectedly, he stubbed his toe—stubbed it in a manner and with a disastrousness that, to a man less buoyant than Roosevelt, might have brought permanent discouragement.

Roosevelt had settled upon Booker Washington as the foremost Negro to encourage and to set up as an example. Washington, born in slavery, had climbed to a leadership role and had enveloped a great Negro industrial school, Tuskegee Institute, in Alabama. By his methods and example he stimulated the Negro to better things, and did not offend whites. All his counsel to his race was that they should not seek social equality, but forget it; that they should strive to gain the respect and good opinion of the whites by industry, thrift, self-discipline, and wholesome family life—just the homely virtues that appealed to Roosevelt. Roosevelt decided he would appoint to office occasionally Negroes recommended by Washington, or who shared Washington's views.

With this purpose in mind, and wishing at once to encourage Washington and to get his advice, Roosevelt summoned him to the White House. Washington, undoubtedly seeing in the invitation an aspect which must have escaped Roosevelt's attention, took pains to make his visit inconspicuous. His precautions, as respects his own actions, were successful. But for a trivial detail of White House routine, the custom of entering the names of visitors in a book, Washington might have come and gone with the unobtrusiveness he aimed at successfully achieved. It happened that a reporter for the *Washington Post*, looking over the day's guest list, saw Washington's name, thought of it vaguely as well known, the sort of public or semi-public name that a reporter should mention, and wrote the kind of item he would have written about any other distinguished visitor. The managing editor of the *Post* either must not have read the item or must have been as unaware as his reporter of just who Booker Washington was; the item appeared the next morning in an obscure position near the bottom of an inside page: "Booker T. Washington, of Tuskegee, Alabama, dined with the President last evening."

Despite the meagerness of the item, and its inconspicuousness among the routine news, its significance was realized by the Washington correspondents of southern newspapers. Their despatches next day led to a fuming of headline and editorial writers that inspired one of Roosevelt's less known but characteristically vivid phrases, "torrential journalism."

Booker T. Washington.

"White men of the South," shrieked the *New Orleans Times-Democrat*, "how do you like it? White women of the South, how do YOU like it?" The *Memphis Scimitar*, prevented by the immensity of its indignation from practicing the keen-edged deftness suggested by its name, grabbed the biggest brick in sight; Roosevelt, the *Scimitar* said, committed "the most damnable outrage ever perpetrated by any citizen of the United States when he invited a nigger to dine with him at the White House." The *Richmond Times* went to grotesque lengths in imputing to Roosevelt ideas that no sane person could believe ever entered his head: "It means the President is willing that negroes shall mingle freely with whites in the social circle—that white women may receive attentions from negro men; it means that there is no racial reason in his opinion why whites and blacks may not marry and intermarry, why the Anglo-Saxon may not mix negro blood with his blood." The *Raleigh Post* jeered in rhyme:

Booker Washington holds the boards—
    The President dines a nigger.
Precedents are cast aside—*
    Put aside with vigor; Black and white sit side by side,
    As Roosevelt dines a nigger.

These were some of the expressions that were printed. In violence they fell short of the anonymous letters that came to the White House, many serving notice that for the rest of his term Roosevelt and all members of his family had better not set foot in the South.

The sincerity of the southern press was as great as its words were violent; nevertheless, most southern editors were cool enough to be shrewd. They recognized that chance had given them the means to combat Roosevelt's purpose to make the South Republican, or bipartisan, and they grasped it, eagerly. They had needed it long before Roosevelt announced his purpose. As early as 1896, the unity of the South for Democracy had been shaken by the "free-silver" platform that Bryan forced upon the party; many of the

*Roosevelt was not the first president to entertain a colored man in the White House. Grover Cleveland invited Frederick Douglass and his white wife to a congressional reception.

best men in the South, their conservatism shocked by Bryan's radical heresies, had helped to form the Gold Democratic Party, and had voted for its candidates, failing, for the first time in their lives, to vote the regular Democratic ticket. As the menace of free silver waned, and the Gold Democratic Party died for lack of reason to exist, these conservative southern Democrats, having gone through an experience of temporary separation from their traditional faith, were susceptible to permanent departure. Much of the South, much of the best of it was fallow for the Republican plow and for Roosevelt's project.

Now, Roosevelt, through the Booker Washington incident, had given the Democratic press of the South material to repel the Republican invader. Cleverly, they made the most of it, phrasing their comment in just the terms which seemed to say finis to Roosevelt's ambition, which served notice on Roosevelt that he could never recover his lost prestige.

Roosevelt's hope of bringing the South to comity with the North, and to tolerance of the Republican Party and of himself, quickly met with reality. By the Booker Washington incident, race became as securely a reason for the South remaining solidly Democratic as at any time since the Civil War.

For once Roosevelt declined a challenge, shrugged his shoulders under a shower of epithets, chose not to match violence with violence. What had

An amusing book, My Negro Policy! A southern cartoon inspired by resentment at Roosevelt's having Booker Washington as a table guest. (L. C. Gregg in the Atlantic Constitution)

Chorus—"There is no South, there is no North, there is no East or West." The South, disaffected since the Civil War, was encouraged by Roosevelt to resume its historic place in the political life of the Union. The cartoonist has here successfully depicted the pleasure of the entire country at the success of one of Roosevelt's overtures to the South. (Reynolds in the Tacoma Ledger)

happened caused no diminution in his zeal to conciliate the South; and he knew that to reply to his detractors, however unjust their attacks, would only jeopardize his permanent purpose.

As part of his determination to have the South understand him, Roosevelt made more journeys into that section than any other president before or since. On his earlier trips crowds gathered, drawn by curiosity; later, under the spell of Roosevelt's personality, they came to be able to cheer, spontaneously, and with the generous heartiness that was the South's characteristic. For the moment, they forgot what Republicanism meant to them, they forgot Booker Washington, they forgot the Civil War. On southern trips that Roosevelt made in 1905, hours before his train was due to arrive, people assembled by the hundreds and thousands, packing the streets about the railroad stations in the cities and congesting the roads leading to country tank stops. On his arrival, even before they caught sight of him, they would break into the noisy tribute that humanity in the mass always renders to a great leader. The roar of greeting they gave him was not a semi-tone less enthusiastic and affectionate than the receptions he got in the West and the North. He was their president, their "Teddy."

Most concrete of all, in 1904, when Roosevelt was a candidate for a new term, he received more votes in the South than any previous Republican candidate; by carrying Missouri he made a sensational breach in the Democratic solid South.

CHAPTER 2

The Railroad Rate Fight

T he railroads in their early days were, with regard to the rates they could charge for transportation, as immune from regulation by government as any other owner of private property; they were wholly free from statutory regulation, wholly free from administrative supervision by government; they were, in their power to fix arbitrarily the price of what they sold (transportation), on the same footing with mill owners, farmers, merchants, ship owners, physicians, and other producers of goods or sellers of services; each had in this respect the same status with respect to government, the broad legend common to all being, "A man can do what he will with his own." The practice, with the railroads, as expressed in a phrase of the day, was to "charge all the traffic will bear."

As respects this immunity from regulation, railroads were on the same basis as other forms of private property. But railroads had a right, a privilege, that other forms of private property had not. Railroads had the right called "eminent domain."

The possession by the railroads of this special right was the reason for the raising of a question about their immunity from government interference with the price at which they sold their services. And the raising of this question is the beginning of the history of railroad rate regulation.

II

F or their rights-of-way, early railroad builders needed narrow strips of land which had to be acquired, in most cases, through purchase. Usually the owner was willing to sell, or even, if he believed the presence of the railroad would be an advantage, to donate the necessary strip of land. But there were occasions when an owner, seeing his opportunity to hold up the railroad, demanded an exorbitant price. And other occasions when a farmer, moved by his affection for the land that was almost a part of himself, or instinctively fearful of the disruption which the railroad would bring to his familiar and beloved ways of life, or suspicious about the city strangers who would be brought to his door, or solicitous for the safety and peace of mind of his cattle and horses that would be terrified by the engine's noise and endangered by its speed, was flatly unwilling to sell at all.

When such cases arose, the railroads went to the courts, called attention

Probably the first locomotive in America driven by steam upon a track. Colonel John Stevens in 1826 invented a multitubular boiler and experimented on his own tracks in Hoboken, near the present Lackawanna terminal. (Courtesy Stevens Institute of Technology)

to their right of eminent domain (granted to them in their charters), and pleaded that the courts, in accordance with that ancient doctrine, should condemn the land, bestow title upon them, and fix the amount of compensation to be paid. The courts always granted the plea (unless there was some defect in the railroad's charter, or other technical legal objection).

Eminent domain traditionally had been a principle associated chiefly with a *public service*, granted to forms of property affected with the special attribute of performing a public service. Eminent domain could only be conferred by government; it was a grant by government of a portion of its own prerogative; it was analogous to the three supreme controls which government exercises over private property: the police power, taxation, and expropriation or destruction during wartime.

Only upon the representation by the railroad promoters that their lines would perform a public service, did legislatures grant, and courts apply, the doctrine of eminent domain for the railroads' benefit.

Without the privilege of eminent domain, the railroads could not have been built—but it was the possession of this privilege that ultimately led to their subjection to public control of their rates. It was the spectacle of railroads exercising the right of eminent domain that caused the public to reason that if the railroads had this extraordinary privilege, it ought to be accompanied by an analogous right on the part of the public.

III

The actions of men who exercised their ambitions and talents in the building and managing of railroads created opportunity for other men, who exercised other ambitions and other talents in the world of politics. Thus there arose, especially in the Midwest, certain political leaders violently antagonistic to the railroads, whose antirailroad agitation, spreading east and west and south, infected most of the country. One among these stood out, not necessarily because of his greater wisdom, more because of certain personal qualities.

Robert M. LaFollette by birth had the temperament of a dramatic tragedian. By the circumstances of his youth he acquired a sense of resentment against cosmos that made him a crusader. Because of the conditions of his time and place, he took the railroads as the object of his crusading zeal. His antirailroad bias came early. "As a boy on the farm," he wrote, "I heard and felt this [antirailroad] movement . . . swirling about me; and I felt the indignation which it expressed in such a way that I suppose I have never fully lost the effect of that early impression."

A dog-eared copy of Henry George's *Progress and Poverty*, loaned to LaFollette by a philosophical blacksmith neighbor, stimulated the youth's grim zest for combat against injustice. At the University of Wisconsin he got the grounding in economics and government that later enabled him to make vivid to farmer audiences the intricacies of the effects of railroad rates on their own fortunes; no public man of his day equaled him in the energy with which he dug into economic data or in the skill with which he made statistics support and confirm his theories.

By about 1895, LaFollette was set in the intellectual, moral, and emotional mold that determined his role in national politics. In whatever stand he took on any issue, he was always dramatic and heroic, ever the crusader against wrong, eternally the champion of the underdog (whom he dramatized as wholly virtuous and always right). He visualized himself, and insisted that his followers regard him, as the faithful servant of the people, the chosen of fate to lead moral causes—most of the moral causes of the time and place being embraced in opposition to the railroads. When he ran for governor, he made the issues mainly regulation of the railroads, heavier taxation upon them, abolition of the passes with which they kept their political power—and a proposal for a novel "direct primary," which should supplant the convention system and thereby render impotent the political bosses.

As governor, LaFollette, after years of denunciation of the boss system, was himself the boss of Wisconsin. He was a boss of a new and utterly different type, who worked always in the interest of the common man as he saw it, who discarded the sordid methods of the older type—and yet a boss, autocratic, imperious, peremptory, practicing toward his apostles a dictatorial insistence upon obedience such as no boss of the older type would ever have dared attempt. Whoever opposed him, whoever disagreed with him, became, ipso facto, one with Lucifer. Whoever, having once been with him, thereafter failed to give 100 percent allegiance to every one of LaFollette's courses, by that fact became guilty certainly of sedition and presumably of corruption, and was exiled and pursued with a ruthlessness even greater than LaFollette practiced against his avowed enemies. He was all grimness. It is doubtful if LaFollette, in his mature life, ever threw back his head and laughed heartily.

Much more than by his official acts as governor, and in a territory that extended far beyond the boundaries of Wisconsin, LaFollette by his campaigns, by the paper *The State* that he and his friends conducted, and by literally thousands of campaign speeches, as well as lyceum and Chautauqua lectures that he delivered up and down the country—LaFollette, with the aid of other leaders, gave to the old Granger antirailroad movement a momentum that by 1906 had reached the proportions and the characteristics of what politicians call—at once a vivid description and an acknowledgment of readiness to run for shelter—a "prairie fire."

As one brand flung off by the now nationwide conflagration, LaFollette himself was elected to the U.S. Senate, where he took his seat on January 4, 1906. LaFollette's arrival in the Senate coincided, almost to the exact day, with the introduction of the Hepburn railroad rate bill in the House, and with Roosevelt's determination to drive that bill through Congress. LaFollette was too new in the Senate, and also too mordantly radical, to have much hand in shaping that legislation. Indeed, his incapacity to cooperate with other men, his suspicion against all men whose notions did not coincide identically with his, made LaFollette a handicap rather than a help to Roosevelt. But the prairie fire of antirailroad feeling that LaFollette had been building in the Midwest over a period of ten years was one of the causes of the public demand for rate regulation that Roosevelt took up. It was also one of the principal agencies that Roosevelt had to aid him in the fight.

IV

Roosevelt, becoming president by accident, found himself head of a party that had not, nationally, taken notice of the country's antirailroad sentiment, a party, indeed, that, except locally in a few states, was sympathetic to the whole nexus of conservative interests of which the railroads composed the principal element. It was the Democratic Party that had taken the antirailroad side, had, in its platforms of 1896 and 1900, demanded and promised relief from railroad inequities. Roosevelt almost immediately began a series of steps with respect to railroads and other corporate business interests, which in their entirety composed one of the historically most important aspects of the Roosevelt era, the gradual separation of the Republican Party from the conservative point of view, its ultimate complete identification, by the time Roosevelt's presidency ended, with a point of view which the political thought of the time denominated "Progressive."

Within three months after his accession to the presidency, Roosevelt, in his first message to Congress, in December 1901, proposed relief from one specific railroad inequity, the granting by railroads of rebates to favored shippers. This Congress, a little over a year later, enacted. In 1904 and 1905, Roosevelt, in several speeches in various parts of the country, laid down a policy of broad and effective regulation of railroad rates.

Characteristically, as an accurate expression of his fundamental and rarely interrupted avoidance of radicalism, Roosevelt surrounded and cushioned and balanced his demand with safeguarding assurances: "I should emphatically protest against improperly radical or hasty action. I do not believe in the government interfering with private business any more than is necessary." Roosevelt's proposal indeed could be regarded as having the purpose of protecting the railroads, and the institution of private property, by warding off demands for more drastic action. "In my judgment," he said, taking account of a type of radical sentiment that Bryan was shortly to propose, "public ownership of railroads is highly undesirable and would probably in this country entail far-reaching disaster."

For his reasonableness, Roosevelt, as is often the fate of one who takes the middle of the road, received bricks from both sides. His action was denounced by LaFollette and other spokesmen of antirailroad sentiment, as a weak expedient, an odious compromise. From the side of the railroads and their allied interests, Roosevelt's proposal was attacked as, in the words of their principal spokesman in the Senate, Joseph Foraker of Ohio, "contrary to the spirit of our institutions and of such drastic and revolutionary character that . . . the consequences are likely to be most unusual and far-reaching."

The railroads and their allied interests charged that Roosevelt's proposal was an assault upon the rights of private property. Because the railroads so interpreted it, the average man regarded it as a rescue of himself and his interests from what he had come to visualize corporate private property and its practices as being—regarded it as his fight against the head, heart, and all the tentacles of organized wealth. The railroads' network of lines up and down the continent composed the picture of far-flung power which the people had been taught to call the "Octopus"; their alliances, through interlocking directorates, with banks, insurance companies and industrial corporations, and the alliance of all these combined with politics, composed what flamed through the political controversy of the time as "The System"; their entrenched advantages, gained and held through their hold on Congress and legislatures, were the "Vested Interests" and, in LaFollette's phrase, "Special Privilege"; their owners, including those who manipulated them, and the bankers who participated, were, in the phrase of the sensational Hearst press, the "Plunderbund."

The sum of which was that to fight the railroads was to fight, practically without exception, all the organized wealth in the United States. Wealth had, as its spokesmen, generals, and lieutenants, much more than half of the Republican membership of the Senate, including nearly all the abler ones and, without exception, all the senators who held the key places of power on committees. Wealth had also on its side, at the beginning, many Democratic senators, some because they were, as much as any Republicans, willing servants of power, and others because they clung to the traditional Democratic policy of opposition to concentration of power in the federal government.

V

Even before the ultimate battle over the rate bill began, as early as August 1905, the newspapers, normally recording the activities Roosevelt engaged in, the events and movements he stimulated, reported "Interstate Commerce Commission Begins Investigation of Combinations Between Railroads and Private Car Lines." On December 5, they reported Roosevelt's message to Congress with its demand for legislation to "prevent unreasonable and unjustifiable rates"; on December 11, that "Attorney-General Moody Directs All United States Attorneys to Prosecute All Railroads Shown to Be Giving Rebates." As the rate bill fight grew hot, investigations that had been initiated months before by Roosevelt or agencies under him, together with court action and miscellaneous movements he had incited, provided from time to time such headlines as PROSECUTE RAILROADS NEXT and AFTER A RAILROAD PRESIDENT: Roosevelt Hopes to Convict One or More.

The cannonade of headlines took on cumulative frequency—occasionally, indeed, two or more jostled each other on the same front page, the general saturation of the atmosphere causing *Life* to remark, plaintively, that "there are a few solvent and respectable persons left in the country who have not yet been investigated."

The president's attacks on the trusts and his demand for railroad regulation dominated the front pages throughout the early months of 1906. But in the newspaper offices on the night of April 18, Roosevelt's latest denunciation encountered collision with a despatch from California. When one looked at the papers the following morning to find the sensational headlines that such a message inevitably called for, one found that instead of Roosevelt-inspired news the entire first page was occupied by a single story—on which the headlines were:

EARTHQUAKE LAYS FRISCO IN RUINS

Entire Business District Burned and Hundreds of Lives Lost

MARTIAL LAW IN CITY

The City Hall and all the Great Buildings Reduced to Debris

PEOPLE FLOCK TO THE HILLS

Great Shock Just Before Dawn Starts a Conflagration

BUILDINGS CRUMBLE AT ONCE

—fulfilling a judgment of the newspaper craft which said that "only an earthquake could drive T. R. off the first page." Roosevelt, to find his own story, was obliged to turn to the back pages.

VI

However resourcefully Roosevelt might use his arts of getting public opinion on his side, all was useless unless he could get a majority in the Senate. That was difficult under the conditions that conservative Republican leader Aldrich had forced upon Roosevelt when he disavowed the bill as a Republican Party measure and made it a Democratic one.

The debate consumed more than sixty hectic days. The opposition to the bill was a kind that, to any one but Roosevelt, would have been dismaying. He had against him practically every important orthodox member of his own party. To combat these, Roosevelt had on his side the Democratic minority, but under what conditions! The minority was small at best, only thirty-three out of the total of ninety. Not all the minority supported the bill—some among the Democrats could be as justly called "railroad senators" as any of the Republican leaders, and a few of the Democrats, old-time "states'-rights" men, opposed the bill on constitutional grounds. Moreover, cooperation between Roosevelt and the Democrats on whom he had to depend was attended with the cumbersomeness and mutual suspicion that always goes with ephemeral alliance between a president belonging to one party and legislators belonging to the other. Finally, the particular Democrat who had charge of the bill, "Pitchfork Ben" Tillman of South Carolina, was Roosevelt's bitter personal enemy.

To supplement the Democrats, Roosevelt had a few Republicans, the beginnings of the group, coming chiefly from the Midwest "Granger" states, who years later made much history as "Insurgents" or "Progressive Republicans." One of the ablest of them at the time of the railroad rate fight was Jonathan Dolliver of Iowa. Another, destined in later years to be outstanding, was LaFollette of Wisconsin; but LaFollette was new in the Senate and utterly without influence. Besides, because of his ultraradical recalcitrancy of temperament, he could be of little help to Roosevelt; indeed, he did not want, either on the railroad bill or ever, to be of help to Roosevelt. LaFollette's ideas about rate regulation were so much more radical than those in the bill as to have little relation of reality to the debate. His attitude,

Senator Jonathan P. Dolliver, a "Progressive Republican" from Iowa. (From a photograph by C. M. Bell, Washington, D.C.)

indeed, created cleavage within the little group of Insurgent Republicans who were part of Roosevelt's slender dependence, causing Dolliver to lament that the bill "had to stand fire from two directions, from its enemies and from the scattered tents of its advocates."

Tillman's contribution to the joint enterprise of Roosevelt and himself proved to be not enough—he had said on April 16 that he "could get 26 Democratic votes and possibly 1 or 2 more"; on April 18, however, a caucus of the Democrats had shown that Tillman could get only 25 votes.

In this state of facts, Roosevelt, on Friday, May 4, sent a message to the Press Gallery at the Capitol saying he would see the newspapermen at three that afternoon. They came, thirty-six of them. Roosevelt told them that he had seen a court review provision for the rate bill—allowing railroads to challenge decisions of the Interstate Commerce Commission—that was satisfactory to him and which he would support. It was known as the Allison Amendment. Allison was a Republican, not less regular than Aldrich but disposed to compromise, partly because Allison's constituency, Iowa, was strongly antirailroad, partly because Allison's habitual caution and unemotional temperament enabled him to see when need of compromise arose, and partly because Allison's role in the Republican senatorial hierarchy was to supply the oil of conciliation for bruises made by Aldrich's imperious dictatorship.

There was enough in the public announcement by Roosevelt of his support of Allison's court review amendment to create a sensation in the country and an explosion in the Senate. The body of Democratic senators, while they did not know that Roosevelt had been working secretly with their leader, saw that he was now working openly with a Republican. They were well aware, as the public was, that Republican Allison's court review amendment differed from that of Democratic Tillman's. They knew it differed in wording, and they assumed it must be, in its ultimate working out in the courts, more generous to the railroads. Most of all they knew, as a matter of politics, that any amendment bearing a Republican name, if incorporated in the bill instead of Tillman's Democratic one, would have the effect of depriving the Democrats of the credit which up to this time they had had. The Democrats, of course, insisted that Roosevelt had not merely compromised but capitulated. Yet the bill passed, and passed only because of the driving force that Roosevelt put behind it. Democrat after Democrat so admitted. Even Tillman combined congratulations with humor in reference to the victory:

> The Pitchfork [Tillman himself], while on duty on the firing line, to use a military phrase, looking around for the ally, saw the tail of his coat hustling to the rear, and . . . the last seen of him he was sliding on all fours between Father Allison's legs. [Nevertheless] but for the work of Theodore Roosevelt in bringing this matter to the attention of the country, we would not have had any bill at all. . . . Whatever success may come from it will be largely due to him.

CHAPTER 3

Two Friends

T heodore Roosevelt and William Howard Taft began their friendship when both occupied subordinate government posts in Washington, from 1890 to 1892, sharing a zeal for public service which Roosevelt expressed as Civil Service commissioner, Taft as solicitor general. They lived near each other, met frequently at the homes of each other and of mutual friends, walked to their offices together occasionally—passing the White House, then occupied by Benjamin Harrison, and turning unconsciously to glimpse its unfailing glamour (though it was Roosevelt alone of the two whose thrill was associated with a personal dream). After advancement in their careers separated them from Washington and from each other, they kept their friendship alive through letters and occasional meetings. As crises arose in Roosevelt's turbulent upward climb, he would, said Taft later, "frequently write me to secure my judgment."

Taft, going forward more ponderously than Roosevelt through paths more serene, passed from the post of solicitor general to become a federal judge and dean of the law school of the University of Cincinnati. In 1900, he went to Manila as president of the second Philippine Commission. When Roosevelt succeeded to the presidency through the death of McKinley in 1901, among the subordinates he inherited was Taft, now in charge of governing our Far Eastern possession.

II

With disturbing unexpectedness there came to Taft in the Philippines late in 1902, from Roosevelt in the White House, a cable saying: "On January first there will be a vacancy on the Supreme Court to which I earnestly desire to appoint you. . . ."

To Taft the offer brought turmoil of spirit. "All his life his first ambition had been to attain the Supreme Bench; to him it meant the crown of the highest career that a man can seek, and he wanted it as strongly as a man can ever want anything," his wife would recollect.

Mrs. Taft, however, "had always been opposed to a judicial career for him," regarding it as "settlement in a 'fixed groove' I had talked against so long." Several of Taft's friends and relatives, including an elder brother, Charles P. Taft, to whom he was devoted, had come to feel that Taft's talents, and the tide of public service upon which he was embarked, were capable of carrying him on to the presidency. Immurement on the Supreme Court would take him out of the current that might lead to the more exalted office.

This ambition Taft himself did not share. For him, the presidency had little allure; the politics incident to the office repelled him. A year before Roosevelt's offer of a Supreme Court berth, Taft had written his brother: "The horrors of a modern Presidential campaign and the political troubles of the successful candidate, rob the office of the slightest attraction for me."

Taft had, however, one reason of his own for forgoing, at this time, the opportunity to go on the Supreme Court. His reason was his feeling of obligation to the Filipinos, the sense of duty which told him he should remain with them until they should be securely on their way to stability. This conviction coincided with Mrs. Taft's preference. Although she "remembered the year of illness and anxiety we had just been through," although she "yearned to be safe in Washington" and "weakened just a little" in her

Roosevelt and Taft on the south portico of the White House just before leaving for the Capitol, where Roosevelt gave up, and Taft took over, the presidency. (From a photograph © by Harris and Ewing)

The Taft figure at a later date—the first of our golf-playing presidents. (From a photograph © by Harris and Ewing)

determination that her husband should avoid the "fixed groove" of the Court, nevertheless her conclusive judgment was that "acceptance was not to be thought of."

Then, in the fall of 1903, Taft received another summons from Roosevelt to larger duties at Washington, which he accepted. Roosevelt's new offer was not to a justiceship on the Supreme Court but to the cabinet post Elihu Root was relinquishing to return to the practice of law. The office of secretary of war, having charge of the Philippines would permit Taft to continue to keep a hand upon their destinies. To Mrs. Taft, this portfolio "was much more pleasing than the offer of the Supreme Court appointment, because it was in line with the kind of work I wanted my husband to do, the kind of career I wanted for him and expected him to have, so I was glad there were few excuses for refusing to accept it open to him."

On February 1, 1904, Taft took the oath of office as secretary of war in Roosevelt's cabinet.

III

Taft was more than secretary of war. Wherever a tension needed the solvent of goodwill, or friction the oil of benevolence; wherever suspicion needed the antidote of frankness, or wounded pride the disinfectant of a hearty laugh—there Taft was sent. He was given prodigious tasks, and the greater the pressure that Roosevelt put upon him, the more effectively he worked. It is difficult to phrase what Taft was to the Roosevelt administration, and to the country. It occurs to one to borrow a term from business, and say Taft was America's "troubleshooter"—but that implies high-pressure explosiveness, and also ruthlessness sometimes, and Taft was neither explosive nor ruthless. It was Roosevelt who was under pressure always and explosive often; Taft was his jovial, never-excited, considerate, smiling associate, partly subordinate, partly partner.

The country liked Taft. They made infinite jests about his fatness—and no one heard or repeated the jokes with greater savor than Taft himself. Making a speech he would pause, with an effect of suspense, just long enough to intensify the audience's attention, then throughout the immense torso and up into the broad features would run little tremors and heavings, rising to a climax in a rumbling chuckle, and Taft would tell a story in which the point was, as he would say in an engaging falsetto, "on me." While he was in the Philippines, disturbing reports about his health caused Secretary of War Root to send a cabled inquiry. Taft cabled back that he was perfectly all right—he had just finished a twenty-five-mile horseback ride and was feeling fine. Root read that, smiled, and sent off another cable of solicitude: "How is horse?" Justice Brewer of the Supreme Court said that "Taft is the politest man in Washington; the other day he gave up his seat in a street-car to three ladies." All the jokes that have been made about fat men since Shakespeare invented Falstaff were brought from their ancient closets and stretched to fit Taft's ample form. New ones emanated from Taft himself. A lady calling on him in the interest of her son's career in the army had received the assurance she wished and, departing, said, as the highest feminine conception of showing appreciation: "Mr. Taft, you're really not near so fat as they say you are."

IV

As the people loved Taft, so did Roosevelt. Whenever Roosevelt mentioned Taft's name it was with an expression of pleasure on his own countenance, a pleasure that was more than mere smiling affection. Roosevelt had regard for Taft's stability and serenity. In cabinet meetings, or at gatherings of friends, to say "Isn't that so, Will?" or "Don't you think so, Will?" was Roosevelt's way of getting what he regarded as the most convincing buttressing of his own opinions—an attitude never modified by the

Secretary of War Taft on one of his trips to the Far East (S.S. Manchuria). *The young woman in front of him is Alice, daughter of President Roosevelt; upon her left (reader's right) is Nicholas Longworth, whom she later married. (From a photograph by Underwood & Underwood)*

fact that at evening gatherings in the White House study, the question would sometimes wake Taft from a nap.

The very ease that Taft had in Roosevelt's presence, his immunity from infection by the latter's eager energy, helped to increase Roosevelt's estimate of the soundness and surefootedness of his judgment. Far from resenting Taft's placid, good-humored indifference to some of Roosevelt's more recondite enthusiasms, Roosevelt valued him the more for it. Instinctively, Roosevelt seemed to sense that Taft's imperturbability was a needed and valuable corrective to his own impetuosity. Taft privately thought of himself as holding on to Roosevelt's coattails to prevent him from going too fast—but publicly always said that whatever Roosevelt did was Heaven's law. Conversely, Roosevelt publicly accepted Taft's benediction as proof that he was right—but privately told friends that sometimes he had to restrain Taft from letting his loyalty carry him too far, from being, in the furtherance of Roosevelt's policies, more Roosevelt than Roosevelt himself.

More than a president to a member of his cabinet, more even than one friend to another, Roosevelt acted toward Taft like a wise father to a son. In this paternal quality of Roosevelt one recognizes the judgment that caused Roosevelt three times to press the Supreme Court upon Taft, and the affection which led him to wish that Taft should have whichever career would most appeal to him.

Out of a conflict between his heart's desire to sit on the Court and the worthy ambition of those close and dear to him, Taft, in the fall of 1906, made a formal statement, its unusual wording and almost backward-leaning spirit reflecting the innate hesitancy of a fine and able man entering a world, politics, that was essentially foreign to him, and a little dismaying:

> For the purpose of relieving the burden imposed by recent publications on some of my friends among the Washington newspaper correspondents of putting further inquiry to me, I wish to say that my ambition is not political; that I am not seeking the Presidential nomination; . . . but that I am not foolish enough to say that in the improbable event that the opportunity to run for the great office of President were to come to me, I should decline it, for this would not be true.

Upon this formal announcement of Taft's candidacy, Roosevelt did not commit himself. On the contrary, some time later he said to Mrs. Taft that he might "feel it to be my duty to be for Hughes"—Charles Evans Hughes, whose investigation of corruption in the insurance industry had catapulted him into the governorship of New York.

Mrs. Taft reported the remark to Taft, who wrote to Roosevelt in a spirit almost of relief and hope: "If you do you may be sure you will awaken no sense of disappointment on my part. . . . You know what my feeling has been in respect to the Presidency." Roosevelt, replying to Taft, said he had merely meant that Hughes might have so much popular sentiment behind him that there would be no course open but to support him.

CHAPTER 4
Selecting a Successor

A s Roosevelt looked forward to the next presidency, his principal concern was to prevent the renomination of himself. He had settled his position by his formal statement, issued a few hours after his election in 1904: "A wise custom which limits the President to two terms regards the substance and not the form, and under no circumstances will I be a candidate for or accept another nomination."

From that position, Roosevelt did not waver, though there was never a day that he was not under pressure, from force of circumstances and clamor of individuals, to revoke his decision. One formidable group, determined to renominate him, invented a distinction between "second term" and "second elective term." They took the ground that the really wrong thing was not for a president to renominate himself, but for a president to interfere with the free will of the people. Declaring that the will of the people was renomination of Roosevelt, they organized a movement to defy Roosevelt's wishes. Roosevelt never formally repeated his early public declaration, though occasion to do so arose practically every week—he knew the interpretation put upon protesting too much. But in letters and statements to friends, frequently in sharp admonitions to them, he declared that renomination of him would be a stain upon his honor. He kept his hand upon the Republican Party machinery until the very hour and minute of the nomination, watchful to prevent any action by what he regarded as his misguided friends. Elimination of himself was Roosevelt's fixed policy throughout the entire four years.

II

T he same instinct that led Roosevelt four times to urge Taft to take a place on the Supreme Court must have inspired him unconsciously to a reluctance, never clearly recognized by himself, to put Taft in the presidency. The reluctance may have been increased by the doubt of Mrs. Roosevelt whether it was wise to push Taft into the presidency, doubt whether the country would be well served, or Taft himself happy. Mrs. Roosevelt did not press her view on her husband; had she done so, much of subsequent history might have been different.

It was not until January 1908, five months before the convention, that

"Passing on the Torch." (Drawing by Lamdin for the Syracuse Herald, *1909)*

Roosevelt decided fully, and then only because his secretary, William Loeb, told him he must act. Loeb's pressure, and Roosevelt's primary decision, was not that he should back Taft but that he should back somebody—because otherwise the convention might renominate Roosevelt himself. "You should have a candidate," Loeb told him one morning. "You are under pledge not to run again. I propose that you make people understand you intend to keep it. Some people believe that a deadlocked convention might force you to disregard it. Others believe you . . . are manipulating things so as to force a deadlock. The air is full of such talk. The way to settle it is to have a candidate."

Roosevelt agreed—"We must have a candidate." After surveying in his mind the possibility of backing Elihu Root, and resurveying Charles E. Hughes, he turned to Taft—with a reluctance only to be explained as the caution of his instinctive question about Taft's adaptability, acting as a brake on the natural impulse of his friendship. Once Roosevelt determined to turn the nomination toward Taft, he went about the elevation of his friend with as much gusto as he would have taken in promoting his own fortunes. To getting the nomination for Taft he devoted all his political resourcefulness, taking in it somewhat the pleasure of a father in promoting the fortunes of a particularly beloved son, somewhat the pleasure that an adept in an art takes in showing off his skill in the presence of and for the benefit of a loved and loyal admirer.

The job really was not difficult in proportion to the éclat that Roosevelt put into it. The act of bestowing the presidency on Taft consisted chiefly of declining to take it himself; more accurately, in preventing its being thrust on him. The only other candidate constituting any impediment to Roosevelt's nominating Taft was Hughes.

III

Hughes, governor of New York, was at high tide of the prestige that had come to him as a result of his investigation of insurance abuses two years before. His availability, his obviousness for the Republican presidential nomination was really greater than Taft's—he was a much more popular figure. Following a characteristically austere conception of propriety, refraining from announcing himself a candidate, hesitant even to allow the use of his name, Hughes came finally to a point where he scheduled a speech to reveal his plans. Anticipation flamed. The New York Republican County Committee endorsed Hughes as their candidate. Similar resolutions or informal steps were taken in New England and elsewhere.

Newspapers, fanning anticipation, said that Hughes would "make plain his views on all important national issues"; and mobilized their facilities to carry to the public the speech which Hughes was

THE MORE HE BOOSTS, THE MORE IT HURTS

(From the Philadelphia Record*)*

to deliver about eight o'clock on the night of January 31. The public, its interest excited, waited in suspense—it was thirteen years before radio broadcasting—to read the speech. The following morning readers picked up their newspapers to find what Hughes had said. They found it—if they looked hard enough. At least, those of them found it whose interest was able to survive what they saw on the first page. In blazing headlines four columns wide appeared, not the name of Hughes but that of Roosevelt.

The headlines epitomized a message Roosevelt had sent to Congress at five o'clock the evening before (after afternoon newspapers had gone to press), the most provocatively sensational utterance of his career; headlines beginning with two words that had become familiar—current humor said the newspapers used to keep these words standing in type—

ROOSEVELT FLAYS . . .

—headlines which shouted:

HOTTEST MESSAGE EVER SENT TO CONGRESS
ULTRA-RADICAL MESSAGE
MESSAGE DAZES
ROOSEVELT'S ONSLAUGHT
"BIG MEN" ROASTED

—headlines followed by the text of the most violent message Roosevelt had ever given out. The epithets, the flaming phrases that blazed from it, were so sensational that an editor of the *New York World* was moved to print them in a double-column box:

Web of corruption.	The strong, cunning men.
Apologists for corrupt wealth.	Law-defying wealth.
Hypocritical baseness.	Vindictive and terrible radicalism.
Criminals of great wealth.	Mammon of unrighteousness.
Powerful wrongdoers.	With envenomed bitterness.
Peculiarly flagrant iniquity.	Notorious railroad combinations.
To shackle cunning.	Bitter and unscrupulous craft.
Laying up a day of wrath.	Very wealthy criminals.
Flagrant dishonesty.	Corruption of organized politics.
Rottenness.	Corruption of high finance.
Unhealthy seeming prosperity.	With frantic vehemence.
Greed, trickery and cunning.	Evil eminence of infamy.
Representatives of predatory wealth.	The death knell of the Republic.
Wealth accumulated by iniquity.	Purchased politicians.
Puppets who move as the string is pulled.	Domineer in swollen pride.
Corrupt men of wealth.	Wealthy malefactors.

The explosive thunders of Roosevelt's message to Congress left little space in the newspapers and only an obscure position for Hughes's speech—the *Chicago Tribune*'s typographical presentation began with two words that constituted a relative rating for its impact—"Hughes also . . ."—HUGHES ALSO HITS RICH EVIL-DOERS: Outlines Platform on Which He Will Make Fight to Become Chief Executive.

Hughes's careful statements about public policy, intended to be his formal declaration of his entrance into the race for the Republican nomination, were not only dwarfed in space and relegated to inconspicuous positions, but were given the effect of pallid feebleness by Roosevelt's savage epithets. Hughes's temperate, sane, well-thought-out discourse could no more compete for public attention with Roosevelt's effulgence than a crystal spring with a volcanic eruption. Hughes's calm advocacy of a commission to revise the tariff and an employers' liability law, his scholarly delineation of the field of federal power compared with state—all that was reduced to a kind of feeble ignus fatuousness by the flaming provocativeness of Roosevelt's torrid denunciations. Against the reverberating thunders of Roosevelt's address, Hughes's scholarly exposition became an unheard whisper. "That," said one journalist, "wound up the Hughes candidacy."

Persons who knew or inferred that Roosevelt must have prepared so important an address several days in advance, and who made further inference from Roosevelt's expert understanding of the mechanics of publicity, charged Roosevelt with having timed the sending of his message to Congress, three hours in advance of Hughes's speech, with the deliberate purpose of blanketing the latter—"Timed to Dwarf Hughes," said the *New York Times* headline. Roosevelt, when friends imputed this adroitness to him, just grinned.

IV

With Hughes out of the way Roosevelt dedicated himself to persuading the country to accept Taft. Resourcefully, persistently, Roosevelt assured the country that Taft was the equivalent of himself, and tried to make his assurance good by attempting to make Taft *be* Roosevelt.

Throughout the campaign Roosevelt gave intimate advice, told Taft just how to make a political speech, how to become a popular campaigner. "Stay in hotels," he advised Taft, instead of the private homes whose hospitality Taft loved, "and give everybody a fair shot at you." When Taft continued his daily golf playing, drawing to that then relatively new game in America the attention that focuses on a presidential candidate, Roosevelt sent word to him to take his exercise in some form more familiar to the plebeian. "It is true," Roosevelt explained to the messenger,* for repetition to Taft, "I myself play tennis, but that game is a little more familiar; besides you never saw a photograph of me playing tennis. I'm careful about that; photographs on horseback, yes; tennis, no. And golf is fatal."

Minutely, Roosevelt instructed Taft in the art of effective political speechmaking. "Don't talk on delicate subjects," he wrote. "Stop citing court decisions, for the moment you begin to cite decisions people at once think it is impossible for them to understand, and they cease trying to comprehend, and promptly begin to nod." "[You] must," he instructed Taft, "treat a political audience as one coming not to see an etching but a poster." "[You] must have streaks of blue, yellow, and red to catch the eye and eliminate all fine lines and soft colors." Taft humbly took the lesson in. "I think," said Roosevelt later, "Taft thought I was a barbarian and a mountebank at first. But . . . he is at last catching the attention of the crowd."

The crowd, nevertheless, saw Taft as what, during the campaign, he was, a not very expertly synthesized Roosevelt, at best the approved heir apparent to Roosevelt rather than a birthright duplicate of the blood. A type of joke became common:

---

*The messenger was Mark Sullivan. Some of these instructions by Roosevelt to Taft were given before the nomination, some after.

"That's a splendid phonograph, old man. It reproduces the sound of Roosevelt's voice better than I ever thought possible. What make?"

"We call it the Taft."

V

When the nominating convention met in Chicago, in June 1908, Roosevelt sent the most expert telegrapher on the White House staff to stand immediately back of Chairman Lodge to flash a message to Roosevelt, and to receive, in case there should be a stampede toward Roosevelt, the imperative refusal, which Roosevelt in the White House was prepared to send.

In another quarter of Washington, across the street from the White House, in Taft's office in the War Department, the convention proceedings were followed in a different mood. Taft had as guests some intimate friends and members of his family. Taft himself, confident and serene, by nature free from suspicion or other form of unhappy apprehension, sat among friends in the middle of the room; at his desk, occupying his official chair, was Mrs. Taft. When Taft's name was placed in nomination and the cheering began, Mrs. Taft remarked, "I only want it to last more than forty-five minutes"—the day before a demonstration at the mention of Roosevelt's name had lasted that long. Taft said, chidingly, "Oh, my dear! my dear!" When a bulletin was handed to Mrs. Taft saying that a large portrait of Roosevelt on the platform had caused a new outburst of cheering, she sat white as marble and motionless. After several painful minutes came a bulletin saying that Massachusetts had cast twenty-five votes for Taft. That, to those who understood, was the signal that Roosevelt's plan to nominate Taft was being carried out successfully, for Massachusetts was the state of Senator Lodge, and Senator Lodge was at once the chairman of the convention and the known spokesman and agent of Roosevelt's wishes. Mrs. Taft's face regained its normal color; she was the personification of a proud and happy wife.

The next day, Roosevelt wrote a letter to a friend:

> Well, the convention is over and Taft is nominated. . . . It has been a curious contest, for I have had to fight tooth and nail against being renominated myself. I could not have prevented it at all unless I had thrown myself heart and soul into the business and had shown to the country that Taft stood for exactly the same principles and policies that I did, and that I believed with all my heart and soul that under him we should progress steadily along the road [my] administration has travelled. He and I view public questions exactly alike. In fact, I think it has been very rare that two public men have ever been so much at one in all the essentials of their beliefs and practices.

And then, in the fine pleasure that comes of a worthy task carried to completion, Roosevelt added a sentence, struck off in the sheer exuberance of its content, which was destined later to bedevil him, destined to be momentous in the presidential campaign of four years later. "Always excepting Washington and Lincoln," Roosevelt wrote, "I believe that Taft as President will rank with any other man who has ever been in the White House."

VI

Now, to electing Taft, Roosevelt renewed his dedication. He collaborated with Taft in composing the latter's acceptance speech—in which Taft said, as his most effective appeal to the American electorate: "Mr. Roosevelt led the way to practical reform. My chief function shall be to complete and perfect . . ."

Painstakingly, and also joyously, Roosevelt took the role of trainer: "Let the audience see you smile always, because I feel that your nature shines out so transparently when you do smile—you big, generous, high-minded fellow," he wrote. "Hit them hard, old man!" When Taft's hitting was not hard enough for his mentor's taste, Roosevelt stepped out of the trainer's corner himself to deliver the needed punch. If it was sympathy and encouragement the candidate needed, the versatile trainer could supply that, too: "Poor old boy," he wrote to Taft, "of course you are not enjoying the campaign; I wish you had some of my bad temper." In Roosevelt's friendly epithets there was, perhaps, just a hint of impatience with his pupil, of dawning disappointment. And, on the other side, if Taft himself was too amiable to resent such intimate urging, others close to Taft may have hoped for the time when Taft would be free of such personal tutoring.

Throughout the campaign Roosevelt guided Taft, far and away the most expert tactician in the party. At all times Roosevelt's manner was the barometer of Taft's fortunes. "Whenever Roosevelt looks worried," his sympathetic aide, Archie Butt, feels "anxious for Taft." But if Roosevelt "is in a rollicking humor," Butt knows all is well with Taft. "We have them beaten to a frazzle" Roosevelt would say when things were going right.

When on election day Taft got 321 electoral votes to Bryan's 162, and 7,678,908 popular votes to Bryan's 6,409,104, Roosevelt was "simply radiant." It was, with one exception, the largest electoral vote and popular plurality ever received by any presidential candidate. With a discriminating prudence relatively rare in statistics, it stopped just short of equaling Roosevelt's own victory four years before—making Roosevelt's happiness complete, perfect.

VII

At precisely the instant when the election returns showed Roosevelt had made Taft president and when Taft had voiced his gratitude to Roo-

President Taft and Governor Hughes on the reviewing stand on the afternoon of Taft's inauguration, March 4, 1909.

sevelt, at that moment, without either realizing it, the relation into which the two had fitted as the mortise to the groove, came to an end and would never be renewed. In the case of Theodore Roosevelt and William H. Taft there was a circumstance that gave to their rupture a resistless inevitability as austere as a Greek tragedy, a circumstance making for disruption so powerfully that only incredible self-restraint and humility, especially on the part of Roosevelt, could have averted it—and Roosevelt did not have incredible self-restraint and humility.

The author of this book called to say goodbye to Roosevelt on the day preceding his departure from the White House, March 3, 1909. As I left, Roosevelt came with me to the door. Something was said about this being the last time we should meet in the White House, and something about the times we had been together there, the battles Roosevelt had fought against the standpatters. As we looked through the glass doors toward the lowering winter sky over LaFayette Park, I asked him, "How do you really think Taft will make out?" "He's all right," Roosevelt said, "he means well and he'll do his best. But he's weak. They'll get around him. They'll"—he came close to me, putting his shoulder in front of my shoulder and pressing gently with an effect of holding me back—"they'll lean against him."

CHAPTER 5
Taft's Four Years

In the argot of politicians and Washington correspondents, there is at the beginning of every administration a "honeymoon period," during which White House and Capitol and partisan press, abjuring politics, radiate an altogether artificial and impermanent sweetness and trust and tolerance toward each other, and especially, on the part of the latter two, toward the new president. In Taft's case, the sentimental interlude was exceptionally sugary. "Never," said the *New York Sun*, "did any man come into the Presidency before with such universal good will."

A survey that probed beneath the surface would have revealed, however, that there had formed within the Republican Party an angry cleavage, an insurgency by a minority West against a majority East.

This insurgency, diverse in its origins, had one root in a feeling on the part of the West that the protective tariff, instituted to foster eastern "infant industries," had overfed those industries until they were now fat and overbearing giants; another in the resentment of the West, composed mainly of individual businesses, chiefly farming, against highly organized business in the East and its great corporations which drew much of their sustenance from the West but paid most of their profits to the East; another in the irritation of the granger West against the mainly eastern-owned railroads, which had gone on from the seventies to the passage of the Railroad Rate Act in 1906; another in the memories of the long controversy over currency, between mainly debtor West and mainly creditor East, which had lasted from soon after the Civil War until 1896; another in the feeling that the remaining free lands, in the West, especially the mineral and oil-bearing ones, were being accumulated in the private possession of eastern-owned railroads and other corporations—this one of the grievances, expressed in a movement called "conservation of natural resources," had many adherents in East as well as West.

All these roots drew sap from a deep undercurrent of American tradition, a spirit of resistance against authority, opposition against organized power, suspicion against vested interests. This truculent independence, now expressing itself acutely in insurgency against the Republican Party, was a dominant trait of the American people, as old as America itself. Politically and socially it *was* America. It had inspired the first settlement of the continent, had caused our separation from the mother country, had dictated the spirit and forms of the new government and institutions we set up. Our earliest settlers, as well as most of our immigrants, had been picked persons, selected by the law of their own natures on the basis of resentment against authority. In Europe in the seventeenth, eighteenth, and nineteenth centuries, the individual who found himself most irked by a stratified society, who most resented organized power, whether of the church or of the system of land-tenure, or of caste of inherited place—any whose instinct urged him toward independence, moved to America. In each succeeding generation, this process of natural selection on the basis of instinct for independence repeated itself. In each generation, the most restless "went West," the first wave to central New York, western Pennsylvania, Kentucky, and Tennessee; the next to Indiana, Illinois, and Wisconsin; the next to Iowa, Kansas, Nebraska, and Missouri; the next to the Rocky Mountains and the Pacific Coast. By the time of Taft's administration or earlier, the people of the West were the result of three or four successive sievings of those most independent in spirit. Also a new condition had arrived; the free land was exhausted. No longer was there any "out West" to absorb those whose nature it was to resist authority, organization, to be made restless by the ruts of settled ways. Deprived of the chance of escape from what irked them, they turned to fight it.

The condition expressed itself in a division of the Republican Party, in the country and in Congress, into mainly eastern "Standpatters" (apt word for conservative contentment with what is) and mainly western "Progressives," translated, by newspaper and popular zest for a fighting word, into "Insurgents."

II

Which group the new president should stand with would be in the popular mind a test of Taft's fidelity to Roosevelt and Roosevelt's policies. Partly a misleading test, for Roosevelt had not really "stood with" the Insurgents; rather, he had used this group as one element of the power which he forged from many sources. Nor had Roosevelt ever completely flouted or directly and permanently opposed the conservative East—them, too, Roosevelt had used as one of the materials out of which he fused his power. But the legislation Roosevelt had brought about was largely in the Insurgent direction, his attitude toward public questions was mainly that of the West, the mainspring of his popularity came from that section. Now the West would instinctively view Taft in the light of whether he stood with them and their representatives in Congress, whether in his official attitudes as well as his informal intimacies he would seem to associate most with the Insurgents in Congress, or with the orthodox Standpatters who held the official places of power and were a large majority of the party.

To Taft it would be a difficult test, for Taft lacked Roosevelt's vigor, which kept both factions subordinate to his own leadership; lacked Roosevelt's diversity of temperament, which used to encourage Standpatters and Insurgents alternately, as each group lent itself to Roosevelt's larger purpose of the moment. Taft lacked Roosevelt's geniality coupled with dominating vitality, which could alternately flout Standpatter or conservative—and then immediately and cheerfully lift the victim to his feet and carry him along in Roosevelt's forward surge. This variousness of temperament, this fecundity of talent for dominance, Taft lacked. Particularly did Taft lack the primitive energy which enabled Roosevelt always to ride the wave, lead the procession. Taft, with his more phlegmatic temperament, his more legalistic mind, would be prevailingly and conspicuously on one side or the other. In Taft's case the outcome of the test would make him seem all black or all white.

The static quality in Taft, his inertia, would bring it about that the label which he should finally bear would be less chosen by himself than fixed upon him by whichever side had the greater energy in surrounding him, pressing upon him, leaning against him.

III

From the time the first Puritan set foot on New England soil, the American idea of what to do about land was to get the Indians off, and settle it. The settlement invariably took the form of private, individual ownership. In all the territory from the Atlantic Coast to the Missouri River, in which the first 250 years of the white occupation of America took place, not one tract of land was reserved for public ownership and common use. (Excepting an acre here and there for a "common" or "green" in a New England village, or for a public school or a church or a state capitol.) Wherever there was unoccupied land, a settler could squat on it, and by occupying it twenty-one years acquire title. In all that stretch of continent there was no equivalent of what later came to be known in the extreme West as a "national park" or a "forest reserve." No one thought of such a thing. The purpose for which land existed was individual ownership.

If the new settler came in the form of a corporation, so much the better—the corporation taking up land would presumably build a railroad, or conduct lumbering operations, or mine coal, or erect a mill or waterpower plant. It was satisfying to the community—the waterpower owner would bring industry, and additional settlers as labor. Corporations acquired waterpower sites on western rivers as informally as early settlers in the East had acquired gristmill sites on tiny streams.

About 1900 came reversal of this point of view. It came through realization that the nation's supply of free land was nearing an end, and that considerable quantities of it in immense tracts had passed into the possession of corporations which through use of "dummy" entrants—a shortcut hitherto good-naturedly condoned—had acquired forests, mineral lands, waterpower sites. Often these corporations oppressed the small individual homesteaders; always, of course, their ownership limited the opportunity of the individual to acquire free land.

Almost overnight, the evasion of red tape technicalities which yesterday

THEN.   NOW.

Gifford Pinchot.

had been a virtue became today a crime. It was one of those shifts of common point of view which prove, among other things, that what are called "moral standards" vary with time as well as with place; and that in some cases morality is closely associated with economics. The change that came in the West in the 1890s found a considerable number of persons midway toward perfecting their titles to public land; many were harassed by the government, and not a few went to jail.

IV

With a fervor almost passionate, idealists dedicated themselves to saving for the people and for posterity such tracts of land as had not yet passed into private ownership. Chief among these was Gifford Pinchot, the young descendant of old New York merchant families, whose dominant inner passion was to flee from the ease that inherited wealth invited him to; almost he seemed to have a terror of the temptation to self-indulgence, seemed always to be fighting it as if it were his most dangerous and malevolent enemy. In a spirit partly of hardening his flesh, partly of crucifying his spirit, he slept on the floor with a wooden pillow, and each morning for his bath had his valet throw buckets of icy water over his sinewy body. With his discipline of the body went a mystic spirituality. Pinchot was of those whose eyes, as they pass through the world, instinctively look about for a hero, and for martyrdom in the hero's service. "Gifford," said Roosevelt, who understood Pinchot perfectly, "truly has an affection for me; it is almost fetish worship, and I have figured it out that Pinchot truly believes that . . . if conditions were such that only one could live . . . I should possibly kill him as the weaker of the two, and he, therefore, worships this in me." As Pinchot sought heroes to worship, so did he seek demons to fight. He found them, in the persons of those who opposed Roosevelt, the Standpatters.

Graduating from Yale in 1889, Pinchot spent three years in Germany and Switzerland, studying there an art, forestry, then unheard of in an America still lavishly rich in wood, though highly developed in old European countries whose supplies needed to be carefully preserved and administered for the common good. Returning to America, Pinchot began, in the privately owned mountain lands of one of the Vanderbilts at Biltmore, North Carolina, the first systematic forest work in America. By 1896, he was the leading spirit in an organization for altruistic propaganda, the National Forest Commission, and a little later head of a tiny "Bureau of Forestry" (later the "Forest Service") in the U.S. Department of Agriculture, of which the annual budget, at the time Roosevelt became president, was only $40,000.

To Pinchot and his cause, as to many other men ardent for new ideas, the accidental presidency of Roosevelt was a gift from the gods. Promptly Roosevelt had Pinchot as a member of his intimate "tennis cabinet," and was preaching to Congress in his first annual message that "the forest and water problems are perhaps the most vital internal problems of the United States. . . . The whole future of the nation is directly at stake."

By 1902, two new words, connoting a new phase of American national affairs, were becoming familiar to an America destined to be made conscious of many new terms for rapidly changing conditions. "Reclamation" meant the fostering of waste land, especially the bringing of water by irrigation to arid desert land; by June 17, 1902, Roosevelt with others had urged through Congress a "Reclamation Act" under which in subsequent years some 160 millions of government money was expended in irrigation. A broader term for the new idea was "Conservation" (of natural resources), which, appearing in Nelson's encyclopedia for 1911 (in a definition written by one of Pinchot's associates, P. P. Wells), meant "foresight and restraint in the exploitation of the physical sources of wealth as necessary for the perpetuity of civilization and the welfare of present and future generations." The word had a social implication leaning toward the philosophy known vaguely as "Socialism," a dogma that the "unearned increment" of the natural resources should be retained for the public. Conservation, Wells said, "was only a means to an end and the end was economic justice."

Associated with "Conservation" were words like "vision," in a literature which rebuked our past wastefulness, warned of impending extinction, and called excitedly for restraint. Pinchot predicted that persons then alive would eat on concrete or metal tables, due to the exhaustion of forests; that at the existing rate of increase of use "our supplies of anthracite coal will last fifty years and bituminous a little over a hundred." Unless we practice conservation, Pinchot said, "those who come after us will have to pay the price of misery, degradation and failure for the progress and prosperity of our day."

To Roosevelt, infected by Pinchot's zeal, stimulated by an approval of crusades that was characteristic of the time, conservation became a holy cause. With high gusto he fought the private interests who were offended by the new policy, the timber, mining, and waterpower corporations whom he designated "land-grabbers." When they undertook to put a statutory curb on Roosevelt's zeal, the subsequent developments constituted one of the most spirited and characteristic episodes of Roosevelt's presidency.

Roosevelt's leverage for practical conservation, his fundamental power to preserve the forests, rested on his authority to withdraw by executive order from entry, and to set aside as forest reserves any part of the public domain which could reasonably be described as forest—Pinchot's young men were constantly ranging the mountains to find land sufficiently wooded to justify Roosevelt in withdrawing it. Senator Fulton of Oregon maneuvered through the Senate, as a "rider" to the Agricultural Appropriation bill, a provision that the president could no longer do this, that future withdrawals must be made, not by executive order but by act of Congress.

Roosevelt knew he must sign the appropriation bill as a whole to keep the Department of Agriculture functioning. While the bill was still in the Senate, Roosevelt and Pinchot conferred. To Pinchot and his subordinates Roosevelt said, in effect, as it was repeated later with possibly some admiring exaggeration: "Bring me maps showing every piece of public domain in those six States that contains a bush." Pinchot's subordinates and his office drafting force worked day and night. Roosevelt, with their maps before him, signed executive orders withdrawing 16 million acres. Then he signed the bill which forbade him to do what he had just done. Grinningly, he wrote years later in his autobiography: "The opponents of the Forest Service turned handsprings in their wrath."

V

This aggressiveness of Roosevelt in behalf of conservation, his assumption, as a broad rule of practice, that the president can and should do anything in the public interest (as conceived by him) that the Constitution did not expressly forbid, gave rise to the atmosphere of angry controversy over conservation when Roosevelt was succeeded by Taft. Roosevelt's official spearhead in the fight had been James R. Garfield, who as secretary of the interior had authority over the public domain. (While Pinchot was the principal inspiration and most earnest zealot, he was, officially, only a subordinate in the Department of Agriculture.) For this reason Roosevelt wished Taft to keep Garfield in the cabinet. Taft did not. From that, the rest followed.

Taft appointed Richard A. Ballinger of Seattle, Washington. Taft may readily have thought that Ballinger was an adequate appointment, for Ballinger had been, up to a few months before, a subordinate in Garfield's department, head of the General Land Office, and as such had seemed to be in sympathy with Garfield, Roosevelt, and conservation. Taft was loyal to conservation, and would not consciously have appointed a secretary of the interior who would reverse the policy.

To Pinchot and the ardent young zealots who had gravitated around him, the dropping of Garfield was complete justification for acute distrust; in their state of mind hardly any successor whom Taft might appoint could fail to be under suspicion. Pinchot was now without the governor that Roosevelt had been to his impulses. With Roosevelt out of touch in Africa, Pinchot became what Roosevelt described him, one "who would expend his great energy in fighting the men who seemed to him not to be going far enough forward."

Ballinger (and Taft) had been in office less than six months when Pinchot put his suspicion into action. To a young subordinate in Ballinger's department, Louis R. Glavis, Pinchot gave a letter of introduction to Taft. Glavis, calling on Taft, charged that his superior, Ballinger, was improperly expediting transfer of 100,000 acres of government coal land in Alaska to a group of capitalists (composed mainly of the Guggenheim family) on claims which, Glavis charged, were in part invalid. Taft sent the charges to Ballinger. Ballinger delivered to Taft a defense and explanation—with buttressing documents it contained upward of half a million words.

Taft addressed to Ballinger a "ponderous, sweeping letter of exculpation and endorsement intended to be a permanent seal of sanctity, to refute all present charges against Ballinger and make future ones impossible."* Taft told Ballinger that he had "examined the whole record most carefully" and that he had "reached a very definite conclusion." Taft's conclusion was that "the case attempted to be made by Mr. Glavis [is] without any substantial evidence to sustain his attack [and] embraces only shreds of suspicions"— this phrase, catching the public fancy, became conspicuous in the subsequent commotion. Taft authorized Ballinger "to dismiss L. R. Glavis from the service of the government for filing a disingenuous statement unjustly impeaching the integrity of his superior officers."

To the support of Glavis quickly came Pinchot. His support took the form in part of having some of his subordinates furnish to the newspapers information from the government files tending to support the charges Glavis had made, tending to reflect on Ballinger and, by this time, inferentially, on Taft. When this activity became known, Pinchot wrote a public letter saying that his subordinates "broke no law and at worst were guilty only of the violation of official propriety."

Pinchot's action was, of course, flagrant insubordination. Taft dismissed him from office. Now, to the support of both Pinchot and Glavis, came *Collier's Weekly*, many newspapers, practically all the cult of conservation zealots, as well as miscellaneous altruists. *Collier's* printed Glavis's charges

*This description of Taft's letter is from a bitterly hostile source, *Collier's Weekly*. It was written, in 1910, by Mark Sullivan. —D.R.

under a headline asking "Are the Guggenheims in charge of the Interior Department?" illustrated by a giant corporate hand reaching out to seize the nation's heritage. Such journalistic exclamations were sufficient excitant to a public which never grasped, to the end of the case or since, the meaning of "clear-listing," "lieu lands," "filing" or the other technical intricacies that made up the substance of the charges and the evidence. The conservation zealots demanded that Ballinger be investigated by a committee of Congress. When the committee met, *Collier's* paid a fee of $25,000 to an able Boston lawyer and reformer, Louis D. Brandeis,* to represent Glavis and in general the forces hostile to Taft.

Within the committee, a majority, Republican, reported that Ballinger was "a competent and honorable gentleman, honestly and faithfully performing the duties of his high office with an eye single to the public interest," that the charges against Ballinger "appear to have had their origin in a strong feeling of animosity created by a supposed difference in policy respecting Conservation." The minority, Democratic and Insurgent Republican, reported otherwise. About everybody agreed that Ballinger was, to put it very mildly, in that state, insecure for a holder of public office, in which his "usefulness was impaired." Ballinger, six months after the report of the committee, resigned.

Pinchot took ship for the White Nile to pour out his tale to Roosevelt, who, by this time, knew that Taft was not expert in administering the government of the United States. He knew, too, that Taft was failing in adequate support of Roosevelt's policies. But Roosevelt also knew Pinchot, knew the touch of fanaticism in him, his disposition to court martyrdom. And Roosevelt knew the rules of conducting an executive office. Remembering his own experiences with Congress, he knew the utter impossibility of having in the executive branch of the government a subordinate who would conspire with men in Congress to embarrass the president. "I am not yet sure," Roosevelt wrote, "whether Taft . . . could have followed any course save the one he did."

Roosevelt's following, however, knowing little and caring less about the question of administrative discipline involved, thought only in terms of conservation, and of Pinchot as a disciple of Roosevelt. Conservation, they felt, had been betrayed by Taft, Pinchot humiliated. The Ballinger case was a prominent ring in the downward spiral of Taft's fortunes.

VI

Taft, at this stage, did a thing of the sort that men in desperation sometimes do when they find the strength of the tide running against them too strong for their mental footing. Not Taft so much as his advisers, for it

*Later Associate Justice of the Supreme Court of the United States by appointment from President Woodrow Wilson.

was not in Taft's nature to do a desperate thing; left to himself he would have let the tide against him go on to whatever fate it might bring him. But some of his advisers suggested that the tide adverse to Taft might be reversed, the Progressives placated, and the Democrats disarmed, by a policy of thoroughgoing prosecution of the trusts. The advice coincided with Taft's fundamental conviction that the law, being on the statute books, should be enforced. In this spirit were started a number of antitrust suits which, in the aggregate of all that were prosecuted in Taft's administration, exceeded by far the number prosecuted in Roosevelt's, or any other—made the Taft administration the outstanding one in American history for prosecution of trusts.

As a spectacular high spot in Taft's prosecution of the trusts, his attorney general, George W. Wickersham, on October 26, 1911, filed a suit for dissolution of the United States Steel Corporation, citing, as one cause for its being a monopoly, its purchase of the Tennessee Coal and Iron Company four years before, and alleging that the act of purchasing had included securing approval from Roosevelt, and that Roosevelt's approval had been procured by deceit.

That suit against the Steel Corporation, with its reflection upon Roosevelt, while it might have seemed the solution of one of Taft's present troubles, was the beginning of a future and a more serious one—was, indeed, the most disastrous act of Taft's political career, and led to the most calamitous episode in the history of the Republican Party.

VII

By the time Taft had been a year in the White House, the fat man jokes about him, which when he was secretary of war had been genial and kindly, began to take on a caustic tang—the 1907 jest about Taft being "the politest man I know because he gave up his seat in a street-car to three women," now supplanted by the 1910 one about a fat woman trying to get off a streetcar: because she was stout, she was obliged to go down the steps backward, but at each stop the conductor and the friendly passengers, seeing her facing forward, assumed she was getting on the car, and by giving her a helpful push facilitated her progress in the direction she did not want to go, so that she was carried past four stops before she could make it clear that it was off, not on, that she wanted to go.

The very things Taft had done to please the crowd, his patting Demos on the head, which had evoked plaudits at the time he did it, was now criticized. He had sat in the bleachers at a baseball game at Pittsburgh, declining to take a box, and had been praised by the press of the country—"he refuses to be exclusive," he is "one of the people." He had made tours of the country and journeys from Washington so numerous as to cause him to conclude privately that "the major part of the work of a President is to increase the gate receipts of fairs." Now, in the changed mood of the country, those excursions and his diversions were turned against him. Too much of his time was "occupied in pleasure seeking, attending baseball games in a number of different cities, frequent attendance at theatres, playing golf and riding around Washington and other places in automobiles."

Inevitably, much of the criticism, whether caustic anger or merely gentle jibing or sad disappointment, took the form of comparison with Roosevelt, as in:

> Dear Teddy, I need you; come home to me quick,
>   I am worried and weary and worn.
> And as hope long deferred only makes the heart sick,
> I am sadly in need of your potent "Big Stick";
>   So, Teddy, please haste your return. . . .

Taft recognized the change in the public mood, and, though brave about it, was distressed. His family and intimate friends "felt as unhappy at the way things were going as Taft himself; I feel so sorry for him I could almost cry," wrote a faithful aide.

It was a pity, and it was unfair. Taft was not a bad president, he was a good one. He had absolute integrity. Considerably less than Roosevelt would Taft relax the highest standards of public service to name a friend to office or pay a debt to a politician. He was clear-minded and discriminating about men, too, and could on occasion exercise a unique power of characterization—one of the Insurgent senators he described as "so narrow he can see through a key-hole with both eyes at once without squinting."

Far less than most presidents would Taft practice hypocrisy, even the relatively harmless political variety, or compromise with it. Anything devious was abominable to him. In all the 330 pounds of him, not a pound nor an ounce nor a gram was deceit. Furtiveness he despised. At his desk, if a politician leaned to whisper to him, Taft's end of the conversation would rise until the windowpanes rattled. Courage he had, too, at all times the quiet kind, and, when roused, the energetic kind. Never did he yield to any organized militant minority—his scorn for that was a chief cause of his downfall.

All Taft's personal failings were immaterial, whether those of inertia before ill-fortune assailed him, or those of irritability later. His tragedy was merely that he was a placid man in a restless time, had a judicial temperament when the country was in a partisan mood, was a static man in a dynamic age. Under other conditions, or in many a four years of the country's history, Taft's elephantine bulk, his good-nature, his easygoing pace, might have commended him to the country, made him a hero at the time and subsequently a legend of gargantua, made him an ideal president. During any period of national quiescence Taft might have been uniquely in tune with the universe. His heartiness, genuineness, and sincerity might have been a tonic to similar qualities in the country. But the people had recently drunk deep of the very different qualities of another personality; having been stimulated by the heady wine of strenuousness, they could not be content with the tepid nectar of Taft's milder qualities.

Taft's chief failing was that he differed from Roosevelt, his chief misfortune that he followed Roosevelt in the presidency. The country had been tuned to the tempo of Roosevelt, and inevitably therefore could only be out of step with the tempo of Taft. To accent the maladjustment, Roosevelt had told the country that Taft was like himself. Taft could not live up to that picture; and to fail to live up to expectations created in others is a sure cause of failure. Taft might be an excellent president in a score of ways; all would do him no good if he was not excellent in the precise way the country had been led to expect. Pathetically, with earnest goodwill, Taft had hoped, had tried, to be what Roosevelt had said he would be. "I do nothing," he had written to Roosevelt as the latter took ship for Africa, "without considering what you would do in the same circumstances, and without having in a sense a mental talk with you over the pros and cons of the situation."

Taft had written that, in all sincerity, during his first month in the White House. He had meant to live up to it. He did not foresee that the role of trying to be Roosevelt involved a pose which his forthright simplicity would not permit him to continue. For Taft, any pose was distasteful to his character, impossible to his nature. He had to be himself. And Taft as himself, placid, easygoing, slow to decide, was a far cry from the strenuous, quick-acting Roosevelt whom the country, with some important exceptions, had come to regard as the model of what a president ought to be.

CHAPTER 6
Roosevelt and Taft: The Break

M eanwhile Roosevelt: On the afternoon of March 4, 1909, he left Washington and the presidency, attended by a whirlwind of comment of which the almost universal characteristic was partisanship, for or against. About Roosevelt while he lived there was hardly such a thing as a balanced judgment. From the day he first became a public character, all America was divided between those who felt the devil had artfully omitted to provide him with horns, and those who justified the saying of a magazine writer, "I still insist that Roosevelt would be applauded for stoning his grandma."

A water buffalo, one of the most dangerous of African big game, killed by Roosevelt. (From a photograph by Kermit Roosevelt)

In the period of private life into which Roosevelt now entered, the first since his early twenties, he was observed with as much affection by the part of the public who loved him, as much acerbity by those who did not, as when he had been in the goldfish bowl that the presidency is. In truth, the phase into which Roosevelt now entered was not "private life." Wherever he might be, whatever role he might be filling, there was that about him which caused eyes to turn to him.

The magnetism he generated was able to reach back across the ocean from Africa. His going as a mighty hunter, as the lion killer, added to him the glamour that the average man has always seen in dangerous adventure. The affection for him, as he sailed out of New York, was so easy to be observed, so strongly felt, as to be almost a thing one could touch—an affection not at all diminished by the jokes about "may every lion do his duty!" a glamour heightened by the strange new words that America became familiar with, "safari," "sais," "mimosa"; the alluring names of the places he went and from which despatches came to American newspapers, Mombasa, Nairobi, Uganda, Gondokuro—to America it was like receiving daily bulletins on the travels of Marco Polo. And the extraordinary names of many of the animals he slew: he, with his son Kermit, killed a total of 512 (Roosevelt 296, Kermit 216), including: 17 lions, 11 elephants, 20 rhinoceroses (9 square-mouthed, 11 hook-lipped), 8 hippopotamuses, 9 giraffes, 47 gazelles, 29 zebras, 9 hyenas, together with miscellaneous numbers of animals whose names contributed an extraordinary, if ephemeral addition to American faunal information—the bongo, the kudu, the dikdik, the wildebeest and the hartbeest, the giant eland and the common eland, the impala, the warthog, the aardwolf, the klipspringer, the great bustard and the lesser bustard, the bushbuck, the waterbuck, and the reedbuck—they were not

Roosevelt at Naples, Italy.

the imaginary fauna of Alice in Wonderland; they were real animals and Roosevelt slew them; many, stuffed, were later to be seen in the National Museum at Washington.

II

Roosevelt returned to America on June 16, 1910, to a lavishness of cere-monial reception, an ecstasy of popular applause, which caused one of his biographers to feel that that day was the "zenith of Roosevelt's fame"— a reception which as respects national politics, and Taft in the White House, expressed itself in a metrical appeal by *Life:*

> Teddy, come home and blow your horn,
> The sheep's in the meadow, the cow's in the corn.
> The boy you left to 'tend the sheep Is under the haystack fast asleep.

Whether or not Roosevelt would "blow his horn" was the common question. The condition—Taft "under the haystack fast asleep"—appealed to the country as one which invited Roosevelt, almost called for him. Every chance word he said, every expression that flickered over his countenance, was spied upon by the microscopes of the press for evidence of political ambition. In the brief address which he could not avoid making in response

The "common people" awaiting "Teddy's" return. (From Herbert Johnson's Scrapbook)

to his welcome back to New York, he had said he was "ready and eager" to "help solve problems." "Ready and eager?" the suspicious press had said. Did this mean willingness to be president again?

Roosevelt at this point could, subject to the law of his nature, make his own fate, and whatever fate he should make for himself would determine the fates of many another—would, indeed, lay out a tangent for his country's history.

Conceivably he might have retired to Oyster Bay, permanently, might have practiced painstakingly the scrupulous self-restraint from active politics that ex-President Cleveland had followed before him, and Calvin Coolidge after him. For the moment, that was his mood. In a spirit that in part was absolutely sincere—yet in part a subconscious seeking of sanctuary from an at-the-moment unpleasing alternative—he looked forward to quiet days at his home, Sagamore Hill.

The nostalgia Roosevelt at all times had for Sagamore Hill was made stronger now by distaste for the alternative of participating in pubic affairs under the handicap put upon him by his relation to Taft. To the swarms of newspapermen who sought to interview him—always with the motive, or the effect, of dragging him into politics—he had nothing to say; and he asked them, almost with irritated abruptness, to stay away from Oyster Bay. The 2,000 invitations to make speeches that had piled up on him while he was in Africa and Europe, and were accumulating at the rate of more than twenty a day, which ordinarily would have pleased and stimulated him, gave him now only irritation. He wished he had remained away from America longer, until after the congressional elections that would be held in the fall. "Ugh!" he had written to Henry Cabot Lodge, "I do dread . . . having to plunge into this cauldron of politics."

That was, for Roosevelt, an extraordinary mood. Normally, prospect of activity was the breath of life to him. But now, when he contemplated participation in public affairs, his mind was obliged to go stumbling about in a maze which balked him whatever way he turned, inhibited all his normal impulses, seared his usual spontaneity, turned his spirit sour. Some motives drew him toward activity, others toward silence, both encountered frustration. Every zest of his normal taste turned to ashes in his mouth.

The heart of the maze, the thing that raised one kind of wall or another against him whatever way he turned, was his relation to Taft in the White House. He had put Taft in the presidency, therefore was responsible for him—that called for support of Taft. But he could not support Taft because Taft had departed from his policies. On the other hand, to criticize Taft would be to apologize for his own act in making Taft president. Not even did silence offer him solution of his perplexity, for silence would be interpreted by some as condonation of Taft, by others as criticism. To be silent about Taft's mistakes was to be disloyal to those policies of his which Taft had departed from, and those friends of his, such as Pinchot and Garfield, whom Taft had flouted or put away from him.

Even if silence could have made Roosevelt comfortable, which it could not, he was unable to be wholly mute, for he had engaged himself (more than a year and a half previous, before leaving the White House) to act as contributing editor of *The Outlook*. He knew the public would expect him to write about public affairs—neither the public nor his publishers would be satisfied by critiques on Irish sagas—and to write about public affairs without mentioning the president of the United States was impossible.

III

Yet throughout all this period Roosevelt had uttered no public word of dispraise for Taft. From the time he left Taft in the White House, March 4, 1909, for two years and eight months, Roosevelt, publicly, made no allusion to Taft that Taft could resent.

Privately, Roosevelt's evolution of thought about Taft took first the form of disillusionment, a disillusionment made possible by distance from Taft's side. Once Roosevelt had taken himself out of an emotional attitude toward Taft, once he became clear-eyed about his former friend, once he put his reason, unclouded by affection, to analyzing Taft's nature, he came to the same conclusion as most of the discriminating public. Taft as a subordinate, Taft when geared to the generator that had been Roosevelt, was one thing; Taft, standing on his own feet, was another. "The qualities shown by a thoroughly able and trustworthy lieutenant are totally different," Roosevelt wrote to Lodge, "from those needed by the leader."

All this was private, to friends. For the first thirty months of Taft's administration Roosevelt said nothing in public critical of Taft.

Nor had Taft said, publicly, anything to give offense to Roosevelt. Privately, he had spoken often, sometimes sadly, sometimes reproachfully, in the earlier days of their separation affectionately, with a sense of loneliness over Roosevelt's absence from his side. "When I hear some one say 'Mr. President,'" Taft said in an intimate moment to his aide, "I look around expecting to see Roosevelt." When circumstances began to make Taft feel that rift was opening, he was reproachful, not yet toward Roosevelt but toward Roosevelt's friends. "I am not criticising Roosevelt," he exclaimed, "but I get rather tired hearing from his friends that I am not carrying out his policies and when I ask for one instance they cannot name one." Later, by the time Taft was obliged to feel that he must be, from Roosevelt's point of view, an unsatisfactory president, he hoped Roosevelt would not come to visit him "because I cannot argue my case with him or before him."

In time, Taft began to let his repining about Roosevelt be heard not merely by his intimate aide but by visitors at his table. As he became less discreet he became less restrained, began to express resentment. "If you were to remove Roosevelt's skull," Taft said, "you would find written in his brain '1912.'" Constantly, "mutual friends"—ironic phrase sometimes!—

were repeating to Roosevelt what Taft had said, to Taft what Roosevelt had said. All remained, however, private, within the circle of personal gossip-carriers, schemers, intriguers.

Newspapers, through the nature of their function, because amity is not drama and quarrel is, kept the atmosphere constantly favorable to rift by assuming or implying, or asserting, in innuendo, quip, and direct averment, that Roosevelt wanted to be president again and would like to take the nomination from Taft in 1912. When Roosevelt took a hand in a political contest in New York in 1910, he was "laying the basis for getting the New York delegation in the 1912 nominating convention." When Roosevelt went on a western speaking trip the same year, he was "after the Western delegates" for the 1912 nomination.

Never, however, from the time Roosevelt left Taft in the White House, March 4, 1909, until November 1911, could any newspaper cite anything said by Taft derogatory to Roosevelt or by Roosevelt derogatory to Taft. All recrimination between them was private, within the circle of their friends and acquaintances.

IV

Then, on the morning of October 27, 1911, Roosevelt read in the newspapers an item that to millions of Americans had only casual interest, the announcement that Taft had the day before begun the dissolution suit against the United States Steel Corporation.

To Roosevelt, the announcement was infuriating.

Hundreds of friends of Roosevelt and of Taft have made surmises about the cause of the split between them, scores of historians have searched to find it, thousands of newspaper articles have assigned one cause or another, millions of the curious have wondered. The Steel Corporation suit was it. To be sure, there was, as in all such cases, no one cause; it was a growth. But so far as one incident contributed more than another, so far as one episode detonated the antagonism into flame, so far as there was any "*the* cause," the Steel Corporation suit was the climax, without which the antagonism might have remained beneath the surface, and events might have taken a different course.

In October 1907, the country had been in a panic. Thousands of shares of the Tennessee Coal and Iron Company had been pledged with important banks in New York. The panic had driven the price of the stock down to a point where it was not equal to the amounts of the loans for which the stock was pledged. If the stock should be thrown on the market, the banks would fail, the panic pass into a worse phase.

In this situation, J. P. Morgan—acting, by common consent, through virtue of his personality and power, as commander-in-chief of the financial community—had sent for Judge Elbert Gary and Henry C. Frick, the two

men who, next to Morgan himself, were the dominant figures in the United States Steel Corporation. To them, after a Saturday and Sunday of practically continuous conference, Morgan suggested—more probably, since Morgan was Morgan, he told them—that they, as heads of the United States Steel Corporation, must buy Tennessee Coal and Iron, that they must buy it before the Stock Exchange opened Monday morning, that they must pay a price roughly twice what the shares were then selling at, a price high enough to protect the loans in the endangered banks and that they must pay for it in Steel Corporation bonds, which, a sound security selling close to par, could be substituted in the banks for stock of Tennessee Coal and Iron.

Gary was willing, but told Morgan that it would be desirable to get the consent of the government at Washington, because otherwise the purchase might be construed as an illegal act in restraint of trade, a violation of the Anti-Trust Act, and the government might enjoin the purchase, in which case the panic would be made worse rather than cured.

Promptly a telephone message to Secretary Loeb in the White House made an engagement for Gary and Frick to see President Roosevelt the next morning; promptly another telephone message assembled a special train of locomotive and Pullman; speedily Gary and Frick made the midnight dash to Washington; eagerly, before Roosevelt had had breakfast they appeared at the White House; anxiously they explained what they wanted to Roosevelt and Elihu Root.

Gary and Frick told Roosevelt that "as a mere business transaction they did not care to purchase" Tennessee Coal and Iron; that "under ordinary circumstances they would not consider purchasing"; that "little benefit will come to the Steel Corporation from the purchase"; that they were "aware that the purchase will be used as a handle for attack upon them on the ground that they are striving to secure a monopoly." But, they told Roosevelt, they "feel it is immensely to their interest as to the interest of every responsible business man to try to prevent a panic, and general industrial smash-up."

Roosevelt "answered that while of course I could not advise them to take the action proposed, I felt it no public duty of mine to interpose any objections."

After the crisis was averted and the country righted, cynics, pooh-poohing, invented the theory that purchase of Tennessee Coal and Iron had not been necessary at all. By a series of ingenious ex post facto hypotheses, they proved the panic would have ended anyhow. Cynically they charged that the Steel Corporation had used the occasion to acquire a valuable property at an exceptionally low price.

Necessarily inherent in these attacks were charges against Roosevelt. One, making Roosevelt out an innocent, said that Gary and Frick had deceived him. The other, making Roosevelt out a conspirator, said that he had consciously connived in the scheme in payment for past favors or expected ones in the shape of political campaign contributions, or because his friendship with Steel Corporation director George W. Perkins. The

Listening. A cartoon based on the artist's suspicion that T.R. may have had a hand in managing some of the events that led to the demand for him as president. (From a cartoon by Ketten in the New York World)

charges the Democrats and every other enemy or critic of Roosevelt took up. Over and over they exploited them. As soon as the Democrats took control of the House of Representatives in 1910 they investigated the Steel Corporation and put Roosevelt on the stand.

Of all the charges ever made against Roosevelt, this one enraged him most. Whenever, wherever, and by whomever it was made, he went to extreme pains to denounce it. He denounced it on the stump, he denounced it before a congressional investigating committee, he denounced it in magazine articles, he took pains to denounce it in his autobiography. His sincerity and indignation led him to such frequency and emphasis of denial as to cause his friends to smile. Defense of himself from this charge became a principal detail of his concern about his place in history. Repudiation of the charge was almost an obsession with him.

Now, four years after the event, here was the Taft administration, which Roosevelt had put in power, asserting to be true, with the authority of a legal document, what Roosevelt had asserted to be untrue; here was the Taft administration declaring that Roosevelt had been deceived, and necessarily implying that if he had not been deceived then he must have consciously connived—"making me out either a fool or a knave," Roosevelt snorted.

V

The Steel Corporation suit had been filed on October 26. The first number of *The Outlook*, a stately gaited weekly, from which Roosevelt

could speak, was the one dated November 16. Angrily Roosevelt repudiated the aspersions upon him. The administration's allegation that "I was misled . . . is not correct. The representatives of the Steel Corporation told me the truth. . . . I was not misled. . . . The representatives of the Steel Corporation did not deceive me. . . . Any statement that I was misled . . . is itself not in accordance with the truth. . . . I reaffirm everything."

In addition to his repudiation of the attack on his honor or his intelligence, he vigorously criticized the principle upon which the suit was based. Big business organizations, he said, should be prosecuted only when they have committed crimes; size alone is not a crime. With italicized emphasis he made himself clear—"nothing . . . is gained by breaking up a huge industrial organization *which has not offended otherwise than by its size*"; such organizations, guiltless of wrongdoing, should be handled by regulation, not prosecution; to do as Taft was doing now about the Steel Trust was an attempt to treat the problem by "destructive litigation" instead of "constructive legislation," "not progressiveness but an unintelligent . . . toryism." With caution, to make certain no one should charge his present outburst with being inspired by approval of trusts, he called the roll of the antitrust suits he had brought. Invidiously he added that when he was president antitrust suits were instituted "only where we felt so sure of our facts that we could be fairly certain there was likelihood of success."

CHAPTER 7
Roosevelt: His Hat in the Ring

Roosevelt's angry public reply to the charges affecting himself in the Taft administration's suit against the Steel Corporation, his public criticism of the governmental policy on which the suit was brought, his private expressions of anger against Taft—repeated in a word-of-mouth transmission that quickly reached about every important person in the country—combined to awake everybody who had wished—hitherto with resignation to disappointment—that Roosevelt might contend against Taft for the presidential nomination. Something electric passed among Roosevelt zealots everywhere, telling their hopeful instincts that Napoleon might now leave Elba, that "his boat was on the sea, his foot was on the shore." There was no radio then, but among the Roosevelt followers the ether of fraternity was enough. From one to another the tidings were relayed as if from beacons on the hills. Eyes that for three years had been dulled by prosaic days lighted up to watch for the fiery torch, alert ears listened for the tocsin.

Roosevelt did not, at first, tell them he would run. For some ten weeks after his November 16 blast at Taft his attitude was one which the *New York American* compressed into a compact question, "T.R.: R U or R U not?" "Almost overnight," said *Current Literature* in January 1912, "has this Roosevelt obsession risen and spread until it has become the dominant feature in the political discussions of the country."

Finally, on February 23, Roosevelt gave the country another of his unforgettable phrases, "My hat is in the ring," adding "the fight is on and I am stripped to the buff." The public, ignoring the terminology of medieval combat, but pleased with the modern, gave the former phrase universal currency. Two days later, in New York, Roosevelt made his challenge formal: "I will accept the nomination for President if it is tendered to me, and I will adhere to this decision until the convention has expressed its preference."

II

In the bitterness that now arose, Taft was driven into a mood expressed by his own unfortunate phrase: "Even a rat will fight when he is driven into a corner." In that mood Taft, on April 25, went to Boston and delivered the most remarkable speech ever delivered by a president about an ex-president.

For two hours Taft stood before his audience denouncing with all the vigor of language he possessed "one whom in the past I have greatly admired and loved." Following an unusually vehement outburst he paused a moment, his great kindly face quivering with emotion, and exclaimed: "This wrenches my soul!" He had been driven to his present course, he explained, by "the unjust, unfounded charges against me . . . that Mr. Roosevelt is now making to the public." Roosevelt had, he declared, attempted to discredit him by "adroit appeals to discontent and class hatred"; had "garbled" his language, "misrepresented" his actions. All this, and more to the extent of ten newspaper columns, Taft charged, with perspiration streaming down his face, in the presence of 10,000 people who sang "We'll hang Teddy's hat to a sour apple tree," under the sponsorship of a presiding officer who declared that "Theodore Roosevelt is following the footsteps of Julius Caesar and Napoleon Bonaparte, and unless we stop him it will be but a question of time when he usurps a dictatorship of the American people"—the setting and manner of the scene accenting the substance of the indictment to a degree which caused the *New York Times* to say, and nearly

"Platform Amenities: President Taft (conductor of the White House Express): 'You can't go on this train.' Colonel Roosevelt: 'If I can't, you shant!' "(From a cartoon by G.R.H. in Punch, *June 26, 1912)*

everybody to feel, that "these damning charges, made by a President of the United States against an ex-President," constitute "one of the most deplorable occasions in the history of our politics."

Twenty-four hours later, and only 40 miles away, at Worcester, Massachusetts, Roosevelt struck back. He had read, in the morning newspapers, the full text of the castigation of him the night before by his onetime friend, and, in a temper defiant alike of the restraining voice of decorum and the placatory counsel of friends, he replied with what stands as the most extraordinary speech ever made in the United States by an ex-president about a president. He had before him an audience of his own partisans, familiar with Taft's speech the night before, and tense with a belligerency that accelerated Roosevelt's own. With fists clenched, head thrust forward from his stocky body, his voice at times hoarsely shrill with emotion loosed from all restraint, his features straining with the anger that blazed within him, he used anathemas about Taft not only sensational as coming from an ex-president, or being hurled at a president, but, according to a Boston newspaper, "such as seldom have been heard on a public platform in this State." "President Taft," Roosevelt said, "has not only been disloyal to our past friendship, but he has been disloyal to every canon of decency and fair play. . . . The assaults made upon me by his campaign managers have been foul to the verge of indecency." Implying that Taft had called him a "neurotic," Roosevelt retorted: "Mr. Taft had better preserve his self-respect by not pretending that it gives him great pain to attack me. No one uses such epithets in pain. President Taft served under me for

Plight of the Republican elephant felled by missiles from both sides in 1912. "I can't stand much more of this!" (From a cartoon by Minor in the St. Louis Dispatch)

over seven years without finding fault with me. He only discovered I was dangerous when I discovered that he was useless to the American people. I wanted from President Taft a square deal for the people of the United States. If he had given the people a square deal he could have counted on my enthusiastic support. I do not believe he has given the people a square deal. I believe that he has yielded to the bosses and to the great privileged interests. Every boss in the country is with Mr. Taft and to deny it is ludicrously false."

Roosevelt's anger carried him to words and actions sensational in the extreme. He denounced as "an unpardonable sin" Taft's reading the night before of an old letter from Roosevelt—and then Roosevelt himself drew from his pocket an old letter that Taft had written to him, and read: "I can never forget that the power I now exercise was voluntarily transferred from you to me, and that I am under obligation to you to see that your judgment in selecting me as your successor and bringing about the succession shall be vindicated according to the standards which you and I in conversation have always formulated." Excoriating Taft's ingratitude, Roosevelt said: "Mr. Taft is President only because I kept my promise in spite of infinite pressure to break it. It is a bad trait to bite the hand that feeds you."

All this, and more to the extent of two hours, Roosevelt said to an audience that cheered: "Hit him again, Teddy! Hit him between the eyes! Soak him! Put him over the ropes!"—the scene and the background causing the *Boston Post* to sum up with sad resignation: "Roosevelt, with his roaring epithets, his prize-fight vocabulary, his complete abandonment to rage; Taft, with his ill-adapted attempts to fight back in kind. . . ."

III

Each man, Roosevelt and Taft, prepared to take their new rivalry to the Republican Convention in Chicago.

At Oyster Bay, June 14, Roosevelt arose early, breakfasted early. In a flurry of instructions to servants and good-byes to neighbors who had come to wish him luck, he climbed into the tonneau of an open car and, with Mrs. Roosevelt, started for New York, 40 miles away. It was noticed by the little group who saw him off that the Colonel's afflatus suggested more militancy, more snap and crackle, than usual, due, in part, to the new hat he was wearing, a hat among hats, big, tan, with a deep crown and a wide brim, having a sombrero effect; the hat of a soldier, of a Rough Rider.

Just before noon Roosevelt reached his office in *The Outlook*. In the corridor outside his door were jammed hundreds of people, through whom Roosevelt shouldered a way, smiling, responding to greetings. As he reached his door, a newspaperman asked a question. Roosevelt turned around, waited for silence: "When am I going to Chicago? I do not know yet. I may return to Oyster Bay this afternoon. But sometimes things move quickly these days." Grinning, he pushed open the door, backed through, and closed it.

In the corridor the hum of excitement went on. Inside, Roosevelt talked over the telephone with his aides in Chicago. The convention was only two days away.

Presently Roosevelt came out, handed around copies of a statement— he was going to Chicago. Reporters rushed to telephones. In the afternoon Roosevelt started.

At Chicago, police had made preparations to control the crowd at the railroad station. The plan, from the moment Roosevelt appeared, evaporated. The sight of the Colonel, teeth agleam, romantic headgear, burly arms waving greetings, was catalytic. A mob, shouting, laughing, cheering, shoving, engulfed the police and took Roosevelt to its bosom. The drive to the hotel was through lines of sensation-mad people, "who greeted him as they might have greeted a successful Roman general returning from the wars." They followed him into his hotel, jammed the lobby, almost crushed the breath from his body. Finally he escaped to an elevator and thence to his headquarters, and ten minutes later emerged onto a balcony and gave a short talk: "It is a naked fight against theft, and the thieves will not win." The crowds in Michigan Avenue and Grant Park roared back, "Soak 'em, Teddy! Give it to 'em!"

To a reporter who asked him a commonplace question about his health and spirits, Roosevelt achieved, in this case without planning it, one of the most potent for effect of all the striking phrases that sparkled along the path of his career. "I'm feeling," he said, using a quite artless simile that came to his mind from his hunting experiences, "like a bull moose"— bringing it about that BULL MOOSE should stalk in heavy black letters across the front pages of 10,000 newspapers (conveying, one wonders, what mystic significance, to a nation in which not one of 100 had ever seen an antlered animal, or could know how a bull moose feels under any set of circumstances). Crudely drawn pictures of the animal appeared in immense posters on the walls of hotels and as placards at the head of improvised parades, the biological details giving some pain, doubtless, to the curator of the Field Museum on Michigan Avenue, but the spirit adequately grasped by Roosevelt's exalted followers. Manufacturers of campaign buttons telegraphed frantically to their factories, where harried artists made unaccustomed demands on local libraries for a picture of "alces Americanus." The name, "Bull Moose," the idea, the spirit, was taken into the national consciousness, became an established thing, a symbol universally understood. Roosevelt's political following was the "Bull Moose Party," a partisan of him was a "Bull-mooser."

IV

The spirit into which Roosevelt at Oyster Bay had whipped the scene and which rose to surround him as he arrived on the field in person, was not what might have been expected from the angry epithets which Roosevelt had been using to stimulate his followers. It was a fighting spirit, of course—it could hardly have avoided that, but the kind of fighting spirit that is described as martial, and the precise shade of martial which verges into religious. Due to the presence of women in large numbers in Roosevelt's ranks, entering into politics for the first time and taking it with exalted seriousness; due to the implications, vague but always elevated, of the phrase Roosevelt had made a slogan, "social justice"; and due perhaps to a certain solemnity, a fatefulness in the fact that the Republican Party, then still remembered as having fought the Civil War and saved the Union, was now in its own grapple of life and death—due to these and whatever causes, the emotion Roosevelt inspired expressed itself in what had already begun to be sung and what became the practically official and universally used battle song of Roosevelt's party, "Onward Christian Soldiers," and the "Battle-Hymn of the Republic."

In that spirit, on the night preceding the opening of the convention, Monday, June 17, Roosevelt made perhaps the most moving speech of his career. The auditorium would hold 5,000—four times that many struggled to enter. Roosevelt began on a high note: "Disaster is ahead of us if we trust to the leadership of men whose souls are seared and whose eyes are blinded, men of cold heart and narrow mind, who believe we can find safety in dull timidity and dull inaction." As for his own fortunes, he offered himself in the spirit of utter sacrifice: "What happens to me is not of the slightest consequence. I am to be used, as in a doubtful battle any man is used, to his hurt or not, so long as he is useful, and is then cast aside or left to die. I wish you to feel this and I shall need no sympathy when you are through with me, for this fight is far too great to permit us to concern ourselves about any one man's welfare." In his peroration he achieved a climax which in emotional intensity equaled Bryan's "crown of thorns, cross of gold," which was comparable to the most elevated oratory in the language—and which made a very old word newly familiar to an America that was beginning to lose acquaintance with its Bible: "We fight in honorable fashion for the good of mankind; fearless of the future, unheeding of our

A characteristic pose of Roosevelt campaigning in 1912. (From a photograph courtesy of Roosevelt House)

individual fates, with unflinching hearts and undimmed eyes; we stand at Armageddon, and we battle for the Lord."

Something about the word "Armageddon," an implication at once mystic and martial, made it overnight part of the language of the street. Embattled righteousness was the meaning commonly ascribed to it; its pronunciation varied with individual preference. Scores of songs and poems were inspired by it, but not all that "Armageddon" inspired was reverent, not all took either the word or its discoverer seriously. Of all the satires and ironies that arose out of the religious flavor which Roosevelt's 1912 crusade took on, the most penetrating came from one unknown to the present historian, or, I suspect, to any other. His performance was of a sort that does not get itself into the official records, nor even into the newspapers. His name is forgotten, if indeed it was ever known. Only the thing he did is recalled.

But I can visualize him strolling down the quieter side of Michigan Avenue, the park side. I can imagine him pausing to observe the Colonel going by, and the crowds that followed. He noticed the rapt quality of them, the visionary gleam in their eyes, the frenzy in some. Seeing it he recalled from his reading the age-long disposition of men to set up heroes, to expect messiahs. Seeing and reflecting, it occurred to him that the scene called for a comment on mankind and his incredible ways. Being a laconic person, his comment took the form of action. Waiting until the crowd had hurried by, he crossed the street, sought a small printer, had a brief order filled, and employed some small boys, with the result that throughout Chicago's streets were scattered thousands of dodgers reading:

At Three o'Clock
Thursday Afternoon

THEODORE ROOSEVELT

Will Walk

on the

WATERS OF
LAKE MICHIGAN[6]

V

From the Roosevelt point of view, all was vain. Parliamentarily, the Taft forces controlled the convention. As for persuasion or intimidation, neither beautiful women in the galleries nor catcalls from the crowd, neither hint of bolt nor certainty of Roosevelt's greater popularity could move the Standpatter forces. They would rather lose the election, even destroy the Republican Party, than let Roosevelt have the nomination. It was in terms of political death that all had come to think—death for the Republican Party and for the two principals, Taft and Roosevelt. "The only question now," said Standpatter Chauncey M. Depew, "is which corpse gets the most flowers."

Roosevelt, when he realized he could not win, announced that his delegates would continue to sit in the convention but not vote nor otherwise participate. When the convention ended he called an informal meeting of his followers, announced a new party, the Progressives, and perfected the organization of it at a new convention two months later. In the election he carried six states to Taft's two, got 4,117,813 votes to Taft's 3,486,316.

But the Democratic candidate, Woodrow Wilson, carried forty states, got 6,294,293 votes, and became president.

The birth of the new party.

VI

W hat was it all about? Apart from the personal aspect, apart from the wish of Roosevelt to be in the White House again and the wish of millions of Americans to have him there, what was the meaning of the Progressive Party? What was the fundamental difference, in terms of governmental policy, between the old Republican Party and the new Progressive one? What, aside from the emotion generated by the angry epithets, "Socialist" hurled by one side, "reactionary" by the other—what differences of principle separated the two? What was decided when the Republicans controlled the convention, and what when the Progressives had the larger popular vote? And what would have been decided had the Republicans under Taft won the presidency, or the Progressives under Roosevelt? And what was decided when the Democrats actually won it?

Only to a comparatively slight extent did the average man think of the conflict in terms of principle at all; he saw it mainly as a duel between personalities, Roosevelt on the one side, Taft on the other. More accurately, the issue was pro-Roosevelt and anti-Roosevelt; for Taft as a personality had no great magnetism, did not attract any large personal following— Taft's role in the fight was largely as a symbol for those who hated Roosevelt, or the smaller number who merely deplored him. The average man, indeed, did not so much *think* about any theories of government involved as *feel* the emotions stirred up by the slogans: those of odium, especially "standpatism"; or those of altruism, "social and industrial justice." The average man in the mass, the whole of the America of that day, was divided— mainly by temperament, by differing responsiveness to certain appeals—into two groups: those whose eyes became rapt in the thrill of singing "Onward Christian Soldiers" behind the banner of Roosevelt, and those who were indifferent to Roosevelt or were moved to acute distaste by his actions and utterances.

When Roosevelt electrified the nation with his "We stand at Armageddon and we battle for the Lord," just what did the average man assume would be the concrete consequences of winning the battle or losing it— other than that in one case Roosevelt would be in the White House and the air would sparkle, while in the other Roosevelt would be at Oyster Bay and the world would be drab?

There was one clear difference of fundamental principle: The Progressive Party and Roosevelt stood for the universal participation of all men and women in all the mechanisms of government (with very slight exceptions, if any). That was new, and far-reaching. Between that and the representative form of government supported by the Republicans, the difference was wide and deep, and the question of national policy thus laid before the country may possibly have been, as the excited disputants on both sides heatedly declared, the most important since the Civil War.

Direct popular government, as expressed in Roosevelt's sequence of "I believe's" in his "Charter of Democracy," embraced: direct primaries for the nomination of all party candidates for all offices, including, as respects candidates for president, direct preferential primaries in which the vote should instruct delegates as to the voter's choice; direct election of U.S. senators by vote of the people—as distinct from the historic method of election by state legislatures; the initiative, whereby the people by petition could initiate laws, could, in effect, command the legislature to enact laws; and the referendum, whereby the people could pass upon laws enacted by the legislature; and the recall, whereby the people could by popular vote remove from office any official, including judges, regardless of the length of term for which he had been elected.

As against that, the Republicans in their platform, with a manner of declining to dignify these upstart innovations by mentioning them, stood

Roosevelt returning from a campaign tour during the 1912 campaign. To the left is Mrs. Roosevelt. (From a photograph by International)

firm for the old way: "We believe in our self-controlled representative democracy."

There was one other deep-reaching difference of principle. Roosevelt and the Progressives believed in the "recall of judicial decisions"—that was Roosevelt's phrase in his "Charter of Democracy" speech. It is doubtful if any political term since "nullification" had so startled the nation. In part the shock was due to popular misunderstanding. When newspapers carried the phrase in headlines, great numbers of people understood Roosevelt to mean that immediately after any judicial decision in any sort of case, criminal trial for murder or civil case of trespass, the public would have the right immediately to act as a court of appeal.

Actually, Roosevelt meant only that in cases involving judicial interpretation of the Constitution the people should have a right to pass upon the decision: "I very earnestly ask you clearly to provide means which will permit the people themselves, by popular vote, after due deliberation and discussion, but finally and without appeal, to settle what the proper construction of any constitutional point is. When a judge decides a constitutional question, when he decides what the people as a whole can or cannot do, the people should have the right to recall that decision if they think it wrong."

Roosevelt's limited, actual meaning, as expressed in the text of his "Charter of Democracy" speech in February, was never able to catch up with the broader, incorrect meaning inferred by the public from the early

Roosevelt making a rear platform appearance during the 1912 campaign. This sort of scene had been characteristic of American political campaigns for a generation preceding 1912 and continued until 1932. (From a photograph by International)

newspaper headlines. After trying to make his meaning clear, and succeeding only in intensifying the opprobrium of the idea, he resigned himself to the rueful conclusion that it is a major error for a man in public life to fail to make himself clear; by the time the Progressives were ready to write their platform in August, they were careful to state the idea with meticulous exactness—and with avoidance of the fatal phrase.

There was yet another difference: The Republicans in their platform, though most of them hated to do it, endorsed the Sherman law making all trusts criminal, pointed with pride to having originated the law in 1889, and congratulated themselves, with some polemic license, upon having "consistently and successfully" enforced it. The Progressives presented the country with a new attitude, advocating not dissolution by prosecution but rather fostering through regulation.

Other important Progressive policies included:

> Effective legislation looking to the prevention of industrial accidents, occupational diseases, overwork, involuntary unemployment, and other injurious effects incident to modern industry; the fixing of minimum safety and health standards for the various occupations, and the exercise of the public authority of state and nation, including the federal control over interstate commerce and the taxing power, to maintain such standards; the prohibition of child labor; minimum wage standards for working women; to provide a "living wage" in all industrial occupations; the general prohibition of night work for women, and the establishment of an eight-hour day for women and young persons; one day's rest in seven for all wage-workers; the eight-hour day in continuous twenty-four-hour industries.

The main tenets of Progressive doctrine, direct participation of all voters in the processes of government, a check by the people upon judicial interpretation of constitutions, and "constructive regulation of trusts instead of destructive litigation," would presumably have made progress had Roosevelt and the Progressives won the election of 1912. Yet it is by no means certain the public was strongly determined upon any or all; actually, during twenty years following, direct primaries made no progress but rather some recession, the recall of judicial decisions acquired no foothold whatever, and trusts in 1932 were treated the same as in 1912. And it is fairly certain that whatever change Roosevelt, had he been elected, might have made along any of these lines would have been unimportant compared to the consequences of his directing the country with respect to the Great War.

The war, lurking just ahead in the corridor of years, utterly unanticipated in 1912, gave a new tangent to everything, making it impossible to say and futile to guess what might have been the future of the Progressive movement in a normal world.

Editor's Note

This is not only the halfway point in *Our Times*, it is also the turning point. For the first half of the book, the figure of Theodore Roosevelt has loomed like a Colossus over our imagination—we as readers, as a nation, and most especially as Mark Sullivan, who must always be numbered among the "we" of *Our Times*. Even when he reflects the consensus, even when he assiduously shares the observations of his legions of witness-correspondents, Sullivan's history is deeply personal.

Some historians may now say that Roosevelt came to the Progressive Movement late, or expediently. Mark Sullivan, one of the original muckrakers, didn't think so. Caught up in the missionary zeal of the movement, and enthralled by Roosevelt's charismatic personality, to which he had uncommon access, Sullivan was a true believer. No one who hadn't seen his highest hopes disappointed could have written Sullivan's study of William Howard Taft. I don't believe any Hollywood movie could have portrayed Taft in more dramatically compelling terms; Sullivan's description of the rift between Taft and Roosevelt startles in its ability to appeal to the reader's emotions—doubtless because Sullivan's own emotions had been so active during these events.

In Sullivan's view, Taft failed to carry out Roosevelt's program as the country (and Roosevelt and Sullivan themselves) had every reason to expect he would. The result was the fatal splitting of the Republican Party and the election of a Democrat, Woodrow Wilson. Wilson believed himself to be, if not a Progressive in the organized, partisan sense, at least a progressive, lower case. He'd been reforming—something, anything—much of his life, and was famous for his reforms as president of Princeton University and as governor of New Jersey. Yet to Sullivan's thinking, Wilson didn't reform the right way. Wilson seemed aloof and patrician, too much the cloistered intellect, and his reforms betrayed a lack of faith in Yankee self-reliance. (Present-day politicians might call some of Wilson's reforms "social engineering"; his contemporaries called them "socialist," and much of the groundwork for Franklin Roosevelt's later, more interventionist reform was laid in the theories and policy of Woodrow Wilson.) Moreover, Sullivan, a Republican, wasn't convinced that it was even possible for a Democrat to be a Progressive. His solution, as a historian, was to omit virtually any reference to Wilson's peacetime domestic policies. Sulli-

van, however, supported America's involvement in the Great War, and in
Our Times he offers grudging approval of Wilson's conduct of that war.

One reason for Sullivan's approval must be that, during the Great War,
America stepped out onto the world stage for the first time as a major
player. According to Theodore Roosevelt's worldview, it was only right
that America command the world, not through imperialism but something
more like Manifest Destiny. America was the smartest, the toughest, the
wisest, and (Roosevelt had no doubt) the elected of God. Lest we forget,
Roosevelt's campaign song in 1912 was "Onward, Christian Soldiers." As
far as Roosevelt's disciples could see, it was the duty of the United States to
lead decadent Europe and uncivilized Africa, Asia, and the Americas. The
Great War provided the United States with the first real opportunity to assume that leadership role, first on the battlefront and then in the negotiations at Versailles. Even a Roosevelt enthusiast who didn't entirely approve
of Wilson might have admired Wilson's Fourteen Points and his vision of a
League of Nations, bringing something like American democracy to the
conduct of global diplomacy and guaranteeing a continued leadership role
for the United States.

The United States, however, would make a quick exit from the world
stage. America refused to join the League of Nations; the League, in turn,
was left powerless to stem the rising tide of fascism in the years to come. If
America had ever cared about such things as Italian incursions into
Ethiopia, now it preferred to ignore these first clear signs of militarism and
fascist dreams of world dominion. America had more pressing business on
Wall Street. Mark Sullivan saw America growing selfish, materialist, shirk-
ing its duties. We were, in his mind, a national illustration of Aesop's fable
of the grasshopper who fiddled away without a thought for winter. By the
time Sullivan wrote, the Great Depression was in full swing, and he knew
that winter was just around the corner from the Jazz Age.

The figure of Theodore Roosevelt dominated the first half of this work.
For the second half, it is his absence that will dominate.

PART IV

Years of Ferment

CHAPTER I
June 28, 1914

Two o'clock in the morning in that vast third of the continental United States that stretches 1,000 miles from the Rocky Mountains to the Pacific Coast. This immense region is deep in slumber, the peaceful stillness only broken here and there by the rumbling of a night train rolling down from Oregon, a lamp in a lonely ranch house where a mother fosters a clamant new life, the droning hum of power plants along streams tumbling down the slopes of the Great Divide. In the cities, what movement goes on is subdued, furtive, "nightlife"—in San Francisco's Chi-

From the front page of the New York Times *of June 29, 1914.*

natown the muffled crackle of dice on baize-covered gambling tables; along the Barbary Coast the tired tinkling of pianos behind closed and curtained windows; a sauntering policeman, twirling his club, yawns. In the far western cities, morning newspapers have just been "put to bed"; their staffs are sleepily gossiping over rolls and coffee before they, too, "call it a day" and go home.

At the same moment it is four o'clock in the morning in the mid-third of the American continent, the great food source of the nation, reaching from the Rockies eastward across endless fertile prairies to Illinois. Smoke is spiraling above the shingled rooftops of a million farmhouses. In kerosene-lighted kitchens, wives and mothers are preparing breakfast on wood-burning stoves; through the open doors and windows pours the fragrance of coffee, pancakes and syrup, frying ham. Men and boys carry milk pails from house to barn; though the day is Sunday, and rural America will rest, morning chores must be done.

At the same moment it is five o'clock in the morning in the eastern third of the continent, from Indiana to the Atlantic seaboard. In the great cities, belated roisterers are homeward bound. A doctor, kit in hand, rubs sleepy eyes as he hurries to answer a night call. From dingy car barns motormen start out on their early runs. Milk horses, trained to their slow-paced routine, clump over cobbled alleys, their clatter the city's chanticleer call to day.

America is abed, sleeping the sleep of the well fed, the carefree, the confident.

At the same moment it is noon in the small foreign city of Sarajevo, capital of Austria-Hungary's newly acquired and sullen province, Slavic Bosnia. The heir to the Austrian throne, Archduke Francis Ferdinand, and his morganatic wife, the Duchess of Hohenberg, are driving to the palace

The arrest of the assassin Gavro Princip.

European news of June 1914 had little effect at the "four corners." (From a drawing by Victor C. Anderson)

from the City Hall, where the Archduke had been given a perfunctory welcome by the burgomaster. As their automobile comes opposite the doorway of a barber shop near the intersection of Rudolph Street, a young Serbian student, Gavro Princip, fires two shots—"the first struck the Duchess low down on the right side, while the second hit the Archduke in the neck near the throat and pierced the jugular vein." The chauffeur drives with panic haste to the garrison hospital. His royal charges, when taken from the car, are lifeless.

Only ten minutes have passed. In New York and Chicago late stragglers continue their way in the cool of beginning dawn. In the Midwest, farmers' wives go on with their lamp-lighted chores. In San Francisco, Chinatown imperturbably gambles on.

America, still asleep on the Pacific Coast, or beginning to arise in the Midwest and East, is unaware of the tragic act of a political maniac 7,000 miles away, has no dream of the consequences to America that are to flow from that mad deed.

II

At the time, the day was merely one in the flow of eventless diurnities. Months later, some who cast their memories back, could only recall it vaguely as a Sunday in early midsummer, associated with newly reaped wheat stacked in fields, cattle knee-deep in shaded pools, hay drying in the sun. Those who tried to remember what they had been doing on the day that was a dividing point in history could identify only their accustomed

"Between the crosses, row on row."

routine of pursuit and diversion; some could recall having gone to church and there to have been in a mood, evoked by sermon, hymn, or ritual, of peace on earth, goodwill toward men. It had been, in the American custom still strong at that time, a day of family dinners preceded by grace, of country drives—with horse and buggy in as many cases as automobile; of evening gatherings of young folks on wistaria-hung porches. The memories of many of the youths of the time associated the day with commencement week in high school or college. It was these who had occasion, later, to realize, poignantly, that June 28, 1914, had contained the tragic omen of events destined to twist and make turbulent the stream of placid future they had supposed to lie ahead; before these awaited the scenes that, for many, ended

> In Flanders fields the poppies blow
> Between the crosses, row on row,
> That mark our place . . .*

III

The youths, for whom that fate was destined, found no hint of it in the world about them. In the American newspapers of June 28 and the day following, there was no suggestion of the "thunder on the left" that was Rome's warning of impending storm, no hint that the day was to be one of the half dozen epochal dates in civilization, dividing modern history into prewar and after. On the contrary, the press from its vantage point of superior wisdom assured the country that the assassination at Sarajevo was merely "another mess in the Balkans." In the American newspapers of June 29, 1914, as surveyed in yellowed files many years later, the assassination at

---

*"In Flanders Fields" was written by Captain John D. McCrae, of Montreal, Canada (killed on duty in Flanders, January 28, 1918).

Sarajevo appears as a temporary intrusion of violence from a distant world and an alien way of life, into an America intent upon the normal concerns of a peaceful country in a particularly peaceful time.

IV

The normal concerns of the America of June 28, 1914, are in most part to be found reflected in the newspapers of that and the following day. To identify and recall them, and to compose a picture of America as it was on that day, the author of this history eighteen years later asked editors in all parts of the country to cull from their editions of June 28 and the day following items characteristic of that time.

The major interests thus revealed included a contest for the governorship of New York and the role played by a political party which the headlines called "Bull Moose"—a newcomer to the curious zoological nomenclature of American political parties, which had emerged full-grown into the arena two years before and for the time seemed equal to the elephant and the donkey in vociferous equipment for longevity. One headline reflected anxiety about the health of a national hero: "Ordered to Rest to Avoid Collapse, the Colonel Refuses"—the character then familiar to everybody as "The Colonel" being, it is necessary to explain to later generations, Theodore Roosevelt. Another headline dealt, somewhat excitedly, with an impending battle between two generals, Mexican, named Carranza and Villa—when newspapers of that time discussed "the war," as they frequently and portentously did, they meant the civil strife in Mexico, and, as to the great majority of newspapers, the danger and undesirability of our becoming embroiled. Another headline (larger in some newspapers than the one about the assassination of the Archduke) recited that "Johnson Retains his Championship, Wins Decision Over Moran"—Jack Johnson being a black prizefighter whose winning the heavyweight championship from Jim Jeffries four years before had added a new facet to America's trou-

Figures in the headlines of 1914 and a few years previous. (From Enright in the New York Globe*)*

"Women will vote by 1917," says Champ Clark. America was stirred, or amused, by news about suffragettes in England. (From Life, *1912)*

bled race relations. Other headlines reflecting the major concerns of the America of June 28, 1914, included: "Suffragettes March on Capitol; Women Will Vote by 1917, Says Clark"—Champ Clark being the Democratic Speaker of the House of Representatives, and his prediction having to do with an amendment to the Constitution giving suffrage to women. (His prophecy was three years too short, since fulfillment did not come until 1920.)

The headlines quoted above, from newspapers of June 28, 1914, reflect the chief interests, the public concerns, of the America of that day. In the press of any one day, however, it is only the publicly important, or the unusual, or the showy, that the larger headlines portray. For a picture of the normal come and go of the day, the spirit and flavor of the time, one will search more fruitfully among the less obtrusive records on the inside pages, including the advertisements, where, as in the living room and kitchen of a home, are to be found a more intimate reflection of the life of the period than is provided by the front porch or the first page.

One intimate aspect of American life as mirrored by those diaries of history, the newspapers, on June 28, was discussed at Indianapolis, Indiana, at a meeting of a women's national medical association, which waged "Hot Debate Over Corset." In Baltimore, a conflict between old ways and new took the form of a debate over a proposal to permit baseball on Sunday. The early Puritan spirit lingered in spots, and among some religious denominations. In Scranton, Pennsylvania, a gospel campaign had recently been conducted by the Reverend "Billy" Sunday, a former baseball player turned evangelist, whose exuberance of exhortation was sometimes called, by persons whose approval of Mr. Sunday was incomplete, "muscular

Christianity" or "strong-arm religion"; one result was a revival locally of sentiment against Sunday baseball.

Growing patronage of public amusements, Sunday and weekday, was the rule. The 176 plays (151 new, 19 adaptations, 6 dramatizations), which the *New York Times* enumerated on June 28 as having been presented in Manhattan during the season just closing, was high tide of the period when the spoken drama had the theater practically to itself. Rapid growth of a humble little Cinderella of the stage, not yet recognized as a competitor, was recorded in the *Register and Leader* of Des Moines, Iowa, where, out of a population of 100,000, fully 20,000 daily "stick nickels or dimes through the ticket-windows of 65 moving picture theatres"; the manager of one said that his "best business-getters are the serials, the stories which are continued week after week"—a very popular one was a lurid melodrama called *The Perils of Pauline*.

A Redfern corset advertisement of about 1914.

Scene from The Perils of Pauline, *a serial movie.*

A headline in the *Cincinnati Enquirer:*

**COUNT OF TEN TO BE TAKEN TUESDAY NIGHT
BY BACCHUS IN PANHANDLE STATE**

Long Dry Spell Coming

DROUGHT WILL BEGIN AS CLOCK STRIKES XII

Treasury Is Deprived of $600,000 Annually—Blue Says
Man May Drink at Friend's Home
If He Doesn't Go There
for That Purpose

would need translation to an archaeologist of the distant future seeking data about the mores of the America of 1914. Interpreted at a time sufficiently near to understand the cryptic combination of the classics of Greece and the numerals of Rome with the slang of the United States, it meant that West Virginia (by a majority of 92,000) had voted prohibition into its state constitution, and that the gods, in a mood of punning, had arranged that the name, as well apparently as the fame, of the head enforcement officer should be Blue. Saloon keepers took the event gaily rather than funereally; placards on the walls and in the corners of the huge mirrors behind the bars warned patrons that "A camel can go nine days without a drink, but after July 1 you will have to beat the camel," and "Don't be alarmed if after July 1 you spit talcum powder." A Wheeling sa-

Opponents of Prohibition predicted unhappy results. "Ha, Ha! Good! Now there'll be lots of bad liquor drunk on the sly." (From Life*)*

Brosnan's Ale House, Fulton Street, one of the oldest in New York. (From a pre-Prohibition photograph)

Buffalo Bill as he was toward the end of his career.

The glory of the Midwest wheatfields. (From a drawing by Edwin B. Child)

loon keeper, August Travert, found solace for the death of his business in the pleasure he derived from contriving his first name into a play on words, at once pun and paradox, which he printed upon cards and presented to his patrons: "July first will be the last of August."

West Virginia was the ninth state that had gone dry on a statewide basis; in some other states many counties had gone dry under "local-option" laws—the country was a mosaic of wet and dry; maps, whether by accident or intended symbolism, represented dry territory as white, wet as black.

All over the country, communities were getting ready for the Fourth of July. The celebration of Decatur, Illinois, announced a balloon ascension, a pie- and bun-eating contest, and a "Jesse James Wild West Show"; one in North Dakota promised "Buffalo Bill in person." Baltimore scheduled "pageants, carnivals, parades, and a sham battle"—but no firecrackers, for Baltimore had been one of the first to adopt the "safe and sane" Fourth.

The *Peoria* (Illinois) *Journal Transcript* stated that it was "a good year for bass." The *Decatur* (Illinois) *Review* reported the capture by John Chrisman of "a 6-pound cat-fish in Stevens Creek about half way between the wagon road and the river, the biggest catch of the season."

Mr. Chrisman, we feel sure, as he ate his catfish at breakfast, June 29, and read in his newspaper of the assassination at Sarajevo, was moved to more than the usual satisfaction which the average American felt with his lot, compared with that of the crowned heads of Europe. From them, and from assassinations and wars, Mr. Chrisman congratulated himself, America was far removed.

CHAPTER 2
New Energy, New Wealth

American national life preceding the Great War was too far-ranging in its vigorous adventuring, too varied in the rich and ever shifting colors it presented to the world, too many-sided in the strongly marked expressions of its robustious spirit, to be confined by any of those adjectival designations, such as the Gay Nineties, or the Tragic Era, with which historians describe, or put labels upon, epochs and eras. Perhaps it would be more accurate to limit this assertion to saying that the present historian is unable to think of any one word or compact phrase that could describe with sufficient inclusiveness or adequate exactness the American years preceding 1914.

Of all designations of eras, those are most nearly possible of justification

The Roosevelt Dam, Salt River, Arizona, completed in 1911 by the U.S. government at a cost of $3,890,000. Roosevelt had much to do with promoting policies of conservation both as to waterpower and other natural resources.

which rest upon association with some dominating personality. The American years preceding 1914 back to about 1900, in their spirit and flavor, had a partial resemblance to the American who was dominant throughout them. If they must be called an epoch and if they must be given a name, the "Roosevelt Era" has some aptness. Yet even here, the era had many qualities differing greatly from those of the man; and the extraordinary variety of the period far exceeded that of even so wide-ranging a spirit as Roosevelt's. Some of the forces which made the America of that day what it was, had come with us from so early a period in our national life, were so invincible in the vital strength of their influence on our national character, that it would be difficult to say, of the years from 1900 to 1914, whether Roosevelt stamped himself upon this American period or whether America stamped itself upon Roosevelt. Of the period as of the man the outstanding quality was energy; energy physical, intellectual, spiritual—and, throughout all, ferment. But not even Roosevelt is an exception to the rule that in any history of a period, heads of state become, to some degree, merely iridescent bubbles on the surface, marking the course of deep streams beneath.

It is futile—worse than futile, misleading—to suggest that the immensity of things happening in America during those years of titanic vitality can be described in one word, or in a thousand. If there must be a condensed characterization, let us say that the time was marked by a prodigious energy, that much of the energy was ferment, and that the whole was infused by an altruism which, taking on the common characteristic, became a dynamic humanitarianism.

The dynamic humanitarianism was directly related to the dynamic ma-

A group of "dynamic humanitarians." From left to right: Robert C. Ogden, President William H. Taft, Principal Booker T. Washington, and Andrew Carnegie.

terialism. It has been asserted by many poets, preachers, and politicians that material enrichment results in spiritual starvation. Of that ancient cant, the America of 1900 to 1914 is sufficient refutation.

II

There had come into the world two new forms of physical energy. To speak of them merely as additions to man's stores of available power would be understatement, for each of the new forms was greater than the sum of all the energy that man had turned to his use in all preceding time; each was far greater—taking into account its mobility, its adaptability to diffusion—than the sum of all the muscles of men, added to all the muscles of horses and oxen, added to all the waterwheels, added to all the windmills, added, even, to the other of man's comparatively recent acquisitions, steam.

The internal combustion engine in its most common form expressed itself in the hands of the average man as an Arabian Nights dream made real; a portable fountain of energy, the automobile, which, weighing only half as much as a horse, would do the work of sixty horses and keep it up without rest for practically an unlimited time.

Electricity was streaking up and down the country, literally like lightning—wires to provide it with a pathway were everywhere being extended, like long nerves of new growth, from central powerhouses, from the city to the suburb, longer and longer capacity for transmission carrying it to distant villages, from the villages to the farm—everywhere ending in a switch,

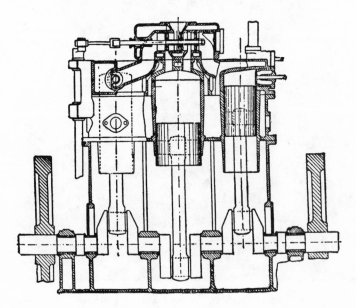

One of the two new forms of physical energy: a three-cylinder compound gas engine.

by the turning of which man could tap for himself a practically limitless reservoir of physical power.

These new forms of energy were wealth; they constituted the greatest additions to man's material enrichment that had ever been created; added to the other forms of wealth which the new energies cumulatively produced, they enriched America to a degree never before paralleled. The very novelty of this new wealth and its abundance had an effect on men, made them openhanded, adventurous.

But the particular quality of this period in America was the diffusion of the wealth that was being created. Not only had that never been paralleled, it had never been to any effective degree attempted. Never before had the producers of wealth thought of wealth as a thing to be dif-

The other new form of physical energy: a hydroelectric power station, Great Western Power Company, Feather River, California.

fused. The old conception had been that wealth is static—things—and therefore to be amassed, stored away, withheld.

Few saw at the time a peculiar and unprecedented quality that had come into the world. The new wealth was not in the form of things, it was in the form of energy, of power of action; it was atoms in motion. Since the new kind of wealth was essentially motion, it did not lend itself to amassing or withholding; it could come into being only through use, and the use of it necessarily enriched the user. The entrepreneurs of the new forms of wealth, the industrial leaders identified with it, could make profit for themselves only insofar as they conferred upon the average man the power inherent in electricity and in the internal combustion engine; they could only enrich themselves by persuading the average man to use, and by enabling him to use, the new forms of energy.

Presently the desire to enable the largest possible number of persons to possess and make use of the new form of wealth became a dominating motive. So far did this new conception go that Henry Ford—and later others

Reo Runabout $500

Folding seat, holding two extra passengers, $25 extra.   Top extra.

A part of the Reo runabout advertisement of 1909 in magazines of the day.

adopting his point of view—came to think of his own laborers, of all workers, not according to the Adam Smith concept, as people to be hired at the
lowest wages they can be persuaded to accept, not as people to leave with
the employer the largest possible share of the fruits of industry, but as people to be paid high wages in order that they might become maximum consumers of the goods Ford and others had to sell. Ford and others came to
see labor not primarily as labor but primarily in the role of consumer, and
therefore to be enriched so that they might consume more. That was a revolution in economic thought and practice.

CHAPTER 3

Henry Ford Emerges, Suddenly

For nearly ten years Henry Ford had been making the largest quantity of the new vehicle that was revolutionizing the country's life, and at a price that made it available to the largest number of people—by 1914 more than half a million Model T's were on the nation's then modest network of highways. Yet Ford as a man had attracted no attention; there were no books about him, no magazine articles. He had not even been deemed eligible for "Who's Who," the national roster of the great, the near-great, and the would-be-great. A baseball player named Napoleon Lajoie was a public character, but not Henry Ford. An actor named Douglas Fairbanks was a public character, and a magician named Houdini; a moving picture actress named Mary Pickford; an Indian athlete named Jim Thorpe and a blind girl named Helen Keller—all these and a dozen others were public characters, their personalities familiar to the country, but Henry Ford was unknown. The name "Ford" was a brand, not a man—merely a proper noun linked with an article of commerce.

Then, in the afternoon newspapers of January 5, 1914, Ford announced that as a way of sharing his profits with his 13,000 employees, he would pay a minimum wage of $5 per eight-hour day.

On the first pages and in the editorial columns of the next morning's papers, Ford's announcement overshadowed the war in Mexico and every other topic of national or local interest. "It was," said the *New York Sun*, groping frantically for a sufficient superlative, "a bolt out of the blue sky, flashing its way across the continent and far beyond, something unheard of in the history of business." "An epoch in the world's industrial history," said the *New York Herald*. Ford became the man of the hour, his plan the topic of the day. Quickly the phrase "Ford idea" became as familiar as the Ford car.

To finding out just what sort of being this strange new Croesus was, at once Midas and Messiah, to satisfying

Advertisement of Ford's Model "T" Coupé. In 1914 more than half a million were on the nation's highways.

Henry Ford, standing beside a racer, as he appeared in the days before he had built his first car.

public curiosity about him, the country's mechanisms of publicity now dedicated themselves. In seven days the press of New York City alone printed fifty-two columns. All over the country, managing editors wired "rush" telegrams to Detroit correspondents, who hastily sent out such casual information as was in their minds about their hitherto comparatively unnoticed fellow-citizen, in despatches to which they appended "more to follow." Overnight, the press, from taking it for granted that Ford was of no more public interest than any other citizen, now combed his present and his past for anything that would help satisfy the public hunger for information about him.

The public learned that Ford liked skating and did not like Wall Street; that after he had become a millionaire he had continued to live in "a plain small house which would probably rent for $50 a month"; that in hiring men he set no extra value on a college education and was tolerant of former prisoners—one of his important executives was an ex-convict; that he liked outdoor recreation and had an adage (he later inscribed it over the open fireplace of his new house) "Chop Your Own Wood and It Will Warm You Twice"; that he did not approve of professional charity—he had a principle, "the best use I can make of my money is to make more work for more men"; that in his business he was himself impatient of routine—though devotion to rigid routine was the very heart of his factory methods.

Ford's hobby and his law of life, the press reported, was to produce a good car at the lowest possible cost; to save a few cents on each car he had dropped the "stripers" who painted a slender ornamental line of yellow on the bodies. When salesmen complained that customers demanded more ornament, in a time when other makes of cars were sold largely on the basis of seductiveness of appearance, Ford's answer had been, "They can have any color they want so long as it's black." This, the press reported, was a basic detail of the process by which Ford had made his fortune. His formula of mass production had been: make a thoroughly good car; make few models and stick to them, thus avoiding the expense, immense in the automobile business, of equipping the factory for new models; make the car as inexpensive as possible by eliminating costly decorativeness, putting all the expenditure into serviceableness only. Sell the car at the lowest price; by that means achieve large sales; by large sales reduce the manufacturing cost of each car; use this reduction of cost to lower the price to the consumer; thereby get larger sales—and so on, in an ascending spiral of expansion, which in 1913 yielded Ford profits of about $20 million. It was this $20 million that Ford now announced he would divide with his workers during 1914 by paying a minimum wage of $5 a day.

The question which everybody speculated about was: Why had Ford decided to pay $5 a day to men he could have had for $2? Whatever may have been his motives before he took the step, and whatever the relative weight of different reasons in the mixture of many motives that commonly lie behind any human action, Ford was now to learn the truth of the worldly counsel, Never give your reasons at the time of an act, because thus you preserve for yourself a mobility which enables you later to adopt any of the motives that others attribute to you, or that which best fits the unanticipatable conditions that subsequently arise. Ford, within twenty-four hours after his announcement, could accept any one of almost as many reasons as there were sources of comment. The head of the rival Chalmers automobile factory attributed socialistic leanings to him, and the *New York Times* sent a reporter to ask him, point-blank and accusingly, whether he was a Socialist, and if it was true that his purpose was to prevent his son from in-

The Ford Motor Company's factory as it appeared in 1903–1904.

heriting a cloying fortune. At the other end of the gamut of imputed motives, a mass meeting of 500 Socialists denounced Ford's act as a detestable trap: "Ford," they unanimously resolved, "had purchased the brains, life and soul of his men by a raise in pay of a few dollars a week"; the Socialist *New York Call,* seeing nothing to praise in any "division of earnings between labor and capital," said it would be interested only "when the working class decides to cease dividing" with capital. Between these extremes of alleged motive ran an infinite range; Ford sought the favor of labor; Ford sought advantage over other manufacturers; Ford sought publicity for himself; Ford sought advertising for his car—and so on.

Ford's own statement of his motive, given to reporters—who called upon him in the spirit of demanding an explanation for having done an unheard-of thing—was that he had taken the step as "a plain act of social justice." This answer was too offhand and simple to be acceptable as a carefully accurate statement of motives which actually must have been complex and must have sprung in part from little understood deeps of human psychology. "Social justice" was a rough-and-ready phrase, at that time much hackneyed by use as part of the creed of the Progressive Party; it would come naturally to anyone's lips, but it was rather too vague to explain so startling and original an act.

Ford sensed or realized that mass production can only exist by being fed with a constantly increasing purchasing power on the part of labor. And if we accept the theory that mass production was a normal and logical step in the development of civilization, then this hypothesis would explain the favor with which the world received Ford and his idea.

At the least, any adequate account of the period this history covers must record, as an important innovation, that there came into the world, origi-

Outside the Ford factory in 1914 , showing the tremendous output of chassis.

Henry Ford. (From a photograph by Brown Brothers)

nating in the United States, widespread understanding of mass production, that to the public Henry Ford was the symbol of it; and that since the public thinks and feels mainly through symbols, its reaction to Ford was its reaction to the thing Ford stood for.

Now, Ford was a public character, an exalted one, in a class by himself, an oracle, with opportunity to be a Titan—and willingness to undertake the role. Accepting perhaps too fully the judgment of the public about himself, he took Olympian responsibility in some matters distant from the manufacture of automobiles. Passing easily from mass production of machines into the notion of mass direction of men, Ford adventured into national and world affairs. Within a year, he, in association with another wizard of the material world, Thomas A. Edison, embarked upon a crusade—"The Cigarette Must Go"; but the millions of copies of a pamphlet of denunciation, "The Case Against the Little White Slaver," were ineffective against the power of advertising that was at the cigarette's command. Within two years he embarked upon an enterprise of stopping the war in Europe, taking ship on December 4,1915 , with a go-getter purpose announced as "bringing the boys out of the trenches by Christmas," which would be about two weeks after his arrival in Europe. When he found the forces boiling along the Hindenburg Line not so amenable to the shortcuts of standardization as the production of automobiles had been, Ford returned with a disillusionment which did not contribute as much restraint as it might have to his further adventuring in fields distant from his experience. Several other attempts to influence public affairs did not add to his stature, but neither did they diminish his permanent position in history, as the outstanding exponent of the most fundamental characteristic of the period, the diffusion of material goods, the enrichment of the average man.*

*The average white, Christian man, that is. Ford's ethnic and religious bigotry have by now weakened his position in history; Hitler found him especially inspiring. —D.R.

CHAPTER 4
New Ways in Industry

The heart of the system practiced in Ford's factory was an "assembly line," a conveyor belt running the length of a long, well-lighted factory nave. Standing along each side are hundreds of workmen, each with his appointed task to perform while the slowly moving conveyor passes by him. Coming in from the sides are "feeder" belts, bearing parts: carburetors, complete and ready for installation; motor blocks still hot from the foundry—forty-eight hours before they were inert ore; screws and bolts, windshields, wheels, batteries, gasoline tanks. At the head of the conveyor belt, deft-handed, quick-moving workers place chassis frames on the assembly conveyor, each at a fixed interval from the next, two or three or more a minute. As the conveyor belt carries the chassis along, workers trained to perfection in their minutely specialized duties attach parts to them, the whole process following a program thought out in meticulous detail in advance, a process in which the human factor is reduced to a minimum.

The process, the speed and precision of it, was symbolized in a popular, and of course apocryphal, legend that a worker who dropped his wrench found, by the time he had picked it up, that fourteen cars had gone past him. The system, as practiced by Ford, and with appropriate variations by manufacturers in many lines, was known as "mass production."

II

Mass production was dependent partly upon, though very different from, another industrial development of the period, a carefully thought out, severely tested philosophy of producing goods called "scientific management." The phrase came to public attention in 1910, when Louis D. Brandeis of Boston, later a Justice of the U.S. Supreme Court, stated, with much attendant publicity, before a congressional committee, that the railroads of the country could save $1 million a day in operating costs if they would adopt scientific management.

An aspect of the new idea that caught the interest of the country, giving rise to much discussion in 1911, was "time studies," conducted with a stopwatch.

To the public, time studies, as pictured (with some sacrifice of facts to picturesqueness) in magazine articles embellished with charts, graphs, and photographs, had the mystic fascination of a witch's incantation. The making of them consisted of observations by a trained engineer—the photographs showed him usually as a well-dressed, alert-faced man in his early thirties, rimless eyeglasses perched on a thin inquisitive nose, stopwatch and other gadgets of his profession in his hands—standing behind a bricklayer or a shoveler in a pit or a machine operator in a factory and making notes on how the workman moved his arms, hands, and fingers. Next the

Brandeis Attacks Price-cutting
Favors Price-maintenance
Under Competitive Conditions

"Price-cutting of the one-priced, trade-marked article eliminates the small dealer, and ultimately ruins the market for the article."

"Encourage price-maintenance under proper conditions of competition, and you will aid in preserving the small dealer against capitalistic combinations."

"The most intolerable of monopolies are those where the price is not a matter of common knowledge, and where the discrimination in prices is used oppressively to annul competition."

Louis D. Brandeis

It takes courage of the highest order to stand firm against uneducated public opinion —for the public's good.

Louis D. Brandeis, the eminent lawyer, has never taken a step in the interest of all the people that will arouse greater comment than the following article.

Many people who have not studied the subject are against price-maintenance. The consumer thinks it a device to make him pay more; the merchant feels that when he buys the goods of the manufacturer they are his, and that it is an infringement of his rights to establish his selling price.

Careful study of the subject, however, shows that the same price everywhere is for the best interests of the buying public, the independent dealer and the independent manufacturer.

Price-cutting on articles of individuality, Mr. Brandeis maintains, would enable men controlling vast combinations of capital to win local markets one by one, and create monopolies on the things we eat and wear, then raise the prices higher than before.

This article is published by a number of the leading magazines in the belief that by giving wide publicity to the views of Mr. Brandeis, the real interests of the enterprising individual manufacturer, the small dealer, and the public will be served.

Half of a two-page advertisement published in a number of leading magazines of 1913, giving publicity to Mr. Louis D. Brandeis's (later Justice Brandeis) views about price-cutting.

engineer was pictured as taking his data and retiring for a period of concentrated thinking. After that, he would emerge with a brand new set of motions which would lessen the number of movements of a bricklayer's right hand from ten to nine, or shorten by so many inches the distance a laborer's hand needed to move drilling a given number of holes in a given time. The objective was economy, labor-saving; the method was specialization, a specialization in which it appeared that the efficiency expert was sometimes willing to require the man to adapt himself to the machine.

That was "time studies" as the average man understood it, after being filtered to his mind through articles in the popular magazines. The average man took "time studies" seriously, as he did all of scientific management, but not so seriously that he would refrain from "kidding" it. He took delight in such extravaganzas as the story of that zealot for scientific management who, having put his mind upon the economical collection of garbage, observed that time could be saved, and rhythm of effective motion attained, if the men on the left side of the cart were chosen from among the left-handed; and that in order to have a supply of "southpaw" scavengers equal to the demand the public schools should train every other child to be left-handed.

Scientific management (of which time studies were but a detail) evolved from many separate origins and was developed by many men. The name

In the Ford plant. What resembles two long stretches of notched floor in this picture are really cooling racks covered with Ford body parts. (From a photograph by Ewing Galloway)

most identified with it, and the man most justly to be credited with pioneering it, was Philadelphia engineer Frederick W. Taylor.

It was not in Taylor's nature, when faced by resistance of conservatism, to make concession of diplomacy. He disdained tact, regarded it as a weakness, a waste of time, and therefore a sin against the code that was his only religion. When he encountered an opinion opposed to his own, he crashed into it, head on like a bull. He browbeat his clients and flaunted his contempt for their opinions. With organized labor, which regarded him with sullen suspicion, Taylor was ever at furious war. He would grow indignant at the charge by labor that his ideas would make men subordinate to the machine and that his system would eventually destroy the livelihood of

An example of industrial efficiency. The building of Grand Central Station in New York City, where excavating, rock-drilling, erecting steel and stone are all going on at once, while train service remains uninterrupted. (From a drawing by Thornton Oakley of October 1912)

multitudes of workers; steadfastly he maintained that scientific management was the solution of the problem of producing goods and that it would in the end lead the worker out of bondage, reduce the hours of man's labor, increase the period of his leisure.

In time, a new generation of workers grew up for whom Taylor's methods involved no change but were themselves the accepted and familiar. Before Taylor died, in 1915, he had the satisfaction of seeing part of organized labor, in the textile and clothing-making trades, swing wholeheartedly to his point of view and voluntarily adopt scientific management on a basis of sharing the increased profits with capital.

A generalized definition of scientific management by Taylor himself said: "The basic principles include: first, the development of a science for each element of a man's work, to replace the old rule-of-thumb method; second, the selection and training of workmen to follow the science laid down; third, the payment of extraordinarily high wages to workmen who approach the standard performance set up, and of ordinary wages to those who take more than the standard time allowance; and, fourth, the dividing of responsibility between men and management on a basis of scientifically determined function."

As science, as efficiency, this was unassailable. In practice, however, Taylorism, or, rather, the corruption of it by efficiency engineers, meant requiring men, often of middle age, to change lifetime ways, to drop motions that had become so instinctive as to be parts of their nature. A hod carrier was outraged to the depths of his soul when told that he could save six seconds of time and eliminate one motion out of ten by picking up a brick with thumb and fingers disposed in a manner minutely specified by an engineer. It is conceivable that some of the acolytes and camp followers of scientific management may have become enamored of system for system's sake; that there were occasions when the workman's instinct was right, the engineer's science wrong—the workman's instinct in accord with nature, the engineer's science a perversion of nature.

To the new vogue, choice by the worker of his own task, and the turning from one to another as his mood suggested, or his tired muscles urged, the determination by the worker of his own pace—to the new all that was wrong. Heresy also was that little excess of motion, the flourish that was the exuberance of spirit in an artisan finding joy in creative work. A worker who would have sung at his task, and made the swing of his tools conform to the rhythm of his song, would have been a startling phenomenon along the Ford assembly line, and would have been regarded by the efficiency engineer as having no place in industry. A village blacksmith forging a shoe for his neighbor's horse inspired a Longfellow to verse, and other poets and singers have been similarly stimulated by the farmer in the dell and the miller by the stream. The poet has not yet emerged who will write a lyric about workman Number 8602 punching hole 69 with drill B-61 in automobile Number 6,841,682.

EFFICIENCY CRANK: *Young man, are you aware that you employed fifteen unnecessary motions in delivering that kiss? (From* Life, *1913)*

The recommendation of scientific management and mass production was that they would permit the workman to reduce the procuring of food and other necessities to a chore of two or three days, leaving the rest of the week free for art or other use of leisure as his soul might summon him to. It is true that hours of labor per day, and days per week, were materially reduced during a period simultaneous with mass production. Believers in it held that the one was the effect of the other, and that the liberation of labor would go farther. The ideal, life divided between work and leisure, with generous emphasis on the latter, work and satisfaction to the soul kept in separate compartments, held out as the ultimate social goal of scientific management, had not, at the time this history was written, fully arrived.

CHAPTER 5
Art Finds a Patron

Hand in hand with mass production went mass distribution. The result enriched the average man, enormously. The processes by which diffusion was accomplished wrought deep-reaching changes in American institutions, points of view, ways of life.

"Scientific management" in production became "scientific salesmanship" in distribution. "Overcoming sales resistance" was professional patter for the process, "sign on the dotted line" the objective of it. This, too, became a school and a cult, its practice a highly developed art, its experts and acolytes a lavishly paid profession. Anyone who possessed in his personality the gift of persuasiveness found the richest market for his talent in the business of influencing men to buy goods. Eloquence, imagination, power of exhortation, magnetism of personality, all those endowments which give to the possessor of them ability to move other men, the talents which in previous ages would have been exercised primarily in the world of ideas and of the spirit, converting masses of men to accept new creeds or abandon old ones, persuading them to support one political party or oppose another—

A double-page advertisement in a magazine in 1909.

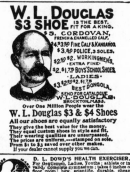

A page of magazine advertisements of the early 1890s. A later development of the Cluett advertisement is shown on the opposite page.

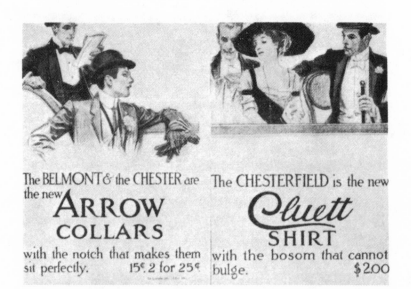

A double-page magazine advertisement of the Cluett, Peabody Company, 1910.

these talents were now dedicated to enticing men to buy more automobiles, more bathtubs, more phonographs, more hats, more shoes, more soap. Talent for exhortation which in former eras taught man to prepare for the next world now taught him to use more goods in this.

Salesmanship evolved a technique more refined than pulpit or platform oratory; advertising became more subtle in method, more concrete in results than any form of proselyting argument. The art which Milton put into selecting words which should make man think about God was excelled by the care with which American writers of advertisements assembled words designed to persuade man to consume more chewing gum. The man, or advertising agency, who wrote an effective selling slogan, such as "It Floats," received far greater compensation than Milton for *Paradise Lost.* And just as the poets and prophets of earlier ages considered that the main concern of man was to think about eternity, so did the Miltons of mass production and advertising come to look upon man as existing for the primary purpose of consuming more goods.

A page of advertisements from the 1890s.

II

Advertising, which preceding the 1890s had consisted of little more than formal announcements, designed mainly to supply the seeker of goods with the name and address of the merchant who had them to sell, was now directed toward inspiring in readers the wish to buy. Advertising became mass stimulation to buy. To provide forums in which it could function, newspapers expanded; periodicals increased in size, multiplied in circulation.

In bringing about this change, the principal agency was the automobile. Here was a new commodity, with an enormous potential market, sold at a price much greater than any other commodity that ever before had had a popular sale. The larger price of the automobile permitted a larger appropriation for advertising than any other advertised goods had ever afforded; an automobile selling for $1,000 could readily allocate as much as $100 for advertising. And here was an immense void, a market wholly unoccupied, which in the quarter century to come would absorb 35 million cars. Manufacturers, sensing the opportunity, could realize that the prizes of the new industry would go, other things being equal, mainly

An advertisement of 1909.

The tingle in the air tells of Fall overcoat-time.

If you are guided by the Kuppenheimer name, you'll get all that an overcoat should be—with style dated far enough ahead to make sure that you will lead.

You'll find our garments at the better clothiers

The House of Kuppenheimer

CHICAGO   NEW YORK   BOSTON

A magazine advertisement in 1909: note the lady's peach-basket hat and the upholstered shoulders of the men.

to those who through advertising first impressed their brands upon the public consciousness. This suddenly expanded demand for advertising space created an immensely broadened opportunity for periodicals and newspapers, and for the authors and artists who supplied reading matter or adornment to them.

A consequence was an arrangement in which, directly or indirectly and in one degree or another, materialism became the patron, art and ideas the protégés, in a function of which the objective was the sale of goods. Newspapers and periodicals became, as to the principal economic base of them, agencies for stimulating the consumption of commodities. Newspapers and periodicals which up to about 1890 had depended for most of their income on money paid by the reader for the ideas, information, or entertainment they contained, now received the major portion of their revenue from advertisers. The advertising, which in newspapers of the 1890s was a rather grudgingly tolerated fringe of simple announcements along the edges of reading matter, or in periodicals was confined to a very few pages in the back, was now expanded and elaborated until it occupied the major portion of the space; while reading matter receded relatively to the position, and the economic status, of in part a frame for the advertising, in part an allurement drawing the reader's eyes to it. Many writers of fiction accommodated themselves to the new basis; the writing of "serials," designed primarily for publication in magazines rather than as books, became a recognized technique in which an observable detail was that the affairs of heroes and heroines came to successive climaxes at points which happily coincided with the end of the installments in periodicals, the spacing thus bringing about a moment of high suspense just preceding the words "To be continued." A novel which omitted thus to adapt itself to serial publication suffered detriment in the literary market, because publication in book form only, where the reader alone paid the bill, was rarely as remunerative as in magazines, where much of the compensation came indirectly in the form of a joint contribution from the advertisers.

The manufacturers of automobiles, ready-made clothing, lotions, soaps, breakfast foods, and other advertised commodities became, so to speak, associated patrons of art and letters. A writer who in eighteenth-century England would have dedicated his book to a noble lord for bearing the expense of publication—and who thereby put himself under obligation to

Bᴇᴛᴛᴇʀ be sure your thin summer clothes are of all-wool fabrics if you want them to hold shape and style.

Hart Schaffner & Marx Good Clothes Makers
Chicago   Boston   New York

Another men's clothing ad of 1909. Though the names of the artists are not given, these advertisements were usually done by capable illustrators of the day.

A joke which pictured the indispensability of advertising to mass distribution during 1900. The man who made the best mousetrap, but didn't advertise, waits for the world to beat a path to his door. (From the Saturday Evening Post; *Nate Collier's cartoon)*

conform to his patron's political and other views—could, in the America of 1914, have appropriately dedicated his book to a joint association composed of General Motors; Hart, Schaffner & Marx; the American Tobacco Company; and the manufacturers of Listerine, Ivory Soap, and Heinz's Baked Beans. The relation did not entail the servility that went with the old form of patronage, and was in respects felicitous. The new type of patron asked nothing of the author except that he please the reader—attention from the reader's eye was all that the advertiser desired. The oversuspicious sometimes found in the arrangement an implied limitation on the writer's freedom of expression. A Socialist and lifelong protestant against what is, Upton Sinclair, wrote *The Brass Check*, in which he pictured literature and art as the "prostitutes" of business. This view surprised and amused or angered both parties to the relation. True, a writer who was a cog in a mechanism for the diffusion of goods could not readily say that diffusion of goods was evil, but few authors ever wanted to say it, and little of the public desired it to be said. And even an advocate of socialism, or an ascetic Gandhi preaching a philosophy of doing without goods, would have encountered no curtailment of his liberty of expression, provided only that he wrote entertainingly. What business in general sought was merely that the reader should be led to read, and thereby notice, the advertising on the adjoining column or page.

The arrangement was fruitful of advantage in many directions. An author who in a $1.50 book might have reached 20,000 readers found in the *Saturday*

Evening Post or *Collier's* several millions. A reader who would not have
brought one book in a year, received, for an annual subscription to the *Saturday
Evening Post*, half a dozen novels and as many as 200 short stories and a similar number of articles. Periodical literature flourished as print had never flourished before. Those that had the largest circulation included in their
contents and carried to millions of readers the best writing of the time.

   To author and artist the arrangement was extremely remunerative.
Writers and painters prospered almost like stockbrokers. "Grub Street" as
an indigent accompaniment of literary life became a quaint antiquarian
phrase. A writer of short stories or serials, who in the early 1890s would
have received $100 from a magazine as his share of what readers paid for
the total contents, received in 1914 ten times that sum as, in the main, his
share of what advertisers* were happy to pay for having a distinguished
and competent author write excellent reading matter alongside which they
could print their announcements. Many artists received exalted compen-

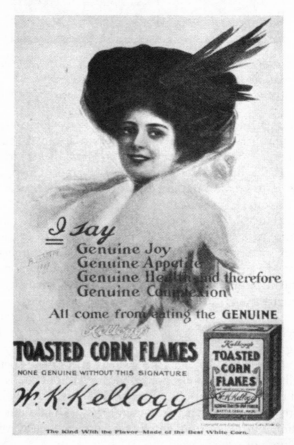

Pictures of pretty girls were in great demand by advertisers throughout this period.

*With the coming of the radio and the development of it as a vehicle for advertising, the subsidiz-
ing of writers (as well as singers and actors) went farther. The performer was paid directly, or often
through an advertising agency.

Old and new (1899 and 1923) in toothpaste advertisements.

sation direct from manufacturers for painting handsome young Adonises who in the advertisements wore Cluett collars or B.V.D. underwear; or alluring young ladies whose beauty, poise, and charm, so the advertisements said, arose from divers cosmetics, corsets, dentrifices, and medicaments. Other artists, including many of the best—Frederick Remington, Maxfield Parrish, Jessie Willcox Smith, Charles Dana Gibson—found a generously remunerative market for their work, not available to artists of previous generations, in the magazine covers or frontispieces of the better class of popular periodicals, and in illustrating magazine fiction. Pictorial and literary art, including the best that was produced, experienced a wide diffusion, riding the same waves of distribution with mass diffusion of goods—hitchhikers, so to speak, upon the progress of the automobile, joyriders upon the one institution that dominated the period, mass production of goods.

III

The mutually serviceable arrangement between materialism and art led to an expansion of the latter, certainly an expansion in quantity. In one field of letters there was an elevation of quality.

Diffusion of goods demanded advertising, advertising called for periodicals as media, periodicals found the short story to be the form of writing best adapted to their use, authors found in periodicals such a market for short stories as had never existed before. The short story, when confined for its market to book publication, had rarely been widely distributed or remunerative. Now editors combed the country for talent that could tell a tale within the length adapted to periodical publication, from 4,000 to 12,000 words. If in America any professional author had a good short story in his brain, there was urgent incentive for him to produce it. Amateurs who had never written before were stimulated to creation by the demand for the short story. Such an infinite variety of topics and situations were treated in the almost universally circulated periodicals that any reader having the faintest urge to create was sure to find, at one time or another, a suggestion stimulating him to construct a story out of something in his own experience. Any fairly good short story from a new author would be followed by a visit from a scouting editor bent on developing the possible mine. Every experienced author had competing editors on his doorstep pleading for more.

The result was a cultivation of American short story talent such as had not existed before and would hardly have taken place without the subsidy of materialism. America in more than 100 years had developed but one outstanding writer of short stories, Edgar Allan Poe. The early 1900s produced more than a score whose output was distinguished. The most popular at the time, O. Henry, who developed a new technique, the surprise ending, became the model most widely followed by young writers. His work was less worthy, however, than that of some others. One, Irvin Cobb, produced, within a mass of output, a few stories not inferior to Poe's.

The short story was the only form of letters that profited through the subsidy by materialism, in the sense of attaining a higher stan-

O. Henry.

dard. The other forms profited in the sense that the public was made widely familiar with them. It was recognized by European critics that the short story had a greater development in America than in Europe. In fact, the short story developed in America more greatly than any other form of literary art. For both these results, a main cause was the subsidy given by materialism.

IV

The flourishing of arts and letters expressed itself, not as conspicuously in the emergence of unusual intellects, nor in outstanding individual achievement, as in the spread of a great quantity of art and letters of average quality, and in increased acquaintance of the masses of people with it. So far as the intellectual energy, the creativeness, of the time expressed itself in distinguished achievements by unusual minds, in really epochal new standards, the advances took place almost wholly within the world of science* or, if among the arts at all, among the utilitarian ones. Hardly any book written by an American author during the period was rated, twenty years later, a permanent or indispensable** addition to literature.

Joyce Kilmer, a "century-plant" among poets.

V

No poem produced in America during the period was rated as high as Emerson, Whitman, or Poe; none was as widely quoted as those of Whittier, Longfellow, Lowell, and Bryant had been when they were creating. The nearest approach to such popularity was attained by a practically solitary poem of Joyce Kilmer, "Trees," of which the opening and closing couplets are:

*This judgment is queried by the very discerning editor of *Poetry*, Miss Harriet Monroe. Advances in science, she says, "give immediate proofs of their rank; the rank of new expressions of art is proved more slowly." This is true; and the condition constitutes one of the handicaps of writing history from a short perspective.
**Miss Harriet Monroe, having read a proof of this chapter, remarks, with some spirit, that 1932 is too early for so confident a judgment.

I think that I shall never see
A poem lovely as a tree. . . .
Poems are made by fools like me,
But only God can make a tree.

"Trees" was the most widely quoted poem produced in America during the period. The quality which causes a poem to be widely quoted may or may not be identical with elevation according to critical standards. Much of America's inclination to memorize verse during this period was absorbed by an English poem, Rudyard Kipling's hymn to steadiness in time of stress, "If," which came to America in 1910.

If you can keep your head when all about you
Are losing theirs and blaming it on you . . .

The first or early appearances of new poets in sufficient numbers made the years 1913 and 1914 a kind of renaissance in American verse. Edgar Lee Masters published a series of autobiographical epitaphs ascribed to persons beneath the tombstone in the cemetery of an Illinois village. Amy Lowell, leading critic of the day, thought the " 'Spoon River Anthology' . . . may very well come to be considered among the great books of American literature." Masters's epitaphs had a grim and acid cynicism, a despairing disillusionment, that was a shock to the spirit of 1914 America but was prophetic of postwar America. One epitaph, written about a Civil War soldier, lent itself to the mood of a later generation who wished to express skepticism about the imputation of glory to the Great War, or any war:

KNOWLTE HOHEIMER

I was the first fruits of the battle of Missionary Ridge.
When I felt the bullet enter my heart
I wished I had staid at home and gone to jail
For stealing the hogs of Curl Trenary,
Instead of running away and joining the army.
Rather a thousand times the county jail
Than to lie under this marble figure with wings,
And this granite pedestal
Bearing the words, "Pro Patria."
What do they mean, anyway?

Other poets of the 1914 renaissance included Robert Frost—the very titles of his poems possessed, to anyone who had ever known and loved New England, the power of a magic carpet, able to carry an exile across seas and continents back to the land of "North of Boston," "The Birches," "The Pasture," "Mowing," "Mending Wall," "Stopping by Woods on a Snowy Evening," "The Thawing Wind," "After Apple-picking," "The Woodpile,"

"The Mountain," "The Hill Wife," "The Gum Gatherer," "An Old Man's Winter Night."

What Robert Frost did for New England was done for Chicago and the Midwest by Carl Sandburg, whose rugged force, however, differed from Frost's gentle serenity about as the Chicago stockyards differed from a New England orchard. Sandburg, in his "Chicago," seemed almost to use words as boulders:

> Hog-butcher for the world,
> Tool-maker, Stacker of Wheat,
> Player with Railroads and the Nation's Freight-handler;
> Stormy, husky, brawling,
> City of the Big Shoulders . . .
>
> Fierce as a dog with tongue lapping for action, cunning as a savage
> pitted against the wilderness,
> Bareheaded,
> Shovelling,
> Wrecking,
> Planning,
> Building, breaking, rebuilding.

Vachel Lindsay, Illinois-born, as American as the Mississippi River, tramped the West reciting a drumming, thumping, rolling type of verse, of which the earliest and perhaps the best were "General William Booth Enters Heaven" and "The Congo." His style is illustrated by "Simon Legree," which, he directed, is "to be read in your own variety of negro dialect":

> Legree's big house was white and green,
> His cotton-fields were the best to be seen.
> He had strong horses and opulent cattle,
> And bloodhounds bold, with chains that would rattle. . . .
> Legree he sported a brass-buttoned coat,
> A snake-skin necktie, a blood-red shirt.
> Legree he had a beard like a goat,
> And a thick hairy neck, and eyes like dirt.

Amy Lowell was at once competent as poet and inspiring as friend of poets. It was a sign of the state of poetry during this period that Lowell was less commonly identified as a poet than as the sister of the president of Harvard University, and through a legend that she smoked big black cigars. A school of verse that flourished during the period was the "Imagist." An eccentric departure vivaciously discussed within the craft, but little known outside, was "free verse," better known, where it was known at all, by the exotic name which marked its alien origin, "vers libre."

" 'September Morn'/Clothed as she was born," was more interesting as nudity than impor-
tant as art. Exhibited in 1912 it gave rise to much discussion and some attempts at repres-
sion. (From a painting by Paul Chabas)

VI

A departure in pictorial art, similarly alien, similarly bizarre, similarly
ephemeral, was called "Cubism," sometimes described as "insurgency
in art," and designated "bedlam in art" by conservative critics who likened
it to the cave ornamentation of prehistoric man. Critic Royal Cortissoz
said it was the trick of "post-impressionism" carried one step farther. A
poet of the day, Harry Kemp, as eccentric in letters as "Cubism" was in art,
after visiting an exhibition of the new genre in New York in the spring of
1913, wrote with an air of being torn between not really liking it and wishing to approve anything that was outré:

> I cannot shake their wild control;
> Their colors still go roaring through my soul, . . .
> Strange cubes evolving into half-guessed forms,
> Cyclones of green, and purple rainbow-storms.
> Thus artists on huge Jupiter might paint
> (Or some mad star beyond the earth's constraint) . . .
> You go out with a whirlwind in your head.
> The thing, at least, is not inert and dead;
> There's life and motion there, and rending force,
> Color-Niagaras thundering on their course,
> Power that breaks like a great wave in spray—
> And what it means we'll let To-morrow say!

A figure—an example of cubist art. (From an abstract painting by Picasso)

By 1932 (the time of this writing), "To-morrow" had arrived—and did not think it worth while to say anything.

VII

The one art that made notable progress was architecture—and architecture is that one of the arts having the largest utilitarian value, most directly integrated into the material world. In this field the one greatest achievement was a building called the Woolworth Tower, erected with profits from the sale of five- and ten-cent articles, and devoted to the housing of lawyers and business offices—a cathedral of trade. Architecture submitted to the limitation put upon it by the spirit of the age, that it must conform to the broad movement of material advance. That limitation, it was thought in the beginning, made beauty impossible. But American architecture, accepting the limitation, accepted also the advantages with which American engineering endowed it, structural steel, concrete, hollow tile, wire cable, and the passenger elevator. Out of these, architecture, with characteristic American adaptability, contrived for itself a revolutionary addition to its scope and variety, actually a new dimension, practically unlim-

The Woolworth Building held the record for height in the early years of the century.

ited verticality. With this addition to its resources, American architecture, incarnating the spirit of the time, created the most distinctively and characteristically American thing in the world, the skyscraper, having the beauty of line as well as the beauty of massiveness and power.

Architecture's release from the limitation of proportions in line and perspective that had been dictated by the need of keeping buildings close to the ground, within heights attainable by climbing stairs, amounted to almost a new art.

VIII

A reflection of the spirit of any age is the new words that come into the language; an index to the era's tempo and energy is the number of the words and the speed with which they come. An epitome of the history of any period could be achieved by an operation in arithmetic: take a dictionary of, say, 1914; subtract from it a dictionary of 1900; the result, the new words that came into being, would be a summary of what happened.

In the supplement to the 1929 edition of *Webster's International Dictionary*, comprising accretions to the language that came into common use between 1909 and 1927, are about 3,000 new words. By classifying a characteristic group of them we can find a clue to the changes taking place during the period, a pattern of the very spirit of the age. Of the 299 words beginning with "A," more than two-thirds, or 221, were in science, physics, chemistry, invention, medicine; and seven more were in the allied world of machinery. Just one word of the 229 was in the world of art, an abstruse new term for an attenuated refinement in music, "atonality."

The emphasis on material things in the new words that came into the language has unmistakable meaning. Equally significant is a new meaning that was acquired by an old word.

The verb "sell" in *Webster's Dictionary* for 1929 was still defined as to transfer goods for a price. But in universal practice, to an extent that the dictionary must soon record, "sell" and the process it connotes had enlarged its domain. To the material world that had been the word's habitat since Christ said, "Go and sell what thou hast and give to the poor," and in a direction different from Christ's admonition, "sell" had invaded the spiritual and intellectual world. To convert a man to a new conviction or point of view was to "sell him the idea." To impress yourself favorably upon another's attention was to "sell yourself to him." The missionary who a generation before would have described his function as to convert unbelievers, might now have described it, or certainly it would have been so described in the common idiom, as to "sell religion to the heathen." A political leader who in the time of Abraham Lincoln would "go to the people" on the question of abolition, or in 1896 would "educate the people" on the gold standard, would at a later date "sell the League of Nations to the country" or the World Court, or the high tariff or the low tariff. And he would have expressed success in the transaction by saying, in terms of conclusion of a deal, that he had "put it over."

If a commercial interest wished professional aid in "putting over" a new idea, it could find paid practitioners of the art, who called themselves "public relations counsel." The word "publicity" had passed through a transition similar to that of "sell," but in the reverse direction. As late as the time of Theodore Roosevelt, "publicity" meant letting in the light. Usually it was used in a sense of disinfection, of destroying something undesirable by making the people see and understand it—Woodrow Wilson thought that "pitiless publicity" would cure many of the ills of government. Almost at once "publicity" was annexed by the material world as part of its jargon for acquiring advantage in the world of the mind. "Publicity" was now mainly an art for causing the world to take notice of, and think well of, goods; or of policies which the makers of goods wished to make popular. The word was coming to be synonymous with advertising.

A word that suffered even greater demeaning was "propaganda." In the 1890s it meant, generically, any institution or function of propagating a doctrine; specifically it was most familiar as the name for an institution in the Catholic Church, the College of Propaganda, founded at Rome in 1622 for the oversight of foreign missions and the education of missionary priests. During almost 300 years the word retained that sacred connotation without taint from the secular world. During the Great War it came to be used for indoctrinating enemy troops or civilians behind the enemy line with ideas designed to undermine their morale—in plain English, to disseminate deceit artfully. Then it came to be used, with "reverse English," so to speak, as a word for disseminating a different sort of falsehood among the home peoples, with the design of stiffening their morale, or stirring them to greater exertions, or to more bitter hatred of the enemy. From its military use, the word during the 1920s passed into political use. Propaganda became, to each side of a controversy, a word to describe ideas expressing the other's point of view. Soon the business world annexed it as in part a new synonym for "publicity."

CHAPTER 6
The Genius of the Age

Things were in the saddle. But this must not be understood to mean that the condition was to the disadvantage of the average man. It meant that America was mainly preoccupied with things, but it meant also that the average man had greater access to things than ever before. With profusion of things, went willingness—more than willingness, eagerness, of those who had much to share with those who had less. Also accompanying the profusion of things was an earnest concern to make the world a better place; with dynamic materialism went dynamic humanitarianism.

As conspicuous as new words like "gasoline" and "airplane" in the material world were some phrases in the area of philanthropy, either new, or now greatly enlarged in use, "social justice," "child labor," conservation, arbitration, juvenile courts, workmen's compensation; and some words of politics, connoting greater power for the average man, such as "direct primary," "initiative and referendum," "recall of judicial decisions."

Whether because of some attribute of humanity inherently associated with the new kind of wealth and the new conception of it, and the new abundance of it; whether because it is in times of well-being that men become kindly and openhanded and only in times of economic depression and spir-

School improvements spread throughout the country. The school pictured here was at Beverly Hills, California. (From a photograph by Ewing Galloway)

itual fear that they become wolfish toward each other—for whatever cause
the period was characterized by concern with the fortunes of fellowmen, a
desire to make the world better, an awakening to the possibility of a finer way
of life, a fervor of many souls to bring in a juster, more lovely era, a super-
sensitive overeager determination like the conscience of a fifteen-year-old
boy—the whole resulting in a budding and flowering of an extraordinary
number, and to an exceptional degree, of those impulses and movements, individual and mass, that are grouped within the words "philanthropy," "reform." This was the outstanding spiritual characteristic of the period.

II

In our determination to bring a better day, we set about our first deliberate alteration of our fundamental plan of political organization, which
for more than 100 years had been regarded as perfected, and had only been
amended before as an incident arising
out of civil war. With one amendment,
adopted May 31, 1913, we changed
election of senators by state legislatures
to direct election by the people—and
felt sure we had taken a considerable
step toward a political millennium.
With another, made effective February
3, 1913, we provided for a tax on incomes, and for the graduation of it on
an ascending scale, so that the rich
should pay not only more but at pro-
gressively higher rates than the well to
do, while those of moderate income
could be exempted entirely. By yet another amendment, just beginning to be
pressed and destined to be adopted in
1920, it was hoped that liquor would be
taken out of politics—put out of exis-

*A pioneer for woman's suffrage, Susan
B. Anthony (1820–1906).*

tence utterly. By yet another, eagerly pressed at this time and adopted in
1921, we proposed to put females upon the same footing as males as respects participation in government.

The movement for woman suffrage had begun as early as the movement to
abolish slavery, and in somewhat the same spirit. It was no more a mass
movement of women demanding their "rights" than the antislavery movement was an uprising of blacks. What happened in both cases was that certain individuals, such as William Lloyd Garrison and John Brown, in the
case of slavery, and Susan B. Anthony, in the case of suffrage, moved by
some mysterious idiosyncrasy of personality, or by some uniqueness of bit-

terness-provoking experience in their own lives, set out to demand rights for masses who had not theretofore felt they were being deprived of anything they particularly desired. It was only after more than three generations that any considerable number of American women came to feel any acute interest in the steps which self-appointed individuals were taking in their behalf. Women, indeed, were as a rule more scornful than men about the movement, being content with their status, including the privileges and the deference which tradition accorded them.

The woman's suffrage movement in America was part of a broader trend, which in the whole of its manifestations was called "feminism," an emancipation of women from ancient taboos of all kinds. Women suffered disadvantage as litigants in courts, as owners of property and heirs to it. A woman author, Mary Roberts Rinehart, when she wrote a play, felt obliged to give herself a masculine pseudonym, "Roberts Rinehart," partly in deference to a doubt in some circles whether it was quite delicate for a gentlewoman to write for the stage, partly to forestall a sentiment that a play written by a woman could not be so good as one composed by a male. Women suffered many such imputations of inferiority. Prominent in feminism was a feeling of rebellion by women—and of sympathy for their point of view by men—against continuance in marriage after the relation had become coercive, merely. The law gave to husbands many rights which made their wives much less than equal, accepted custom gave the husbands yet other privileges. Against all this, feminism arose. The movement, in America, achieved rapid momentum through methods which at no time invited the forceful attention of the police. So far as there was controversy between old ideas and new, it took place in the field of forensic debate, and in ex-

When Women Vote. Mrs. Jones officially notified of her election as sheriff. (From New Cartoons, *by Charles Dana Gibson, copyright by Charles Scribner's Sons)*

change of barbed quips. A suffragette lecturer appealed to reason with an argument saying: "I have no vote, but my groom has; I have great respect for that man in the stables, but I am sure that if I were to go to him and say, 'John, will you exercise the franchise?' he would reply, 'Please, mum, which horse is that?' "

The opposition to suffrage, like the advocacy of it, took to a great degree the form of good-natured jibing. "Imagine," said the humor magazine *Puck*, "a long line of skimpy skirts tackling an election-booth—each one having to stop and powder her nose, and fix her hair, and adjust her belt, and look through her handbag, and wonder who the occupant of the next booth is voting for; the elections would have to be held 'the first two weeks in November,' or perhaps longer." Even those more aggressive assertions of feminism which demanded complete participation in all roles hitherto assigned to men, excited no opposition more determined than could be expressed in humor. "Is Man coming to this?" asked another magazine, as it pictured the male of the species saying to his wife, "Mary, I am positive there is a woman under the bed." Triumph of the cause and accepted superiority of the female were portrayed in:

> Peter, Peter, pumpkin eater,
> Had a wife and tried to beat her;
> But his wife was a suffragette,
> And Peter's in the hospital yet.

The aim of feminism was equality. In its final phase it seemed to go a little beyond, or for other reasons to shock us. One of the earliest and most loyal devotees of the movement was William Allen White. By 1914, he observed, a little ruefully, and with the deliberate exaggeration of humor, that he had "supposed 'feminism' meant giving a latch-key to mother," but had found it meant "taking the latch-key away from father."

Woman suffrage, many felt confident, would introduce into politics the presumed-to-be superior ethics of women; and into the business of government their housewifely traits and other desirable qualities. A few skeptically doubted whether mere doubling of the electorate would necessarily increase its capacity to function.

III

Diminution of sale of intoxicating liquors was making progress along lines of statutory enactment. Diminution of consumption of them—a somewhat different concept—was making progress along lines of voluntary temperance in use, or, in many cases, total abstinence. An accurate index was embodied in an observation in which the writer Elbert Hubbard recorded his experiences during the winter 1913–14: "During the last six months I have attended forty-seven banquets. Sixteen were dry. Eighteen were semi-arid; these have started with a cocktail and stopped there. The rest, thirteen, were the old-fashioned kind beginning with cocktails, running into wine, and often there were beer and whiskey."

Gradual progress in self-imposed moderation or voluntary abstinence was too slow for the breathless reform that was in the air. That spirit included a disposition to do good to one's fellowman without always consulting the latter about what he regarded as his best good, a trait reflected in a quip which interpreted W.C.T.U. (Women's Christian Temperance Union) as "We see to you."

This aggressive benevolence accounted in part, though only in small part, for the organized effort to settle the liquor problem by complete, nationwide prohibition of its manufacture or sale. Much more, however, that movement, and the Anti-Saloon League that crusaded for it, arose as reaction against the political power exercised, arrogantly and ruthlessly, by the organized liquor interests. They exercised their power not only to end or neutralize temperance movements, not only to resist and defy attempts at regulation; they went into politics in a broad way, setting up in states and cities political machines which dominated public business.

That extermination of the commercialized liquor business would result in depriving the individual of the legal right to buy and drink liquor was a condition which did not weigh heavily. The conviction among the majority who at that time came to accept the idea of total prohibition was that even if the individual must sacrifice his right legally to drink, nevertheless the commercial liquor business must be extirpated. The commercial exploitation of liquor was too flagrant an agency against good, too stubborn a combatant against betterment, to escape the spirit of reform that was in the air.

IV

Energetically and confidently, and with the accompaniment of considerable melodrama, we attacked some aspects of evil associated with "the most ancient profession in the world." Some amelioration was achieved—how much by statute and how much by other influences would be difficult to apportion. The current excitement expressed itself in an inflammatory phrase "white slavery." The thing that "white slavery" originally and literally meant had an actual though extremely limited existence, a commercialized business, very loosely organized, of procuring young women chiefly in Europe and shipping them to houses of prostitution in seaport cities of North and South America, mainly the latter.

The phrase, when it appeared in newspaper headlines, had great potency to excite crusading minds, and also minds with an appetite for pornography. Investigations by grand juries and other official or altruistic organizations sprang up everywhere. A former head of the New York police wrote the book *The Girl That Disappears*. Magazine articles were numerous. Minneapolis set up a Vice Commission; Syracuse, New York, a Moral Survey Committee, and Chicago a commission whose report, "The Social Evil," was exceptionally thorough and exceptionally useful.

Agitation about the evil led to exploitation, by some parts of the stage, press, and films, of the sensational possibilities associated with the idea, an exploitation as commercial in motive as the traffic itself. There were "white slave" plays, "white slave" motion pictures. This in turn led to a popular hysteria which believed that "white slavers" procured victims by carrying a "poisoned needle" with which they stupefied young women beside whom they, in the artful pursuit of their business, seated themselves in streetcars. So prevalent became the vague but sensational accounts of mysterious disappearances that it became prudent for the press, some of which had incited the hysteria, to quiet it by procuring from physicians authoritative testimony to the practical impossibility of drugging an unwilling person by injection from a hypodermic needle in a crowded streetcar.

The curative statute passed by Congress, called the "White Slave Traffic Act" or Mann Act, included in its prohibitions an embracing phrase "or for any other immoral purpose"; with the result that enforcement descended not only upon the professional procurers and shippers of white slaves in the true sense, but also upon many philanderers who incautiously paid the railroad or taxicab fare of a lady across a state line, and thereby made themselves liable to prosecution later by a woman scorned, or by one who had planned blackmail from the beginning.

Other legislation by Congress successfully wiped out a "red light" district in Washington, on a site which had been the camp of General Hooker's division in the Civil War, and which under the colloquial term "the division," had been a place of disorderly houses during the nearly fifty years since Hooker's soldiers had left. In states and cities, vice districts were broken up. There was, beginning about 1910, a diminution, almost a disappearance, of the form of vice which, once common in every city under the name "houses of prostitution" had included a kind of semibondage on the part of inmates. It would not be safe to say that the quantity of unsanctified or nonlegalized relations between unmarried persons became less, but those odious aspects of it which included commercialization by entrepreneurs, and a degree of forced detention of prostitutes in houses, disappeared in many cities. The reasons were not wholly confined to statutes enacted by legislatures, or raids by police, or crusades by vice societies. They included a rise in the economic status of women, an extension of the occupations opened to them, an elevation of their pay.

What might have been the next stage of the America that was on June 28, 1914; what direction might have been taken by the evolution of that combination of materialism, diffusion of the fruits of materialism, and crusading altruism—all that became, by the shot at Sarajevo, one of the "ifs" of history. It is fair to surmise that this interruption of the course upon which America was intent constitutes the greatest of all indictments against war.

CHAPTER 7
New Influences on the American Mind

The average man found himself thinking differently, or in a greater number of cases, found his children thinking differently from himself. The man who was adult between 1900 and 1925 had acquired his stock of ideas* some decades before, through association as a child with his family and through school life during the 1890s, 1880s or 1870s. Many of these ideas had become, by the 1900s, so antiquated as to seem, to the newer generation, humorous or quaint, or in some cases odious—ancient fogyisms, to be laughed at, or amiably tolerated, or savagely attacked, according to the attitude of any individual youth toward his elders.

The sources of the new ideas, and the channels through which they found their way into the American mind, were as various and intricate as the fabric of civilization. Neither source nor channel was commonly known by the average man. Indeed, he did not ordinarily recognize that his point of view had undergone change. As for the young, the new ways came to them not as new but as part of the world about them, as taken for granted as the air they breathed. Any reflective person, however, upon reviewing even a brief span of years, could observe that what had once been shocking, such as talk about sex, was now accepted; what had been taboo, such as smoking by women, was now general; what had been authoritative, such as permanence of marriage, was now ignored or questioned; what had been an imperative requirement, such as chaperons for young women, was now passé; what had been universal custom, such as grace at meals and family prayers, was now rare; what had been concealed, such as women's legs, was now visible.

Conventions which had been respected, traditions that had been revered, codes that had been obeyed almost as precepts of religion, had been undermined or had disappeared. In their place had come new ways, new attitudes of mind, new manners. The sum of the changes had a deep-

---

*What is commonly called, loosely, a nation's culture includes the points of view a person has about individual conduct and social relations; his attitude toward government and toward other peoples; his habit of mind about the family, the duty of parents to children and children to parents; his standards of taste and of morals; his store of accepted wisdom which he expresses in proverbs and aphorisms; his venerations and loyalties, his prejudices and biases, his canons of conventionality; the whole group of ideas held in common by most of the people. This body of culture comes to every individual mainly through well-recognized channels, through parents and elders who hand it down by oral traditions, through religion, through schools, and through reading, of books and of newspapers and periodicals.

In 1909, the chaperon was still in vogue. (From a drawing by A. B. Walker in Life*)*

reaching effect on the generation that was young as the Great War began; coupled with the war, it made a different America.

The sources of the new, the causes of the change, the routes by which the new came, were in most cases vague, indirect, and not readily recognizable. To find the springs and trace the paths of all the new ideas would be impossible. A few, including some of the more important, are susceptible to the process of historical investigation; they came from such concrete sources and by such direct routes as to lend themselves to exact identification.

II

The largest single group of new ideas, and the ones that were most fundamental in the changes they wrought, appeared in America between 1909 and 1914. They had originated in Europe, some thirty years before.

About 1881, in Vienna, a physician named Sigmund Freud (his practice was mainly with the mentally ill) evolved some startling new theories about personality and conduct, which denied every existing hypothesis about human behavior.

Freud claimed that the personality is divided into two parts, the conscious and the subconscious or unconscious, the latter in turn divided into the true subconscious and the censor. Between the conscious and the subconscious, Freud asserted, there is constant war, with the censor acting as a busy little mediator.

Freud's theory held that the conscious is that respectable and superficial part of the personality which presents itself to the world as a civilized and self-disciplined human being, but that the subconscious is the fundamental part, the irrepressible part, the primitive personality; that the conscious is the well-ordered parlor of the personality, while the subconscious is the cellar of caveman passions; that between conscious and subconscious there is constant struggle, the subconscious striving to carry out its animal impulses and instincts, the conscious engaged in a continuous process of repressing, or else camouflaging with a veneer of civilization, the tendencies of the powerful subconscious—a never-ending strife between subconscious as the caged beast and conscious in the role of keeper and only partially successful tamer.

Freud held that in the subconscious, and therefore in the personality as a whole, the fundamental and universal basis of all human action is the sex urge; that within every individual, the biologic urge to reproduce and perpetuate is the sole driving force that inspires all emotions, impulses, and actions; that our strivings, and our exultations in achievement—which the world theretofore had called ambition and let it go at that—were really expressions of sex impulse, of the cosmic urge to perpetuate the human race; that where actions seem spiritual, it is merely a case of the personality "sublimating," putting a better color on, a process which in the subconscious remains always savage and always sex; that the sex urge exists, functions, and is in evidence from the moment of birth—indeed, some of the Freudian school asserted its beginning to be prenatal, "intrauterine."

A corollary of the Freudian theory was that religion is merely "an unconscious transference of love energy from human to divine objects . . . a symbolic satisfaction for hidden impulses and primitive emotions, a forcing of unconscious desires into forms acceptable to the moral consciousness." Another corollary was that dreams are the vicarious gratification, sometimes symbolic or indirect, of suppressed wishes—the subconscious escaping from the tyranny of the conscious, going on the loose and taking its fling in time of sleep, while conscious the keeper is off guard.

The Freud theory came to the United States first through medical journals, the earliest mention in an article entitled "The Psychopathology of Everyday Life," by Boris Sidis, in the *Journal of Abnormal Psychology* in 1906. By 1909, medical periodicals had much of it. In September of that year, Freud came in person to deliver a series of lectures "Concerning Psychoanalysis," at Clark University, Worcester, Massachusetts. By 1910, allusions to the new concept of psychology began to appear in the lay press, usually with angry disapproval. "So far," said the *American Magazine* in November 1910, fingering the subject rather gingerly, "no other leading psychopathist has accepted this sweeping and audacious theory." Two years later, *Scientific American* spoke, with repugnance, of Freud's "disgusting and wild interpretations."

That was the average normal layman's reaction to initial acquaintance with a theory which was utterly contrary to religion and subversive of every existing conception of romantic love. To the average American of about 1910, it would be difficult to imagine anything more repellent. A not too imaginative reader would have interpreted Freud's theory to mean that a devotee kneeling before the Cross is unconsciously satisfying a sublimated form of desire of the flesh, and does not differ from a pagan bowing before

a phallic symbol; that every baby in his cradle is a leering philanderer; that
a boy-child throwing his arms about his mother is an incestuous libertine;
that every girl-child has an incestuous love for her father accompanied by a
murderously jealous hate of her mother; that protective tenderness shown
by an adult toward a child of the opposite sex is a scandal; that a Romeo
sighing beneath his Juliet's balcony is merely the two-legged and more musically voiced equivalent of any male cat yowling to his tabby on a backyard
fence—some of the early and zealous converts to Freudianism would have
implied that the tomcat was on the whole the more laudable, since he practiced no debasing dissimulations or indirections.

The new theory did not come to the average man directly nor in its stark
form; the average man, indeed, rarely heard the name Freud, and never
grasped the meaning of "Freudian" even after the word got into the 1927
edition of *Webster's Dictionary*. Nevertheless, the world about the average
man, the books, magazines, and newspapers he read, the plays and motion
pictures he saw, the manners and point of view of the people about him, including ultimately his own, were profoundly modified by the ideas of the

Sigmund Freud.

Viennese physician of whom he knew nothing, coming to him through processes of which he was never aware.

The medium through which Freud's ideas were impressed upon the country and altered its standards, consisted mainly of the novelists, dramatists, poets, critics, college teachers, and a type of intellectual called, somewhat condescendingly, "high-brows." These, seizing upon the new "ism" avidly, were soon talking animatedly in its outré terminology: "Psychoanalysis," meaning the study of man's subconscious motives and desires, or the act of a practitioner in analyzing the subconscious mentality of an individual; "sublimation," meaning the diverting of sexual energy into intellectual channels or creative work; "fixation," meaning the unconscious arrest and crystallization at an early age of a subconscious tendency, for example, the affection, alleged by Freud to be wholly or mainly sexual, of a child for a parent; "repression," meaning the keeping from consciousness of primitive desires or mental processes that would be painful for the conscious to admit; "complexes," meaning obscure mechanisms arising in the subconscious as a result of the tyranny of the conscious or of the outside world—a series of associated ideas, the touching of any one of which stirs the whole series into action; "libido," meaning originally sexual hunger but broadened to include what the philosopher Henri Bergson termed the "vital impetus" and becoming almost synonymous with all forms of instinctive energy.

Chatter of all that stirred the air wherever intellectuals met; by the 1920s, there were more than 200 books dealing with Freudianism. Among intellectuals as well as high-brows and those who were impressed by them, it became a fad to be psychoanalyzed, abbreviated to "psyked." To meet the demand, practitioners arose. Lucrativeness attracted charlatans; at the height of the vogue, advertisements offered to psychoanalyze by mail.

The dramatists, novelists, and poets, by accepting the new theory, caused practically the whole of previously written English literature, so far as it dealt with love or religion, to become, as they said, old-fashioned. A novel such as Nathaniel Hawthorne's *Scarlet Letter*, dealing with the struggle between conscience and conduct, became, to these intelligentsia, valueless unless interpreted in terms of the Freudian formula. Romantic love, as it had been described by novelists like William Thackeray, or poets like Alfred, Lord Tennyson, was considered a sentimental glossing over of animal instincts. "He for God alone, for God in him," would have been analyzed by an American intellectual of about 1914 as a "father fixation" suffered by each lover. The romantic tradition in literature came to be regarded as passé, and was jeered at. The Puritan tradition both in literature and morals began to be derided. Hardly any intellectual revolution in history was more complete than the transition from reverence for Emersonian Puritanism up to about 1910, to fierce jibing at it subsequently. It was a denial, by American authors, of the most American standard, almost the only American standard, we had—a rejection of the austere morality of a New

England philosopher to make way for the biological theory of an Austrian physician to diseased minds. The new novels and plays written from about 1914 until about the middle of the 1920s took the Freudian thesis, in one degree or another, and by that name or under the designation "realism," as the basis of the love episodes they contained. Eugene O'Neill, considered during the 1920s to be the ablest American dramatist, followed the Freudian concept starkly, almost slavishly.

Through all this, romantic love, not only in literature but in life, had a rough time. A generation of youth, made familiar by novels and the stage with the exclusively biological explanation of love, came to be a little ashamed of romantic love, or became heretics denying its existence.

Interest in Freud and his theory removed the taboo upon sex as a topic susceptible of discussion in what used to be called "mixed company"; once sex as a subject of conversation became permissible, it became general, to the considerable embarrassment of persons aged thirty or more, who could recall when the word "leg" was questionable, and the word "sex," for example, not questionable at all but strictly forbidden. By 1915, one journalist was moved to remark, "It's sex o'clock." The phenomenon, until we got used to it, was acutely disturbing; the *New York World* spoke of "our present popular hysteria, sex-madness"; a Philadelphia author distinguished, if somewhat cloistral, in her personality and in her art, Agnes Repplier, spoke of it as the "repeal of reticence."

Freudian influence in the theater. A scene from Eugene O'Neill's play Desire Under the Elms.

Much of the new thought about love was sincere, some was a mere rushing to adopt the novel, not a little was meretricious. In literature and the drama, and especially in moving pictures, there were some who used the new theories as an excuse for moneymaking pornography. A joke of the period represented a motion picture magnate as saying "two and two make four, four and four make eight, sex and sex make millions."

The movement left some enduring effects. Such valid residuum of it as was able to withstand criticism, modified greatly the science of psychology, both the medical aspect of it and the teaching of it in colleges. It revolutionized the treatment of the mentally ill. Freedom from self-consciousness about talking of sex between the sexes led to evaporation of some false sentimentality about women. The mere experience of acquaintance with a new point of view, of seeing an ancient and accepted convention brought under attack, had an intellectual effect of "shaking up" even where the new view was rejected. Some of the new frankness and the new understanding had partial value. There was much validity in the supporter of Freud who said of the older order that "sending the young out into life with such a false psychological orientation was as if one were to equip people going on a polar exploration with summer clothing and maps of the Italian lakes."

Between those entranced by Freud and those outraged by him, battle raged for more than twenty years. "The ideas of no other living man are so directly responsible for so many printed pages," wrote Joseph Jastrow in 1932. The controversy could have no conclusion. The basis of the Freudian theory was not within the world of proof or disproof; it was not the end of a syllogism, but the beginning; it was a premise, upon which many conclusions, sound or fantastic, were built, by which many practices, good or bad, were justified.

III

Most of the new ideas came from across the sea, from Freud in Austria, Shaw and Wells in England, Nietzsche and Schopenhauer in Germany, Tolstoy and Gorki in Russia, from Omar Khayyám in Persia and nine centuries ago. Such idol-wreckers as arose in America as a rule owed what conspicuousness they achieved to their adeptness and quickness as adopters and adapters of new thought that came from abroad; America had no really important image-smasher of its own. During the 1870s, 1880s, and 1890s, Walt Whitman had originated new ideas and new forms of poetry; Henry George had made familiar a new theory of organized society; Robert ("Bob") Ingersoll had made agnosticism familiar though decidedly not popular. Minor iconoclasts of religion were Elbert Hubbard with his bizarre little magazine, *The Philistine*, and a fiercely belligerent atheist who reached the average man with a fiery, cheaply printed, paper (often consumed in bonfires by angry believers), called *Brann's Iconoclast*. At all times,

especially in church and university circles, there was querying of some portions of orthodox religion. "Higher Criticism" was a euphemism, devised
as armor against accusation of heresy, for attempts made by churchmen
and collegians to construct an intellectual bridge between religion and
Darwinism. Darwin's *Descent of Man*, published in England in 1871, was, of
course, the source of practically all modern questioning of the Bible. It
never reached the average man directly, though the effects of it seeped
down to him from colleges.

The seeping was slow; as late as 1925, the outstanding sensation of the
country for a month was the trial of a Tennessee schoolteacher, John
Thomas Scopes, for giving instruction in biology which included Darwin's
theory—contrary to a statute of Tennessee which banned the teaching of
evolution.

For the exceptional responsiveness of America to new ideas, and exotic
ones, for the fact that foreigners became popular in America long before
they were accepted in their own countries, there were reasons easily identifiable. America, as a people, did not have deep roots in the soil upon which
it lived; the oldest community in the United States was, in 1914, but little
over three centuries old, the average less than 100 years—merely a morn-
ing-hour of sunrise compared to the length of continuous life and unbro-
ken tradition among European peoples. America had no separate body of

Count Tolstoy.

Immigrants at Ellis Island, New York, waiting to be passed for entry into the United States.

culture that had germinated here; such traditions as we possessed had come to us with early settlers or with waves of immigration, and had experienced arrest of growth by transplanting, had suffered attenuation in the new soil, and attrition by rubbing against differing traditions from other sources. America presented to the assaults of change no such crystallized front of long accepted, indigenous culture as did older peoples. American culture was still in the melting pot, still in a flux into which new ideas could be thrown and become part of the whole.

This fluidity of the American body of ideas, this receptivity to the new, was kept alive by constant waves of new immigration. The immigrant, because of the equality of mind that led him to migrate, was susceptible to change; one who of his own impulse had sought the new, was pliant to the new when it came to him from any source.

IV

A fundamental fact about America, constituting a special cause for its quick receptivity to new ideas, and necessary to be taken into account in any thoughtful attempt to understand the country's culture and its social history, is a unique relation that existed between America's metropolis and America itself.

In every country, changes in culture originate in the metropolis and from there spread out. One reason is the tendency of the provinces to regard whatever is done in the great city as "the thing," and to imitate it. Another reason is that, in any country, the largest city, because of its aggregation of wealth and other conditions, is, so to speak, the culture cap-

Ellis Island Immigration Station, New York Harbor, as seen from an airplane.

ital. A more direct reason is similar to one of the laws of mass production in the material world: The metropolis of a nation is the densest and most easily accessible market for all those forms of art and culture which are the ve-

Above left, interior of a dairy barn of an electrically equipped farm. Below right, government scientist testing milk.

Through the introduction of vacuum cleaners, choking clouds of dust have become relics of barbarism.

"Why stir up the Dust Demon to a frenzy like this?" (From Theatre Magazine, *September 1908)*

hicles of new ideas for new plays, new books, new music, including new popular songs. The purveyors of these aim at the population of the metropolis for their primary market. Innovations of every kind, including new styles in clothing and new vogues in manners, commonly sink their first roots in the metropolis. What the metropolis adopts is certain to spread out through the country; the influence of a metropolis on a nation's culture is irresistible.

But about the metropolis of the United States there was a unique condition making it, and the country tributary to it, peculiarly susceptible to innovations. The metropolis of the United States was made up mainly of peoples different from the country whose culture it modified. Nowhere, either in the present world or in history, was another case of a city exercising the influence of a metropolis on a country without being made up of people of that country.

New York during the period this history covers had come to be made up, to an increasing extent, of immigrants—almost exclusively immigrants if we include the first generation born in America. Of greater consequence in its bearing on cultural change, a rapidly growing preponderance of the new immigrants came from countries which had not before contributed to the makeup of the American people. The new immigrants, in many respects culturally different from the older stock, came from Italy, Russia, Poland, Austria-Hungary, and the rest of southeastern Europe.

Had the immigrants brought their native cultures with them, and held to them, New York might have been, as respects culture, a polyglot city. To a slight degree this took place. There were Yiddish theaters and an Italian press, as well as a German theater and newspapers in some twenty-three tongues. These, however, catered only to successive groups of newly arrived immigrants. They did not tend to perpetuate in New York the cultures of the peoples who made up the city. The trend was against New York becoming a polyglot city in the sense of being made up of separate peoples and separate cultures existing side by side. The trend, very strong, was toward New York becoming a "melting pot" city.

What happened was that the immigrant, as he arrived at Ellis Island, was moved, in a rather fine spirit, to drop his native culture, to cease to be an Italian, Russian, or Pole, to become an American. But if he stayed in New York he had little opportunity to become American in the sense of taking on a traditional American culture, traditional American ways; he found about him only uprooted Europeans like himself. As for the children of immigrants, their wish to drop the ways of their parents was self-conscious and aggressive—they tended to be a little ashamed of their parents' ways, often in rebellion against their parents' codes. They were determined to be American, or what they understood to be "American"; but they, like their parents, found about them only uprooted orphans of culture like themselves. It was the common observation that what the younger generation in New York picked up as "American ways" was tragically inferior to what their alien parents had possessed as inherited and cherished traditions.

The consequence was, New York, while exercising the influence that a metropolis inevitably has upon a country's culture, did not itself have a traditional American culture, nor a polyglot culture, nor any standard of culture at all. New York was a culture void. To the new it presented no resistance of indigenous custom or native tradition. To any chance seed brought by the wind, it opposed no granite of crystallized tradition, but rather gave the febrile welcome of a hothouse. Such a soil is one in which new ideas, new points of view, new ways of life, can easily take root. The city, naked of tradition or ancient standard, was subject to infection by any ephemeral vogue that might arise from any source, whether generating spontaneously, or coming from abroad, or thrust upon it by commercial entrepreneurs. If, from time to time, it should generate momentary standards, they would be something new and hybrid, not felt to be kin to any nation that is homogeneous or has traditions.

New York dominated the theater. Plays either were written for New York or were dependent for their survival on suiting the taste of New York. If New York liked them, they were successful and were sent with road companies to impress themselves on the taste of the rest of the country. The motion picture business (though operated in California because of conditions of sunlight*) was dominated from New York, and productions were aimed at New York audiences as their primary market. New York was the largest market for books. Of the sales of an average book, more than half would be made in the metropolitan area. Most of the critics whose applause or disapproval had influence on the success of books either lived in New York or reflected the New York spirit. The newspapers of New York,

---

*All early motion pictures were filmed in sunlight, since adequate electrical lighting had not yet been developed. —D.R.

A well-known Washington landmark, thirty years ago. The New Jersey Avenue Station of the Baltimore and Ohio Railroad, as it appeared after successive remodelings.

A modern terminal, from the air. This photograph of the Union Station at Washington shows the arrangement of tracks.

From 1900 to 1914 many railroad terminals were rebuilt, including the Grand Central and Pennsylvania in New York. These pictures show the contrast between the old Baltimore and Ohio Station at Washington, D.C., and the new one which houses all the lines entering Washington.

Theater time in New York—once.

Theater time in New York—now.

(From the New York Herald Tribune, *December 23, 1928)*

written necessarily to meet the taste of that city, became the models for the press of the rest of the country. Practically all the country's forms of art, almost all its vehicles for the introduction of new ideas, took their color from New York.

On the one hand, the country was clinging with instinctive affection to its old standards; on the other, it was turning to a metropolis which generated fitful gusts of change, hectic successions of vogues. With one instinct, that of imitation, entertained chiefly by the young, the country tended to accept the innovation from the metropolis just because it was new, "the latest thing." With a deeper instinct, the country resented and resisted. Frequently, the opposition was organized, formal, statutory, expressing itself in such devices as censorship of motion pictures by towns or states. Practically always, however, for good or ill, the new prevailed, until supplanted by another new from the same spring.

V

Those whose profession is words, historians as well as critics, essayists, and other literary artists, frequently assume, perhaps through pride of calling, that new ideas, changed habits of thought, come into the world only or mainly through words. They assume that of all the sights that pass into man's mind through his eyes, the ones that work changes in his thinking are black marks upon white paper. It is tenable to suggest that the intellectual innovations which came to America during the period this history covers were due more to changes in the material world about him than to anything that came to him through the pens of intelligentsia; that the aver-

Louis Bleriot leaving France. He was the first to cross the English Channel in a monoplane, July 25, 1909.

age man's mind was modified more by the automobile than by any so-called leader of thought; more by Wilbur and Orville Wright than by the author of *Origin of Species* or of *The Interpretation of Dreams.*

The automobile acquainted the average man's mind with rudiments of physical law, to an extent that formal education as practiced at that time never would; working with gasoline, oil, and electricity gave to his thinking the greater exactness, the better understanding of cause and effect, which accompanies even elementary acquaintance with chemistry and physics.

Use of the new vehicle brought man freedom from old-world limitations, from ancient subjections to circumstance. It modified time and distance. What had been an hour became five minutes, what had been 10 miles became one. Before the motorcar came, the market in which man could sell his labor was limited to the area he could reach on foot or by horse, or to the lines of railroad or streetcar along which he lived. With the motorcar, man could choose the buyer of his labor anywhere within a radius of 30 to 50 miles. By its gift of quickly achievable distance, the automobile released man from subjection to small and stratified circles of public opinion. If the radius of a normal unit of community hegemony and interdependence had been 5 miles, it became, with the motorcar, 30 to 60. The automobile actually broke up the old cell of organized society, substituting an enlarged one. The process, going on for more than thirty years, gave rise to ferment and flux in every area of life.

The average man, by the new scenes to which the automobile carried him, by the new sights brought before his eyes through the motion picture, by the immensely increased quantity of reading matter brought to him through the growth of newspapers and periodicals and the increase of books and spread of libraries—the average man cerebrated, within his limitations, as he had not before. By these causes and by the diffusion of pictorial and literary art, as well as information, the intellectual energy of the period, looked upon as a quantity or in terms of intensity, was measurably increased and speeded up. But—excepting in science, invention, and related fields—it expressed itself not conspicuously in the emergence of unusual intellects, nor outstanding heights of individual achievement, but rather in an enlargement of the intellectual functioning of the average man in the aggregate; a quickening of the speed with which he thought, within his limitations, and an enlargement of the field in which he thought, again within his limitations. By the necessity put upon him of dealing with a more complex and faster moving world, and of handling familiarly some intricate embodiments of physics and science, his mind was quickened. The older American who could nod upon the back of his horse, or let the lines lie slack upon the dashboard of his buggy while his mind occupied itself with reflection or revery, was succeeded now by one whose brain must be every minute upon the steering wheel and pedals, his sense alert for signals and for danger. Man's mind was sharpened, though not necessarily deepened.

* * *

The new was accompanied by some illusion. The quantity of new facts brought before man by increase of printed words, the sights brought by the motion picture, the words brought by the later-invented radio, did not necessarily bring him more wisdom. The ability to distill wisdom from experience remained what it had always been, a quality varying with the individual's ability to assimilate and reflect. And reflection, under the new order, became less possible. The speed of the new ways, the quantity of voices and sights rushing in upon man from the world, the enforced obedience to signals on the road, the summoning of bells in office and the home, reduced the time for reflection, made the mood for it difficult. The value of a message coming over the radio was not increased by the distance over which it came; that remained dependent upon the mind at the microphone. The effect of many of the inventions and new ways was to make man less an individual, more a unit in the herd. The act of picking up a newspaper and, even more, of turning on the radio was in effect the slipping of a clutch which geared the individual into the common emotions, the mass thinking of the crowd, making him more subject to slogans, more responsive to stimulus, by those who wished to move the mass for their own ends. Man, surveying some of the results of the new, might reasonably have asked the inventors and innovators to reverse, for a while, their talents and direct themselves to a new need, insulation and isolation.

VI

To catalogue the changes that came to men's minds would be to survey the whole of civilization. Much of the changed direction took the form of releases, chiefly releases from fears.

Man was freed from fear of hell—the notion of a literal hell of fire and brimstone receded to the backwaters of primitive sects in isolated communities. Man was freed from fear of divine wrath—God as a god of vengeance largely disappeared from men's minds. To some extent man was freed from fear of sin and sense of guilt—states of mind previously regarded as sin, such as doubt about literal interpretation of Scripture or some other religious dogmas, now became a virtue, at least in the world of intellect. Man was released from many arbitrary imperatives, from authoritative "thou shalts" and also "thou shalt nots." A command, whether its source was religion, government, or public opinion, unless it appealed to the reason of the individual, or to the accepted standards of those whose opinion he happened to respect, was often ignored and could always be questioned without sacrifice of society's esteem. With the command not to doubt passed the command to have faith—men had faith, perhaps as much as ever, but it was a faith that germinated within himself and was maintained by inner conviction rather than outer rule.

Intellectually, and to a large extent in religion, it was the "Why?" era.

Michael Pupin. (From a photograph © Underwood & Underwood)

Many of man's ancient speculations had been answered by science, many of his apprehensions dissipated. With the answers came freedom from many forms of dread, from dread of what, because it had not been understood, was supposed to be supernatural. By increased acquaintance with cause and effect, by new understanding of natural phenomena, the world, or certainly America, was almost wholly released, in many cases within a lifetime, from superstition. A physicist of the period, Michael Pupin, who in his maturity became America's outstanding authority on the laws of sound, had been taught in his boyhood that thunder was the noise of Jehovah's car as he careened about the heavens.

VII

Whether the new was in every case better than the old is merely matter for philosophical dissertation; whether the convention of women smoking was better than the convention of women not smoking; whether any of the new ways was better or worse than that which it displaced, is neither here nor there. The fact of history is that the new conventions came in great numbers, and in every area of life.

Whether the average man, the world, was happier for the changes, is a question only to be answered adequately by answering inconclusively; by remembering that the "average man," while a useful abstraction for historians and statisticians, does not exist in fact. There is no such thing as a "world" that feels happiness or lacks it; the world is made up of flesh-and-blood human beings of every variety of temperament and predilection. Probably the number who entertain the delusion that all the old was golden is roughly equal to the number who believe the fallacy that all the new is good. Some like change; others feel always the need of stability and security, of fixed anchorages of faith, authority, rule, command, familiar paths, fixed ways, appointed hours, the protecting walls of rutted courses. These had a rather unhappy time. "Mr. Dooley," speaking for some of them, recalled the time when "half th' congregation heard mass with their prayer-books turrned upside down, an' they were as pious as anny." For himself "Th' Apostles' Creed niver was as con-vincin' to me afther I larned to r-read it as it was whin I cudden't read it, but believed it."

However one viewed change—with regret or excitement—it was a time of endings and beginnings, of the commotion that goes with clash of old against new, the momentum of the innovation against the inertia of the established. The most cultivated American scholar of that day, Henry Adams, writing his autobiography in 1906, felt, he said with gentle resignation, like a man who had come down from centuries before. His education (which he had received in the 1850s and 1860s at the best American and European sources) had fitted him well to live in the time of Julius Caesar—but not at all to live in the time of Theodore Roosevelt. The figure of speech was not too far-fetched; the changes that took place within a single lifetime spanned centuries in terms of culture; the number and importance of the changes in the material world alone that took place during the life of Theodore Roosevelt were greater than the sum of those that had taken place during 2,000 years preceding.

CHAPTER 8
Popular Songs

To the historian, some songs constitute an index to manners, vogues, even morals, the events and subjects that engaged national interest, economic, social, and cultural changes. Others are comparatively slight in their relation to contemporary events:

> Meet me in St. Louis, Louis,
> Meet me at the Fair

obviously referred to the World's Exposition at St. Louis, 1904. "He'd Have to Get Under"* (1913) referred to an incident of motoring, practically unknown to drivers of the foolproof cars of later years, but very familiar in the days before the wayside garage became common, and when part of the equipment for a ride consisted of a "duster" or a pair of overalls with which one could transform oneself into a mechanic when caught by trouble with gear or transmission. "Come Take a Trip in My Airship" (1904) was an attempt by a song artisan to take advantage of the current talk about aviation.

Popular songs identify trends, conditions, eras. Future historians will know that "Her Golden Hair Was Hanging Down Her Back" (1894) must have been written in the prebobbing era. They will know, too, that the change from long hair to short accompanied a change in the attitude of women toward the world, and of the world toward women.

To identify the causes of any change, in any field, small or great, is a task which historians undertake with a confidence out of proportion to their success. Sometimes they make long-armed deductions, in which they may confuse mere sequence of events, or coincidence, with cause and effect. To the shortening of women's skirts, many agencies contributed—it was a symbol of, and a part of, a movement broader and more diverse than feminism, a movement that expressed itself, one way or another, in practically every field of human affairs, and in every quarter of the globe. The process of modernization, considered in the light of all its causes, effects, and associations, was important, and can hardly be fully dealt with as one facet of a comment on popular songs.

*In this chapter, in every case, the figures in parenthesis after song titles are the year of copyright. In some cases the period of the song's greatest vogue was one, two, or more years subsequent to its copyright.

With these very broad qualifications, it is worthwhile to call attention to what is at the least a coincidence, and may be more. The striking elevation of the lower hem of women's skirts began about 1910, in which year it advanced from about the knob of the anklebone upward as far as the shoe top. In the same year, the automobile self-starter was perfected and put on the market. So long as automobiles had to be cranked by hand, it was taken for granted that women generally could not be drivers or owners. With electric self-starters came realization by automobile manufacturers that their market might be increased by persuading women they could now drive. When women began to move their feet about the pedals of a car, long skirts became an inconvenience.

In proportion, as legs in the flesh became visible, so did the word become permissible in conversation, and also in song and in books. And in proportion as the word became permissible, so did it cease to provide occasion or material for jokes and stories of the sort whose point and interest depended upon suggestiveness of wickedness. The situations in song and story that constituted a double entendre moved upward with the skirts, or, to put it in political terms, far over toward the radical left. In the Victorian 1880s a typical double entendre song, "Aching Heart" (1880), depended for its point upon the unmentionability and unprintability of a detail of woman's dress which, by the 1920s, was utterly familiar to every eye, completely casual in common talk. The song alluded to the nursery tale of Hickory Dickory Dock, about a mouse that ran up a clock, and added:

> But the case that I refer to is particularly shocking.
> The clock that this old mouse ran up was on a lady's st—

In proportion, as the area expanded over which a lady might become sunburned, so did a host of songs, jokes, and stories come into the light whose circulation previously had been confined to furtive word of mouth, and to adolescents of all ages. In the field of song, every popular favorite had always had its obscene variation, for rendition in barrooms and at parties of "men only"; and songs of the "Frankie and Johnny" sort had flourished for generations in the musical underworld. By the 1920s, "Frankie and Johnny" was freely sung at mixed gatherings of young folks. In 1929, a volume entitled "Songs My Mother Never Taught Me" stood in the windows of sedate bookshops alongside the *Life of Abraham Lincoln* and *The Meditations of Marcus Aurelius*.

Until the 1900s, "double-meaning" songs, or songs that had only the ribald meaning, had been rigidly excluded from public performance in ordinary theater and vaudeville houses. Unsanctioned relations between men and women could be mentioned only if attended by a wholesome moral, as in "She Loved Not Wisely But Too Well" (1894)—"now she's fled to hide her shame." By 1907, "Be Good" took the tone of advising, not goodness for goodness's sake, nor goodness as a quid pro quo for a harp in heaven, but rather the appearance of goodness for artfulness's sake, and carefulness for safety's sake:

> Be good, very, very good . . .
> If you can't be good, be careful.

Other songs lending themselves to the requisites of double meaning or suggestiveness included "Mary Took the Calves to the Dairy Show" (1908), "This Is No Place for a Minister's Son" (1909), "If You Talk in Your Sleep, Don't Mention My Name" (1910).

The movement was not wholly meretricious in motive, nor necessarily unwholesome in effect. This, like the change in women's dress, like feminism, like a new attitude about religion, was interlocked with other developments, in a mesh far too intricate to permit any historian safely to assert any sure relation of cause and effect—too intricate, also, to permit any moralist dogmatically to say how much of the new is evil, how much good. The area of the discussable was enlarged not only in songs and novels but everywhere.*

The coming of the day when women and children were employed in great numbers in factories, oftentimes supplanting men, made it inevitable that fathers of families should have more leisure, enforced or otherwise, than when they were the sole breadwinners. This shifting of burdens was signalized by a song in which the son or the daughter of the family complained:

> Everybody works but father, and he sits around all day,
> Feet in front of the fire, smoking his pipe of clay;
> Mother takes in washing, so does Sister Ann,
> Everybody works at our house but my old man.

Most of those who sang "Everybody Works But Father" (1905) thought of it merely as a good song. It had economic and social pointedness, however, in circles where the relationship of the daughter-worker's paycheck to the family budget was the occasion of some tartness about the whole obligation of breadwinning being on the father. Whether it was the duty of a good daughter to "bring the pay-envelope home unopened" on Saturday night was a question occasionally mooted in not a few families. Apart from economic asperities, "Everybody Works But Father" coincided with the beginning of an attitude toward parental dignity which in the year of this

---

*The world had become alarmed at the ravages of two familiar diseases mainly associated with sex, whose spread had been partly facilitated by the refusal of common print and speech to acknowledge their existence; it was about 1910 that the world was permitted to read warnings against them, with the names of them used. Similarly, the world had been shocked by the existence of commercialized sex relations on an organized scale in large cities, involving odious semibondage for some women; exposure and cure of the conditions involved familiarity with the word "prostitution" in newspapers and common speech.

song was merely good-humored irreverence, but by 1930 had become out-right flouting tempered by affectionate condescension.

II

The popular songs that had their brief blooming between the turn of the century and the Great War were, for the most part, almost as ephemeral as the emotions they evoked. Few had the robustness to endure; none concerned itself with anything so hardy as a will to survive. A few of them dainty, many merely antic, all fragile—they sang the youths of their day into love, and themselves succumbed to the vicissitudes that at all times beset them. Each was jostled by the next newcomer; whole groups were elbowed aside by new vogues in song and in manners.

Several friendly collaborators who searched the attics of their memories to ascertain which of the songs of 1900–1914 lingered most lovingly in the affections of those who as youths had sung them, agreed that the rusts of a quarter century had been best resisted by a melody whose theme and name was "In the Good Old Summer Time" (1902), beginning

> There's a time in each year
> That we always hold dear . . .

"In the Good Old Summer Time" achieved glamour by a metrical listing of the more agreeable phenomena of the season it extolled. In the cataloguing, difficulty was encountered, through the disinclination of some familiar words to accommodate themselves to rhyme, resulting in such disconcerting assonances as "breezes" and "trees-es." That duplication of a sibilant syllable may seem awkward to generations who will know the song only in cold print; on persons sensitive to locution it may have the effect of a deliberate false start, as if the verses were meant to be burlesque; or it may seem an interruption, as if the singer had stuttered and momentarily changed his vocal step, and his mood. Actually, to the zestful generation that sang the air in its pristine freshness, the "trees-es" was an added lusciousness. One accented it, feelingly, with volume; it became a vocal springboard from which one swung with accelerated momentum into the lilting sweep of sentiment about young love, young love at a time when

> Strolling thro' the shady lanes with your baby mine;
> You hold her hand and she holds yours . . .

was as daring as a popular song was likely to be—some fifteen to twenty years before expressions like "petting" and "necking"* ogled their way into permitted speech.

The appeal of "In the Good Old Summer Time" lay partly in its senti-

*The 1900s equivalent for these words was "spooning."

mental motif. It evoked rural scenes and summer scents, half remembered or wholly dreamed, expressed the mood of "spring fever," suggested vacation, voiced the longing of dwellers in dreary city canyons for the wide bright fields of country-bred childhood. The adult city people of the early 1900s had for the most part been born and reared on farms or in villages, either in America or abroad, and had been drawn into urban life by the fast-growing industrialization of that day. Their rural background made them poignantly susceptible to "In the Good Old Summer Time's" suggestion of the unshadowed sunniness of country meadows, the scents of ripening orchards, and the other allurements, real or dreamed, of country life.

A similar tug on the same heartstrings was made by "In the Shade of the Old Apple Tree" (1905). A chorus that asked no aid from summer, buzzing bees, or apple trees, that sang of love only and put concentrated sentiment into the drawn-out, almost wailing, tenor echoes on which it chiefly depended for its effect, was "Sweet Adeline" (1903). For the vogue it enjoyed, it received help from a most unusual source. The mayor of Boston in 1906–1907 and 1910–14, John Francis Fitzgerald, earlier a member of Congress, used to sing this song on occasions when the more usual expectation from a politician would have been a speech—a laudable consideration for audiences which contributed to his being called "Honey Fitz," and facilitated a locally successful political career*:

> In all my dreams (in all my dreams),
> Your fair face beams (your fair face beams);
> You're the flower of my heart, sweet Ad-e-line (sweet Ad-e-line).

The height of "Sweet Adeline's" vogue was about 1906. Many a youth in college during the 1920s, taught by modern teachers curious new theories about eugenics and the laws of mating, about "fixations" and "complexes," could have learned from his parents that a considerable element in the determination of his immediate ancestry had been the fortuitous conjunction of a spring night, a full moon, and "Sweet Adeline"—followed in due course by "Oh, Promise Me" and the "Wedding March."

III

The period covered by this chapter, 1900 to 1914, spanned, in music, two extremes, from the tranquil "Rosary" to blatant ragtime, the former a vogue in 1900, the latter a rage by 1914. Between those two, about the only characteristic in common was that both were written in musical notes—a more complete revolution could hardly be. Beneath the revolution, however, and serenely undisturbed by it, continued sentiment, and the expression of sentiment in song. The love songs of the early 1900s were neither greater nor less in proportionate quantity, neither better nor worse

*Fitzgerald is now best remembered for his daughter, Rose, matriarch of the Kennedy clan.—D.R.

in quality, than those of the decades that preceded or succeeded. There was possibly a greater emphasis on permanence, in contrast with a later tendency to emphasize exclusiveness of possession, or intensity of passion.

Love in wedlock, fireside love, romantic love as a continuing accompaniment of marriage, love associated with home, was quite within the imagination, and, in spite of mounting divorce statistics, commonly within the practice, of the early 1900s. "Little Grey Home in the West" (1911) was the song of the home-faring husband; "Just a Wearyin' for You" was of the waiting wife:

The generation that lived through this period was sometimes described by its descendants as having been oversentimental. It took sentiment as it took its other moods, as it took the seasons and the weather—in their natural place and proportion. One of the richest men in America, an ironmaster named Henry C. Frick, who bought fine old paintings and endowed an art gallery, had in his mansion a pipe organ proportioned to his wealth, from which, in his hours of ease, it was his custom to have "Dearie" (1905) summoned*:

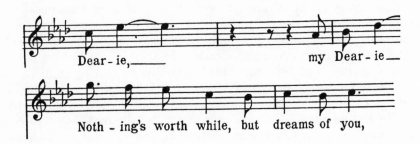

> . . . For I dream of you all the day long,
> You run thro' the hours like a song . . .

> Dearie, my dearie, nothing's worth while but dreams of you,
> And you can make ev'ry dream come true; dearie, my dearie!

*Visitors to the Frick Gallery in New York City can still see the pipe organ. —D.R.

Not classifiable in any ordinary grouping, not romantic because it had nothing to do with love, hardly even sentimental in the ordinary sense, but powerful to move many hearts, was "The End of a Perfect Day" (1910), described by one who liked it as "the story of an aching heart in music." "The End of a Perfect Day" was written as the spontaneous expression of a sincere emotion evoked by beauty and an experience of fine pleasure. The author, Carrie Jacobs-Bond, had been motoring with friends: "Arriving at Riverside, California, late in the afternoon, we traveled to the top of Mt. Rubidoux, sat down and watched the sunset. . . . That night, while dressing for dinner, I sat down and wrote a few verses on little cards used as placecards for the dinner. It didn't take me more than ten minutes; at dinner I read them, and my friends were all pleased":

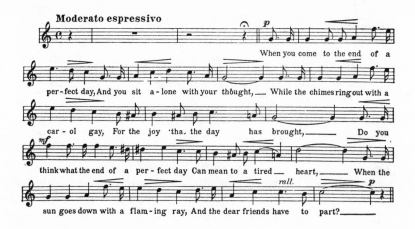

More than 5 million copies were sold, more, perhaps, than of any other American song except "Home, Sweet Home"; it drew royalties from twenty-nine manufacturers of phonograph records, player-rolls, and other forms of mechanical music; and enriched the woman who, by an unusual combination of talent, wrote both words and music—a widow, who, before this success, had kept lodgers, painted china, made dresses, and sung at church entertainments to eke out the income of the hall-bedroom shop in which she carried on a small business in sheet music. "The End of a Perfect Day" evoked moods of peace and repose for literally millions of average Americans. The wife of President Warren Harding (she had much need of peace) cherished it as her favorite song, often asking official musicians to play it as the closing number on White House programs. One of them, remembering, played it at her funeral.

There were songs in which the dividing line between sentiment, and satire on sentiment, was made deliberately narrow; songs that could be sung soulfully and received in the same spirit—or sung and received as conscious burlesque. (Awkwardness occurred only when the singer and the audience had conflicting moods.) For example, concentrated dolefulness, yet with the wink of a pun, was in

> Annie Moore, sweet Annie Moore,
> We will never see sweet Annie any more;
> She went away, one summer's day,
> And we'll never see sweet Annie any more.

Similarly,

> Ev'ry morn I send thee violets

could be taken with extreme seriousness, or it could give rise to harsh remarks about bleating tenors. It was much the same with a group of ballads about lost love, or unrequited love, or love frustrated by circumstances. One could indulge in a mood of melodrama, or one could smile at melodrama, as in:

> She was happy till she met you,
>   And the fault is all your own.
> If she chooses to forget you,
>   You will please leave her alone!
> She is with her dear old mother;
>   In this world she has no other,
> There is no-o place like home, sweet home!

Another ballad of affection misplaced, in which love became involved in unhappy complications through trying to bridge an economic chasm, was told in words and music designed to make hearers feel very sad:

> She's only a bird in a gilded cage,
>   A beautiful sight to see;
> You may think she's happy and free from care;
>   She's not, though she seems to be.
> 'Tis sad when you think of her wasted life,
>   For youth cannot mate with age.
> And her beauty was sold for an old man's gold,
>   She's a bird in a gilded cage.

"A Bird in a Gilded Cage" (1900) could not have been written or become popular in the America of a quarter century later. The picture would be so different from the new conditions as to seem too far-fetched even for burlesque. Economic and social changes had given a young woman too many careers alternative to selling her beauty "for an old man's gold." A woman of 1930 who married for money and found the bargain unsatisfactory did not seek sad sympathy in a song—she stepped out briskly to the divorce court, and exchanged the clanking chains of matrimony for the gayer jingle of gold in the form of alimony.

IV

One can imagine the learned societies of Mars having commissioned one of their number to make, in the most scientific spirit, a meticulously literal record of the musical sounds with which the inhabitants of Earth gave expression to their various emotions; one can picture the expert, as he approached the surface of the United States, on January 1, 1900, for his fourteen-year vigil, holding his notebook ready with scholarly care to take down in order each vocal sound as it reached him in the upper air, his aural tentacles alert, his recording apparatus poised—a little pedantic, perhaps, but finely faithful to the spirit of scholastic inquiry; one can imagine him painstakingly recording every shred and fragment of sound as it floated upward—and one can visualize, later on, the Martian learned societies patiently endeavoring to untangle the melodic jumble, and from it make erudite deductions about the emotional nature of the average American, about the aspects of life that moved him to song, the kind of event that he considered of sufficient importance to write a song about. Such application of scientific methods to the interpretation of melodic vocal sounds would have presented exceptional difficulty in a period, 1900–1914, when song titles and lines from songs with which America expressed its moods at one time or another, composed a peculiarly chaotic babel. The medley would yield rather more to the average American who lived through the period, to whom not only meanings but memories, happy emotions, old associations would be evoked by "I Hear You Calling Me" (1908), "On a Sunday Afternoon" (1902), "By the Light of the Silvery Moon" (1900), "Could You Be True to Eyes of Blue if You Looked into Eyes of Brown?" (1902), "Will You Love Me in December as You Do in May?" (1905) written by James Walker, later mayor of New York City, "Next to Your Mother Who Do You Love?" (1909), "Rip Van Winkle Was a Lucky Man But Adam Had Him Beat a Mile" (1909), "Why Did I Pick a Lemon in the Garden of Love?" (1906).

Most of these songs were mere tiny bubbles of iridescence on the surface of the time. To regard them as landmarks, musical or social, would be the last thing those humble little ditties would ask of history. To future generations they will be no more than quaint or amusing or otherwise entertaining reflections of the sentiments and manners of the America of the early 1900s. They meant more to those who as youths sang them than they ever will mean again.

They made no pretentious claims for themselves; so far as they had merit it was more in the melody than in the words, hence some injustice is done by a recital of them that can appeal only to the eye. The mass of them were composed in a febrile region of New York called, by one obliged to hear the sounds from it, Tin Pan Alley. The denizens of that district, in the period this chapter covers, reversed the art of the old-time ballad writer, whose first concern was to tell a story. The aim of the later generation of song artisans was to hit upon some new combination of sounds, or some rearrangement of an old combination, that would fall agreeably upon the human ear. With the melody accomplished, the finding of words was a secondary consideration, facilitated by the amiable disposition of some words associated with sentiment to unite euphoniously with each other in rhyme—love and dove, coo and woo, heart and part, tune and croon, you and true, moon and June, as in:

> Honey moon, keep a shining in June,
> To my honey I'll croon love's tune . . .

—the final union of the words to the melody being achieved in a spirit which said, in the words of one popular song of the day:

> So the tune has a right good ring
> It doesn't much matter what words you sing.

The Martian observer might have made a not too wide-of-the-mark guess had he said, as to the mass of the fragments of harmonious sounds floating upward, that they were the love sounds, the equivalent of dove calls, availed of by the unfeathered and songless bipeds of earth during the period of susceptibility to mating.

The youths of any generation, when the adolescent imagination is burgeoning, do not commit the cold-blooded atrocity of passing critical judgment on the popular songs of their time; to them any song heard under any fortuitous conjunction of romantic circumstances has an aura that endures so long as they live. From the critical or historical point of view, the successive cycles of songs that happen to be popular during successive generations of adolescents are as ephemeral as the moods with which they were associated. To have a longer life than the love-time of one particular age group, a song must have, in some degree or other, the quality that makes the *Iliad* immortal. Either there must have been in its authorship some elevation of enduring genius, or the song itself must have some musical "it,"* some of the essence of universality, which gives it protection "'gainst the tooth of time, the 'rasure of oblivion."

V

One song popular during the period this chapter covers, "The Rosary," touched hands with the most exalted in poetry and in music; it stands out in this record of popular songs like a solitary tall lily in a garden rather given to marigolds and zinnias. As to its words, it was one of the few songs

*A term that came into popular use about 1924, meaning, among other things, a charm of personality, or exceptional magnetism.

of sentiment that would parse; as to its music, it was one of the rare American popular songs of which the composer had a background of sound training in classical music. The author of the words, Robert Cameron Rogers,
could have had a high place among American poets. That he fell short was
due to a cynicism about his function, a disdain toward his own best, which,
whether real or a pose, is usually a corrosive of talent; and to an intellectual
curiosity about fields other than his own, an interest in other pursuits,
which made perseverance and concentration unlikely. Another handicap
this poet had was not within himself: Inherited wealth, canceling the obligation of hard work, made of his life an easy schedule of tomorrows that
proved ever pleasant but ever barren of yield, a masterpiece of genial laziness. The most compact explanation of Rogers's frustration is to be found
in the humorous cynicism, the too great self-tolerance, which he compressed into an epitaph he wrote for himself, while still in his twenties:

> He was patient in the pursuit of pleasure,
>   and ambitious for his father.

In 1894, Rogers wrote "The Rosary," saw it when set to music acquire
the greatest current vogue of any American poem, saw it become the inspiration of a sentimental British novel whose sales went over a million—and
lived until 1912 enduring the irony of seeing the world adore his popular
song while ignoring what he regarded as by far his better poetry.

"The Rosary," published in a magazine, caught the eye of a chance
woman reader, who happened to be writing to a friend, an American composer named Ethelbert Nevin; with her letter she enclosed the verses. By
that incident, the poem came to another artist whose career, more typically
American, had had the stimulus of poverty and stern discipline, as Rogers's
had had the opiate of inherited wealth.

The words of "The Rosary" reached Nevin one evening while at home
with his family. He read them, came under their spell, and walked up and
down the room repeating them until he had them by heart:

> The hours I spent with thee, dear heart,
>   Are as a string of pearls to me;
> I count them over, every one apart,
>   My Rosary, my Rosary.
>
> Each hour a pearl, each pearl a prayer,
>   To still a heart in absence wrung,
> I tell each bead unto the end,
>   And there a cross is hung.
>
> O memories that bless and burn!
>   O barren gain and bitter loss!
> I kiss each bead, and strive at last to learn
>   To kiss the cross;
>   Sweetheart! to kiss the cross.

Next day, Nevin, arriving home from his studio, handed his wife the penciled music for the song—he had written it, said Mrs. Nevin, "in less than an hour, and never changed a note." Notwithstanding his speed, he had practiced expert craftsmanship, subtly combining the emotions of love and religion in a melodic outline in which the eighth notes of the music suggest the manner in which the smaller beads of the Rosary slip through the fingers of a pious devotee, while at the end of each phrase of the music comes a long note and a pause, corresponding to the larger beads that divide the Rosary into tens. Upon audiences, singers observed, the song had always the same effect. As the listeners caught the first familiar phrase there was a spontaneous burst of applause.

"The Rosary" was first sung publicly in Boston in 1898. Almost a generation later, in 1925, the critic Alexander Woollcott could write: "Every publisher's ear is strained to catch the first notes of another 'Rosary,' for

Part of the original score of "The Rosary."

they all doff their hats to a song that is still in great demand at the beginning of its second quarter century."*

VI

Irving Berlin (born Israel Baline) was destined to have a wide and elevated fame, to excel every other American composer of popular music
during his generation, in the sense
of writing the largest number of
good songs on the widest variety
of themes, having his songs sung
by a larger number of Americans,
and—particular cause of his importance—exerting a greater influence upon American popular
music. As a part of his versatile
talent, Berlin was to show a capacity for writing exquisite songs of
sentiment,   beautiful   waltz
rhythms—of being, indeed, extremely sentimental.

That Berlin had within him the
capacity to achieve such variety
was due to his possession of that
attribute of genius which is able to
take on the atmosphere of its surroundings, to "sense" the spirit of
its locale, and having sensed it, to
express it in art. And Berlin's surroundings when he came into

Irving Berlin.

conjunction with ragtime had been the surroundings in which ragtime at
that stage was likely to be; his background and experience up to that time
illustrating the sad limitation which too often constitutes America's careless
welcome to its immigrants.

Berlin, brought from Russia when he was four years old, deprived of his
father at eight, was thrown into the welter that was New York. He sold papers, carried telegrams, sang songs in saloons for such pennies as the senti-

*The yearly sales of all arrangements of "The Rosary" in the United States from its first year were:

1898	1,990	1906	39,808	1914	228,324	1922	80,170
1899	18,410	1907	48,665	1915	184,946	1923	90,690
1900	32,500	1908	46,459	1916	103,847	1924	93,157
1901	37,500	1909	72,743	1917	98,020	1925	87,015
1902	36,655	1910	71,288	1918	59,201	1926	73,207
1903	35,945	1911	199,780	1919	67,011	1927	68,096
1904	23,332	1912	264,561	1920	71,296	1928	48,735
1905	33,094	1913	287,267	1921	69,738		

GRAND TOTAL   2,673,450

A colored jazz orchestra in action.

mental would chuck on the sawdust at his feet. He slept where he could get a bed for ten cents a night; changed his name for a time to an Irish one, Cooney; became a "busker"* on the Bowery; "plugged" songs from the balcony of Tony Pastor's Music Hall for $5 a week; became a singing waiter in a Chinatown restaurant, "Nigger Mike's Place," where he swabbed the floor foul with cigar butts; and took advantage of occasional moments of leisure to pick out, imitatingly, on the black keys of the piano, the tunes he had heard the day before on the barrel organs of Chinatown. Then, at twenty-three, he wrote the song from which ragtime really dates, "Alexander's Ragtime Band."

With "Alexander's Ragtime Band," Berlin lifted ragtime from the depths of sordid dives to the apotheosis of fashionable vogue. The suddenness of the transformation was sensational. "This was the first full free use of the new rhythm which had begun to take form in the honky-tonks where pianists were dislocating old melodies to make them keep step with the swaying hips and shoulders of [black] dancers" wrote Woollcott. "New York was soon noisy with the boom and blare of the song which was promptly caught up by bands and orchestras and cabaret singers in endless succession. It infected other songwriters. It smote its day and generation as few songs have."

"What was needed," said Gilbert Seldes, a New York critic, "was a crystallization, was one song which should take the whole dash and energy of rag-time and carry it to its apotheosis. With a characteristic turn of mind Berlin accomplished this in a song which had no other topic than rag-time itself. 'Alexander's Ragtime Band' was . . . utterly unsentimental and the whole country responded to its masterful cry, 'Come on and hear!' "

*A singer who seeks his audiences on the streets, or where he can.

Come on and hear,......... Come on and hear............ Al - ex - an - der's rag-time band,........ Come on and hear.......Come on and hear,.......... It's the best band in the land,...........

The triumph of ragtime was not merely a case of one type of music succeeding another. It was a case of conquest, achieved, as if by assault, accompanied by a kind of truculence toward older types, an example of what Gilbert Seldes calls "frank destruction of sentimentality." Ragtime drove to the front in the spirit of overthrow, of revolution. It consciously jeered at the older music, always in spirit, often in words, as in "Alexander's Ragtime Band" itself:

> Come on and hear, come on and hear Alexander's ragtime band,
> Come on and hear, come on and hear, it's the best band in the land. . . .
> And if you care to hear the Swanee (*sic*) River played in ragtime,
> Come on and hear, come on and hear Alexander's ragtime band.

"Swanee River" was only one that ragtime lampooned. "Everything that could be syncopated, and some that could not, paid their quota to ragtime," wrote Seldes. The "ragging" (i.e., transposing into ragtime) of other songs had been, from the beginning, the essential technique of the new syncopation. The resulting travesty, with its effect of jeering, was part of ragtime's method of conquest.

In this technique, the solemn "Rosary" was made the subject of "When Rag-time Rosie Ragged the Rosary." John McCormick's lovely "Mother Machree" became "Mother Machree looked like a chicken to me"—the outstanding example, the pinnacle (if that is the right word) of the ragtime spirit. Even psalms did not escape the cacophonic Herod. When a ragtime tune parodied the hymn held in highest affection by most Americans, a New York teacher of music stirred the newspapers with her indignation, charging that artisans of the new music "stopped only a few inches short of setting the Bible to rag-time. . . . The most absolutely irreverent burlesque I have ever heard lies in the tune built upon 'Nearer My God to Thee.' The young folks think it is funny. A halt should be called before this system of ridicule shatters our every tradition and ideal." The burlesque to which she objected began: "Nero, my dog, has fleas."

VII

To such conservatives as had a feeling for the more formal type of music, the ragtime syncopation was unpleasing enough, but the words thrown together to fit the syncopation were even more distasteful. The idea that a popular song should tell a story was dismissed. In "Tin Pan Alley"—where nine-tenths of the country's popular music came to be produced—hectic artisans, hurrying frantically to take advantage of the new vogue, threw together words having no pretense of narrative, or logic, and only as much poetry as the assonance of love with dove, moon with June, or attained by main force, tune with soon, or maid with said. In the ragtime songs, the words were merely a series of ejaculations, the music a sequence of panting gasps.

If the words were banal, the utterly revolutionary ragtime dances that came with the new music were no less than shocking. Some achieved the effect of double entendre by motion. If what cannot be said can be sung, ragtime discovered that what cannot be sung can be danced. An early one of the impish series was celebrated in a song that Berlin wrote, a song which partly described the not very intricate motions—motions rather than steps—of the parvenu dances, and partly placated scruples against it, the placation consisting of what was coming to be sufficient justification for a good many things, "Everybody's Doin' It Now" (1911):

> Honey, honey, can't you hear funny, funny, music, dear? . . .
> Can't you see them all, swaying up the hall?
> Ev'rybody's doin' it, doin' it, doin' it.

The Turkey Trot and the Grizzly Bear. Modern dances barred from dance halls but popular in society, drawn by A. B. Walker in Life.

See that ragtime couple over there,
Watch them throw their shoulders in the air,
Snap their fingers, honey, I declare,
It's a bear, it's a bear, it's a bear! There!
Everybody's doin' it now!

The spawn of new dances that ragtime begot, called, generically, "animal dances," included the fox trot and the horse trot, the crab step and the kangaroo dip, the camel walk and the fish walk, the chicken scratch and the lame duck; the snake, and the grizzly bear; and—especially common, in both senses of the word—the turkey trot.

VIII

The ragtime dances, at first, made even New York a little squeamish. Battle raged. William R. Hearst's *New York American*, taking a shot at a double target, the new dances and "society," recorded that "New York and Newport society are just at present manifesting a craze for the disgusting and indecent dance known as 'Turkey Trot.' " The *New York Sun* asked: "Are we going to the dogs by the rag-time route?" and hurled harsh phrases, "decadent drivel," "rhythmically attractive degenerator which . . . hypnotizes us into vulgar foot-tapping acquiescence."

In the end, the new dances won. Not only did they win in the ordinary dancing circles of the city, but they carried their conquest into areas of life where dancing had been dropped with the passing of youth. The "dancing age" leaped as high as the sixties; the "frontiers of senescence," as the journalist Elmer Davis put it, were "pushed back forty years."

With universality came condonation. *Life*, with a complacence which felt sure that whatever New York approved, the country would accept, frowned upon "the disturbance which is proceeding about the prevalence in this city of modes of dancing which do not commend themselves to the guardians of our manners and moralities. The 'turkey trot,' the 'bunny hug,' and the 'grizzly bear' spread up and down and far and wide through our metropolitan society. Little Italians dance them in Harlem, polite cotillions at Sherry's have been diversified by them, and they flourish above, below, and between. Dancing masters are besought to teach them; the cabaret performer of a Broadway restaurant who is thought to be most proficient in them is said to be overrun with demands for instruction from learners out of fashionable families. The dancing set in our town must be at least half a million strong, and it makes a difference how it dances."

IX

With approval by the metropolis began inundation of the country. Rural communities and cities other than New York offered resistance. All over the country, newspapers charged that ragtime was vulgarizing the young, undermining respect for sacred things, and was "responsible for deterioration of manners, taste, and right thinking. . . . The real danger to the community is the songs that give young folks a false and perverted impression of love and romance, which hold a pure and romantic sentiment up to slangy ridicule." In Philadelphia, uncompromising disapproval by a conscientious guardian of young women was reflected in an episode reported in a newspaper dispatch which described the turkey trot as "taboo at the office of the Curtis Publishing Company; fifteen young women were dismissed to-day after they had been detected enjoying the suggestive dance at lunch time by Edward W. Bok, editor of *The Ladies' Home Journal*." A Paterson, New Jersey, court imposed a fifty days' prison sentence (as the alternative to a $25 fine) on a young woman for dancing the turkey trot. At Millwood, New York, Grace Williams, eighteen years old, was arraigned on complaint of former Justice of the Peace Ogden S. Bradley, who charged that she was guilty of disorderly conduct in frequently singing "Everybody's Doin' It Now," as she passed his house, and dancing the turkey trot. "Squire" Bradley said that he and his wife thought that both the song and dance were highly improper and that they had been greatly annoyed. Lawyer Stuart Baker demanded a jury trial. Williams said she sang the song because she liked it, and danced because she could not help it when she heard the catchy tune. Lawyer Baker volunteered to sing the song in court. The prosecuting attorney objected, stating this would make a farce of the trial. Judge Chadeayne overruled him and told Baker to go ahead. The lawyer, who had a good baritone voice, sang the ditty. When he reached the chorus, "Everybody's doin' it, doin' it, doin' it," spectators joined in. The jurors called for an encore. Again taking out his tuning fork to pitch the key, the lawyer sang the second stanza with more feeling and expression, and as he sang he gave a mild imitation of the turkey trot. The jurymen clapped their hands in vigorous appreciation, and after five minutes' deliberation found Williams not guilty.*

X

It was said, after ragtime (and its descendant, jazz) had proved that nothing succeeds like success, that this was a "peculiarly American product"; that it was the spirit of America; that it was "the national idiom"; that it is "our one original and important contribution to music" and that it contains "the true American spirit"; that it "seems to fit the nervousness of our climate and our people"; that "the dash and vim of it is in the American blood"; that it is "the rhythmical and melodic expression of life in the modern United States."

---

*So was born a cultural constant of this century: white fears that youth would be corrupted by black music. Almost every popular style—jazz, bebop, blues, rock, and rap—with origins in black communities has in turn been denounced, usually with the sobriquet "jungle music." Youth has danced more than it heeded—for generations. —D.R.

Maybe. The writer of this history does not know, but doubts. Perhaps someone with sympathetic understanding of the deeper subtleties of our national psychology, and of the conflict between New York City standards and older American ones, might say that the triumph of ragtime and jazz was merely another case of a new vogue taking root like a weed in the heterogeneous welter that the American metropolis was, and from there inundating the country; and that the genuinely American thing was not ragtime but the instinctively defensive—and pathetically futile—effort of the older generation in the rural parts of the country to ward off this assault on the older American melodies at which ragtime jeered. Can one imagine ragtime springing up spontaneously and indigenously on the prairies of the Midwest or on the farms of New England, as the old outdoor dances sprang up on the village greens of England, "Annie Laurie" in the glens of Scotland, "Garryowen" at the country fairs of Ireland, the "Volga Boat Song" on the steppes of Russia, or "El Manicero" ("Peanut Vender") in the purlieus of Havana, or "O Sole Mio" on the canals of Venice?

CHAPTER 9
An Emancipation

On December 4, 1902, a convention of physicians at Washington, D.C., listened, with the tolerance of pundits for a neophyte, to an address by a very youthful-appearing man of science, Dr. Charles Wardell Stiles, described on the program as chief of the division of zoology of the U.S. Public Health Service. Stiles naturally, since his audience were specialists in preventive medicine, used the language of technical men. The physicians present followed him with understanding, but to one listener, apparently, much of the lecture might as well have been in Sanskrit. In a front seat, just below the speaker's platform, sat a rotund, moon-faced young man whose head at short intervals would sink slowly to his breast, while his increasingly heavy breathing approached so close to a snore that the question whether he would or would not became an occasion for acute suspense, surpassing, from time to time, interest in the more formal program. Whenever the sleepy auditor mobilized all his resources of attention, his reviving faculties were again driven into retreat by such opiatic phrases from Dr. Stiles as "ancylostoma duodenale" and "uncinariasis americana."

Dr. Stiles, under the compulsion of a natural law with which public speakers are familiar, found his attention drawn to the spectacle that was a rival to himself. More exactly, Dr. Stiles's mind divided itself into two, half of it concerning itself

Dr. Charles Wardell Stiles in 1930. (From a photograph by Science Service)

with the speech he was making, half turning anxiously to the disturber. With each slow descent of the latter's chin, each resumption of the cumulatively slow breathing of approaching slumber, Dr. Stiles passed through a corresponding cycle of suspense, wondering if this time the snore would really come. Who was he, anyhow? Stiles asked himself. Why was he here? Why should he be in this audience, embarrassing an earnest young scientist with an exceptionally passionate wish to have the attention of his listeners?

Suddenly, to Stiles's relief, and also to his mystification, the young man shook off his lethargy and began scribbling furiously on a pad. Now, perversely, Stiles's bedeviled mind flashed back and forth from his speech to a new speculation. What had caused the transformation? Had it been something Stiles had said, some solecism or impropriety, perhaps? Stiles had been talking about the hookworm parasite, which he had recently found to be widely prevalent in several southern states. The portion of his speech that had coincided with the drowsy auditor's sudden revitalization had dealt with the effect the hookworm has of causing in its victims an extreme disinclination to labor. The so-called poor white trash of the South, Dr. Stiles had said in substance, were probably not inherently lazy; their energy was being consumed by hookworms. What was there in that statement to galvanize a lethargic young man?

After the lecture, the sleepy young man—he was a newspaper reporter— took himself off into the night, leaving for history no explanation of his abrupt emergence from sleepiness—whether the startling thought had struck him that his own proneness to somnolence might be due to hookworms in his internal anatomy, or whether his interest had been awakened by the implications in the thought that so common a human trait as laziness might be caused by a microbe. In the anonymity that was the almost universal rule of newspaper writing in America during the early years of the century, the young man's name disappeared into the limbo of that quite large number of persons whose contributions, in the course of the day's work, to the wit of the time or its enlightenment, or its wisdom or emotion, are unacknowledged by fame.

Stiles, the congratulations of his scientific colleagues tingling pleasantly in his ears, went home to a quiet night's rest, undisturbed

---

GERM OF LAZINESS FOUND?

DISEASE OF THE "CRACKER" AND OF SOME NATIONS IDENTIFIED.

Dr. Charles Wardell Stiles, Discoverer of the Hook Worm Disease, Describes Its Curious Effects to the Sanitary Conference of American Republics

WASHINGTON, Dec. 4.—The Sanitary Conference of American Republics closed its sessions to-day with a declaration almost sensational in its significance. Dr. Charles Wardell Stiles, Zoölogist of the Bureau of Animal Industry of the Agricultural Department and well known in the medical world as the discoverer of uncinariasis,

A headline that made history. Printed in the New York Sun, December 5, 1902, its whimsicality set the world a-laughing and, by focusing attention on an obscure scientist, helped make possible a great victory over disease.

by any dream that the day's occurrences had unleashed forces destined to make him, in turn, first, the target for newspaper and stage humorists the world over; next, the object of scorn and vituperation in all the region south of the Potomac River and east of the Mississippi; and, finally, years later, one of the heroes of medical science in his generation.

II

The following evening, Stiles, after a routine day in his laboratory, went to the Cosmos Club for dinner. Afterward, while looking over the newspapers in the club library, his eye was caught by a headline in the *New York Sun:* "Germ of Laziness Found?" Chuckling, he was about to turn the page when his own name seemed to leap out of the type at him. Aghast, Stiles read a description of his own speech at the preceding day's meeting of the Sanitary Conference, written by the young man whose drowsiness had so troubled him. The despatch, in effect, declared that Dr. Stiles had found the germ responsible for that widespread human failing, chronic indolence.

Next day began the flood. On the authority of the *Sun's* despatch, accounts were telegraphed throughout America and to Europe. Some of the newspaper treatment was serious, taking the form, in part, of interviews with physicians. That, however, was minor compared to the explosion of facetiousness.

In glad celebration of science's acquittal of sloth, editorial writers, professional jokesmiths, and cartoonists pressed the starter of imagination; newspaper rhymesters took up the challenge to their ingenuity inherent in the technical name of the new disease:

One of the pictorial jokes inspired by Dr. Stiles's lecture on Uncinaria americana, *renamed by the* New York Sun *"Germ of Laziness."*

THE MICROBE OF SLOTH

I for long had believed that, concerning my case,
   There existed much popular haziness;
I for years had felt sure it was grossly unfair
   To regard as a failing my laziness;
Now, the truth has come out, thanks to good Doctor Stiles,
   And 'tis proved how unjust a strong bias is,
For I, if you please, for my idleness scorned,
   Have been suffering from uncinariasis!

Of course, I've been lazy—who wouldn't be so
   Who has known what the "hookworm's" fell trail meant?
Who wouldn't, I ask, who's endured all his life
   A confounded six-syllable ailment?

Such "hookworm verse" became a recognized category of contemporary doggerel.

Among the thousands of jokes, cartoons, comic strips, and the countless parasangs of hookworm hectameters and dactyls, it was an editorial in the *Salt Lake City Herald* that most accurately expressed the precise American shade of humor—mild jeering, softened by tolerance, touched indeed almost with envy:

> Are you troubled with "that tired feeling"? Have you a settled aversion for getting up in the morning to start a fire in the kitchen range? If you have, folks say you are lazy, don't they? Well, they are wrong. The trouble with you, although you may not have known it until now, is that you have uncinariasis.
>
> Uncinariasis? Yes; it's a disease. Dr. Charles Wardell Stiles is the discoverer. He has just returned from a sojourn among the laziest people in the world, the "crackers" of the South. Lazy? We beg their pardon. Those fellows are suffering so terribly from uncinariasis that they wait for the apples to fall off their trees, and then ask somebody to pass the fruit along. . . . Almost any fair day you can see on the corner of Main and Second South Streets whole droves of men who are in the very last stages of uncinariasis. Day after day the poor fellows stand around, stand around, looking at other people work. At intervals they go home and eat, provided the neighbors have sent in anything, but the rest of their time they put in just standing around.

All of which, while it added to the gaiety of nations and portrayed an agreeable aspect of the American spirit, had a manner of forgetting about Stiles, though Stiles's name ran, of course, through the newspaper comment. Jokes lampooned him, and some of the serious comment chided him for a "sensationalism" for which the newspapers themselves, not the modest scientist, were responsible.

III

Stiles, returning to the United States in 1891 after studying medical zoology in Europe, had received an appointment as a consulting zoologist in the Bureau of Animal Industry of the Department of Agriculture at Washington. His duties as custodian of the helminthological collections of the National Museum, coinciding with his intellectual curiosity about everything in the field of zoology, led him to make a careful examination of the parasite collections under his charge. The mass of what he found was, after his extensive European experience, familiar; he was surprised, however, at not finding any specimen of hookworm of the species that infects man. No American scientific collection contained any hookworm specimen of this type; no American scientific body presumed the existence of hookworm in this country. A study by Stiles of American medical literature for many years back revealed no definite assertion of the existence of hookworm disease in the United States. As late as the year 1901, hookworm disease, recognized as such or by that name, was unknown in the United States.

But if there was no hookworm disease, by that name, there were countless thousands of cases of a disease variously referred to as "chronic anaemia" and "continuous malaria," of a type associated with dirt eating, medically "malacia." In whole regions of the South it was endemic. Dirt eating, it was literally that, because it was so horrifying a contrast to normal human behavior, had a fascination for the kind of popular curiosity catered to by the "shocker" sections of Sunday newspapers. Frequent articles about

Dispensary group, Jacksonville, North Carolina. They came 20 and 30 miles by boat, train, and private conveyances. (From the report of the Rockefeller Sanitary Commission)

"dirt eaters," "clay eaters," "brick eaters," "resin chewers" dwelt upon the revolting symptoms and effects of the morbid diet habit, usually with the implication that a moral stigma went with it. Occasional newspaper articles told of cultivated persons, formerly fastidious, who after affliction with this disease pathetically adopted furtive devices to conceal their revolting habit. As a rule, however, the disease was thought of in connection with an unhappy class in the South called "poor white trash," "crackers." Much of the writing about "dirt eating," medical as well as popular, assumed that the unnatural diet was, in some cases, deliberately adopted as a means of bringing about a physical condition which would justify avoidance of labor.

To Stiles, the references to dirt eating in the South had the illuminating effect of a searchlight. Dirt eating, he recalled from his education abroad, was regarded in European medical circles as a concomitant of hookworm disease; in European medical experience, dirt eating and hookworm were inseparable. To Stiles, it was clear that American medical opinion about malacia had mistaken effect for cause; he was confident that the dirt eating found in the southern states was not a disease but a symptom. The disease, Stiles felt sure, was hookworm, the existence of which in the United States was not even suspected by American medical science.

Stiles, when he recited his theory in American medical circles, encountered sometimes polite skepticism, sometimes raucous disbelief. He was, in the eyes of physicians, merely a zoologist, a student of animals and small bugs, and therefore not as qualified to know about human disease as men who devote their lives to clinical medicine.

In October 1901, Stiles read in a medical journal that a Texas physician, Dr. Allen J. Smith of Galveston, had found eight cases of hookworm among some eighty-odd medical students of the University of Texas. This, to Stiles, was illumination; in effect, definite proof. The cases could not compose a local infection brought from abroad; since university students come from scattered localities, the infection must be endemic and more or less widespread throughout Texas. Stiles wrote the Galveston physician requesting specimens of the worms. When these arrived, Stiles put them under his microscope. They were hookworms—not identical, he discovered, with the old-world hookworm. He named the new species *Uncinaria americana, Necator americanus*—"American Murderer."

IV

Up to this time, Stiles's opportunities had been limited by his routine duties as a subordinate in the Bureau of Animal Industry; his study of hookworm had been carried on as an avocation outside the scope of his official tasks. Since he was without private wealth he could not give up his post to devote himself to the travel that was necessary for the investigation upon which his heart and mind were intent. What might have happened under these conditions to a man of Stiles's zeal and concentration, what explosion of his temperament, or stunting of his talent, is hard to guess. It is not, however, necessary to guess. Fate interposed a beneficent hand by transferring him to the U.S. Public Health and Marine Hospital Service, in which hookworm was as proper a subject for investigation as any other disease. The head of the Public Health Service, Surgeon General Walter Wyman, happened to be one of those men whose contributions to scientific discovery are sometimes only less great than those of the discoverers themselves. General Wyman's temperament inclined him to regard men of one idea not as cranks but as possible harborers of the divine spark of genius; he believed in his subordinate, and he gave Stiles permission to do what he had long wanted to do, make a trip through the southern states to determine by personal observation if his long-held theory was correct.

In September 1902, Stiles set out. Now began one of the strangest odysseys ever recorded in the annals of any people. Indeed, such odysseys as Stiles's are rarely recorded in history, for that art, so far as it deals with travel, confines itself usually to the marches of warriors, the treasure hunts of Argonauts, or the crusades of religion. Stiles had much of the temperament and some of the ways of a religious pilgrim. To the matter-of-fact persons with whom he came in contact in the southern states of America, however, in the early years of the twentieth century, he could have been explained only as a person demented. Here was a man carrying little baggage besides a microscope—to most of the communities he visited the microscope was novel; a man who, judged by accepted interpretations of human motives, was obviously seeking something valuable, perhaps signs of gold or jewels, but jewels with an extraordinary setting, for his quest, his inquiry at each place to which he came, was for human ordure. Little wonder that at the Cumnock mines in Chatham County, Virginia, Stiles was subjected by the miners to the process described as being "run out of town"—leaving behind him, one feels sure, among those simple folk, extraordinary surmises that one would enjoy hearing told in the hillside cabins, tales that must have composed an extraordinary legend.

At Richmond, Stiles's examination of some of the 1,200 convicts in the state penitentiary revealed no hookworms or hookworm eggs. In the brickyards at Camden, South Carolina, Stiles found hookworm eggs in night soil, but no person he could be sure had the disease. In 500 miles of travel, chiefly in cities and in the clay lands, south from Washington, Stiles, though he examined many people from among those classes who, according to his theory, should be infected, had found no convincing evidence to support his hypothesis.

In a mood of brooding doubt, Stiles's mind, winding backward over his past researches and reading, recalled that in several of the cases of hookworms in animals which he had studied, there had been repeated allusions to a soil condition which had not, until now, seemed significant. Alaskan seal pups infected with hookworms had been found on sand rookeries, sheep and goats infected with the parasites had been found in sandy pastures, an outbreak of the disease among dogs had occurred in a sandy yard.

Stiles, his mind now on soil as a possible factor, "learned that the land near the Haile gold mines in South Carolina was chiefly a granite sand."

He went there, and for the first time found evidence of widespread infection; entire families of plantation workers tested positive for the parasite.

Continuing his journey, Stiles found cases of hookworm disease in Charleston, in the neighborhood of Macon, Fort Valley, and Albany, Georgia; Jacksonville, Ocala, and other places in Florida. In one rude cabin he found an emaciated farmer and his wife and five stunted children. Uncared-for graves in the yard marked the resting places of ten other children whose hookworm-debilitated bodies had been unable to survive the handicap of disease and poverty they had borne from birth.

V

Jubilant, Stiles returned to Washington. He had established the identity of one of the most common diseases in the South, a disease hitherto undiagnosed, hitherto regarded as incurable and unpreventable, hitherto accepted as an inevitable and unarrestable deterioration of hundreds of thousands of persons. Stiles had proved it to be hookworm, and hookworm was curable by a brief and simple treatment costing less than fifty cents. Stiles was justified in feeling that measured in terms of curing those already afflicted and preventing future infection, his achievement would rank as one of the great medical triumphs of all time.

Back in Washington, he rushed forward a preliminary report of his journey for publication as a bulletin of the Public Health Service. What he needed now was public attention for the disease. He could envisage the fruits of his report—the country would be stirred, an aroused country would galvanize Congress, Congress would provide the sinews for the kind of war Stiles contemplated—not cannon nor battleships nor regiments of troops, but tons of thymol and epsom salts, and flying squads of sanitarians.

Stiles's report, printed as an official document of the U.S. government, created scarcely a ripple; there was hardly a sign even that anyone had read it, let alone comprehended its significance. Sadly, Stiles concluded that his report, which he felt was the most important thing printed in the United States in 1902, which he had counted upon to awaken the country to the condition of wholesale sickness in the South, was not going to help him. If there was any concrete result, it was an invitation to address the Pan-American Sanitary Conference on December 4.

At the conference the sleepy newspaperman, whose precarious foothold on a gypsy occupation depended upon a facility with words, wrote a report of Stiles's discovery, upon which a headline writer struck off, as a spark of his day's work, the phrase "germ of laziness." Overnight came not exactly the publicity Stiles had hoped for but publicity all the same. He was a robust fellow, and he took the goods that the gods provided. If the public attention he sought, for the opportunity to exterminate hookworm, had to come with the accompaniment of ridicule for himself, that partial misadventure was better than complete public indifference.

*　　*　　*

The jeering with which Stiles's discovery was now surrounded made it impossible to hope for organized action to relieve the South; nobody would take the idea seriously. Stiles began single-handedly. In him were combined two types of public benefactor. Many a scientist would have regarded his discovery as a sufficient climax, would have left the public to make such use of it as public intelligence might devise, and for himself would have turned to further research in his laboratory for some new scientific triumph. In Stiles, however, was a trait having no relation to the scientific part of him, a characteristic American quality, a missionary streak, the better part of Puritanism, a zeal to carry healing to the afflicted, combined with an urge to exhort, to preach, to recruit converts and apostles to a good cause. In a series of journeys out of Washington over a period of eight years, journeys made possible by the sympathetic support of his chief in the Public Health Service, Surgeon General Wyman, the idea-driven scientist made himself a lone exhorter, bringing together audiences in schools, clubs, and colleges, to whom he lectured.

In other trips out of Washington, southward, Stiles carried his own kit of salts and thymol. Rural folk in remote districts found occasion to wonder at the purpose of a traveler who showed an extraordinary interest in their insides. Suspicious of "furriners," especially of "city" people, they eyed him coldly. Occasionally, on approaching the cabin of a "hillbilly," he found himself waved on his way with a shotgun.

VI

In 1908, Stiles's familiarity with conditions in the rural South caused him to be assigned as an attaché to a Commission on Country Life, appointed by President Roosevelt to make a nationwide survey of rural living conditions. Members of the commission included Walter Hines Page, editor of *World's Work Magazine*, and Henry Wallace, editor of an Iowa periodical, *Wallace's Farmer*. One morning, when the commission's train was traveling through the South, Stiles, Page, and Wallace happened to be together in the smoking car when a stop was made at a small country station. On the platform they noticed a miserable figure, a type hardly to be recognized as human, misshapen, his dwarfish body small in proportion to his apparently elongated limbs and fingers and unnaturally swollen joints; shoulders hunched and pointed, neck attenuated like that of a very old man, his dropsically pro-

Walter H. Page—One of the most useful Americans of his generation.

tuberant stomach forming a hideous contrast with his pathetically emaciated, unnourished frame; skin the greenish-yellow tint of tallow, shriveled
and parchmentlike, eyes like a fragment of faded rag, nose almost transpar-
ent, mouth sagging; his attitude, if he could be said to have an attitude, that
of a three-fourths empty sack supported by contact with the station wall.
To Page, as a southerner-born, the sight was all too familiar, all too common, and all too tragic; but to Wallace, coming from Iowa, it was arresting.
There ensued a conversation, which Stiles recalled years later to have run
as follows:

> WALLACE: What on earth is that?
> PAGE (*sadly*): That is a so-called poor white.
> WALLACE: If he represents southern farm labor the South is in poor
> luck.
> STILES: That man is a "dirt eater." His condition is due to hook-
> worm infection; he can be cured at a cost of about fifty cents for
> drugs, and in a few weeks' time he can be turned into a useful
> man.
> PAGE (*astonished*): Is that really a hookworm case? Can he really be
> cured? You can make a healthy man out of that wreck? Good
> God! Stiles, are you in earnest?

Now occurred the very essence of history: the juxtaposition in a smoking car of two travelers, of whom one, Stiles, had a scientist's information
about hookworm, while the other, Page, had a passion about bettering the
South; the detonation of the mind of the first by the spectacle of a chance
figure dawdling on a station platform, coupled with the eagerness of the
mind of the second, set great events upon their way.

The hookworm, Stiles told Page, is about as thick as a pin and about half
as long. By means of hard structures in its mouth—curiously and, when
seen under the microscope, hideously adapted to the purpose—it fastens itself, in clusters of several hundred, on the mucous wall of the small intestine of its victim. There it spends its adult life, sucking the blood of its
human host and ungratefully discharging into his system enervating poi-
sons. Its eggs, passing out with the bodily wastes, hatch in any warm, damp
soil. The new generation, so tiny as scarcely to be perceptible to the naked
eye, lie in wait, sometimes as long as six months; to the sole of the next
barefooted passerby they attach themselves and bore through (causing an
irritation known as "ground-itch," "dew-itch," "toe-itch," and by a multi-
tude of other names in different communities). Entering the bloodstream,
the worms pass through the heart and lungs and eventually settle in the
small intestine, where a new cycle begins.

The victim of hookworm, Stiles told Page—and Page recognized each
symptom and effect as ones he had observed a thousand times—becomes
inert, mentally incapable of ambition, physically incapable of application.
He does not always die from hookworm disease directly, but he becomes
useless to himself or to society, and he is an easy and early victim to tuber-

culosis, pneumonia, typhoid, or any other disease. If the hookworm victim is young, and the infection severe or long-standing, physical and mental growth is inhibited; boys and girls twelve years old, look six; adults have the mental and physical development of a child of twelve, the appearance of either a young child or a very old person, often that of an elderly dwarf.

Diagnosis, Stiles told Page, though easy when the process is understood, had in the past always been mistaken; usually the hypothesis had been chronic anemia or continuous malaria, always something chronic, about which nothing could be done. But diagnosis of hookworm, once the "knowhow" was grasped, was one of the simplest possible operations of the laboratory; only a microscope was necessary, and identification of the disease consisted merely of finding eggs in the victim's excrement.

Cure, Stiles told Page, was equally simple, utterly inexpensive, and infallibly certain: a few repeated doses of thymol, which would cause the worms to relax their grasp on the intestines of their unwilling host, followed by doses of epsom salts to eject them. If the work of cure and prevention were organized, if it were carried far enough and long enough, the hookworm could be completely exterminated—a new generation growing up would be free of the menace of it.

To all Stiles said, Page listened with the fascination of one in whom a speaker's words inspire visions—how much of the South's past did Stiles's theory explain! How much for the South's future did it promise! Page's ardent spirit took fire. His interest in all sorts of good causes had given him the acquaintance and confidence of everybody in the North interested in philanthropy or given to benevolence. Once Page was convinced of the soundness of Stiles's theory and the dependability of Stiles as a man, messages flew North that set wires of altruism in motion.

VII

Stiles and the rest of the Commission on Country Life, returning from their tour, stopped at Cornell University. At a reception in their honor Stiles heard a voice booming behind him, "Where is Stiles?" He turned and was introduced to a plump, jolly-looking man, Wallace Buttrick, at that time secretary of the General Education Board, an organization through which John D. Rockefeller carried on some of his philanthropic activities. Buttrick told Stiles: "Walter Page says you know something which I must know immediately; let us go to my room." Stiles and Buttrick talked hookworm almost all night.

Back in Washington, Stiles was settling into the routine of his office when a telegram came to him from Dr. Simon Flexner, director of the laboratories of the Rockefeller Hospital for Medical Research. The telegram invited Stiles to New York for a conference. Stiles went, armed with specimen case, microscope, drawings, photographs, and statistics. At Rockefeller's office Flexner introduced Stiles to Frederick T. Gates, Rockefeller's

John D. Rockefeller.

chief adviser in his philanthropies. Stiles told his story, Flexner and Gates listening quietly. After about forty minutes Gates interrupted, rang for a messenger, and sent for Starr J. Murphy, whose place in the Rockefeller hierarchy of benevolence was described as "personal counsel and benevolent representative." When Murphy appeared, Gates said: "This is the biggest proposition ever put up to the Rockefeller office. Listen to what Dr. Stiles has to say. Now, Doctor, start from the beginning again and tell Mr. Murphy what you have told me."

After several more conferences, Gates called Stiles to his home one night and told him: "The Rockefeller office will support this work."

VIII

The announcement, early in November 1908, that Rockefeller would give $1 million to combat hookworm, started the newspaper humorists on a second installment of the gibing with which they had greeted Stiles's "germ-of-laziness" address six years before—with the South substituted for Stiles as the chief victim of the jeering. The spectacle of hardheaded old John D. Rockefeller cooperating with a scientist-discoverer to make war on laziness was pictured as very, very funny.

To much of the South, Stiles, with his Rockefeller backing, "appeared in the light, not of a deliverer but of another dam Yankee bent upon holding the South up to ridicule. And they abused him with the proud fluency of which only a self-righteous Southern rhetorician seems to be master," wrote the *Baltimore Sun* in 1927.

Of all the abuse heaped by the South upon Stiles, as well as Rockefeller, the most violent came from Florida. There was a special reason.

One of the thousands of southern children examined by the Rockefeller Sanitary Commission. (Photograph by courtesy of Dr. C. W. Stiles)

Stiles, in accounts of the symptoms of hookworm, had enumerated what had been called by other observers before him "Florida complexion." To a community just beginning to think of itself as a winter health resort that was infuriating. The editor of a Tampa newspaper attacked Stiles in an editorial and threatened him with lynching if he ever set foot in that state. Somebody sent a copy of the paper to Stiles, who read it, packed a valise, and left at once for Tampa, went to a hotel and registered under his own name. For a week he loitered about the streets, and visited nearby rural schools, accosting people who to his practiced eye appeared to be suffering from hookworm disease, and getting them to allow him to make microscopic examinations. When he had incontrovertible evidence of the existence of the disease in and around Tampa, he sent word to the editor who had attacked him, relating what he had been doing and what the results of his investigation had been, and added: "The lynching may begin when you are ready."

The editor called on Stiles, dined with him, spent half the night talking hookworms, and became a convert. The next day his paper published a generous retraction.

IX

The first formal work done through Rockefeller's beneficence was a careful survey under Stiles's technical direction, during the early part of 1909, to determine the geographical extent of the hookworm infestation and the approximate number of sufferers. Before this was completed Rockefeller called a joint meeting of scientists and southern leaders of thought, to whom he turned over $1 million to be used in a five-year war on the hookworm.

The Rockefeller Sanitary Commission for the Eradication of Hookworm Disease began, largely, with activities designed to have the effect of ingratiation and education—lectures, demonstrations, talks with individuals and with local groups, items prepared for southern newspapers, tactful enlistment of cooperation by local physicians, careful selection of local state directors to carry the work to every infected county. During the first year about 102,000 persons were examined in nine southern states, of whom 42,945 were found to have hookworms. More convincing than the statistics were example after example of whole local communities cleaned up. A community known to their neighbors as "Forkemites" (because of their location in the fork of a creek) had seemed for generations to live under a curse; they were poverty-stricken, they were sickly—and they were called lazy; few of them could read and most of them were believed to be of a low order of mentality. During the first April of the Rockefeller commission's work (1910), a local physician, aided by the commission, began treating them for hookworm. In one school he found thirty-eight of the forty pupils infected, while forty-five of their brothers and sisters were too sick of the disease to go to school. A year later the teacher of the school said to a visitor: "Children who before the treatment were listless and dull are now active and alert; children who could not study a year ago are not only studying now but are finding a joy in learning. They have a new outlook on life. There is a new spirit in the school. Most of the forty-five who were sick at home are now well and coming to school."

In a southern orphan asylum, many of the children, when watched too closely to get dirt to eat otherwise, would gouge out the mortar between the bricks of their dormitory and swallow it. After treatment, the children blossomed luxuriantly. From horrible, heart-rending caricatures of children, they were changed—it seemed almost overnight—into chubby, rosy, exuberantly healthy boys.

Such striking examples, occurring in community after community, carried conviction to whole neighborhoods. The commission's work became easy. By 1914, half a million schoolchildren and 392,765 grown persons had been examined, 382,046 of whom had been found infected and had been treated.

Nevertheless, when the Great War combed the South for young men, from 12 to 33 percent of the draftees were found to have the disease; it was estimated that there were still approximately 2 million hookworm patients and carriers in the South. By 1927, however, after about 7 million persons had been treated, the annual report of the International Health Board (into which the commission had been merged) was able to declare: "At the present time it is fair to say that hookworm disease has almost disappeared from the United States and is rapidly coming under control in many parts of the world."

X

During the thirty-nine years, from 1891 when Charles Wardell Stiles returned to the United States with the best scientific education obtainable in Europe, to the year in which this history was written, 1930, eight presidents rode in swaying barouche or shining motor from Capitol steps to White House door; seventeen Congresses ground out thousands of statutes and millions of words of what is called history; two victorious armies returning from foreign wars paraded up Pennsylvania Avenue; some scores of generals and admirals and captains were borne on flag-draped caissons across the Potomac River to graves in the Arlington Memorial Cemetery. Upon it all, Stiles looked out from the dusty windows of a division of a bureau of a government department—if indeed he ever took time to look at all, if ever there was an occasion when even for a quarter-hour the spectacle of pomp or pageant was as alluring to him as the quaint creatures that wiggled beneath his microscope. After 1914, when he could see the work of hookworm extermination so organized as to be certain to succeed, he retired to his laboratory, allowing his great discovery to slip to the rank of a mere episode in his concentrated life. As he withdrew more and more continuously into his laboratory, devoted himself more and more to the work of his mature years, one thought of him as a man who had taken youth's fling in the form of an immense adventure in altruism. He had been but twenty-three when he first began his investigations of hookworm, thirty-four when he identified *Necator americanus*, and barely over forty when his rich and persistent vitality set the work of extermination upon its way. By the time he was fifty, he had receded from public consciousness in both North and South; the immense outburst of publicity and ridicule about the "germ of laziness" had become, to a new generation, merely an unimportant detail of the long-gone past—to them, one with Nineveh and Tyre—prewar America.

PART V

Over Here

ARMAGEDDON
1914–18

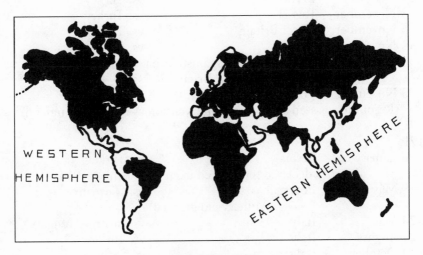

WESTERN HEMISPHERE

EASTERN HEMISPHERE

THE WORLD WAR.

The parts of the Earth's land surface shown in black are those of countries which in one degree or another were involved, most of them taking a part in the fighting. The small number of countries which stood off from hostilities are shown in white. Of these, a few, such as China, declared war but did not contribute fighting troops; others severed diplomatic relations.

DECLARATIONS OF WAR

CHRONOLOGICAL LIST

1914

28 July	Austria-Hungary	vs. Serbia
1 August	Germany	vs. Russia
3 August	France	vs. Germany
3 August	Germany	vs. France
4 August	Germany	vs. Belgium
4 August	Great Britain	vs. Germany
6 August	Austria-Hungary	vs. Russia
6 August	Serbia	vs. Germany
7 August	Montenegro	vs. Austria-Hungary
8 August	Austria-Hungary	vs. Montenegro
9 August	Montenegro	vs. Germany
12 August (midnight)	France	vs. Austria-Hungary

1914, cont.

| 12 August (midnight) | Great Britain | vs. Austria-Hungary |
| 22 August | Austria-Hungary | vs. Belgium |

(Received by Belgium 28 August)

23 August	Japan	vs. Germany
29 October	France	vs. Turkey
3 November	Russia	vs. Turkey
5 November	Great Britain	vs. Turkey
11 November	Turkey	vs. Allies

(Spoke of it as a holy war against Serbia and her allies—
France, Great Britain, Russia)

| 23 November | Portugal | vs. Germany |

(Resolution passed authorizing intervention as an ally of England)

1915

| 8 January | Serbia | vs. Turkey |

(Treaties declared terminated from 1 December 1914)

| 19 May | Portugal | vs. Germany |

(Military aid granted)

24 May	Italy	vs. Austria-Hungary
21 August	Italy	vs. Turkey
14 October	Bulgaria	vs. Serbia
14 October	Serbia	vs. Bulgaria
15 October	Great Britain	vs. Bulgaria
16 October	France	vs. Bulgaria
19 October	Russia	vs. Bulgaria
19 October	Italy	vs. Bulgaria

1916

| 9 March | Germany | vs. Portugal |
| 27 August | Romania | vs. Austria-Hungary |

(Allies of Austria also considered it a declaration of war)

28 August	Germany	vs. Romania
28 August	Italy	vs. Germany
29 August	Turkey	vs. Romania
1 September	Bulgaria	vs. Romania
24 November	Greece	vs. Germany

(Provisional Government)

1917

6 April	United States	vs. Germany
7 April	Cuba	vs. Germany
7 April	Panama	vs. Germany
2 July	Greece	vs. Bulgaria

(Government of Alexander)

2 July	Greece (Government of Alexander)	vs. Germany
22 July	Siam	vs. Austria-Hungary
22 July	Siam	vs. Germany
4 August	Liberia	vs. Germany
14 August	China	vs. Austria-Hungary
14 August	China	vs. Germany
26 October	Brazil	vs. Germany
7 December	United States	vs. Austria-Hungary
10 December	Panama	vs. Austria-Hungary
16 December	Cuba	vs. Austria-Hungary

1918
20 April	Guatemala	vs. Germany
7 May	Nicaragua	vs. Germany
8 May	Nicaragua	vs. Austria-Hungary
23 May	Costa Rica	vs. Germany
12 July	Haiti	vs. Germany
19 July	Honduras	vs. Germany

Prologue

"Now tell us what 'twas all about,"
 Young Peterkin he cries;
And little Wilhelmine looks up
 With wonder-waiting eyes.
"Now tell us all about the war,
 And what they fought each other for."

"But what good came of it at last?"
 Quoth little Peterkin.
"Why, that I cannot tell," said he;
"But 'twas a famous victory."

—"The Battle of Blenheim," Robert Southey

In the pleasant midsummer of 1914, a local banker in Monterey, California, Charles D. Henry, went with some friends on a fishing trip into the remote heights of the California Sierras. A few weeks later, on his way down the slopes in early August, he was hailed from across a ravine by an in-going party who called out, "Any news of the war?" Henry, puzzled, asked the stranger to repeat. Again came the question, "Have you any news of the war?" Henry, mystified, turned queryingly to his companions. They all concluded they were being subjected to a not particularly funny attempt at "kidding." Thereupon Henry, entering as fully into the spirit of the occasion as his appreciation of its wit would permit, groped among his materials for repartee, recalled a phrase of his boyhood in Civil War times, and shouted back, "All's quiet along the Potomac." With that he dismissed the incident. Not until he and his friends had reached a town several days later did he learn of the outbreak of the Great War.

The coming of the war to Charles Henry—he was an average American, not distinguished* from millions of others and he does not figure again in this history—was, in its unexpectedness and its casualness, typical of its coming to America as a whole.

*Except that some years later it happened that his son-in-law, Herbert Hoover, became the thirtieth president of the United States.

II

The war did not come to America as it came to Europe. No Oregon rancher working in his field of a peaceful afternoon was disturbed by an odd whirring in the sunny air, and looked toward Mount Hood to see an airplane spitting fire upon his neighboring village. In no New England town did children huddle in the windows and peer at exultant Uhlans prancing down the maple-shaded street. No Maryland farmer from his hilltop field saw a thing that sent him hurrying to the house to gather his children into his cart and take to the road in fear. No city of ours walked for days in anxiety, listening to the rise and fall of a fateful cannonade. War did not thunder at our doors as at the forts of Liège.

It was not in the shape of violence of any sort that the war, in its early phase before America became a belligerent, came to us. Its coming took a form hardly physical at all; it came as newspaper despatches from far away, far away in distance and even farther away in spirit. The despatches were as

AUSTRIA DECLARES WAR, RUSHES VAST ARMY INTO SERVIA; RUSSIA MASSES 80,000 MEN ON BORDER

GERMANY DECLARES WAR ON RUSSIA; FRANCE PREPARES TO JOIN HER ALLY; ITALY QUITS THE TRIPLE ALLIANCE

U. S. TRANSPORTS FOR RELIEF OF MAROONED AMERICAN TOURISTS

LATEST NEWS OF THE WAR

Berlin, Aug. 1.—The German Emperor declared war on Russia at 7:30 p. m., two hours after signing an order mobilizing the army. The last line of reserves has been called up, bringing the strength of the Kaiser's forces to close upon four million men.

KAISER MOBILIZES TO HIS LAST MAN; 4,000,000 IN ARMS

BRITISH ULTIMATUM TO GERMANY; JOHN BURNS QUITS THE CABINET; GERMANS ADVANCE THROUGH BELGIUM

RUSSIAN FLEET DRIVEN BACK; 1 SHIP ASHORE; THREE TOWNS SEIZED

LATEST NEWS OF THE WAR.

London, Aug. 3—John Burns, the ex-Labor leader, resigned from the British Cabinet, indicating that the war party is in the ascendant. Berlin, Aug. 3—The invasion of Russian Poland by German

INVASION OF THE LUXEMBURG BY KAISER'S TROOPS SWIFTLY COUNTERED BY SIR E. GREY

How America learned of the war through headlines.

if black flocks of birds, frightened from their familiar rookeries, came darting across the ocean, their excited cries a tiding of stirring events. The despatches, printed under heavy black headlines smudged across the first page of the country's newspapers, gave an impression as if Europe by some dark enchantment had become a witch's cauldron brewing mephitic shapes which, flying westward in an unending black slash across the clean skies of the Atlantic, came to roost in the newspapers of America.

Despatches came giving accounts of the leaving for the front, the march toward the battle line, early clashes, refugees. In the yellowed newspaper files of many years later these despatches and headlines appeared as vivid facets of the picture that the America of 1914 saw:

GERMANY GOES
SINGING TO WAR

In Trains Labelled "Special to Moscow," "Excursion to Paris"

Scheveningen, Holland, August 7.—The Germans are going to war in the liveliest good spirits, smiling, singing, and cheering. "Die Wacht am Rhein" and "Deutschland, Deutschland über Alles" echoed unceasingly from them.*

KITCHENER'S CALL
BRINGS LEGIONS

Rush of Volunteers to Army Surpasses Anything in England's Military History

SWAMP RECRUITING OFFICES

Men in Silk Hats Stand Shoulder to Shoulder with Laborers in Waiting Throngs**

FRENCH SINK CRUISER
PANTHER OFF
ALGERIAN COAST†

London, August 7.††—There is a queer and touching mixture of enthusiasm and pathos in the scenes at the departing Continental trains taking French and Belgian reservists. The termini are packed with cheering crowds, while wives and daughters of the men leaving break down utterly and have to be led away by their friends.

*New York Times, August 8.
**New York Times, August 8.
†New York World, August 5.
††New York World, August 7.

By mid-August and toward September first, longer despatches began to come, detailed descriptions, narratives of battle. The best American war correspondents, hurrying to Europe by what means they could find, had arrived at the front or near it. Their accounts, in weekly periodicals as well as daily newspapers, were eagerly received by the mounting American appetite for pictures of the incredible scene.

Of the American correspondents who covered the war, Richard Harding Davis of the *New York Tribune* had an extraordinary gift of vividness. His picture—it was almost literally pictorial—of the entry of the German army into Brussels was eagerly read by the America of that day, and deserves to be regarded as classic among accounts of the war:

> The entrance of the German army into Brussels has lost the human quality. It was lost as soon as the three soldiers who led the army bicycled into the Boulevard du Régent, and asked the way to the Gare du Nord. When they passed the human note passed with them.
>
> What came after them, and twenty-four hours later is still coming, is not men marching, but a force of nature like a tidal wave, an avalanche, or a river flooding its banks. At this minute it is rolling through Brussels as the swollen waters of the Conemaugh Valley swept through Johnstown.
>
> At the sight of the first few regiments of the enemy we were thrilled. After, for three hours, they had passed in one unbroken steel-gray column, we were bored. But when hour after hour passed and there was no halt, no breathing time, no open spaces in the ranks, the thing became uncanny, unhuman. You returned to watch it, fascinated. It held the mystery and menace of fog rolling toward you across the sea.
>
> The gray of the uniforms worn by both officers and men helped this air of mystery. Only the sharpest eye could detect among the thousands that passed, the slightest difference. All moved under a cloak of invisibility. Only after the most numerous and severe tests at all distances, with all materials and combinations of colors that give forth no color, could this gray have been discovered. That it was selected to clothe and disguise the German when he fights is typical of the German staff in striving for efficiency to leave nothing to chance, to neglect no detail.
>
> After you have seen this service uniform under conditions entirely opposite, you are convinced that for the German soldier it is his strongest weapon. Even the most expert marksman cannot hit a target he cannot see. It is a gray-green, not the blue-gray of our Confederates. It is the gray of the hour just before daybreak, the gray of unpolished steel, of mist among green trees.
>
> I saw it first in the Grande Place in front of the Hôtel de Ville. It was impossible to tell if in that noble square there was a regiment or a brigade. You saw only a fog that melted into the stones,

Richard Harding Davis (left), American war correspondent, whose account of the Germans entering Brussels was a classic.

blended with the ancient house fronts, that shifted and drifted, but left you nothing at which you could point.

Later, as the army passed below my window, under the trees of the Botanical Park, it merged and was lost against the green leaves. It is no exaggeration to say that at a hundred yards you can see the horses on which the Uhlans ride, but cannot see the men who ride them.

If I appear to overemphasize this disguising uniform it is because, of all the details of the German outfit, it appealed to me as one of the most remarkable. These men passing in the street, when they have reached the next crossing, become merged into the gray of the paving-stones and the earth swallows them.

Yesterday Major-General von Jarotsky, the German Military Governor of Brussels, assured Burgomaster Max that the German army would not occupy the city, but would pass through it. It is still passing. I have followed, in campaigns, six armies, but, excepting not even our own, the Japanese, or the British, I have not seen one so thoroughly equipped. I am not speaking of the fighting qualities of any army, only of the equipment and organization. The German army moved into this city as smoothly and as compactly as an Empire State Express. There were no halts, no open places, no stragglers.

This army has been on active service three weeks, and so far there is not apparently a chin-strap or a horseshoe missing. It came in with the smoke pouring from cook-stoves on wheels, and in an hour had set up post-office wagons, from which mounted messengers galloped along the line of column, distributing letters, and at which soldiers posted picture postcards.

The infantry came in in files of five, two hundred men to each company; the Lancers in columns of four, with not a pennant missing. The divisions of quick-firing guns and field pieces were one hour at a time in passing, each gun with its caisson and ammunition-wagon taking twenty seconds in which to pass.

The men of the infantry sang "Fatherland, My Fatherland." Between each line of song they took three steps. At times two thousand men were singing together in absolute rhythm and beat. When the melody gave way, the silence was broken only by the stamp of iron-shod boots, and then again the song rose. When the singing ceased the bands played marches. They were followed by the rumble of siege-guns, the creaking of wheels, and of chains clanking against the cobble-stones, and the sharp, bell-like voices of the bugles.

For seven hours the army passed in such a solid column that not once might a taxicab or trolley-car pass through the city. Like a river of steel it flowed, gray and ghostlike. Then, as dusk came and as thousands of horses' hoofs and thousands of iron boots continued to tramp forward, they struck tiny sparks from the stones, but the horses and the men who beat out the sparks were invisible.

At midnight pack-wagons and siege-guns were still passing. At 7 this morning I was awakened by the tramp of men and bands playing jauntily. Whether they marched all night or not I do not know; but now for twenty-six hours the gray army has rumbled by with the mystery of fog and the pertinacity of a steam-roller.

Davis also wrote, from the window of a car in which he was held prisoner by the Germans, a description of the destruction of Louvain.

For two hours on Thursday night I was in what for six hundred years had been the city of Louvain. The Germans were burning it, and to hide their work kept us locked in the railroad carriages. But the story was written against the sky, was told to us by German soldiers incoherent with excesses; and we could read it in the faces of women and children

Belgian civilians made prisoners by the Germans, entering Brussels under German guard. (© Underwood & Underwood)

The German entry into Brussels. For twenty-six hours the gray army rumbled by with the pertinacity of a steamroller. (Photograph by Underwood & Underwood)

being led to concentration camps and of the citizens on their way to be shot.

The Germans sentenced Louvain on Wednesday to become a wilderness, and with the German system and love of thoroughness they left Louvain an empty, blackened shell. The reason for this appeal to the torch and the execution of non-combatants, as given to me on Thursday morning by General von Lutwitz, military governor of Brussels, was this: On Wednesday, while the German military commander of the troops in Louvain was at the Hôtel de Ville talking to the burgomaster, a son of the burgomaster with an automatic pistol shot the chief of staff and German staff surgeons. Lutwitz claims this was the signal for the Civil Guard, in civilian clothes on roofs, to fire upon the German soldiers in the open square below. Fifty Germans were killed and wounded. For that, said Lutwitz, Louvain must be wiped out. . . .

Money can never restore Louvain. Great architects and artists, dead these six hundred years, made it beautiful, and their handiwork belonged to the world. With torch and dynamite the Germans have turned these masterpieces into ashes, and all the Kaiser's horses and all his men cannot bring them back again.

When by troop train we reached Louvain, the entire heart of the city was destroyed and fire had reached the Boulevard Tirlemont, which faces the railroad station. The night was windless, and the sparks rose in steady, leisurely pillars, falling back into the furnace from which they sprang. In their work the soldiers were moving from the heart of the city to the outskirts, street by street, from house to house. . . .

On the high ground rose the broken spires of the Church of St. Pierre and the Hôtel de Ville, and descending like steps were row beneath row of houses, roofless, with windows like blind eyes. The fire had reached the last row of houses, those on the Boulevard de Jodigne. Some of these were already cold, but others sent up steady, straight columns of flame. In others at the third and fourth stories the window curtains still hung, flowers still filled the window-boxes, while on the first floor the torch had just passed and the flames were leaping.*

III

Thus—first by brief despatches, flashes of startling news, later by vivid narratives and descriptions in periodicals and newspapers, accompanied by photographs of soldiers marching, cities ruined, men in trenches, tragedy at sea—did America learn of the war. It gave rise among us to many

*Not too much a stretch to point here to Davis's influence on the greatest correspondent of the next World War, the broadcast journalist Edward R. Murrow. In prose, styles, and perceptions, the two men are often strikingly similar. —D. R.

The early photographs of trench life, which were widely printed in American newspapers, interested everybody because of this novel aspect of this war. (© Underwood & Underwood)

mods, expressed in Isaiah-like sermons with Europe's "insanity" as text, pontifical editorials which combed the dictionary for synonyms of "senseless," "barbaric"; man-in-the-street debate, cigar-store oraculation. Present among the echoes, sure to appear in any American reaction to any event or condition, was a characteristic national humor, compounded of wit and pungent sageness, the newspaper quip. "This European war," said the *Buffalo Courier*, "suggests that maybe the white man's burden is the white man himself."

Quips that went deeper, reflected a fundamental American feeling, prov-

After the first call to the colors. French soldiers marching to the front along vineyards in which the civilian population continued busy. (© Underwood & Underwood)

An early photograph of a scene destined to be duplicated throughout much of France and Belgium. (Photograph from Underwood & Underwood)

ing that jest may contain many a true word, were in the vein of the *Chicago Herald*'s, "Peace-loving citizens of this country will now rise up and tender a hearty vote of thanks to Columbus for having discovered America." That was the humorous way of putting what was the universal serious feeling and expression of America's attitude toward the war—"Thank God we are not mixed up in it!" Perhaps the most accurate and comprehending reflection of the American attitude—the more characteristic because it was voiced by a Midwest, small-town newspaper, was that of the Wabash, Indiana, *Plain Dealer:* "We never appreciated so keenly as now the foresight exercised by our forefathers in emigrating from Europe."

CHAPTER I

War Knocks at Wilson's Door

To President Woodrow Wilson, the contentions and responsibilities, domestic and foreign, which came with the war, were a rude intrusion. Wilson's way of treating an unwelcome intruder, if an individual, was to assume a manner of gazing at the stars over the offender's head. But the war could not be snubbed.

To deal with the problems the war raised was, in the early phases, uncon-

Something New for the Barbarians to Look At

The early inclination of President Wilson was to snub the war, turn his back upon it. He had disdain for the war, regarded it as barbarous, a thing with which America should have nothing to do. As this cartoon suggests, Wilson's attitude was approved, during the early days, by much of America. (Darling in the Des Moines *(Iowa)* Register and Leader.)

genial to Wilson's temperament. It was a kind of duty distant from what he had in mind when he sought the presidency. He resented the war, tried to put it away from him, not in a spirit of timorousness but rather of irritation.

Yet it came to be that the war was Wilson's greatest responsibility; and, later, that Wilson was, in the whole world, the figure about whom the war raged and the peace swirled. For some five years, 1914–1919, the history of the United States, as respects the Great War, was mainly the history of Woodrow Wilson's mind. For the last two years, 1917–1919, the history of the whole world was the history of Wilson's mind. And the results of Wilson's acts lay upon the world for more than a decade after the end of the war. For years after his death the world was racked by ideas that Wilson had introduced; steps that he had taken or attempted continued to be the concern of statesmen, the preoccupation of nations and of peoples.

Wilson's mind, the evolution through which it passed, was the largest single factor in the war. And the first phase of Wilson's attitude toward the war was distaste for it, a wish to keep it at arm's length, as something shameful to the world, odious to him personally.

During the early part of Wilson's administration, before the war broke, Wilson was engaged with a legislative program of business and financial reform which he called "The New Freedom." (Ketten in the New York Evening World, *© Press Publishing Co.)*

II

Wilson had been elected with a mandate almost limited to, certainly with heavy emphasis on, internal reform—a series of policies, chiefly economic and all domestic, called by Wilson the "New Freedom," meaning freedom for the average man against big business and high finance.

In fulfillment of his domestic program, Wilson, taking high satisfaction in the process, sponsored and aided in getting through Congress a bill reorganizing the banking structure of the United States into the Federal Reserve System, designed to frustrate what he and the Democrats called the "Money Trust." He brought about creation by Congress of the Federal Trade Commission, to prevent unfair methods of competition in business and to aid in executing the antitrust laws. He initiated and pressed through Congress a farm loan act setting up government and quasi-government banks to loan money to farmers at rates lower than 6 percent (in practice 4 to 5½ percent) as against preexisting rates of private local bankers sometimes twice as high. He broadened the scope of the Sherman antitrust law of 1889 by the Clayton Act, which prohibited the selling of commodities at different prices to different purchasers when such discrimination tends to lessen competition, and in other ways curbed unethical business practices. He initiated, and successfully pushed through Congress, a downward revision of the tariff. He brought about the enactment, as an amendment to the Tariff Bill, of a measure imposing a graduated tax on incomes. He advocated and had enacted into law a measure limiting the workday of interstate railroad employees to eight hours. He encouraged the passage of the Seaman's Act, written by Senator Robert M. LaFollette, which in the judgment of its advocates "freed the men in the forecastle from the tyranny of the bridge." (But in the judgment of its critics, "prescribed such rules for wages, food, and accommodations of sailors as made it impossible for the United States to compete with foreign shipping.")

This program of domestic legislation was practically finished before the war began. Wilson, confident and serene, was able to say to Congress, in his message of December 8, 1914: "Our program of legislation with respect to business is now virtually complete. . . . The road at last lies clear and firm before business."

III

Into this preoccupation of Wilson with domestic affairs, agreeable to his temperament, congenial to his talent and experience; into this complacency with its completion and assurance about the future, intruded the war.

It found him by the bedside of his sick wife. She died August 6, 1914, without knowing war had broken out. Her death, and the coming of the war, combined to a peculiar degree to make a break in Wilson's life, tragic in the personal sense, having far-reaching consequences in the public

*President Wilson and his first wife, Ellen Axson Wilson. She died August 6, 1914, just af-
ter the war began, and her death had a material effect on the spirit in which Wilson met
the impact of the war in Europe.*

sense. One who knew Wilson well thought the death of his wife had an effect on the spirit with which he met his and the world's crises: "There was
never a time when Wilson so needed the steadying influence of Ellen Axson as the months that immediately followed her death. And the world
needed it even more. . . . Who can say how the death of this modest, self-
effacing, self-denying woman affected the future of the world?"

August 6, Wilson attended to his other routine function, issued the formal
proclamation of neutrality, the customary American formula, devised in the
administration of George Washington: Americans must not enlist in the
army of either belligerent nor aid in fitting out any armed vessel to be used
in the service of either belligerent. Belligerents in their turn must conform
to our status as a neutral, must not permit their vessels of war to engage in
hostile operations within the waters of the United States, nor make use of
our ports to facilitate attack upon their enemy.

These formalities attended to, Wilson, following his wish rather than
his reason, looked upon the war as a distant event, terrible and tragic, but
one which did not concern us closely in the political sense.

But the war pressed upon him nonetheless. He was beset with contra-
dictory advice. The man who perhaps was the wisest American of his time,
Dr. Charles W. Eliot, president emeritus of Harvard University, wrote
him:

Has not the United States an opportunity at this moment to propose a combination of the British Empire, the United States, France, Japan, Italy, and Russia in offensive and defensive alliance to rebuke and punish Austria-Hungary and Germany for the outrages they are now committing by enforcing against those two countries non-intercourse with the rest of the world by land and sea? . . . The proposal would involve the taking part by our navy in the blockading process.

On the other side, the principal man in public life other than the president himself, ex-President Theodore Roosevelt, wrote: "We should remain entirely neutral and nothing but urgent need would warrant breaking our neutrality and taking sides one way or the other."

To both kinds of advice and all kinds, and to everybody, Wilson replied August 19, with a proclamation: "My Fellow Countrymen: I take the liberty of addressing a few words to you . . . to urge very earnestly upon you [that] we must be impartial in thought as well as in action. The United States must be neutral in fact as well as in name."

Finally, he decreed a Peace Sunday, and his proclamation was very generally carried out. "Whole nation prays for peace," and the *New York Times* headline of October 5. "The response to the President's call for a day of prayer could not have been more general or more fervent. . . . Enormous numbers of persons went to the doors of the churches at an early hour: thousands tried in vain to obtain admission." Secretary of State Bryan went to New York to speak in the morning at Carnegie Hall, in the evening at Broadway Tabernacle. In Chicago, Governor Dunne of Illinois observed, with a slight touch of self-righteousness, that "if this Republic can live in peace, others ought to be able to do the same." About the reaction on the battlefields to Wilson's "Peace Sunday," there is no record, except that the lists of dead and wounded did not diminish.

To Congress, when it came into its first session following the beginning of the war, Wilson spoke with a manner of petulance against those who felt we should take notice of the war by preparing for the eventuality that we might be drawn into it: "This is the time above all others when we should wish and resolve to keep our strength by self-possession. . . . [To engage in preparedness], permit me to say, would mean merely that we had lost our self-possession, that we had been thrown off our balance by a war with which we have nothing to do, whose causes cannot touch us."

Wilson felt strong, superior, felt that the right is so mighty it can look after itself without exercise of physical might. Wilson at this time, in this attitude about the war, was even more the intellectual aristocrat than usual.

It was an attitude of proud detachment—the war was a barbarous thing, indecent, with which America and Wilson should have nothing to do. The attitude of America was parallel with that of Wilson. The country, without quite sharing Wilson's high disdain, felt that the war was, in the colloquial phrase, "none of our business."

CHAPTER 2

America Looks On at the War

A merica was self-contained and self-contented. Our sense of remoteness from Europe, habitual at all times, our preoccupation with our own conditions and concerns, had been accentuated during several years by an enthralling adventure we were making toward social altruism, expressing itself in movements toward forbidding labor by children, limiting employment of women in factories, prohibiting absolutely the manufacture and sale of alcoholic drinks, giving women the suffrage, enlarging the direct participation of all citizens in the mechanisms of government through direct primaries, direct election of U.S. senators, initiative and referendum, recall of judicial decisions.

All that, and more like it, and controversies arising out of it, engaged American interest to a degree and in a manner which we thought of as having a martial quality of its own. The fight between Republican and Progressive, now three years old, was what America in August 1914 understood to be Armageddon.

II

We had heard, with only listless attention to its ominousness, the shot at Sarajevo; we had read the despatches, sketchily brief in most American newspapers, especially in the interior, about exchanges of angry notes, ultimatums, threatened mobilizations of troops; and we had been aware, rather dimly, that several European nations—we were not quite clear just which ones—were "giving each other the dog-eye." Even when the first of the declarations of war came, July 28, we thought of conflict between Austria and Serbia as little more than "another mess in the Balkans," of a sort that had been intermittently chronic as long as any of us could remember. When Germany declared war on Russia, August 1, and the New York Stock Exchange appraised its significance by closing for the first time since 1873 (for a period that lasted more than four months—it was reopened on December 12), a few of the more sophisticated among us were impressed, but even yet many Americans paid only casual attention to it, as something far away, and not necessarily conclusive—at all times we thought of most of the European nations, especially those east of the Rhine, as constantly shaking mailed fists at each other. American newspa-

Belgians, retreating in front of the German invaders, left their addresses penciled on bulletin boards for the information of their families. (Photograph by Underwood & Underwood)

pers had a phrase, "saber-rattling," with which they were accustomed to explain that sort of thing, and dismiss it.

It was not until newspaper headlines the morning of August 4 described German troops actually marching into Belgium on their way to France that we realized something formidable and portentous was really under way.

III

The average American saw Germany's invasion of Belgium in the simplest possible terms, as a big dog pouncing on a little one. In such a contest it was an American trait to take, rather aggressively, the side of the smaller and under dog—that was a quality of our temperament and a tenet of our national traditions. Recalling our own earliest experience as a nation, a small people fighting for independence against a powerful one, we had usually sympathized with the little contendent against the invader or oppressor: with Ireland against England, with the Boers against the British, with Cuba against Spain, with all the Latin American peoples against Spain and Portugal, with Greece against the Turk. When we read that Germany's invasion of Belgium was something even more flagrant than wanton attack upon a small nation, that Germany was a guarantor of Belgian neutrality, had been bound by specific treaty (with France and Britain) to respect Belgium as neutral, that deepening of the offense, and the indignation that arose against the German chancellor's scornful reference to the treaty as a "scrap of paper," added little to the American feeling which had already flamed up against Germany. America's attitude had been fixed the hour that

Germany's army projected the first stiff goose step of its vanguard's toe across the boundary line of Belgium. With average Americans all the legalisms about right and wrong, all the arguments about original responsibility, weighed little. The average American did not look farther into the evidence than the simple newspaper picture of the opening blow, a powerful, militarist nation sending a great army into a country we knew was small and believed to be peaceful. That, and Belgium's gallant defense, followed by her succumbing to overwhelming force, fixed American opinion or emotion, crystallized it for the duration of the war, adverse to Germany.

IV

It need not have been so. Had Germany realized, as in her confidence she did not, that the war would be so prolonged as to make American opinion as important as armies and navies, had Prussian insight into American psychology been as accurate as Prussian military science was expert in estimating the quickest path to Paris—in that event Germany might profitably have given up the military advantage of a shortcut through Belgium, for the moral advantage of avoiding alienation of American opinion.

The natural disposition of America was to think well of Germany. Had anyone on August 3, 1914, or a week or a month or a year before, said to a group in a cigar store that in any European war, with Germany on one side and France and Russia on the other (as the lineup stood August 3), America would participate, he would have been jeered at. Had the prophet convinced his audience of what then seemed fantastically improbable, and had he asked for a cigar-store plebiscite about which side America would take, the response in most cases would have said that in such a lineup America would stand with Germany, against France and Russia.

Every American had neighbors of German birth or ancestry. Germans had been with us in large numbers since the immigration of 1849, and we liked them. Each of us knew a Gus or a Hans, a Heinie or a Rudolf, and had affection and respect for him. Every American, farmer in Iowa or clerk in New York, knew the Germans in America as good citizens and friendly neighbors.

With the French, on the other hand, most Americans had little acquaintance. Vaguely we knew from our school days that Lafayette had fought for us in our war for independence, but that had been a long time ago, and considerations having to do with our early history had begun to become less potent as determining influences on American thought. There were few French among us; and so far as the untraveled and little-read American knew the French by reputation, he thought of them vaguely as having ways he did not approve—in the lower strata of American folklore, for some reason not easily traceable to its origin, the adjective "French" carried implications of gilded sin rather than of any particular culture or philosophy. To the average American, a French picture meant one you were more likely to see in a barroom than in a home. "Slightly Frenchy" meant slightly risqué,

Many Americans arrived at their view of the French as somewhat "risqué" from maga-zines such as this.

or as the common man would have expressed it, "slightly off-color." Certainly "French" did not connote anything you would fight for. As for Russia, we thought of that as pretty far away and a little barbaric.

The Germans on the other hand we thought of as kin to us. Words and phrases of theirs, such as "Gesundheit!," had passed almost into our own speech, certainly into our consciousness far enough to carry implications of likable German traits. Some of the music that was at once the best and most familiar in America was German, such as "Stille Nacht, Heilige Nacht." Much of our tradition about Christmas had come to us from Germany. German standards of education were models for many American teachers and colleges. The cleanliness and order and discipline which the Germans called "Ordnung" they had brought with them to America, not to so rigid a degree as to repel us but, rather, sufficient to cause us to think of their ways as somewhat preferable to our own comparative easygoingness. So far as their Kaiser and their military system carried discipline to an extreme that was repugnant to our conception of government, and to our ideal of individualism, we thought of those German institutions as absurd, to be laughed at—not by the most fantastic stretch of imagination did we think of German autocracy or German militarism as things we should ever go to war to destroy.

Immediately after the opening of the war, German reservists in New York (as well as French reservists) made their way to the war. This photograph pictures a parade of German reservists. Under the law it was necessary to carry the American flag when the flag of another nation was displayed. (Globe Photograph)

V

Though Germany's invasion of Belgium made us partisan (and anti-German), we were still very distant from thinking of the struggle as a thing we should have any part in. As Germany pressed on into France, and into Russia on the east, we took the role of fans in the bleachers, regarding the Allies like the home team, to be sure, and cheering them on, but with no more thought of becoming participants than of descending on the diamond to take part in the game. In this spirit during the early weeks, the war was discussed in corner-grocery forums, on the street and in the home, displacing argument about the relative merits and capacities of Red Sox versus Chicago Cubs, Jack Johnson versus Jess Willard, Democratic versus Republican, Roosevelt versus Wilson.

Presently, as a kind of newspaper record of the progress of the game, came daily maps with a heavy black line to show the long battlefront from Switzerland to the sea, first-page equivalent of the baseball score on the tenth page. The crude small newspaper maps were supplemented soon by large colored ones hung from the walls of business offices, accompanied by a little tray of pins with which could be marked the wavering of the line from day to day, pins with blue heads for the Allies, red ones for the Germans. Many an American carried for years, as a vivid recollection of the Great War, the emotion, in most cases sad, with which he set blue pins back, red ones forward, until September 3, when soberly he set the blue pins of the Allies almost on the borders of Paris, and read that the French government had removed the capital to Bordeaux. Thereafter, beginning September 6–10, he enjoyed for several days in succession the exultation of setting red pins farther and farther back toward Germany. Toward Germany, but not into Germany. Not until after the armistice did the Allies on the west set foot on German soil.

VI

Adequate expression of our interest in the struggle was handicapped by difficulty of pronouncing places of battles and names of generals—it dawned upon many Americans that another reason for self-congratulation lay in the democratic simplicity which had led us to fight our American battles at places and under generals having names easily pronounceable by any lips. Bunker Hill and Gettysburg, George Washington and Robert E.

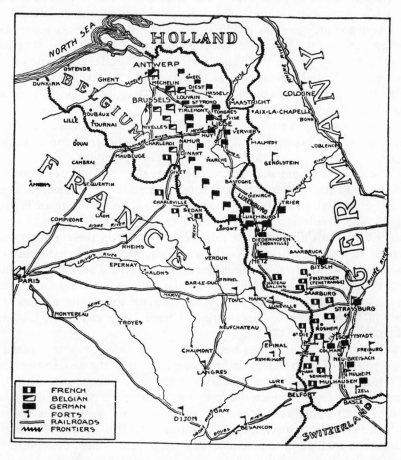

The battle line as it stood on August 19, 1914. Maps like this were in every American newspaper and enlarged ones were on the walls of many offices. This map appeared in the New York Times.

Provincial American difficulty in understanding war terms was cartooned in the Jacksonville *(Florida)* Metropolis.

Lee, did not require Americans to twist their tongues into unaccustomed contortions.

German names gave us little trouble. Von Kluck and von Hindenberg, von Moltke and von Falkenhayn, von Bulow and von Mackensen, were easy to the American tongue. But a cigar-store partisan, charged with emotion about the greater right on the side of the French, or their superiority in strategy, found the flow of his eloquence cramped when obliged to stumble at "Joffre" or "Foch," "Amiens," or "Rheims"—after the name of that town and cathedral newspapers tactfully added, "pronounced 'Hrans,' " which really did not help much. There was no way by which the ordinary American equipment of lips, tongue, and larynx could achieve some of the French consonants; in attempting them it became common, as a humorous confession of our inadequacy, to pinch the nose between thumb and forefinger.

Presently, in the informal forums of barber shop and grocery store, unwillingness to see freedom of discussion hampered by an immaterial detail of phonetics, arrived tolerantly at standardized approximations of French, Belgian, and Polish names, which, however they might have surprised the respective nationalities, became valid verbal tender in the cigar-store exchanges. Among the atrocities of the war not undeserving of mention were the varied violences of mutilation practiced upon the word "Ypres," which some impish god decreed should be the place where the battle line crystallized roughly for most of the war, hence the one town most necessary to mention. Only slightly less incommoding were Mons and Aisne, Oise and Ourcq.

As for the scenes of battles between Germans and Russians, a material factor contributing to the lesser American interest in the eastern front was the difficulty of expressing convictions or emotion in sentences compelled to include "Przemsl," which became, during the early part of the war, almost as much a landmark on the east as Ypres on the west. It was not reasonable to expect Americans, even those with the most wide-ranging interests, to include in their concerns a battlefront which, as reported in the *New York Times* on September 1, 1914, "extends through Przmyslany to Brzozdovitza."

VII

Many new words, essential vocabulary of the struggle, we could not ignore. They came across the ocean to us in every despatch. To read about the war we had to learn them; to talk about it we had, difficult job for most of us, to pronounce them: "bosche" for German soldiers, later varied by "Fritzy"; "junker" for German caste arrogance; "All-highest," a jeering designation of the Kaiser; "Hun," generic word for all Germans, conveying an implication of barbarism; "poilu" for French soldiers, "Tommies" for British—the last derived from Kipling's "Here's to you, Tommy Atkins." "Allies" for one group of contendents, "Entente" for the other group, became familiar in the printed form, but timorousness about pronouncing them led us to use the term "Germans" for all the Central Powers. "Carry on," British term for "close ranks," coming later to signify cheerful endurance under hard circumstances; "cheerio," British word of greeting, meant in part to convey the effect of an encouraging slap on the back. "Shrecklichkeit," German word for frightfulness, used by their enemies and critics, and to some extent by themselves, to describe their means of reducing to meekness the civilian populations of the Belgian and French

A worldwide view about "Kultur" as reflected in an Italian periodical, which pictured "Kultur" as a plant which must be watered often with blood.

towns they occupied. "Der Tag," to which Germans dranks toasts, as the day when they should attain their "place in the sun." "Kultur," spelled, according to German usage, always with a capital *K*; a sinister quality attributed to the words was suggested by a magazine article to which Professor Frank Jewett Mather, Jr., of Princeton University, gave the caption, "Kultur versus Culture." "Deutschland über Alles," denoting German ambition or German exultation. "C'est la guerre," shoulder-shrugging explanation of anything that went wrong, any interruption of the accustomed routine of peace. "Somewhere in France," dictated by military authorities as the only permitted dateline on news despatches or letters, since greater exactness might enlighten the enemy about the location of troops. "Zeppelins," "blimps," "communiqué," "sector," "propaganda."

VIII

Almost instantly with the outbreak of the war came recognition by both sides that American public opinion constituted a sector of the battle-front rather more important to capture than Mons or Verdun. To win American opinion, propaganda arose; it came from all the combatants; we

The first press agent's war, pictured in the Baltimore Star, *October 8, 1914.*

Berlin Accuses France of Atrocities.

Protests Against Mutilation and Killing of Wounded German Soldiers, Charges French Troops
Fired on Ambulances and Physicians in the Field, Invaded Hospitals, Arrested
Clergymen and Otherwise-Disregarded the Rules of War.

From the New York Herald, *October 22, 1914.*

were drenched with it. We did not at first call it by that name. Hitherto "propaganda" had been a rather technical word, residing mainly in the world of religion, describing the process and institutions by which churches, especially the Catholic, sought to propagate the Christian faith in non-Christian nations. Such attempts by interested parties to shape public opinion as we had been familiar with in America had come mainly from the world of business and had been called "publicity." It was by that name, or in that way, that we thought, at the early stage, of the attempts of the European combatants to influence us: "This," said a *New York Times* editorial, September 9, 1914, "is the first press agents' war."

"Press agent," however, was recognized instinctively as too lowly a term to describe the personages who presently made us the beneficiary of efforts to influence our opinions. They were very exalted indeed, as exalted as possible, for capture of American public opinion was recognized by every head of state involved to be a major objective of the war. Kaiser Wilhelm, King Albert of Belgium, King George and Foreign Minister Grey of Britain, President Poincaré of France, all bestowed upon us repeatedly gestures or messages designed to attract us to their respective sides.

From the heads of state down, varied groups were called to the literary colors, or volunteered. Fifty-three British authors, including Kipling, Galsworthy, Hardy, Masefield, Barrie (Barrie came to visit us), united in a statement assuring us of the "righteousness" of the Allied cause, "its vital import to the future of the world." Germany countered with twenty-two heads of German universities who sent out a "German appeal to civilized nations against the campaign of systematic lies and slander." One hundred and fifty British professors exchanged literary volleys with "34 German dignitaries . . . thinkers, moralists, philanthropists," who proclaimed "the Truth about Germany, Facts about the War." Forty-five British artists and art lovers were pitted against ninety-six German professors, "representatives of German art and science" who protested "to the civilized world against the lies and calumnies" of the Allies.

In the competition to capture American favor, Britain had many advantages. British and other Allied propaganda, wrote one historian, was much "more general than that of the Teutons, and more adroit." Also, Britain, with France, controlled all the cables. Britain cut the only German cable as one of her first acts in the war. By the British control of cables, German communication with the United States was confined to wireless, then still new and imperfect. The two receiving stations in America were taken over and censored by the American government; Germany was permitted to communicate in cipher with its ambassador in Washington provided a copy

American opinion was unanimous in regarding as outrageous and intolerable Britain's in-terference with our commerce with European countries other than the Allies. The author of this cartoon, McCutcheon, of the Chicago Tribune, *aptly labeled it: "The Atrocities Still Go On." The sitting figure is, of course, John Bull.*

of the code was deposited with the State Department. Anyhow, German messages flying through the air were subject to not difficult picking up and deciphering by the extremely expert British secret service. The only real means left Germany to communicate with the United States was by mail, much too slow for the speed with which events moved. Besides, Britain, by reason of her incomparable advantage, control of the sea, was able to assert the right and exercise the power to seize, and hold long enough for exami-nation and censorship, mail between the United States and Germany, even mail directed via neutral countries and mail originating in neutral coun-tries, including America. Britain was ruthless about it. She seized and opened official letters addressed to our consuls.

As one result of control of cables by the Allies, the bulk of the news America got, whether of battle or of other developments, came from or via London or Paris, and took on the color of the route it traveled. American correspondents at the front were almost always with the Allied troops, since only from there would they get their accounts to America promptly. Correspondents not at the front were usually at one of the Allied capitals; inevitably they took much of their news from the British and French press—what they did not get from that source, they necessarily could only get from British and French officials. Moreover, practically everything they sent was censored. What the Allies did not want sent to America was not sent.

Most of all, Germany was eclipsed in American favor by England through the possession by America and England of a common tongue and common ways of looking at things, a common background of literature and institutions. Milton and Wordsworth, Shakespeare and Shelley were as much a part of the fiber of American emotion as of English. As the war got under way one could realize that without any planning, without any intention of propaganda, with a force that made propaganda a fantastic superfluity, every little red schoolhouse in America where on Friday afternoon children recited Gray's "Elegy Written in a Country Churchyard," had been through generations a recruiting post which now produced sympathy for Britain; and every prairie courthouse where judges and lawyers dealt daily with Blackstone and Coke and Magna Carta, had been an unconscious breeding-ground for the conviction that British institutions must not be destroyed.

All this crystallized when Britain entered the war, when the lineup became, in American eyes, mainly Britain versus mainly Germany. We followed the fortunes of the first British Expeditionary Force almost as closely, as poignantly, as if it had been our own; took almost as much pride as the British themselves in turning into a designation of honor the term in which the Kaiser was said to have expressed his jeering scorn of them, "the Contemptibles." When cables told us the British in France, as they marched, sang a ditty that had been current in London music halls when they entrained, America took up the tune almost as universally as the British themselves—"Tipperary" during the fall and winter of 1914–1915 was sung in America, and whistled, hummed, danced to, and applauded in public places where "Die Wacht am Rhein" would have led to a riot.

IX

Propaganda, at first chiefly that from the Allies, projected "atrocities," in a special meaning, into our rapidly increasing vocabulary of war. Allied propagandists charged that German soldiers had cut off the breasts of Belgian women, the hands of Belgian babies; that London hospital cots contained scores of the maimed Belgian children; that German soldiers had crucified Canadian soldiers, with bayonets stuck through hands and feet; that the Germans, as a detail of efficiency, salvaged all the corpses on battlefields, tied them into bales, and shipped them back to Germany to be made into soap, grease, and fertilizer.

Germans, with equal inventiveness, charged that the Allies gouged out the eyes of German prisoners; that the French put cholera germs in wells

TOURIST SAW SOLDIER WITH BAGFUL OF EARS

American Salesman Bluffs His Way to Front and Sees Real Fighting.

Super-Dum Dums Inflict Awful Injuries on Victims

Wounds of Soldiers in Hospitals in Belgium Cited as Proof of
Use of Prohibited Bullets by Prussians—German De-
nials and Accusations Ready When War Begun.

N. Y. Herald, Oct. 5, 1914.

Lif

(New York Herald, October 5, 1914)   (Life)

in territory occupied by the Germans; that a Belgian priest wore a chain of German finger rings around his neck; that French priests offered to German soldiers coffee poisoned with strychnine; that a Belgian priest put a machine gun behind the altar to spray German Catholic soldiers who came to Mass.

Life, July 25, 1915.

There was much propaganda to the effect that prisoners were mutilated and that the Germans took delight in torturing the weak and helpless. (Life, July 25, 1915)

"To Your Health! Civilization!" Louis Raemaeker's cartoons furnished the most graphic evidence of the barbarity of war. (By courtesy of the Century Company)

America, prevailingly, being pro-Ally, believed the stories of German atrocities and rejected those about the Allies. Many, one felt, seemed to get a perverse pleasure in believing the story about the Belgian children without hands. It persisted for the duration of the war. In 1918, an Iowa orator making speeches to stimulate purchase of Liberty bonds told the story as a personal experience: A childless couple, he said, friends of his, who had sent to Belgium for two children for adoption, found the tots, when they arrived, handless. A Des Moines newspaperman, skeptical, directed a photographer to find and photograph those children regardless of expense. They were never found. They did not exist. The orator finally admitted he had averred his personal knowledge of the story as an invented contribution to stimulate emotion which should express itself in buying more Liberty bonds.

By five years after the war ended, practically every atrocity story from either side had failed, upon investigation, to yield proof. "A lie," said Sophocles, "never lives to be old." But for these atrocity stories, to live for the duration of the war was, as regards effect, to live forever.

X

Even atrocity stories could not deflect the common American impulse "to keep out of it." Prediction said this would be easy. Much of the prophecy—there were floods of it—had to do with duration; the common estimate of the length so devastating a war could last was three to five months. Equally frequent among the prophecies was the word "certain" or "permanent" accompanying self-congratulation over America's immunity, our "permanent good-fortune" in not being mixed up in it.

"Our isolated position and freedom from entangling alliances," said the *Literary Digest*, putting the common attitude into words, "inspire our press with the cheering assurance that we are in no peril of being drawn in to the European quarrel." The *New York Sun*, confidently and somewhat complacently, asserted that the United States would "suffer inevitably to some extent from the waste and destruction abroad, but it had permanent cause for gratitude in its insulation from the worst." Any timid souls dubious of the soundness of this conviction had reassurance from the professors, the historians, like the eminent one who wrote:

> Needless to say, the European war will not involve the United States in actual hostilities. It is highly improbable that either our army or our navy will see service. We are too distant from the seat of war; too entirely devoid of interests the combatants might seriously injure, too completely incapable of aiding or abetting one or the other in arms to cause them to assail us. Even were we not a nation of a peaceful disposition, even had we not a President blessed with a singularly clear head and able to keep his temper, we should still stand little chance of going to war.

CHAPTER 3

The Lusitania

O f all the motives, the dark emotions and clear-thought purposes
that incited Germany to war, of all the envies that tormented her
into fighting for her place in the sun, the most concrete was England's dominance, naval and commercial, on the sea. Of all the conditions
that now tortured the German soul, the most biting was the consciousness
that every ship of hers that had sailed the seas was now in frightened hiding
in German ports or interned in neutral ones, while British ships imperturbably carried on: On any day, from the beginning of the war to the end,
any American traveler could go down to the Bowling Green section of
New York, walk into a British steamship office, talk with a placid English
clerk, and get passage to Europe—while, next door and across the street,
the Hamburg-American and other German offices were idle. (Except as the
Hamburg-American served as a center for propaganda and other furtive
activities.)

Of all the lines and routes that composed England's worldwide fabric of

---

SPECIAL ANNOUNCEMENT

*In view of the uncertainty of the
present European situation, we have
decided to postpone sailings of the S. S.
Vaterland from New York; Amerika
from Boston, August 1st, and Im-
perator from Hamburg, July 31st. For
the same reason we have also ordered
the S. S. President Grant, which sailed
from New York yesterday, to return.*

HAMBURG-AMERICAN LINE

---

*A material factor in the war was the practically complete paralysis of German shipping while
British shipping imperturbably "carried on."* (Philadelphia Ledger, *August 1, 1914*)

commercial dominance, proudest and oldest was the Cunard, special pride of the British nation, special concern of the British Admiralty. And of all the ships that flew the Cunarder flag, queen of the fleet was the *Lusitania.*

The *Lusitania* was a splendid ship. A four-stacker, 30,395 gross tons, 755 feet in length, and 88 in breadth, the largest ship afloat when launched, first four-propellered turbine steamship, with accommodations so ample and luxurious for her capacity of 3,000 souls (passengers and crew), that ship designers said one-third of her space was prodigal gratuity to comfort. She was the first vessel in the world to be called a "floating hotel." The Cunard were proud of that phrase, and prouder still of her speed record. She was the first ship to steam for twenty-four hours at a higher average speed than twenty-five knots—she did twenty-six and a third. And their cup overflowed when they recalled that the *Lusitania* had fulfilled her British builders' intention by wresting the ocean speed record from the North German Lloyd's *Kaiser Wilhelm II* on Friday, September 13, 1907, a time when Germany had been content to make her attempt at dominance by honest competition in skill. The *Lusitania* had been built to be empress of the seas, and she was.

Superbly conscious of this prestige, then, on April 30, 1915, the Cunard's accustomed advertisement—simple and dignified as befitted their traditions—announced the sailing of the *Lusitania* for the following morning.

Directly beneath the Cunard announcement of sailing appeared on Saturday morning, May 1, 1915, the "Notice" reproduced on this page. It excited attention; the Associated Press sent the text of it as a news despatch to papers in the interior.

15

OCEAN STEAMSHIPS.

CUNARD

EUROPE. VIA LIVERPOOL
LUSITANIA
Fastest and Largest Steamer
now in Atlantic Service Sails
SATURDAY, MAY 1, 10 A. M.
Transylvania, Fri., May 7, 5 P.M.
Orduna, - - Tues.,May 18, 10 A.M.
Tuscania, - - Fri., May 21, 5 P.M.
LUSITANIA, Sat., May 29, 10 A.M.
Transylvania, Fri., June 4, 5 P.M.

Gibraltar–Genoa–Naples–Piraeus
S.S. Carpathia, Thur., May 13, Noon

NOTICE!

TRAVELLERS intending to embark on the Atlantic voyage are reminded that a state of war exists between Germany and her allies and Great Britain and her allies; that the zone of war includes the waters adjacent to the British Isles; that, in accordance with formal notice given by the Imperial German Government, vessels flying the flag of Great Britain, or of any of her allies, are liable to destruction in those waters and that travellers sailing in the war zone on ships of Great Britain or her allies do so at their own risk.

IMPERIAL GERMAN EMBASSY
WASHINGTON, D. C., APRIL 22, 1915.

An advertisement, extraordinary in character, which made much history.

It excited attention—but no one heeded it. The word "unthinkable" is commonly used after an event, as an epithet, an expression of strong disapproval, a synonym for horrible. In this case "unthinkable" had an exact meaning in advance of the event. No one believed the German government could seriously intend to do the thing this warning implied. No one of the 1,257 passengers booked to sail on the *Lusitania*, so far as there is any record—and subsequently this and every other aspect of the event was subjected to minute scrutiny—considered canceling his sailing. No member of the *Lusitania*'s crew of 667 gave it a thought. If any had, he would have ignored it.

The warning diminished not at all the gaiety and eclat that accompany embarkment on one of the crack liners of the world. The scene was at once festive and distinguished; the passengers included several leading figures in the national life of the time: Charles Frohman, principal American theatrical producer, patron and friend of nearly all the important actors and playwrights of the English- and French-speaking worlds, now off to look after some of his London productions; Alfred Gwynne Vanderbilt, best-known member, because of his interest in horses and sports, of a famous American family, sailing to look over his London racing stable; Elbert Hubbard and his wife—Hubbard was known to all America as head of the "Roycrofters," a school of genial iconoclasm expressed by Hubbard in incessant popular lecturing and in a pungent, humorous little periodical, *The Philistine*; Justus Miles Forman, an author just coming toward the top rank—a recent play of his, *The Hyphen*, had irritated German-Americans; Charles Klein, leading playwright, producer of the *Music Master*, and now contemplating production of *Potash and Perlmutter in Society*; Herbert Stone, son of Melville Stone, head of the Associated Press; other persons eminent in business, the arts, and professions. The *Lusitania*'s passenger list was a microcosm of Americans well known, well liked.

The Lusitania, *premier ship of the British passenger service at this time, called, fairly,* "Empress of the Seas."

Passengers and friends of passengers crowded dock and decks. Messenger boys carrying flowers, baskets of fruit, and books rushed up the gangplank. The ship's musicians played the latest fox-trots and one-steps. As the hawsers of the great liner were cast off and a dozen puffing tugs maneuvered her into midstream, crowds lining the pier waved and shouted good-byes, not at all in the spirit of parting, but, as usual, in the spirit of cheering the fortunate travelers on to a happy voyage.

The trip across was exceptionally agreeable. Except for a few hours of fog the second morning out, the weather was perfect, the sea smooth. For six soft sunny days the passengers enjoyed an exceptional experience of the pleasure of a transatlantic voyage on the most luxurious liner afloat. Nights, the portholes were closed and lights on deck forbidden—any passenger who struck a match for his cigar found his arm seized by a steward, deferential and polite but firm, who reminded him he was breaking a ship's rule. That, however, had become the universal and commonplace precaution of wartime travel on the sea and, if commented on at all, was used only as a peg upon which to hang a witticism. Within, in the parlors and smoking rooms, passengers danced, played cards, drank cocktails and champagne, made bets on the day's run; with no thought of insecurity, they enjoyed an ocean trip under the most agreeable conditions afforded by the modern world.

Friday, May 7, passengers finishing lunch came on deck to see, some 8 or 10 miles away, the green fields, sloping hills, and white-washed cottages of the southern point of Ireland, the Old Head of Kinsdale. They called to each other to look. Between expressions of pleasure at the sight of one of the most alluring bits of land in the world, there were occasional allusions, nearly all humorous, to the possibility of submarines now that the *Lusitania* had reached British waters. There had been momentary expectation that fast British destroyers would appear to escort the *Lusitania* into port, as was the custom. Indeed, failure of a convoy to appear suggested assurance that danger from submarines was past. Elbert Hubbard, feeling relief over the *Lusitania*'s safe passage through the submarine-infested waters farther out, spoke with humor to a fellow passenger of a personal reason the Kaiser had for "getting" him—Hubbard had written and published in *The Philistine* an article about the Kaiser and the war bearing the suggestive title "Who Lifted the Lid Off Hell?"

Suddenly, there was a sound, heavy, muffled; and a shock, a tremor through the ship, the smash of glass from portholes. The bow began to dip, forward and to the side.

Of the total of 1,924 aboard, only 726 were saved. Among the 1,198 lost were 63 infants and children. Out of 35 babies only 4 were saved. One family of eight was completely wiped out. Americans aboard numbered 188; 114 were drowned.

Survivors gave the newspapers vivid eyewitness accounts.

Robert Rankin, of Washington, D.C.:

> We saw what looked like a whale or a porpoise rising about three-quarters of a mile to starboard. We all knew what it was, but

no one named it. Immediately a white line, a train of bubbles, started away from the black object. It came straight for the ship. It was obvious it couldn't miss. It was aimed ahead of her and struck under the bridge. I saw it disappear. We all hoped for the fraction of a second it would not explode. But the explosion came clear up through the upper deck, and pieces of the wreckage fell clean aft of where we were standing. We ducked into the smoking-room for shelter from the flying debris. The boilers exploded immediately. The passengers all rushed at once to the high side of the deck—the port side. There was such a list to starboard that all boats on the port side swung right back inboard and could not be launched.

Ogden H. Hammond, of New York:

The man at the bow of the lifeboat let the rope slip through his hands, while the man at the stern paid it out too slowly. The situation was terrible. We were dropping perpendicularly when I caught the rope and tried to stop the boat from falling. My hands were torn to shreds, but the boat fell and all in it were thrown into the water—a dense struggling mass. I went down and down and down, with thirty people on top of me. I thought we never would come back to the surface. I must have been partly unconscious then, for I can only remember getting almost to the surface and then sinking back, and doing this three or four times. Finally, I was hauled into some boat, but no one else from the boat that fell was ever seen again.

Then there is the account of a St. Louis man, a salesman probably—his name was not given in the cable that transmitted his story—whose Missouri sense of humor was so sinewy that it stayed by him throughout all the horror of the *Lusitania*'s sinking:

We had been playing poker ever since the trip began, and some one had just ordered a round of beer. As we started to drink, one of the fellows said: "What would you do if a torpedo hit us?" I said: "I am unmarried, and I'd finish my beer." Just then the torpedo struck and the others bolted, but I finished the beer and went over to the bar and called for another bottle and said to the bartender: "Let's die game, anyway." But he said: "You go to hell," and bolted, leaving me all alone. I had another drink, and just as I was finishing it the boat turned over. When I woke up I was being hauled into a small boat.

Watches recovered later from floating bodies were stopped at a few minutes after half past two. Allowing twenty minutes for the sinking of the ship and the drowning of the passengers, the time when the torpedo struck was eight minutes past two: 2:08 P.M. of May 7, 1915. That was the precise moment—more nearly than the inception of most wars can be fixed—when war between America and Germany became inevitable.

THE ANNOUNCER.

GERMAN EMBASSY'S ADVERTISEMENT
GAVE WARNING ONE WEEK AGO

The American press printed hundreds of such angry cartoons as these. The one above was printed in the Brooklyn Eagle *on the anniversary of the* Lusitania's *sinking, May 8, 1916. The one bottom left was printed in* Life, *May 27, 1915. The one bottom right in the* New York Herald *the day after the* Lusitania's *sinking, May 8, 1915.*

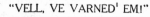

"VELL, VE VARNED' EM!"

II

The average American, after reading his newspaper at breakfast Saturday morning, May 8, looked about hoping to see a German whom he could fight, or at the least express his opinion to. The immediate feeling was reflected in the *Des Moines Register and Leader* an editorial which began: "The sinking of the *Lusitania* was deliberate murder" and ended impressively with the same affirmation: "The sinking of the *Lusitania* was deliberate murder."

That was the emotion of America as a whole. No event since the sinking of the *Maine* had so stirred the country. The phrase used by a distinguished historian to describe the country's emotion, "mingled horror and rage," was not too strong.

Popular anger was increased by the attitude of the German-American press, which had a manner of shrugging its shoulders and saying, "War is war"; by stories that groups in German-American restaurants had broken into cheers at the news and drunk toasts to the U-boat commander and sung "Deutschland über Alles"; by other stories that in Germany schoolchildren had been given a holiday and that a medal had been struck off to commemorate the sinking; and by the indisputedly authentic remark of an official German representative in America, Dr. Bernhard Dernburg—ironically his official function was one of mercy, he was the head of the German Red Cross work in America: "The death of the Americans might have been avoided if our warning had been heeded; we put in advertisements and were careful to put them next the announcements of the Cunard Line's sailing dates; anybody can commit suicide if he wants to."

Medal struck off in Germany in celebration of the Lusitania *sinking.*

As resentment rose and surged, all thoughts, all eyes, turned to President Wilson. Here, every one thought, was the thing—worse than the thing—he had warned Germany against when he had said he would hold Germany to "strict accountability." It was now "inconceivable we should refrain from action," said Theodore Roosevelt; "we owe it not only to humanity but to our own national self-respect."

III

It happened that Wilson some time before had made an engagement to speak in Philadelphia, Monday, May 10. The fact that the audience was to consist of some 4,000 foreign-born persons recently naturalized aroused expectation that Wilson would speak in the vein of patriotism. Now, with the speech coming three days after the *Lusitania* sinking, anticipation was confident and excited.

Wilson made the speech. He did not use the word "Germany." Conspicuously, he did not use the word "*Lusitania*," nor make the remotest allusion to what was in every American mind. The nearest he came to alluding to anything controversial was an appeal to the newly naturalized citizens that they should not think of themselves as "groups," meaning, by implication—he did not use any word so provocative as "hyphenated"—that they

The Destruction of the Lusitania

A Marching Song.   (Tune: Upidee, Upida.)

By RUDOLF KUHN.

I.

Carrying shameful contraband,
From New York to the English land,
Bearing thousands, on she came:
But the U-boat sniffed its game.

II.

Sailed the Lusitania gay
Further on her felon way;
Off Ireland's coast the U-boat peers,
See the course her quarry steers!

III.

Passengers from every shore—
English, Greek, and Dutch galore,
Americans and sons of France
Sail along to death's fell dance.

IV.

Ah! The U-boat's aim was good;
Who doesn't choke, drowns in the flood.
Vanderbilt was there that day,
The only one we missed was Grey.

V.

Each one gives his nose a wrench
At the gases' awful stench.
"They're our shells, our very own,"
Cries the Yankee Mr. Kohn.

VI.

The old water-nymphs below
Straight begin to curse and blow;
"What chuck ye then so carelessly
On the bottom of the sea?"

VII.

There lay the dead in Neptune's jaws,
Most of them with scalded paws—
Sons of England with their wives;
Ne'er so still in all their lives!

VIII.

Chant we now the funeral chant,
More U-boats is what we want.
To a chill grave with the enemy!
Till he stop bothering Germany.

Exultation by German sympathizers over the sinking of the Lusitania *contributed to inflaming American emotions. This doggerel asserts that the* Lusitania *carried "shameful contraband." That the* Lusitania *carried "contraband" in the broad sense, is true, for "contraband" had come to describe a wide variety of goods. As to whether the* Lusitania *carried munitions there has been prolonged dispute. There is some evidence that her cargo included a small quantity of materials for munitions, such as unfilled cartridge cases.*

should not think of themselves as British-Americans, nor Swedish-Americans, nor Irish-Americans, nor German-Americans. Wilson did not use

Reproduction of a picture postcard sold by the millions in Germany following the sinking of the Lusitania. *In the inset is Admiral Von Tirpitz, author of Germany's submarine campaign. The inscription, translated, reads: "Queenstown, May 7, 1915. The Cunarder* Lusitania *has been torpedoed and sunk." (International Film Photograph)*

these terms, only the generalization "groups." His speech was not about the war, his topic was Americanism in an idealistic sense. Without having the war in mind, he expressed an ideal of his own. To be mixed up in fighting is a thing that a proud man disdains. Expressing that ideal, Wilson used a phrase that startled every ear:

> The example of America must be a special example. The example of America must be the example not merely of peace because it will not fight, but of peace because peace is the healing and elevating influence of the world and strife is not. There is such a thing as a nation being so right that it does not need to convince others by force that it is right. . . . There is such a thing as a man being *too proud to fight.*

Press and public, having anticipated drama in Wilson's speech in the form of allusion to the *Lusitania,* and having failed to find that, now made drama of "too proud to fight." To those who wanted to go to war with Germany, it was poltroonery on Wilson's part, national humiliation on the part of America—in huge type the *New York Herald* exclaimed: "What a Pity Theodore Roosevelt is Not President!" But to those who did not want war, "too proud to fight" was magnificent self-restraint. Persons and parts of the country who were normally for peace but had been moved to willingness

"SO SAY WE ALL OF US"

A cartoon from the Cleveland Leader *which reflected a view widely held in America, especially the rural portions, that Wilson was right in treating the* Lusitania *sinking not as an immediate cause for war but as a matter for diplomatic protest.*

for war by the *Lusitania* sinking, now, through Wilson's silence and through his "too proud to fight," were swung back to peace. The *Des Moines Register and Leader*'s editorial "Deliberate Murder" of May 9, became on May 13, "Trust the President." "It is because the President has the courage to hold himself in restraint and not because he is wanting in courage, that everybody turns to him. . . . Trust the President."

By Wilson's silence and his "too proud to fight," the momentary impulse of the nation to go to war was turned back to cautious waiting. "Trust the President," "Sit Tight," became the majority state of mind.

As respects the evolution of his mind, Wilson had now passed from an original passive neutrality to an active, affirmative, determined neutrality. He would not allow the war to touch us, he would fight it off.

CHAPTER 4
Evolution of American Thought

It was commonly said later, and frequently at the time, that Wilson, the day after the *Lusitania* sinking, could have carried America into the war. The German ambassador to the United States thought so, and he should have been a good judge: Wilson needed only to "nod to induce his country to fight after the *Lusitania*."

But this should be added: It was on the Atlantic seaboard mainly, and perhaps only, that willingness for war prevailed to a degree sufficient to make a declaration by Wilson practicable. The East was the section, principally, that expressed itself in execration of "too proud to fight." For whatever reason, whether because of the greater quantity of war news in the eastern big-city newspapers, whether because of greater nearness to the scene, or the larger number of persons who had direct associations with England and France, it was a definite and important fact in the evolution of American thought about the war that the East arrived at readiness to enter long before the rest of the country.

This cleavage between the East and the remainder of the country was but one of several divisions into which the country had fallen. The cleavages crisscrossed each other intricately.

II

Even without being pro-war, so general was pro-Ally sentiment in America that many of us came to feel that not to be pro-Ally was to be not patriotically American. In our overwhelmingly pro-Ally emotion, our conviction that Germany was in the wrong and should be defeated, our latent impulse to help, if only vicariously, in the pro-Ally cause—in that condition the pleas of German-born professors to see the virtues in the German cause gave us something concrete to complain against, something occurring on our own soil.

Complain many of us did, and presently we extended our complaint to include our German-American citizens generally. They, in natural resentment against being treated so, and partly on account of the spokesmanship given them by the German professors, partly on account of the sum of all the conditions, became self-consciously pro-German, vocal, and organized. Some of them acted through the National German-American Alliance,

The Fatherland
FAIR PLAY FOR
Germany and Austria-Hungary

Edited by
GEORGE SYLVESTER VIERECK
FREDERICK F. SCHRADER
European Representative:
LOUIS VIERECK, Berlin, Suedwest Korso 8.

A weekly published and owned by The International Monthly, 1123 Broadway, New York City. Telephone, Farragut 9038. Cable Address, Viereck,
New York. President, George Sylvester Viereck; Vice-President, Joseph
Bernard Rethy; Treasurer, M. Binion; Secretary, Curt H. Reisinger. Terms
of Subscription, incl. postage in the United States and Mexico $2.00 per
year; $1.00 for six months. In Canada, $2.25 per year; $1.25 for six
months. Subscription to all foreign countries within the postal union, $2.25
per year. Single copies, 5 cents. Newsdealers and Agents throughout the
country supplied by The International News Company. Manuscripts,
addressed to the Editor, if accompanied by return postage, and found un-
available, will be returned. The Editor, however, accepts no responsibility
for unsolicited contributions.
Copyright, 1914, by The International Monthly, Inc.   Entered at the
Post Office, New York, N. Y., as Second Class Matter.

When you have finished reading this number,
don't lay it aside, but pass it on to your American friends who may be anxious to know the
other side of the great European conflict.

LIES, LIES, LIES.

IF we are to believe the mendacity mills of St. Peters-
burg and London, the German Army is bent on carrying out on a large scale the theory of a pessimist philo-

again and again in official reports from Paris and London. It was not until the 19th of September that the
German dispatch was verified by London. The Sayville
station is the only source of reliable information.

GREAT BRITAIN REPRIMANDS PRESIDENT WILSON.

SIR LIONEL GARDEN, formerly Great Britain's
representative in Mexico, now on his way to his
new post in Brazil, severely reprimands President Wilson for his order withdrawing our troops from Vera
Cruz. The British diplomat does not hesitate to characterize President Wilson's action as "a shame." The
interview is printed in the New York Sun and is
vouched for by one of that newspaper's ablest reporters
and two of his colleagues. The subsequent perfunctory denial by Sir Lionel isn't taken seriously by any
one acquainted with the editorial integrity of the New
York Sun, and this minister's past record for impert-
inence toward the President of the United States.

English warships have seized and destroyed the mail
of American citizens addressed to Germany without regard to neutrality, in flagrant violation of the conventions
of international law. This act of piracy is almost a
casus belli.

Evidently British statesmen look upon the United
States as a province of the British Empire.
Else they would not dare to strain to the break-
ing point the neutrality proclaimed by President Wilson.

The German side of the argument as presented by The Fatherland.

which urged German-Americans to "organize press bureaus and combat
the attitude of the English language press." A conspicuous American of
German parentage, George Sylvester Viereck, conducted a weekly paper,
"*The Fatherland*, devoted to Fair Play to Germany." The quite considerable
German language press in America, hitherto a rather innocuous medium of
news from the homeland and of neighborhood items for German immigrants and their descendants, became aggressively pro-German. Many,
though not all, ministers of Lutheran churches called meetings, adopted
resolutions: "We German-Americans" protest "against the common
calumnies against the head of a nation friendly to us . . . [brand as false the
charge] that Germany and its Emperor have sought and forced this war."

Between German-Americans and pro-Germans and, on the other hand,
anti-Germans, academic war, kept within oral and polemic limits, went on
constantly. Friends of Germany, thinking mainly in terms of the German
people, pointed to their kindliness, quoted their poets, cited German
achievement in science. Anti-Germans, thinking mainly in terms of the
German ruling caste, the Hohenzollerns, the militarists, and the *Kultur*
they had fastened on the people, pointed to the Kaiser's bombast, cited
some of the German philosophers and about all the German authors of
treatises on military science, the *Schrecklichkeit* they preached or condoned.
Philosopher Friedrich Nietzsche, through quotations from his "Will to
Power" and other works, became almost as familiar a name as that of the
contemporary holder of the highest batting average in professional baseball.

As the tension grew, activities of some pro-Germans went to a point inconsistent with our neutrality, inconsistent indeed with loyalty to the

In the 1916 campaign the political parties at one and the same time desired and looked askance at the German vote (personified in this Life *cartoon as a dachshund).*

United States. They established connections with the German government, received money which they spent on propaganda, in some cases on criminal conspiracy, even criminal violence. This, as it became known, excited strong feeling. The cleavage between pro-Germans and the rest of the people became tense.

The Germans were joined by some Irish, comparatively few but very much moved and extremely vocal; the beginning of the Great War had happened to coincide with an acute outbreak of the seven-centuries-long struggle of the Irish against England. An organization of Irish Nationalists, meeting in Philadelphia, "pledge ourselves to do all in our power . . . to bring Irishmen and Germans together to fight for a common cause, the national welfare of Germany. . . ." One Irish organization that became active and resourceful in pro-German propaganda was called the American Truth Society. At many an exalted meeting "The Wearing of the Green" mingled, rather incongruously, with "Die Wacht am Rhein."

As feeling grew, ethnic consciousness became infectious. In the bedeviling cleavages by which America was thus beset, an intricate line of division separated various foreign groups each from each: Italian-Americans, Irish-Americans, Polish-Americans, Russian-Americans, Hungarian-Americans, and other groups from the peculiarly polyglot Austro-Hungarian Empire. All began to organize, take sides, and express their emotions in foreign-language newspapers, including demands that their adopted country should take one side or the other. Thus arose another war-created term, "hyphenated American." The phenomenon disturbed us, caused many to wonder if our policy of unrestricted immigration had been wise, whether America was really a nation, or just an international boardinghouse. It was not a happy time for average Americans—occasions arose when they were obliged to wonder whether they existed, whether there was such a thing as "the average American." Some, conspicuously Theodore Roosevelt, then ex-president, took the situation very seriously, started movements for "Americanization"—Roosevelt popularized a phrase, "hundred percent American."

III

A long another line, there was cleavage between preparedness advocates and pacifists. Both these groups, however, must be subdivided.

Some preparedness partisans aimed at universal military training, others merely at having a larger army and a quite strong navy.

Pacifists were divided between two factions. One opposed preparedness for this war—these were to some extent identical with or parallel in their aims with the pro-Germans. The other group, pacifists in the more exact sense, opposed preparedness on principle, opposed it for any war at any time with anybody, the peace-at-all-times-and-at-any-price people. Argument and quarrel between pacifists and preparedness advocates was rather less violent than that which had its origin in ethnic affiliations. Preparedness advocates could as a rule satisfy their emotions adequately by speaking of their meek opponents as "milk-faced grubs." Pacifists retorted, "jingo" and "bloody-minded militarists." Millions of individual arguments posed the question, "Would you fight if a foreign soldier struck your mother?" Much of the emotion of the pacifist-preparedness jibing centered about a song, its sentiment taken perfectly seriously by those who liked it, fiercely jeered at by those who did not: "I did not raise my boy to be a soldier!"

IV

T he cleavages that beset the country were far more intricate than could be described as three pairs of antitheses: preparedness advocates versus pacifists, pro-Germans versus pro-Allies, and East versus West. One lists the groups only with much qualification; each line of division was cross-cut by other lines.

At all times there was a large group, the largest of all, into which the lines of cleavage did not penetrate. The people in this group were comparatively detached about the war; they either mildly favored the Allies or took neither side; so far as they reflected at all upon what we should do, their instinct said we should stay out of it, the war was none of our business. To mind one's own business was a traditional American attitude of mind, a corollary to our strong individualism; it had almost the force of folklore. Now it was expanded from a personal rule of life to a national one. Only upon some extremely strong incentive, such as assurance from Wilson that we should fight, would the majority of Americans consider entering the war.

CHAPTER 5

Henry Ford Takes a Hand and a Ship

T he more ardent pacifists took it for granted that the United States would never enter the war—that would be too shocking. Feeling confident about this, some of the more earnest dedicated themselves to bringing the war in Europe to an end.

With this fine altruistic purpose, some of the most high-minded persons in America, led by David Starr Jordan, head of the American Peace Society and president of Stanford University, and Jane Addams, leading welfare worker, head of Chicago's Hull House, organized what they called an Emergency Peace Conference, and joined at the Hague an International Conference of Women—called impishly by the American ambassador to Britain Walter Page the "Palace of Doves"—which would unite with others in carrying on what Addams called "Continuous Mediation."

Their aim, no less, was to labor directly with the heads of the European governments at war. They did labor with them. Addams and some companions called on Foreign Minister von Jagow in Berlin, Foreign Minister Grey in London, and other foreign ministers of the belligerent nations. Wilson's canny adviser Col. E. M. House said that Addams "accumulated a wonderful lot of misinformation," that the foreign ministers with whom she talked "were not quite candid with her," and that she "has a totally wrong impression."* Addams, however, and the women who accompanied her, were sure that all the heads of states desperately wanted peace, were only deterred from saying so by fear of "losing face," and would ardently welcome peace if pressed upon them from outside.

A sheaf of confidential statements of what the ministers of belligerent states were alleged to have said to the peace-making ladies was turned over to a Hungarian woman, Rosika Schwimmer. Schwimmer, carrying the alleged statements in what newspapers later referred to as a "little black bag," came to Washington to lay her information before President Wilson and to solicit him to take the steps toward peace which, she asserted, the belligerents would welcome. Wilson was cordial, interested, but noncommittal—he had been warned by Colonel House to be cautious.

While waiting for some action by Wilson, Schwimmer went about the

---

*Colonel House's skepticism about Addams's efforts may have reflected the depreciation that men are prone to feel about activities of women in public affairs, common at a time when woman was still a newcomer, and an interloper, in politics. The Colonel would have been especially subject to this sentiment; he was elderly, he was an old-fashioned man, and he was a southerner.

Jane Addams, distinguished American leader in good works, whose Emergency Peace Conference partly inspired Ford to try to "get the boys out of the trenches by Christmas."

country delivering lectures in the interest of peace. On a day in early November, 1915, she arrived in Detroit and found the newspapers there excited about something that had occurred the day before in the office of Henry Ford.

II

Ford had been impatient with the war from its opening in 1914, often used his advertising space in newspapers to decry the folly of it and gave out interviews to the same effect. On a day in the fall of 1915 he happened to see in the war news a definite figure and a concrete fact—in the fighting of the preceding twenty-four hours, 20,000 men had been killed. That struck Ford as shocking, the inhumanity of it, the economic waste. With a manner that implied "This thing has gone on long enough," he strode into the hall outside his office exclaiming something to the effect that he would be willing to spend half his fortune to shorten the war by a single day—Ford had a good deal of practical faith in the power of half his fortune. A reporter jumped from his bench and snatched out his pencil. His story, quoting Ford's remark, naturally made the first page of the *Detroit Free Press* and was broadcast by the news associations. Immediately Ford was deluged with letters pleading with him to lead the way.

Schwimmer went and saw Ford. She stayed to lunch. It was the psychological moment; he was eager for her persuasions. Next day was even better; he approved heartily of the mediation plan and promised not only to support it but to go to Europe himself and take part in it. Ford was on fire. "All we know," he said, "is that the fighting nations are sick of war, that they want to stop, and that they are waiting only for some disinterested party to step in and offer mediation."

III

Ford's impulse was not unique and not necessarily impracticable. Millions of Americans shared it—to stop the war was indeed the prevailing American wish. Many Americans of elevated position were actually active in the purpose in one way or another. Ford differed from them only in his possession of great facilities. He was absolutely sincere—never more so— his action was by no means the gaudy gesture of a money-confident man bent on getting his name into history; whatever Ford's shortcomings, showy display was not among them. He may have been overoptimistic, doubtless he underestimated the difficulties of the task he set himself. But who, in view of Ford's record, could place a limit on what it might be possible for him to achieve? Ford, following his own methods, had accomplished the impossible in business. In the field of economics he had evolved and put in practice a new principle—if he could defy the old ways of economics, why not the old ways of statesmanship? With his record of successful innovation, perhaps the most important since the beginning of the Industrial Era, and with the moral support of the overwhelming majority of the American people, who looked upon Ford as the evangel of a new and better world, Ford had reason to feel hopeful in his new purpose. The war, in Ford's eyes, was a wholly mad and evil reversion to savagery, needless to tolerate. For the ways of orthodox diplomacy, statecraft, he had a disdain

Henry Ford with Rosika Schwimmer, who largely persuaded Ford to take his expedition on the "Ark of Peace." (Photograph by Underwood & Underwood)

The common newspaper attitude toward Ford's expedition was one of extreme satire. In this cartoon by Chamberlain, which appeared in the New York Evening Sun, *Ford is pictured as saying to the whole war, "Now you stop!"*

equal to that in which he held the orthodox economics. He had seen the statesmen fail, ignominiously, disastrously. Ford's own approach to a problem was the antithesis to that of statecraft. He was directness, simplicity, decision, intelligence, originality personified. If buffoons pirouetted across the world stage in 1915, they were not Ford and the half dozen who participated with him in the project of halting the madness of Europe; the buffoons were the rulers and statesmen and diplomats whose inability to maintain peace among civilized nations stood as the most tragic failure in all the annals of humanity.

IV

In a few days Ford went to New York, took a suite at the Biltmore, and moved at once to join a group at the McAlpin in which were Schwimmer and Addams, together with several other earnest pacifists—"militant pacifists," one might call them—including: Oswald Garrison Villard, editor of the *New York Evening Post* (subsequently editor of a liberal weekly, *The Nation*); Paul Kellogg, editor of an organ of social workers, *The Survey;* and Professor George W. Kirchwey of Columbia University. Schwimmer remarked that it would be pleasant to have a ship for the delegates. Ford had been a bit lost amid the generalities of their pacifist theories, but "ship" meant something in his line, graphic and tangible: "We'll get one!" he said; immediately he phoned for agents of the steamship lines to come to the hotel.

At about this point the press took up the enterprise and irrevocably transformed its nature. What was in essence a not necessarily infeasible idea became, in the eyes of the newspapers (and by that token in the eyes of the public), a bandwagon for extravagant hopes, a grotesque circus for the delectation of the man in the street. Ford's secretary had toppled the structure in this direction; his last act before following Ford to New York had been to give the Detroit papers a statement in which he said: "We'll get the boys out of the trenches by Christmas"—and this was almost December 1! The newspapers leaped on the phrase. Schwimmer, having a clearer sense of the ridicule appropriate to such an impossibility, was said to have fainted when she heard it. After that phrase the "Peace Ship" had not the slightest chance for serious credence. It was natural enough that the editorial writers, humorists, cartoonists, and columnists should make Roman holiday; what they had to work on scarcely needed exaggeration—the facts of the succeeding days were sufficiently entertaining to sustain any extravagance of newspaper jeering.

Ford had himself introduced to the group of shipping agents as "Mr. Henry." After they had amply shown they thought a man crazy who wanted to charter a whole steamship, he relished their delighted surprise at finding the demented one was a man amply able to charter a ship, or a fleet. Ford ordered the *Oscar II* of the Scandinavian Line for December 4. Then he summoned a corps of stenographers from the Long Island branch of his company, settled them at the Biltmore, and proceeded to send out invitations for the trip. Among others asked were all senators and congressmen, all state governors, and a student-delegate from each university. The sole governor to accept was the one of North Dakota, and since he confessed he was an advocate of military preparedness, one presumes he went for the ride. Ex-Congressman Bartholdt of the German section of St. Louis, likewise unique, accepted the invitation and then withdrew on being told that

Ford was pro-Ally. Margaret Wilson, the president's daughter, sent regrets. Jane Addams pleaded illness. David Starr Jordan declined. William Jennings Bryan, who had recently resigned as Wilson's secretary of state in protest against what he saw as a pro-Ally tilt in the administration, said he could be of greater use remaining at home to oppose large increases in preparedness expenditure.

Ford, seeking official sanction, went to Washington, met Wilson, told him a Ford joke, and came away in a huff because Wilson declined to give countenance to the expedition. A cablegram to Rome asked the blessing of the Pope; that it was addressed to "Pope Pius VII," who had died in 983, is an index of the confusion that reigned in the Biltmore suite.

If the invited guests showed no hurry in accepting, volunteers and miscellaneous gate-crashers were innumerable. Ford and his peace secretaries were besieged night and day. The president of the Anti-Smoking League considered his theories had a bearing on the problem and demanded passage. An engaged couple with a romantic wish to be married at sea were hopeful that the *Oscar II* would provide the opportunity. A woman was enraged that she, who had "torn ten thousand bandages for the Belgians," had not been invited. The author of the song "I Didn't Raise My Boy to Be a Soldier" was hurt when he found himself outside the list. The Biltmore suite was jammed with star-eyed enthusiasts, as well as cranks, fanatics, butters-in, and joyriders of all sorts. In the shuffle genuine delegates got mislaid, lost their heads and tempers. So great was the turmoil it was difficult to make out order or purpose.

V

But the scurry and flurry of preparation was mild comedy in comparison with the sailing of the *Oscar II* from Hoboken on the afternoon of December 4, 1915. Fifty-four newspaper and magazine correspondents, three newsreel men, Ford's personal staff of twenty, and sixty-odd delegates (the number is even yet indeterminate) had to be winnowed from a crowd which blackened the ship and the pier. The captain swore he would sail by two, passengers or no passengers; as he watched the proceedings he swore harder. It was a carnival, in the slang of the day "a scream." A German band alternated with several other providers of musical well-wishing. A young Jewish man stood in the bows and bantered the crowd in Yiddish. The Reverend Dr. Jenkin Lloyd Jones of Chicago offered prayer from the rail amid hoots and yells at his splendid white beard. Bryan came sailing through the mob in his wide hat, to be greeted with cheers.

Presently the tumult died down a little as Thomas Edison, acutely embarrassed, pushed toward the ship—followed by a man in a derby hat and a fur-trimmed coat, on whose "colorless face . . . there was drawn tight the smile of a sick man who didn't quite know what to do about something, but who surrendered himself to the thing he was caught up in," an eyewitness later recalled. It was the proprietor of the show. An actor, Lloyd Bingham,

The Scandinavian liner Oscar II, *better known as the "Peace Ship." (International News Photograph)*

in beret and Windsor tie, waited until Ford stood beside him at the rail, and then led "three cheers for Henry." The noise broke out redoubled. Some one shouted: "Why don't you start?" Bingham called back: "You know it's a Ford!"

An hour late, amid a din of steam whistles, yelling and cheering, and the fanfare of bands, the *Oscar II* drew up the gangplank and got under way. Someone on board threw roses to the crowd. On the dock, Bryan sat precariously on the end of a pile and shouted his blessing. A man jumped into the water and tried to swim after the ship, only to be picked up by a tug; he was a spectacular welfare worker of the time who called himself "Mr. Zero." The Peace Ship headed down the Narrows, bearing Ford; Schwimmer; Samuel S. McClure, the magazine publisher; Ben B. Lindsey, judge of the Denver Juvenile Court and energetic participant in all good causes—he allowed no progressive parade to pass without getting on the bandwagon; Helen Ring Robinson of Colorado, the first woman state senator; Inez Milholland, known as a militant suffragist and a beautiful woman; the Reverend Dr. Jones, the Reverend Dr. Charles F. Aked of San Francisco, and other "consecrated spirits," engaged in the greatest mission ever before a nation—thus the delegates were described in Ford's letter of invitation. It may or may not have been that in Ford's estimate all the delegates fitted that ecstatic description. In the eyes of the newspapermen, some at least of the delegates were of a sort that caused them to speak of the *Oscar II* as the greatest squirrel cage in history—it contained so many "nuts." There were

As part of the fierce satirizing of Ford's Peace Ship, the "comic strip" figures "Mutt and Jeff" were represented daily as taking part in Ford's attempt to bring about peace. (Fisher in the San Francisco Chronicle)

two vicarious passengers—"Mutt and Jeff" went along; Bud Fisher, the car-toonist, sketched them as peace delegates every day in the comic strip that was printed in hundreds of newspapers.

VI

The trip was a disaster. The delegates bickered among themselves, and the belligerent governments would have nothing to do with them. Ford came down with a cold in Norway and, without announcing it, left for home the day before Christmas (when the boys were to have been "out of the trenches").

Back within the comfortable cordon of the Ford Motor Company, he was asked what he had really got out of the peace expedition. "I didn't get much peace," he replied. "I learned," he added, "that Russia is going to be a great market for tractors."

As respects the belligerent governments, the sum and essence of their views was that Ford was an excellent manufacturer of automobiles.

The Ford Peace Expedition had one serious result, directly counter to the purpose with which it started. After its failure, dying down to an echo of gigantic and exhausted laughter, it deprived every other peace move-ment in the country of force and conviction. The dove of peace had gone forth a Ford and come back a flivver—flivver and peace movement were one, it appeared. It put pacifists on the defensive against a weapon more deadly to them than guns—laughter.

CHAPTER 6

Preparedness

In the movement for preparedness the outstanding spokesman was the one man who shared Wilson's elevation in American national life, ex-President Theodore Roosevelt.

For Roosevelt, the war brought revival, not a "come-back" in the colloquial sense, but emergence in a new role which included some of the qualities of an Old Testament prophet, a minatory one, thundering reproof and warning, an Ezekiel. His new emergence started from what was perhaps the deepest depth of Roosevelt's mature career. After trying unsuccessfully against Taft for the Republican presidential nomination in 1912, Roosevelt had organized the Progressive Party. When both the Progressives and the Republicans lost to Wilson, Roosevelt was under guilt of having split the Republican Party and could hardly hope ever to be taken back by its embittered leaders and members. At the same time he knew, though not all the Progressives shared his expertly sure judgment, that he had not succeeded in creating a new party. He had received many votes, much more than the Republican Taft, and he had carried many states. But it was Roosevelt who had carried them, not the Progressive Party. Roosevelt knew this and would gladly have had it otherwise. The test was that only a tiny handful of Progressive candidates had been elected to the Senate or House, or to governorships or other offices. There was no real Progressive Party, there was only Roosevelt as a magnetic individual. He was unhappy, miserable. He had no party; he could hardly hope ever again to get a nomination for the presidency—and in 1914 he was only fifty-six.

Throughout Roosevelt's exile from politics and to some extent from popular favor, his sorrow's crown of sorrow was that by the same act which had brought him down, he had contributed to placing in the White House a man whose conduct of the office distressed Roosevelt utterly. His distaste for Wilson as president was shared to one degree or another by the Republicans and most of his own Progressive following. So long, however, as Wilson's actions had to do only with domestic matters, the common dislike of him was not sufficient to overcome the dislike of Republicans and Progressives for each other. But when the war came, and after Wilson's attitude toward it developed, there arose among Republicans and Progressives a sense of need for common leadership in opposition and criticism of the administration. Roosevelt's was the obvious voice to rally to. Reconciliation came about. Roosevelt and Taft embraced, publicly. The reconciliation,

Wilson's attitude toward the war and preparedness led to this cartoon advising Uncle Sam to watch his step. (Marcus in the New York Times*)*

however, had not progressed far enough in 1916 to bring the Republicans to consider nominating Roosevelt for the presidency; but after another defeat of the Republicans in that year, after realization that Wilson would have another four years in the White House, Republicans and Progressives, everyone opposed to Wilson's policies and actions turned toward Roosevelt as spokesman.

In the very early months of the war, Roosevelt had shared the common impulse toward neutrality. But in proportion as it was our duty and self-interest to be neutral, so was it the more important we should be able to defend and enforce our neutrality. "When giants are engaged in a death wrestle," he wrote prophetically three weeks after the war began, "as they reel to and fro they are certain to trample on whomever gets in the way." The war was to Roosevelt, therefore, argument for his lifelong policy of a strong army and navy. Powerfully he pleaded for preparedness. In time his advocacy of preparedness merged into advocacy of our entering the war on the side of the Allies. In behalf of the double cause Roosevelt carried on against Wilson a crusade that ranged through invective, irony, and loftily solemn warning and appeal.

Because Roosevelt was Wilson's rival, had run against him for the presidency and been defeated, he was subject to the charge that his advocacy of preparedness, his attacks on Wilson on all counts, were political in motive. That charge served Wilson and the Democrats as a partial protection against Roosevelt's thunderings. It is true that Roosevelt, after he had been in the White House, found it hard to endure seeing another man there, any other man, especially one who, he felt, was filling the office less capably than he himself could have done—and Roosevelt would have felt that way about almost any president.

The force of Roosevelt's attacks on Wilson was further diminished by the public's recent memory of his similar attacks on Taft. Many, who recalled and resented the fulminations against Taft some five years before, charged that Roosevelt's present attacks on Wilson put him in the category of an habitual scold. He had lost the conservatives among his following by the radicalism of his 1912 proposals; later he had seen some of his Progressive following drift away to Wilson because of Wilson's domestic policies.* Consequently, Roosevelt, in the early part of his campaign for preparedness, had but little following, and it included some whose adherence did his cause little good. The sum of all was that Roosevelt began his crusade for preparedness from an unfortunate start and under great handicaps.

Wilson knew all this, and because he knew, felt the safer. Wilson ignored Roosevelt. Wilson knew not only how to be subtle with words but how to be subtle with silence. His attitude toward Roosevelt's attacks was one of seeming not to know the attacks or the man existed. Once Wilson said to a friend, "The way to treat an adversary like Roosevelt is to gaze at the stars over his head."

But in truth never was Roosevelt more earnest, more deeply stirred about a cause. His crusade satisfied two passions, his belief in preparedness and his detestation of Wilson.

Roosevelt's hatred of Wilson was not political—certainly not political merely. Roosevelt would have disliked Wilson personally had he never had any controversy with him politically. In practically every detail of temperament and personality, as well as in conceptions about conduct of the coun-

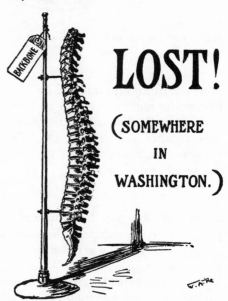

The demand that Wilson accept preparedness was expressed in violent cartoons. (Rogers in the New York Herald)

try's affairs, Wilson was as near the antithesis of Roosevelt as one man can be of another.

Publicly, Roosevelt's denunciation of Wilson was hardly less mordant than in his private letters and conversations, though in his public writings and addresses he put his condemnation not so much on the ground of Wil-

*Note Sullivan's reluctance to acknowledge Wilson's own brand of Progressivism as in any way comparable to Roosevelt's. —D.R.

son's personal traits as on the public issues involved. Mainly these were at all times preparedness and, as our relations with Germany grew more tense, demand that Wilson should make war.

In these public attacks, personal dislike or political motive played little part. Roosevelt was solemnly sure that Wilson was leading the United States, and later the world, in a direction that must end in disillusion and tragedy. Of all the axioms of personal and national conduct that Roosevelt held to be imperative, perhaps the basic one was that neither a man nor a nation should ever hold out words, whether of promise or of threat, unless it is certain the words both can be and will be translated into action—some early experience or other must have taught Roosevelt that as an ineradicable lesson; he came back to it in a thousand conversations, speeches, and public writings. And a deep trait of prophetic understanding told Roosevelt that Wilson, especially after he began to advocate the "concert of powers" which was the embryo of the League of Nations, was holding up before the world ideals which could not be fulfilled, and which therefore must bring disappointment and bitterness. On this count, "elocution not backed by deeds," and on a score of other indictments, Roosevelt thundered against Wilson in speeches, public statements, articles in the *Outlook*, the *Metropolitan Magazine*, the *Kansas City Star*, with a solemnity and earnestness which, in spite of the occasional caustic harshness, achieved a kind of grandeur and set Roosevelt on a height among the public men of his time.

II

The military strength of the United States on the day the Great War broke out consisted of:

	Officers	Men
Regular Army	3,441	77,363
Organized Militia	8,323	119,087
Totals	11,764	196,450

And that was absolutely all. Indeed, that is much more than all. To consider the Organized Militia, improperly styled the National Guard, as effective "military strength" was to assume they would all respond to a call to arms, "in other words, upon a miracle." It involved an assumption that such of the Organized Militia as should take arms would be, at once, effective soldiers. Effective soldiers! All the training required of such militia—required but not always enforced—consisted of twenty-four drills a year, including a summer camp.

Not only that. The 80,804 officers and men authorized for the Regular Army were not all effective "military strength" in the sense of being available to defend the United States or act as a mobile army. Nearly half were in, and were needed in, the Philippines, Hawaii, Panama Canal Zone,

Puerto Rico, China, and Alaska. The total of regular troops within the United States was 2,577 officers and 50,445 men. Of these, in turn, nearly half were needed to man the Coast Artillery defenses. The total "mobile army" in the United States was 24,602—smaller than at any time since the Civil War.

It was a good little army. British and German military attachés said they "had never seen a finer body of troops, superior discipline, less intoxication, or such perfect sanitary arrangements in camps." But it was very small. The regiments were almost skeletons, scarcely more than half their war strength—a company of infantry, which should have a war strength of 150, had 65; a troop of cavalry had 71, as against a war strength of 100; a battery of artillery, 133, as against 190.

III

In the organized movement for preparedness the man of action was General Leonard Wood. By far the outstanding figure in the army, Wood had had a brilliant career, had filled the army's most responsible posts—in Cuba as military governor, in Washington as chief of staff, in the Philippines as governor-general. Before the country his standing depended only slightly on his army record; in any career Wood's force of personality would have given him the position he had as a leading figure of his generation.

From the opening day of the war in Europe, Wood believed that we should be drawn in, felt we "could not avert it by good intentions, nor pro-

Leonard Wood.

A cartoon which, putting Roosevelt's criticism of the Wilson administration into a form easy for anyone to understand, cast ridicule on Wilson's early opposition to preparedness. (Wilson in Seattle Post Intelligencer)

tect ourselves by exhortation." Moved by that feeling, he made speeches, gave interviews, inspired books and magazine articles, talked at public and private dinners.

Presently, success of Wood and others, and resulting public uneasiness about the small size of our army, brought frowning attention from President Wilson, who, in his message to Congress in December 1914, declared: "We shall not alter our attitude toward the question of national defense because some amongst us are nervous and excited. . . ." Difference between the commander-in-chief of the army, and the best-known soldier in the army, about national military policy, was a serious matter. Eager pacifists told Wilson he should take disciplinary notice. Because, in the preparedness campaign, Wood was backed up by Theodore Roosevelt, and because both were old friends and Republicans, Wood's differences with the administration could be charged by the suspicious with having partisan implications. It was on this ground, partially, that Secretary of War Garrison put his tactful rebuke: "It would be wise for Wood, for the present, to decline all public expression."

Wood abated little of his activity, kept up his speechmaking to universities, chambers of commerce, any gathering that was appropriate. Prepared-

Richard Harding Davis (left) at Plattsburg. (© Underwood & Underwood)

ness organizations sprang up. One university after another adopted military training. Samuel Gompers conferred with Wood about a summer training camp for labor. Wood became patron saint, guide, and inspiration of the National Security League, the American Defense Society, and the American Legion, Inc.* The American Legion, Inc., inspired by Wood and endorsed by Theodore Roosevelt, proposed to establish an unofficial reserve enrolling men of military age who had had military training or possessed peculiar qualifications which might be turned to use in case of war—automobile drivers, telegraph and telephone operators, bridge builders, mechanics of all sorts; in time of peace a list, and nothing more; in time of war a source not impossibly of 300,000 or 400,000 volunteers.

Commotion arose. Suspicion continued on the part of the administra-

---

*Not to be confused with the later "American Legion," composed of veterans of the Great War, founded in Paris, March 1919.

tion that the activities of Wood and Roosevelt were political. Wood was called on the carpet, was ordered to evict American Legion, Inc., from the Army Building in New York. Secretary Garrison issued an order—addressed to all officers of the army, but well understood to mean Wood—forbidding the "giving out for publication any interview, statement, discussion or article on the military situation."

Wood, obeying the letter of the order by not "giving out" statements for publication, continued to disobey its spirit, flagrantly. He inspired a "business men's camp" for military training at Plattsburg, New York, at which a most incongruous group of some 1,200 men touched shoulders in "fours left," "fours right."

To Wood at the Plattsburg camp came a telegram from Roosevelt saying that Roosevelt would make a speech to the "rookies" and that "I request . . . that it be made out of camp, at a time when the men are not on duty," and "if possible the men should be in citizen's clothes." Wood, warned of brimstone, thought it prudent he should edit Roosevelt's speech in advance, and did. That evening, however, several hours after the speech, Roosevelt said to newspaper reporters the things which he had omitted from his speech, to the effect, chiefly, that "standing by the President" was a fetish that could be overworshiped. The country, right or wrong, yes; but not the president—let men stand by him when he was right, against him when he was wrong. "To treat elocution as a substitute for action," so Roosevelt's statement to the press concluded, "to rely upon high-sounding words unbacked by deeds, is proof of a mind that dwells only in the realm of shadow and of shame."

This denunciation Roosevelt supplemented with an improvised

A machine-gun squad at drill in a preparedness camp at Lansdowne, Pennsylvania. (International News Photograph)

metaphor, inspired by a friendly Airedale terrier which, feeling regret on bumping into Roosevelt, rolled over on his back, his paws ingratiatingly limp in the air. "That is a very nice dog," said Roosevelt in hearing of the reporters. "I like him—his present attitude is strictly one of neutrality."

Sensation in the newspapers. More commotion in Washington. The secretary of war, under impulsion from the White House, sent Wood a sharp rebuke: "There must not be any opportunity given at Plattsburg or any other similar camp for any such unfortunate consequences [as Roosevelt's statement]." Wood replied: "Your telegram received and the policies laid down will be strictly adhered to." Wood, frustrated, found momentary satisfaction in a cutting quip. When a newspaperman told him that the botanist Luther Burbank had announced himself as an opponent of all military preparedness, he became contemplative. "Isn't he the man who developed spineless cactus?"

One would like to say that the Plattsburg camp, and the other results of Wood's and Roosevelt's campaign, contributed as much to our military strength as they did to the zest of life in America during 1915 and 1916; but the training for five weeks of a few hundred men, many of them middle-aged, was but as a drop in the bucket to an army which, when war came, had to muster 4 million. As influence, however, as stimulus to sentiment for preparedness, the Plattsburg camps and the "Plattsburg idea" were important. They, with other influences, increased preparedness sentiment to a point where it was politically dangerous for Wilson to fail to take account of it.

The preparedness movement proved to be the swan song of Theodore

A class in field telegraphy at the Women's National Service School Camp near Washington, D.C., 1916. (© International News)

Roosevelt. When America entered the war, he desperately urged Wilson to let him lead a regiment. Wilson, remembering Roosevelt's attacks and doubting his military value, refused. Less than two months after the Armistice, having watched another president win the war, the Rough Rider was dead.

CHAPTER 7
Wilson Changes His Mind

P reparedness aimed directly toward war with Germany Wilson would not have—that would have interfered with his larger purpose of keeping the United States out of the conflict. But preparedness which seemed inspired by and appropriate to our difficulties with Mexico, now recurrent for some three years; or preparedness having the color of

Wilson's veering around to preparedness, after long opposing it, was pleasing to the public. The artist here pictures Uncle Sam in a smiling mood as Wilson starts to play the song now popular, "Johnny Get Your Gun." (Marcus in the New York Times*)*

precaution against the state of the world in general—that would not interfere with the program that had begun to crystallize in Wilson's mind. If a
considerable section of public opinion demanded a limited preparedness,
Wilson was tolerantly willing to go as far as seemed necessary to keep his
hold on the people—and also willing, one surmises, to regard himself as
the head of a political party, with a duty to keep his party in power by taking account of currents of popular emotion. Personally he did not like the
notion of a large military establishment, but if a formidable public opinion
favored preparedness, he could yield without impairing the project that
had become his chief aspiration.

By the meeting of Congress in December 1915, Wilson was willing to
go so far as to recommend an increase in the standing army to 141,843
rank and file, and a reserve force of 400,000 volunteers, to be built up by
giving two months' training a year for three years. "So much," Wilson said,
"by way of preparation for defense seems to me absolutely imperative
now." This was, on Wilson's part, a middle ground. The ardent preparedness leaders wanted to adopt General Wood's plan for universal, compul-
sory, military training of all young men between eighteen and twenty-two
for two months a year for four years. Congress, as it turned out, was unwilling to go even so far as Wilson advocated. At all times, until war actually came, the majority sentiment of Congress was against preparedness, or

At the time Wilson got around to accepting a policy of partial preparedness. (Webster in the
New York Globe)

reluctantly assented to a smaller preparedness than even Wilson thought desirable.

Wilson, to bring pressure on Congress, made a tour through the country. At the opening speech, New York, January 27, 1916, he was candid in announcing his change of step. He admitted that a year before he had told Congress that "this question of military preparedness was not a pressing question." "But," he went on, "more than a year has gone by since then and I would be ashamed if I had not learned something in fourteen months. The minute I stop changing my mind, with the change of all the circumstances of the world, I will be a back number."

On the tour, he spoke for preparedness, and as audiences cheered him increasingly, so did he talk with increasing force; by the time he reached St. Louis he advocated "a great navy second to none in the world." But never did he say anything that would compromise his inner and primary determination to avoid war with Germany. Always his plea for preparedness was coupled with an equally strong affirmation of determination to remain at peace. With his extraordinary skill in phrasing he carefully tied the two purposes into the same sentence: "This country should prepare herself, not for war . . . but for adequate national defense."

After the close of Wilson's preparedness tour, Roosevelt erupted:

> In the fourteen months from December 8, 1914, to February 10, 1916, there were fifteen messages, letters, and speeches of President Wilson's which I have read. In those fifteen messages, letters,

President Wilson speaking, from the rear of his train, on behalf of preparedness at Waukegan, Illinois, in February 1916. (International News Photograph)

and speeches President Wilson took 41 different positions about preparedness and the measures necessary to secure it; and each of these 41 positions contradicted from 1 to 6 of the others. In many of the speeches, the weasel words of one portion took all the meaning out of the words used in another portion, and those latter words themselves had a weasel significance as regards yet other words. He argued for preparedness and against preparedness.

If Roosevelt could not understand Wilson, the public did. Wilson knew the mass mind deals less with argument than with feeling. He was intent not on syllogistic argument but on making an impression. And the public got precisely the impression Wilson meant it should get.

It is true Wilson used words adroitly; no other statesman in the world had his skill. More than that, he used ideas adroitly. For his art he had much need. He was looking forward to an immense enterprise, and he was obliged to be always, as one writer said, "shifting his pace, like an expert boxer, to match the dexterity of the most cleverly adroit diplomats in Eu-

Too many cooks threaten to spoil the preparedness broth. Wilson, recently converted, still differs from Roosevelt, while Bryan, Congress, and Uncle Sam make diverse comments. (De Ball in the Chicago Post*)*

rope." Wilson knew, from his ambassadors and other agents abroad, the kaleidoscopic changes constantly taking place in the European situation, and was always adjusting himself to it. He had determined, when the right time should come, to take hold of it, dominate it, and bend it to an idealistic purpose he had conceived. To accomplish this purpose, it was desirable that America should not enter the war. And it was imperative, of course, that Wilson should still be president when the war should come toward an end. To be reelected in 1916, it was expedient that he should guardedly endorse preparedness, and otherwise take account of the varied and shifting currents of feeling in America. He was obliged to be for preparedness and also against going to war. He was obliged to be for preparedness far enough to avoid wholly alienating the moderate believers in preparedness, but not far enough to alienate those who feared preparedness might take us into the war. To manage all that took some art with words, but by no means so much as Wilson possessed. To Wilson it was easy. He was destined to have occasion, before the war ended, to show what he could really do with words.

Meanwhile, it was imperative he be reelected.

II

Wilson ran in 1916 under the slogan "He kept us out of war." As campaign strategy, it was superb. It placed Charles Evans Hughes and the Republicans in a dilemma and kept them there. But in doing that Wilson, one observer remarked, "unquestionably promised the nation there would be no war. While he did not expressly pledge it, his words are open to no other interpretation, and the election was clearly won on that issue." Wilson, it is not too much to say, by implication, committed himself to a promise, a literal contract: Elect me and you will be kept out of war.

He was elected, very narrowly. Election night he went to bed believing he had lost. The doubt lasted three days. The electoral score was, Wilson 277, Hughes 254.

III

Secure in the presidency for another four years, Wilson was now able to proceed with his plan. He had just married a new wife. Personal ambition coincided with the spirit of high adventure in idealism.

There had developed in America, even before the Great War broke out (during the period of militance for peace that had been part of the atmosphere of the Progressive movement), a plan for avoiding all wars called "The League to Enforce Peace." A parallel suggestion had arisen in Europe. This nebulous idea Wilson now took hold of, made it his own, expanded it.

Wilson's plan contemplated that he should act as a peacemaker, not only

President Wilson's reelection promised the continuation of the hum of industry. (Godwin in the Pittsburgh Dispatch)

as peacemaker to end this war but as a super-peacemaker—he would use this war as a war to end all wars, by setting up an organization, a concert of powers (it later came to be called the League of Nations).

On January 22, Wilson appeared unexpectedly and dramatically before the Senate with an address meant more for the belligerents in Europe than for the Senate—and not only for the belligerents but for the world. He was acting, he said, "on behalf of humanity."

Speaking "for the silent masses of mankind everywhere," he adopted the manner of an outsider addressing, rather imperatively, the two sets of belligerents who were making the world a miserable place to live. To the belligerents, he had the air of saying that this fighting must stop. But, he said, it should stop in a particular way. It must end in a "peace without victory." He admitted "it is not pleasant to say this." But "victory would mean peace

Much of the comment stirred up by Wilson's proposal of "Peace Without Victory" was ironic and resentful. (Nelson Harding in the Brooklyn Daily Eagle*)*

forced upon the loser, a victor's terms imposed upon the vanquished." Such a peace "would be accepted in humiliation, under duress"; it "would leave a sting, a bitter memory"; it would "rest upon a quicksand." Therefore, Wilson proposed that the peace should be one "without victory," for "only a peace between equals can last."

If the belligerents were willing to come to this kind of peace, he said, the United States would participate in the making of it. Therefore, he proposed, in order to make the peace permanent and universal, there should be a "definite concert of powers which will make it virtually impossible that any such catastrophe should ever overwhelm us again." In this permanent concert of powers, if created along lines Wilson laid down, the United States would be willing to participate—"it is inconceivable that the United States should play no part in that great enterprise." The United States, he asserted (with what later proved to be too much confidence) would "add their authority and their power to the authority and force of other nations to guarantee peace and justice throughout the world."

IV

Eight days after Wilson had startled the world with his peace address to the Senate, while the contrapuntal discord of plaudit and execration was still crescendo, German Ambassador von Bernstorff, on January 31, 1917, delivered to the State Department, and the State Department delivered to Wilson, a note from Germany. Germany would begin, on February 1, absolutely unrestricted submarine warfare: "All sea traffic will be stopped with every available weapon and without further notice."

The German note announced that Germany "has so far not made unrestricted use of the weapon she possesses in her submarines," but that now she proposes to use them to "the full." She would now "forcibly prevent" any vessel of the United States (or of any other nation) from going to England except—and the exception was what made the announcement peculiarly intolerable, it would have been less offensive had the embargo been absolute: The United States would be permitted to send one passenger vessel once each week to England under very restrictive conditions.

Wilson was utterly shocked. As he read the German declaration, the

The Kaiser presents Uncle Sam with a pass good for one trip of one ship per week to England. (Rogers in the New York Herald)

flight of swift emotions across his features was observed by his secretary, Joseph Tumulty—"first blank amazement, then incredulity, then gravity and sternness, a sudden greyness of color . . ."

All that, Wilson had supposed, was safely behind him. Nine months before by a triumph in diplomatic dialects he had maneuvered Germany, after the *Lusitania* sinking, into agreeing not to sink except in accord with international law; for nine months, there had been no unlawful sinking. That condition, suspension of unlawful sinkings, was essential to Wilson's plan to make peace as a neutral. The situation in which he had been proceeding to enforce peace as a neutral dictating to both belligerents was now shattered.

V

A president may be sad, depressed; but inexorable time, imperious events, will not wait for the mood to lift. Saturday, February 3, was the regular day for cabinet meetings. The members came realizing "that we might be facing the most momentous issue in our experience and in the history of the nation." As Wilson entered, his manner, the droop of his shoulders, the tired flatness of his voice as he spoke to them, caused the

Colonel House and President Wilson during the period of their great intimacy. The mourning band on Wilson's sleeve is for his first wife. (Photograph by Underwood & Underwood)

Wilson's cabinet at the time America entered the war. Rear row left to right, Secretary of the Navy Daniels, Secretary of Labor Wilson, Secretary of War Baker, Attorney General Gregory, Secretary of the Interior Lane. Front row left to right, Secretary of Commerce Redfield, Secretary of State Lansing, Secretary of Agriculture Houston, President Wilson, Secretary of the Treasury McAdoo, Postmaster General Burleson. (© Harris & Ewing)

more sensitive to look at him closely. His opening remark was startling. He asked what should be done—"Shall I break off diplomatic relations with Germany?"

The following day, Wilson went before Congress:

> I think you will agree with me that this government has no alternative consistent with the dignity and honor of the United States. . . . I have therefore directed the Secretary of State to announce to his Excellency the German Ambassador, that all diplomatic relations between the United States and the German Empire are severed and to hand to His Excellency his passports.

Wilson's address to Congress was at two in the afternoon. Within a few minutes afterward, passports and note of dismissal were handed to Von Bernstorff. The German consuls scattered over the United States and their families were summoned to Washington and, on February 14, the ambassador and his party, 149 persons, sailed from New York on a Danish vessel.

*   *   *

February 26, Wilson again went before Congress. He was not, he said, "proposing or contemplating war or any steps that may lead to war." He was merely requesting that Congress give him "the means and authority to safeguard in practice the rights of a great people, to supply our merchant ships with defensive arms should that become necessary, and with the means of using them, and to employ any other instrumentalities or methods" necessary to protect our ships and people in their rightful pursuits on the sea.

In response to Wilson's request a bill was at once introduced authorizing the president to supply arms, ammunition, and the means of using them to American merchant ships, and to appropriate for the purpose $100 million. Congress proceeded, somewhat leisurely, to debate the measure. There was real opposition. Sentiment against going to war, or doing what might precipitate war, was still strong. There was doubt whether Congress would give Wilson the authority to arm merchant ships.

VI

On February 24, Wilson, still not sure he could carry Congress and the country into war—indeed, on the contrary, he was quite doubtful whether he could get from Congress even authorization to arm merchant vessels—received a message from Ambassador Page in London. Page said that the British Secret Service had intercepted and decoded a message sent

Sinking of U.S.S. President Lincoln. *She was one of the two vessels of the cruiser and transport service to be sunk by submarines. All but twenty-six aboard her were saved. (From painting by Marshall, May 31, 1917. Courtesy of the Navy Department)*

by an under secretary of the German Ministry of Foreign Affairs, Alfred Zimmermann, to the German minister to Mexico. The message read:

> We intend to begin on the first of February unrestricted subma-
> rine warfare. We shall endeavor in spite of this to keep the United
> States of America neutral. In the event of this not succeeding, we
> make Mexico a proposal of alliance on the following basis: make
> war together, make peace together, generous financial support and
> an understanding on our part that Mexico is to reconquer her lost
> territory in Texas, New Mexico, and Arizona. The settlement in
> detail is left to you. You will inform the President [that is, President
> Carranza of Mexico] of the above most secretly as soon as the out-
> break of war with the United States of America is certain.

To Wilson, as to everyone else when it became public, this instruction by the German government to its ambassador in Mexico seemed so fantastic as to justify suspicion that it might be a hoax. Certainly it was likely that the public would think it must be a hoax. The State Department spent several days verifying the message and getting the original German text.

Thus buttressed, Wilson, on February 28, permitted the Associated Press to print the message. The Senate, astounded, passed a resolution asking the president if the message as published in the newspapers was correct. The president, through the secretary of state, replied: "I have the honor to state that the government is in possession of evidence which establishes that the note referred to is authentic." Next day came further verification in the shape of an admission volunteered by Zimmermann, that he had sent the note. Naively, Zimmermann emphasized that "the instructions were only to be carried out after declaration of war by America"—an explanation doing more credit to Zimmermann's legalism and morals than to his intelligence.

Stimulated by the Zimmermann note, the House passed by a vote of 403 to 13 the bill for arming merchant ships. In the Senate, opposition was kept up by eleven senators, led by LaFollette. With the end of the session three days away, they filibustered. (They had the double motive of wanting an extra session and of opposition to the armed ship resolution.)

In a way, the incident was a godsend to Wilson, giving him opportunity for an emotional catharsis. The anger he was

Germany promising Texas to Mexico. (Cassel in the New York Evening World. © *Press Publishing Co.)*

Senator Stone of Missouri surrounded by newspapermen following a conference on the bill for arming American merchant ships. (Photograph by International News)

not yet ready to express fully against Germany he poured out on the eleven recalcitrant senators, inventing a phrase that became famous, "a little group of willful men":

> In the immediate presence of a crisis unparalleled in the history of the country, . . . Congress has been unable to act either to safeguard the country or to vindicate the elementary rights of its citizens. More than 500 of the 531 members of the two Houses were ready and anxious to act. But the Senate was unable to act because a little group of willful men, representing no opinion but their own, had determined that it should not. [They] have rendered the great government of the United States helpless and contemptible.*

The session adjourned with the armed ship resolution not yet passed. But Wilson had seen that Congress and the country favored the proposal. He asked the attorney general whether he had power to arm merchant ships without specific authorization by Congress. The attorney general—

---

*The incident, and Wilson's angry denunciation, had one important effect. Under the pressure of public opinion, on March 8, 1917, the Senate, which never in the whole course of its existence had laid any restraint on the length of debate, adopted a rule providing that whenever two-thirds of the Senate wish a measure brought to a vote, they may so express themselves, and thereafter each senator may debate the measure not more than one hour. Thus cloture, of a very limited sort, came to the Senate.

an office which usually finds it legal for a president to do what a president wants to do—told Wilson he had the power. Wilson directed that guns and gunners be placed on merchant ships, and an announcement was made on March 9 that this would be done.

VII

By about this time, early March 1917, Wilson was clear-minded again and confident, knew once more what he wanted to do. His distraction over receiving Germany's announcement of unrestricted submarine warfare had not been timorousness—there was nothing of that in Wilson. His depression and nervousness had been due to the utter disruption of his plan to enter the situation as a neutral and from that vantage point press down upon the belligerents—not only the belligerents but the world —the kind of peace he had planned. Prospect of going to war, as such, disturbed him some. But taking up the role of belligerent put him out of the role he had formerly conceived for himself. Since he must fight at all he must fight on to victory. That meant there could not now be the "peace without victory" which had been fundamental in his plan. That mishap to his grandiose plan was the sufficient cause of his distraction and hesitancy throughout February 1917.

That, and one other cause. Wilson must now modify his plan fundamentally. That is, he must perforce modify his role of neutral, though not his plan. Abandonment of his plan he never considered. But change his own role he must. He must now be a belligerent against Germany, and in that role must work out the achievement of his plan. The situation involved considerable adjustment within his own mind, and that adjustment, the gestation of his modified plan, was a contributing cause of his February of distraction.

In the modification forced upon him, he must now: (*a*) Take America into the war— and that was not easy, though Wilson had no doubt he could do it; (*b*) in cooperation with the Allies, crush Germany's arms—he had no doubt about that either (though he might have if he had had at this time the information he later received about the success of submarine sinkings); and (*c*) make peace and set up a League of Nations according to his original plan.

Fighting Germany was the new factor. To that, how best to do it, how best to fight Germany and beat Germany thoroughly but at the same time impair himself least for his role at the peace table—upon these and collateral considerations, Wilson now bent his powerful and flexible mind.

CHAPTER 8

War

On March 9, 1917, Wilson, with his plan clear in his mind once more, his vigor renewed, summoned a special session of Congress to meet April 16.

A few days later came news of an overt act by Germany. Three overt acts. Three American vessels—American built, American manned, American owned—the *City of Memphis,* the *Illinois,* and the *Vigilancia* were sunk by U-boats. Dramatically, Wilson advanced by two weeks the special session of Congress; it would meet, he now announced, April 2, "to receive a communication concerning grave matters."

II

To every person present, from members of the cabinet and Justices of the Supreme Court in the front row, to observers in the remote seats in the gallery, that evening was the most-to-be-remembered of their lives. Years later Secretary of the Treasury William G. McAdoo, with a touch of poetry moving even his active and practical mind, recalled, as a detail that stood out in his memory, "the pouring rain, a soft fragrant rain of early spring; the illuminated dome of the Capitol stood in solemn splendor against the dark wet sky."

Wilson was more than the master dialectician of the age. His command of ideas and the expression of ideas, his exercise of them in the speech he now delivered, made him the master strategist of the war.

What had caused Wilson's speech of two months before (to the Senate proposing to dictate peace to both belligerents and set up a League of Nations) to be de-

President Wilson delivering his war message to Congress, April 2, 1917. (Photograph by Underwood & Underwood)

scribed in superlatives was mainly the sensational quality of his proposal, the audacity of it. The speech he now made, calling on Congress to declare war against Germany, better deserved the superlatives. It was great in many ways, had several different arts compressed into it; was obliged to include several different purposes, including the not too easy task of taking America into the war, which involved persuading or otherwise moving an only half-willing Congress and country. The speech contained many phrases destined to become historic: "vessels ruthlessly sent to the bottom without warning and without thought of help or mercy for those on board" . . . "reckless lack of compassion or of principle" . . . "It is a war against all nations" . . . "The challenge is to all mankind" . . . "the rights and liberties of small nations" . . . "The world must be made safe for democracy."

The outstanding quality of Wilson's war speech was a new and subtle feature of his plan as a whole, which he now injected.

He would, as a master detail of strategy, military no less than dialectic, drive a wedge between the German government and the German people. Actually he would, though adroitly yet no less forcefully—and, as it turned out, successfully—solicit the German people and German army to turn against their government. Holding out amity toward the German people (as distinguished from their government) would at once help Wilson win

New York   **Tribune**

First to Last — the Truth: News · Editorials · Advertisements

| 7,706 | [Copyright 1917— The Tribune Ass'n.] | TUESDAY, APRIL 3, 1917 |

The President Calls for War Without Hate

the war and later cause the demoralized Germany, which Wilson envisaged, to be sympathetic to his plan for a League of Nations.

It was, as an agency for victory and for Wilson's larger purpose, superb strategy; from the point of view of the enemy it was outrageous, the sort of thing that often caused Wilson's adversaries in politics, national or college, to charge him with polemic deviltry.

In his speech, in his very first allusion, he spoke of the enemy he was about to fight as "the Government of the German Empire." America's purpose would be "to bring the Government of the German Empire to terms and"—here, as the concluding clause of his sentence, he used words which he knew would sound well to the war-sick part of the German population—"and end the war."

Having dropped this verbal depth-bomb he receded, dealt for several paragraphs with other matters. With little dialectic forays he came back from time to time to his subtle purpose, dropped phrases like "Prussian autocracy," "dynasties," "rulers," "autocratic governments." What he proposed to fight against was "autocratic governments backed by organized force which is controlled wholly by their will, not by the will of their people."

In due course he became explicit, drove the wedge like a military tank between Kaiser and people, held out the olive branch in plain sight before the German people:

> We have no quarrel with the German people. We have no feeling towards them but one of sympathy and friendship. It was not upon their impulse that their government acted in entering this war. . . . [The war was] provoked and waged in the interest of dynasties accustomed to use their fellow men as pawns and tools. . . . We are, let me say again, the sincere friends of the German people.

Holding out concrete assurance, he told the German people that, "We seek no indemnities . . . no material compensation; we desire no conquest, no dominion. We have no selfish ends to serve. . . ."

Finally, with magnificent combination of subtlety and audacity, he held out solicitation to the German people to turn from the Kaiser to Wilson himself, no less! Alluding to his major purpose, a League of Nations, a "concert for peace," the "ultimate peace of the world," he promised "the liberation of [all] peoples, the German peoples included."

But the masterpiece of Wilsonian art lay quite unnoticed in the concluding four words of his speech. Departing from overt allusion to Germany, dealing with the decision America must make, the path America must fol-

Wilson forging the sword with which he was going to do battle. (Morris, in Puck)

low, he built up an eloquent, moving peroration, ending: "God helping her, she can do no other."

Probably not one of a hundred of his American hearers recognized that paraphrase of Martin Luther's declaration, immortal to every German Lutheran, "Ich kann nicht anders" (I can do no other). And Germans, in America as well as Germany, who felt the sentimental pull of it, did not recognize the Wilsonian art of it.

Against hostile armies, Germany had prepared well; soldier for soldier she was at all times superior. She was now to face a foe who fought with ideas. Ideas more dynamically explosive, more subversive to the German military machine than all the shells the Allies ever fired.

III

Vaguely, but as yet only vaguely, America realized that war on Germany involved something more grim than the thrill of hearing the declaration. Somebody must fight the war. A number of young men would be glad

Americans living in Paris, in the early days of the war, organized a volunteer regiment to fight with the French. The photograph shows recruits off to camp. (Photograph by Underwood & Underwood)

to—about the proportion that in any war would volunteer, the adventurous, the romantic, those who found their ordinary life dull, those having associations they would be glad to get away from, those without jobs, those who preferred the routine of military life above the self-responsibility of civil life—in any country in any time there is always a ratio who will volunteer in any war. In America at this time the proportion to volunteer would be smaller than normal, for nearly three years of watching the western front had brought realization that war under modern conditions meant hardship, dirt, and death, and very little glamour or romance. As for economic motive, there was none; every man in America who wanted a job could have one, and at high wages—America was furiously busy turning out munitions for the Allies. Moreover, of those who would normally volunteer, a considerable proportion had already gone forward. A few, the most dashing, had gone early in the war to Canada, and managed to get into the fighting. Many had enlisted in our own regular army or navy or national guard in the moderate expansion which Congress had authorized at Wilson's request a year before. Those volunteer enlistments had been slow. It was not likely that a call for volunteers to fight Germany would bring numbers adequate for this major war. There must be conscription, but art would be needed to lead the country to accept it, an art with which both President Wilson and Secretary of War Newton D. Baker were exceptionally endowed.

*   *   *

The fact that an attempt at a draft during the Civil War had led to riots in New York caused Secretary of War Baker and President Wilson and the army heads to be apprehensive and to be careful in the methods they used to bring about conscription for the Great War. (Leslie's Weekly)

The 1917 draft begins. Men waiting to register in downtown New York. Our Allies in the war were astonished at the speed and orderliness with which America's draft army was raised.

General Enoch H. Crowder. (© Underwood & Underwood)

Wilson personally did not like conscription; he preferred the spirit of volunteering. In his early discussions of preparedness he had emphasized the volunteer system and his faith in it. He also knew that America as a whole did not like conscription—indeed, it never occurred to the masses of the country that conscription would be attempted. Conscription, in the American mind, was associated with autocracy. Never in any war of ours had conscription been suggested at the outset; only once had it been tried at all, and when, after two years of the Civil War, an attempt had been made to draft, rioting mobs in New York had sacked the provost marshal's office, burned and smashed the wheels and lists and the other paraphernalia for taking Americans to war against their wills. In this war, not only would there be the usual American repugnance, but 13 percent of our people were of German birth or descent, and a considerable percentage more were of peoples embraced in the Austrian Empire. In the war in Europe so far, the precedent we most respected had been against conscription—Britain had relied on volunteers for the first eighteen months, her government unwilling or afraid to attempt conscription.

   All this Wilson knew. But Germany had flouted him and America; he had a high purpose in which, since Germany had forced him to it, crushing German arms was now the first and indispensable step. Wilson could be hard; "like most reformers," said Dr. Charles W. Eliot, "Wilson had a fierce and unlovely side."

*   *   *

Wilson's decision to conscript America was made before he called on Congress to declare war, and more than two months before Congress, after vehement debate, passed the act that legalized the draft. By agreement, kept secret, of Wilson, Secretary of War Baker, and Judge Advocate General (later Provost-Marshal) Enoch H. Crowder, the colossal machinery for enforcing the draft was set up and made ready long before the country knew there would be a draft—while, indeed, the country continued to take it for granted that only the volunteer system would be used.

Anticipating that the country would be shocked, that it might refuse to submit to conscription, a procedure was devised that would be least offensive to the people, that would indeed give the process to some extent the color of volunteering. The direct act of taking young men from their homes would not be done by army officers in uniform; the process would be carried out by civilians, so far as possible by neighbors of the conscripted man. And that is how the process went. As soon as Congress passed the act, all men of draft age registered at the place in the local precinct where it was their custom to vote. Out of those thus registered—every male of draft age—local civilian officials picked those to be turned over to the army for service, said who was exempt, who had to go. The process was one, not of the army walking into the draftee's home but of civilian officials, mainly neighbors, delivering the draftee to the army. It was supervised by civilian sheriffs and governors, officials holding their of-

Registering in a district where many of the registrants were Chinese born. (© American Press Association)

fices by popular vote. But the draftee reached the army just as surely as if the army had come and taken him.

June 5, 1917 was Registration Day. Baker's wide-flung, high-powered propaganda campaign to make the day a "festival and patriotic occasion . . ." had succeeded in stirring up a national sentiment which dispelled or intimidated any remaining reluctance to accept the draft. To the polling places went nearly 10 million young men, the very heart of the country's vitality, a cross-section of its variety—ore-passers in Ashtabula, lumbermen in Bangor, cowpunchers in Cheyenne, cotton farmers in Dallas, miners in Leadville, shoe workers in Lynn, sophomores in New Haven, grocery clerks in Syracuse, apple growers in Walla Walla, city boys from Third Avenue, country boys from Main Street and Bear Notch, youths white, black, and of foreign birth, every type and condition of man between twenty-one and thirty-one to be found in the country. Each set down the data required of him: his name, address, age, physical features, occupation, and reason, if any, for claim of exemption. Each received the small green card certifying his registration. Without disturbance anywhere, almost one male out of every five in the country had shown his readiness to be tested for the army.

Now, from these 10 million men, the government wanted 687,000 soldiers at once. This quota must be chosen from among those physically fit

Secretary of War Baker drawing the first number of the draft lottery. (Photograph from U.S. Army Signal Corps)

and without need of exemption. The provost-marshal decided upon a lottery as the fairest method.

At Washington on the morning of July 20, 1917, a distinguished group of officials, senators, congressmen, and high army officers gathered in the public hearing room of the Senate Office Building around a large glass bowl containing 10,500 black capsules with numbered slips inside. Rarely has human eye been so privileged to see fate engaged in concrete functioning, the gods of the machine in operation. The gods, for once, made a formal ceremony of their distribution of destinies.

At 9:49 A.M., Secretary of War Baker, blindfolded, put in his hand and drew out a capsule—it was number 258. Flash powder boomed, cameras clicked, reporters sprang for the door. By telephone and telegraph the number "258" sped over the country to waiting newspaper presses, to stock tickers, to crowds standing before the bulletin boards of draft offices. In each of 4,500 local villages and precincts man number 258 was chosen to fight—he had now to go to camp or show cause why he should be exempt.

The lottery went on until after two the following morning; one blindfolded man took out the capsules, three tellers verified the number, and six tallymen recorded the list, one on a large blackboard which was photographed and reproduced on front pages everywhere. That day there was more excitement throughout the country than on the day of declaring war, for the lottery told each registrant how close he was to battle. War in general had become war personally.

IV

In every town and village in America, from Eastport, Maine, to Coronado Beach, California, occurred an event almost as standardized as an army uniform.

The train drew in. On the station platform were the draftees, wearing their civilian clothes for a time which would be the last for many months, in some cases the last forever. Accompanying them were wives and mothers whom they kissed good-bye; sweethearts, friends, and acquaintances with whom they exchanged farewells half-gay, half-solemn—the emotion of the whole scene was of the sort that is delicately balanced between smile and tear. The local band played patriotic airs, rather avoiding the music of parting such as "Auld Lang Syne." In country villages in the North the airs included many Civil War ones, particularly "Marching Through Georgia"; in the South, where that would not do, there was "The Bonnie Blue Flag"—and everywhere, always, "Dixie." As the engine bell rang, they picked up their suitcases and the pies and cakes and doughnuts pressed upon them by the Red Cross Committee or the Ladies' Aid, and climbed into day coaches decorated with flags, bunting, and huge signs which read: "We're off to lick the Kaiser!" or other facetious expression of exalted purpose. Camp was the next stop.

*   *   *

Their first army clothes. (© Underwood & Underwood)

The whistle blew, the band played a last tune, the crowd increased its shouting, the train pulled its length of flags and bunting, its freight of "draftees," suitcases, pies, and cakes, out of the station.

Then the men sat back. It had begun; they were on their way. Each man

Two-day rookies at Camp Meade, Maryland. (Photograph from U.S. Army Signal Corps)

squared his shoulders, thought what he would do to the first Bosche he met. Only when in the exaltation of celebration someone started to pass a bottle did they discover another side to this adventure; a tall man, one of their own number, stepped up with "Cut it out! You're in the Army!" He was the "draft leader"—order and discipline began at the first turn of the engine's

Above, noncommissioned officers training at Camp Hancock, Georgia. Below, in the firing trench at Camp McClellan, Alabama. (Photographs from U.S. Army Signal Corps)

wheels. Yet they were still heroic, glorious. Cheers floating in the window at every village they passed told them so, benevolent ladies who boarded the train at every stop to distribute candy and cigarettes made it plain. The men felt like veterans, already victorious, glory already achieved, until the train drew up at its last stop and they saw olive drab step forward to meet them. The army in the flesh was something new to each man.

There followed bewildering events: loud-spoken orders, getting on trucks or buses, getting off before an expanse of bare wooden buildings; more orders, officers at tables inside demanding draft cards, other cards to be filled out, a doctor's curious thumping on their chests once again (those who failed in the camp physical examination were returned home at once), standing in weary yet jocose line while the sergeant rummaged through piles of olive drab and flung out coats and breeches. Not until he emerged into sunlight, a service hat over one eye, his arms filled with strange-looking apparel, could the "draftee" catch his breath. He was no longer miner, bookkeeper, grocery clerk; he was, in one of the most familiar cantonment phrases, epitome of all that was different from civil life—he was "in the army now."

The cantonment day began, as days everywhere commonly do, with getting up in the morning, and about that there was a remarkable army song written by a sergeant at Camp Upton, who was named Irving Berlin, and who, preceding his army life and after, was America's greatest contemporary composer of popular songs. Berlin's civilian life would never have given him the materials with which to compose this song, his personal favorite. It "could only have been written by one who knew what it was to hate a bugler," remarked Alexander Woollcott.

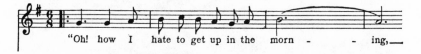

Oh! How I hate to get up in the morning,
Oh! How I'd love to remain in bed;
   For the hardest blow of all
   Is to hear the bugler call—
   "You've got to get up,
   You've got to get up,
   You've got to get up this morning!"
Some day I'm going to murder the bugler,
Some day they're going to find him dead;
   I'll amputate his reveille
   And step upon it heavily,
And spend the rest of my life in bed!

Little wonder that song delighted the rookie. It stated plainly his opinion of the one large, inescapable, and never-to-be-forgotten fact of army life—that the bugle blew at 5:45 in the morning. Loud and clear in the dawn it shrilled:

I can't get 'em up,
I can't get 'em up,
I can't get 'em up in the morning.
I can't get 'em up,
I can't get 'em up,
I can't get 'em up at all;
Corp'rals worse than privates,
Sergeants worse than corp'rals,
Lieutenants worse than the sergeants,
And the Capt'ns worst of all!

Only those who had come from farms thought this was an easy rising; to the rest it loomed sign and token of the immediate strangeness of the army's ways.

Fifteen minutes after first call the men "stood reveille," assembled in line before their barracks to answer the roll. Mess call sounded for breakfast at 6:20:

Soup-y soup-y soup
Without a single bean;
Pork-y, pork-y, pork,
Without a streak of lean;

Mess at the Pelham Bay Naval Station.

>Cof-fee, cof-fee, cof-fee,
>The weakest ever seen!

At 6:45 came sick call; men who felt that they ought to have a doctor's attention reported to the orderly room.

>Come and get your quinine, come and get your pills;
>Come and get your quinine, come and get your pills!

If the regiment were cavalry or field artillery, the stable call was given at 7:00.

>Come all who are able and go to the stable
>And water your horses and give them some corn,
>For if you don't do it the colonel will know it
>And then you will rue it as sure as you're born!

Otherwise the men returned to quarters to "police up" by making their beds and arranging their kits.

They assembled at 7:30 for the start of the day's serious work. There-

ABC's of the Manual of Arms, Camp Devens, Massachusetts.

after for four hours the men were drilled in the intricate technique of the soldier. Mess call sounded dinner at noon—for once the bugle fell upon willing ears. At 1:00 came another assembly call for more drill or fatigue duty (general labor), which lasted until 5:00. Assembly for retreat occurred at 5:25—the men in formation presented arms, the band played the national anthem, and the flag came down (it had gone up at 7:30 A.M.). Mess call for supper came at 5:45. At last assembly was often gathered at 7:00 for an hour and a half of school—lectures and theoretical instruction—but this

Above, teaching a group of depot engineers how to pick up and carry a wounded man, at Camp Grant, Illinois. Below, machine-gun training at Camp Devens, Massachusetts.

was sometimes omitted. A man then had free time until the call to quarters at 9:45, and at 10:00 came lights out and Taps. If he had never in his adult life gone to bed at 10:00 before, he was ready to sleep now.

We're in the army now.
Mail time at Spartansburg (International News), and every man his own tailor and barber (© Underwood & Underwood).

*   *   *

A million soldiers meant a million young men taken out of their homes; at the very entrance of America into the war, the army realized this side of the problem and set up the Commission on Training Camp Activities to provide, as well as it could, normal relations of life, "to rationalize the bewildering environments of a war camp." The commission dealt with all sides of a soldier's recreation. It erected thirty-four Liberty Theaters in as many camps; each had a capacity of from 2,000 to 10,000 men and showed current movies every night as well as plays and vaudeville performances. (Vaudeville and actors' associations donated their services to the army, both here and abroad, with fine liberality.) It supplied dramatic managers for amateur theatricals. It appointed forty-four athletic directors, thirty boxing instructors, and fifty-three song leaders to oversee these activities in the camps; they had many assistants. And it provided full equipment for all activities and sports.

All the efforts of the C.T.C.A. to fill the soldier's free hours seemed but little more than a drop in the bucket compared with the semi-private enterprises which came forward. Every benevolent association in the country, apparently, found some facet of a soldier's life to aid and comfort. The Red

Depositing money with the Y.M.C.A. secretary at Camp MacArthur, Waco, Texas.

Cross went further than supplying lint bandages and crutches; it built club-
houses, put on vaudeville shows, gave Christmas parties. The Y.M.C.A.
had secretaries in every camp to carry out its varied program; at Camp

*Above, Y.M.C.A. hut in one of the camps. Below, class in English for non-English-speaking
soldiers, 126th Machine Gun Company, Camp MacArthur, Waco, Texas.*

Boxing match in the "Y" auditorium at Camp Devens, Massachusetts.

Dodge alone, ten buildings bore the red triangle on circle, international insignia of the "Y"—each with fireplace, piano, phonograph, movie projector, complete sets of athletic goods, 1,000 books, current magazines, hometown papers, easy chairs and writing desks, free notepaper, postal facilities, and sitting rooms for visiting ladies. The Knights of Columbus (National Catholic War Council) and the Jewish Welfare Board provided similar facilities. The Salvation Army, the Y.W.C.A., and the Travelers' Aid also helped at the camps; the American Library Association collected books and magazines, the Playground Association of America organized adjacent communities with respect to recreation for the men.

If the drilling, the sentry duty, the regularity of reveille and K.P. grew monotonous for the soldier, this was so completely balanced by baseball, football, boxing bouts and track meets, movie stars such as William Farnum and Mary Miles Minter on the screen, vaudeville legends such as Elsie Janis and Harry Lauder in the flesh, pool tables, songfests, phonograph records, magazines, ice-cream sodas, and cigarettes, then he could almost forget he was a soldier in a war camp. It did not, for a while, even seem that war was serious business.

V

It is just as essential," said General Leonard Wood, seriously or casually—perhaps apocryphally—"that a soldier know how to sing as that he should carry a rifle and know how to shoot it." Probably the general did not really say "know how to sing." The "knowing how" was neither essential nor universal. But the singing was universal. In cantonment, literally everyone sang, whether it were a lone tenor in a barrack-lined street lifting his voice in "Good-bye Broadway, Hello France" and "Dearest, my heart is dreaming, dreaming of you," or 10,000 soldiers led by a divisional song leader shouting "Men of Harlech" on the drill ground of an evening.

There were, of course, the almost formal songs of soldiering. Much more spontaneous and rather more characteristic of the citizen army were many songs that were being sung by everybody at the time and were brought into camp by the draftees, and some other songs that sprang up in the cantonments, and yet others that came back from the front. These composed a gorgeous galaxy, gay and appealing at the time, glamorous to recall. Some faded, almost disappeared; some lived on in gatherings of men on Saturday night and were revived at meetings of veterans.

The stammering song "K-K-K-Katy, Beautiful Katy," popular before we entered the war, gave rise to many soldier parodies, among them an expression of harsh opinion about "K.P.," "Kitchen police":

> K-K-K-K. P.,
> Dirty old K. P.,
> That's the only Army job that I abhor;
> When the m-moon shines over the guard-house,
> I'll be mopping up the k-k-k-kitchen floor!

> C-C-C-Cootie,
> Horrible cootie,
> You're the only b-b-b-bug that I abhor;
> When the m-moon shines over the bunkhouse,
> I will scratch my b-b-b-back until it's sore!

A not too serious apprehension about the effect of martial experiences on the distribution of population was expressed in:

> How 'ya gonna keep 'em down on the farm, after they've seen
>   Paree?
> How 'ya gonna keep 'em away from Broadway,
> Jazzin' a-roun', and paintin' the town?

The soldiers bade the folks at home keep their courage up in

> Keep the home-fires burning, while your hearts are yearning;
> Though your lads are far away, they dream of home.

Then they turned around and sang a like message of cheerful fortitude to themselves. The English "Pack Up Your Troubles in Your Old Kit Bag, and Smile, Smile, Smile" was adopted by the American doughboys without

K.P. at Camp Grant, Illinois.

a blink at its alien "lucifer" for match and "fag" for cigarette. More native, more homely and pungent, was "The Last Long Mile," the Plattsburg Marching Song in 1917:

> Oh, they put me in the Army and they handed me a pack,
> They took away my nice new clothes and dolled me up in kack;
> They marched me twenty miles a day to fit me for the war—
> I didn't mind the first nineteen but the last one made me sore:
> Oh it's not the pack that you carry on your back,
> Nor the Springfield on your shoulder,
> Nor the five-inch crust of khaki-colored dust
> That makes you feel your legs are growing older;
> And it's not the hike on the hard turn-pike
> That wipes away your smile,
> Nor the socks of sister's that raise the blooming blisters—
> It's the last long mile!

"Long Boy," the picture of the country lad going off to battle the German army, tickled everyone's risibilities:

> Good-bye, Ma! Good-bye, Pa!
> Good-bye, Mule, with yer old hee-haw!
> I may not know what this war's about,
> But you bet, by gosh, I'll soon find out;

An' O my sweetheart, don't you fear,
I'll bring you a King for a souvenir,
I'll git you a Turk an' a Kaiser too—
An' that's about all one feller can do!

Earliest of the war songs was "Tipperary"; it was widely sung in America from the time, late in 1914, when despatches from the front said it was the marching song of the first British Expeditionary Force:

It's a long way to Tipperary; it's a long way to go;
It's a long way to Tipperary, to the sweetest girl I know!
Good-bye, Piccadilly, farewell, Leicester Square,
It's a long, long way to Tipperary,
But my heart's right there.

Knights of Columbus canteen.

A soldier's glimpse of "No Man's Land," was in Lieutenant Rice's

"Keep your head down, Fritz-ie Boy, Keep your head down,

> Keep your head down, Fritzie boy,
> Keep your head down, Fritzie boy—
> Late last night by the star-shell light
> We saw you, we saw you,
> You were mending your barb-wire
> When we opened rapid fire—
> If you want to see your father
> In your Fatherland,
> Keep your head down, Fritzie boy

But the soldiers' song of songs was "Mademoiselle from Armentières," sometimes called "Hinky Dinky Parley-Vous." It became the folk song of the army. It was sung in the trenches; in places of recreation behind the lines it was universal; among soldiers on leave in Paris it was decidedly more familiar than the "Marseillaise"; it came to America with returning veterans and, with its flavor of the front, eclipsed in popularity the familiar American tunes. Literally every soldier sang it; and years after the war, veterans moved to song found expression for every mood, solitary or gregarious, in one or another of the countless narratives of the charms and the adventures of the lady from Armentières. She was, to each soldier, what each soldier dreamed her to be. Anyone seeking to reconstruct a coherent history of the lady from the thousands of versified accounts of her would be obliged to give up. A version of the song that was somewhere fairly near to its origin pictured Mademoiselle as one who spent her days working in a laundry and her high-spirited evenings in a café frequented by American doughboys:

> Oh, Mademoiselle from Armentières, parley-vous?
> Oh, Mademoiselle from Armentières, parley-vous?
> Oh, Mademoiselle from Armentières
> Will you wash a soldier's underwear?
> Hinky Dinky, parley-vous?

More probable, whether more authentic or not, was the version which pictured Mademoiselle as a barmaid:

> Mademoiselle from Armentières
> Won't you bring me a bottle of beer?

One version pictured Mademoiselle as aged and acid:

Mademoiselle from Armentières
She hasn't been kissed in forty year.

That slander must have originated with some doughboy in a pique of disappointment or jealousy; by the evidence of hundreds of other versions, Mademoiselle was distinctly kissable, and rich in experience. She had, in one version or another, every experience of every girl since Eve.

Not only did "Mademoiselle from Armentières" recite the innumerable adventures of the heroine. The tune was a vehicle for the telling of any story, the expression of any opinion:

> Oh, the Medical Corps, they held the lines; parley-vous?
> Oh, the Medical Corps, they held the lines; parley-vous?
> Oh, the Medical Corps, they held the lines
> With C. C. pills and iodine.
> Hinky Dinky, parley-vous?
>
> Oh, the General got the Croix de Guerre; parley-vous?
> Oh, the General got the Croix de Guerre; parley-vous?
> Oh, the General got the Croix de Guerre,
> But the son-of-a-gun was never there!
> Hinky Dinky, parley-vous?

> O, the French they are a funny race,
> They swipe your francs
> And lie to your face . . .
>
> The little marine he grew and grew,
> And now he's hugging and kissing 'em too . . .
>
> Froggie, have you a daughter fine?
> Fit for a marine, just out of the line . . .
>
> O, oui, I have a daughter fine,
> But not for a Yankee just out of the line . . .

Of all the American war songs, the two that divided top honors alike among soldiers and civilians were "Over There" and "The Long, Long Trail." The latter, with its gentle melancholy and suggestion of distant adventure, provided almost perfect solace to the mood of the soldier contemplating service:

> There's a long, long trail a-winding
>   Into the land of my dreams,
> Where the nightingales are singing
>   And a white moon beams;
> There's a long, long night of waiting

(Drawing by Captain John W. Thomason, Jr.)

Mad-em-o'-elle from Ar-men-tieres par - - lez vous.... Mad-em-ois-elle from Ar-men-tieres par - - lez vous..... Mad-em-ois-elle from Ar-men-tiers. She has-n't been kissed in for-ty years. Hink-y dink-y par-lez vous.........

Until my dreams all come true;
Till the day when I'll be going down
That long, long trail with you.

George M. Cohan's "Over There," partly because of its high-spirited, quick-stepping imperativeness, and even more because of its simple bugle melody, had the effect of a recruiting song:

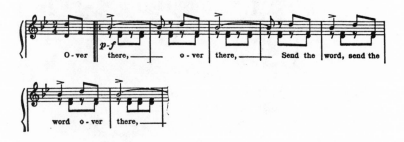

Over there, over there. Send the word, send the word over there,
That the Yanks are coming, the Yanks are coming, the drums rum-
    tumming everywhere.
So prepare, say a pray'r. Send the word, send the word to beware,
We'll be over, we're coming over, and we won't come back till it's
    over over there.

VI

The training in the cantonments hewed to its purpose. In due course, out of ten ports, 2,086,000 soldiers sailed for France.

In late 1917, transports were taking 50,000 men a month. By early 1918, after interned German liners had been pressed into service, the rate rose steeply; May saw 245,000 men shipped across, July 306,000—more than 10,000 a day. By July 1, the first million men had reached France, the second million landed before the end of October. It was an overwater troop movement far greater than any in history.

What had permitted this transportation of 2 million men across 3,000 miles of ocean in so short a time was, of course, an immense production

Heartaches and cheers at parting. (Above: © Underwood & Underwood; below: U.S. Army Signal Corps)

The spirit of the 10 million. (© Underwood & Underwood)

and conscription of ships. Even so, 49 percent of our soldiers had to be carried in British bottoms. Further, due credit must be given to the rapidity of "turnabouts"—the time between the day when a ship with cargo aboard

Red Cross canteen workers served coffee any hour of the day or night to troops en route.

Just a few of America's 10 million. (Photograph by U.S. Army Signal Corps)

sets sail, and the day, after it has crossed, discharged cargo, returned and taken on another, when it is ready to sail again. In 1917, the average "turnabout" of a troopship was fifty-two days; in 1918, it fell to thirty-five.

In spite of the vulnerability of so thick a traffic, only 200,000 tons of transports were lost—142,000 tons of this by torpedoes. No troopship was lost on an eastern voyage, with one exception, the *Tuscania*, torpedoed off the Irish coast, with the loss of 100 out of the 2,000 troops she was transporting to France.

The division, any division, was still drilling in camp after five, six, seven months. Then one day the rumor spread from barrack to barrack like wildfire: "Tomorrow we move!" Every man's heart lifted and beat quicker; here was real war at last.

Orders multiplied. The division packed. Perhaps the men, with full equipment, boarded a train at night and woke up next morning at the embarkation camp behind Hoboken. Transports were ready in the Hudson, or across the bay in Brooklyn, and the troops marched aboard. Fantastic with camouflage, the ship moved down the bay and met other transports; together they headed toward open sea. Somewhere in the Atlantic they would pick up their convoy of gray, rake-lined destroyers.

Ten days on a transport was misery. The men crowded into the hold, where bunks jammed to the ceiling; when the ship rose, swayed, and fell,

So this is Paris!

seasickness became contagious, epidemic, the quarters almost unbearable. Officers forbade smoking on deck, ordered all lights covered. There was nothing to do but shoot craps or play poker, until, entering the war zone, one could look for submarines—every piece of driftwood, every breaking wave, became a periscope. Perhaps, one morning, doughboys lined the rail to watch the white wake of a torpedo slide by the stern and see the destroyers, belching smoke, dash in to drop a depth bomb. In the geyser of foam which boomed up were scraps of metal, and oil spread on the water. The stands cheered as if Ty Cobb had stolen home.

At dusk they met another convoy, homeward bound. "Hospital ships," said someone, and men talked late into the night about wounds, death, and battle, and reckoned up their chances until the sarge shouted from the hatch, "Stow it down there!" Next morning early there was a fog and then, suddenly, before them, around them, lay high rocky islands on the gray sea. The gray clot on the hillside ahead, growing clearer moment by moment, was Brest.

It was all a thrilling experience, to be remembered and told to grandchildren. A few, for differing motives, chose to miss it or ignore its spirit— the "slackers" and the "conscientious objectors."

CHAPTER 9

Wilson Organizes for War

Wilson, with the war upon him, retired further into himself. Not in the sense of refuge or brooding, but rather that he might function the better. He visualized the war as one of ideas, he was the principal source of ideas on the Allied side, and he guarded the delicate mechanism of mood and mentality of which his ideas were the fruit.

It was fortunate for Wilson and the country that for the conduct of essential activities of the war, he found, or there gravitated to him, at least four men who in their personalities combined temperaments tuned to his own, together with high executive capacity for the tasks Wilson gave them.

One was Newton D. Baker, secretary of war; Baker could always smooth the quirks out of Wilson's spiritual commotions—once, when Wilson, angry, was about to write a letter "bawling out" a cabinet member, Baker suggested: "Let me take on that quarrel; a row between two Cabinet members is no harm but a row between a Cabinet member and the President would be bad." Another was Bernard M. Baruch, extraordinarily endowed with energy and decisiveness coupled with intuition and considerateness—upon Baruch's entering the room, the barometer of Wilson's spirit, if previously disturbed, would subside a degree or so toward serenity. Similarly endowed was Herbert Hoover, whose talents for organization matched, and perhaps even exceeded, Baruch's. A fourth, utterly different from Baruch, Hoover, and Baker, but sharing with them, in his own way, the capacity to make Wilson comfortable, was George Creel. Creel's appeal for Wilson lay in his robust vitality, from which Wilson could absorb some for his own habitually depleted stores; Creel was entertaining; sometimes he was entertaining

Bernard M. Baruch. (Wide World Photograph)

when he did not try to be—the furies of his indignation, the mordancy of his denunciations amused Wilson rather more than they convinced him; and Creel was superbly entertaining when he tried to be. He was one of the best storytellers in Washington, had gifts for humorous and accurate characterization of the exalted persons who came and went, and had an art of mimicry as great as that which Wilson himself practiced when in moods of humor and intimacy. By the nature of this war, and especially in the way in which Wilson conceived and directed it, the four principal agencies were Baker as secretary of war, Baruch as chairman of the War Industries Board, Hoover as head of the Food Administration, and Creel as chairman of the idea-disseminating, emotion-rousing function that went with the Committee of Public Information.

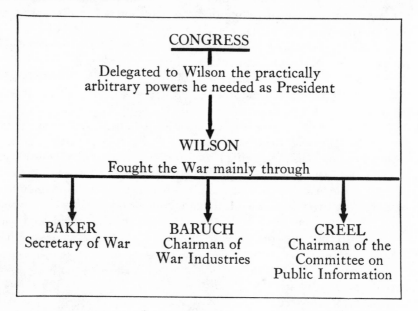

CONGRESS

Delegated to Wilson the practically
arbitrary powers he needed as President

WILSON

Fought the War mainly through

BAKER
Secretary of War

BARUCH
Chairman of
War Industries

CREEL
Chairman of the
Committee on
Public Information

II

The job of Bernard M. Baruch, as chairman of the War Industries Board, was, to express it in one figure of speech, to operate the whole United States as a single factory dominated by one management, with the relation of the departments to each other worked out as smoothly as in Henry Ford's factory; to achieve as coordinated a production of material for war as Ford achieved for automobiles. By another figure, the job was to bring the whole industrial structure of the United States into one organism, similar to the human body, with materials flowing along the arteries, veins, and capillaries in quantities and at a speed regulated and adjusted by a single intelligence.

The "single intelligence" was Baruch, except that Baruch, in the exercise of the many-sided wisdom he possessed, realized that no one intelligence could possibly be enough, and to put away from himself and from the job all notion of autocracy, in fact or in spirit. The men with whom Baruch surrounded himself were an elite of industry. Not that he merely turned to a blue book of business and drafted a list of men who had already come to the top—that would have brought him, for the present purpose, not a few stuffed shirts. Rather he carefully selected men who at once had experience in their fields, together with flexibility of mind, imagination, force, and the qualities of temperament that commended them for a unique, enormous, and intricate job.

One could visualize the stream of materials, minutely intricate in detail, massive in the aggregate, which, from the finished shell on the front, ran back to the ultimate mines and factories in which they were produced: a trickle of copper from a Utah mine brought into conjunction with another trickle of manganese from Georgia, and other trickles of chemicals and metals coming through arteries and capillaries from a score of widely separated sources; the flow of each, and their junction points regulated as nearly watchlike as was attainable by Baruch and his aides at Washington.

In the hot little cubicles of emergency war buildings they never compared either the hard work or their dollar a year from the government with the comfort and large incomes of their private callings. They enjoyed it hugely. The judgment of one historian was not extreme: "It was undoubtedly the greatest gathering of able business men into a single public enter-

Women workers placing powder in shells in a munition plant. (Photograph by U.S. Army Signal Corps)

prise necessitating energetic and continuous effort by each and all that this country and indeed the world has ever known."

For their talent as a group, much was due to the fact that Baruch selected them; for their success, much was due to the radiations that came to them from Baruch's personality. He had made a fortune as a Wall Street speculator. The fortune gave him independence; the manner of his making it—by the exercise of his individual judgment, without association with any banking group, or with any industry—gave him freedom to deal with all industries and all bankers impartially; "he had no past favors to reward, no future benefits to cultivate." That sounds as if he were grim, puritanical. Actually, he was gay, humorous, gallant, fond of company, boyish, simple—except when circumstances gave him occasion to draw on his incredible resources of subtlety. His quick insight into human beings told him instantly whom to cajole, to whom to be fatherlike and patient, with whom to be firm; his blue eyes—their normal softness and variety of expression suggested an artist as much as a businessman—could become cold steel toward a manufacturer who tried to profiteer. Between him and his associates on the War Industries Board there was an intimacy and informality like that of a college fraternity. They were all unusual, all had salient personalities; and there was a quality about them that made the sum of them, when they were together, greater than the arithmetical addition of each to each. They understood each other by intuition, resolved themselves into teamwork by instinct, generated high spirits both in accomplishment at their work and in the gay camaraderie which, at Baruch's home in the evening, was the chief reward of their labors.

Making shells in an ammunition factory at Bethlehem, Pennsylvania. (© Underwood & Underwood)

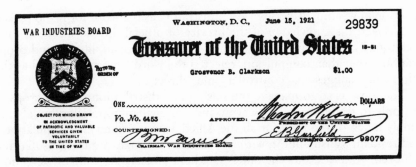

Check to a "Dollar-A-Year Man."
The payee of this, Grosvenor B. Clarkson, was executive director of the Council of National Defense. The check is signed by Woodrow Wilson, and in this case countersigned by B. M. Baruch, chairman of the War Industries Board. A U.S. statute, for some reason, prohibited accepting services without pay—hence the "Dollar-A-Year." Those who gave all their time and their high talent to the government during the war on this basis included most of the country's leading businessmen, such as Charles M. Schwab; Alexander Legge, head of the International Harvester Co.; Robert S. Lovett, head of the Union Pacific Railway; Samuel M. Vauclain, head of the Baldwin Locomotive Works. A complete roster would be a Blue Ribbon list of American industry.

When their task was finally done, they performed one last and exalted service. When the armistice came, or as quickly thereafter as each could cut off the tag ends of his war work, they went home—stopping at the Treasury to get the check for $1 which they would frame for their homes and pass on to their children. They had had no taste for bureaucracy, and their experience with power and with Washington had infected them with none. Every wartime control, regulation, priority, or other form of rule was tossed in the wastebasket. American business went back to its basis of individuality as completely as if it had never been interrupted.

III

To organize the country's food supply, Wilson's choice was predestined. Herbert Hoover may be termed a benevolent casualty of the war; caught up in it by accident, a young mining engineer comparatively unknown outside his profession, he came out at the end, as a London paper put it, "the biggest man who has emerged on the Allied side during the war." The rise of such a figure, its combination of quality in the man with adventitious circumstance, is always a fascinating aspect of history.

Hoover's rise began before America became a belligerent. An engineer stationed in Europe, he took on the difficult job of coordinating efforts to provide food and clothing to ravaged Belgium.

When America entered the war, management of Belgian relief by an American must perforce end; by the same act Hoover became the obvious man to take on the administration of food which would be a necessary function in wartime America. "Administrator" as the word for it was picked by Hoover; his knowledge of the brevity of official life of European food dictators, as well as his strong instinct for individualism, liberty, and cooperation rather than compulsion, rejected the word "dictator" as well as the minor titles suggested, "controller" and "director."

The job was so to manage the raising and distribution of food crops as not only to feed our own new army and our civilian population but also to supply much of the food for all the Allied armies and civilian populations. As President Wilson put it, with a vividness of homely phrase Wilson often achieved, America and the Allies, soldiers and civilians alike, were now "eating at the common table." The catering must be accomplished mainly by a country in which much of the manpower on farms would now be diverted to the army and more to ship-building and other essential wartime activities.

As respects food manufacturers and dealers, Hoover was given authority by the law, with power to coerce if he chose; all (except those whose business was less than $100,000 a year) were licensed and Hoover could take away the license of any who profiteered or otherwise violated regulations. Very rarely, almost never, did Hoover impose the penalty; his practice with flagrant violators was to exact a contribution to the Red Cross, equivalent of a fine, and let them continue in business on good behavior. Mainly, however, he secured conformity by innumerable conferences with groups of dealers, in which they were shown the need and were moved to cooperate in spontaneous goodwill.

As for the 105 million American consumers, Hoover reached them with a vast mechanism of organization and vocal and printed urging, designed and expressed in a temper which caused housewives and children and men

Food supplies were eked out by "war gardens" in the cities.

to feel a glow of pleasure in helping toward a process which Hoover called "food conservation," but which the millions of loyal participants in sacrifice preferred to call "Hooverizing"—the word was used for anything that helped about food, mothers serving no more than was necessary, girls planting gardens, boys working in the fields, children wiping their plates clean. There will be Americans in the year 2000, venerable nonagenarians then, who will have forgotten Foch and Joffre, Pershing and von Hindenburg—but will recall a time when their mothers told them, "Chew your food," to please a deity of their childhood, vaguely associated with omnipotence, who was called "Mr. Hoover."

To be economical with food became a vogue with the smart, with the simple and sincere almost a prayerful rite. Hoover's appeals were read out from pulpits and in schools, thrown on the screen in motion picture houses, printed in newspapers. At all times, before the eyes of all, on poster, placard, and billboard was kept the slogan, "Food Will Win the War."

Hoover's directions were numerous and specific; a comprehensive one on January 26, 1918, included, in the phrases the public came to express them in, wheatless Mondays and Wednesdays, meatless Tuesdays, porkless Thursdays and Saturdays, and use of "Victory bread," which contained more of the wheat grain than ordinary white bread. February 11, 1918, he forbade the killing of hens until May 1. March 29, he suspended his meatless order for thirty days. May 26, he proposed a limit of two pounds of meat per person per week. October 12, twelve rules for public eating places were given out, including: no bread until after the first course, only one kind of meat, one-half ounce of butter per person, no sugar bowl—such sugar as was served was in small cubes, only two pounds of sugar for every ninety meals served.

The citizen who was suspected of having more than his share of prunes. A Life *cartoon on the rationing of food.*

The spirit in which Hoover asked it led to serious ardor in the carrying out of it, or, with the humorous, gay geniality: "Do not permit your child," said *Life*, "to take a bite or two from an apple and throw the rest away; nowadays even children must be taught to be patriotic to the core."

Translating Hoover's appeals into rhyme, *Life* printed a burlesque of a polite diner-out thanking his hostess, a wartime "bread and butter letter":

> I cannot thank you for your bread,
> Because there wasn't any,
> Nor any butter, either, though
> Its substitutes were many.
> But your pecan and fig croquettes;
> Your muffins, flour- and eggless;
> Your beef-steak, raised in window-box;
> Your mock duck, wing- and legless;
> Your near-fish, wheedled from oat-meal;
> Your butterine, from apple;
> Your catnip salad, dressed with lard;
> Your porkless, parsnip scrapple
> Composed a menu so conserved
> That Mr. Hoover'd better
> Commend my cheer in sending you
> This meatless, wheatless letter!

IV

Wilson, early in the war, while he was still wrangling with Congress over the War Resolution, while he was busy organizing the country, while he was rushed with conferences dealing with manpower, dreadnaughts, munitions, food supplies, all the matters commonly considered to be of first importance to a nation at war—while in the midst of all that, Wilson turned aside for a moment to bring into being an agency which, while classifiable among war activities, bore no remotest resemblance to the conventional and traditional methods of bringing an enemy to submission. Indeed, this creation of Wilson's, the Committee on Public Information, was so different in its function from any war activity ever before engaged in by any country at any time that it may be regarded as an American contribution to the science of war.

Like most institutions, the committee was the shadow of a man; and the man was not Wilson, it was George Creel. Wilson officially initiated it (as a different thing from what it became); Wilson took advantage of it and in his war purposes profited by it greatly. But it was the incredibly efflorescent imagination of George Creel, his fertile ingenuity, his prodigious energy which, beginning with a perfunctory clearinghouse for day-to-day information about government activities, developed it into something new in war, new and very formidable.

When we entered the war, the question of censorship came up. Army and navy urged on Wilson the usual thing, the strict limitations found by the Allies to be necessary. American newspapers felt that a nation 3,000 miles from the battlefront need not be so rigid about publishable news. While the controversy was on, George Creel wrote a letter to Wilson. Characteristically, Creel had a new conception, proposed an innovation; characteristically also, he expressed it violently, by paradox. No censorship of war news at all, said Creel, except such as the newspapers would voluntarily impose on themselves after receiving explanation of the need. What is wanted, Creel said, is not suppression but expression—"unparalleled openness," a spreading abroad among our own people of information about our activities in the war and especially about our purposes, to the end of arousing a war emotion, a morale that we did not yet have. It was, as Creel saw it, "a plain publicity proposition, a vast enterprise in salesmanship, the world's greatest adventure in advertising." Such a proposal lay within the field of propaganda; but, Creel told Wilson, let there be no propaganda in the sense in which it was practiced by the combatants in Europe, no false claims of victories, no concealment of defeats—in short, no lies of any kind, no lies either to deceive the enemy peoples or to allay the home population.

Wilson, receiving Creel's letter, sent for him, turned the whole nebulous idea of censorship, and of propaganda of whatever sort, over to him.

Creel's imagination was literally boundless. Within a week he conceived himself—and lived up to his conception—as having a mission to make America war-conscious. In that enterprise he mobilized under his direction just about every spring or avenue of publicity, imagination, or other attention-compelling activity that there was in America. As the war spirit spread, persons of many arts or callings were moved to do their bit. When they came to Washington, Creel became the man for them to see.

Creel mobilized the artists. Painters, sculptors, designers, illustrators, and cartoonists, as Creel put it, "rallied to the colors." Under the chairmanship of Charles Dana Gibson, they became what Creel called—military terminology was the order of the day—his "Division of Pictorial Publicity." Commending his subordinates as a good general should, he declared that "no other class or profession excelled them in devotion that took no account of sacrifice or drudgery." "America," Creel exclaimed, "had more posters than any other belligerent, and they were the best." They were, too. Some of the work that Gibson, Harrison Fisher, Howard Christy, Wallace Morgan, Charles Bull, Montgomery Flagg, Joseph Pennell, and others did under the inspiration of war was among their finest.

Creel mobilized the advertising forces of the country—press, periodical, streetcar, and outdoor, including a special species of the advertising genus known as "idea men"—in a vast patriotic campaign which thundered on the consciousness of every person in America who could read or under-

James Montgomery Flagg drawing a poster as an incident of a drive to get recruits for the Marine Corps, July 1918. (Photograph by U.S. Army Signal Corps)

stand a picture. From the walls of subway stations, from billboards, from barns along the highways, Creel's artists shouted exhortations for a united front against the enemy—"The Battle of the Fences," he called it.

Creel organized a motion picture division to stimulate American interest and morale by showing in every city and village pictures made under the direction of his committee: *Pershing's Crusaders, America's Answer,* and *Under Four Flags.* As time went on this branch of the committee's work expanded to take in every phase of photography. "Stills" by the thousand were sent out to the newspapers, great quantities of stereopticon slides were made and distributed, scenario departments were formed, comedy films especially adapted to the entertainment of troops were prepared and sent to cantonments.

Creel mobilized the oratorical talent of the country, chiefly amateur, 75,000 voices strong, into an organization called the Four Minute Men— the relation was obscure between this designation and the unlimited Minute Men of the Revolutionary War, or perhaps those were only One Minute Men.

Creel's talkers were introduced to the public mainly at motion picture theaters, where, during the performance, a slide would appear on the curtain saying:

4 MINUTE MEN 4
(Copyright, 1917. Trade-mark).

. . . .

(Insert name of speaker)

**will speak four minutes on a subject
of national importance. He speaks
under the authority of**

THE COMMITTEE ON PUBLIC INFORMATION
GEORGE CREEL, Chairman,
Washington, D. C.

From motion picture theaters the service was expanded to lodge meetings, grange meetings, schools, churches, synagogues, Sunday schools, sessions of labor unions—it became difficult for half a dozen persons to come together without having a Four Minute Man descend upon them. The supply of talent being generous, the service reached out to lumber camps. "Indian Reservations," Creel wrote in his report, "furnished some of the largest and most enthusiastic audiences."

By the end of the war, the 75,000 Four Minute Men had delivered a grand total of 7,555,190 speeches, to audiences aggregating 314,454,514. And they had elicited from the press, Creel said in concluding satisfaction, 900,000 lines of publicity commending their work.

Creel also mobilized the singing voices of the country, prepared a bulletin of songs specially selected to incite patriotism, and appointed a corps of song leaders to take charge of motion picture theater audiences.

Creel mobilized novelists and dramatists, including Booth Tarkington and Mary Roberts Rinehart; he mobilized historians and college professors to write articles and pamphlets. Creel mobilized . . . but let us cease detail, and merely say Creel assembled leaders of about every group in America whose occupation or function was in the field of imagination, creative art, or publicity.

The sum of Creel's activity was prodigious. Only one branch of it lends itself easily to statistical estimate—the words of his orators were as the winds of the world; the posters and pictures he put out, as the leaves of the forest. The number of printed words he inspired and distributed reached a point at which, the Government Printing Office proving unable to keep step with his imagination, he developed his own machinery for printing and distribution. Of one pamphlet, "How the War Came to America," the printing was 5,428,048; editions for the foreign-born in Swedish, Polish, Italian, Spanish, Czech, and Portuguese brought the total to 6,775,892. This was the most widely distributed of the pamphlets—it contained Wilson's speech to Congress calling for declaration of war, and Creel's judgment, as well as his personal affection, put emphasis always on circulating Wilson's speeches. Of

Wilson's Flag Day address he distributed 6,813,340 copies. Of other pamphlets, booklets, leaflets he circulated a grand total of some 60 million.

Creel's work had deluged America, saturated it; the country was as war-
conscious as it could become. But Creel was an artist, had to an extraordi-

War posters by American artists.
Top left, Liberty Loan poster by Howard Chandler Christy. Top right, recruiting poster by
Herbert Paus. Bottom left, poster drawn by Charles Dana Gibson to glorify workers in
shipyards. Bottom right, recruiting poster by James Montgomery Flagg.

When Creel was deluging Germany with Wilson's speeches, the German government tried to prevent the speeches from reaching the army or the civilian population. (Knoxville Journal and Tribunal)

nary degree the floreating quality that dreams huge projects. And Creel was in a position, had a freedom from limitations, such as no artist ever knew. He had access to as much money as his most expansive dream could call for. While Congress had limited his appropriation to $1,250,000 (and in subsequent anger threatened to curtail the amount), Creel could draw on a "President's fund" of $50 million which Wilson had been given to lay out in his discretion. Wilson let Creel have $5 million of it.

More than money, Creel had, without cost or at very little, such help as money could never command. All the writers, artists, and other persons of imagination, practically all the country's genius, were on fire to help win the war, and would throw into Creel's projects such talent, inventiveness, fervor, and devotion as probably was never before assembled. Creel's own generous description of his aides was not extravagant, "all that was fine and ardent in the civilian population came at our call."

Finally, Creel had Wilson. Wilson would do about anything Creel suggested, would O.K. anything Creel proposed—Wilson's signature to documents beginning "I hereby create under the jurisdiction of the Committee on Public Information"—was a familiar sight, and, of course, a potent one.

Thus equipped, it occurred to Creel to conquer the world—and this became the activity that made Creel seriously important in the war. His own phrase for what he now undertook was "a world-fight for the verdict of mankind." Including—this was the daring and subsequently decisive part of it—a fight for the minds of the German people. Some of Creel's lieutenants in his advertising division would have called it "selling America to the world," that is, selling America's part in the war, especially America's war aims. And since America's war aims were Woodrow Wilson's ideas, Creel's enterprise became mainly one of "building up" Wilson, causing Wilson's ideas to dominate the mind of the world, including Germany, including even the minds of Germany's armies in the field.

A former newspaperman, Creel saw the propaganda value of a "snappy" statement of Wilson's ideas and approached the president. Wilson consulted his closest adviser, Colonel House, and the two boiled Wilson's war aims and peace terms down into what, within a little while, was known from Archangel to Patagonia as the "Fourteen Points."

The president put his epitomized Fourteen Points into a speech which he delivered to Congress on January 8, 1918, labeled as a "statement of the War Aims and Peace Terms of the United States." This was not merely for Germany; it was for the world. One point or another appealed to practically every small people aspiring to independent nationality, and to every existing nation. The sum of the Fourteen Points enlisted behind Wilson most of the opinion or emotion within practically every nation of the world, big or little, Allies or enemy, or neutral. The Fourteen Points (with Wilson's other terms) were not merely a peace proposal to the nations at war; they were directed to the whole world, an appealing charter of a new order, glamorous to all; they constituted Wilson's promise to the world of what he would cause the peace to be, and the world to become:

1. Open covenants of peace, openly arrived at. . . .
2. Absolute freedom of navigation upon the seas. . . .
3. The removal, so far as possible, of all economic barriers and the establishment of an equality of trade conditions among all the nations. . . .
4. Adequate guarantees given and taken that national armaments will be reduced to the lowest points consistent with domestic safety.
5. A free, open-minded, and absolutely impartial adjustment of all colonial claims based upon a strict observance of the principle that in determining all such questions of sovereignty the interests of the populations concerned must have equal weight with the equitable claims of the government whose title is to be determined.
6. The evacuation of all Russian territory and such a settlement of all questions affecting Russia as will secure the best and freest co-operation of the other nations of the world in obtaining for her an unhampered and unembarrassed opportunity for the independent determination of her own political development and national policy. . . .
7. Belgium must be evacuated and restored. . . .
8. All French territory should be freed and the invaded portions re-

stored, and the wrong done to France by Prussia in 1871 in the matter of Alsace-Lorraine . . . should be righted. . . .

9. A readjustment of the frontiers of Italy should be effected along clearly recognizable lines of nationality.

10. The peoples of Austria-Hungary, whose place among the nations we wish to see safeguarded and assured, should be accorded the freest opportunity of autonomous development.

11. Rumania, Serbia, and Montenegro should be evacuated; occupied territories restored; Serbia accorded free and secure access to the sea; . . . international guarantees of the political and economic independence and territorial integrity of the several Balkan states should be entered into.

12. The Turkish portions of the present Ottoman Empire should be assured a secure sovereignty, but the other nationalities which are now under Turkish rule should be assured an undoubted security of life and an absolutely unmolested opportunity of autonomous development, and the Dardanelles should be permanently opened as a free passage to the ships and commerce of all nations under international guarantees.

13. An independent Polish state should be erected which should . . . be assured a free and secure access to the sea. . . .

14. A general association of nations must be formed under specific covenants for the purpose of affording mutual guarantees of political independence and territorial integrity to great and small states alike.

CHAPTER 10
Over Here

For the services that were urged upon noncombatants—women, elderly folks, invalids, and children—by slogans and appeals from the Food Administration, the Red Cross, Belgian Relief, the Fuel Administration, and other organizations, a phrase became current—it was borrowed from the British—"doing your bit"; one patriotic lady thought the phrase implied too little, suggested "doing your all." The number and variety of such organized and sloganized urgings reached a point where, in an apotheosis of organization it was proposed that a "What Can *I* Do? League" (emphasis on the "*I*") be organized.

The war, coming at a time when the feminist movement was making an immense surge forward, led to a vast broadening of the activities in which women took part. They served as nurses and in the other fields which tradition had sanctioned. But they also did work that women had never done before. They became messenger "boys" for the telegraph companies, operated elevators, acted as streetcar conductors, labored as full-time and able-bodied operatives in munitions factories, railroad repair shops. Girls who in groups worked on farms were called "farmerettes." When bu-

When women took over men's jobs. Left, Washington, D.C.'s first female traffic cop. Center, the first of ten women letter carriers on the job in New York City. This mail carrier holds a whistle, not a cigar, in her mouth. Whistles were used to signal residents that mail had been delivered and that the carrier was available to receive outgoing mail (or even to sell stamps). Whistles were once standard issue for all postal carriers. Right, college girls in woman's land army raised crops for Uncle Sam. (© Underwood & Underwood)

reaus in the naval establishment appealed for clerks and stenographers, but found there was no appropriation for the hiring of civilians, Secretary of the Navy Josephus Daniels asked: "Is there any law that says a yeoman must be a man? Then enroll women!" he ordered. The women "Yeomen" (it was not permitted to call them "Yeomanettes") numbered 11,000; the women marines (popularly called "Marinettes") were 269.

II

"Under modern conditions of warfare," said the journalist and historian James Truslow Adams, "hate becomes almost as essential as ammunition, and hate is manufactured." In our manufacture of verbal hatred, clergymen helped much. Dr. Newell Dwight Hillis of Plymouth Church, Brooklyn, contributed a brand: German "soldiers [are] sneaking, snivelling cowards. . . ." The Reverend Dr. Henry van Dyke (American minister to Holland during the war) invented a new epithet for the Kaiser, the "Werewolf of Potsdam," more literary, if less alliterative, than the "Beast of Berlin." Dr. Van Dyke would "hang every one who lifts his voice against America's entering the war." Dr. S. Parkes Cadman, pastor of Central Congregational Church, Brooklyn, dealing also in figures of speech, declared that the Lutheran Church in Germany "is not the bride of Christ, but the paramour of Kaiserism." The Reverend W. Bustard stepped out of the pulpit manner long enough to say, succinctly, "To hell with the Kaiser!" The

Reverend Dr. Billy Sunday, invited to deliver a prayer in the House of Representatives at Washington, began: "Thou knowest, O Lord, that no nation so infamous, vile, greedy, sensuous, bloodthirsty ever disgraced the pages of history."

In the concoction of hate, college professors contributed as generously as clergymen: Dr. Louis Gray, of the University of Nebraska, judged that "The Prussian is a moral imbecile, an arrested development." Dr. Joseph Jastrow, of the University of Wisconsin, was credited with a new literary and scientific term, "Mania Teutonica." Professor William H. Hobbs of the University of Michigan called Germany "the nation which sold itself to the devil." Dr. William Roscoe Thayer, historian, poet, biographer of John Hay and Theodore Roosevelt, onetime president of the American Historical Association, wrote "Volleys from a non-Combatant" "to prevent the total pollution of our people by letting loose of the Prussian moral sewers." Melancthon Woolsey Stryker, president of Hamilton College, put his emotion into verse:

> The clock has struck! The death-smeared double vulture
> Shall swoop no more adown the insulted skies,
> To spill the venomous bacterial Kultur. . . .

III

A "spy fever," natural fruit of wartime psychology, given official encouragement by the stringent law against enemy espionage and seditious utterances, set everyone to watching out for German agents. The official "Intelligence Section" of the army was ubiquitous, meticulous. In addition to the Intelligence Section, civilians were asked to keep their ears and eyes open, report disloyal utterances or suspicious activities. To the amateur detectives, "suspicious activities" became a broad term. One of the functions was to investigate the antecedents and associations of persons of German birth or associations. Employers were asked to furnish data about employees having German names, and to be responsible for their loyalty.

Those who had authority from the Army Intelligence Section were supplemented by volunteers, even more zealous, even less discriminating, proving once more Carlyle's saying, "Of all forms of government, a government by busybodies is the worst." A lamp kept lighted all night anywhere within sight of the sea was a signal to German submarines. A street conversation in German, or in any language other than English, even a sentence or a word, was likely to bring trouble. It became dangerous to say "Prosit!" or "Auf wiedersehn!"

It was asserted, and in theory was true, that five German spies, taking up points of strategy and acting simultaneously, could paralyze the city of New York: One, placed at the right point, could by bomb or otherwise interrupt the telephone service for days; another the electric light system; another the gas plant; another the water supply. Some ten German agents, acting simultaneously, could stop indefinitely all railroad traffic entering New York, by dynamiting all the railroad bridges over the Harlem River, the Delaware, and the Hudson. This condition was indisputable and was recognized by the government. At each end of every bridge stood, during the war, a soldier. On trains, travelers who sat on the rear platform were asked, on the approach to a bridge, to step inside; it would be easy to drop a bomb that would paralyze a trunk line railroad.

The spectacle of actual danger guarded against gave rise to grotesque mare's nests. It became a hysteria. Whispers predicted, or asserted as actu-

RED CROSS BANDAGES POISONED BY SPIES

Startling Plot Reported by Director Staub in Urging Precautions by Philadelphia Workers.

Special to The New York Times.

PHILADELPHIA, March 28.—Albert W. Staub, Director of the Atlantic Division of the American Red Cross, addressing the local Red Cross organization today, said:

"You women of Philadelphia must clean house. Go over the list of your members and make sure of the loyalty of every one. Under no circumstances allow any one in your board rooms unless you know who they are. Keep persons out of the workrooms who have no right to be there.

War hysteria. (New York Times, *March 29, 1917*)

ally having happened, armed uprisings in Milwaukee, St. Louis, Cincinnati, or other German-American centers. Trifling epidemics of diarrhea proved that German spies had put germs in the local water supply. An individual illness unduly prolonged was related to the German name of the apothecary who made up the prescription. Failure of a cut in a child's hand to heal quickly was due to germs placed in the bandage supplied by German agents. Any interruption of the flow of munitions from a factory was due to a German saboteur who had tampered with an essential mechanism.

The night before Wilson delivered his speech asking Congress to declare war, he talked with Frank Cobb, editor of the *New York World:* "Once lead this people into war, and they'll forget there was ever such a thing as tolerance; to fight you must be brutal and ruthless, and the spirit of ruthless brutality will enter into the very fibre of our national life, infecting Congress, the courts, the policeman, the man in the street."

The wartime laws against espionage and sedition, passed June 15, 1917, amended May 16, 1918, prescribed penalties for speaking, printing, or otherwise expressing contempt for the government or the constitution or the flag or the uniform of the army or navy; using language calculated to aid the enemy's cause, using words favoring any country with which the United States was at war, saying or doing anything likely to restrict the sale of U.S. bonds. The postmaster general was empowered to deny the mails to anyone deemed by him to be violating the act.

Under this law, 1,532 persons were arrested for disloyal utterances, 65 for threats against the president, 10 for sabotage. William D. Haywood and 94 other members of the I.W.W. (Industrial Workers of the World),

after a trial lasting 138 days, were sentenced to prison terms. Two prominent Socialists, Eugene V. Debs and Rose Pastor Stokes, were convicted
and sentenced to long terms as well.

The number charged informally with plotting, or suspected, was legion.
After the hysteria died down, a federal judge, George W. Anderson of
Boston, who during the war had been a U.S. attorney and otherwise in intimate personal association with the men charged with the responsibility of
discovering, preventing, and punishing pro-German plots, said, "I assert,
as my best judgment, that more than 90 per cent of the reported pro-
German plots never existed; I think it is time publicity was given to this
view." To the same effect, Alice Roosevelt Longworth said: "I personally
know of not a single case in which anything was proved."

With volunteer spying by Americans on alleged German spies went volunteer censorship, informal punishment of persons suspected of lack of loyalty. On a streetcar in Cleveland a man of foreign appearance was seen
angrily to pull from the rack above him a Liberty Bond poster and tear it
up. Super-loyal Americans, taking him from the car, handled him roughly.
When someone who could speak the man's language pressed forward, it
developed that he could not read English, and that what had excited his
rage was not the words of the poster's appeal to buy Liberty Bonds but a
drawing of the Kaiser which the artist had injected into the poster as a
stimulus to patriotic generosity. Search of the man's pockets, revealing two
Liberty Bonds, completed his vindication.

The mob spirit emerged in quarters more elevated than a streetcar
crowd. The Poetry Society of America and the Author's League felt they
were demonstrating the superiority of American culture to German, and
helping to win the war, by expelling from membership a German-American poet named George Sylvester Viereck. (One should add that Viereck
had been pretty offensive as a propagandist for Germany, a panegyrist of
the Kaiser.) Opera singers were made to understand that German birth
made their voices less musical than they had been accepted as before the
war. Demand was made for removal of the German-born conductor of the
most famous orchestra in America, Karl Muck, and he was taken into custody as an enemy alien. The patriotic mayor of East Orange, New Jersey,
would not permit Fritz Kreisler, outstanding violinist, formerly a lieutenant in the Austrian army, to play in a concert. Brown University helped
to win the war by revoking an honorary degree it had previously conferred
on German Ambassador von Bernstorff. In the ranks of business and elsewhere, zealous Americans demonstrated their patriotism by calling for removal of German-born clerks. German-born individuals were not the only
victims. Any who failed to share the current hysteria were crucified by it.
Two boys in Madison, Wisconsin, one destined to become a senator, the
other a governor, saw their father, Senator Robert M. LaFollette, burned
in effigy.

When Czechoslovakians in America organized, not to help Austria but

Above, Douglas Fairbanks urging a New York throng to buy Liberty Bonds. (Photograph by U.S. Army Signal Corps) Lower left, Arthur Guy Empey, war hero and author of "Over the Top," aiding a Liberty Bond selling rally. (© Underwood & Underwood) Lower right, a character of the day known as "King of the Hoboes," urging a street crowd to buy Liberty Bonds. (© Underwood & Underwood)

to incite rebellion against her by their brothers at home, they encountered violence. In Iowa and Nebraska, meetings to rally recruits for the Czechoslovakian army were broken up by patriotic Americans whose cause for zeal was their lack of understanding of the Czechoslovakian tongue. In Seward County, Nebraska, the local council for national defense required all the churches in the district to conduct their services in English except one, for persons at once too old either to be German soldiers or to learn English. German and Scandinavian communities desiring to hold Liberty Loan or Red Cross rallies found it prudent to meet secretly. No distinction was made, the language of Allied and neutral countries being under the ban as well as enemy languages. The governor of Iowa gave out rules—

> First. English should and must be the only medium of instruction in public, private, denominational, or other similar schools.

> Second. Conversation in public places, on trains, or over the telephone should be in the English language.

> Third. All public addresses should be in the English language.

> Fourth. Let those who cannot speak or understand the English language conduct their religious worship in their homes.

Some lost not only their tolerance but their sense of humor. The word "sauerkraut" was tabooed as German, but since we did not care to banish so agreeable a food we continued to eat it as "liberty cabbage." Cincinnati ruled pretzels off the free-lunch counters of local saloons. In some parts of the West the name of a familiar ailment was changed from "German measles" to "liberty measles." Dachshunds became "liberty pups."

In the crusade, one act of resistance stood out: November 5, 1918, citizens of Berlin, New Hampshire, by a vote of 933 to 566, decided that the name of their town was not so humiliating as to demand change.

Associated with the spirit of censorship and suspicion was the spirit of compulsion. Cruelties practiced in northwestern communities, where Germans and Scandinavians were a majority of the citizens, left scars which remain livid for generations to come. In Ontagamie County, Wisconsin, a farmer, John Derul, barely escaped lynching when a mob came to his house and demanded that he give more than the $450 he had already subscribed to the Liberty Loan campaign.

IV

The social and economic effects of the war were deep, far-reaching, and intricate. The active ferment which was at all times the condition of American society was now greatly speeded up. Not only individuals but groups rose or fell. Change in the purchasing power of money (caused

Girls loading rattan on freight cars tracked in the Bush Terminal Docks, Brooklyn, New York. (© Underwood & Underwood)

largely by expansion of credit as an incident of war financing and wartime business activity) sent some classes upward in the world, others downward. The rearrangement was visible. The type of person that had composed for a generation almost the exclusive patronage of expensive hotels and of Pullman cars on the railroads was diluted by a class to whom these luxuries were new.

One stratum of the rich were made relatively poorer. Those who lived on the income from mortgages and bonds saw the purchasing power of their dollars go as low as forty cents. These were the most conservative class of the well-to-do, persons who had inheritances of gilt-edged mortgages: widows, beneficiaries of trust funds, teachers in colleges whose fixed salaries came from endowments—after the war it became necessary to conduct "drives" to increase college endowments and raise faculty salaries. So far as this class were the principal custodians of taste, the possessors and practitioners of learning and of interest in art and the like, their lowered status was unsettling to tradition, played a part in the general overthrowing of accepted standards that came soon after.

Another class of the rich benefited enormously. These were the owners of factories, the participants in active business, the stockholding class as distinguished from bondholders and the land- and goods-owning class. These benefited by the increased valuation of their properties as expressed in dollars, and benefited extravagantly by the profitable manufacture of munitions and the supplying of goods to meet the needs of a war-paralyzed Europe. "War millionaires" became a current term for the new rich; "war babies" was a Wall Street term for corporations that became suddenly fat.

As the European reservist was called to the colors, the Negro waiter was called from the South to fill his place. (New York Telegram, *August 7, 1914*)

In proportion, labor benefited most of all. So great was the war demand for goods, both in America and from Europe, and so restricted the supply of workers due to diversion of manpower to war, that labor could command almost any wage it chose to ask—indeed, what actually happened was not demand by labor but furiously competitive up-bidding by employers. As a rule, sudden ease about money expressed itself in free spending. Arrival of workmen at the factory Monday morning wearing silk shirts, an incident probably overemphasized in proportion to its novelty, was much talked about by those who held the fixed view that workmen did not know how to handle money. The free spending for luxuries, hitherto commonly bought only by the well-to-do, in turn accelerated the profits of manufacturers.

Scarcity of labor, and therefore elevation of labor's economic status, was accentuated by practically complete cessation of immigration. For the year that ended June 30, 1914, immigration amounted to 1,217,500. With the mobilization in Europe, the number fell to 315,700 in 1915 and continued to fall until less than 20,000 a month entered this country, of whom a large number came from Mexico and the West Indies. Thus the war brought about a result which many Americans had begun to think desirable. As the war came to an end, and it became apparent that millions of soldiers disbanded in a poverty-stricken Europe would at once flood to fat America, the check on immigration, which war had been, was made statutory; in the early 1920s, America adopted a restrictive policy which was the reversal of its practice since the earliest times. The social and economic consequences, and even the ethnic effect, first of immigration and then of its restriction, were so fundamental and so complex as to be almost incalculable.

With cessation of the immigration that had long been the supply of cheap unskilled labor, and with the increased need for such labor, industrialists in the North sent agents into the southern states. To the Negro in the cotton fields and on the levee the labor agents sang a siren song: undreamed of wages, steady jobs, political equality, no race discrimination, better housing, good schools for the children, free transportation north and frequently money for food while on the way. The song fell on willing ears. A large percentage of the South's Negroes were living on hunger wages. The boll weevil was virulent, crops had been bad for several consecutive years. Floods in 1916 had done great damage in Alabama and Mississippi. Many of the plantations paid but 50 to 75 cents a day, and this only when there was work; $1.25 to $2.00 were high wages and went to only a few men in the cotton-oil mills and the sawmills. Housing and schools were inferior; "Jim Crow" cars, political inequality—the combination made the Negro eager to go.

The South, complacent at first about the social result of diminution of Negro majorities, began to be alarmed by other effects: the disappearance of field hands essential to plantation life, of house servants held in affection, of factory workers indispensable to industry; the breakup of a familiar and cherished social order. The *Macon Telegraph* printed a plaintive warning: "Everybody seems to be asleep about what is going on right under our noses—that is, everybody but those farmers who waked up mornings recently to find every negro over twenty-one on their places gone—to Cleveland, to Pittsburgh, to Chicago, to Indianapolis."

V

Of the effects of the war on America, by far the most fundamental was our submission to autocracy in government. Every male between eighteen and forty-five had been deprived of freedom of his body—for refusing or evading the surrender, 163,738 were apprehended and disciplined, many by jail sentences. Every person had been deprived of freedom of his tongue, no one could utter dissent from the purpose or the method of war—for violating the sedition act, 1,597 persons were arrested. Every businessman was shorn of dominion over his factory or store, every housewife surrendered control of her table, every farmer was forbidden to sell his wheat except at the price the government fixed. Our institutions, the railroads, the telephones and telegraphs, the coal mines, were taken under government control—the list was complete when, after the war and preceding the Peace Conference, Wilson took control of the transatlantic cables. The prohibition of individual liberty in the interest of the state could hardly be more complete.

And it was not merely that we had passed through the experience of enforced submission or voluntary surrender or both. The results remained with us. Government had learned that we could be led to do it, had learned the technique of bringing the individual to give up his liberty, the cunning of propaganda, the artfulness of slogans, and the other methods for inciting

mass solidarity and mass action, for causing majorities to insist on confor-
mity by minorities.

The purpose for which we did this, as described by the one who urged
us to it and led us into it, was "the destruction of every arbitrary power
anywhere," "to make the world safe for democracy," to save the peoples of
all nations—including and especially Germany—from autocratic government, to have the individualist ideal of society (France) triumph in a struggle against the ideal of regimentation (Germany).

That purpose, viewed in the light of what had happened in the world fifteen years later, seemed very ironic indeed—Germany and Italy under dictators, Russia under a dictatorship called proletarian but equally extreme in
its deprivation of individual liberty.

CHAPTER 11
Peace

I n America, after just more than a year and a half of participation, expectation of the end of the war had been created by many events reported in the newspapers: on November 3, 1918, Austria surrendered to the Italians; in Germany, sailors at Kiel mutinied openly, troops revolted, the line of battle fell back faster and faster—in plain sight of the world, Germany was going to pieces. In America, in every city, town, and village, in every family, in every heart, there was tension, a feeling of emotion tugging to explode.

The detonant came in early afternoon newspapers of November 7, in the shape of shrieking headlines based on a despatch received through United Press from Brest:

```
UNIPRESS  NEWYORK
   PARIS URGENT -- ARMISTICE ALLIES SIGNED
   ELEVEN SMORNING ["cablese" contraction for
   'this morning"] -- HOSTILITIES CEASED TWO
   SAFTERNOON -- SEDAN TAKEN SMORNING BY
   AMERICANS.
                        HOWARD -- SIMMS
```

New York went wild. It happened to be a day of noticeable sunniness and serenity, the heart of lovely Indian summer. To rend that calm, seeming to tear the very atmosphere to rags, came the din of sirens, factory and ship whistles, auto horns, and church bells. Universal holiday was assumed and not questioned. Crowds stampeded out of offices and factories. No traffic could move. Confetti and ticker tape rained from office windows. The crowds resolved themselves into informal processions, people forming arm to arm, no one cared who, no one cared where. A melting, exulting, half-sobbing, half-heart-lifting mood seized upon a whole city. Moist eyes looked out above ineradicable smiles. Here and there the crowds formed little knots. In front of the Sub-Treasury cheers went up for all the Allies. A crowd sang before the Waldorf. At Columbia University, students rushed out of classrooms, snake-danced on the campus. The Stock Exchange closed at 2:30 instead of 3:00. Between 1:00 and 3:00 the telephone company carried more calls than in any two hours of its history. The wave of feeling struck every one as it did the barber in Park Avenue who left a customer half-shaved, folded his razor, and exclaimed to his assistant, "Finish

TWELVE PAGES | **NIGHT FINAL**
Postscript | **Postscript**
Full Closing Market Reports | *Full Closing Market Reports*

The Evening Post

FOUNDED 1801.—VOL. 117.NO. 102.   NEW YORK, THURSDAY, NOVEMBER 7, 1918.   2 CENTS.

REPORT ARMISTICE SIGNED; CITY IN WILD DEMONSTRATION; STATE DEPARTMENT AT 2:15 P. M. DENIES REPORT; AMERICAN TROOPS IN SEDAN; ENEMY LEAVING GHENT

him and then shut up shop. Me? I'm going home to cry with my wife! That's where I'm going!"

After several hours of this came a spirit of disturbing doubt. It came first, and most poignantly, to the offices of the United Press—they had had an exclusive story, the most sensational in modern times, but after it had remained exclusive for some four hours they began to feel uncomfortably that it was "too damned exclusive." No other newspapers followed it up. The doubt, spreading from newspaper offices, expressed itself to the crowds in failure of late editions to have further details. At 4:00 P.M., Secretary of War Baker said he had no word of an armistice. The Associated Press, after labored inquiry, reported that Paris and Washington knew nothing of an armistice. Little by little people looked at each other, realized their delusion. The heart went out of the excitement. Said an editorial in the *New York Tribune* on November 8: ". . . One of the famous fakes of history. . . . A sky full of paper, parades, horns, madness! Well, in America it has been a people's war throughout. The people made it; they fought it. Why shouldn't they go mad at the thought of German surrender if they want to?" The next day, rather wistfully, the *Tribune* headed an editorial "The Thief of Joy" and said, "When the real news of peace arrives shall we have another celebration as good and joyous as those first hours? Hardly, we think. The edge has been taken off."

II

The armistice celebration of November 7 had been false, yet only premature. From events reported in every issue of newspapers, everybody knew the end was near: On November 9, the Kaiser abdicated; the Allied battle line pushed forward furiously to less than 18 miles from German soil. On November 10, revolutionists seized Berlin; the Kaiser crossed into Holland; the French army, fighting on land it had not seen since 1914, was astride the Belgian border; the British army had almost reached Germany; Pershing's First and Second Armies advanced on a front of 71 miles between Sedan and Moselle. The end could not be long delayed.

In the early hours of November 11, in the still, sleeping town of Emporia, Kansas, an editor of the local paper dozed in his office under a lone light. A dog barked far away over corn lands, the street below his window lay silent in shadows. At 2:22 A.M., the telephone startled him; Topeka was calling. What the far voice said shook him broad awake—with husky, excited words he called the Fire Department. Gongs clanged out in the night. A whistle blew and kept on blowing. All over town men and women jumped anxiously from bed and looked out. By 3:30 A.M., fully 200 people had gathered in Commercial Street. Bonfires spurted up at every corner. When morning came, business was suspended for the day. The judge of the District Court set over every case on the docket and excused the jury. At 10:00 an impromptu parade started off—the longest and largest in Empo-

Wall Street, New York, on Armistice Day.
A sky full of paper, parades, horns, and madness. (© International News Photos, Inc.)

New York Tribune   EXTRA
7 A. M.
First to Last—the Truth: News·Editorials·Advertisements
Vol. LXXVIII No. 26,293   MONDAY, NOVEMBER 11, 1918

GERMANY HAS SURRENDERED;
WORLD WAR ENDED AT 6 A. M.

ria history—led by a band of thirty pieces, its auto section more than a mile long. "Wild-cat whistles" screeched from fire trucks, one Ford towed four tin washtubs with monstrous racket. An old horse-drawn hack went by labeled "There ain't no Kaiser!" The war was over in Emporia, and in 50,000 towns and cities from coast to coast.

In Detroit, where Taps had been bugled every day on the City Hall steps at 4:00 P.M.—the exact hour when Taps sounded in France for "our boys"— last Taps for the war rang out above exultant crowds. In Newport News, soldiers and sailors took riotous possession of the city, wrecking streetcars, raiding restaurants, breaking windows, building bonfires in the street from smashed delivery wagons. There were no casualties. In Atlanta, crowds thronged Five Points, Peachtree, and Whitehall. In Hartford, the greatest celebration in its history included a parade of 10,000, taking two hours to pass the reviewing stand. Someone who preserved a whimsical spirit noticed that of all the celebrants the loudest noise was made by the employees of the Maxim Silencer Company. A butcher's truck bore a stuck pig with one word on it, "Kaiser." In Boston, the 160-year-old State House bell rang out.

In San Francisco, ten minutes after the flash arrived at 1:00 A.M., huge

Des Moines, Iowa, turned out in costume to parade. (Courtesy of the Des Moines Register*)*

bonfires laid by the Fire Department were burning on Twin Peaks, Scott's, and Telegraph Hill. Later, a monster parade moved down Market Street to the Ferry Building and back to the City Hall. This celebration had a strange aspect—every person wore a white cloth over his nose and mouth, protection against an influenza epidemic which raged over the country. The effect touched the height of incongruity, but the spirit was not marred; the Health Office lifted for the day the ban on music and dancing, and Tait's and other restaurants and the Palace and St. Francis hotels were jammed.

In Washington, Wilson gave out his proclamation at 10:00 A.M. Shortly after noon, he rode down Pennsylvania Avenue amid an immense ovation to address Congress, reviewed the United War Work Campaign parade (scheduled for the day by chance, thereby gaining tenfold significance), altogether appeared five times before jubilant crowds. In the evening, forty-nine bonfires lit up the Ellipse between the White House and the Potomac River.

In New York, the first Associated Press flash arrived shortly before 3:00 A.M. Presses whirred, and newsboys shrieked "Germany surrenders!" to late stragglers in Park Row who shouted, pounded each other on the back, and danced over the street in the dawn.

Lights sprang out on the Statue of Liberty. Air-raid sirens blared. Noise increased, multiplied, traveled along the waterfront; ships and tugs tied down their whistles, lit all their lights, ran up flags; sailors tossed calcium-burning flares on the dark water. Munitions factories across the Hudson took up the chorus. Newsboys were crying themselves hoarse as far as the Bronx. Minute by minute the wave of clangor deepened over the city. No

Crowds in Washington, D.C., who had fought to obtain newspapers revealing news of the Armistice, gladly hold them up to a news photographer. (© International News Photos, Inc.)

one could sleep. Men and women snatched a bite of breakfast, seized noise-makers they'd bought during Thursday's celebration, and jammed subways and streetcars headed downtown. Until far after midnight New York celebrated; this, at last, was "the day!"

III

W ilson continued to be at his best up to October 23, when he sent the last of several notes setting the terms for Germany's surrender. His thought was never more exact, his expression never more lucid, his judgment never more clear, his grasp never more comprehensive. That series of notes was the apotheosis of the functioning of Wilson's extraordinarily able mind. If, immediately thereafter, he became less than his best, it is not unusual that this kind of letdown should come at the end of long years of high-strung strain, the climax which Germany's surrender was. And, since Wilson was then sixty-two years of age and had been frail always, it is not surprising that the letdown should go farther than the normal resilience of a younger man would have recovered from.

Beginning about the last week of October 1918, Wilson made mistake after mistake, made them in fields in which ordinarily his judgment was subtly sure.

On the suggestion of the more political-minded among his advisers, he appealed to the country to elect a Democratic majority to Congress in the election of November 6, so that he might "be your unembarrassed spokesman at home and abroad." Much of the country felt hurt, saw in the action ingratitude for the united support the nation had given him, saw vanity in it and imperativeness. Especially did they see, in one of the reasons Wilson gave—"A Republican majority would be interpreted on the other side of the water as repudiation of my leadership"—a wish on Wilson's part to dominate the world at the coming Peace Conference. The Republicans denounced his appeal and capitalized on it, fomented public distaste for it. The country elected a Republican majority.

Wilson announced that he would go to the Peace Conference in person. To the country that seemed confirmation of the suspicion of egotism. From the point of view of Wilson's effectiveness at the Conference, it was generally recognized by those equipped to judge, his presence at Paris would be a serious detriment to the purpose he had most dearly in mind. Wilson sitting across the table from the European statesmen—wiliest of traders and diplomats—would be obliged to answer questions, to make instantaneous decisions, to commit himself. Every person experienced in conferences or in business knew that Wilson would now be obliged to trade, and he was a poor trader—it was contrary to his nature. Wilson's way was to say, at once, openly and fully, what he considered the right course, and then to stand on that as a principle. To give and take as traders do, and especially to ask in the beginning for more than he expects to get, in order to have something to "trade with"—which is the essence of negotiation—all that was foreign to

Wilson's nature. He would not attempt it, and if he should he would be beaten at it. On the other hand, Wilson in Washington, with representatives under his direction at Paris, would be able to preserve the serenity and detachment which, in his case, were peculiarly indispensable requisites for his functioning well. He would have time to think his decisions out. He would be able to continue to appeal to the world from the same high Washington pulpit which had served him so well thus far, would be able to make use of world opinion, which was the fulcrum that had given him his enormous prestige and success. Wilson at Washington, with his emissaries at Paris referring questions back to him for decision, would have been ideal. His going to Paris in person was one of the major mistakes of his career.

IV

At first, it did not seem that way. He arrived in Paris on December 13 and was feted there—his entry was more that of a conquering hero at the close of a victorious war than in the case of most military leaders. There had hardly been such scenes since Napoleon. "Vive le Président Wilson!" "Vive l'Amérique!" Over the street where the procession passed waved a great banner, "Honor to Wilson the Just."

This sign flashed a welcome to President Wilson on the rue Royale, Paris, on his way from the station. (© Underwood & Underwood)

He was flattered by the great, sought by the humble. Waiting for him, almost standing on the steps of the house he was to occupy, or arriving soon after, were delegations from the little peoples in Europe and Asia who had been stirred by his promise of "self-determination." "Oppressed nationalities" that for centuries had renewed in each generation, persistently though hopelessly, the dream of independence, had during the war taken Wilson's promise in full faith, looked upon him as the deliverer, the redeemer.

The Peace Conference would not begin until January 7. In the meantime, Wilson was deluged with pressure to accept honors—and confer them; to be the guest at great celebrations, to visit the crowned heads of the other Allies; Britain, Italy, and Belgium would be hurt if, visiting the French capital, he failed to visit them also.

He resisted pressure to visit the devastated territory because he felt he might be harrowed and thereby stirred into a mood in which it might be less easy for him to maintain a just point of view toward Germany. But he reviewed the American army. He visited King George at Buckingham Palace and made a tour of England, speaking at the Guildhall in London, at Manchester, at Carlisle. He visited Italy, made speeches at Turin and Genoa and Milan and Rome.

Everywhere he was the idol of the masses. "The mass of European peasantry, shopkeepers, and day laborers looked forward to his arrival as men looked in medieval times to the second coming of Christ."* Not since Peter the Hermit had Europe so blindly, so eagerly followed one leader. It was a frequent saying during late December 1918 that Wilson could overturn any government in Europe by an appeal to the people as against their rulers.

That was apotheosis of Wilson's fame and prestige, of the glamour and power he had come to have in the world. And that was just five days in advance of the opening of the Peace Conference in Paris. Thence on was downward.

V

Wilson had already, as an incident of the Armistice, made a fatal error. His Fourteen Points had been put forward in the war as a tender to Germany, and had been repeated in Wilson's correspondence with Germany leading up to the Armistice. By Germany's acceptance, they became a contract. But some of the Allies, who were Wilson's partners in the contract, now raised qualifications to some of the points.

It was by this act and at this point, so far as such a matter can be asserted with definiteness, that the world got off the track. Failure to live up to the Fourteen Points and the other assurances Wilson had held out was the starting point of much that bedeviled the world for years. To attempt to say

*Quoted from *Woodrow Wilson and His Work*, by William E. Dodd.

Queen Elizabeth, President and Mrs. Wilson, and King Albert, taken at the King's Palace in Brussels, Belgium. (Photograph by U.S. Army Signal Corps)

what course the world would have taken had Wilson's contract with Germany been lived up to, his assurances to the world carried out, is of course to deal with one of the "ifs" of history. We know that failure to do so led to consequences definitely identifiable and very unhappy.

The British raised one qualification about Point number 2, freedom of the seas. The British and French raised another about Point 8, the amount of damages (later called "reparations") Germany must pay. All along, one judges, some of the Allies' leaders had regarded the Fourteen Points not as Wilson regarded them, not as a sincere tender, but rather as a ruse of war designed to lure the German people to surrender and overthrow their government. The early assent of some Allied leaders to the Fourteen Points had been with their fingers crossed. Now they had a manner of surprise that Wilson should really have meant them.

Wilson, the new Wilson that was less than Wilson, made not only the mistake of permitting qualifications by the Allies to the Fourteen Points, but within his own mind he made what was for such a man the most tragic of lapses. He compromised with his own intellect and conscience, said to himself it would do no harm to let the Allies make qualifications to the Fourteen Points, because he would be sure to set up his League of Nations, and that, when in operation, would carry out the Fourteen Points and correct all other errors. The League of Nations, he thought, was the only indispensable thing. More and more he sank deeper and deeper into that pit of his own making, the relaxation of intellect and conscience which said that his other promises did not matter, that he need only stand by his promise of the League of Nations, and the League, when in operation, would make his other promises good.

On the fourth of March, one of Wilson's earlier mistakes came back upon him. He had ignored the Senate in selecting his Peace Commission, and he had flouted the Republicans by his appeal for a Democratic Congress. Thirty-nine members of the new Senate which on that day came into power—and thirty-nine was more than the one-third that could prevent ratification of a treaty—signed a round-robin saying they would have no League of Nations; let Wilson negotiate a simple peace treaty ending the war and come home; if Wilson set up a League of Nations, the Senate would not ratify it. That was notice to the world; especially, it was notice to Wilson's adversaries in the Peace Conference.

Wilson, in adjusting himself to meet this threat from the Senate, was for a moment the old Wilson. With his familiar skill in dialectics, his Napoleonic instinct for the unexpected in strategy, he tied the Covenant of the League of Nations into the treaty of peace and knotted the two firmly so that it would be impossible to have a formal ending of the war without adopting the League of Nations. That was possible. But at once Wilson lapsed. The fundamental art of such a move is to let it speak for itself; Wilson, however, talked about it. While in America for an interval he told a public audience that "When that treaty comes back, gentlemen [in the Senate] will find the Covenant not only in it, but so many threads of the Treaty tied to the Covenant that you cannot dissect the Covenant from the Treaty without destroying the whole vital structure."

As defiance that was dramatic. But to reveal strategy, to announce motive, as an incident of indulging in the emotion of defiance—that was far from the subtlety and self-control of the Wilson of his best days. Defiance for defiance's sake begets defiance in the defied. Wilson's act strengthened the senators in their determination, brought them sympathy from quarters which otherwise might have remained indifferent. "Very well, then," said the senators in effect, "we will prevent ratification of the whole treaty."

Wilson had supposed that to be unthinkable, and his thus supposing was another mistake. The senators proceeded to resist the treaty as a whole. Congress, to bring the state of war technically to an end somehow, felt obliged to pass a simple joint resolution. Wilson vetoed it as a disgrace to American honor.

VI

Wilson determined to make a direct appeal to the people, to make speeches from coast to coast. His physician and devoted friend, Admiral Grayson, opposed it, asked Secretary Tumulty to help prevent it, intimated to Tumulty that the president might pay with his life. Mrs. Wilson joined them. Tumulty, feeling that Wilson was "plainly on the verge of a

Senator Hiram Johnson and Medill McCormick, arriving in Chicago, September 12, 1917, as they trailed Wilson, arguing against his plea on behalf of the League. (© International News Photos, Inc.)

nervous breakdown," asked him, instead of the speechmaking trip, to take a long rest away from Washington. Wilson pushed him aside. "I know I am at the end of my tether," but "the trip is necessary to save the Treaty. . . . No decent man can count his own personal fortunes."

So, he went. Day after day for twenty-two days Dr. Grayson saw continuous brain fatigue, violent headaches. At night, in his speeches, Wilson was at times bitter; at Des Moines he called his adversaries "jaundice-eyed bolsheviks of politics." Other times he was despondent, moody; frequently in his speeches he exalted the nobility of death in a great cause. From one night to another he forgot the substance of speeches he had already delivered. In proportion as he was ill, and because he was now old and determined, he was more meticulous than ever to keep every engagement, to appear at each meal in the dining car, to respond to every call from wayside crowds for additional train platform speeches. In an excess of an old man's grimness, he even planned to extend the trip, carry the fight into the enemy's country, Senator Lodge's New England.

During his speech at Pueblo, Colorado, September 25, 1919, he broke into tears—to so slender a store of nervous stamina had he come. Afterward, during the afternoon, Mrs. Wilson had the train stopped; and, to give him such recreation as was possible, walked with him upon a dusty country road. When he returned to the train, he had a temperature. Dr. Grayson gave him a narcotic.

Late that night (about four o'clock in the morning of September 26), Dr. Grayson knocked at the door of Tumulty's compartment in the sleeping car, asked him to dress quickly, the president was seriously ill.

In the president's drawing room Tumulty found Wilson fully dressed. His face was pale, one side of it had fallen. When he tried to talk he could not articulate clearly. Tears running down his face, he said to Tumulty: "My dear boy, this has never happened to me before. I do not know what to do." Tumulty of course proposed to cancel the rest of the trip. Pleadingly, almost childishly, Wilson said: "Don't you see that if you cancel this trip Senator Lodge and his friends will say that I am a quitter and that the Western trip was a failure and the Treaty will be lost?"

Impulsively Tumulty took hold of both his hands: "What difference does it make what they say? Nobody in the world will consider you are a quitter, it is your life we must consider." Wilson tried to move nearer to Tumulty to press his argument. His left arm and leg refused to function.

Tumulty and Grayson announced to the newspapermen that the rest of the trip was off. The train, instead of stopping for the scheduled speech at Wichita, was switched round the city. With drawn blinds it hurried eastward.

VII

The endings of wars, the periods succeeding them, have roughly a common pattern attended by the same emotions, including hate. In this lies a parallel between Wilson and Lincoln.

Lincoln during the Civil War promised fairness to the enemy, "with malice toward none, with charity toward all." And as the Civil War ended, Lincoln, to fulfill his promise, proposed generous terms for the South, general amnesty for those who had fought, reconstruction of their state governments by their own people. At once he was reviled by those who insisted on a more radical reconstruction. Before the attacks on him reached full momentum, Lincoln had the good fortune to die, five days after the surrender of the Confederates at Appomattox. His death, coming at the peak of his military success and his fame, silenced his enemies, intimidated calumny, made his place in history unassailable.

Wilson, in the Great War, promised fairness to the enemy. When the war ended Wilson, to fulfill his promise, tried to form a League of Nations and otherwise live up to the promises he had held out to the German people. At once he was reviled and pulled down by those bent on revenge, the "Hang the Kaiser!" and "Make 'em pay!" partisans in France and Britain, the "unconditional surrender" partisans and "isolationists" in America.

Wilson, to have shared Lincoln's good fortune, would have had to die five days after the Armistice ending the Great War. Had he done so he might have been today, in popular estimation, one with Lincoln.

And had Lincoln lived, as Wilson did, for five years after the war, probably that part of the parallel, too, would have been carried out.

There was parallel in their careers but not equality in the men. Had Wilson been, in nature, as great as Lincoln, his stature in history would have been immeasurably taller, for the scope of Wilson's functioning was infinitely broader, the stage upon which Wilson acted was literally the world.

What, then, was Wilson's lack? At what point, and how, did he fumble? You must not expect the answer in an epigram. His physical and intellectual deterioration at the end of the long strain of the war had much to do with it. Aside from that, much of his failure was predestined.

It had been part of his polemic technique to get assent to a principle, and to refuse to discuss details until the principle was agreed to. Now he had got the world's consent to the League of Nations as a principle, as an abstraction—and when he came to fill in the details, one of them had to be the use of collective force—and that America would not have. Of all the tragedies that man may bring upon himself, and to those who build their hopes upon him, one of the saddest is to excite expectations which he cannot live up to. When the ideals that Wilson had set up were not realized, as they faded into mist, the world fell into the worst disillusionment the world as a whole had ever had, a universal disease, a sickness of spirit from which almost the whole human race suffered for years.

VIII

The rest of Wilson was very sad. In the White House ten days after his breakdown at Wichita, he had a second stroke, was found semi-conscious on the bathroom floor. Those about him believed death certain. He could not be shaved; for weeks, lying in bed, he had a scraggly white beard and mustache. He was kept secluded. Only Mrs. Wilson and Dr. Grayson had access to him. Not even Tumulty was admitted, except rarely, and then with Mrs. Wilson standing back of the head of the bed to put her finger to her lips and shake her head if Tumulty brought up anything likely to excite the president. The wife and physician not knowing what to do about the public aspect of the situation, wondering whether to have the vice-president take over the government at once, but thinking how terrible that would be to Wilson if he should recover, fearful of letting the public know how ill he was lest that might lead to demand that the vice-president be inaugurated—all had the result of making a mystery of it, led to frightful gossip and innuendo. On some of the White House windows were bars, put there years before when Theodore Roosevelt's children playing ball broke the glass; the bars were now pointed to with whispers—there was a madman in the White House. In the Senate there was discussion whether the technical condition had not arisen that called for action.

After some four months he was materially improved. One of the specialists who had been called in declared the president was "organically sound, able-minded, and able-bodied." After some seven months he began occasionally to hold cabinet meetings.

He resumed a fitful and rigid insistence on the League of Nations. Enough of him was left to give him authority as Democratic leader, but not enough of him was left to lead wisely, and he refused to consider reserva-

President Wilson meeting with his cabinet for the first time after his illness. He "looked old, worn, and haggard; his jaw tended to drop on one side, his voice was very weak, and strained; it was enough to make one weep." (© Underwood & Underwood)

tions proposed by the Republicans—the Democrats left to themselves would have accepted the reservations and taken America into the League. At Paris he had compromised with Europe when he ought to have stood firm; now, at Washington, in his illness, he was obstinate against America when he ought to have compromised.

Along with fits of brooding and occasional lapses of memory were occasional brief periods of bright interest in public matters, of strength pulled together to perform a duty. When it came time to leave the White House, he rode with his successor, Harding, to the Capitol. When Harding, embarrassed, making conversation, told him some irrelevant story about a baby elephant, he broke into tears. At the ceremony, fate had it that his ancient enemy, Lodge, the man who had led the fight to defeat Wilson's beloved League, should be the one to announce adjournment of the Senate and ask him the usual formal question: "The Senate and House have completed their work and are prepared to receive any further communications from you." Wilson turned glassy eyes upon him, then looked into space and said: "Senator Lodge, I have no further communication to make. Thank you, good day, Sir!" and stumbled away on his cane. Behind him, as Harding took the presidential oath, the band played "Hail to the Chief"— to Wilson, recessional.

The final years were spent in a house on "S" Street in Washington. He died February 3, 1924.

PART VI

The Twenties

CHAPTER I
The World in 1920

O f all the nostalgic longing for the past that man has experienced since theology first taught him to look back toward Eden, hardly any was greater than the homesickness with which much of the world of 1920 looked back toward the world of 1914, in vain. That homesickness was responsible for many of the votes that Warren G. Harding got when he ran for president of the United States in 1920; of all the speeches he made in his campaign, the three words that most appealed to the mood of the country, the one phrase for which he was most applauded, was "back to normalcy."

Yet the wish, as the average man felt it, as it arose from his particular circumstances, was not for the return of any specifically visualized time or scene; rather it was a discontent with the postwar commotion, the turbulence and unsettlement, that surrounded him and fretted him; it was a wish for settled ways, for conditions that remained the same long enough to become familiar and therefore dear, for routine that remained set, for a world that "stayed put." It was a yearning for "the time of peace wherein we trusted"—not meaning merely for peace in the sense of absence of war, but for peace in the sense of serenity, for a state of things in which it was possible to feel trust, to rely upon permanence.

As always, under the worst of circumstances, the average American kept some humor for the condition that beset him. He had a phrase for it, not so much a resentful epithet as a baffled acknowledgment of what could not be denied, a verbal shrug of the shoulders, a resigned shaking of the head: "the cockeyed world."

Yet if we were to describe the state of the world after the Great War as frivolous slang described it, we should be obliged to use terms implying greater infirmity than a mere congenital misdirection of one of the organs of vision. To say, as cartoonists did, that the world walked on crutches, with its arm in a sling, and that it had besides several dislocated ribs and a fractured skull—all that would be too mild a portrayal of the degree of temporary decrepitude in which the war left the world. We should add, that it was shell-shocked besides; that term, as an item in a description of the postwar world, would be no figure of speech, it would be literal, the condition was patent.

Even that was not the whole of it. "Wounds" may be a convenient expedient with which to describe what had happened to the world. But to imply that the world was merely suffering from injuries, which could be restored, would be to mislead, seriously. Some were wounds, curable by the beneficent processes of nature or by the intelligence of man, if that should happily be present, in sufficient quantity and in the right places. But some of what had occurred was fundamental alteration, from which we would never go back.

Let us list, partially, the changes that had taken place in the world during some seven years prior to March 4, 1921, when Harding became head of its leading country. The process of identifying the changes might be conceived as an exercise in arithmetic: Take the world as it was in 1921, and subtract from it the world as it was in 1914—the difference would be the changes that had occurred between. But perhaps it should be the other way around; it may be that of the two the world of 1914 was the larger, or at least the more amply satisfactory; hence the process should consist in subtracting 1921 from 1914. In any event, let us set the two side by side and observe the differences; the operation, supplemented with the benefit of hindsight, will enable us to see what were the conditions facing the statesmen of the world at the time Harding became head of its most powerful nation. It is not enough to say merely that the world had endured the greatest war of all time; that statement resounds oratorically to the ear but does not help us to know what statesmen were called upon to take account of, or ought to have taken account of had they been more nearly omniscient than any of them turned out to be. We must identify the respects in which the world had changed, at least the more important of them.

II

Of all the changes there was one that went deepest, and included many of the others. Preceding the Great War, the world had had a status, an equilibrium. Fundamental in that status—and fundamental in the status of the world during almost every period—was the existence of one nation more powerful than any of the others. For more than a century this position had been occupied by Britain, latest in a long and colorful line of dominating nations that went back through France and Spain and Holland all the way to Tyre.

The role of a dominating nation includes giving stability to the status quo; the status quo may be desirable or not, relative to past periods or succeeding ones; whatever the status quo is, the mere fact of the existence of one dominating nation tends to give it balance, and preserve it.

Britain, measured by power of arms, power of wealth, and power of ideas, was the center about which the world, in most respects, revolved. This position, Germany envied. Germany called it the "place in the sun," coveted it, and tried to take it. She had not succeeded, but she had weakened Britain seriously.

When a leadership long held by one nation ceases, and there is failure of any other nation to step into the succession, a period of chaos appears historically to be the rule. This accounts for the frequency with which scholars and statesmen apprehensively compared the period following the Great War to the period following the fall of Rome—predictions of a new Dark Ages, a prolonged interruption of civilization, were common during the 1920s, and came from exalted sources.

In the course of nature, America should have stepped into Britain's vacated dominance. We emerged from the war by far the world's richest and most powerful nation. By analogy to what had happened in past eras, we should have become the most important mercantile nation, become the greatest lender, put the dollar in the place of the pound in international trade, built the largest navy, and accepted the role that fate thrust toward us. But America did not care for the power, or did not know how to use it; she did not take the responsibility.

For a time, the world considered a proposal that no longer should there be any dominant nation, no longer should the world be organized on a basis of, so to speak, national individualism; that instead we should have a federated world, a League of Nations. That, too, America rejected.

The result was two fundamental, world-embracing uncertainties. We did not know whether the world was to go forward on the basis of federation, or on the old basis of national individualism. And if the latter, we did not know which was the dominating nation, did not indeed know if there was to be a dominating nation. Any status, long preserved, gives a sense of security. Any abrupt change to a different status brings a sense of insecurity. When the change is from a long stable status to no status at all, the sense of insecurity is greater, and tends to increase.

Out of this condition, more than any other, arose the confusion, and the apprehensions of worse, that bedeviled the world in 1920 and for many years following.

III

A ssociated with this cause of insecurity was another. There had come into the world a new conception of society and government. In Russia, some aggressive exponents of new thought about society, taking advantage of the chaos arising out of the collapse of the old regime, imposed on that country a conception of government that not only was novel but ran counter to every pattern of society the world had ever experienced. The new ideal of society denied most of the things which governments are founded to secure; it denied the right of the individual to own property; it denied practically every right of the individual—the individual had no privilege or right that the state was bound to respect; it denied the validity of many of the social and family relationships that in other countries were sanctified; it denied religion, it not merely denied the right of the individual to practice religion according to his conscience or tradition, it actually barred the existence of religion, extirpated it.

The nation in which this new conception of society was set up had some

170 million people; measured by manpower and resources it was the most potentially powerful unified nation in the world. If this nation should choose to arm, it could be a formidable contender for the position Britain had lost, which America put aside, and which now was vacant. To this, actually, the leaders of Russia aspired; they began energetic efforts to cause the rest of the world to accept their theory of society.

Additional causes, or details, of the confusion that beset the world in 1920 included:

Every great trade route in the world had been interrupted; many completely paralyzed. Some would never recover, at least not within any foreseeable future, for the nations which were the termini of them had been so reduced in commercial power that the trade of the world would have to beat new paths, determined by the new relations of the nations to each other. It was as if the whole web of international trade, patiently woven through centuries, composed of sea-lanes intricately crisscrossing, had sunk beneath the water, and must be rewoven. By another figure of speech, these trade routes were the links which bound the world together, and now many of them had been broken.

The currencies of the principal nations of the world were either in process of devaluation or were destined to be devalued, even the currency of the United States. Among other effects, these changes in the values of currencies, taking place in differing ratios in different countries, made international commerce difficult, accentuated the disruption of trade routes.

The wealth of the world had been destroyed to a degree almost immeasurable. For periods of eighteen months to four years, in most cases the latter, all the great nations had concentrated their energies upon the destruction of the wealth of the others. Much tangible wealth had been ruined, and that part of wealth which consisted of goods in motion, goods in transit and in process—civilization as a "going concern"—had been ruined to an even greater extent.

Every great nation had borrowed enormous amounts. The money had been borrowed not for the normal, fruitful purpose of creating more wealth, nor had it been borrowed for purposes of mere waste; it had been borrowed for the direct, affirmative purpose of destruction, of bringing it about that there should be less wealth in the world. The borrowings were beyond any possible capacity of the borrowers to repay.

Three great nations—Russia, Germany, and Austria—and some smaller ones, had passed through revolutions in their forms of government.

One great nation, Austria-Hungary, had been disrupted. Parts of it had been set up as political entities which did not have the economic basis to make their political autonomy possible.

Elsewhere throughout Europe, new nations, and new autonomies and hegemonies, had been set up, with new economic structures which, in many cases, had not the basis to endure. The number of separate nations in Europe when the World War began was seventeen; at the end the number was twenty-six.

A wholly new conception of government had secured a foothold in the world, communism in Russia. And the condition was such that yet another new conception, fascism, was destined to emerge in Italy, to be followed, after ten years, by Nazism in Germany.

In all the leading nations, ancient moral concepts had been shattered. Youths who in home and Sunday school had been taught that murder is sin, had now been retaught that murder is virtuous if done by sanction of the state. This was merely the most vivid of many examples of ancient moral standards for individuals coming into conflict with different moral standards for the state. Everywhere the tendency was for the state standards of morals to supplant the individual ones.

The effect of the strain was greatest on growing children; consequently it would affect the peoples for many years to come. In one nation, Germany, the war strain was intensified, and the effect on children increased, by malnutrition, by lack of sufficient food, or of the right kinds of food.

The altered conditions came not only as a direct consequence of the war. After the war had come the peace treaty, as after death comes judgment. The peace treaty had sought to put a straitjacket on the changed world, had sought to "freeze" it as it was, and had thereby made impossible whatever might have been the healing courses that nature would have taken. The peace treaty had fixed national boundaries that did not conform to nature; had imposed on the principal loser in the war, Germany, reparations she could not possibly pay, and had forbidden the exchanges of goods with which any large degree of payment could be made.

Using the hypothetical reparations as a base, the victorious nations fixed, among themselves, intergovernment obligations which must be defaulted so soon as Germany should default.

IV

Some of the changes were peculiar to America. We were affected, of course, by the universal changes, more affected than we were intelligent enough to see, or flexible enough to admit. But some of the changes had greater application to us than others, and some were local to us.

America, like other nations, had gone deep into debt. In 1914, our national debt was $1,188,235,400; in 1921, it was $23,976,250,608.

Our economic structure had been seriously warped (though for the time being made seemingly more powerful). We had greatly enlarged and speeded up our factory capacity, first to supply the war needs of Europe, and later our own; as a result, our capacity to produce was greatly beyond our peacetime capacity to consume, and greater than we could find markets for abroad, as soon the other nations should return to normal production.

Similarly our agricultural production had been stimulated and greatly expanded to feed the peoples of warring nations who previously had been supported by their own fields, and now would again turn to their home acres. In the process (and for other causes associated with the war) prices of farm products and farmland, especially the latter, had risen to fantastic heights. This had been attended by much buying of land at prices the land would not be able to support, as soon as prices for crops should descend to normal. In the speculative buying, great quantities of mortgages had been given, which would be impossible to pay as soon as prices of crops should fall.

America had ceased to be a debtor nation and become a creditor one, had paid off some $3 billion which before the war it had owed to Europe, and assumed a creditor relation in which Europe owed America some $10 billion. That reversal of position rendered it necessary that other changes, far-reaching ones, should be made in our relations with the world, and in our domestic economy, changes which required reversals in many of our ways of thinking about trade. The reversals of thought, it turned out, were difficult to make, and were not made soon enough.

Every male in America between eighteen and forty-five had been registered for the army; some 4 million had actually been taken into military camps and nearly half sent abroad. The psychological effect of this experience varied, of course, with the temperaments of the men. Large numbers who previously had accepted and practiced, each according to his limitation, the American ideal of self-help and reliance upon individual initiative, had learned, through their army experience, to prefer a status in which decision is made for them, their routine of life prescribed for them, their needs provided for; they had learned to like immunity from responsibility, to prefer regimentation.

The war had accelerated the economic and social ferment that is always at work in America; had wrought a change in the status of large numbers of persons, whole groups and classes of them. There was a "new rich" side by side with a "new poor." By wartime inflation the purchasing power of the dollar sunk from a normal 100 to 45. Those who had fixed incomes, who lived upon the returns from bonds, mortgages, and rents—and these had been a large portion of the wealthy—had become the "new poor." Their fate was shared by those who lived on fixed salaries, government employees, schoolteachers, college professors—all these were reduced in economic status. The "new rich" were those whose wealth was in lands, goods, shares in corporations, and who therefore profited by the rise in prices. To a degree not very significant the "new rich" included labor, whose wages rose greatly. This dislocation of groups from former economic and social positions was, as always happens with changes in the value of money, a cause of much discontent. The former rich, those of them who lived on income from bonds, had been, to some degree, the custodians of culture, and of standards of manners. With their lapse from economic elevation, their standards came to have less authority. Reduction in the real income of college teachers—who continued to receive the same salaries but found themselves unable to live as amply, who found in many cases artisans able to live better—was one of the causes of a questioning of the American form of society which became common among intellectuals during the 1920s.

V

I have been speaking of changes that had accompanied the Great War, changes that had occurred during some seven years preceding 1921. These were accentuated and made more difficult to meet by another group of changes. The latter group were the advanced stages of developments that had been under way, with cumulative force, for decades. We can conveniently suggest them by the device of making a partial list of the innovations and inventions, mainly scientific and mechanical, that had come into the world during the lifetime of the man who became president of the United States in 1921. Harding had been born in 1865. In the year in which he became president he was fifty-five years old. During that half century and a little more, greater changes had come into the world than in all recorded time previously. The things which in the year of Harding's birth did not exist, but which in the year of his inauguration were as commonplace as the weather, make a list which is the picture of more than a changed world, almost a new one.

Within Harding's lifetime had come electric power, with electric light and all its other manifestations. In the year of his birth, the only sources of power available to man (other than his own muscles and beasts of burden) had been the wind, falling water, and steam—and the steam engine was still crude. When Harding was born, there had been no gas power or oil power—the first oil well was only six years old. During Harding's lifetime had come all the devices for transmission of the human voice—the telephone had been invented in 1875 and by 1921 was universal in America; Harding during his presidency would participate in a ceremony initiating the first undersea telephone. The radio, in 1921, was being developed to the stage of practicability—Harding's successor in the presidency would deliver his inaugural speech direct to the whole nation. Within Harding's lifetime had come the motion picture, fruitful agency for the rapid dissemination of information and ideas. At the time of Harding's birth there had been no transcontinental railroad; had Harding as a child been taken from Ohio overland to California, part of the journey would have been by covered wagon. Within Harding's lifetime had come the automobile and the airplane. Harding had been seven years old when, in 1872, Jules Verne entertained Europe and America with a fantasy of the impossible, *Around the World in Eighty Days;* by 1921, with the airplane, it was possible to circle the globe in less than ten days.

These innovations in the material world had many effects. The one appropriate to point out here is the increased rapidity of communication as respects both goods and ideas. The world had been made smaller, peoples and nations brought closer together. A result, one of the many important ones, was that dislocation at any point would more quickly and more surely bring repercussions elsewhere. Whoever was head of the United States would be obliged to take account of, and be to some degree at the mercy of, developments in the state of the world outside the United States. The area of what could be called purely domestic affairs was narrowed; domestic affairs and foreign relations tended almost to merge with each other.

CHAPTER 2
Harding

H ad Warren G. Harding been left free to follow his own wish, he probably would never have left the United States Senate. The honor of it was as much as he ever wanted, more than he had ever hoped. The work of it was largely what he chose to make it. He could look forward to days of ease and honor, nights of peace. He was completely happy.

But fate and his old crony, Harry Daugherty, had another use for him. Daugherty, ever since the two had met back home in Ohio, had carried in the back of his mind the idea that Harding would make "a great President"—sometimes, unconsciously, Daugherty expressed it with more fidelity to exactness, "a great-*looking* President." And to Daugherty, since he was in the political game and was by nature a player for the highest stakes, making a president would be the apotheosis of his career. Yet it was only as a remote possibility that Daugherty carried his dream. He never mentioned it to Harding seriously, and when he mentioned it facetiously or tentatively, Harding turned it aside. It was, in the early days of the vision certainly, just a thing that might conceivably come about, as one chance in a thousand, only possible to happen through some extraordinary contribution of accident to other favoring conditions.

In the early winter of 1920, accident contributed the conditions that turned Daugherty's dream into the possibility of reality. It was a situation, and a sequence of developments, of the sort that make politics fascinating. The Republican state organization in Ohio was in the control of Harding and Daugherty, Harding remote and titular, Daugherty active. They were threatened by a rival group. The rival group, taking advantage of the fact that it happened to be a presidential year, was backing General Leonard Wood for the Republican presidential nomination. Since Wood had much popularity in Ohio, the rival group were likely to be able to elect delegates pledged to Wood. And if they did, they would acquire for themselves control of the Ohio Republican organization. The menace was especially serious because Harding, later in the year, would come up for renomination to his seat in the Senate; if he and Daugherty should lose control of the organization, Harding might not get the renomination to the Senate.

Briskly, Daugherty described the situation to Harding; resourcefully, he suggested a countermove. They must put forward an Ohio candidate for the presidential nomination, a "favorite son." The gesture was one familiar in politics. The "favorite son" candidacy would be, not so much in hope of getting the presidential nomination as merely to garner the Ohio delegates and enable Harding and Daugherty to keep their Ohio leadership. For the role, Harding himself was the obvious man.

Harding shrank from it. He did not like the turmoil of it, he cherished his ease, the leisure for whist and poker, and golf, and long sojourns in Florida. "I found him," said Daugherty, "sunning himself, like a turtle on a log, and I pushed him into the water." The water, Harding understood, would not be deep, nor the pool big. Harding was not actually to try seriously for the presidential nomination; he was merely to run for the purpose, mainly, of getting the Ohio delegates.

Even so, Harding was reluctant. But he realized the force of Daugherty's suggestion. To seem to try for the presidential nomination was the best way of actually assuring his return to the Senate. Perfunctorily, Harding permitted his candidacy to be announced and began to make speeches, the first one at a dinner of the Ohio Society of New York City, followed by others in Ohio.

But Ohio was suspicious of the good faith of the Harding candidacy; much of Ohio really wanted General Wood and set about electing delegates for him. In this situation, Daugherty explained to Harding that as a matter of strategy Harding must seem to show good faith by running in some states outside Ohio—not many states, just enough to seem to be a bona fide candidate on a nationwide basis. Harding consented, though reluctantly. Without dreaming there was much real likelihood of the nomination descending on him, thinking he was only serving Daugherty's and his own desire to keep their hold on the Ohio state machine, Harding extended his speech-making to a few other states.

II

But Daugherty's adventurous, far-ranging mind had foreseen something which, as yet, he kept to himself. He foresaw, but he did not yet tell Harding, that Harding might really get the nomination, might get it, not by effort on Harding's part, for Harding would not make the effort, but by the fall of the cards in the convention.

There were two principal candidates, General Wood and Frank O. Lowden. Daugherty's shrewd mind foresaw a typical situation arising: The followings of the two principal candidates would be roughly equal. As the battle progressed, each following would come to hate the candidate of the other more than it would hate any third candidate—the two principal candidates would, as Daugherty put it, "fight each other to a frazzle"; they would, in the political phrase, "kill each other off." The prize would go to some third candidate, to someone who had not been conspicuous enough or aggressive enough to arouse antagonisms.

Quietly, subtly, Daugherty arranged his cards. The essence of his subtlety was that he did not, as yet, let Harding fully know; if Harding really thought there was any chance—"any danger" Harding would have called it—of his getting the presidential nomination, he might back out of the situation into which Daugherty had maneuvered him.

In two rooms of a dingy old hotel in Washington, Daugherty set up Harding headquarters. To a newspaperman* who called there, Daugherty explained his strategy. With a candor that was part of his intellectual armory, to be used where his instinct told him candor would serve him best, and with a pictorial vividness of speech that was part of his rich endowment of imagination, he said: "I won't try to fool you; you can see what we've got here, it's only a shoestring. I'll tell you, in confidence, what's in my mind. All I'm doing is getting in touch with the leaders and delegates who are for Wood and Lowden, being friendly with them. When the convention comes, those two armies will battle each other to a standstill. When both realize they can't win, when they're tired and hot and sweaty and discouraged, both the armies will remember me and this little headquarters. They'll be like soldiers after a battle, who recall a shady spring along a country road, where they got a drink as they marched to the front. When they remember me that way, maybe both sides will turn to Harding—I don't know—it's just a chance."

Toward the newspapers generally, and the public, Daugherty practiced a finesse that was the ultimate refinement in subtlety. For the sake of Ohio looking on, he had to seem to be pushing the Harding candidacy seriously. But if he actually pushed it seriously, he would destroy the only chance he had, by antagonizing the major candidates and their delegates. However, to be between the devil and the deep sea was a familiar experience with Daugherty. He enjoyed it and spent most of his life in that exhilarating strand, or in pulling clients out of it. His present dilemma was no great tax on his resourcefulness.

To Daugherty almost alone (among important persons) did it seem possible Harding might be nominated. For a brief time, early in Daugherty's promotion of Harding, he had some encouragement, tentative and rather furtive, from some powerful Republican senators, "elder statesmen," so to speak, of the party. But it was a friendly blessing rather than active help, or even serious expectation. Their principal motive was that Harding was their Senate crony, they liked the idea of putting a colleague in the White House, especially one with Harding's amiability and amenability.

Whatever slight notion the senators ever had of backing Harding for the nomination, they abandoned when he made little progress in getting delegates, especially when he did not get all the delegates from his own state, and when his manager, Harry Daugherty, was defeated as a candidate for delegate. Promotion of Harding rested almost alone on Daugherty and his scanty organization.

*Mark Sullivan.

III

As the convention neared, the time came when Daugherty had to take Harding completely into his confidence, had to tell him that, in Daugherty's judgment, there was really a chance of his being nominated for president, and that Daugherty intended to push the chance to the limit.

The tensity of opposition between the two foremost contenders which Daugherty had been hoping for, upon which he had built all his own plans, had developed as Daugherty had foreseen. Beginning with the earliest primaries for the election of delegates, there had been strong rivalry between the camps of Wood and Lowden—rivalry which had soon turned to bad feeling and to overeagerness, expressing itself in competitively lavish organizations and expenditures.

These expenditures and the bad press they produced about Wood and Lowden increased the likelihood that their mutual feud would have its natural result, and that some other candidate would win.

For Daugherty, nursing along Harding's candidacy with consummate care, the turn events had taken was tremendously heartening; he recognized, though hardly anyone else did, that now there was a real chance for Harding to win. Harding's term in the Senate was ending; and there was a crucial date ahead, when, under the Ohio law, Harding would be obliged to say whether or not he would be a candidate for another term in the Senate. Harding had taken it for granted that before that date came, his pro forma candidacy for the presidential nomination would be over, and he would be free to run for the Senate seat which he loved and knew he could get again. Now Daugherty told him he would have to take his chance on the presidential candidacy and forgo the senatorial one. He must, Daugherty told him, "go into the big circus."

Harding had one of his rare bursts of anger. Profanely he swore he would do no such thing. The incident occurred in Harding's Senate office. Daugherty, unable alone to compel Harding, sent for Mrs. Harding. She was an alert, sharp-voiced compound of energy and a kind of nagging ambition for her husband. "The two of us," said Daugherty later, "backed him against the wall and made him stick."

In the end, however, the decision was to file for the senatorial nomination; an agent was sent on to the state capitol at Columbus, and at 11:58 P.M., Friday night, two minutes before the deadline, he filed Harding's name.

To Harding the whole episode had been acutely displeasing. He had felt from the beginning of the discussion about whether he should file for the senatorship or not, that to be running for two offices at once would be unsportsmanlike, "unbecoming," the thing his inner spirit most disliked to be. That it "wouldn't seem right" had been, in all the discussions, his argument against running for both presidency and the Senate at the same time.

Throughout the whole week of the convention his manner, as he walked about the hotel corridors, was noticeably dejected. Some of the time he spent alone in a hotel suite with a young friend. To the young man he talked much about his early days in rural Ohio, the loveliness of the country roads in spring, the charm of the old-time one-room schools. Whenever he mentioned the battle for the presidential nomination raging a stone's throw away, it was to express a hope that he would not get it.

While Harding waited, aloof and gloomy, Daugherty was a dynamo of nervous force. For him, it was an occasion that comes only once in a lifetime, and to many, never—an occasion that all important politicians live for, and ninety-nine out of a hundred never see.

IV

From the opening day of the convention, Daugherty drew his talents tense. Emanations from his personality penetrated into every hotel where delegations stopped, almost into every convention seat. By intuition and experience, by the information he had acquired during the weeks before, and through scores of scouts who now served him, he knew the mind of every leader, almost of every delegate. Better than many of them knew themselves—for it is the way of leaders and delegates passionately devoted to a candidate to think their choice must win and to give no thought to any alternative—Daugherty knew what leaders and delegates would do as soon as it should be apparent that their candidates could not win. He knew not only their probable second choices but their third and their fourth. Most useful of all, he knew what they would do when all their choices had lost, when they were disappointed, tired, disgusted, and had no wish other than to nominate somebody, anybody, and go home.

While the delegates were Daugherty's main concern, he gave shrewd and subtle thought to all the aspects of his project. Throughout, his aim was to make the convention have a friendly feeling about Harding, to create what Daugherty called a "sweet atmosphere." With a major contender that would be impossible, for a major contender inevitably inspires rivalries, enemies, partisan resentment. But for a candidate who had few delegates, whom no one expected to win, Daugherty could make friends everywhere. He brought from Columbus a glee club of seventy-five voices. Ordinarily the function of such a club would have been to parade up and down the streets, and push through the crowded hotel lobbies, singing and shouting, truculently and raucously, something like, "We want Harding!" Not so with Daugherty's singers. His instructions to them were to visit the headquarters of all the other candidates and serenade them.

The convention, as Daugherty had hoped, came to a deadlock. With only one day left, the party elders decided to act. In a Chicago hotel suite— the "smoke-filled room" of political legend—they chose Harding as their compromise candidate. At ten o'clock the next morning, when the convention came together, the elders took hold of the situation. Not too firmly or too openly. They did not need to do that. All they needed, as respects the early ballots of the day, was to let events take the course which they knew to be predestined. It would be a mistake, a detriment to their later purpose and a possible damage to the party, for them to seem to be responsible for eliminating Wood and Lowden. They must let Wood and Lowden mutually eliminate each other, as was bound to happen. Happening that way, there would be no resentment on the part of the third of the convention who were for Wood or the third who were for Lowden. That is, of course, no resentment except as against each other; there would be no resentment against the party leaders nor against the candidate who must ultimately be chosen. And so there were several ballots which were partly the natural development of the situation and partly the shrewd directing of the elders, designed for window dressing, face-saving, and other desirable effects.

By the ninth ballot all the amenities and anticipatory prudences had been taken care of. It was late Saturday afternoon, forty-six minutes past 4:00; it was time to conclude. On this ballot Harding was given 374½ votes—his highest preceding had been 133½. That ballot was notice to all that Harding was the man; notice to all who desired to ride on the bandwagon that the wheels were about to roll. The delegates rushed for it. On the tenth ballot, Harding's total was 692⅕ and he was nominated.

Daugherty, during the afternoon, when the strain was tensest, had come up behind Mrs. Harding, seated in a box, and leaned over to whisper to her that on the next ballot her husband would be nominated. Mrs. Harding, by the sudden start she gave, drove two hat pins into Daugherty's side. He felt the pain, felt what seemed the trickling of blood down his side, and was a little alarmed. Characteristically, he said nothing to Mrs. Harding. Characteristically, he did nothing—the next ballot would be the crisis and climax of his career. As he hurried about he felt the queer swish of liquid in his shoe. After all was over, late that night, he tottered to his room, took off his shoe and found it full of perspiration.

V

Harding, nominated, told the Republican managers he would make the campaign from his home at Marion; he would, in the phrase made familiar by the practice of an Ohio Republican candidate of a quarter century before, William McKinley, "conduct a front-porch campaign." Some advisers and Republican managers demurred; times had changed, they told Harding; the presidency, like other goals of ambition, must be gone after; it must be sought in the modern manner and tempo, by "go-getter" methods. The people, they told Harding, might resent a front-porch campaign, might think it "high-hat," "snooty." But just because the front-porch method was more dignified, Harding clung to it. It appealed to a trait that was strong in him, his regard for seemliness, becomingness. He made few speech-making trips, and those reluctantly.

The front-porch method brought the ends of telegraph wires to the house next door to Harding's, and a swarm of newspapermen to Marion. These learned, and through them the country, the personality, antecedents and background of the little-known former newspaper publisher who was proposed as head of a nation of 120 million people.

Harding was the town's leading citizen, and one of the most well-to-do, but was no more pretentious than when he used to carry a pail of newsboys' pennies to the bank. He still, on frequent occasions, took off his coat and "made up" the paper, or set some type, doing it merely for the pleasure of recalling his younger years, mingling with the men, and enjoying the agreeably acrid smell of printer's ink. At the Marion Club of evenings he played whist and poker with old friends and cronies. For thirty years his morning walk from home to office had been a refrain of "Hello, Jim!" "G'mornin', Bill!" He was utterly modest, wholly without egotism, incapable of making the faintest effort to create an impression.

In the strong light that now beat upon him, this native unpretentiousness did not evaporate. Rather, it was increased, became a quiet humility. He had a task—he set his face to it and he would go through with it; he would work at it with earnestness because being earnest is part of the task, but he would not pretend to be more than he was. Outwardly, Marion saw no change in him.

Marion thought of him as one of them, and liked him, extravagantly. By every superficial appearance he was one of them. Yet some of the newspaper correspondents and others, who had had wide experience with men, and who now focused their minds intently upon understanding a man who might be president of the United States, felt that Marion did not fully know Harding. He was baffling to classify; he did not conform to any familiar pattern.

Physically, he was a distinguished person—that was the most patent fact about him. Probably he was aware of his advantage of appearance—he was aware of most things about himself—but he showed no faintest disposition to parade this distinction, or capitalize on it, nor any other consciousness except perhaps some quiet care about his clothes. The physical distinction was not—not on first acquaintance, certainly—borne out by his mind. In offhand talk he was commonplace, often crude, sometimes banal. Yet, observing him among his friends and neighbors, one was aware that they, after a lifetime of acquaintance, had a regard for his mind and his judgment. In any Marion group, Harding's word weighed more than that of any other. The atmosphere would be one of completely relaxed camaraderie, but there would also be unconscious deference.

The most available measure of Harding's personality was the institution that was his reflection; rarely has any relation between man and work so fully lived up to Emerson's rule that every institution is the elongated shadow of one man. The *Marion Star* was Warren Harding. It had been Warren Harding from the time of his taking hold of it as a derelict infant to its present very considerable eminence as a prosperous property covering its field as few newspapers do, its circulation in proportion to the population of the town hardly exceeded by any other paper in the country.

Stories sent out from Marion during the campaign, inspired more by zest for the dramatic than regard for the literal, said that much of the *Star*'s success, and of Harding's, was due to his wife. She was pictured as the vibrant dynamo who kept an inert husband going. There was little to that. It is true that for fourteen years after their marriage she had gone daily to the *Star* office, at a time, beginning in the early 1890s, when a woman in an office was novel. It was this conspicuousness, perhaps, that gave rise to the legend that the active and aggressive and talkative woman who bustled about the *Star* office was the source of much of its growth, and of Harding's. Passersby on the street had seen, on a thousand hot summer afternoons, Harding's outstretched feet reposing on the windowsill of the editorial sanctum on the second floor, and an equal number of times had seen Mrs. Harding chattering at the newsboys whom she managed in the first-floor office. From the contrast, some had deduced incorrect conclusions. The repose of Harding's personality, the reflective quality of his mind, his easygoingness of spirit, coupled with his common sense and his touch with the common man, were precisely what had enabled the *Star* to become what it was. A thousand acts of quiet, offhand judgment, a thousand refrainings from actions urged by the impetuous, a thousand waivings of what seemed immediate self-interest, had entered into the institution Harding had built, and the place he had made for himself in the community. Marion was a growing town, the *Star* needed only to grow with it; its guiding spirit needed little more than to have calm judgment, avoid mistakes, and keep the common touch.

The contrast between Harding's zest for physical exercise and his almost torpor when in repose, between his trenchant vigor of body and his poise of spirit, was but one of his many puzzling qualities. Marion thought Hard-

Home of Harding's newspaper, the Marion Star. *(From a photograph by Brown Brothers)*

ing's kindliness was undiscriminating, a little soft, one with his unwillingness to see an ant stepped upon, almost a fault and certainly a weakness. To the more experienced persons who now put Harding under close observation, his kindliness seemed one facet of a personal philosophy which had generated within himself, by which he guided himself—and which he kept to himself. He seemed to have an inner life, which he did not permit to extrude upon his Marion surface. It was as if his daily touch with his neighbors had planed and smoothed his exterior to slide smoothly along his Marion contacts, while within himself, and to himself, he kept judgments and standards and points of view that were individual to himself, as if, beneath the smooth and placid surface, a considerable intensity of emotional life might go on.

In most respects he was as much a part of Marion as Main Street, and the dry-goods store, and the courthouse steeple, and the crowd at the post office Sunday mornings. In other respects he seemed like something exotic, something slightly Buddhic dropped into this commonplace American community. What in other men might have been natural casualness seemed in Harding an innately developed philosophy. When his friends warned him against some who had hitched themselves to his rising public fortunes, and who had so maneuvered as to put Harding under a seeming obligation to accept association with them, Harding's reply was, "They won't cheat me." The head-shaking friends thought it was fatuous weakness, and in the outcome it led to tragedy, but I felt it was a conscious philosophy about human nature that Harding had worked out for himself and taken for his guide. When a Marion wisecracker asked him, "Do you know the difference between you and George Washington? George Washington couldn't tell a lie and you can't tell a liar"—I felt that maybe Harding could tell the liars, but chose not to. In politics, the liars and frauds sometimes have other characteristics which make them, as wholes, more trenchant in personality, more able for many purposes, or more amusing and engaging, or more generous and tolerant, and better companions for hours of ease, than some whose virtue is their only, and somewhat chill, appeal. And some who in politics are frauds and liars, are in other relations of life completely dependable, and—this would have appealed to Harding—generous and likable.

However we might explain and understand Harding's tolerance, we wondered uneasily if a trait that was harmless and even laudable in a small town's leading citizen might become a handicap and danger in a nation's president. One of the legends about him quoted the remark made to him by a friend sterner than himself, "Warren, your weakness is that you always treat everybody as good 'til you find them bad." A president of the United States, if Harding should become that, would need to be more hard-boiled. We were troubled, too, by his emphasis on loyalty. "God," he was quoted as having exclaimed, when he was urged not to yield too much to an unworthy friend, "God, I can't be an ingrate!" A sense of fraternity, of standing by one's own gang, may be harmless in the politics of a small community, but may be deadly in the White House. We knew that some

At the residence of President Harding, Marion, Ohio, August 12, 1920. Harding in a characteristic pose and action on his front porch at Marion during his campaign for the presidency. The little girl to whom Harding has given a piece of chewing gum is Narcissa Sullivan; the larger girl is Sydney Sullivan. The woman looking on from the steps is Mrs. Harding. The man to the left is Mark Sullivan. (From a photograph © by Edmonston)

who had helped Harding toward the presidential nomination, who had put him under what his code felt to be an obligation, were men who might be dangerous, if Harding should, through fear of seeming ungrateful to them, do what they asked.

Though he had a reticence which, we recognized, kept some of his personality hidden from the world, there was no dissimulation in him; indeed, some deep inchoate sense of taste, coupled with a natural honesty, led him to shun forms of pose which, in politicians and other public men, are taken for granted. When a currently well-known writer arrived in Marion on a Sunday morning, sent by the Republican campaign managers to go to the Baptist church with Harding and describe the candidate as a worshiper, Harding vetoed the exploitation, explaining gently that he was not really as religious a man as this kind of publicity would make him seem to be, that this was Communion Sunday, and that, while he was a member, he doubted whether he was good enough to take part in the communion. His refusing caused him some pain, for it wounded one of his other qualities, his wish to be accommodating. The incident disturbed him, he spent much of a valuable day in being friendly to the writer; he did not like the fellow, felt an inner disdain for one who would exploit religion, but he had made the man's errand fruitless, and felt he owed him something.

One of the town stories about him did not seriously impress us at the time; we felt it was a fiction, having the nature of a cartoon; one of those synthetic stories which, like an artist's drawing, is invented as frank exaggeration, not meant to be taken as fact. The story purported to be about the last occasion when Harding's father punished him corporally. The old gentleman was still alive, still vigorously moving about Marion to call on his patients. Our acquaintance with the father, the flavor of him, his strong common sense, the respect we had for him, all added to the piquancy of the story about him and his son. When the incident occurred, the boy had been about fifteen. The trouble he had got into and that had made his father angry with him was some boyish escapade, not any real fault of his own, but due to his "going along" with his gang, boys of greater initiative and daring than himself. In the ensuing rendezvous with his father in the woodshed, the physical punishment was accompanied, as was usual on such occasions, with verbal reproach. Between descents of the strap, old Dr. Harding remarked, "I suppose I ought to be thankful for one thing, that you're a boy; if you'd been a girl, by this time every boy in town would have had his way with you."

Harding on his front porch addressing one of the gatherings of visitors that were almost daily, and sometimes more than daily, incidents of the front-porch campaign. (From a photograph by Underwood & Underwood)

CHAPTER 3

The Election of 1920
and the Postwar Mood

To run against Harding, the Democrats nominated a man having much the same background (though quite different qualities of mind), a small-city editor and publisher, James M. Cox, who had spent two terms in Congress and was now governor of Ohio.

Cox, when he was nominated, was at his home in Dayton, Ohio. As his first act in the role of candidate, with the country watching intently to learn about his views and personality, he made a journey to Washington to call on President Wilson in the White House. It was, for Cox, a fateful journey; the atmosphere of the time gave to it the color of a pious pilgrimage, an act of devotion and dedication. That, to the public mind, identified Cox with Wilson, and with Wilson's ideals. And Wilson's ideals, to much more than half of America, had come to the stage in which early popular fervor was succeeded by disillusion, bitterness.

Wilson had presented the war to us as a fine spiritual adventure—and the 4 million Americans who participated had found it, most of them, disillusioning. Wilson had told us it was a "war to make the world safe for democracy"—and America had already begun to sense the decline of democracy that had begun with communism in Russia in 1917, and was destined to put democracy on the defensive everywhere. Wilson had told us it was a "war to end all wars"—and America had begun to feel that that promise, too, would fail. Wilson had committed America to membership in a League of Nations—and America had become suspicious that that meant commitment of America to send troops abroad on future occasions, repetitions of the experience that was already, and recently, dust and ashes in our mouths. Wilson, in short, was the symbol both of the war we had begun to think of with disillusion, and of the peace we had come to think of with cynicism. And Cox, by identifying himself with Wilson, took on Wilson's liabilities.

II

Rarely has any national mood been so definite or so nearly universal as the American one which followed on the heels of the Great War. A

The Democratic nominees in 1920, James M. Cox (right) for president, and Franklin D. Roosevelt for vice-president. The photograph was taken on the grounds of the White House on the occasion of Cox's visit to President Woodrow Wilson. (From a photograph © by Keystone View Co.)

word-of-mouth story of the day—one of that type of narrative that never happened but spontaneously generated as the epitome of a condition, a story whose essential truth lay in the delighted recognition with which hearers received it, rather than in fidelity to any actual event—was about a soldier returning from Europe on a transport. As the ship reached that nearness to home shores where it permitted the soldier to see the Statue of Liberty in New York Harbor, her face looking out toward Europe, he gazed rapturously at that first outpost of home shores, and solemnly vowed, to the statue and to the world, "Lady, once I get behind you, I promise I never will look at your face again."

That was not merely the returning soldier's homesickness for his familiar America; it was repugnance for his recent experience. That his repugnance was not very vocal, that he put his occasional expressions of it sometimes in terms of humor, was a characteristic American trait, and did not lessen the disrelish which the returning veteran felt.

He had gone to France thinking war romantic, glorious. That notion had come to him through the toys he played with and the ditties he had learned as a child; it had come to him from the stories and poems and orations about war and patriotism in his school "readers." It had been made fresh and personal to him, when, as a child about the turn of the century, he had thrilled at the sight of soldiers marching off to the Spanish War or to the Filipino Insurrection, the bands playing "Good-bye Dolly Gray," and the home folks singing,

> Don't you hear the tramp of feet, Dolly Gray,
> Sounding through the village street, Dolly Gray?
> 'Tis the tramp of soldiers true, in their uniforms of blue . . .

War as a romantic adventure had been impressed upon him by the Memorial Day parades of the Grand Army of the Republic in the North or the Confederate veterans in the South, by the tales he had heard from his father and grandfather about the Civil War. That war was fine and glorious had been impregnated into his spirit by the Civil War songs that were familiar in every family, sung at every gathering, songs of sentiment and glamour, and of war as a nostalgic memory: "Tenting Tonight on the Old Camp Ground," "When I Fit Fur Gineral Grant," "The Bonnie Blue Flag," "John Brown's Body," "Marching Through Georgia," "The Battle Hymn of the Republic," "Rally Round the Flag, Boys"—those airs, familiar to him throughout his boyhood, had been repeated by the bands that played him off to France. Practically all the literature about war that was familiar during the boyhood of those who grew up to cross the ocean with the American Expeditionary Force had pictured war as an adventure, as sentimental, as not-to-be-missed, as falling in love.

Exalted by that sentiment about the wars in which his older brothers and his father and grandfather had fought, and by the whole literature that war had produced since writing about war began, the young American had gone to France and to the front—but had found something very different from the skirmish which his school reader had called the Battle of Lexington, and nothing to remind him of Henry the Fourth's leading his soldiers "Once more unto the breach, dear friends." This was not a war of gallant dashes and cavalry charges, there was nothing like Sheridan galloping up from Winchester 20 miles away. This war was a thing of machinery and poison gas, of trenches, dugouts, mud.

Many conditions contributed to the young American's disillusion. The glow of high emotion about saving France had dulled upon acquaintance with Frenchmen en masse and in person—it was a common saying that American soldiers who after the Armistice occupied German territory had found the order and kindliness of the Germans, their *Ordnung* and *Gemütlichkeit*, more appealing than any qualities they found in the French. A story that went up and down the lines in France and trickled back to America was to the effect that the French charged the Americans rent for the land upon which the Americans dug trenches to defend France against the enemy. The story was not true, but, like many inventions, it reflected a prevailing mood.

The mood of exasperation, of expectations unfulfilled, of high emotion trickling out to disappointment, was accentuated by the manner of the war's ending. The inconclusive outcome did not conform to human nature. It was not a clean fight to a finish. About the time the Americans had got into the full heat of fighting spirit, the Germans quit. The Germans did not have the emotion of being beaten, the Americans did not have the emotion of winning—and that lack of the normal end for a fight was bad for both, led in both nations to distortion of nature's course. The fighting mood of the Americans, frustrated, deprived of its natural fulfillment, turned sour. Then, after the fighting ended with the armistice of November 11, 1918, most of the Americans were kept in Europe throughout nearly all the tedious length of the Peace Conference. By the time they could get back to America, their mood about their recent experience, and about Europe altogether, was "Never Again!" So also felt, as a rule, the young veteran's sister and his mother and his aunt, and his brother and his father.

Not much was said of it yet; we still felt obliged to pretend to ourselves that the war had been a fine experience; the returned soldier hated to forgo one of war's rewards, the thought of tales he would tell his children, like those his grandfather had told him about the Civil War. This subconscious unwillingness to acknowledge disillusionment, even to ourselves, did not rob the mood of its force; rather the unconsciously enforced self-repression gave the country a kind of fretful sullenness. It is to be observed that after the Great War we set up no heroes, no equivalent of Grant or Sheridan or Sherman or Lee or Jackson. And when books and plays about the Great War began to emerge, such as *What Price Glory*, and the bitterly sardonic *Plumes*, they emphasized not war's glamour but its grimness. The postwar literature, the "war books," not only reflected and expressed American disillusionment about the war, they had a far-reaching effect on our national thought in many respects.

If to the people, a large majority of them, the war was merely distasteful, the peace, the League of Nations, was odious, a menace. Wilson, after the Senate had wrangled for months over the treaty and the League, and after he had become bitter and sick, had said the election of 1920 should be "a great and solemn referendum." This declaration by Wilson, Cox endorsed. He made the issue clear, declared unequivocally what he would do if elected. "The first duty of the new administration," Cox said, "will be the ratification of the treaty. . . . The League of Nations is in operation. The question is whether we shall or shall not join. As the Democratic candidate I favor going in."

To which the Republican answer, if translated into the slang of the day, would have been, "Oh boy! Go to it!" The Republicans were sure a majority of the voters opposed our adhering to the League and disliked Wilson. In addition to the general disapproval of Wilson, specific groups of voters disliked him for specific reasons, all associated with the war or with the peace: German-Americans disliked Wilson because he had made promises to the German people which the Peace Conference did not keep; Italian-Americans disliked him because at the Peace Conference he had prevented Italy from getting Fiume and other territory to which Italy thought she was entitled; Austro-American voters disliked him because of the dismemberment to which the Peace Conference had subjected their unhappy homeland. Irish-American voters disliked him because of an episode at the Peace Conference; he had refused to give audience to an Irish delegation which wished to present claims to that "self-determination of small peoples" which Wilson had proclaimed for all—but which it was inexpedient to give to a dependency of Great Britain at a time when Britain's Lloyd-George was Wilson's associate in the Peace Conference. Nearly every group of foreign-born voters (except the Poles) had some such reason for disliking Wilson, something Wilson had done at the Peace Conference, some shifting of a national boundary in Europe, some denial of ethnic aspirations. And on all this the Republicans capitalized.

III

The campaign was extraordinarily unexciting. After it was three-quarters over a Minnesota great-grandfather among politicians of the day wrote, "I haven't heard of anybody getting mad and punching somebody else on the nose over a political argument this year yet." The editor of *Collier's* asked a journalist* of the time to answer the question, "Why is it that at this late day, with only four or five weeks left to go, nobody is taking much interest in the election?"

One reason lay in the recent passing of a group of great personalities from American politics. The gods had gone, and, compared to them, those who took their places, the present presidential candidates, were hardly even half-gods, barely quarter-gods. For more than a generation, three great personalities—Wilson, Bryan, and Theodore Roosevelt—had dominated the American political scene. That all three were immense personalities everyone would concede; as to any one of them, a partisan might like or not like the kind of personality, but could hardly fail to concede the quantity of it. In every presidential election for twenty-four years, since 1896, one of these had been a candidate, and sometimes two; and when any of them was not a candidate, he was active, sometimes overtowering the candidate. Now all three had passed to one kind or another of desuetude. Theodore Roosevelt lay in a hillside grave at Oyster Bay. Wilson was broken physically and politically—in the Democratic convention of 1920 his name had figured in one ballot of the forty-four, and he received the votes of two delegates out of a total of 1,094—he who less than two years before had truly bestrode the world.

Bryan, with his extraordinary vitality, though he had come to the front of American politics earlier than the other two, was still active, still had

*Mark Sullivan.

much prestige, still exercised some power. At the Democratic convention of 1920 he had been the most impressive figure, had made by far the most stirring speech, a plea for a "dry" plank in the platform. The convention listened respectfully, paid him complete deference—but did not adopt his plank, and Bryan, leaving the convention and taking a train for the North, bade a poignant farewell, "My heart is in the grave." The words were regret over the failure of the Democrats to be as "dry" as Bryan thought the party should be; but also, I think, he really felt old, and was giving expression to a mood deeper than the public knew. "My memory went back to the slender, black-haired, gallant, flashing, vital, resonant Bryan of 1896, and I had a somber feeling of the inexorableness of time. One thought of Bryan at that 1920 convention as an elderly uncle who comes to visit, wearing his black alpaca coat and his starched white shirt and his narrow black tie. He read us the Bible every night, he said grace at every meal, he quoted a good deal from Isaiah and the prophets, and he exhorted us to morality and virtue. We were all glad to see him; we listened to him very respectfully; we paid him the greatest deference; we treated him altogether with genuine and unstudied affection; but when he got around to telling us what we should do about our business, we gently and kindly, but firmly, elbowed him aside."*

The Titans had gone; and a generation that had known the strong wine of Bryan, Wilson, and Theodore Roosevelt could hardly be stirred by Harding and Cox. It was put succinctly by a senator when explaining on the evening of Harding's nomination the reason why Harding had been chosen—the senator was one of the most cultivated men in public life, a graduate of Yale, but he chose to be colloquial: "There ain't any first raters this year. This ain't 1880 or any 1904; we haven't any John Shermans or Theodore Roosevelts; we've got a lot of second-raters and Warren Harding is the best of the second-raters." Neither was Cox, it may be added, a Wilson or even a Grover Cleveland.

IV

The one sensation of the campaign, a story that Harding had Negro blood, exploded during the last few days before the election. It emerged first in whispered word of mouth. Then circulars appeared, anonymous of course, directly stating that Harding had Negro blood and supporting the assertion with a pseudogenealogical table. Two hundred and fifty thousand of the circulars were discovered in the mails at San Francisco—the Post Office Department at Washington, under Democratic President Wilson, ordered them destroyed and forbade postmasters to receive more. No one charged the national Democratic campaign management with giving any countenance to the thing. One minor Democratic worker in Pennsylvania, charged with distributing some of the circulars,

*Mark Sullivan in *Collier's*, October 9, 1920; here partly paraphrased.

"The Titans Had Gone."
*Top, Roosevelt's grave at Oyster Bay. (Underwood & Underwood) Bottom left, Wilson, in
his broken old age. (Wide World) Bottom right, Bryan, at the Dayton, Tennessee, trial
of John Scopes; a few weeks after this photograph was taken, Bryan died. (United
Newspictures)*

was arrested for libel. An attempt to distribute the circulars on suburban
trains running into Chicago resulted in a small riot. Tens of thousands
were slipped under doorways at night.

The Republican Party management, consisting mainly of one man,
probably the most vigilant and energetic national chairman either party

ever had, Will H. Hays,* had received information that this charge might be made, and had prepared for it. Promptly, Chairman Hays issued an authentic family tree, compiled in part by the historical society of Wyoming, Pennsylvania, where a generation of the Hardings had stopped on their way westward to Ohio, from which it appeared that Harding's blood was composed of the best strains from Pennsylvania, New York, New Jersey, and Connecticut. Harding's personal manager, Harry M. Daugherty, declared, with some pontifical pomposity, that "No family in the state [Ohio] has a clearer or more honorable record than the Hardings, a blue-eyed stock from New England and Pennsylvania, the finest pioneer blood, Anglo-Saxon, German, Scotch-Irish, and Dutch."

While some might smile at the inclusiveness of Daugherty's assertion, might say he was practicing the familiar political device of claiming everything, and might humorously suggest that had he thought of the electorate in Minnesota he would have added Swedish and Norwegian strains to Harding's lineage, yet no one gave serious credence to the charge that Harding had Negro blood; it was with humor, mainly, that the charge was received—though Frank Munsey, then owner of the *New York Herald*, screamed in his paper phrases about "dastardly conspiracy," "insidious assertion," "villainous undertaking," "foul eleventh-hour attack."

The charge, in its most concrete form, appeared in a circular calling itself "An Open Letter" addressed "To the Men and Women of America" and containing what purported to be five affidavits. The principal affidavit had at the bottom the facsimile signature, "W. E. Chancellor." A man bearing this name was at the time a member of the faculty of Wooster College, located not far from Marion. The affidavit represented that the man whose name was attached to it had authoritative qualifications: "I have studied ethnology in America and in Europe . . . I have measured the heads and carefully observed the other physical features of many thousands of persons. In Washington, where I was city school superintendent for several years, I had the opportunity of dealing with the largest colored population of any American city."

Basing its authority on these qualifications, the affidavit asserted that "Warren Gamaliel Harding is not a white man." With scientific precision, the affidavit particularized: "He is not a creole, he is not a mulatto, he is a mestizo." For which reason, the affidavit prayed "May God save America from international shame and from domestic ruin."

Such tangible origin as the story had was run down by newspaper correspondents at Marion. It went back some seventy years to a schoolyard quarrel of children, one side of which, after exhausting the effectiveness of tongue stuck out and thumb to the nose, and after using up the more familiar epithets of "scum" and "trash," had the inventiveness to think of "nigger." As it happened, this particular quarrel did not have the fortunate evanescence of most schoolyard flare-ups. An incident of physical violence

*Later famous in Hollywood as the author of "The Hays Code," guidelines for moviemaking that prohibited depiction of sex, vice rewarded, or much other human experience.—D.R.

To the Men and Women of America

AN OPEN LETTER

When one citizen knows beyond the peradventure of doubt what concerns all other citizens but is not generally known, duty compels publication.

The father of Warren Gamaliel Harding is George Tryon Harding, second, now resident of Marion, Ohio, said to be seventy-six years of age, who practices medicine as a one-time student of the art in the office of Doctor McCuen, then resident in Blooming Grove, Morrow County, Ohio, and who has never been accepted by the people of Crawford, Morrow and Marion Counties as a white man.

attended it and this led to a neighborhood feud that included grown-ups. "Nigger" became an epithet which one side hurled at the other; for generations the epithet remained alive; whenever Harding had run for office, the innuendo was whispered; persons who for any reason hated Harding used the epithet.

V

Harding was elected president of the United States. Some of his emotions were those that would come to any man, some were the fruit of Harding's particular temperament, upbringing, and environment. None were unworthy. Among the earliest was a sense of personal romance. It was not grandiose self-complacency—that Harding never had. But he would now be able to confer on old friends such elevations as they had never dreamed.

That a president should give a cabinet post to the author and manager of his campaign is a first law of politics. When intimate friend and political manager are one, the compulsion is doubly binding. Failure of Harding to put Harry Daugherty in his cabinet would have been a pointed exception to political practice, a pointed personal rebuff—and Harding was not the man to violate either the code of politics or that of friendship.

Had Daugherty happened not to be a lawyer, the situation would have been simpler; in that case Harding could have made him postmaster general, with fidelity to the rule that this post commonly goes to a political manager, and without offense to a public opinion that condones the rule. But Daugherty was a lawyer. Under the circumstances, to give him less than a legal post would have been only a little less pointed than to give him none. And the only legal post in the cabinet was an exalted and exacting one, attorney general. The appointment ought to go to a lawyer of the highest standing—and Daugherty, far from that, was, so to speak, outstanding in the dubiety of his standing. The situation was one to make a headache for Harding; and for Daugherty, too—if Daugherty had not been immune to headaches from that kind of cause.

From the time public discussion of cabinet possibilities began, newspapers watched and wrote of what Harding would do about Daugherty, the discussion being almost universally to the effect that Daugherty was not, either as man or as lawyer, a fit selection for attorney general. One journalist* of the day wrote pointedly and strongly about Daugherty's unfitness; suggested that Harding's sense of obligation might lead him to tender the office to Daugherty—but that if Daugherty was as good a friend as he claimed to be, he would decline the proffer. The *New York World* carried on a campaign against Daugherty, called him a lobbyist, unfit for that or any other high office; published sustained attacks on him, printed accounts of his career which laid emphasis on his lobbying. To Daugherty, the *World*'s assaults were as water on a duck's back, his integument had long been indurated to that sort of thing; to be the center of a swirling whirlpool of controversy was, for Daugherty, to be in his habitual habitat. To Harding, however, the *World*'s campaign against Daugherty was infuriating, he felt Daugherty was being crucified by a Democratic paper because of loyalty to him.

Finally, at a conference with the newspaper correspondents, Harding noticed the *World* correspondent who had written many of the attacks on Daugherty. Harding, growing red, let his anger force his own hand. He broke out—even in anger there was about Harding's words an aura of old-fashioned formality: "I am ready today to invite Mr. Daugherty into the cabinet as my Attorney-General; when he is ready there will be an announcement, if he can persuade himself to make the sacrifice; . . . if I can persuade him to accept the post. And"—pointing his finger at the *World* correspondent and recalling from his own experience a technical newspaper term—"you can set that up in a block on your first page."

A few minutes later, Daugherty coming down the steps, saw at the foot the other of his two principal newspaper critics, the author of this history. As he came face-to-face with me I assumed, I suppose, what manner of smile a man can summon up for such an occasion, and held out a congratulatory hand, saying: "Well, you're going to be Attorney-General!" Daugherty, with a manner that was one of his assets as a politician, the ability to preserve friendly relations with opponents and critics—Daugherty said, with complete good humor, "Yes, no thanks to you, goddam you."

About the time Harding had completed roughly half his cabinet selections, he passed through one of those sudden emotional elevations that brought out the best in him—some of his friends used to think of them as "camp-meeting conversions," though in fact they came to Harding when he was most alone. To an acquaintance who saw him in his Marion home early in January 1921 he said, with a manner which to a sensitive observer seemed poignant, "You know, before I was elected President, I thought the chief pleasure of it would be to give honors and offices to old friends—I thought that was the one big personal satisfaction a President would get. But you

*Mark Sullivan.

Harding's cabinet as first appointed. Seated from left to right, Secretary of War John W. Weeks; Secretary of the Treasury Andrew W. Mellon; Secretary of State Charles E. Hughes; President Harding; Vice-President Coolidge; Secretary of the Navy Edwin Denby. Standing, left to right, Secretary of the Interior Albert B. Fall; Postmaster General Will Hays; Attorney General Harry M. Daugherty; Secretary of Agriculture Henry C. Wallace; Secretary of Commerce Herbert Hoover; Secretary of Labor James J. Davis. (From a photograph by Globe)

know"—here Harding put his hand on his heart and his features took on a kind of solemn grief—"you can't do that when you're President of the United States; you have to get the best men."

And in that altered mood Harding, combing the country for talent, appointed three of the best men ever in any cabinet, men who had no personal relation to Harding at all: Charles E. Hughes to be secretary of state, Andrew W. Mellon to be secretary of the treasury, and Herbert Hoover to be secretary of commerce.

But the demons boiling the brew that was to be Harding's destiny knew they did not need to feel disturbed. One of the commonest contributions to tragedy is a moral decision, made too late.

CHAPTER 4

The United States, When Harding
Became President

The America in which Harding became president suffered from not only the worldwide dislocations and distresses caused by the war, but also from domestic turbulence and rancor, mainly the outgrowth of the war, domestic expressions of the worldwide condition. In America, the coming to an end of wartime emotion and of the spirit of national unity (partly fomented artificially) that had accompanied the war, was succeeded by a swing to the other extreme. The lifting of wartime controls over industry, the ending of war-achieved compactness, together with the cessation of wartime demand, followed by descent from wartime prices of food and other goods, led to severe economic dislocations which increased the harsh and discordant mood of the people. The resulting phenomena conformed, roughly, to a cycle. Wartime prices continued to rise for two years after the war ended—the peak was almost exactly November 1920. Consequently, the years 1919 and 1920 were a period of strikes, not only strikes to get increased wages but also strikes against high costs of living, "buyers' strikes," "rent strikes." About November 1, 1920 began descent in the prices of goods (rising value of money) which led to different but equally disturbing phenomena—failures in business, foreclosures of mortgages, distress on farm, reduction in wages, unemployment.

The two sets of clashing phenomena, with the many expressions of them in emotions of rancor, met and overlapped during the two years preceding the inauguration of Harding, and the ensuing swirling of untoward forces was at its worst when Harding became president. The sum of them composed the background in which he took responsibility for the country's well-being. The nation of which Harding became president was not happy, and forces were under way which seemed likely, unless arrested, to bring more serious unhappiness.

¶I

A long series of strikes and lockouts began January 9, 1919, with a strike of harbor workers in New York. . . . January 21, 35,000 dress and waist makers in New York, mostly young women, struck for a forty-four-hour week and a 15 percent increase in pay. . . . February 6, the country was shocked by the calling of a "general strike"—always an ominous thing—in Seattle, in support of striking shipbuilders. . . . February 17, threatened strike by 86,000 packers' employees was called off when the packers agreed to a wage increase amounting to $13 million for the year. . . . March 12, every car of the Public Service Railway Co., which ran through 141 New Jersey cities and towns, ceased operation at 6:00 P.M.; company officials explained that they preferred to give up service for the night rather than risk violence from their employees, who, 4,500 strong, had walked out at 4:00 A.M. . . . April 11, demands of railroad workers for higher pay were conceded by Director General Hines (the railroads were still under government control), who ordered advances amounting in their sum to $65 million a year. . . . July 17, 30,000 cigar makers struck in New York City. . . . July 18, 30,000 construction workers were locked out in Chicago. . . . August 1, 70,000 railroad shopmen in the Chicago district quit work; a strike of streetcar, elevated, and subway workers in Boston and Chicago partially paralyzed transportation in those cities. . . . Letter carriers appealed, August 3, to President Wilson for wage increases. . . . August 4, 4,500 railroad shopmen at Washington, D.C., and vicinity quit work. . . . August 6, Brooklyn's surface, subway, and "El" lines shut down at 10:00 P.M. because of violence attending a strike; during the day flying squadrons of strikers had halted cars, beat motormen, conductors, and policemen, and fled in automobile trucks. . . . August 7, actors walked out in New York, closing most of the city's theaters; on the same day a walkout of New England railroad shopmen caused the suspension of 102 passenger trains. . . . September 5, a strike of engineers and firemen forced

Left, a strike on the Brooklyn Rapid Transit lines led to use of bicycles. Right, a strike scene in Chicago. (From a photograph © by Western Newspaper Union through Underwood & Underwood)

Chicago Race Riots of 1919.
Negro residence after a crowd of whites had attacked it (see page 626). (From a photograph by International News Photos, Inc.)

tenants of the Metropolitan Building in New York to walk up forty-five flights of stairs. . . . September 19, at Chicago, 15,000 carpenters who had been on strike since July 18, forcing 80,000 other workers out, won their strike for $1 an hour, the highest wages paid carpenters in the United States. . . . September 30, a lockout of pressmen by printing shops started a strike which spread until more than sixty periodicals which normally were printed in New York had transferred to other cities. . . . A strike beginning October 31, which closed every bituminous coal mine in the country, causing everywhere a crippling of industry and transportation, was sustained until December 6, when President Wilson effected a compromise settlement.

III

The coming of the greatest strike of the year was foreshadowed August 27 when Judge Elbert H. Gary, head of the United States Steel Corporation, refused to deal with leaders of a newly formed union of steel workers organized by the radical wing of the American Federation of Labor. September 10, the mill employees of the Steel Corporation set September 22 for a general strike. September 17, Judge Gary reiterated his determination to stick to the open-shop policy at whatever cost; in the

Children of the Lower East Side doing picket duty during the rent strike in New York. (From a photograph by Underwood & Underwood)

Chicago district strike signs were posted on the walls of mills. September 18, a request by President Wilson that the strike be postponed was rejected by the leaders of the union. September 22, the great steel strike began. At the end of the first day union leaders claimed that 279,000 out of 350,000

An incident of the actors' strike in New York. (From a photograph by Underwood & Underwood)

workmen had quit. The companies said that not more than 20 percent of the men had left their jobs. At Pittsburgh the bulk of the workers remained at work, but in Chicago most of them walked out. Trouble occurred between strikers and mill guards at Homestead, Pennsylvania, and at New Castle five men were shot. September 23, at a Buffalo plant, two strikers were killed and fifty wounded by mill guards. At Farrell, Pennsylvania, two were killed and several wounded. At Chicago and Youngstown the strike spread. September 29, the Bethlehem Steel Company having rejected the demands of the union, a strike was called and about a quarter of the workers walked out. At Chicago, the Jones and Laughlin plants were forced to close, and 4,000 men quit at Clarksburg and Weirton, West Virginia. October 6, General Leonard Wood and Federal troops took charge at Gary, Indiana. The strike dragged to its end January 8, 1920, when the American Federation of Labor conceded defeat. William Z. Foster, radical leader of the strike, was compelled to resign his post with the union.

IV

In the excited state of mind that had been induced among American workers one item of news about a labor development abroad found a favoring ambient. August 2, 1919, a cable from London recited that 1,000 police at London and 929 at Liverpool had gone on strike. Among American police the idea of organizing into unions, though long discussed, had never taken hold. In 1919, of all wage earners the police had most cause for complaint. During the war their salaries had increased little if at all and the greatly higher prices for food, clothing, and housing had made it increasingly difficult for them to make ends meet. From the reports they read about the police strikes in England, they took hope that by organizing unions they could improve their condition. Several police unions were formed, among them one in the city of Boston.

The Boston union, chartered on August 15, 1919, and affiliated from the start with the American Federation of Labor, quickly ran into difficulties with the city officials. August 26, nineteen patrolmen, leaders in the union movement, were summoned before a trial board and charged with disobeying a ruling by the commissioner of police, Edwin U. Curtis, forbidding organization. In the meantime, a Committee of 34, appointed by Mayor Andrew Peters, conducted an investigation and presented a conciliatory report suggesting that the men be permitted to retain their union provided it be divorced from any connection with the American Federation of Labor. This solution Police Commissioner Curtis refused to accept. Thereupon the union officials called a strike for 5:00 P.M. Tuesday, September 9. At that hour, 1,117 patrolmen out of a total force of 1,544 walked out. For the first time a great American city was left without protection, completely at the mercy of the lawless. Merchants, frightened, closed and locked their shops and prepared to make armed defense of their property. At 11:00 P.M., with not a policeman on the streets anywhere, looting began;

The Boston police strike, 1919. (From a photograph by International News Photos, Inc.)

all night long, Boston witnessed such scenes as had never before occurred in an American city in peacetime.

On September 10, Mayor Peters called on the militia for police duty, and the soldiers, trying to put down lawlessness, became involved in fights with rioters which resulted in the killing of two persons and the wounding of many more. The next day, with the strike still on but with disorder diminishing, Governor Calvin Coolidge took command and issued an edict calling on the citizenry of the state to uphold the forces of the law. That was the turning point. September 12, the places of the striking police were filled by new men, including a number of war veterans, and the trouble was over.

But though Boston was again serene there was still to happen an event both dramatic and historic. A plea by President Gompers of the American Federation of Labor that the defeated strikers be allowed to return to their jobs was denied by Governor Coolidge, who replied in a telegram which, when printed in the newspapers, brought him a message of congratulation from President Wilson, applause from the public, and the vice-presidency in 1920: "There is no right to strike against the public safety by anybody, anywhere, any time."

V

Some of the strikes and other violence connected with labor had their origin in the I.W.W. and other radical organizations. The radicals, regarded with repugnance by many Americans, were, in 1919, looked upon with more than ordinary dislike. The fear of disorder that followed the war inspired a crackdown on "Reds."

February 4, following a declaration by Senator King of Utah that the Russian Bolsheviks were conducting propaganda for the overthrow of the American and other capitalistic governments, a Senate committee was appointed to investigate Bolshevik activities in the United States. . . . February 11, the Department of Justice brought fifty-three Reds from the far West to Ellis Island for deportation. . . . A month before, on January 8, Congressman Victor L. Berger and other socialists and radicals had been convicted by a federal jury at Chicago of sedition and disloyalty under the Espionage Act. . . . February 20, a jury at Hammond, Indiana, after deliberating two minutes, acquitted Frank Petroni, naturalized citizen whose patriotic emotion had led him to shoot and kill Frank Petrich, an immigrant, for yelling: "To hell with the United States!" . . . March 10, the U.S. Supreme Court unanimously sustained the conviction of Eugene V. Debs, four times Socialist candidate for president, found guilty of violating the Espionage Act through statements made in a speech at Canton, Ohio, in June 1918, and sentenced him to ten years imprisonment. Debs, two days later, in a farewell public address at Cleveland, praised the Bolshevist rule in Russia and referred to Lenin and Trotsky as the "foremost statesmen of the age." Debs said the judges of the Supreme Court were "begowned, bewhiskered, bepowdered old fossils who have never decided anything." Entering prison April 13, 1919, to begin serving his sentence, Debs was made clerk in the hospital. . . . April 14, a group of I.W.W., attempting to hold a meeting at Farrell, Pennsylvania, were driven out of town. . . . April 30, what was asserted to be a nationwide plot by Reds to celebrate May Day with wholesale assassinations of jurists, cabinet members, and other public officials was thwarted by the discovery of sixteen packages in the General Post Office in New York containing dynamite bombs. Throughout the country a total of thirty-four infernal machines, addressed to public officials, all of the same make, were seized in the mails or after delivery. Among those who received bomb packages, or were marked for death in some other way, were: Justice Oliver W. Holmes of the Supreme Court; Postmaster General Burleson, federal judge K. M. Landis, Governor Sproul of Pennsylvania, Secretary of Labor Wilson, Attorney General A. Mitchell Palmer, Mayor Hylan of New York. . . . May 1, upward of 400 soldiers, sailors, and marines, including some Victory Loan workers, raided the office of the *New York Call*, a Socialist newspaper, beat several editors, and damaged the plant. . . . May 5, the I.W.W., holding a convention in Chicago, were denounced by the Board of Aldermen. . . . May 7, Governor Alfred E. Smith of New York signed a bill forbidding a display of red flags in New York State. . . . June 2, a bomb wrecked the residence of Attorney General Palmer, arch-foe of the Reds, in Washington; a man thought to be the bearer of the bomb was blown to pieces. . . . June 17, the American Federation of Labor convention at Atlantic City rejected the I.W.W. plan for one big union, and passed a resolution condemning Bolshevism. . . .

The wholesale deportation of alien agitators from the United States in 1919 and 1920, and the presumably not very comfortable lot of the deportees after their return to Russia, supplied the inspiration for this cartoon. (© George Matthew Adams)

October 7, 118 immigrants, steel strikers belonging to the I.W.W., were forced to kiss the American flag by police at Weirton, West Virginia. . . . November 7, the Department of Justice, alleging a revolutionary plot had been uncovered, began a nationwide raid on radicals, arresting more than 200 in New York City alone. . . . November 10, the House of Representatives, by 309 votes to 1, unseated Socialist Congressman Victor L. Berger of Milwaukee. . . . November 11, at Centralia, Washington, three ex-service men, members of the American Legion, attempting to raid I.W.W. headquarters during an Armistice Day parade, were shot to death. One of the alleged shooters was lynched. . . . December 2, President Wilson in a message to Congress urged action for the curbing of Reds. . . . December 21, the U.S. transport *Buford*, with 249 radicals, among them the feminist and anarchist Emma Goldman, marked for deportation, sailed for Russia. January 7, 1920, the New York State Legislature refused to permit the seating of five Socialists elected to the Assembly from New York City. Alfred E. Smith, governor of New York, protested: "Although I am unalterably opposed to the fundamental principles of the Socialist Party, it is inconceivable that a minority party, duly constituted and legally organized, should be deprived of its right to expression so long as it has honestly, by lawful

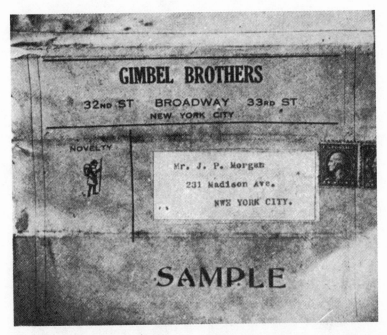

One of the many bombs addressed to public men in a nationwide dynamite conspiracy during 1919. The paper in which the bombs were wrapped had either been stolen from or was a counterfeit of paper in which packages were sent out by a well-known New York department store. (From a photograph by Underwood & Underwood)

methods of education and propaganda, succeeded in securing representation, unless the chosen representatives are unfit as individuals."

VI

On April 15, 1920, carrying $15,000, the payroll of the shoe factory for which they worked, Frank Parmenter and Alexander Berardelli, paymaster and guard, were shot and killed on a street in South Braintree, Massachusetts. They had gone to Boston at noon to get the payroll and had returned on the train, reaching South Braintree at 3:00 P.M. Leaving the station, they were almost at their destination when an automobile drew swiftly up beside them and two of five men riding in it, according to stories told by eyewitnesses, started shooting with revolvers. Parmenter and Berardelli slumped to the ground, killed instantly. The murderers, brandishing their weapons, leaped to the sidewalk, seized the payroll, and sprang back into their car, which dashed around a corner and disappeared. Numerous persons who saw the crime told the police that the murderers and their companions were swarthy of complexion and appeared to be Italians.

Three weeks after the murders, two Italian workmen, Nicola Sacco and Bartolomeo Vanzetti, were arrested at Brockton and charged with the crime. In the trial, presided over by Judge Webster Thayer, the men

The R Street, Washington, home of A. Mitchell Palmer, attorney general in Wilson's cabinet. The house was wrecked by a bomb thrown by an unknown person who was killed by the explosion. (From a photograph by Western Newspaper Union)

protested their innocence. Both furnished alibis. A clerk in the Italian Consulate at Boston testified that Sacco had been in his office on April 15 at about the time the crime was committed. Vanzetti, according to several witnesses, had spent the day selling fish in Plymouth, 35 miles from South Braintree. Evidence against the men was largely circumstantial. Judge Thayer, when charging the jury, said, "There is a most strenuous dispute as to the identity of the murderers; the real issue you must determine is" their identification. The jury brought in a verdict of guilty and Judge Thayer sentenced the two men to death.

Before their arrest neither Sacco nor Vanzetti had been convicted of a crime. Sacco was a shoe worker and watchman, and one employer testified to his honesty. Vanzetti had done menial work. For some months prior to his arrest he had made a living peddling fish in the Italian colonies near Boston.

Both men were radicals. Shortly before their arrest they had been leaders in arranging a mass meeting of protest against the alleged brutality of Department of Justice agents toward a fellow radical, who had leaped to his death from the New York offices of the Department of Justice while undergoing questioning. Both Sacco and Vanzetti were active in strikes, though not as paid organizers.

With the arrest of the two Italians, friends and sympathizers formed a

Nicola Sacco and Bartolomeo Vanzetti. (From a photograph by International News Photos, Inc.)

Funeral of Sacco and Vanzetti in Boston, following their execution in the Charlestown Prison, August 23, 1927. (From a photograph by International News Photos, Inc.)

A demonstration in Union Square, New York, by radicals and other sympathizers with
Sacco and Vanzetti, against the execution of the two men; 12,000 persons were in the
crowd. (From a photograph by Underwood & Underwood)

"Save Sacco and Vanzetti" committee, which raised a defense fund and for
years after the trial agitated for the release of the prisoners. Radicals everywhere in the world affiliated themselves with the cause. Joined with the
radicals were numerous other persons of high standing who believed that
the two Italians had been "convicted by atmosphere, not evidence." Sacco
and Vanzetti were executed on August 23, 1927, at the Charlestown, Massachusetts, state prison.

VII

When, on February 17, 1919, a large body of black soldiers, returning
from France, marched up Fifth Avenue in New York, they were
given as fine an ovation as any white troops had received. That was the last
time returning Negro soldiers were cheered by white people. Trouble between the races broke out in several places. At Washington, D.C., in late
June 1919, for several days the nation's capital witnessed street fighting between blacks and whites almost on the scale of a small civil war. At
Chicago, a racial clash occurred July 28 and lasted for three days, during

which thirty-six persons were killed. Equally serious trouble occurred in Arkansas and St. Louis. Throughout the South and Midwest, racial feeling ran high, stimulating the growth of the Ku Klux Klan and adding one more to the rancors and class conflicts that beset the country.

VIII

"The government," said the periodical *The New Republic*, "during the next four years will have to deal with a group of political and economic problems of altogether exceptional stubbornness and difficulty. Only once before in the history of the nation, in the years immediately preceding the election of Washington, has the American people been confronted with the necessity for an equally grave and complicated group of decisions. In reaching these decisions the next President must for good or ill play the leading part. The government and public opinion can obtain leadership from no other source."

For meeting these tasks and responsibilities, Harding had a method—not so much a consciously worked-out method as a simple expression of his personality. Its spontaneousness, its naturalness, as an emanation of Harding's personality, was not altered by the artificiality of the phrases in which his editorial training had led him to put it, in a speech at Boston in May 1920: "America's present need is not heroics, but healing; not nostrums but normalcy; not revolution but restoration . . . not surgery but serenity."

CHAPTER 5

The Harding Tragedy

A t all times, when a new president comes into office, many classes of persons seek to find out who is close to him, who knows his inner mind. The good seek to learn in order that they may know through whom they may most advantageously present the diverse plans of bettering the world that they wish to promote. Newspapermen seek to learn in order that, by association with the president's intimate, they may find out the president's thoughts. Politicians seek to learn in order that, by dropping suggestions to the president's friend, they may hope the suggestions will later reach the president. Office seekers and sponsors of office seekers want to learn in order that commendation poured into the ear of the intimate may find ultimate lodgment in the ear of the president.

To one class, knowing who is close to the president—who is "next," this class would put it—is a career, a business. The more elevated among them are lobbyists in the familiar sense, the more sordid are an inferior caste. Lobbyists in many instances have places in clubs, are met at dinners; the objects for which they pursue acquaintance and influence are, while selfish, nevertheless legitimate; their work in many cases is helpful to Congress and the government departments, and useful to the country. The more sordid agents have purposes which are on the borderland of the sinister, attainable as a rule only by the evasion of law or the perversion of authority. Their pursuit of their objectives has some similarity to the stalking of prey. Lynx-eyed, they sit in hotel dining rooms to observe who lunches with whom. Ingratiatingly they inject themselves into the semi-public conversations of hotel lobbies. Casually, but sharp-eyed, they stroll the streets in the neighborhood of the White House and the cabinet departments. Obsequiously, they make acquaintance with anyone who seems to have a place in the hierarchy of power. Within a few months after a new administration is in office, they know the lines of friendship and acquaintance that lead up to the president, know the relations of minor satellite to major in the orbit of which the White House is the sun; know who is the friend of the President, who is the friend of the friend, who the friend of the friend of the friend, to the nth degree of consanguinity of power. Not always, indeed only rarely, can they get direct advantage from their knowledge—but often they can use it to impress the dubious seekers for illicit advantage, or the scared seekers of safety who are their clients.

To everybody, the knowledge was universal that in the Harding administration, Harry Daugherty was closest to the president, and Jess Smith was the satellite of Daugherty. All, all varieties, every shade in the spectrum, from altruists seeking action by Harding that would bring the millennium and pacifists wishing to lay before Harding the plan that would infallibly bring permanent peace, down through rich men seeking to be made ambassadors or ministers and politicians promoting appointment of a friend to office, and still farther down to the lobbyists for great interests, and yet farther down to the fixers for small and sometimes corrupt interests—all these gradations of suppliants for good causes and promoters of bad ones knew that Daugherty, more than any other man, had the ear of Harding, and presumed that Jess Smith had the ear of Daugherty.

II

A man of Smith's nature was sure to be liked, and one having his position was sure to be flattered and favored. Persons having no immediate ulterior motive paid attention to him—the deluxe suite in a hotel for a nominal price or none, a free trip on a steamship, his check for services returned to him with a receipted bill and the compliments of the management.

Among it all he was sure to be sought by the fixers and lobbyists, and so naive a person as Jess was sure to fall for them. Presently he was besought to get a pardon for this one, a liquor permit for that one, and soon tender of compensation was made to him, at first perhaps a case of pre-Prohibition whiskey, a tip on the stock market, but later, compensation more substantial. Smith became an occasional visitor to a greenstone house on K Street with a magnolia bush in the small front yard; it had been leased by an Ohio politician come to Washington as a lobbyist, and it became known (when subsequently commotion arose), as the "little green house on K Street." Here and elsewhere Jess became associated with persons expediting deals for large fees. He began to introduce lawyers having cases before government departments to the officials in charge of the cases—and to such lawyers, an introduction from a person having Smith's position was a valuable commodity.

Soon Jess learned that if he had thought the ordinary politics of Washington, D.C., to be much the same as the ordinary politics of small-town Ohio, he was much mistaken. The sinister politics of Washington was much more intricate and formidable. Smith found himself beyond his simple depth. In his progress in sophistication, he was carrying large margin accounts in stock brokerage offices, and they went the way the stock speculations of the inexperienced often do. Losses in this quarter led to desire for more money. A small fee taken for questionable services "just this once" became a precedent for larger fees taken for services more questionable. He was obliged to hold somber secrets about himself, and this was corroding to his expansive nature. Smith became uncertain, nervous, dazed, then frightened. His mental condition was aggravated by illness; he had diabetes, and when he had an appendicitis operation, the diabetes prevented the wound from healing. Between physical illness and mental distress, Smith became a desperately unhappy man.

III

Daugherty, too, for different reasons, was under strain, but he was of stouter fiber than Jess Smith; in Daugherty frazzled nerves took the form of irritability. His work as attorney general was strange to him; he knew there was mistrust of him because of the newspaper criticisms of his earlier career. Always he was under fire, from newspapers, from individuals and committees in Congress. Aside from these harassments of his own, he was troubled about some ominous developments he knew were arising within the Harding administration, and some close to himself. He was especially concerned about his old friend Jess.

Daugherty and Smith decided to go to Ohio for a rest. But the change of scenery did not relieve the strain. When Jess woke Harry from a nap one afternoon, Daugherty flew into a rage and abused Smith unmercifully. The following night, Jess took the train back to Washington. At the apartment

Attorney General Harry M. Daugherty (right) and Jess Smith. (From a photograph by Acme Newspictures)

he and Daugherty shared he was alone—Daugherty had moved into the White House. The following night Daugherty asked his secretary, Warren F. Martin, to stay in the apartment with Smith—Daugherty was worried about him. The next morning Martin heard a crash, he thought it was a door slamming or that a waiter had dropped a tray; but he could not get to sleep again and he went into the sitting room. Looking into the other bedroom, he saw Jess Smith slumped on the floor his head in an iron wastebasket and a revolver in his right hand.

That night, as usual, Daugherty—still a guest of the White House—dined with the Hardings. Mrs. Harding, as if she sensed the gloom that must be upon the two men, with their intimate memories of Smith and happy times, invited two guests from outside, a couple who were close friends of the Hardings. The device did not help much. The guests, far from being able to bring cheerfulness to the table, were suffused with the numb despair of the hosts; for the rest of their lives the two guests—they happened to be a sensitive couple—remembered that night. At the dinner table, only fragmentary sentences were spoken. Afterward, a private showing of a motion picture in the upstairs hall furnished no real diversion—but did happily provide a darkness to five harassed souls, a darkness that saved each countenance from sight of the others. No one spoke. Only from one person came any sound; from time to time Daugherty uttered a long-drawn-out "O-o-o-o-o-o-o." For the ordinary blows of fate, Daugherty had stoicism unlimited, but this wound to his affections broke his defenses. At the end of the motion picture, the guests shook limp hands with white-faced hosts.

IV

For Harding's distress at Jess Smith's suicide, there was enough reason in the personal affection he had had for him, the old associations, and the very great affection which Harding knew Daugherty had felt for him.

There was justification for another reason: Harding had heard that Smith had been keeping company a man in his position ought not to keep, that he was much with lobbyists and fixers, that there was ominous talk about it. Harding had told Daugherty that he must send Jess away from Washington, and Daugherty had told Jess he must go back to Ohio. Now Harding could not know how much Smith's suicide might be due to humiliation over Harding's saying he must leave Washington—Harding, more than almost any other man, would have hated to think that. Harding could not know how much Smith's suicide might be due to that, how much to ill health, and how much might perhaps be due to guilty conscience in Smith—to what degree Smith might have become seriously involved with the lobbyists and fixers and might have been in fear of exposure.

But Smith's had been the second suicide in the Harding circle within three months; and in connection with the other one, Harding had convincing evidence that there were dubious conditions in an important department of his administration.

V

Of all the appointments Harding had made on a personal basis, from among his own circle of friends and acquaintances, he had taken almost the greatest pleasure in giving the office of head of the Veterans' Bureau to an acquaintance he had made on a trip to Honolulu, Colonel Charles R. Forbes. Harding later took pride in Forbes's work. Forbes was a bustling, energetic person, with a glib and convincing tongue; he kept telling Harding how fast he was getting hospitals built—Congress had appropriated $36 million for the purpose and Forbes was making the money fly; these reports Harding used to repeat to newspapermen at his press conferences. One observed during the early months of Harding's administration that whenever he mentioned Forbes's work he looked pleased; here was one part of his administration, Harding felt, that was clearly making good.

One day, Harding's personal physician, Dr. Charles E. Sawyer, whom Harding had brought from Marion and who was alert for Harding's interest, heard information that made him suspicious about Forbes. Sawyer looked into it enough to become more suspicious, and then went to the other old friend who was watchful for Harding, Attorney General Daugherty. Sawyer told Daugherty facts which suggested strongly that Forbes had corrupt relations with the contractors to whom he let out the building of hospitals, and with others, to whom he was selling excess supplies left over from the war.

Daugherty decided to tell Harding. He hated to, he knew it would hurt

Charles R. Forbes. (From a photograph by Keystone)

Harding. But he went to the White House. As he had predicted, the president was stunned, then irritated and depressed.

Harding sent for Forbes and had an interview with him (from which Harding returned to sit through a dinner with friends in the White House without saying a word); he arranged with Forbes that the latter should go abroad, and while abroad should resign; this Forbes did. Within a short time, the gossip about Forbes reached a point at which a Senate investigation of the Veterans' Bureau was inaugurated. Twelve days after the investigation was authorized, Forbes's closest assistant, legal adviser to the Veterans' Bureau, Charles F. Cramer, asked his wife one night to take the midnight train to New York with a message Cramer said was important. The next morning, Cramer's cook, surprised by his not coming down to breakfast, found him on the bathroom floor, shot, a suicide. To Harding, suicide of a person high in the Veterans' Bureau and close to Forbes at the time investigation of the Bureau and Forbes was beginning, could not help but be ominous.

The incidents had not, as yet, made much impression on the public; they were chiefly subjects of gossip in small circles. But Harding had begun to learn something of the conditions they implied.

One of the few photographs of Harding and Coolidge together. As the photograph suggests, Harding, but for a fatal streak of softness, was the bigger man, the larger personality. As between the two, it was Harding who looked the president. The qualities that enabled Coolidge to make the better record were caution, coldness, a canny shrewdness. This photograph was taken shortly before Harding started on his ill-fated trip to Alaska in June 1923. At this time, as the expression of strain on his face indicates, he was well on in his via crucis. (© by Edmonston)

VI

To only a slight degree was Harding temperamental; life did not translate itself to him in terms of being happy or unhappy. But the presidency weighed on him. The work of it was more arduous and continuous than he had been accustomed to. The hard work, the limitations on his ease and freedom, wore him down. As he worked harder, he pursued his diversions harder, golf two or three times a week, poker and whist at night. The speed, the tempo, was so contrary to Harding's nature that it alone was enough to weaken him physically, distress him spiritually.

He was conscientious, according to his own standards—which is the only way anybody can be conscientious; and he was irked, a little shamed, by the compromises he had frequently to make between what he liked to do and what his office obliged him to do, or what he felt was due to his office. Once, after he had sent for me and we had sat on the South Portico of the White House, talking about a serious railroad strike, he wished to offer me a drink. He, with Mrs. Harding, took me into their bedroom, saying they felt that since national prohibition was in effect, they ought not to drink in the ordinary rooms of the White House, nor offer drinks to their friends, but that in their bedroom they might properly follow their personal standards.

Of all Harding's escapes from weariness, the one he liked best was to go out into the country and make speeches. He felt he spoke well; it was the sole thing he was vain about. Modest to the degree that he blushed when other accomplishments were attributed to him, he would say, to friends sufficiently intimate, "I really think I know how to deliver a good speech." The ability to please his audience and the response, the sympathy he got from the crowd, stimulated him. So he liked to do it, he had a word for it; his expression was, "I like to go out into the country and 'bloviate.'"

Some of this feeling moved him, in the spring of 1923, to plan a trip to Alaska. As the time approached, it happened that he completed negotiations begun by two men who had wished to buy the *Marion Star.* The price was large, for the *Star* was a fine property, and the contract included an arrangement by which Harding, when he should complete his presidency, would write for it. To close up the negotiations and write the contract, he had Daugherty in the White House for a day. It was the day before he was to leave for Alaska. He took advantage of Daugherty's presence also to have him write his will.

VII

At the start, the crowds meeting the train in cities and towns were small and apathetic, but as Washington was left farther behind they grew in size and enthusiasm. Had the circumstances of the trip been different,

Harding would have got enjoyment from it. As it was, he was miserable. Physically, he was tired out, tired beyond the point where recuperation would be possible short of a long period of absolute quiet and rest. And matching his physical discomfort was mental unease. The president was distraught, restless. He disliked being alone. The train, after reaching the Midwest, struck a heat wave which lasted all the way to Denver. Dr. Sawyer, concerned, urged Harding to relax, take things easy, but at every town and village where the train stopped, Harding appeared on the rear platform, made a speech, shook as many hands as he could reach, posed for photographers, stood bare-headed in the sun's glare.

Before leaving Washington, Harding had written a number of speeches for delivery along the way. By 1923, the radio had developed to the stage where it was an adjunct to oratory; in some of the places where Harding talked microphones and amplifiers were installed. These were new to Harding and it was noticed that using them cost him a double expenditure of effort. He was irritated, felt that his delivery was made ineffective. That distressed him. His delivery was the one thing he was proud of.

In Alaska, travel proved to be more of a strain than had been anticipated. The president grew more and more tired. A plan to return by way of the "Richardson Trail" was given up in favor of the route by rail, which was more direct and would more quickly get Harding to the quiet and rest of the sea trip aboard the transport *Henderson*. But the few days at sea on the *Henderson* were too short. At Vancouver, where the party landed on July 26, tremendous crowds welcomed them; but Harding's effort to respond to their enthusiasm was pitiful. The next day, at Seattle, he spoke in the stadium, bare-headed, under a burning sun. Members of the party observed that several times he faltered, as if about to collapse. By now everybody on the presidential train felt acute concern; everybody except Harding thought that the trip should now be given up.

That night from the president's room a hurry call was sent out for Dr. Sawyer, who found Harding in great pain. He thought it due to ptomaine poisoning caused by eating tainted crabs. Others had eaten the crabs but had not been made ill.

Harding insisted that the journey be resumed. On the way to San Francisco, he remained in bed in his stateroom. Repeatedly he expressed distress because of the disappointment he was causing the crowds by not being able to show himself.

San Francisco was reached on Sunday morning, July 29. Harding dressed himself and walked unaided through the station to the street. Reporters said in their stories that he looked "gray and worn."

At the Palace Hotel, Harding went at once to bed, but sent out word that after resting he would be all right and that he would surely deliver an address he had scheduled for the following Tuesday. Over the weekend he failed to improve. A doctor called in for consultation wrote: "His acute illness came to a peak on Monday night with the rapid development of a bronchial pneumonia. The quick, irregular, and labored breathing dis-

The last photograph of Harding, taken at the end of the Alaskan trip as he was entering the Palace Hotel in San Francisco, from which he was to be borne out on a bier. There is a melancholy interest in comparing this with earlier photographs of Harding on preceding pages. (From a photograph by Underwood & Underwood)

tressed him and when, by stimulation, he had been relieved after a sharp attack of breathlessness, he said, 'I feel much relieved, but, oh, so very tired.'" On Tuesday he was seriously ill. The doctors said his heart was weak. Wednesday he showed "remarkable improvement," was able to sit up in bed, read the papers, take solid food. Wednesday afternoon Dr. Sawyer announced that the crisis had passed and that the president was on the road to recovery. Thursday the bulletins announced continued, though slow, improvement. Thursday evening at about half past seven, Mrs. Harding was reading aloud to him an article about himself by Samuel G. Blythe in the *Saturday Evening Post*—the editors had captioned it "A Calm View of a Calm Man." When Mrs. Harding paused a moment, Harding said, "That's good! Go on, read some more." As he uttered the words, a shudder passed through his body. Then he relaxed.

Harding was the first president to die in office in twenty years, since McKinley, and the fifth in the history of the country. The event provided one of the rare occasions America has for national emotion. The circumstances—the death in San Francisco, the long journey of the funeral train across the continent, the ceremonies at Washington, the journey from the capital back to Ohio, the burial at Marion—prolonged the emotion as few emotions are, enabled scores of separate communities to have a direct part in it, and made of the whole an event not before duplicated and not in the future likely to be.*

The itinerary of the cross-continental run had been arranged in advance on a fixed schedule, and newspapers had given wide publicity to it. Thus it was possible for people living long distances from the route to be on hand to see the train as it passed by. Multitudes came—estimates put the number as high as 3 million. The spectacle was a unique one. Newspapermen aboard the train, some of them veterans who had witnessed most of the important happenings in America during the prior twenty years, said they had never seen anything to compare with it.

In towns, as the train passed through, practically the whole population assembled at the stations. In cities, so vast were the crowds at the stations and along the tracks that the train could only creep along. Even in the open country there was hardly a mile of the continentwide journey without its fringe of onlookers.

In a way, Harding was fortunate to die when he did. The outpouring of grief was genuine; the crowds had wanted "normalcy" when they elected him, and normalcy he had given them. Though he lacked the equipment for the office, his presidency was not without its accomplishments. Under the leadership of Secretary of State Charles Evans Hughes, the Washington Conference for the Limitation of Armament agreed on a reduction in the navies of the major powers. The Harding administration negotiated the eight-hour day in the steel industry. And in the spirit of normalcy, of putting to rest the bad feelings engendered by the war to rest, the president pardoned the Socialist leader Eugene V. Debs. These accomplishments— and the calm integrity of Harding—filled the thoughts of the mourners who witnessed the journey of the funeral train. Not until after Harding rested in the ground would the public's view of his administration begin to change.

*Unfortunately, Sullivan was wrong. The deaths in office of Presidents Franklin Roosevelt and John Kennedy would provide Americans with more opportunity, and perhaps more cause, for mourning. At Kennedy's death, television would reach more communities than Harding's funeral train ever did. —D.R.

CHAPTER 6

The Scandals

Calvin Coolidge was in the White House. Harding was in his grave. Dying, he had known that some of his friends and appointees, some that were closest to him personally, had betrayed him, that scandal was brewing and must in time explode. Hardly had grass taken root above him when, through a long series of congressional investigations and criminal trials—installments of them continued as late as the 1930s—the country saw one after another of Harding's appointees, some his close friends, brought under accusation of crime, three convicted of crime.

II

In telling the tale that came to be known for an American decade as the "oil scandals," we may begin with an obscure citizen of Wyoming, his name buried somewhere in dusty files, whose part consisted merely in writing a letter to his senator. His motive was self-interest. Self-interest, indeed, in varying degrees of praiseworthiness—or the opposite of praiseworthiness—is, in this narrative, the practically uninterrupted motif. It would be difficult to find another drama in which any kind of disinterestedness is so rare.

The Wyoming citizen was in the oil business. In the circles where his calling took him he heard, early in April 1922, gossip that certain oil land belonging to the government and known as Teapot Dome—that odd and vivid name of a queer-shaped Wyoming hill was destined to ease the daily stint of many a cartoonist and newspaper paragrapher—was being leased by the secretary of the interior to a private corporation, that the leasing was being done secretly, and that the private beneficiary of the lease was a corporation called the Mammoth Oil Company, which was, in effect, a corporate alias for a bold and successful oil producer and promoter named Harry F. Sinclair.

That the story should provoke curiosity was natural. The government had held the oil lands for many years; why should it now part with them? And why should the negotiations be secret? The usual way of the government, imposed by law as a rule, is to conduct such transactions by public bidding. The negotiations on the side of the government were being carried on, so the story said, by Secretary of the Interior Albert B. Fall—why should that be? It was for the navy that the oil lands had been set aside; if

The shape of a butte on the oil reserve leased by Fall to Sinclair provided the name for the reserve and provided opportunity for cartoonists. (Page in the Louisville Courier Journal*)*

they were to be leased at all, why should not the secretary of the navy do the leasing?

Thomas J. Walsh of Montana was made head of a Senate subcommittee to investigate the oil leases. With quiet deliberateness, Senator Walsh went about the work. To examine the evidence, to familiarize himself with so technical a subject, and otherwise prepare for public hearings would take time—it turned out to be a year and a half.

He was left to do the work in quiet. Newspapers and public forgot the early flare-up.

So far as the administration was concerned, President Harding ended the matter with a brief assertion of rectitude: "The acts," he declared, "have at all times had my entire approval." That, at a time when the administration was still comparatively new, and high in favor and respect, was sufficient.

Newspapers printed, without unusual conspicuousness, such items of news as bore on the lease. When outsiders protested Sinclair's occupancy of Teapot Dome, the Navy Department, through Assistant Secretary Theodore Roosevelt, Jr., sent a detachment of Marines to eject trespassers and protect the Sinclair Company in developing the field. Meanwhile, Fall completed another lease of oil lands—at Elk Hills, California—to Edward L. Doheny of the Pan-American Petroleum and Transportation Company.

The oil leases were taken for granted, as an accepted thing, presumably a worthy and useful thing. Many felt that Fall, coming from the West, might share a common view of that section about public lands; that he might, by reason of his associations and background, be unsympathetic to the policy of conservation; that he might hold the view that the public domain was meant to be opened up to private development. Indeed, Fall, being rather truculent about his views, might conceivably have leased the oil fields partly as a flaunting gesture of defiance to the conservationists, as a sign that the policy was to be modified. That, many assumed, might be the explanation of Fall's leasing the oil reserves, if explanation were needed.

III

The men involved in the oil scandal, those who began it and those drawn into it; those who caused it, like Fall, as well as those who exposed it, like Senator Walsh; those who were tempted and fell, and those who were tempted but were too virtuous, or too worldly wise, to fall; those at the bottom of it, like Sinclair and Doheny, and those blamelessly touched by the flying spray of it, like William G. McAdoo and George Creel, both of whom had briefly been on Doheny's payroll; those whose role was sinister, and those whose role was innocent—all had one quality in common, an indigenous trait of outstandingness. As each stepped onto the witness stand, all who watched recognized that here was an exceptional personality—the quality of the personality might be one thing or the other, but the quantity of it was undeniable.

In the fauna of American society, they belonged among the genera of the grizzlies and the bison, the Hereford bulls and the timber wolves, including that species which American slang calls the bear-cat. No three-hour drama on the stage could have accommodated such a parade of characters. From the aggregate of them one could select, from here a trait and there a trait, the materials to assemble a gallery that would include much of Napoleon and St. George, Cromwell and Clive, Machiavelli and de' Medici. Sinclair in a different era and place might have been a Cecil Rhodes, Walsh a St. Ignatius Loyola. Those who were weak were spectacularly weak, those who were strong a little too strong for an age that has left the Napoleons behind it. The liars were magnificent liars; the truth-seekers were similarly eminent on the side of virtue.

IV

Walsh, opening the Senate hearings, called the government official who made the leases, Fall, and uncovered nothing. He called the two beneficiaries and uncovered nothing from either.

But in prosecuting the investigation, Walsh was favored by one condition, a condition that never fails to emerge in similar circumstances, a condition familiar to every committee chairman who ever conducted an investigation, to every lawyer who ever prosecuted a sensational case, to every editor who ever conducted a newspaper crusade.

Whichever way we look at it, whether the righteous see it as a beneficence aiding the operation of punitive justice, or the cynical see it as a manifestation of a less lovely part of human nature—in either case, it is the experience of all who ever conducted a cause célèbre that once the victim is on the rack, once the mills of exposure are set in motion, the materials to keep them going come in from every quarter. So surely does this occur that a prosecutor with experience will sometimes begin an inquisition without having the key evidence in hand, trusting to chance that the needed stone for his arch of proof will come to him some day in a telephone call from a stranger, or a letter, or a whisper from a caller. Once the newspaper headlines begin to send accusation out upon the winds, volunteer offerings of evidence blow in from every point of the compass. From a wide variety of persons it comes, and through many kinds of motive, from furtive busybodies writing anonymous letters, to vain exhibitionists eager to get in the limelight that shines upon a witness stand. Much of it, of course, is chaff; yet in some such way, in many a famous case, has come the particular bit of evidence that made the difference between conviction and acquittal.

From such volunteers there came to Walsh's office evidence that Fall had lately experienced an excess of affluence not explainable by any apparent source of legitimate income. Two years before, an editor in New Mexico stated of his personal knowledge, Fall had been "broke."

Some of the signs of Fall's new affluence were comparatively trivial; they turned out to be material for a smile, or at the most, unconvincing evidence of corruption. Some blooded stock had appeared among the flocks and herds on Fall's New Mexico ranch, stock of a lineage more high-bred than Fall had hitherto owned. The number was small, only—as it turned out when their association with crime subjected them to precise enumeration—fourteen heads extraordinarily assorted, six hogs, a stallion, six heifers, and a bull. And the total value was only some $1,400. But there was information that the freight car which had brought the animals across the continent had begun its journey at Ramapo Hills, New Jersey, where there was a stock farm owned by Harry F. Sinclair. And there was information that Sinclair and his wife had been visiting at Fall's ranch not long before the blooded stock arrived.

Sometime after that evidence came out, a rather distinguished volunteer witness appeared. Archibald B. Roosevelt was a son of the late Theodore Roosevelt; it was immaterial to the case, but provocative of added interest, that young Roosevelt's brother, Theodore Roosevelt, Jr., was assistant secretary of the navy. Young Roosevelt, pale and nervous, asked to be allowed to take the stand and make a statement. He was, he said, or had been until the day before, an employee of Sinclair, vice-president of a subsidiary of Sinclair's oil company. His sudden termination of the connection had been, he said, of his own accord; he had resigned because of a remark that had been made to him by another Sinclair employee. Sinclair's confidential secretary had hinted to him that "somebody might have lent Mr. Fall money," and had mentioned a payment of $68,000 to the foreman of Fall's ranch.

The next day, Sinclair's secretary appeared on the stand. It was true, he said, he had talked with young Roosevelt about Fall and Sinclair. But he denied ever having mentioned $68,000. Roosevelt had misunderstood him. He had spoken about "six to eight cows"—not "sixty-eight thous'."

The incident, at the time, led to not much more than expressions of cynicism about the accuracy of the secretary's enunciation, coupled with smiles at young Roosevelt's panic over an innocent association with sin.

But some of the statements about Fall's new affluence were more convincing. From the treasurer of Fall's county in New Mexico came information, later put in affidavit form, that, in 1922, Fall had paid the back taxes on his ranch, some of them in arrears for ten years. From neighbors of Fall in New Mexico came information that he had bought a ranch adjoining his own for $91,500, and other land costing $33,000, and had installed a $40,000 electric light and power plant on his ranch, and made other expenditures, for repairs to buildings, new construction, fencing, and the like, the whole approximating an outlay of $175,000.

V

At first Fall seemed to have a convincing explanation. He claimed he had received a $100,000 loan from Ned McLean, scion of a rich Washington family. Under Walsh's relentless pressure, however, McLean confessed that he had never made the loan—that he had written checks as a cover for Fall, but that no payments on the checks were ever made. McLean's confession forced Edward Doheny to come forward and recant his earlier testimony. Doheny now testified that he had made the loan to Fall.

On the night of the day this testimony was made public Fall arrived in Washington. To reporters he said only: "I am a very sick man." The next day a subpoena was served on him. February 2, Fall faced the committee. That was one of the most tragic spectacles Washington ever saw, a former senator appearing before his former associates under what amounted to a charge of crime; a former cabinet officer already plainly guilty of a lie and by all appearances guilty of having accepted a bribe.

Fall entered the committee room piloted by Senate attendants who elbowed a path through the dense mass of avid spectators that overflowed the room, crowded the doorway, and milled in the corridor. He leaned on a cane—in his best days he had carried one, but then jauntily, as an ornament for virility; now it was a support for feebleness. His blue serge suit was creased and baggy, the outer surface of inner demoralization. As he approached the witness chair, he almost tottered; all the lines of his features and figure bent downward, the bars of his gold-framed spectacles made a downward line from his ears to his eyes; the ends of his mouth drooped, his cheeks hung limp, everything about him sagged. Around him his lawyer bustled, almost as much nurse as lawyer. Pulling himself together

Former Secretary of the Interior Albert B. Fall and his wife at the opening of his trial. (From a photograph by Underwood & Underwood)

for a moment Fall read, in a voice that was clear enough but totally without resonance, a statement that his lawyer had prepared. With the opening words every senator and lawyer recognized the words of the traditional legal form and knew what it signified: "I decline . . . to answer any questions, on the ground that it may tend to incriminate me, and on the further ground . . ."

Concluding, he did not look at his fellow senators or at anyone else. Eyes looking downward, he turned, took the arm of his lawyer, and moved slowly toward the door. The crowd, turning to watch him, was so silent that the tapping of his cane could be heard as, with shuffling feet, he moved slowly down the corridor.

VI

Walsh said—and who could know better—that "it was Fall's parading of his new-found wealth among his neighbors in New Mexico that led to the exposure."

That was not only the immediate cause of his exposure, it was a clue to the remoter and fundamental cause of his tragedy. Not that Fall was especially ostentatious. But his whole personality was a curious combination of façade that seemed one thing and reality that was another. He was a synthesis of integrated ostensibles. He was ostensibly a rich man but actually not; he was ostensibly courageous but actually a coward; ostensibly he seemed a man with an exceptional code of pride, including what is commonly called honor, but actually he was a liar.

The ostensible part of him, the façade, was convincing. Men who for six years sat beside him in the Senate, and lounged beside him in the cloakroom, exceptionally shrewd and worldly men whose careers in politics had depended in large part on their insight into other men, had taken Fall as what he appeared to be. Some of the ablest men in America, who for two years had sat around the table with him twice a week at Harding's cabinet meetings, accepted him at the valuation that seemed to go with his exterior. Perhaps the reason they were misled was that by reason of his background, the Southwest and the desert, he was an unfamiliar type. Coming from

Two "old prospectors," Albert B. Fall (left) and Edward L. Doheny (right), with their lawyer, Frank J. Hogan, taken at the time of the trial of Fall and Doheny. (From a photograph © Underwood & Underwood)

New Mexico, wearing the soft felt hat of an older West, having the mannerisms and locutions of the vanished frontier, telling stories of early prospecting days, describing himself as "engaged in farming, stock raising and mining," men thought of him as a survivor from the West of the past, and credited him with the glamour and the ruggedness and the code of the pioneer. Perhaps Fall romantically thought of himself as what he was not, and thus became more convincing to others.

His façade had made him; it was his reality that destroyed him. Had he had true pride, he would not have sought or accepted money from Doheny to parade in false pride as a lord of lands and herds. Had he had courage he would not, when exposure threatened, have told the lie about getting it from McLean, but would have told the truth. And had he told the truth at that time he might have saved himself. Had Fall told the very version that Doheny told later, the picture of two old friends and fellow prospectors, desert bedfellows under blankets spread beneath the stars, of whom one became rich and the other remained poor; and of the rich one wishing to make it easy for his former companion to live in ease and dignity—had Fall told that story, the country might have accepted it, might even have felt sentimental.

VII

Events were now hurrying at a pace far beyond that when Walsh had been able to give a year and a half to preliminary exploration before calling his first witness. No longer, in the flow of rumor that flooded his office, did he carefully sift innuendo from fact, and the absurd from the probable. Without adequate preliminary examination he sent subpoenas for all against whom the most irresponsible fingers pointed and permitted almost any exhibitionist volunteer to go on the stand.

An ex-train robber turned reformer, Al Jennings of Oklahoma, took the stand to assert that a rich and vulgar Oklahoma oil promoter, Jake Hamon, now dead, had told him that he, Hamon, had spent a million dollars to nominate Harding for president. Once that was in the record, a considerable portion of the male population of Oklahoma had to be called, some to support

"Jake" Hamon, a newly rich oil operator in Oklahoma, whose alleged actions and utterances figured in the oil investigation. Hamon was murdered under sensational circumstances by a woman. (From a photograph by International News Photos, Inc.)

the tale, others to denounce it as a fantastic yarn. The residuum of truth seemed to be adequately described by one witness who said that "when Jake had a few drinks of scotch he talked pretty big."

Walsh came to the point where he really thought Harding personally might be involved, and even Harding's successor, now in office, Coolidge. Coolidge's secretary, Bascom Slemp, was called on to explain that a Christmas trip he had taken to Florida had been for recreation only and had not had any connection with the Fall case; the committee had to satisfy itself that the trip had not been to see Ned McLean and stiffen his backbone to stick to his story about having loaned $100,000 to Fall. Walsh summoned the White House secret service man, Colonel Starling, to explain a telegram he had sent to McLean—it was about a private employee of McLean whom Starling had recommended. Walsh summoned the head telegrapher at the White House, E. W. Smithers, to explain his employment during evenings as a telegrapher for McLean's newspaper—it was to eke out his salary of $2,500; he needed the money. Walsh summoned the White House doorkeeper, "Pat" McKenna, to explain a telegram he had sent to McLean—it was an innocent message of routine sort informing McLean that Bascom Slemp was leaving Washington and would arrive at Palm Beach at a certain hour.

VIII

By now, public emotion was beginning to be sated a little with the sight of victims on the rack, bored a little with a bizarre that could not become more bizarre. Part of public opinion turned to distaste for the extravagances of some of the Senate committee's divagations. There was, in some quarters, something like approval for Sinclair when, called again before the committee, he refused to answer questions. Sinclair did not give the reason that Fall had given. Fall had put his reason in a familiar formula of law, "on the ground that it might tend to incriminate me." That reason amounted almost to confession of crime and made it practically certain that Fall would later be in the criminal courts; but it was a complete excuse for Fall as respects the Senate proceedings—the committee could only let him go.

But Sinclair did not say that. Sinclair specifically refrained from saying that. Sinclair said: "I do not decline to answer any questions on the ground that my answers may tend to incriminate me, because there is nothing in any of the facts or circumstances of the lease of Teapot Dome which does or can incriminate me."

Having made that clear, Sinclair stated just why he declined to answer the Senate committee's questions. He said that he would "reserve any evidence I may be able to give for those courts to which you and your colleagues have deliberately referred all questions of which you had any jurisdiction and shall respectfully decline to answer any questions propounded by your committee."

Harry F. Sinclair. (From a photograph by Brown Brothers)

Ten times, Walsh asked Sinclair a question. Ten times Sinclair replied, "I decline to answer on advice of counsel."

For that Sinclair was subject to contempt. The committee itself could not punish him. It could only report Sinclair's recalcitrant taciturnity to the Senate. This the committee did. The Senate, by a vote of 72 to 1, cited him for contempt. "Citing" meant that Sinclair was turned over to the criminal courts, charged with refusal to answer questions asked by a duly authorized committee of the U.S. Senate. In the criminal courts, Sinclair was indicted for contempt of the Senate and released on $1,000 bail.

There followed much argument in the courts, and appeals from court to higher court, on the right of the Senate to ask the particular questions they had asked Sinclair, on whether Sinclair's refusal was contempt of the Senate, and on whether contempt of the Senate under these circumstances constituted a crime. In the end, Sinclair was tried on the contempt charge, convicted, and sentenced to pay a fine of $1,000 and spend three months in jail. He was confined in the District of Columbia jail, where he reverted to the occupation of his youth, making up pharmaceutical prescriptions for prisoners, who came to like him.

In the wisecracking of the time, Sinclair was given a curiously inverted eminence and credit. He had proved the negative, so the epigram said, of an aphorism that had long been serviceable to cynics and radicals, the assertion that "you can't put a million dollars in jail."

Sinclair had another minor distinction. He served his sentence for contempt of the Senate. Then, later, he was put on trial for the real criminal charge involved in the oil scandal, the charge that he and Fall had conspired to defraud the government. In the course of that trial, Sinclair employed detectives to shadow the jury. This was discovered and reported to the court, which regarded Sinclair's action as contempt of court, and sentenced him to six months in jail. By that, Sinclair achieved a unique eminence; he was the only man who ever succeeded in getting himself in jail twice for contempt of two separate bodies, the U.S. Senate and the courts of justice.

Fall, Sinclair, and Doheny were indicted on June 5, 1924, in the District of Columbia Supreme Court, Fall and Doheny charged with conspiracy, Fall and Sinclair charged with conspiracy, and Fall and Doheny charged with bribery. On April 3, 1925, Chief Justice McCoy dismissed the indictments on a technicality. On May 27, 1925, new indictments were returned. Doheny and Fall, tried on the charge of conspiracy to defraud the government, were acquitted on December 16, 1926. On November 1, 1927, during a trial of Sinclair and Fall before the District of Columbia Supreme Court on the charge of conspiracy to defraud the U.S. government, Prosecutor Roberts presented affidavits showing that the jury was being shadowed by detectives employed by Sinclair. A mistrial was declared. A retrial of the case resulted, on April 21, 1928, in the acquittal of Fall and Sinclair. In October 1929, Fall, after a long delay, was put on trial for having accepted a bribe. On October 25, the jury after deliberating a day and a night brought in a verdict of guilty but with a recommendation of mercy. Fall was sentenced to a year in jail and fined $100,000. After many delays Fall went to jail in July 1931, serving until May 1932, when he was released, his sentence shortened by his record of good behavior while a prisoner. He had the ignoble distinction of being, in the whole history of the United States, the first cabinet officer to go to jail. In March 1930, Doheny was acquitted, following a trial by jury before the District of Columbia Supreme Court, on the charge of bribing Fall.

IX

Other scandals followed. During 1927 there appeared in the advertising offices of New York newspapers copy submitted as advertisements for a book called *The President's Daughter*, written by Nan Britton, and published by the "Elizabeth Ann Guild, Inc." In one case the advertisement, going through routine channels under the eyes of clerks too busy to more than glance at it, appeared in print.

Inquiry led to hurried consultations by editors and business managers. Where the advertisement had not been originally refused it was dropped after one or two publications. Editors of book review departments debated whether to review the book; whether they were excused from that function by the fact that the organization putting it out was not a standard publishing firm, whether it belonged in the category of books in the conventional sense. In the channels where books are sold there was similar perturbation; many booksellers, horrified, refused to handle it; such as did hid it on lower shelves beneath the counter, like contraband.

Readers to whom the book came spoke of it in horrified whispers—whispers penetrating enough, however, to give the book ultimately a circulation of some 90,000—and probably never did a book have so large a number of readers in proportion to the number sold, for the volume was passed from hand to hand, was abstracted from a drawer of the desk in the sitting room to be read by adolescents away from the parental eye; or was devoured by eager-eyed servants in the absence of the family. At such libraries as acknowledged they had it, or were willing to handle it as they did ordinary books, there were waiting lists. One way or another *The President's Daughter*, by the time it had been out for about a year, had probably been read by more persons than commonly read the most widely and openly circulated best-sellers.

The book had as its frontispiece a photograph of a little girl some six years old, upon which readers, after they had absorbed the book, looked intently to see if they could find likeness to Warren Gamaliel Harding. There was a

DEDICATION

THIS BOOK IS DEDICATED
WITH UNDERSTANDING AND
LOVE TO ALL UNWEDDED
MOTHERS, AND TO THEIR
INNOCENT CHILDREN WHOSE
FATHERS ARE USUALLY NOT
KNOWN TO THE WORLD. . . .

NAN BRITTON

and a prefatory declaration of "the author's motive" which, according to the author, was, of course, completely high-minded. She had written the book, she said, for the Cause (capital *C*), the Cause of illegitimate children everywhere, that of all such "the name of the father be correctly registered in the public records," that every child born in the United States of America be recorded as legitimate, whether born within or without wedlock.

In the book Britton recited:

That she had been brought up in Marion, Ohio, the daughter of a physician; that when she was fourteen—and Harding a more than middle-aged man, nearly fifty, running for governor of Ohio—she had conceived an infatuation for him; that she used to phone his house frequently hoping he might answer the phone; that she decorated her bedroom with photographs of him cut from campaign posters bound in frames the child bought at five- and ten-cent stores; that she used to stand in a doorway across the street from the office of the *Marion Star*, watching Harding in his office on the second floor—Harding's habitual pose, she wrote, was with his feet on his desk; when she saw his feet leave the desk she knew he was about to walk home, and she would follow him at a distance; that Harding at this time was completely unaware of the child's long-distance adoration of him and never spoke to her except as he might casually greet the not very distinctly recognized child of a neighbor.

She recited that after the death of her father she went to work in New York in 1916; that she wrote a letter to Harding, then in the Senate, asking him to find her a position; that Harding replied that he would do so and, on a trip to New York, told her to come and see him at his hotel; that at once the relation was put upon a sentimental basis; that Harding decided he should get her a position in New York rather than in Washington, as in New York he would be under less observation; that Harding got her a position with the United States Steel Corporation at $16 a week; that once when Harding was making campaign speeches at Indianapolis and Rushville, Indiana, Britton accompanied him, being registered at the hotel and introduced by Harding to his friends as his niece; that Harding visited her many times in New York, the two stopping at various hotels; that she used to receive letters from him as much as sixty pages in length (though no love letter, nor any part of one appeared in the book); that she made frequent visits to Washington to see Harding, and that the two met at the Ebbitt House or in apartments that Harding borrowed for the day from various friends; that once she visited him in his Senate office.

On October 22, 1919, Britton declared in her book, when she was twenty-three and Harding fifty-four, she had a baby, born at Asbury Park, New Jersey; that Harding treated her generously, sending her $100 to $150 every week or so; that in June 1920, when Harding was in Chicago at the convention at which he was nominated for the presidency, he visited her several times at her sister's apartment; that after Harding was nominated she went to the Adirondacks for a rest, leaving her child in Chicago; that while she was in the Adirondacks and Harding was campaigning for the presidency, Harding sent her money, the money being brought by a secret service man to whom Britton gave the name Tim Slade (a pseudonym easily decoded by anyone familiar with the secret service staff at the White House). After Harding was elected, Britton said, she visited him secretly at Marion, where Harding gave her three $500 bills; she said that after Harding was in the White House, she, in June 1921, made a trip to Washington and met Harding at a tryst in the White House; that she corresponded with Harding constantly, the letters being sent in care of the secret service man whom she called Tim Slade; that in January 1922, Britton's child was formally adopted by her sister and her husband; that Harding had never seen the child; that Britton continued to pay occasional visits to the White House; that in 1923 she took a trip to Europe, Harding bearing the expense, and was in France when Harding died.

Shortly after Harding's death, Britton said in her book, she married a Swedish ship captain. Soon the two separated. Britton said she began to make inquiry as to whether Harding had made any financial provision for her and her child. "Tim Slade" was unable to discover anyone to whom Harding had entrusted any such fund. Thereupon, Britton said, she decided she should approach Harding's family; she said that she wrote many letters to Harding's sisters, Daisy Harding and Mrs. Heber Votaw. At first, she said, Daisy Harding was sympathetic, gave her, on different occasions, sums amounting to a few hundred dollars, but rather abruptly ended the gifts when Harding's brother, Dr. George Harding, took hold of the situation. Dr. Harding met Britton, so she complained in her book, with a cold eye, a notebook on his knee. He asked her for letters—she had none; Harding, she said, had asked her to destroy them, and she could produce only a few impersonal notes. Dr. Harding remained "stonily impassive." He asked her for dates, places. "When was that?" "Where did that meeting take place?" Britton "wondered vaguely at his wanting these so definitely." At the end Britton thanked him for the interview. Dr. Harding showed impatience. She did not see him again. The Harding family did not give her the $50,000 she asked.

X

Upon Harding's reputation, upon the memory of him—he was three years in his grave—the effect was terrible. The Nan Britton book, coming after exposures of financial corruption on the part of members of his administration, made Harding's memory almost a rag in the gutter.

A cartoon famous during the presidential campaign of 1924. The oil scandal had been exposed and the Republicans were necessarily in the position of promising future honesty. The theme was taken from a song widely known at the time "It Ain't Goin' to Rain No Mo'."

Omitting the Nan Britton book, listing only the proved crimes or undisputed facts, the country saw:

Harding's friend and appointee as secretary of the Interior, Albert B. Fall, convicted of accepting a bribe and sentenced to jail.

Harding's friend whom he had appointed to be head of the Veterans' Bureau, Charles R. Forbes, convicted of defrauding the government and sentenced to jail.

Harding's appointee as Alien Property Custodian, Thomas W. Miller, convicted of accepting money to influence an official action, and sent to jail.

Harding's intimate associate, the promoter of his presidential nomination, his appointee as attorney general, highest law officer of the government, Harry M. Daugherty, accused, indicted, and put on trial for faithlessness to duty. Even though Daugherty had not been convicted, the incident was sufficiently sordid.

An intimate of the Harding entourage, Jess Smith, revealed as having accepted more than $50,000 to facilitate a case before the Alien Property Custodian; Smith had committed suicide, and everybody felt the self-destruction had been in anticipation of exposure.

The bald, proved facts were awful enough. Because of circumstances associated with some of the cases, rumor expanded even beyond the facts. The suicide of Jess Smith, intimate of Attorney General Daugherty, the suicide taking place in Daugherty's apartment, led to stories that he had been murdered to still his tongue about tales he might tell, and that Daugherty had been party to the murder. The fact that another suicide, Charles F. Cramer, assistant and counsel to Forbes in the Veterans' Bureau, had had a financial transaction with Harding—he had bought from Harding the Washington house Harding had occupied when a senator and his suicide took place in this house—gave rise to suggestions that Harding himself had been involved. In the inflamed state of the public mind, sufficiently shocked by the facts and even more appalled by the rumors, the story that Harding had been involved personally was given momentum by publication of a statement that Mrs. Harding, before she died in 1924, had destroyed his private papers.

Presently, many of the rumors began to center around Harding, especially after they began to include "woman stories" about him. Word-of-mouth whisper said the president had killed himself, other whispers said he had been murdered. A book, *The Strange Death of President Harding*, plainly implied that Mrs. Harding had poisoned him—not all who read the book, or heard similar stories, knew that the writer, Gaston B. Means, was the most monumental liar and facile criminal of his time. Another book, *Revelry*, by a reputable author, Samuel Hopkins Adams, who did not purport to write more than fiction based on the facts and rumors of the Harding administration, added momentum to the story that Harding's death had been suicide. *Revelry* was made into a play and a motion picture.

By this time, the Harding scandals were a conspicuous feature of the time. Everybody heard them. Some cynically believed all. Others, their finest sensibilities wounded, hating to believe but unable to deny, refused to talk about them or listen to them. The effect on the country's morale was definite, visible, and most damaging. Some of Harding's friends had undertaken to erect a great memorial at his grave in Marion; confident in their faith in his public integrity, they loyally went through with it, but much of the public smiled wanly and some newspapers felt they were discreet in not giving much space to accounts of the project.

On June 16, 1931, nearly eight years after Harding's death, after the memorial to him at Marion had been long completed but had for several years stood undedicated, President Hoover, with former President Coolidge also present, performed the duty of a living president to the memory of a dead one; he paid just tribute to the fine qualities in Harding, and said:

> We came to know that there was a man whose soul was being seared by a great disillusionment. We saw him gradually weaken not only from physical exhaustion but from mental anxiety. Warren Harding had a dim realization that he had been betrayed by a few of the men he had trusted, by men he had believed were his devoted friends. It was later proved in the courts of the land that these men had betrayed not alone the friendship and trust of their stanch and loyal friend but they had betrayed their country. That was the tragedy of the life of Warren Harding.

It was Harding's tragedy, but the country's also. Harding's ended with his death; a nation is a constantly developing organism, wounds to a national spirit may modify its ethos for a long time. The injury to the national morale by such conditions as arose in Harding's administration could not be wholly cured by the austere disinfectant that the administration of Coolidge was. When, in the early 1930s, depression came; when depression caused discontent, and discontent expressed itself in the discrediting of government by plays, books, and the intellectuals—in that condition the willingness of the public to tolerate the demeaning might have been less but for the recollection of the Harding scandals, which seemed to justify it.

CHAPTER 7
Literary and Cultural Trends During the Twenties

That the war should give rise to books and plays was natural. That the output would be large was to be expected—the age was vocal. What constituted a phenomenon was that the "war books" unanimously took one view of the war, the bitter view. All pictured war grimly—a horrible, destructive experience for those who lived through it; a loathsome, useless death for those who died. The figures, whom literature about former wars had made to seem romantic, glamorous—Kipling's dashing young subalterns, Richard Harding Davis's gallant captains, even Rupert Brooke's eager young patriots—all these seemed a thousand years away from the stony disillusionment expressed in the novels and plays about the Great War.

When the war books turned out to be very grim, and yet best-sellers, there was argument about what inference should be made, what the phenomenon might portend. Some, pacifists especially, believing that the wide reading of works picturing war in its most horrible aspects might mean popular hatred of war, thought, too sanguinely, that the revulsion would bring permanent world peace. Others, too gloomily, inferred that, since authors wrote war books because the public liked to read them, it must be that the public liked war.

Somewhere between those two extremes lay the correct interpretation. It was nearer to the former. True, the average person enjoyed war books avidly—the sales proved that; books treating war with unrelieved realism were immensely popular. But it is possible to enjoy art without necessarily wishing to experience what the art portrays. Many a reader of war books reflected, "So that is war! Thank God I wasn't there!" And the average reader said further—this was one contribution of the war books to national policy—"We must see to it that America gets into no more wars."

This disillusionment, the unanimity of it, and the force with which it was expressed, gave to the war books as a group an importance unique in the literature of the time. The importance had no relation to the literary value of the books. The importance was not in the field of literature; it was in the world of national point of view. The war books at once expressed and helped to create the national thought about a national question; they had weight in determining the country's attitude about its relations with the world, and about some phases of domestic policy.

II

Apart from their importance in expressing and determining national thought, it happened that many of the war books were good as literature. *All Quiet*—so the title was abbreviated—by a German, Erich Remarque (read in America more than any war book by an American), managed to convey the most revoltingly loathsome details of life in the trenches with a philosophical, an almost tranced detachment, infinitely more moving than indignation. The spirit of the book, comparable to the calm center of a cyclone, was conveyed in the solemn rhythm, the sardonic irony of its title *All Quiet on the Western Front*, a title most fortunately retained when the book was made into a very successful film, where its influence on national thought was expanded.

There were very few novels in the early twenties which had not some war episodes or background, but *Three Soldiers*, by John Dos Passos, was probably the first outstanding American novel written entirely about the Great War and life in the army. This record of what one reviewer called "the seamy side of experiences with the A.E.F." was obviously autobiographical in part—Dos Passos, as an ambulance driver, had seen the worst of war. The three soldiers he selected for artistic presentation of war's horrors were types of the A.E.F.—a city boy, a country lad, and a musician. They had gone into the war gaily, in the spirit of another Dos Passos character who wanted to get in quickly "before the whole thing goes belly up." But soon: "'Fellers,' Fred Summers was saying, 'this ain't a war, it's a goddam madhouse.'"* Still later: "I can't explain it but I'll never put a uniform on again." Their final desperation, the strain that passed the stage where war's horrors were intolerable and reached a point where even the routine of army life was unendurable, was expressed, with appealing poignance, in, "I've got to a point where I don't give a damn what happens to me; I don't care if I am shot or if I live to be 80; I'm sick of being ordered around; one more order shouted at my head is not worth living to be 80."

A play about the war, *Journey's End* by R. C. Sheriff, achieved its somber spirit without stressing

John Dos Passos.

*Quoted from Dos Passos, *1919*.

"War—sure—is—hell."
One of Captain John W. Thompson, Jr.'s, drawings for his book of the war, Fix Bayonets.

war's physical horrors; there were no sordid details to be, so to speak, risen above; Sheriff's art, suggesting the Greek classics, made the very fact of war seem more tragic and terrible than any mere wounds to the physical body or any sights of carnage. The struggle between man and the terrific forces that were utterly beyond his control, and between man and the varying facets of his own nature when under the strain of war—all that Sheriff portrayed with a verity, and a beauty of writing and characterization, which achieved something close to greatness.

Another play dealing entirely with the war, *What Price Glory*, by Maxwell Anderson and Laurence Stallings, achieved prominence by genuine gusto and merit—and also achieved notoriety by the profusion and pungency of the soldier profanity pressed into service by the authors. A joke current during the vogue of *What Price Glory* was about two old ladies who, when they went to see the production, were as ladylike as old ladies should be, but who entered into the spirit of the play so thoroughly that, at the end, one said to the other, "Shall we get the hell out of here?" "Not," replied her elderly companion, "till I find my goddam glasses."

Of all the American writers influenced by the war and articulate in varying degrees, the one who was most acclaimed as the historian of the generation that reached maturity during the war, the one who summed up with final authority and greatest effectiveness the judgment of the most sensitive of that generation, was Ernest Hemingway. His early stories, beginning about 1925, although obviously a result of postwar disillusionment and of a passion for naturalism fed by the war, did not deal explicitly with war experiences. His later pronouncement about the war itself, coming ten years after it had ended, in 1929, was *A Farewell to Arms*. The story begins in the Italian army where the hero, an American, is an officer in an ambulance

A scene from the motion picture made from What Price Glory.

unit. He is wounded and falls in love with a nurse. He deserts and they go to Switzerland where they pretend to be married and where the nurse dies in childbirth.

As to the war:

> You did not know what it was about. You never had time to learn. They threw you in and told you the rules, and the first time they caught you off base they killed you. . . . I was always embarrassed by the words "sacred," "glorious," and "sacrifice," and the expression "in vain." We had heard them sometimes standing in the rain almost out of earshot, so that only the shouted words came through, and read them, on proclamations that were slapped up by billposters over other proclamations now for a long time, and I had seen nothing sacred, and the things that were glorious had no glory and the sacrifices were like the stockyards at Chicago if nothing was done with the meat except to bury it. There were many words that you could not stand to hear, and finally only the names of places had dignity. Certain numbers were the same way and certain dates, and these with the names of the places were all you could say and have them mean anything. Abstract words such as glory, honor, courage or hallow were obscene beside the concrete names of villages, the numbers of roads, the names of rivers, the numbers of regiments and the dates.

When Hemingway spoke thus of the war he spoke not only for himself and for other writers whose temperament led them to express themselves differently, perhaps less poignantly. He spoke also for hundreds of thousands of men, white and black, who shared to the full his emotion. Some were unable to read or write, most of them would have found that passage completely unintelligible, but translated into their terms they would have agreed. Hemingway spoke for an era.

III

The direct effect of the war on the generation that lived through it was not the whole consequence. The war affected every aspect of their lives, it would continue to affect them until they died; it affected and would continue to affect the whole national spirit.

The war, carried on by draft on the whole country, took in a representative cross-section of every class, every type, every temperament. Some were exceptionally sensitive; among these would be the generation's writers, artists, and playwrights. As such they would—and during the twenties did—at once reflect the mood of the generation and in part create it. Into the books they wrote they put the effects of the war on their own acute sensitiveness, and also the point of view about the world and society which their revulsion to war had caused in them; the books, being read, stimulated the same point of view in others. The writers and artists were not the whole of the generation; many, differing in temperament, did not share their emotions during the war, nor after the war share their disillusionment, sense of frustration, and cynicism. Great numbers, an overwhelming majority, indeed practically all of the generation, lived lives normally contented.

But the writers and artists, though numerically only a tiny fraction of the generation, had an influence greater than their numbers. With perhaps too much confidence in their franchise to speak for all, and with some Byronic self-consciousness and romantic self-pity, they called themselves "the lost generation." That phrase was invented and applied to them, so gossip among writers said, by one of their idols, Gertrude Stein, in a conversation with Ernest Hemingway. And Hemingway it was who, in *The Sun Also Rises*, wrote the most complete expression and description of the "lost generation." For the func-

Ernest Hemingway. (From a photograph by Helen Breaker taken in Paris during the late twenties)

tion, Hemingway was especially equipped, by temperament, by the reaction of his temperament to his own experiences in the war, and by his style (a greatly simplified and articulated derivation from Gertrude Stein's early principles, which, though it becomes occasionally monotonous, has an individual rhythm and power. Like a surgeon in a sardonic mood, Hemingway cut away ideals, introspection, analysis, subtlety, national or class roots, and left his characters reduced to the simplest terms. He believed in a world in which the only conceivable good is an intensification of stoicism, courage to endure rather than courage to do. Of this rather primitive attitude *The Sun Also Rises* is the outstanding expression. It deals with a group of expatriates in Paris—Jake, Bill, Brett Ashley, Robert Cohn, and their friends—artists and writers who feel that life is too complicated to think about and who endlessly pursue some unobtainable anodyne for their bored and rootless spirits. Terse and quick-witted, they drink incessantly, sobering up occasionally only to get drunk again as soon as they realize that the world about them is still too much with them—and for them. Any diversion which will prevent thought is desirable. Introspection is absolutely useless, to be avoided at any cost.

Those who, like the characters in *The Sun Also Rises*, were made by the war into neurotics, were a small number. The writers who wrote about them were an even smaller number. But the historian must always consider the right of the current books of any period to be accepted as the reflectors and records of the period, as well as its guides and teachers. Rather more in the 1920s than in other periods did books clearly establish the inevitability of their inclusion in an adequate history of the times. An author might take refuge in an ivory tower to avoid the rub of the world, yet he could not help reflecting the world. Even less could he avoid influencing it. Permeation of his ideas was facilitated by new mechanisms for the spread of the written word. A book was written; by highly organized business methods it was spread and sold; accompanying distribution as a book, it was disseminated far and wide by serial publication in newspapers and periodicals; if successful it was imitated; the imitations were put through the same processes; both original and imitations were made into motion pictures. By the sum of these processes, ideas in books spread out, during the 1920s, to a larger proportion of the population than in any other country or time. Indeed, dissemination of the ideas in any really popular book was close to universal. Many a father had to tolerate a conversation overheard in the sitting room between eighteen-year-old Nelly and her beau, a conversation which shocked the old gentleman—because a man he never heard of named Hemingway wrote a book he never heard of called *The Sun Also Rises*.

IV

The average thoughtful American had, when the World War broke out, reached a place where he had attained enough material prosperity to enable him to have the leisure to reflect on the world about him. This release from the stress of making a living and gaining security for himself and his children was interrupted by the war. Not only was his leisure taken from him by the stress of world problems, but his inclination to think of himself was taken from him by the daily reading matter of tragedy, by the vitalness and the starkness of the life that the daily press placed in front of him for four years or more.

When the war and its problems seemed to have been temporarily shelved, he found that he had more leisure than he had had before, and that he could give his children the opportunity for education and development that he himself had been deprived of by the exigency of making a living. He could give his children some protection from the necessity of making a living until they had obtained a college education, in some cases until they had attempted to find their place in the world through extra postgraduation years at universities; in remarkably many cases he could keep them from the necessity of facing the workaday world until they had had a chance to travel extensively through the civilized world. Of course, this was not true of a majority of the fathers of families in the United States, but it was true to some degree for a large part of the young generation maturing between 1919 and 1929.

Youths who, if born a generation before, would have been behind the plow at fifteen, remained in high school until seventeen, or in some cases went to college until twenty-three, or even to postgraduate school until close to thirty. The prosperous condition of the entire American business world made it possible for many young men and women, whose families formerly could not have supported them after they were through high school, either to earn their way through college, or borrow the money, or acquire scholarships. Many could earn their way to Europe, either as stewards on transatlantic liners, or by playing musical instruments for the entertainment of other young people traveling "Students Third," or by conducting the children of wealthier parents to Europe, or by working for the numerous American business concerns that needed young people to handle the affairs of fellow Americans traveling on the Continent.

Also after the war an emphasis was placed on the young, simply because they were young, that has probably never been equaled in the history of the world. Anthropologists say that the more highly developed forms of animal life can be distinguished, among other marks, by the length of the period in which they protect their young. If this analogy can be carried over to a society that prolongs the care of its young, then the 1920s was a period of an exceptionally high civilization. Partly because of the number of youths lost through the war; partly because of the emphasis that psychology and psychoanalysis placed on training the individual when he is young, before his habits are set; partly because of the premium that the inventions of the machine age placed on the younger person—it was difficult for an older man to adjust himself to the dexterity demanded in handling new machinery—partly for these reasons, but mainly because of the wish and the means to gratify it, this generation gave its youth unheard of opportunities for education and advancement. The decade was the decade of the young. It was

"It's broccoli, dear."
"I say it's spinach, and I say the hell with it."

This illustration, printed in the New Yorker, *became famous. The firmness and definiteness of the child's expression of opinion, together with the forcefulness of language, was accepted as the complete picture of the mental attitude of the "younger generation."*

natural that the literature of the period would be occupied, more than is generally the case, with the contrast between an older and a younger generation.

It was natural that youth, having the advantages that the parents had not, would measure the parents by a new standard and find them lacking. Youth felt superior. Always youth is a little defiant, always it has an adolescent conviction of its own importance; and the American youth of the twenties found in the world about him many circumstances that tended to confirm this conviction. Pathetically, in many cases, the parent fed the natural arrogance of the youth, subscribed to the superiority which youth claimed for itself. The twenties, reversing age-old custom, biblical precept, and familiar adage, was a period in which, in many respects, youth was the model, age the imitator. On the dance floor, in the beauty parlor, on the golf course; in clothes, manners, and many points of view, elders strove earnestly to look and act like their children, in many cases their grandchildren. The egotism thus stimulated was increased by the ease with which young folks could achieve economic, and therefore to a large extent moral and intellectual, independence. Everywhere, youth was flattered. And there was one supreme cause for the ascendancy of youth: youth had fought the war. No matter what his years, any male who had gone through the war was a man, chartered to talk, think, and write like a man.

An opening gun in the pro-youth, pro-freedom, and anti-Puritanism campaign was fired in 1920, with the publication of *This Side of Paradise,* a book

which had the distinction, if not of creating a generation certainly of calling the
world's attention to one. The author was
F. Scott Fitzgerald, aged twenty-four.
While it was felt that the book was not
literally autobiographical, still, alarmed
elders felt that Fitzgerald knew of what
he wrote. It was a curiously chaotic and
formless novel, with almost every fault
except lifelessness. The central character,
Amory Blaine, a young man of great
beauty and sensitivity, finds himself facing a world in which all gods are dead, all
wars fought, and all faiths in man shaken.
Worldweary as he considers himself to
be, he manages to enjoy several love affairs of extraordinary subtlety and sophistication. The theme gave Fitzgerald

F. Scott Fitzgerald, author of This Side of Paradise.

an opportunity to record college life in the jazz age without falling into either of the two great errors, belligerent hedonism or comstockery. But
Fitzgerald's readers were unable to preserve so detached a point of view.
Young people found in Amory's behavior a model for their conduct—and
alarmed parents found their worst apprehensions realized.

The interest created by *This Side of Paradise* stimulated imitation. Lynn
and Lois Montross wrote lightly mocking stories of life in a small coeduca-
tional college in the West, where their protagonists had formed themselves
on Fitzgerald's model; the principal character was Andy Protheroe, a per-
petual senior. Charles Wertenbacker, with a novel called *Boojum*, caused a
sensation, as limited geographically as it was intense emotionally, by his description of life and liquor at the University of Virginia, where, according
to this author, alcohol for the time had taken the place of the ideals of
Thomas Jefferson and snobbishness had replaced chivalry.

V

Supremely, the artist of youth in the jazz age, in words as well as drawings, was John Held, Jr., whose sardonic sketches of "flappers," "jelly
beans," and "drugstore cowboys" were a caricature gallery of the youth of
the period. Held's drawings became a proof of Oscar Wilde's contention
that nature imitates art far more than art imitates nature. As the Gibson
girl and the Gibson man had been the ideal for the youths and maids of the
1890s, so Held's drawings were the archetype of the late twenties. On every
street corner was the Held male, buried in a raccoon coat, with patent
leather hair, wrinkled socks, and bell-bottomed trousers. Frantically bidding for the superior creature's attention was the Held flapper—stubby
feet, incredibly long and brittle legs, brief and scanty skirt, two accurate

John Held, Jr.'s, drawings of the younger generation for Scott Fitzgerald's Tales of the Jazz Age.

circles of rouge just below the cheekbones, and a tight little felt hat like an inverted tumbler. The apotheosis of an attitude heralded its passing.

VI

The attitude of the twenties' younger generation was not caused wholly by the war, nor was it as new with them as they thought. The causes went as far back as Darwin in the 1860s, and included the doctrines of Freud about sex which came to America in 1910, the reading of the hedonistic quatrains of Omar Khayyám about the same time, the jeering at conventionality that Bernard Shaw had kept up for more than a generation, the novels of H. G. Wells. All these influences and many others, growing cumulatively, came to a climax in the twenties. To these were added the effect on young American minds of seeing what was happening in Russia. Here was being put into practice a new conception of society and government, a conception which not only ran counter to, but denied, opposed, and regarded as its enemies nearly everything that, in other forms of society and government, were regarded as fundamental. The new Russian conception fought religion, called it the "opium of the masses," exterminated private property, introduced new and startling practices about marriage and family life.

The ferment of all these influences in the world could not help but affect young Americans greatly. The "younger generation" in combination with the "lost generation" took the new ideas, and themselves, most seriously. A group of them—authors, poets, playwrights, and artists—inhabited a purlieu of New York, a modern American version of Bohemia, called Greenwich Village. Some so-to-speak cousins of them lived in the Latin Quarter in Paris. The ideas they advanced, the convictions they held, amounted, about 1920, to a doctrine, a system, which, one* of them said years later, "could roughly be summarized as follows":

1. *The idea of salvation by the child.*—Each of us at birth has special potentialities which are slowly crushed and destroyed by a standardized society and mechanical methods of teaching. If a new educational system can be introduced, one by which children are encouraged to develop their own personalities, to blossom freely like flowers, then the world will be saved by this new, free generation.
2. *The idea of self-expression.*—Each man's, each woman's, purpose in life is to express himself, to realize his full individuality through creative work and beautiful living in beautiful surroundings.
3. *The idea of paganism.*—The body is a temple in which there is nothing unclean, a shrine to be adorned for the ritual of love.
4. *The idea of living for the moment.*—It is stupid to pile up treasures that we can enjoy only in old age, when we have lost the capacity for enjoyment. Better to seize the moment as it comes, to dwell in it intensely, even at the cost of future suffering. Better to live extravagantly, gather June rose-buds, "burn our candle at both ends."

"*But Mater, this is life in the raw.*"

This cartoon, "But Mater, this is life in the raw," pictured another form of self-expression on the part of the youngish generation. (A drawing by Van Buren in the New Yorker)

*Malcolm Cowley. The statement, here condensed, is taken from Cowley's *Exile's Return.*

The child's request, "Mother, when you're dummy, will you hear my prayers?" was a biting satire on the vogue of bridge and the devotion of parents to pleasure. (From a drawing by Alice Harvey in the New Yorker)

5. *The idea of liberty.*—Every law, convention or rule of art that prevents self-expression or the full enjoyment of the moment should be shattered and abolished. Puritanism is the great enemy. The crusade against Puritanism is the only crusade with which free individuals are justified in allying themselves.
6. *The idea of female equality.*—Women should be the economic and moral equals of men. They should have the same pay, the same working conditions, the same opportunity for drinking, smoking, taking or dismissing lovers.
7. *The idea of psychological adjustment.*—We are unhappy because we are maladjusted, and maladjusted because we are repressed. If our individual repressions can be removed—by confessing them to a Freudian psychologist—then we can adjust ourselves to any situation, and be happy in it. . . .
8. *The idea of changing place.*—"They do things better in Europe." England and Germany have the wisdom of old cultures; the Latin peoples have admirably preserved their pagan heritage. By expatriating himself, by living in Paris, Capri, or the South of France, the artist can break the Puritan shackles, drink, live freely, and be wholly creative.

The influence of the intelligentsia went far. One of the Greenwich Villagers, Edna St. Vincent Millay, a distinguished poet, wrote a stanza which became a battle cry of freedom for young people from the Atlantic to the Pacific:

> My candle burns at both ends;
> It will not last the night;

But ah, my foes, and oh, my friends,
It gives a lovely light.

That, during the early 1920s, could be recited by more young persons than could repeat the formalized codes of more orthodox authorities.

If all this seems pretty jejune, a justified answer on behalf of the young American intellectuals might say they had a right to be surprised at their moderation. Their sincerity, their effort to pass the new ideas through the prisms of their own minds, to reflect upon them and reduce them to credo was a credit to them. They had recovered from the immediate war mood of Dos Passos's soldier, "I don't give a damn what happens to me." They cared very much what happened to them; they cared very much what happened to the world, and with complete sincerity wished to make the world over according to what they conceived to be a better pattern. But this charitable and consoling reflection did not occur to many parents, who merely knew that, as it was often put, the twenties were a hard time for raising children. Young persons in school and college, too immature to understand the new ideas fully or reflect on them or examine them as a code, merely said, with a kind of diffident defiance, "I have a right to do anything that doesn't harm anyone else"—that was heard often by parents in the twenties, it was a kind of slogan of the adolescent. With maturity, the young folks learned it is not easy to live by so simple a formula, not easy for an individual to be sure what acts of his will or will not harm others, not easy indeed to be sure what acts will or will not harm himself. Both to individuals and to the "younger generation" as a group, passage of a little time brought clear thinking, sobriety, and a sense of responsibility. The casualties attending the impact of new ideas about morals were not more numerous than under the old code. Indeed, I think that at any time during the twenties the essential standards, and the practices under them, were on the whole rather more wholesome than in the past.

VII

The practice of writing is in actuality a profession like any other, in spite of the efforts of some practitioners to make it seem special or even supernatural. As among lawyers there are shyster lawyers, as among physicians quack physicians, so there are literary quacks, men who, having some slight or even marked talent for writing, seize on literary trends and fads, and capitalize them. To such facile artisans, the twenties were a period peculiarly favorable. A great demand for books of all degrees of merit, and many new and strongly marked developments in the field of literature, gave them an unparalleled opportunity, and they took it.

In 1919, an honest artist, Sherwood Anderson, wrote *Winesburg, Ohio*, and in all earnestness and sincerity recorded the life of a midwestern American village as he believed it to be, its inhabitants preoccupied either consciously or unconsciously with sex. Contemporary with Anderson, and

A drawing by Helen Hokinson for the New Yorker, *showing that the older generation was not unsusceptible to the vogue of sex novels but felt it proper to practice a little Victorian hypocrisy.*

sharing his sincerity, several others—notably Theodore Dreiser and John Dos Passos in America, and Somerset Maugham and D. H. Lawrence in England—wrote about sex with fidelity to artistic integrity and to the validity of factual and emotional realism.

Taking advantage of the honest pioneering done by these valid artists, came the quacks. Warner Fabian, in *Flaming Youth*, made three motherless sisters the puppets about which he wove an improbable tale almost exclusively concerned with sex and alcohol, its high spot a moonlight bathing scene. It is most unlikely that Fabian believed that such characters existed anywhere in the length and breadth of the United States, but he knew the bans had been raised and that all through the country men and women, who would not read Anderson's sober and troubling book, would devour with lascivious excitement Fabian's glib and highly spiced account of the improbable and erotic adventures of incredible people. In a second novel, *Unforbidden Fruit*, Fabian, using college life as a background, achieved an even greater apotheosis of pruriency, and a second time made the bestseller list.

Of all the sex books, the one that attracted the most attention, one that for a time had the ecstatic adulation of much of the intelligentsia, was *Jurgen*, by James Branch Cabell. Upon its publication in 1920, it was suppressed. Moved perhaps by anger toward the authorities, or possibly by regard for the painful efforts at a style which the book showed, the literati of the United States hailed a masterpiece—though not without dissension even within the ranks of the elect. While one critic praised it as written "with phallic candour" another felt that it had been written "with a smirk"—precisely between those two characterizations lies the line that

separates honest realism from deliberate lasciviousness. On the whole, the
group who insisted that *Jurgen* was honest "phallic candour" won the day,
until they rather lost interest when the book was released for free circulation in 1923. The book is the story of the adventures of a young man
named Jurgen in "the heaven of his grandmother and the hell of his fathers" and a great many other strange and exotic regions as well. Examined
with more detachment several years later, there seems little unique about it
save a curious use of rather strained erudition; *Jurgen* is an elaborately
veiled and long-drawn-out smoking room story which proves practically
nothing save that Cabell had some acquaintance with the works of Anatole
France. The book could, for the purpose of any examination of the literary
trends of the era, be entirely disregarded save for two facts. The first is that
it proves the self-consciousness of the breakdown of former reticences, and
the second is that *Jurgen* was to some extent the forerunner of a curious little group of novels characterized by an immense and blasé cynicism and a
fevered preoccupation with sex for sex's sake.

Sex, the subject of universal interest since time and man began, had an
additional fascination for a generation recently and abruptly released from
the prohibitions of Victorianism. Eagerly, certain types of writers catered
to the demand. To satisfy it came sex in Paris as portrayed in Victor Mar-

When James Joyce's Ulysses *was barred by the censors from sale in America, Americans
hunted for it in Paris bookstores. (Drawing by Helen Hokinson in the* New Yorker*)*

guerite's *The Bachelor Girl*, with its extremely liberal heroine and the apartment in which she played hostess in extraordinary episodes; sex in college as portrayed in the career of Hugh Carver in *The Plastic Age*; sex on the desert as portrayed in *The Sheik*, with its scenes of passion between a young English woman of title and an amorous Arab; sex in high-life London as portrayed in the luxurious milieu and sophisticatedly casual affairs of Iris March in Michael Arlen's *The Green Hat*—the vulgarity was increased by the author's awed admiration for the titled and the wealthy.

Eric Dorn, by Ben Hecht, was a story of neurotic people written in a choppy exotic style; when the same author the following year published *Gargoyles*, even the advanced minority group of the intelligentsia could find little to praise and contented themselves by mentioning that the characters were obsessed with sex. *Peter Whiffle*, by Carl Van Vechten, was a tenuous story of an idler among the sophisticated, a story so very attenuated and removed from ordinary life that it scarcely existed at all. *The Tattooed Countess* by the same author described the extremely dull seduction of a young boy in a Midwest town by a countess with the appropriately gaudy name of Ella Nattatorini. *Blackguard*, by Maxwell Bodenheim, a poet of some ability, and the same author's *Georgie May*, the story of a prostitute in a southern city,

Elinor Glyn, author, who introduced a new meaning for the pronoun "it"; and Clara Bow, who became known as the "it" girl in motion pictures. (From a photograph by Underwood & Underwood)

showed marked peculiarities of style and subject matter, subject matter which if treated differently would have been as permissible as any other, but which, as treated by Bodenheim, indicated a neurotic tension.

One novelist who dealt almost exclusively with manifestations of the sexual impulse, but who, due possibly to a less "high-brow" attitude, found a far wider audience than the others, was Elinor Glyn. All her books were utterly worthless, and all were tremendously popular. A perfectly fair sample of the Glyn dialogue is taken from *Man and Maid* in which the hero murmurs thoughtfully to the heroine, "You have had immense experience of love, Coralie, haven't you?" Glyn's most lasting achievement was in a field not necessarily literary; like the man who had "quiz" written on all the walls of Dublin, like the unfortunate Captain Boycott, like the estimable Mrs. Bloomer and the industrious Macadam, Glyn added a word to the English language. Rather, she added a meaning to the simple pronoun "it," transmuting that neutral little word into a noun and making it, for the younger generation at least, a symbol for the most desirable thing the gods could give. Glyn used the word, with these special connotations, for the first time in a short story called "The 'It' Girl" to indicate a tremendous attraction for the opposite sex. In schools and colleges, classes voting upon which of their members was most likely to succeed, gravely included in their tests of distinction the choice of the fellow-student fortunate enough to possess the most "it," sometimes translated as "sex appeal" and abbreviated as "S.A."

VIII

All "lost causes," if they are lost definitely enough, whether by clear-cut decision or by the passage of time, become objects of romance and glamour. Bonnie Prince Charlie is a storybook hero, William of Orange a dull figure in history; Napoleon is a superman, Wellington just another general; Lee a legendary knight, Grant a drab president. Inaccurate as these estimates are, they are the snap judgments of the average man, or his spontaneous feelings, and they would have to be greatly changed before the love letters of the victorious Duke of Wellington would be published serially in the newspapers—as the defeated Napoleon's were in 1935.

Of this tendency to exalt the vanquished, the South, after the Civil War, was one beneficiary. In imagination and in literature, the great houses became greater, the lovely women lovelier, the chivalrous men more chivalrous, the faithful slaves happier.

This legend was accepted not only in the South but perhaps even more wholeheartedly in the North. O. Henry observed that when the band played "Dixie" in a New York café about the turn of the century, the man who leaped into the air with a wild yell, waved his hat and then buried his face in his hands and burst into tears—such a man, said O. Henry cynically, is usually an inhabitant of Keokuk, Iowa. "Dixie" was not alone the song of the South, it was a symbol of romance for the whole country.

An illustration by C. K. Linson for In Ole Virginia, *by Thomas Nelson Page, depicting life in the older, romantic South.*

This disposition of the whole nation to cherish the southern legend was natural. We were a new country, our heritage of tradition was relatively scant, we lacked romantic associations, we had no sagas. We hungered for glamorous tradition, for legends of "home scenes and places and familiar names." To feed our hunger we accepted the tradition about the South and magnified it.

As for the South, its circumstances drove it in the same direction. Prevented by superior force from actual secession, it sought solace in spiritual secession. Completely impoverished, the best of its manhood gone, the one way of life it knew destroyed, the South turned its face backward and created a legend of the past. For half a century, southern authors—Thomas Nelson Page, F. Hopkinson Smith, George W. Cable, Mary Johnson, Joel Chandler Harris, even the "Little Colonel" books and the "Elsie Dinsmore" series—created, added to, and intensified a vision of life in which crinolined maidens, hanging on the arms of gallant soldiers, walked forever beneath magnolia trees; where white-mustached and always courtly colonels drank an eternal julep brought to them by their devoted bodyservants, where the laughter and the singing of the slaves was only interrupted to listen to the softer singing of birds.

The first modification of this picture was brought by Ellen Glasgow. Born in Richmond, Virginia, self-educated there and remaining there, she

A scene from the stage presentation of Erskine Caldwell's Tobacco Road, *dealing with "poor whites" in the new South in literature.*

became, in literature, a bridge between the old South and the new, the novelist of transition. Knowing the old South and loving it, yet seeing it clearly, she looked with equal clearness upon the coming of the new. Her *Deliverance* was the story of the passing of a plantation from one of the old families, the Blakes, incompetent to adjust themselves, to one of the new, wealthy families, the Fletchers. Glasgow treated both with objective fairness.

It was Glasgow who, precisely through her artistic objectiveness, did most to shatter the sentimental tradition of the South; certainly she was the first to crack it. Then, in 1915, a younger author—he happened to be a relative of Glasgow—James Branch Cabell, wrote a novel whimsically entitled *The Rivet in Grandfather's Neck*, in which he told Richmond some quite unpleasant home truths. This was the beginning of the almost complete breakdown, so far as contemporary literature was concerned, of the legendary South.

Presently, a critic, Henry L. Mencken, was hurling bricks, almost literally, at the Virginia legend: "Not a single contribution to human knowledge has come out of her colleges in twenty-five years; she spends less than half upon her common schools, per capita, than any Northern state spends. In brief, an intellectual Gobi or Lapland."

It was in this spirit that the new South, in the person of its own writers, began to deal with the homeland. While the better ones preserved much of what was fine and true in the old picture, the South as a whole had the feeling of being subjected in literature, to what in politics and economics, in the North of twenty years before, had been called "muckraking." Some of the new southern writers seemed to take a sadistic, perverted pleasure in what an old phrase described as "fouling his own nest."

Taking the Deep South as background, William Faulkner wrote, in *The Sound and the Fury*, of a family in which one member was an idiot, one a prostitute, and one committed suicide; in *Sartoris*, of a returned soldier who after several unsuccessful attempts, manages to accomplish, by his own suicide, the wiping out of a worthless and degenerate southern family; and in *As I Lay Dying*, the journey of an insane and revolting family of degenerates as they cart a putrefying corpse half across the state to bury it. A less authentic artist, Erskine Caldwell, again with the Deep South as background, achieved what would seem to be the ultimate in horror writing. In fact the horrors described by Caldwell were so extreme as to border on the grotesque. After reading one of his stories the exclamation of the average reader, uninfluenced by the idea that any pronouncement on art was necessary, would probably be, "Oh, now, honestly!" uttered in a tone of indifferent incredulity. In an effort, presumably to give some order to the chaotic and obviously overdrawn world that he created, Caldwell injected a little of the fashionable "class-consciousness" of the early depression years into his work—without, however, bringing his efforts any closer to literature.

Not all the realistic writing about the new South was sordid. Much of it merely applied correction to the earlier picture. DuBose Heyward in *Porgy and Mamba's Daughters* wrote of Negroes as complicated characters rather than puppets; and Julia Peterkin in *Green Thursday, Black April,* and *Scarlet Sister Mary,* which won the Pulitzer prize for 1929, did the same with greater realism. In 1929, Thomas Wolfe published a book having its background in North Carolina, which should rank as a great American novel, *Look Homeward, Angel.* The sense of time and the universe, the beauty of writing and the deeply rooted Americanism made the book great, at once a best-seller and a favorite with the critics. No reader of the book could forget the vitality of the Pentland clan, the howling imprecations of W. O. Gant, the laconic and hidden love of Ben for his young brother Eugene, and the pathos of the little school that Eugene

Thomas Wolfe.

attended. So faithful was the book to the city of Asheville that it was said that touring buses conducted *Look Homeward, Angel* tours about the city, pointing out the scenes described in the book.

IX

Sinclair Lewis was a tall, lean, freckle-faced, red-haired young man with a temperament akin to the color of his hair. He had been born in a characteristic American small town, Sauk Centre, Minnesota; had gone through the local high school and through the other boyhood experiences of the community with a nervous, restless, rebellious mind. He went to Yale University, learned much there, but was in constant irritation against many of the student body's conventionalities; went to a Socialist and Utopian colony in New Jersey, where he stoked the furnace and ran the patent washing machine; passed some ten years, in different cities, in newspaper reporting and editorial work to which he was unsympathetic and at which he was neither very good nor very successful. Having by nature a mind that saw things in lights and colors different from those in which the average and complacent youth sees them, and having an innate distaste for the usual, the accepted, in way of life or point of view, Lewis, by the time he was thirty, had acquired a considerable number of rasping experiences, and a quite fat mental portfolio of keenly observed American types, many of them, to him, irritating. These he put into a number of novels. Since Lewis had an extraordinary gift for mimicry, the characteristic types in his novels were universally recognized, by themselves with resentment, with hilarity by those who disliked them. Lewis's novels became the most discussed fiction of the twenties.

In *Main Street*, Lewis introduced a gallery of typical characters of a small American town—the doctor, the undertaker, the storekeeper, a score of others—all painted unsympathetically except one, the doctor's wife, Carol Kennecott, a misfit dreamer whose sensitiveness brought out the contrast with the self-satisfied provincialism of the others.

In *Babbitt* (George Follansbee Babbitt, leading realtor of Zenith), Lewis caricatured the small-city businessman; he ridiculed Babbitt's pride in his city, his pride in his association with prominent persons of his small world, his pride in his up-to-date-ness, his pride in his automobile, his pride in his white-tiled bathroom—and, as a symbol of all that Babbitt represented, ridiculed his pride in his membership in Rotary. In *Elmer Gantry*, Lewis lashed out at the clergy; inventing one whose major interest in his profession was material, and sensual; whose eye constantly moved from the sermon on his lectern to the figure of the most susceptible choirgirl; whose religion consisted of the art of showmanship; whose career was a constant juggling between his undisciplined desires and the necessity for deceiving his parishioners. In *The Man Who Knew Coolidge*, Lewis achieved a composite of many types; Lowell Schmalz, oracularly pontificating to a group of fellow Americans in a Pullman car, "does not stop talking after describing his intimate relations with Mr. Coolidge; he tells what he considers a funny story; he holds forth on women, California, relatives, touring, birth control, psychoanalysis, undertaking parlors and cafeterias."

Lewis's novels were prodigiously talked about; many who never read the books came to know the characters. "Babbitt" passed into the common tongue, like Hamlet, Don Quixote, and Sherlock Holmes; in American print and talk of the twenties, "Babbitt" became almost a common noun, almost it could be spelled with a small *b*; the derivation "babbittry" was frequent. The term "Main Street" was recognized and used, by persons who never heard of the book, as a generic term for small-town ways, institutions, and personalities.

Sinclair Lewis (left) and James Branch Cabell.

Of the types that Lewis satirized most fiercely, many were mainly in the world of business, the "go-getter," the smug success, the "human dynamo," the "mixer," the man who could "sell himself," the one who could "put his message across." As a consequence of the satires by Lewis and others—combined with several contemporary actualities, overemphasis on salesmanship, overrespect for business success—and also some contemporary scandals in business and politics, it resulted that some American types formerly treated with deference, even in some cases awe, found themselves, by the end of the 1920s, occupying pedestals lower than those to which they had been accustomed. The process went hand in hand with the debunking of history which was also a characteristic of the period.

X

To write of Henry L. Mencken as a literary figure is completely appropriate and accurate—yet inadequate. He was a national character, and the magazine he edited, the *American Mercury*, a national institution, one with an influence projecting into the future, for, said a teacher at the University of Chicago, an elderly conservative alarmed for youth, "the one thing that makes me fear for the future is the number of our students who read the *American Mercury*; on the campus you see it under every arm; they absorb everything in it." And a clergyman, the Reverend S. Parkes Cadman of Brooklyn, appealed to "pastors and orators" to talk at colleges, that students "be saved from the beliefs preached by H. L. Mencken." Another clergyman, the Reverend Louis L. Neuman of San Francisco, partly in satire, partly in unwilling concession, gave to Mencken and his magazine the rank of a cult: "Mercurianity is the name of a new religion, the Bible of which is a green-covered monthly magazine."

Mencken was a Baltimorean by birth and, as he reiterated in his diatribes against New York, by preference. Even during the some fifteen years he edited magazines published in New York, he commuted twice a week or so from Baltimore, retaining, by his residence in the latter city, a contact with a more average American background, an immunity from infection by the metropolis, a detachment from the influence of New York's literary cults and fads, which fortunate dissociation was part of his uniqueness and his strength. His innate ruggedness hated the aesthetic pose; while he knew intimately the most elevated stratum of professional writers, and held their exceptional confidence in his taste and judgment, yet by instinct he spent many of his hours of diversion, much of that part of his time not devoted to writing and editing, in the company of persons remote from the esoteric. Once he told me he had never attended a "literary tea" (Prohibition era euphemism, partly sarcastic, for a literary cocktail party). He maintained his connection with workaday newspaper circles, kept his hand in by regular contributions to the *Baltimore Sun*; at political conventions he was present as a working reporter. By instinct he stood apart from the rather effete or neurotic self-styled "intelligentsia" of the period; when they were writing about sex and shrieking against Puritanism, and clamoring for more freedom, Mencken thought they "have just about as much freedom as is good for them," as much as their literary horsepower could make good use of. Mencken was too vital to have any kinship with the defeatists who wrote much of the fiction of the "lost generation," too normal and wholesome to have much communion with the neurotics who wrote many of the novels of the "younger generation."

One other immunity Mencken had; he had never gone to college, and thus he became an outstanding one among those occasional personalities that are the better for not having been subjected to formal academic training, "a good brain not spoiled by education." As a youth and as a young man working on the *Baltimore Sun*, his native instinct for excellence led him to find standards of his own; his mind, curious, acquisitive for knowledge, and virile and conscientious, grew sturdily, with a confidence, and ultimately a surefooted facility, that might not have come to him had his information and standards, and his art, been handed down to him. With Mencken, information, knowledge, standards of taste, judgment about books and about men; these grew, with Mencken, as with a coral, through slow acquisition accompanied by sure digestion into an integral possession of his own. The understanding of words, prosody, style, which many college students fail to acquire from a score of teachers and textbooks, Mencken distilled for himself from one self-found book, Sidney Lanier's *Science of English Verse*. He became one of the most skilled craftsmen of his time. As a stylist, his every sentence was firm and intelligible; he had a genius for the striking word and the effective phrase, an instinct for musical sentences; he knew how to make punctuation an effective accessory to his art, he used it perhaps more meticulously than other writers of the twenties; he achieved the most forthright, clear, and provocative writing done in America during his time. His style was a complete expression of his personality, and was therefore brilliantly effective for what he had to say.

Meeting Mencken, sitting down opposite him at table (usually there would be a stein of beer or a bottle of wine between), one would, if given twenty guesses about his occupation, have said businessman, or lawyer, or doctor, or any other of seventeen. In appearance he was stocky, almost chunky, his head round, his eyes blue-gray and direct, his mouth humorous.

H. L. Mencken

That physical averageness was accompanied by intellectual normalcy; Mencken was the normal American, essentially an American archetype—energetic, logical, entirely practical, curious, unbiased, loving liberty and scorning sentimentality and hypocrisy. In short, he applied to literature those habits of mind usually employed by Americans in the pursuit of business. A steel manufacturer would weigh no more impartially a proposition for doubling production than Mencken weighed the ideas current in his time. He loathed nothing more than "an endless series of false assumptions and non sequiturs—bad logic piled recklessly upon unsound facts." He was in incessant warfare upon "hampering traditions of any sort." He was a firm believer in self-help and self-reliance as the only necessities for personal advancement, as firm a believer in them as were any of the Rotarians whom he zestfully jibed at. He stood for progress, deploring the tendency of the mob to cling to its delusions; he was an individualist, believing that the rewards for extraordinary efficiency should be without limit; he was an admirer of the early heroes of America, because, among other reasons, "The Fathers of the Republic . . . not only sought to create a governmental machine that would be safe from attack without; they also sought to create one that would be safe from attack within; they invented very ingenious devices for holding the mob in check, for protecting the national policy against its transient and illogical rages."

He distrusted Idealism—that is, self-conscious Idealism, Idealism with a capital *I*—which Mencken called "bilge." He hated prudery, and the censorship with which prudery seeks to protect itself; the contemporary symbol of prudery and guardian of it, Anthony Comstock, Mencken called a "damn fool," an "imbecile." He hated slipshoddiness, in work, in morals, in thinking, in style; the speeches of President Harding drove him to fury: "Harding writes the worst English I have ever encountered; it reminds me of a string of wet sponges; it is so bad that a sort of grandeur creeps into it." But equally Mencken hated meaningless mellifluousness; turning from Harding to his predecessor in the White House, Mencken wrote: "Almost I long for the sweeter song, the rubber stamp of more familiar design, the gentler and more seemly bosh of the late Woodrow." Even more did Mencken dislike Bryan: "Bryan was the most sedulous fly-catcher in American history and in many ways the most successful; his quarry, of course, was not *musca domestica* but *homo neandertalensis;* for 40 years he tracked it with coo and bellow up and down the rustic back-waters of the Republic."

Mencken attacked moralists, progressives, reformers, patriots, boomers; from the beginning of his career, he said, his general aim had been "to combat, chiefly by ridicule, American piety, stupidity, tinpot morality, cheap chauvinism in all their forms."

The particular disapprobation that brought Mencken most attention was that which became familiar through his newspaper reports of the Scopes trial. Mencken thought of Fundamentalism as largely one with Prohibition and the Ku Klux Klan, and at these he fired his biggest guns. Mencken's was not a fight against religion so much as one in behalf of tolerance; it was a fight largely in behalf of religious minorities—including that minority which believes in no religion:

> After all, no human being really *knows* anything about the exalted matters with which all religions deal. The most he can do is to match his private guess against the guesses of his fellowmen. For any man to say absolutely, in such a field, that this or that is wholly or positively true and this or that is utterly false is simply to talk nonsense. Personally, I have never encountered a religious idea— and I do not except the idea of the existence of God—that was instantly and unchallengeably convincing, as, say, the Copernican astronomy is instantly and unchallengeably convincing. But neither have I ever encountered a religious idea that could be dismissed offhand as palpably and indubitably false. In even the worst nonsense of such theological mountebanks as the Rev. Dr. Billy Sunday, Brigham Young and Mrs. Eddy, there is always enough lingering plausibility, or, at all events, possibility, to give the judicious pause. Whatever the weight of the probabilities against it, it nevertheless *may* be true.

Mencken's reports from the Scopes trial, his attacks upon Fundamentalism, Prohibition, and the Ku Klux Klan, his thrusts at the rural sections, especially the southern sections—he called the South "the Bible-belt" and its people "the boobery"; as individuals, "boobus Americanus"—caused him to be noticed by a wider audience than would have observed his more purely literary productions. His victims fought back, with blistering ferocity.

In the combat, necessarily the weapons had to be words; and, compared to Mencken's arsenal, his adversaries were poor in vocabulary. They managed, however, to find a considerable number of simple, primitive epithets, which they used with a force that, they hoped, would offset Mencken's superiority in artistic deftness. Many of the epithets were taken from the terminology of the less esteemed species of the animal kingdom. The aggregate of these zoological appellations—had Mencken been at one and the same time all the animals his adversaries called him—would have composed a truly terrifying creature. To the *Tampa Times*, Mencken was, by a curious misalliance of disparate parentages, at once "this maggot, this buzzard." To the *Jackson* (Mississippi) *News*, he was "a howling hyena." To the *San Francisco Chronicle* he was, simply, "a pole-cat." Charitably, the *Philadelphia Inquirer* said that "perhaps society needs Mencken as nature needs mosquitoes." To the *Minneapolis Journal* he was, strange achievement in mongrelism, "wasp and pole-cat purely." To the *Norfolk Virginian-Pilot* he was, with some aptness, "the literary man-eating tiger." The *Diapason* (Chicago) compared him to "flies that gather about the garbage in summer, and delight in what they can discover." To the Nashville *Tennessean* he was a "mangy ape"; to the Iowa *Legionaire*, "a mangy mongrel." The Knights of the Ku Klux Klan of Arkansas formally "Resolved: that we condemn in the strongest possible language the vile mouthings of this writer, to whom virtue, patriotism and decency are only a subject upon which to expend the venom of a poisonous pen, and that we protest against the calumny as too degrading and false to come from the heart of one who is not himself a moral pervert."

All of which, and some 130 printed pages of similar epithets and miscellaneous objurgations, Mencken, with the humorous gravity that was one of his charms, collected and published in a volume which he called *Menckeniana, A Schimpflexicon*, saying suavely, in a prefatory note, that "this collection is not exhaustive, but an effort has been made to keep it representative."

But one observed that Mencken's hospitality to his enemies was not broad enough to include in his *Schimpflexicon* what many thought the sharpest arrow ever aimed at him. When he, and a literary partner he had for a time, were at the height of their vogue; and when they seemed, to fellow-craftsmen, in some danger of accepting too seriously the role of omniscience that current valuation set on them, a young woman deft with words, intent upon saving Mencken and his partner, George Jean Nathan, from self-overestimation, wrote a biting couplet:

> Mencken and Nathan and God;
> Yes, probably, possibly, God.

XI

They said the twenties was a material age, that it was dominated by business, that much of the imaginative in man and the spiritual had been diverted into making business "go-getters"; that what the twenties meant by "a man with a mission" was a man with a mission to sell more automobiles, more chewing gum, more shaving soap.

They said these things, and these things were true. They said also—foreigners said it and Americans said it—that the triumph of industrialism in America had been at the expense of art; that life in America was so bleak, so lacking in intellectual depth, so lacking in encouragement for the artistic life, that the few sensitive, refined minds America produced were forced to flee to Europe to escape spiritual starvation. They had been saying this for a long time. A distinguished author of American birth had said it; one of the highly developed intellects that had escaped the American wilderness to the security of England, Henry James, had written: "One might enumerate the items of high civilization, as it exists in other countries, which are absent from the texture of American life, until it should become a wonder to know what was left: No sovereign, no court, no personal loyalty, no aristocracy, no church, no clergy, no army, no diplomatic service, no country gentlemen, no palaces, no castles, no manors, nor old country-houses, nor parsonages, nor thatched cottages, nor ivied ruins; no cathedrals, nor abbeys, nor little Norman churches; no great universities nor public schools—no Oxford, nor Eton, nor Harrow; no literature, no novels, no museums, no pictures, no political society, no sporting class." Henry James had said that during the late nineteenth century, and it continued a highbrow thing to say until the 1920s. What they implied was that without the accessories Henry James catalogued, art could not thrive.

Yet the fact is that during the period following the war, the poetry written by Americans was more important than that written by the poets of any other country. And the renascence of poetical writing was accompanied by spread of popular acquaintance with it.

For the emergence of an unusual number of exceptionally talented poets, one would hesitate to venture a reason. It is not the sort of phenomenon that can be explained. Historically we can say there had been a prolonged period of sterility, and that abundance followed. The burgeoning began about 1912. It came after almost half a century of sterility. The New England poets who had created the nineteenth century's golden age of verse had ceased to be productive about the time of the Civil War. There followed a quarter century during which the only American poets of any consequence were Walt Whitman and Emily Dickinson. From 1890 for a score of years there was only Edwin Arlington Robinson in his early phase. Then, for about five years, from 1912 to 1917 came a spate: Vachel Lindsay, Amy Lowell, Robert Frost, Edgar Lee Masters, Carl Sandburg, Ezra Pound, and Edna St. Vincent Millay. These all continued to produce into the 1920s; so did also Edwin Arlington Robinson, improving always. They were joined, during the 1920s, by Elinor Wylie, e. e. cummings, T. S. Eliot, Conrad Aiken, Archibald MacLeish, Stephen Vincent Benét, William Rose Benét, and the young Negro poet Countee Cullen.

These, not recognizing fatal handicap in the lack of Henry James's "no palaces, no manors, nor thatched cottages nor ivied ruins"—these American poets found adequate inspiration in familiar American scenes:

Robert Frost in the New England countryside:

> The woods are lovely, dark and deep,
> But I have promises to keep,
> And miles to go before I sleep,
> And miles to go before I sleep.

Edwin Arlington Robinson in the ruin of a farmhouse on a New England hill:

> They are all gone away;
>   The House is shut and still.
> There is nothing more to say.
>
> Why is it then we stray
>   Around that sunken sill?
> They are all gone away.
>
> There is ruin and decay
>   In the House on the Hill.
> They are all gone away—
> There is nothing more to say.

Carl Sandburg in the life and language of the Midwest:

> A code arrives; language, lingo; slang;
> behold the proverbs of a people, a nation:
> Give 'em the works. Fix it, there's always
> a way. Be hard boiled. The good die young. . . .
>
> Good morning, America!
> Morning goes as morning-glories go!
> High noon goes, afternoon goes!
> Twilight, sundown, gloaming—
> The hour of writing: Good night, America!
> Good night, sleep, peace, and sweet dreams!

T. S. Eliot in a skeptical interpretation of a certain New England culture:

> When evening quickens faintly in the street,
> Wakening the appetites of life in some
> And to others bringing the *Boston Evening Transcript,*

I mount the steps and ring the bell, turning
Wearily, as one would turn to nod good-bye to Rochefoucauld,
If the street were time and he at the end of the street,
And I say, "Cousin Harriet, here is the *Boston Evening Transcript.*"

Vachel Lindsay in scenes in the Mississippi valley:

Booth led boldly with his big bass drum—
    (Are you washed in the blood of the Lamb?)
The Saints smiled gravely and they said:
    "He's come."
    (Are you washed in the blood of the Lamb?)

Among writers of light verse there was one who achieved supremely
what light verse (of the ironic kind) is supposed to do. Here was an age intent upon striving, regarding diligence as the most worthy of virtues, giving to optimism almost the standing of religion, making a god of success.
About all that, Dorothy Parker wrote verses which began with apparent
sharing of the universal reverence:

If I should labor through daylight and dark,
Consecrate, valorous, serious, true,
Then on the world I may blazon my mark—
And what if I don't and what if I do?

More direct was the thrust—the twenties would have called it a "swift
punch"—that Parker delivered upon her own and related professions, in
which, during the period, many of the practitioners tended to be more self-
conscious than talented:

Authors and actors and artists and such
Never know nothing, and never know much.
Sculptors and singers and those of their kidney
Tell their affairs from Seattle to Sydney.
Playwrights and poets and such horses' necks
Start off from anywhere, end up at sex.
Diarists, critics and similar roe
Never say nothing, and never say no.
People Who Do Things exceed my endurance;
God, for a man that solicits insurance!

One of Parker's distinguishing traits was an application to the art of
verse of the O. Henry trick-ending technique, long familiar in short stories. She gave delight to college students with a rondelle in which she
dwelled sentimentally and demurely on the theme "She's passing fair," and
then ended,

> But if the passing mark be minus D,
> She's passing fair.

She wrote a conventional, fairly charming lullaby, addressed to a lovely young lady—but in the last two lines reveals the reasons for her tender solicitude:

> When you're awake, all the men go and fall for you,
> Sleep, pretty lady, and give me a chance.

Integral in Parker's art was a talent for titles. Under the caption "Two Volume Novel," she wrote merely:

> The sun's gone dim, and
> The moon's turned black;
> For I loved him, and
> He didn't love back.

XII

In the judgment of many persons of reflective temperament, the best autobiography ever written by an American (some thought it the best ever written by any one) appeared in 1919. (There had been a private publication some years before.) That it remained on best-selling lists for eighteen months is a tribute at once to the quality of the book and to the taste of a large segment of American readers—compensation for the popularity conferred upon many trivial or foolish volumes, even undesirable ones. It remained several years later among the few books of the 1920s that seemed most likely to endure, or the best deserving to endure. One might use, as a test of the cultural standard of Americans having some elevation of taste, two questions: Did they read and appreciate *The Education of Henry Adams*? And did they know, actually or in pictorial reproduction, and were they moved by, the bronze statue of "Grief" in Rock Creek Park, Washington, D.C., which Henry Adams had the sculptor Saint-Gaudens make as the tombstone for his wife?

Henry Adams came of the best stock America possessed, received the best education America afforded, experienced the most cultivated associations and followed one of the most elevated careers. Grandson of one president of the United States, great-grandson of another, member of the American family that has had the most sustained vitality and has contributed the largest number of members to the public service, he was born under the shadow of the State House in Boston; spent much of his youth with his grandfather, the sixth president, in retirement at Quincy; was educated at Harvard, where his teachers included the scientist Louis Agassiz and the poet James Russell Lowell; was further educated in Germany;

The Memorial to Mrs. Henry Adams, in Rock Creek Park, Washington, D.C., by Augustus Saint-Gaudens.

served as secretary to his father, Charles Francis Adams, when the latter was American minister to Great Britain during the stirring period of our Civil War; taught history at Harvard; edited the *North American Review* when it was the most distinguished literary periodical in America; wrote authoritative books in a wide variety of fields—*Essays on Anglo-Saxon Law, Life of Albert Gallatin, Life of John Randolph,* a nine-volume *History of the United States,* a study of medieval life and philosophy called *Mont-Saint-Michel and Chartres;* wrote two novels under a pseudonym; traveled—often, extensively, and thoughtfully—throughout Europe, in the Caribbean, in the South Seas; and spent his later years in Washington as the closest friend of John Hay and a familiar in a group of similar spirits. More than any other man of his generation, Henry Adams had known the finest and most thoughtful minds in America and Europe, had known them intimately; more than any other man, he had participated in the most elevated intellectual and artistic life of his day; more than any other, he had had variety and depth of intellectual experience.

Out of that experience, in a spirit of seeking to distill what he had seen and felt and participated in, trying to find some lesson in it, seeking to extract from it some design for living—or the reason for lack of a design—

Adams wrote his autobiography. What grandiose self-complacency a man of ordinary clay would have made of it, one can surmise. The mood in which Adams went about it is suggested by his eliminating the pronoun "I," writing it in the third person, and calling it *The Education of Henry Adams*. In the book, the events and conditions he saw and shared, the exalted experiences he had, are used by him as merely the framework upon which he builds the record of his intellectual development. In a man of Adams's type it could not be otherwise. More truthfully than any man of his generation, he could have said, though his diffidence would have prevented him from saying: "Cogito, ergo sum." His life was a life of the mind. All his years he had searched, and now in his confession he recorded his search, for the laws of life, to discover them and apply them.

The autobiography resolved itself, in large part, into an account of the difference between him and his environment, between his mind and the time he lived in, between his spirit and the spirit of the age. His mind had been determined by his education, the education he had received through contact with the elders of his family, and the formal education he received

A photograph of Henry Adams taken by himself in his study in Washington about 1903. (In the possession of Mrs. Ward Thoron)

in the schools that were dominated by the same Puritan spirit. His ancestors had, almost literally, worshiped duty as the "Stern Daughter of the Voice of God." This austere conception of life and duty was transmitted almost unchanged to the sensitive son who was torn by doubts unknown to them. The very landscape and familiar scenes of Henry Adams's childhood, the granite hills and stone-walled fields of New England, imposed austerity, assumed a world in which right and wrong were always and clearly distinguishable. The sobriety of the New England scene, the temperament of the Puritans, the severity of a classical education, the consciousness of duty to himself and to his family, all these had led Adams throughout his life, in spite of Hamlet-like doubts and questionings, toward one pattern of life. The education he had received through heredity, from the conscious intent of his parents, and from his early environment, was to fit him to live in a world in which the right course of action for a responsible man was ascertainable, and the only problem was to follow this right course through the vicissitudes and temptations of circumstance. But Henry Adams felt and saw clearly that the world in which he spent his life was one in which values and criteria were in such flux as to make the education he had received obsolete. Not only had the standards changed, they constantly continued to change; almost each day he awoke in an altered world. The horizons of man's knowledge had been extended more rapidly than man's ethics could keep pace with. The change from the world in which his grandfather, President John Quincy Adams, consumed six weeks in traveling from Boston to Washington, to the world in which Henry Adams made the same journey in one day, had brought corresponding disruption in the intellectual and spiritual pattern of life.

So, at the end, Adams felt that he had failed, that he had been obliged to fail. His conclusion, possibly too broad, possibly too large a generalization from one individual's experience, was that, "In plain words, chaos was the law of nature, order was the dream of man." Probably it is best to regard Adams's *Education* as one man's confession of futility rather than to accept it, in the way some have, as an affirmation of defeatism in the sense of a universal philosophy.

CHAPTER 8
Tunes of the Twenties

Serious acceptance of the theory that "the history of a country is written in its popular songs" would lead to distortion of a sort not uncommon when history is made to conform to a formula, and facts ingeniously mobilized to support a theory. But, accepting popular songs as a facet of the times, we might say, without too much straining, that the decade of the 1920s had as its overture the serene and confident "Smiles," that it rose to a fortissimo which might be expressed in a paean of exuberant affluence, "My God, How the Money Rolls In," and that it ended, after the panic of 1929, with a crashing finale—"crashing" is in this connection an especially apt adjective—the universally familiar and uniquely appropriate song of indigence, "Brother, Can You Spare a Dime?"

For a song to express the boom-peak of the decade, we should be obliged to go back to an old ditty which during the twenties experienced a revival and an adaptation. "My God, How the Money Rolls In," sung with exuberant gusto, was an accurate expression of the late 1920s, but the original words had been written many years before:

> My sister she works in the laundry,
> My father he fiddles for gin,
> My mother she takes in washing,
> My God! how the money rolls in!

By changing the second line to "My father sells bootlegger gin" or "My father makes synthetic gin," the twenties gave to the song a timeliness which related it to the "easy money" phase of the decade, and also made it appropriate to another aspect of the period. The allusions to specifically described sources of easy money provided humor to a generation just becoming familiar with outlawed, but not successfully exiled, substitutes for liquor. A good many Americans of 1920 and subsequent years never heard the word "synthetic" except as an adjective describing gin.

Change of yet another line of "My God, How the Money Rolls In" introduced an additional modern allusion, and gave to the adaptation that attraction which the younger generation during the twenties seemed to find in songs (and novels) about an area which their parents described as "low-life"—partiality of "high life" for "low life," a wish of the former to seem

the latter, was one expression of the pose of daring which was a vogue of young folks during the twenties.

For the full understanding of the 1920s version of "My God, How the Money Rolls In," it may be desirable to explain that "snow" was argot for cocaine, and "snow-birds" for its addicts. Since sale of the former to the latter was illegal, the traffic was remunerative; it became one of the ways in which "easy money" was achieved. The enumerated sources of revenue in the twenties' version ran:

> My sister sells snow to the snow-birds,
> My father makes bootlegger gin, . . .
> My mother she takes in washing,
> My God! how the money rolls in!

II

A period which made its money in the spirit of "My God, How the Money Rolls In," spent it, naturally, in the spirit of "Makin' Whoopee." As the former reflected economic exuberance, so did the latter express spiritual recklessness. The words of "Makin' Whoopee" were merely some cynical, gay verses about marriage, divorce, and alimony; it was the music that expressed the whole spirit of noise, abandon, recklessness, and excitement which were implied by the song and were characteristic of large segments of life. The phrase "makin' whoopee" became a part of the common tongue; any person or group who dismissed restraint and threw themselves with loud and feverish gusto into any area of activity—a visitor spending freely in a nightclub, a farmer "on a tear" in the city, a husband on the loose, a politician starting an insurgent movement, a banker banking recklessly, a businessman imprudently expanding—all were "makin' whoopee." Nearly everybody did it; few, during those flush years, escaped the infection that made men act with an impulsiveness which did not sufficiently calculate the consequences:

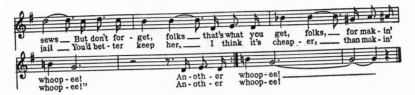

sews ___ But don't for - get,   folks ___ that's what you   get,   folks, ___ for mak - in'
jail ___ You'd bet - ter   keep   her, ___ I   think   it's   cheap - er, ___ than mak - in'

whoop - ee!   An - oth - er   whoop - ee! ___
whoop - ee!"   An - oth - er   whoop - ee!

> Picture a little love-nest
> Down where the roses cling
> Picture the same sweet love-nest—
> Think what a year can bring:
> He's washing dishes and baby clothes,
> He's so ambitious he really sews.
> But don't forget folks
> That's what you get folks,
> For makin' whoopee.

"Making whoopee" was associated with nightclubs, features of city life, especially New York City life, which sprang up as incidents of national prohibition—institutions designed to provide illicit and therefore alluring access to stimulation by alcoholic beverages, accompanied by associated

Texas Guinan, nightclub hostess, as she sailed with her entertainers for London. (Underwood & Underwood photo)

Helen Morgan, a torch singer well known on the stage and in the nightclubs of the period. (De Mirjian photo)

forms of gaiety. The most lavish patron of nightclubs in New York, the one who provided most conspicuously the wherewithal upon which and for which whoopee was made, was the rich visitor from out of town; his role was recognized with disarming audacity by a famous nightclub hostess, Texas Guinan, whose technique was to address loudly the prospective spender as "Hello, Sucker!" So strange was the spirit of the time that the customer was pleased by the conspicuousness, and proceeded to act the part which the hostess had conferred on him. Generically, the free spender, especially if elderly and a little obese, became known as a "big butter and egg man"; geographically he was usually described vaguely as "from the West." About him a song was written:

CHORUS

1. The   big   but-ter and egg man   from   Crack-er- town   P   A

> The big butter and egg man from the West,
> He carries his produce on his vest . . .
> He turns the city upside down
> And drinks up all the wine in town.
> He just throws his dough away . . .
> He bought a chorus girl a pup,
> Next day the price of cheese went up.

III

From almost every lip in 1923 one could have heard a song about a humble fruit, the banana, a song expressed in a locution so contorted that hardly any amount of grammatical diligence on the part of a foreign visitor would have enabled him to understand just what this ditty meant, or why it was sung.

About the origin of the phrase "Yes, we have no bananas today," there is dispute, the final arbitration of which would consume time which in this book it seems best to reserve for issues more simple to solve. Some said the phrase came into existence as the response of a Grecian vendor of fruit, or perhaps an Italian one, whose regretted inability to supply the particular fruit requested by a customer was expressed in a phraseology designed to soften disappointment with graciousness. After the phrase became familiar, it served as the point of many quips that amused the early twenties. One of these purported to repeat a laconic conversation, alleged to have taken place in that fecund source of much American folklore and slang, the mess kitchen of an army post, a conversation in which the captain undertook to impress on the private that punctilio of army life which requires that the reply of a subordinate to a superior must end with "sir":

CAPTAIN (*sternly:*)Do I understand there is no dessert today?
PRIVATE: Yes.
CAPTAIN: Yes, what?
PRIVATE: Yes, we have no bananas.

"Yes, We Have No Bananas," during 1923 and soon after, was sung infinitely more often than "The Star Spangled Banner," and more often than all the hymns in all the hymnals of all the churches combined. If European visitors assumed it to be the national anthem, maybe they were not wholly wrong; perhaps the song which during any period is the most generally sung deserves to be regarded, for the time, as the musical expression of some temporarily forward phase of the national spirit. What queer momentary aberration of the American national ethos the banana song may have reflected is beyond the ability of this historian to say. Indeed, to say anything about "Yes, We Have No Bananas" is futile surplusage. It so fully speaks for itself. To paint the lily, to add gilt to gold, would be justifiable adornment compared to adding yellow to the banana song. I reproduce it, with its strange and inexplicable bizarreries of spelling and lettering, just as it was printed on the millions of sheets of it that were sold during 1923 and for a short time after.

What the banana song signified as a phenomenon; whether Sigmund Spaeth could in this case prove his generalization that popular songs "often reflect the spirit, the atmosphere, the customs, the manners and morals of the day"—about all that I am unequipped to be authoritative. Possibly America sang "Yes, We Have No Bananas" to disprove any suspicion of cultural effeteness—that instinct for a kind of flaunting earthiness was widely current during the twenties, especially among young folks.

IV

In accepting, so far as we dare accept, the theory that popular songs reflect the spirit of the age, we must always bear in mind that in any age there may be a surface spirit, and also an inner one. If during the 1920s, any ordinary artisan of tune had set out merely to imitate the music of the day and push the current vogue to a greater height, he would have been likely to give his creation a rapid tempo, and fill it with noise—he would have tried to out-whoopee whoopee. Many did that, and wrote ordinary songs, destined to ephemeralness followed by desuetude. One person, however, seeing more of the age than its surface, wrote a song which, years after it was composed, had a degree, and kind, of appreciation which seemed to forecast for it an enduring position in the classics.

To compose a song that adequately reflects the spirit of an age is rare and distinguished. But to compose one which probes through the surface spirit down to a mood that the age itself has not yet recognized—to accomplish that calls for such prophetic insight, such instinctive understanding, such kinship with the inner soul of a generation as is indisputably genius.

The late 1920s was the peak of the boom, a time when, any ordinary observer would have said, the spirit of America was supremely one of concern with things, possessions, buildings, and bonds and barter; with size and speed, a time when the ambition of every American was to acquire, by processes faster and faster, more and more of whatever material accumulation was his private zest, and a time when the more and more seemed so easy of attainment that all were, or thought they were, happy in the achievement.

Into the very vortex of that whirling-dervish time came, in 1927, a song of longing for repose and peace, a song which exalted detachment from the hurly-burly, contentment with little:

    Ol' man river, dat ol' man river, he must know sumpin', but don't
       say nuthin',
    He just keeps rollin', he keeps on rollin' along.
    He don't plant 'taters, he don't plant cotton, an' dem dat plants
       'em is soon forgotten
    But ol' man river he jes keeps rollin' along.
    You and me, we sweat and strain, body all achin', an' racked wid
       pain.

"Tote dat barge ! Lift dat bale!"
Git a little drunk an' you'll land in jail.
Ah gits weary an' sick ob tryin', ahm tired of livin' an' feared of
  dyin',
But ol' man river he jes keeps rollin' along.

Doubtless "Ol' Man River" is timeless; no doubt it would have taken
high place had it emerged in the time of Thomas More or Christopher
Marlowe or Horace; and no doubt fifty years hence or a hundred it will
have its place among that very small number of permanent classics of popular song, in which high musical merit goes hand in hand with the tuneful-
ness that appeals to the mass. But can anyone doubt that the instantaneous
and universal appreciation which "Ol' Man River" received in 1927 was
due to a special condition, a reason deep in the spirit of the times? Perhaps
a beginning disillusionment with the material abundance that was supposed to be the pride of the age, a disrelish for the hurry and fret with
which that material abundance was achieved, a questioning of the complexity and the feverish tempo that the twenties imposed, a longing for the
serenity and imperturbability, the self-sufficient philosophy of "Ol' man
river, he jest keeps rollin' along." Almost with the dignity of an Old Testament prophet, "Ol' Man River" stood up before an America frantic with
hurry, and told it what was its true heart's desire.
  To "Ol' Man River" several of the best talents of the time contributed:
One of the great storytellers of the generation, Edna Ferber, wrote a novel
of life on the Mississippi, *Show Boat*; the most expert showman of the time,
Florenz Ziegfeld, adapted the novel into a musical play; the words of the
lyrics were written by Oscar Hammerstein II, the music by Jerome Kern.
One other contributor there was, one who, curiously, did not see the song
nor hear it sung until it was completed, but whose personality had been in
the mind of the composer from his first inspiration, a great Negro singer,
Paul Robeson, who, Kern had hoped, would have a role in the play, but was
unable to do so in the original production.*

V

The type of music that was supposed to be essentially characteristic of
the twenties was jazz. And in truth, one of the definitions of jazz,
"brazen defiance of accepted rules," would have served equally well to describe the spirit of much of the generation. The eccentricity of syncopation
which jazz achieved is suggested by the happily apt title of a piece written
in 1921 to adapt jazz to the piano, "Kitten on the Keys"—in which the startling effect was achieved by triple rhythm with the right hand against double rhythm with the left. And the public favor for jazz was proved by the

*Robeson played Joe in London and in the 1936 MGM film of *Show Boat*—and continued to sing
the song until his death. —D.R.

eagerness with which "Kitten on the Keys" was received by the early twenties; "probably no other piano solo ever leaped into such widespread popularity in so short a time," claimed one writer. Similarly expressive was the title of another widely popular jazz creation, "Crazy Rhythm," some words of which described the insidious and conquering pervasiveness of the bizarre cacophony:

> Every Greek, each Turk and each Latin,
> The Russians and Prussians as well;
> When they seek the lure of Manhattan,
> Are sure to come under your spell.
> Their native folk songs they soon throw away . . .

The fantastic syncopation of jazz was neither the accident of a kitten on the piano keys nor the haphazard aberrations of the mad. Jazz never made the apology of the reproved member of an orchestra who explained that he had "played the fly-specks." The unusualness of notation was deliberately sought, and attainment of the most outré of cacophonic combinations was the jazz composer's triumph. Erratic syncopation, eccentricity deliberately planned, was only one of the characteristics of jazz. It was rapid, feverish, excited, and exciting.

To write fully and adequately about jazz would be to write the history of much of the generation. The word passed into common use; to "jazz" or "jazz up" became a transitive verb, used to describe the introduction of speed and excitement into any activity of life, the operation usually being regarded as praiseworthy. To "jazz it up a bit" was the common recommendation for anything whose tempo had failed to keep up with the times.

"Let's have the Schubert Serenade and get some dirt into it."
To "Jazz up" the classics meant, in many cases, to play them with a touch of salaciousness.
(A drawing by Leonard Dove in the New Yorker)

Some composers and purveyors of jazz took it seriously, seriously in the sense of approving it, creating it, and performing it. A composer of high standing, George Gershwin, defended it: "Music should be a product of the time in which it was produced. . . . The old masters reflected in their music the spirit of their ages: isn't it up to us to do the same?" A successful orchestra leader, Paul Whiteman, said, "I sincerely believe that jazz is the folk-music of the machine age."

Others took it seriously in the sense in which they took pestilence seriously, or as the hind takes the wolf seriously. An English musical critic addressing the National Union of Organists' Associations condemned "that cursed American form of music," and the London *Times* solemnly repeated the malediction. Another English critic, Ernest Newman, called it "musical insanity," a product of "brainlessness and boredom." One eminent modern Italian composer, Pietro Mascagni, composer of *Cavalleria Rusticana*, made a statement which a Philadelphia headline writer epitomized as "'Jazz Sounds Death-Knell of Opera,' Says Mascagni."

But it turned out that an American composer, at the time wise and old, was at once more calm and more accurate than the Italian and English ones. "Jazz," said John Philip Sousa in 1928, "does not truly represent America. . . . It will, I am positive, some day disappear."*

Essential to jazz was the saxophone—"it was the heart, soul, mind, body and spirit of the jazz orchestra." It was not new, it had been invented some eighty years before by a Belgian instrument maker named Saxe. But it was in the 1920s that extraordinary use, leading to widespread vogue, came to this curious hybrid. (The saxophone is the only reed instrument made of brass, the other reeds—the clarinet, the oboe, and the bassoon—are of wood; the saxophone player could be at one and the same time both string band and woodwind.) Like all virile invaders the saxophone was ruthless; roughly it elbowed the gentle violin out of its dominance in orchestras.

The very shape and appearance of the saxophone was striking; a player standing up with one to his lips could by dipping and swinging its long length, by sudden starts and rigidities and tremors, by swoops and swerves, give to the instrument an effect of sentience; could create, by the motions he gave it, expressions which supplemented the music, the union of music to the ear and motion to the eye having an extraordinary capacity to create effects of comedy, surprise, dismay, satisfaction, or whatever other emotion the music was designated to convey.

As for the sounds that a skilled saxophone player could achieve, there was almost no limit to them. The saxophone could be onomatopoetic as no other instrument could. Even an amateur, a boy—as many a parent discovered during the twenties—could evoke sounds which the household would have pre-

---

*It may seem to us that Mascagni was more correct than Sousa (or Mark Sullivan) on the subject of jazz. Yet this section seems especially valuable as a gauge of contemporary misunderstanding of jazz, the degree to which an American of Sullivan's comprehension could miss the point. Or, as Louis Armstrong might say, "If you have to ask what jazz is, you'll never know."—D.R.

Cartoonist J. N. Darling (Ding), in the New York Herald Tribune, *illustrates the contrast between Secretary of the Interior Wilbur reproving the social diversions of some of his Indian charges and the Caucasian diversions that were current at the same time.*

ferred to be absent. The saxophone could imitate the yowl of a cat, the moo of a cow, the baa of a calf, the whinney of a horse. Parents imprudent enough to yield to a boy's begging for a saxophone as a Christmas present found by New Year's that their home was housing the entire animal kingdom, a menagerie of wild animals and a barnyard of tame ones, a lunatic asylum in which were segregated victims given especially to maniacal laughter, together with a wide variety of other sources of noise, chiefly unwanted ones, banging doors, howling winds, honking automobiles. The saxophone could, and in the hands of prankish boys did, reproduce, with rather greater effectiveness than the actual thing, human sounds whose reproduction is not universally desired, a yawn, a grunt, a belch. A skillful player with an acrobatic tongue slapping against the reed, his fingers fluttering over the score of keys, could achieve titillating arpeggios, glissandos, every sort of musical coruscation; he could toot and he could tootle, he could blare and blast, could bleat and blat, he could chatter, he could coo. Especially could he coo; there was wide complaint, where there was not approval, that the saxophone was sensuous, that it was "music in the nude." It was the instrument of the twenties—and it was a long way from the pipes of Pan.

VI

The decade was cordial to change, at times seemed to prefer strangers to old friends. Many innovations rushed to take advantage of the period's zest for the new. One of the novelties was "crooning." It was developed by a young man who had been born in Vermont, reared in Maine, and educated at Yale—that New England background, especially the Maine and Vermont part of it, seemed somehow incongruous with the art the young man practiced, for crooning was on the verge of being regarded as soft, as almost effeminate. Born Hubert Prior Vallee, he came to be called "Rudy"; that abbreviation seemed also a transition in the direction of the sentimental. Crooning heard directly, by one in the same room, made somewhat the slightly disconcerting impression of a male human being making sounds like those a mother makes to a very young child. The microphone, however, and the ether waves seemed to transmute sounds of mother-love into sounds having seductive appeal and gave to crooning over the radio some sort of magic.

By his art, Vallee, with other crooners, revived some old songs, made many new ones familiar—among the latter, "Good-Night, Sweetheart," and "When It's Springtime in the Rockies."

Another innovation was called, for whatever reason, "torch singing." The woman most identified with it was Libby Holman, a professional

Libby Holman, whose deep-throated husky voice made her popular as a torch singer. (From a photograph by Hal Phyfe)

singer who happened to have a voice with a wide range and an agreeably husky, throaty quality. The general effect, both of the manner of singing, and of the songs, was lament about life, self-pity. The titles of the songs suggested the spirit of them: "Moanin' Low," "Body and Soul," "Am I Blue?" Another torch singer, Helen Morgan, asked, with husky doleful-ness, "Why Was I Born?" Her manner implied that there wasn't any good reason. Another ditty that lent itself to the throaty self-pity of torch singing was "Ten Cents a Dance," plaint of a girl who made her living by dancing on a commercial basis with the customers of dance halls.

Hardly an innovation, not much more than a mannerism associated with one personality was the "boop-a-doop" singing of Helen Kane, a cute, pert little vaudeville performer who discovered she could achieve fame by in-serting irrelevant and meaningless syllables, such as "boop-a-doop," here and there in the words of her songs. Sigmund Spaeth called it, with some lack of respect, "sillysyllabic singing." Kane's ditties included a satirically solicitous ditty called "Button Up Your Overcoat," and "Thank Your Fa-ther, Thank Your Mother," "I Wanna Be Loved by You," "That's My Weakness Now."

VII

Another feature of the twenties, a kind of gargoyle on the cathedral of American music, Negro in origin, was the "blues" (not to be confused with "spirituals" which were religious. A "blue," though the word was never used in the singular, was originally a lament rhythmically wailed by a Negro who felt badly; he had the blues and chanted a "blue":

> Gwine to de river, take a rope an' a rock,
> Gwine to de river, take a rope an' a rock,
> Gwine to tie rope roun' my neck and jump right over de dock.

Originally, the laments were spontaneous, a gloomy emotion put into moaning, rhythmic words. An early one, and one that became best known, was the "St. Louis Blues," in which a black woman mourned the loss of her lover and considered how to get him back:

> I hate to see de ev'nin' sun go down,
> Hate to see de eve-nin' sun go down,
> 'Cause my baby he done lef' dis town.
> Feelin' tomorrow lak Ah feel today,
> Feel tomorrow lak Ah feel today,
> I'll pack my trunk, make ma getaway.
> St. Louis woman wid her diamon' rings
> Pulls dat man 'roun' by her apron strings
> 'Twant for powder an' for store bought hair,
> De man I love would not gone nowhere.

Got de	St.	Lou-is	Blues	jes	as	blue	as—	Ah—	can	be ————
I—	loves	dat	man	lak	a	school	boy—	loves-	his	pie ————
A—	black	head-ed	gal	make	a	freight	train-	jump-	the	track ————
Lawd a	blonde	head-ed	wom-an	makes	a	good—	man—	leave the	town ————
Oh	ash-es	to	ash-es				and	dust	to	dust ————

Got de St. Louis Blues, jes blue as Ah can be!
Dat man got a heart like a rock cast in the sea,
Or else he wouldn't gone so far from me.
[Spoken] "Doggone it!"

Been to de gypsy to get ma fortune tole;
Been to de gypsy to get ma fortune tole;
'Cause I's wild about ma jelly-roll.
Gypsy done tole me, "Don't you wear no black!"
Gypsy done tole me, "Don't you wear no black!"
Go to St. Louis, you can win him back."
Help me to Cairo, make St. Louis myse'f;
Git to Cairo, fine ma old friend Jeff,
Gwine to pin myse'f close to his side;
If I flag his train I sho can ride.

The "St. Louis Blues" was composed by a black man, W. C. Handy. White imitations or adaptations came forward in the "Limehouse Blues" and "Birth of the Blues." Apotheosis, a long distance from the Mississippi canebrakes, came when George Gershwin composed *Rhapsody in Blue*, played by the New York Symphony Orchestra under Walter Damrosch. It

Two of the steps of the Charleston as illustrated by Arthur Murray, New York instructor in the modern dance.

was not a "blue," but was about blues, a composition written with high symphonic dignity.*

A Negro innovation in dancing was the Charleston, followed and made more ultra in the black bottom. Both were acrobatic, the dancing equivalent of the frenzy of a jazz orchestra. They were the manifestation of the Negro influence on American ballroom dancing, the farthest distance that the jazz period went from the stately waltzes and decorous polkas of the older generation. "Nice" people did them only as an occasional stunt under special circumstances; they were a means by which the younger set at the country club would have shocked the chaperones—only, by the twenties, there were no chaperones.

VIII

No account of popular songs during the 1920s, and such fragile relation as they have to history, could pretend to be adequate—it would not be even a skipping from high note to high note—if it failed to mention the conspicuous revival of an old song of three decades before. The renascence came about through the political prominence of a three-time, and each time excellent, governor of New York upon whom his parents, and the Catholic priest who baptized him, had conferred the names Alfred Emanuel, but whom America preferred to call by an affectionate abbreviation, "Al." Al Smith had been born on the East Side of New York. About the time he reached the age in which interest in girls goes hand in hand with, and partly accounts for, interest in song, it happened that the popular song of the period—it was during the early 1890s—was one called "The Sidewalks of New York," in which the most familiar lines were,

East   side,   West   side,   all   a-round the town,___   The

> East Side, West Side,
> All around the town . . .
> Boys and girls together,
> Me and Mamie Rourke,
> Tripped the light fantastic
> On the sidewalks of New York.

The fortuitous conjunction of the name of the song, its locale, and the fact that Smith had been born and brought up in the same section of New York, brought it about that when Smith ran for president in 1928, this song, more than thirty years old, was played more often, and heard by more people, than any of the current songs of the day. In vain did the harried artisans

---

*One sincerely hopes not. —D.R.

of ephemeral hits pound the drum and blow the saxophone of jazz against the greater appeal of a thoroughly old-fashioned song, one that was utterly sentimental, and because of that, in the judgment of the sophisticated, outmoded and banal.

"The Sidewalks of New York" was more closely associated with Al Smith than any other song had ever been with any candidate or president. Some instinctive sense that Smith in his personality had qualities of homeliness, simplicity, and directness similar to those of the old-fashioned, sentimental waltz caused the combination of song and candidate to appeal strongly to the country; it made friends for both man and song.

174 South Street, New York City—birthplace of ex-Governor Alfred E. Smith and locale of the song "Sidewalks of New York."

Four years later, in 1932, when Franklin D. Roosevelt was a presidential nominee, some of those interested in his candidacy, perhaps remembering the happy association of Smith with "The Sidewalks of New York," and carrying on the old tradition that every candidate should have a campaign song, put forward for Franklin Roosevelt "Happy Days Are Here Again."

> So long, sad times!
> Go along, bad times!
> We're rid of you at last . . .
> Happy days are here again,
> The skies above are clear again, clear again,
> Let's sing a song of cheer again,
> Happy days are here again.

In "Happy Days Are Here Again" as the Franklin Roosevelt campaign song of 1932, there was logical aptness, for the country was in the depth of depression, and the implication was that Roosevelt, if elected, would bring good times. But just because in this case the association between candidate and song was artificial and forced, it was less successful than in the case of Smith and "The Sidewalks of New York," in which the association was natural and honestly sentimental.

IX

In the twenties, the new popular songs, like almost everything else, experienced an accelerated ephemeralness. After the radio came, a new air might be sung the first time at some New York nightclub at 3:00 A.M., or in a new musical play, and, if recognized as a "hit," might by seven o'-clock the ensuing evening be flying on the ether waves to practically every home in the country, pushed on its feverish way by a hundred instrumentalities of high-pressure business organization. And if, the following morning in another nightclub, a hit was made by some still newer song, the later favorite might, by the same process of practically instantaneous diffusion, crowd into beginning obsolescence the favorite of twenty-four hours before.

One thought of how the songs of an earlier time had made their way: "The Last Rose of Summer," sung in a London drawing room, heard by someone who after days of slow travel carried it to Liverpool, picked up and memorized by a ship captain or sailor who brought it a six weeks' journey across the Atlantic, sung in a Philadelphia tavern, heard and memorized by a Conestoga wagoner who carried it with him as he traveled westward toward the Alleghanies, singing it in each tavern where he stopped overnight, and repeating it for the benefit of listeners who learned it and in turn carried it upon their various ways. Between the first singing of a song by Robert Burns or Stephen Foster, and the complete familiarity of all America with it, years must have elapsed. In that earlier time, a person heard a song and, if he liked it, learned it, committed it to memory, made it a part of his personality, had for it the affection that goes out to that which is at once dear and familiar.

But in the 1920s "the thing," the vogue, was to know not the old songs but the new ones—to know the latest "hit" was one mark of the sophistication that was universally desired. And since new was so soon displaced by newer, hardly anyone tried to learn a song. Little more of it was known than a line or two of the chorus, a phrase or two of the music. The musical possessions of the average person became not four or five songs well-learned and permanently remembered, but a mere jumble of melody lines.

X

In the newer way of things, the ballad, the narrative song, the song that told a story, disappeared utterly—I doubt if any important new one emerged during the 1920s. More and more, popular songs tended to be the mere repetition of a phrase, not pretending to tell a story, hardly even to make sense. They were abbreviated almost to a series of vocal ejaculations, depending, for the attraction of the words, almost wholly upon reiteration of such simple consonances as June with moon. The appeal of the ultramodern songs was to emotion almost wholly. Ignoring the mind, their purpose was mainly to evoke a mood, which can be achieved by mere sound, regardless of the intellectual content of the words; indeed, a state of mere revery in the listener is the more easily evoked if his mind is not called upon to be active or even to pay attention.

This almost exclusive emphasis on the evoking of a mood left a need unmet; man is more completely pleased when both his emotions and his mind are stirred, as is done by a combination of agreeable music with words that move toward some kind of destination.

Man's primitive and age-long liking for a story, a ballad, was unsatisfied. Groping to satisfy this desire, many old-time American ballads were revived. The southern Appalachians and the Ozarks were combed for "hillbilly" tales in simple verse and music. Cowboy ballads, tales of derring-do on the western prairies, became a vogue in the drawing rooms of eastern cities; a collection of them, which pleased the tuneful and also won the esteem of scholars, was made by a teacher at the University of Texas, John A. Lomax—who thus enabled many a smartly tuxedoed and ultrasophisticated representative of golden youth to make a hit in Park Avenue penthouses by singing "The Cowboy's Lament":

> As I walked out in the streets of Laredo,
> As I walked out in Laredo one day,
> I spied a poor cowboy wrapped up in white linen,
> Wrapped up in white linen as cold as the clay . . .
>
> "Go gather around you a crowd of young cowboys,
> And tell them the story of this my sad fate;
> Tell one and the other before they go further
> To stop their wild roving before 'tis too late." . . .
>
> We beat the drum slowly and played the fife lowly,
> And bitterly wept as we bore him along;
> For we all loved our comrade, so brave, young, and handsome,
> We all loved our comrade, although he'd done wrong.

The old ballads thus or otherwise made available may have given the 1920s as much pleasure, and a pleasure with rather more substance, than did the current hits. It is quite possible that those who composed the younger generation, when they became the older one, recalled the time-tested old ballads they sang as vividly as the hits of the day.

In convivial gatherings during the twenties, after the songs of the moment had had their precedence, someone would turn to the old-time ballads; and it was to be observed that though the current songs might hold the guests together until ten or eleven o'clock, it was the ballads that kept the party going until two or three in the morning. After a party had reached the point at which normally it would break up, someone would step to the piano and begin one of the old ballads.

Young folks of the twenties, when they turned to ballads, often liked those that had the added attraction of low life:

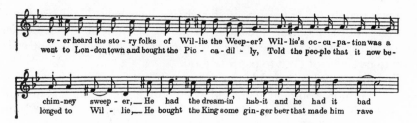

ev - er heard the sto - ry folks of Wil - lie the Weep - er? Wil - lie's oc - cu - pa - tion was a
went to Lon - don town and bought the Pic - ca - dil - ly, Told the peo - ple that it now be-

chim - ney   sweep - er,__ He had the dream - in' hab - it and he had it   bad
longed to   Wil - lie,__ He bought the King some gin - ger beer that made him   rave

Did you ever hear tell about Willie the weeper?
Willie the weeper was a chimney sweeper,
Had the dope habit and had it bad,
Listen while I'll tell you 'bout the dream he had. . . .

The ballad that the younger generation liked best and sang oftenest was
"Frankie and Johnny," a raw tale of life in the underworld which any time
before the twenties would have been strictly confined to stag parties, but
which, under the changed standard of manners, was sung freely and frequently in what the older folks used to describe as "mixed company":

Frankie and Johnnie were lovers.
O my gawd how they could love,
They swore to be true to each other,
Just as true as the stars up above,
He was her man, but he done her wrong.

*John Held's drawing of "Johnny and Frankie," from a song collection of the era. (Published
by Macauley, reproduced by permission of the artist)*

Frankie's station in life was made plain by the vernacular candor of the designation of the place in which she carried on her occupation: "Frankie lived down at the crib-house." The relation Johnny had to her was made clear:

> Frankie she was a good woman,
> And Johnnie he was her man.
> And every dollar Frankie made
> Went right into Johnnie's hand.
> He was her man, but he done her wrong!

Johnny was faithless; the money Frankie gave him he spent upon the ladies of a rival establishment:

> He spent it all on those call-house girls,
> He was her man, but he done her wrong.

Frankie, naturally, was resentful:

> Frankie went down to the call-house,
> She leaned on that call-house bell,
> "Get out of the way, all chippies and fools,
> Or I'll blow you straight to hell;
> I want my man who is doing me wrong."

> After she shot him she was sorry,
> And it wrang her poor heart sore,
> To see her loving Johnnie
> Stretched across that hotel floor.
> But he was her man and he done her wrong! . . .

In the springtime of 1927, observers of the come-and-go of street phenomena noticed that in New York and other cities hawkers were selling great numbers of a ditty called "Hallelujah, I'm a Bum." Since the song was not new, there arose discussion about the reason for its apparently spontaneous reemergence—the *New York World* printed a learned editorial speculation about it, without, however, being able to come to a conclusion. The song had been well known in the West about 1915 as the "hymn of the Wobblies"—Wobblies being a corruption, derisively intended, of I.W.W., the Industrial Workers of the World.

In its earlier existence, "Hallelujah, I'm a Bum," as sung by the I.W.W.'s, had been defiant, threatening, almost sinister; the I.W.W.'s were perhaps the most radical labor organization America had ever known. In choosing the tune for their song of defiance, they had turned, with deliberate irreverence undoubtedly, to one of the most venerated hymns of the evangelical churches, "Hallelujah, Thine the Glory; Hallelujah, Amen," and to that solemn music had written words of contempt and scorn for capitalism and the accessory institutions of American society.

Subsequently, the I.W.W. had ebbed, and with it their hymn. "Hallelujah, I'm a Bum" had been forgotten for years. Then, in the spring of 1927, it turned up in eastern cities, with, however, new words, words that implied no great truculence toward society, but pictured, rather, the freedom and pleasure of a vagabond life. It was in this incarnation that the song became popular during the late twenties. Could it have been that the popularity was a sign of reaction from the conditions of intense economic activity of the boom days? That singing "Hallelujah, I'm a Bum" gave a sense of vicarious release to men who felt themselves bound tighter and tighter into the meshes of business at high speed? One could imagine that a businessman, especially one still young, riding in the Pullman from care in New York to care in Chicago, could look with some longing at a group of carefree hoboes about a pot of stew beside the railroad track:

Hal-le - lu-jah, I'm a   bum   Hal-le - lu-jah, bum a - gain,   Hal-le -

> Rejoice and be glad, for the springtime has come,
> We can throw down our shovels and go on the bum.
>   Hallelujah, I'm a bum,
>   Hallelujuh, bum again,
>   Hallelujah, give us a hand-out to revive us again.

It was, of course, prosperity that allowed such romantic feelings about hand-outs and bums. Three years later, with millions unemployed, the romance had faded. Homelessness no longer seemed free, pleasurable, or so far away for many Americans.

CONCLUSION
An Essay on Optimism

Here Mark Sullivan brings his history lesson to a close. In the original edition of *Our Times*, each of the six volumes ended with a timeline spanning the period covered in that volume. Together, the six timelines are as long as a seventh book. Anyone who has ever enjoyed a popular history yearbook or picturebook, such as any in the *Time-Life* series, will be familiar with the form Mark Sullivan used. The stories Sullivan gleaned from dozens of American newspapers are briefly sketched, often funny, and truly offbeat. There is, however, a liability: They either reiterate material provided in the main body of the text, or are genuine trivia. It was a wrenching decision, but I have omitted all the timelines for reasons of space.

We are left then not with a bang but with a song. Mark Sullivan conducts another of his dazzling tours of popular culture, in this case the survey of American popular song that brings this editor up to the music he loved best in childhood. The other closing images may be disturbing or sad: Mark Sullivan in bitter disappointment at the broken hopes of his younger years; a poignant nostalgia for an era of giants; memories of a time of carefree abundance—written in a time of Depression and despair.

Yet these are not the images that linger. What one takes away from this book is an image of the United States in irresistible upswing, bursting with confidence, pride and optimism, when no problem seemed a match for American know-how and destiny beckoned this nation to glory. In its rich detail, Mark Sullivan's personal optimism persists and pervades in spite of everything.

It is almost impossible to imagine any history today being written with such a buoyant spirit or with such goodwill toward its subjects. A century after the beginning of this history and a half-century after its author's death, Our Own Times are not noted for optimism. Historians and sociologists tell us that some melancholy is natural at the turn of any century. If that's so, we shouldn't be surprised that today's surveys and studies show Americans prey to every kind of cynicism, melancholy, despair, and, perhaps above all, pessimism. The only surprise in all this may be that registered by newspaper and broadcast editorial writers, forever shaking their heads in wonder at the "sudden" enormity of public cynicism.

And don't we have cause to be cynical? In recent years, America has suffered many blows to public morale, to the Constitution itself. In Vietnam we fought a protracted war no one wanted, until no one was able to justify it any longer; political and military leaders lied to cover up their own blunders and to persuade the American people that such a war could be won without significant sacrifice on the home front. A few years later, the vice president of the United States, Spiro Agnew, resigned in the disgrace of a bribery scandal. Shortly thereafter, his president, Richard Nixon, facing impeachment, also resigned, after proof was found that he and top-level members of his administration had engaged in criminal conduct. Then, under President Jimmy Carter, the mighty superpower of America was taken hostage by an upstart Islamic republic, Iran. A few years later, presidential impeachment was again a threat, as we found that top members of the Reagan administration had formed a blatantly unconstitutional shadow government, secretly, at least partially, selling millions of dollars of this country's best weapons to Iran, that same sworn enemy and terrorist state, in order to fund an illegal war in Nicaragua. We would ultimately learn that President Reagan and his vice president, George Bush, were involved in some aspects of the arms sale; we would never learn where all the money went. In other cases, the bright light of television was believed to burn public figures to a crisp. Yet in the meantime, the public became more aware of the methods of some elements of American journalism. They grew more convinced that reporters saw themselves not as watchdogs but as lapdogs—or, worst of all, attack dogs. Thus, according to conventional wisdom, the American people were less inclined to believe even the most dire reports about malfeasance by elected officials. According to such observers, the American people, instead of responding with outrage and calls for swift justice in the Iranian arms scandal, responded with cynicism, self-interest, or apathy.

Cynicism has become chic today, pessimism a mark of intelligence. To look on the dark side is to be "realistic." Perhaps it was ever thus. But that is not the kind of country Mark Sullivan describes in *Our Times*.

Sullivan describes a nation consumed by optimism, an absolute confidence in American know-how as the solution to any kind of problem. He sees pride in our shared past and no doubts in the wonders of our anticipated future. The very nature of this history—one that sets daily life and the "average American" alongside presidents, senators, and captains of industry—is quintessentially American, and may even be a leap of faith in the grandest tradition of the American experiment, whose inventors dared trust that "We, the People" would indeed be wise and strong enough to lead the new nation.

Sullivan's own optimism remains resilient even when confronted by the disappointments that characterize the second half of his history: the decline of the Progressive Movement, the retreat of the United States from the world arena, and the death of Theodore Roosevelt. Certainly, the Great Depression is a mess, Sullivan might say, but it's no match for American energy and spirit (and probably could have been avoided if we'd stayed more true to our duty—or elected leaders more like Teddy).

This attitude extends beyond the "can-do" spirit we heard praised by our grandparents; it exceeds the nationalistic fervor that informed the Spanish-American War. It is nearer to the bravado shown by the kind of legendary, Mark Twain-y frontier American who bursts into London or Paris (or New York, for that matter) ready to lick any man who says "Boo," proudly declaring himself the equal, if not the better, of the crowned heads of Europe.

Sullivan was less boisterous in his optimism but nonetheless remarkable. The leading political reporter of his day, he could look on the leaders of the U.S. government, most of whom he knew personally, and yet summon what appears to be boundless admiration, especially for Roosevelt. Sullivan is capable of skepticism: No reporter can have been a muckraker, as he was, without a healthy dose of that. But he is never cynical. It is his writing about Roosevelt that best illustrates the generosity, the guilelessness of Sullivan's optimism and the absence of cynicism in his nature.

Sullivan identifies, analyzes, and praises Roosevelt's use of "balanced sentences," the way T.R. seldom addressed one view without also allowing for its opposite. Today's reporters might well describe that as waffling not balance, a sign of weakness, not one of comprehension (even though many reporters, especially those for television and radio networks, are often required to employ exactly the same kind of balanced sentences). Teddy Roosevelt, Sullivan observes, can't resist a challenge: throw down the gauntlet, and he will pick it up. Today, we might call that dangerous, hot-headed, or thin-skinned at the least. Yet again and again Sullivan demonstrates that the qualities Roosevelt brought to public office—intelligence wedded to emotion, seriousness of thought coupled with swiftness of action—were exactly those that served him and the country well.

The reader of the late 1990s must, however, question whether Roosevelt could have succeeded if his constituents, including Sullivan, had not also been endowed with certain qualities amenable to his own, including that willingness to appreciate and admire the best intentions and best efforts of a public figure. Did Teddy Roosevelt have "spin doctors" who told Sullivan just how wonderful the president was, or did Sullivan arrive independently at that conclusion? How much does hindsight, ours as well as Sullivan's, improve Roosevelt's appearance? And how much would we benefit from (or be betrayed by) adapting Sullivan's attitudes toward our own leaders?

After reading *Our Times*, we may wonder why Mount Rushmore contains portraits of any president other than T.R. Even without Sullivan's help, he has become a beloved character in our national folklore—the teddy bear and the grin saw to that. Yet much as we may love him in retrospect, how would we have felt listening to his Bull Moose campaign song, "Onward, Christian Soldiers"?

In Our Own Times, one failed candidate for president rocked the Republican National Convention when he called for a "a jihad," "a cultural war" to "retake our cities" in a manner that was disturbing to many even before the terrorist attack on the Murrah Office Building in Oklahoma City, April 19, 1995. (In reflecting on the use of phrases such as "retake our cities," one must always ask who the speaker means by "our," as one never need ask of Mark Sullivan and *Our Times*.) Other politicians active today promise to force their religious or cultural beliefs (or lack of same) on the rest of the country. Would Sullivan's old-fashioned optimism protect us sufficiently from politicians who *aren't* as nice as Teddy?

I am often struck by how we have forgotten how that same optimism once protected us—at the very time *Our Times* was written. It is easy, too easy, to forget how close the United States came during the Great Depression to domination by the forces of fascism and communism, forces that came not from any foreign threat but from within our own borders. Economic hardship brought desperation and a desire for quick, easy solutions; fascism and communism seemed like such solutions. Charismatic leaders offered well-turned speeches, preyed upon fears and hatreds, and offered salvation at the low cost of our liberty. Liberty always seems least valuable when it hasn't been lost. Yet Americans, overall and in the main, resisted the demagogues and the seductive charms of authoritarian rule; we couldn't believe things had gotten so bad that we would actually need to abandon democracy. We remained true to our principles, and we survived. Only a fundamental confidence in our institutions, and optimism for our future, could have seen us through the Great Depression.

Perhaps it was easier for the generations who endured the Great Depression to retain that spirit, since they were closer to the golden age of Theodore Roosevelt and Mark Sullivan, and closer also to the ages of Washington, Jefferson, and Lincoln. The lessons of history were still fresh to them, the "good old days" were a living memory, and the disappointments of today had not yet been visited upon them. In less complicated times, it is easier to preserve one's optimism. In more complicated times, some would say that optimism is no longer feasible, and may even be harmful.

Some would point back to the same list of disillusionments: Vietnam, Watergate, the Iranian hostage crisis, and the Iranian arms conspiracy. I reported every one of those disillusionments. As White House correspondent for CBS News during the Nixon administration, I missed several important early leads and exclusive stories, because I was reluctant to believe that this country's highest officials could be guilty of such widespread criminal activity. I had been brought up with an abiding faith in my country's leaders, and a tremendous respect for the presidency. Only when brought face-to-face with extensive, irrefutable documentary evidence did I come to accept the repellent truth. Doubtless thinking of such incidents, in which the faith of the citizenry is abused by the leadership, today's cynics insist that Americans cannot afford optimism, even if we could regain it.

But I disagree. We cannot afford to do without optimism. Most of us have never lost it. We have been sorely disappointed, but optimism has, if not softened the blows, at least shown us the light at the end of the tunnel. My faith in this country's system of government was confirmed at the time of the Watergate scandals, the very time when my faith might have taken its worst bruising: Although one president resigned in disgrace, another stepped in peacefully, lawfully, hopefully. It was not only our legal Constitution but also our spiritual constitution that carried the day—exactly as all our antecedent optimists hoped they would.

Our lives are surely more complicated than the lives of *Our Times*. We haven't the luxury of time that our ancestors, or even our former selves, once had in abundance. A proliferation of communications media distributes information, factual or not, more widely than our forebears would have dreamed possible. We have more information, or more kinds, through more means than ever before. And it is no longer possible even for latter-day Mark Sullivans to pretend that ours is a nation composed of white males. We cannot help but see a rainbow of faces, hear a chorus of voices, when we consider our America today. That diversity provides energy and strength, but it can also make more difficult the teaching of valuable lessons. The prescriptions of the Founding Fathers may have saved our skins during the Watergate crisis, but those men two hundred years ago were white slaveholders who denied their wives and daughters the right to vote and whose sons would oppress the native population across the continent. Knowing all these things, as we now know them, it is more difficult to hold up as paradigms the persons, or even the words and feelings, that built this country.

Admitting that optimism is valuable, how can we encourage it, how can we teach it to our children, when our history tells of disillusionment and schism, of demoralizing events and shaming truths? A school district in Florida recently came up with a suggestion: Teachers would be required to tell students that the American culture is superior to all others. The proof of this superiority, they said, was that America had outlasted all other cultures, meaning presumably the Soviet Union. (The ancient Egyptians, whose culture lasted thousands of years, would surely be amused by the idea of a two-century-old culture's having "lasted.") It seems a poor method, but we were told that the Florida curriculum was born of a sincere concern. How can young Americans be expected to defend their country in time of war, for example (although some critics said the Floridians' greater fear was of attack not by foreign armies but by immigrants and nonwhites from within our own borders); how can young Americans stick to our institutions in time of economic instability, or perform any of the other deeds of heroic belief for which our predecessors were so often called upon? Schoolchildren today learn so many horror stories of oppression by the dominant cultures in American history; so many tales of scandal are repeated, so many heroes tarnished in the classroom. Never mind that it's all more or less true. Today there's less of the kind of values education we see in the old McGuffey Readers, and you won't see slave-owning, mistress-keeping, false-tooth-wearing George Washington held up for the kind of adulation he once commanded. And don't forget that George never cut down the cherry tree, nor did he stand in the prow of the boat when he crossed the Delaware. Can we be certain that our children will have the faith and strength our grandparents had, when they turned down fascism and communism at the height of the Great Depression?

The solution is a kind of informed optimism—retaining some skepticism, refusing to accept every word of every story as pure truth, always wanting to keep an eye on those in power anywhere, but always willing to rally to support the neighbors, the needy, and the nation as a whole. The solution is shown in Mark Sullivan.

In examining the legend of George Washington and the cherry tree; and all the wise, well-behaved, and well-spoken farm animals in the fables; and all the other homely pieties taught in McGuffey's Readers and other schoolbooks, Sullivan writes nervously that such stories may have encouraged cynicism in American schoolchildren, since they were so often called upon to repeat and believe what they knew perfectly well to be untrue. And yet those same cynics-in-training served their country in the Great War, endured the Great Depression, resisted fascism and communism, and (in some cases) served their country yet again in the Second World War. This is the very generation held up to us today as exemplars of the best kind of American patriotism. If they were cynical, it doesn't seem to have interfered much with doing their duty as Americans. Perhaps the worst cynics after all are those who disbelieve the optimism of the young, who think the young need dictating to before they'll do the right thing. At any rate, this kind of doubting is not a new trend in American society.

The temptations to despair are many, the cynics and the naysayers numerous; yet the United States of America remains a landmark of civilization. Capable of error but also capable of recognition and regret. Strong and proud, and unrivaled in history for its attempt to build and govern a society of multiethnic, multireligious, multiracial equals under the law. In Our Own Times, we have endured many dark hours. Yet the American experiment is no less worthy, and no less successful today than it has ever been. How Mark Sullivan would have loved to witness and write it all!

Index

Page numbers in *italics* refer to illustrations.